Dynamic Reconfiguration

Architectures and Algorithms

SERIES IN COMPUTER SCIENCE

Series Editor: Rami G. Melhem
University of Pittsburgh
Pittsburgh, Pennsylvania

DYNAMIC RECONFIGURATION
Architectures and Algorithms
Ramachandran Vaidyanathan and Jerry L. Trahan

ENGINEERING ELECTRONIC NEGOTIATIONS
A Guide to Electronic Negotiation Technologies for the Design and
Implementation of Next-Generation Electronic Markets—Future
Silkroads of eCommerce
Michael Ströbel

HIERARCHICAL SCHEDULING IN PARALLEL AND CLUSTER
SYSTEMS
Sivarama Dandamudi

MOBILE IP
Present State and Future
Abdul Sakib Mondal

OBJECT-ORIENTED DISCRETE-EVENT SIMULATION WITH JAVA
A Practical Introduction
José M. Garrido

A PARALLEL ALGORITHM SYNTHESIS PROCEDURE FOR HIGH-
PERFORMANCE COMPUTER ARCHITECTURES
Ian N. Dunn and Gerard G. L. Meyer

PERFORMANCE MODELING OF OPERATING SYSTEMS USING
OBJECT-ORIENTED SIMULATION
A Practical Introduction
José M. Garrido

POWER AWARE COMPUTING
Edited by Robert Graybill and Rami Melhem

THE STRUCTURAL THEORY OF PROBABILITY
New Ideas from Computer Science on the Ancient Problem of
Probability Interpretation
Paolo Rocchi

Dynamic Reconfiguration
Architectures and Algorithms

Ramachandran Vaidyanathan

and

Jerry L. Trahan
Louisiana State University
Baton Rouge, Louisiana

Springer Science+Business Media, LLC

Library of Congress Cataloging-in-Publication Data

Vaidyanathan, Ramachandran.
    Dynamic reconfiguration: architectures and algorithms/Ramachandran
Vaidyanathan, Jerry L. Trahan.
        p.   cm. — (Series in computer science)
    Includes bibliographical references and index.

    1. Computer architecture.   2. Computer algorithms.   I. Trahan, Jerry
L. II. Title.   III. Series in computer science (Kluwer Academic/Plenum
Publishers)

QA76.9.A73V35 2004
004.2'2—dc22

                                                                    2003064000

ISBN 978-1-4757-7769-7   ISBN 978-0-306-48428-5 (eBook)
DOI 10.1007/978-0-306-48428-5

©2003 Springer Science+Business Media New York
Originally published by Kluwer Academic/Plenum Publishers, New York in 2003
Softcover reprint of the hardcover 1st edition 2003

To

Sudha, Shruti, and Deepti

and

Suzanne, Dana, and Drew

Contents

List of Figures

Preface

Computing with dynamic reconfiguration has developed into a mature area, with a rich collection of techniques, results, and algorithms. A dynamically reconfigurable architecture (or simply a reconfigurable architecture) typically consists of a large number of computing elements connected by a reconfigurable communication medium. By dynamically restructuring connections between the computing elements, these architectures admit extremely fast solutions to several computational problems. The interaction between computation and the communication medium permits novel techniques not possible on a fixed-connection network.

This book spans the large body of work on dynamically reconfigurable architectures and algorithms. It is not an exhaustive collection of results in this area, rather, it provides a comprehensive view of dynamic reconfiguration by emphasizing fundamental techniques, issues, and algorithms. The presentation includes a wide repertoire of topics, starting from a historical perspective on early reconfigurable systems, ranging across a wide variety of results and techniques for reconfigurable models, examining more recent developments such as optical models and run-time reconfiguration (RTR), and finally touching on an approach to implementing a dynamically reconfigurable model.

Researchers have developed algorithms on a number of reconfigurable architectures, generally similar, though differing in details. One aim of this book is to present these algorithms in the setting of a single computational platform, the reconfigurable mesh (R-Mesh). The R-Mesh possesses the basic features of a majority of other architectures and is sufficient to run most algorithms. This structure can help the reader relate results and understand techniques without the haze of details on just what is and is not allowed from one model to the next.

For algorithms that require additional features beyond those of the R-Mesh, we highlight the features and reasons for their use. For example, having directional buses permits an R-Mesh to solve the directed graph reachability problem in constant time, which is not known to be (and not likely to be) possible for an R-Mesh with undirected buses. In describing this algorithm, we pinpoint just where directed buses permit the algorithm to succeed and undirected buses would fail.

Although most of the book uses the R-Mesh as the primary vehicle of expression, a substantial portion deals with the relationships between the R-Mesh and other models of computation, both reconfigurable and traditional (Chapters 9 and 10). The simulations integral to developing these relationships also provide generic methods to translate algorithms between models.

The book is addressed to researchers, graduate students, and system designers. To the researcher, it offers an extensive digest of topics ranging from basic techniques and algorithms to theoretical limits of computing on reconfigurable architectures. To the system designer, it provides a comprehensive reference to tools and techniques in the area. In particular, Part IV of the book deals with optical models and Field Programmable Gate Arrays (FPGAs), providing a bridge between theory and practice.

The book contains over 380 problems, ranging in difficulty from those meant to reinforce concepts to those meant to fill gaps in the presentation to challenging questions meant to provoke further thought. The book features a list of figures, a rich set of bibliographic notes at the end of each chapter, and an extensive bibliography. The book also includes a comprehensive index with topics listed under multiple categories. For topics spanning several pages, page numbers of key ideas are in bold.

Organization of Book

The book comprises four parts. Part I (Chapters 1–3) provides a first look at reconfiguration. It includes introductory material, describing the overall nature of reconfiguration, various models and architectures, important issues, and fundamental algorithmic techniques. Part II (Chapters 4–7) deals with algorithms on reconfigurable architectures for a variety of problems. Part III (Chapters 8 and 9) describes self and mutual simulations for several reconfigurable models, placing their computational capabilities relative to traditional parallel models of computation and complexity classes. Part IV (Chapters 10 and 11) touches on capturing, in the models themselves, the effect of practical constraints, providing a bridge between theory and practice. Each chapter is reasonably self-contained and includes a set of exercises and bibliographic notes.

The presentation in this book is suitable for a graduate level course and only presupposes basic ideas in parallel computing. Such a course could include (in addition to Chapters 1–3), Chapters 4–8 (for an emphasis on algorithms), Chapters 4–6, 8, 9 (for a more theoretical flavor), portions of Chapters 4–6 along with Chapters 8, 10, 11 (to stress aspects with more bearing on implementability). This book could also serve as a companion text to most graduate courses on parallel computing.

Chapter 1: Principles and Issues
This chapter introduces the idea of dynamic reconfiguration and reviews important considerations in reconfigurable architectures. It provides a first look at the R-Mesh, the model used for most of the book.

Chapter 2: The Reconfigurable Mesh: A Primer
This chapter details the R-Mesh model and uses it to describe several techniques commonly employed in algorithms for reconfigurable architectures. It also develops a palette of fundamental algorithms that find use as building blocks in subsequent chapters.

Chapter 3: Models of Reconfiguration
This chapter provides an overview of other models of reconfiguration with examples of their use. These models include restrictions and enhancements of the R-Mesh, other bus-based models, optical models, and field programmable gate arrays. It describes relationships among these models based on considerations of computing power and implementability.

Chapter 4: Arithmetic on the R-Mesh
Unlike conventional computing platforms, resource bounds for even simple arithmetic operations on reconfigurable architectures depend on the size and representations of the inputs. This chapter addresses these issues and describes algorithms for a variety of problems, including techniques for fast addition, multiplication, and matrix multiplication.

Chapter 5: Sorting and Selection
This chapter deals with problems on totally ordered sets and includes techniques for selection, area-optimal sorting, and speed-efficiency trade-offs.

Chapter 6: Graph Algorithms
Methods for embedding graphs in reconfigurable models are described

in the context of list ranking and graph connectivity. Along with other techniques such as tree traversal, rooting, and labeling, these techniques illustrate how methods developed on non-reconfigurable models can be translated to constant-time algorithms on reconfigurable architectures.

Chapter 7:   Computational Geometry & Image Processing
This chapter applies the methods developed in preceding chapters to solve problems such as convex hull, Voronoi diagrams, histogramming, and quadtree generation.

Chapter 8:   Model and Algorithmic Scalability
Normally, algorithm design does not consider the relationship between problem size and the size of the available machine. This chapter deals with issues that arise from a mismatch between the problem and machine sizes, and introduces methods to cope with them.

Chapter 9:   Computational Complexity of Reconfiguration
This chapter compares the computational "powers" of different reconfigurable models and places "reconfigurable complexity classes" in relation to conventional Turing machine, PRAM, and circuit complexity classes.

Chapter 10:   Optical Reconfigurable Models
This chapter describes reconfigurable architectures that employ fiber-optic buses. An optical bus offers a useful pipelining technique that permits moving large amounts of information among processors despite a small bisection width. The chapter introduces models, describes algorithms and techniques, and presents complexity results.

Chapter 11:   Run-Time Reconfiguration
This chapter details run-time reconfiguration techniques for Field Programmable Gate Arrays (FPGAs) and touches upon the relationships between FPGA-type and R-Mesh-type platforms. Towards this end, it presents an approach to implementing R-Mesh algorithms on an FPGA-type environment.

Acknowledgments.   We are grateful to the National Science Foundation for its support of our research on dynamic reconfiguration; numerous results in this book and much of the insight that formed the basis of our presentation resulted from this research. Our thanks also go to Hossam ElGindy, University of New South Wales, for his suggestions on organizing Chapter 2. Our thanks go to numerous students for their constructive criticisms of a preliminary draft of this book. Most importantly, this book would not have been possible without the patience and support of our families. We dedicate this book to them.

R. VAIDYANATHAN

J. L. TRAHAN

PART I

BASICS

Chapter 1

PRINCIPLES AND ISSUES

A *reconfigurable architecture* is one that can alter its components' functionalities and the structure connecting these components. When the reconfiguration is fast with little or no overhead, it is said to be *dynamic*. Consequently, a dynamically reconfigurable architecture can change its structure and functionality at every step of a computation. Traditionally, the term "reconfigurable" has been used to mean "dynamically reconfigurable." Indeed, most dynamically reconfigurable models (such as the reconfigurable mesh, reconfigurable multiple bus machine and reconfigurable network) do not employ the attribute "dynamic" in their names. We will use the terms "reconfigurable" and "dynamically reconfigurable" interchangeably in this book. In Chapter 11, we will discuss a form of reconfiguration called run-time reconfiguration (RTR) in which structural and functional changes in the computing device incur a significant penalty in time.

One benefit of dynamic reconfiguration is the potential for better resource utilization by tailoring the functionality of the available hardware to the task at hand. Another, more powerful, benefit stems from the agility of the architecture in adapting its structure to exploit features of a problem, or even a problem instance. These abilities, on one hand, allow dynamic reconfiguration to solve many problems extremely quickly. On the other hand, they raise new issues, such as algorithmic scalability, that pose no problems for conventional models of parallel computation.

The notion of an architecture that can dynamically reconfigure to suit computational needs is not new. The bus automaton was one of the first models to capture the idea of altering the connectivity among elements of a network using local control. Subsequently, the reconfigurable mesh, polymorphic torus, the processor array with a reconfigurable bus system (PARBS), and the, more general, reconfigurable network (RN) were introduced. Several implementation-oriented research projects further promoted interest in reconfigurable computing. The resulting research activity established dynamic reconfiguration as a very powerful computing paradigm. It produced algorithms for numerous problems, spawned other models, and, to a large extent, defined many important issues in reconfigurable computing.

Research has also explored reconfiguration in the setting of Field Programmable Gate Arrays (FPGAs). Originally designed for rapid prototyping, FPGAs did not emphasize rapid reconfiguration. Subsequently, ideas such as partial reconfiguration, context switching, and self-reconfiguration made their way into an FPGA-type setting, giving rise to the notion of run-time reconfiguration or RTR (as opposed to reconfiguring between applications or prototype iterations).

Dynamic reconfiguration holds great promise for fast and efficient computation. As a dedicated coprocessor (such as for manipulating very long integers), a reconfigurable architecture can deliver speeds much beyond the ability of conventional approaches. For a more general environment, it can draw a balance between speed and efficiency by reusing hardware to suit the computation. Indeed, several image and video processing, cryptography, digital signal processing, and networking applications exploit this feature.

The purpose of this chapter is to introduce the notion of dynamic reconfiguration at the model level and the issues that it generates. We begin in Section 1.1 with two examples as vehicles to demonstrate various facets of dynamic reconfiguration. For these examples, we use the segmentable bus, an architecture that admits a simple, yet powerful, form of dynamic reconfiguration. Subsequently, Section 1.2 extends the segmentable bus into a more general model called the *reconfigurable mesh* (*R-Mesh*), the primary model used in this book. Chapter 2 discusses the R-Mesh in detail. Section 1.3 touches on some of the issues that go hand-in-hand with dynamically reconfigurable architectures.

1.1   Illustrative Examples

Consider the *segmentable bus* architecture shown in Figure 1.1. It consists of N processors connected to a bus. Each processor can write to and read from the bus. In addition, the bus contains N switches that can split the bus into disjoint sub-buses or bus segments. For $0 \leq i < N - 1$, setting switch i segments the bus between processors i and $i + 1$. Data written on any segment of the bus is available in the same step to be read by any processor connected to that bus segment. Assume that all switches are initially reset so that a single bus spans all processors.

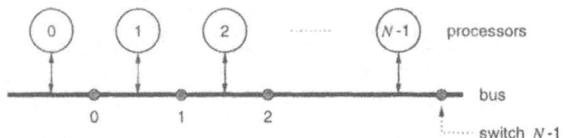

Figure 1.1. An N-processor segmentable bus.

For $0 \leq i \leq j < N$, denote the portion of the segmentable bus from processor i to processor j by $Seg\_Bus[i : j]$. Thus, $Seg\_Bus[0 : N - 1]$ denotes the entire segmentable bus.

We now illustrate the salient features of the segmentable bus architecture through two simple algorithms for (a) finding the sum of N numbers and (b) finding the OR of N bits.

Illustration 1: Adding N Numbers. For $0 \leq i < N$, let processor i initially hold input a_i. The object is to compute $a_0 + a_1 + \cdots + a_{N-1}$. We use the well-known binary tree paradigm for reduction algorithms to reduce N inputs at the leaves of a balanced binary tree to a single output at the root. Let $N = 2^n$, where $n \geq 0$ is an integer. The following recursive procedure implements this approach on $Seg\_Bus[0 : N - 1]$.

1. Set switch $\frac{N}{2} - 1$ to segment the bus between processors $\frac{N}{2} - 1$ and $\frac{N}{2}$.

2. Recursively add the elements in substructures $Seg\_Bus[0 : \frac{N}{2} - 1]$ and $Seg\_Bus[\frac{N}{2} : N - 1]$; let processors 0 and $\frac{N}{2}$ hold the two partial results.

3. For each $0 \leq i < \frac{N}{2}$, reset switch i to reconnect the bus between processors 0 and $\frac{N}{2}$, then add the partial results of Step 2 on $Seg\_Bus[0 : N - 1]$ and store the final result in processor 0.

Since the algorithm implements the balanced binary-tree approach to reduction, it runs in $O(\log N)$ time and can apply any associative operation (not just addition) to a set of inputs. Figure 1.2 illustrates the bus structure for the algorithm with $N = 8$.

Illustration 2: Finding the OR of N Bits. For $0 \leq i < N$, let processor i hold bit b_i. The aim here is to compute the logical OR of bits $b_0, b_1, \cdots, b_{N-1}$. One way is to use the binary tree algorithm of Illustration 1. The approach we use here differs from that of Illustration 1 and is unique to dynamically reconfigurable architectures. Unlike the

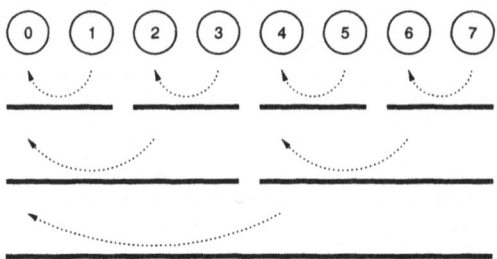

Figure 1.2. Bus structure for a binary tree algorithm. The figure shows the lowest level of recursion at the top. For each bus segment, the dotted arrow indicates the flow of data.

algorithm of Illustration 1 that applies to any associative operation, this method exploits properties specific to OR. The idea is to have a processor i with input bit $b_i = 1$ inform processor 0 that the answer to the OR problem is 1. If processor 0 does not hear from any writing processor, then it concludes that the answer is 0. The following algorithm finds the OR of N bits on $Seg\_Bus[0 : N - 1]$ in constant time.

1. For $0 \leq i < N - 1$, if bit $b_i = 1$, then set switch i to segment the bus between processors i and $i + 1$; if $b_i = 0$, then reset switch i to fuse the bus between processors i and $i + 1$.

2. For $0 \leq i < N$, if bit $b_i = 1$, then send a signal on the bus. Processor 0 receives a signal if and only if the OR of the N input bits is 1.

Figure 1.3 uses a small example to illustrate the bus structure and flow of information for this algorithm. Notice that Step 1 creates a unique

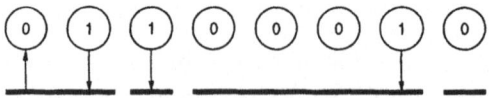

Figure 1.3. Bus structure for finding the OR on a segmentable bus. The numbers within processors are the input bits held by them and arrows indicate the signals.

bus segment for each 1 in the input. Step 2 simply informs the first processor of the presence of the 1 in the first segment. (Notice that at most one processor writes on each bus segment.) The presence of a 1 in the input, therefore, guarantees that the first processor will receive a signal. If the input contains no 1, then no writes occur in Step 2, so processor 0 does not receive a signal. Thus, processor 0 receives a signal if and only if the OR of the N input bits is 1. Since each of the two steps runs in constant time, so does the entire algorithm.

Illustrations 1 and 2 underscore some important features of dynamically reconfigurable architectures.

Communication Flexibility: Illustration 1 shows the ability of the model to use the bus for unit-step communication between different processor pairs at different steps. In this illustration, processor 0 communicates with processor 2^i, for each $0 \le i < \log N$. Other processors communicate similarly.

- On a fixed (non-reconfigurable) model, the wiring needed to meet the communication requirements of Illustration 1 would occupy $\Omega(N \log N)$ area. The segmentable bus, on the other hand, reuses its communication fabric to connect different processor pairs at different times and occupies $\Theta(N)$ area.

- An N-processor linear array that directly connects processor i only to processors $i\pm1$, for $0 < i < N-1$ has a diameter[1] of $N-1$, while the segmentable bus can directly connect any pair of processors; that is, its diameter is 1.

- A simple "non-segmentable" bus also has a diameter of 1, but it can support only one communication on the bus at any point in time. In contrast, all segments of a segmentable bus can simultaneously carry independent pieces of information.

- A point-to-point topology with constant diameter would require a large (non-constant) degree. On the other hand, each processor has only one connection to the segmentable bus. Indeed, most reconfigurable models use processors of constant degree.

Although a single bus (segmentable or not) can reduce the diameter and facilitate easy broadcasting, it is still subject to topological constraints such as bisection width[2]. The segmentable bus has a bisection width of 1. Therefore, for bisection-bounded problems such

---

[1]The *diameter* of an interconnection network is the distance between the furthest pair of processors in the network.

[2]The *bisection width* of an interconnection network is the smallest number of cuts in its communication medium (edges or buses) that will disconnect the network into two parts with equal (to within 1) number of processors.

as sorting N elements, a solution on a system with one segmentable bus will require as much time as on a linear array, namely $\Omega(N)$ steps.

Computational Power: The constant time solution for OR in Illustration 2 reveals some of the computing power that dynamic reconfiguration holds. The problem of finding the OR of N bits requires $\Omega(\log N)$ time on a Concurrent Read, Exclusive Write (CREW) Parallel Random Access Machine (PRAM)[3]. A Concurrent Read, Concurrent Write (CRCW) PRAM, however, can solve the problem in constant time by exploiting concurrent writes (as can a "non-segmentable" bus with concurrent writes—see Problem 1.1). The algorithm in Illustration 2 requires only processor 0 to read from the bus and at most one processor to write on each bus segment, thereby using only an exclusive read and exclusive writes. (Note that the algorithm of Illustration 1 also restricts the number of reads and writes on a bus segment to at most one.) In Section 3.3, and more formally in Chapter 9, we establish that an R-Mesh, a model featuring dynamic reconfiguration, has more "computing power" than a CRCW PRAM.

Local Control: A reconfigurable bus tailors its structure to the requirements of the problem, possibly changing at each step of the algorithm. Processors can accomplish this by using local information to act on local switches. In Illustration 1, for instance, buses are segmented at fixed points whose locations can be determined by the level of recursion alone. Therefore, processor i can use its identity and the level of recursion to determine whether or not to set switch i. This implies that no processor other than processor i need have access to switch i. Similarly, for Illustration 2, the only information used to set switch i is input bit b_i; once again, only processor i need have access to switch i.

This local control has the advantage of being simple, yet versatile as processors have "connection autonomy" or the ability to independently configure connections (or switches) assigned to them.

Synchronous Operation: Since a reconfigurable bus can change its structure at each step with only local control, a processor may have no knowledge of the state of other processors. Therefore, to ensure that the reconfiguration achieves the desired effect, it is important

---

[3] A CREW PRAM is a shared memory model of parallel computation that permits concurrent reads from a memory location, but requires all writes to a memory location to be exclusive. Some PRAM models also permit concurrent writes (see Section 3.1.3).

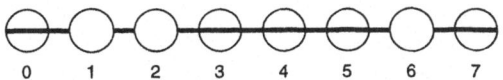

Figure 1.4. An example of an eight-processor, one-dimensional R-Mesh. The bus structure matches that of the segmentable bus in Figure 1.3.

for processors to proceed in a lock-step fashion. A synchronous environment obviates the need for expensive bus arbitration to resolve "unpredictable" concurrent writes on a bus. In Chapter 3, we will permit the R-Mesh to perform concurrent writes on buses. This situation differs from the unpredictable conflict arising from asynchrony, and is easier to handle; Section 3.1.3 discusses details.

1.2 The R-Mesh at a Glance

In this section we offer a glimpse at the reconfigurable mesh (R-Mesh), the primary model used in this book. The purpose of the discussion here is only to provide the reader with a general idea of the R-Mesh and the computational power it holds. Chapter 2 presents a more formal treatment.

One could view a one-dimensional R-Mesh as a linear array of processors with a bus traversing the entire length of this array through the processors. Each processor may segment its portion of the bus. Figure 1.4 shows an example in which processors 1, 2, and 6 have segmented their portions of the bus. Clearly, this structure is functionally similar to the segmentable bus. In general, one way to view the R-Mesh is as an array of processors with an underlying bus system that traverses the processors. Each processor serves as a "interchange point" that can independently configure local portions of the bus system. A one-dimensional R-Mesh allows each processor to either segment or not segment the bus traversing it.

A two-dimensional R-Mesh arranges processors in two dimensions as a mesh where each processor has four neighbors. Many more possibilities exist for configuring the bus system; Figure 1.5 shows the different ways in which each processor can configure the bus system. This ability of the two-dimensional R-Mesh to produce a much richer variety of bus configurations (than its one-dimensional counterpart) translates to a greater computational power, as we now illustrate.

Consider the R-Mesh shown in Figure 1.6. If each column of this R-Mesh holds an input bit, then it can configure the bus system so that a bus starting at the top left corner of the R-Mesh terminates in row x of the rightmost column if and only if the input contains x 1's. That

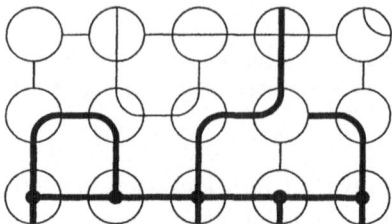

Figure 1.5. An example of a three-row, five-column, two-dimensional R-Mesh. The 15 processors in the figure show the 15 possible ways in which each processor can configure its portion of the bus system. (Notice that each processor connects its four ports in a different way.) One contiguous portion of the bus system resulting from the processors' configuration is in bold.

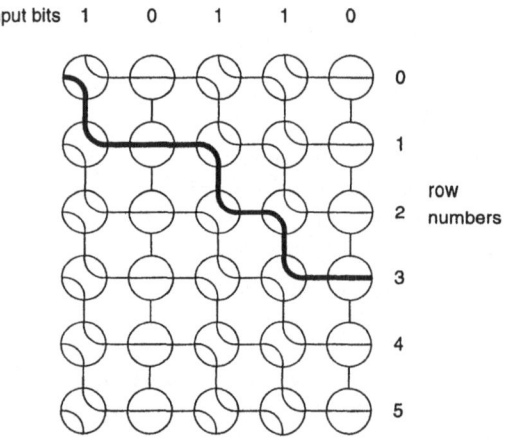

Figure 1.6. Using a six-row, five-column R-Mesh to count the number of 1's in a sequence of five input bits (shown one per column). The bus shown in bold sets up a path from the top left corner of the R-Mesh to the processor in row 3 of the rightmost column as there are three 1's in the input.

is, one could use this bus configuration to count the number of 1's in the input. Notice in Figure 1.6 that all processors in a column with a 0 input bit hold the same configuration. In this configuration, a signal entering the column at some row i exits the column at the same row i. Similarly, all processors in a column with a 1 input bit hold the same configuration in which a signal entering the column at row i exits the column at row $i + 1$ (if it exists). Thus a bus that starts in the top left corner in row 0 steps down a row for each 1 in the input, ending at row 3 at the right hand side of the R-Mesh. In general, the method of Figure 1.6 translates to a constant time algorithm to count N input bits on an $(N + 1)$-row, N-column R-Mesh; we elaborate on this algorithm and the underlying technique in Chapter 2.

In the above algorithm, the R-Mesh configures its bus system under local control with local information (as in the case of the segmentable bus). Unlike the segmentable bus, however, the R-Mesh can solve many more problems in constant time, including the counting bits example of Figure 1.6; it is possible to prove that the segmentable bus (or a one-dimensional R-Mesh) cannot count N bits in constant time.

1.3   Important Issues

As the illustrations of Section 1.1 show, dynamic reconfiguration holds immense promise for extremely fast computation. They also show that computation on a reconfigurable model requires a different perspective. In this section we touch upon some of the issues of importance to dynamic reconfiguration and approaches to addressing these issues. An algorithm designer must bear these considerations in mind while weighing various options during the design process.

Algorithmic Scalability.   In general, a parallel algorithm to solve a problem of size N is designed to run in $T(N)$ time on an instance of size $P(N)$ of the underlying model, where $T(N)$ and $P(N)$ are functions of N. For example, an $O(\log N)$-time PRAM algorithm to sort N elements could assume N processors. In a practical setting, however, problem sizes vary significantly while the available machine size does not change. In most conventional models, this mismatch between the problem size and model instance size does not pose any difficulty as the algorithm can scale down while preserving efficiency. (For the PRAM example, a sorting problem of size $N' \geq N$ would run on the N-processor PRAM in $O\left(\frac{N'}{N} \log N'\right)$ time. Put differently, one could say that a PRAM with $M < N$ processors can sort N elements in $O\left(\frac{N}{M} \log N\right)$ time.)

Unlike non-reconfigurable models, many dynamically reconfigurable models pay a penalty for a mismatch in the problem and model sizes as no method is currently known to scale down the model to a size called for by an algorithm while preserving efficiency. The standard approach to algorithmic scalability is by *self-simulation*. Let $\mathcal{M}(N)$ denote an N-sized instance of a parallel model of computation. A self-simulation of $\mathcal{M}$ is a simulation of $\mathcal{M}(N)$ on a smaller instance $\mathcal{M}(M)$ (where $M < N$)

of the same model. If the self-simulation of an arbitrary step of $\mathcal{M}(N)$ requires $\Theta\!\left(\frac{P(N)}{M}F(N,M)\right)$ steps on $\mathcal{M}(M)$, then $\mathcal{M}(M)$ can run any $T(N)$-step algorithm designed for $\mathcal{M}(N)$ in $\Theta\!\left(\frac{P(N)}{M}\cdot T(N)\cdot F(N,M)\right)$ steps, where $F(N,M)$ is an overhead. Ideally, this overhead should be a small constant. While this is the case for some models with limited dynamic reconfiguration ability, other models incur non-constant penalties (based on the best known self-simulations) that depend on N, M, or both. In designing reconfigurable architectures and algorithms for them, it is important to factor in trade-offs between architectural features (or algorithm requirements) and their impact on algorithmic scalability.

Chapter 8 discusses self-simulations and algorithmic scalability in detail.

Speed vs. Efficiency. Another facet of algorithmic scalability holds special significance for reconfigurable architectures. Many algorithms for these models are inefficient at the outset because their primary goal is speed rather than efficiency. Ideally, the best solution is both fast and efficient. Inefficiency, however, is the price often paid for extremely fast (even constant-time) algorithms that are possible with dynamic reconfiguration. Thus when speed is paramount, efficiency must often be sacrificed. A constant scaling overhead causes the scaled algorithm to inherit the (in)efficiency of the original algorithm.

One approach is to use different algorithms for different relative sizes of the problem and model instances. A better approach is to design the algorithm to accelerate its efficiency as it transitions from the computational advantages of a large model instance to the more modest resource reuse ability of a small instance. The ability of the algorithm to adapt to different problem and model instance sizes is called its *degree of scalability*. A designer of algorithms for reconfigurable models must therefore keep an eye on its degree of scalability, in addition to conventional measures such as speed and efficiency.

Chapter 8 further discusses the degree of scalability.

Implementability. The power of dynamic reconfiguration stems from the architecture's ability to alter connections between processors very rapidly. To realize this ability, the underlying hardware must generally implement fast buses with numerous switches on them. The cost and feasibility of this implementation depends on various factors such as the "shape" of the bus and the number of processors it spans. As a general rule, the more restricted the reconfigurable model, the easier its implementation. Thus, an algorithm designer must carefully balance the power of dynamic reconfiguration with its implementability.

In this book we do not directly address hardware design details or technological advances that impact implementation. Rather, we will direct our discussion towards identifying and developing approaches to address this issue. In Chapter 3, we describe model restrictions that favor implementability. Chapters 8 and 9 present simulations between various models that allow algorithms on less implementable models to be ported to a more implementable platform. In Chapter 11, we describe implementations of the segmentable bus and of a useful restriction of the R-Mesh.

In the meanwhile, we will direct our discussion towards developing fundamental reconfiguration techniques and identifying approaches that lend themselves to a reasonable hardware implementation without getting bogged down in details of hardware design and technological constraints.

In the next chapter, we will describe the R-Mesh in detail and present many techniques to exploit its power. Chapter 3 discusses variants of the R-Mesh and provides a summary of the relative powers of various models of computation, both reconfigurable and non-reconfigurable. Subsequent chapters build on these ideas and explore particular topics in depth to reveal the broad range of applications that benefit from dynamic reconfiguration.

Problems

1.1 Consider a (non-segmentable) bus to which N processors are connected. Each processor has an input bit. If more than one processor is permitted to write (the same value) to the bus, then design a constant-time algorithm to find the OR of the input bits.

1.2 If the OR of N bits can be computed on a model $\mathcal{M}$ in T steps, then show that the same model can compute the AND of N bits in $O(T)$ steps.

1.3   How would you add N numbers on an architecture with one or more non-segmentable buses? What, if any, are the advantages and disadvantages of this architecture when compared with the segmentable bus architecture?

1.4   Let $b_0, b_1, \cdots, b_{N-1}$ be a sequence of N bits. The *prefix sums* of these bits is the sequence $s(0), s(1), \cdots, s(N-1)$, where $s(i) = \sum_{j=0}^{i} b_j$.

Adapt the algorithm for counting N bits in constant time on an $(N+1)$-row, N-column R-Mesh (Section 1.2) to compute the prefix sums of the input bits. The new algorithm must run in constant time on an $(N+1)$-row, N-column R-Mesh.

1.5   One of the problems with implementing buses with many connections (taps) is called *loading*. An effect of increased loading is a reduction in the bus clock rate. Supposing a bus can have a loading of at most L (that is, at most L connections to it), how would you construct a "virtual bus" that functions as a bus with $N \geq L$ connections? What would be the clocking rate of your virtual bus (in terms of the clocking rate of a loading-L bus)?

1.6   As with a non-segmentable bus (see Problem 1.5), detrimental effects also exist in a segmentable bus with a large number of processors (and segment switches) connected to it. Repeat Problem 1.5 for a segmentable bus. That is, assuming that at most L segment switches can be placed on a segmentable bus, construct a "virtual segmentable-bus" with $N \geq L$ segment switches on it. How fast can this segmentable bus operate?

Bibliographic Notes

Li and Stout [181], Schuster [291], Sahni [286], and Bondalapati and Prasanna [34] surveyed some of the early reconfigurable models and systems. Moshell and Rothstein [219, 285] defined the bus automaton, an extension of a cellular automaton to admit reconfigurable buses. One of the earliest reconfigurable systems, Snyder's Configurable Highly Parallel (CHiP) Computer [303] allowed dynamic reconfiguration under global control. Shu *et al.* [296, 297, 298] proposed the Gated Connection Network (GCN), a reconfigurable communication structure that is part of a larger system called the Image Understanding machine [352].

Miller *et al.* [213, 214, 215, 216] proposed the "original" reconfigurable mesh (RMESH) and basic algorithms for it; the reconfigurable mesh (R-Mesh) model adopted in this book is slightly different from that proposed by Miller *et al.* Li and Maresca [179, 180] proposed the polymorphic torus and a prototype implementation, the Yorktown Ultra Parallel Polymorphic Image Engine (YUPPIE) system. They also coined the term "connection autonomy" (the ability of each processor to independently configure connections (or switches) assigned to it); this is an important feature of reconfigurable systems. Wang *et al.* [348] proposed the processor array with a reconfigurable bus system (PARBS) and introduced the term "configurational computing" that refers to the use of a (bus) configuration to perform a computation, for example, as in Illustration 2 of Section 1.1.

Bondalapati and Prasanna [34], Mangione-Smith *et al.* [197], and Compton and Hauck [61] described reconfigurable computing from the FPGA perspective.

Ben-Asher and Schuster [21] discussed data-reduction algorithms for the one-dimensional R-Mesh. They also introduced the "bus-usage" measure to capture the use of communication links for computation. Thiruchelvan *et al.* [314], Trahan *et al.* [325], Vaidyanathan [330], Thangavel and Muthuswamy [312, 313], Bertossi and Mei [29], and El-Boghdadi *et al.* [93, 94, 96, 95], among others, studied the segmentable bus (one-dimensional R-Mesh). The technique for finding the OR of input bits is called "bus splitting" and is one of the most fundamental in reconfigurable computing; it was introduced by Miller *et al.* [213, 215, 216]. The $\Omega(\log N)$ CREW PRAM bound for the OR problem is due to Cook *et al.* [63].

The binary tree technique for semigroup operations is very well known. Dharmasena [81] provided references on using this technique in bused environments.

The use of buses to enhance fixed topologies (primarily the mesh) has a long history [81, 261, 305].

Jang and Prasanna [148], Pan *et al.* [260], Murshed [222], Murshed and Brent [224], and Trahan *et al.* [316, 320] addressed speed-efficiency trade-offs in specific reconfigurable algorithms. Vaidyanathan *et al.* [333] introduced the idea of "degree of scalability" that provides a more general framework to quantify this trade-off. Ben-Asher *et al.*

[17], Berthomé *et al.* [25], Matias and Schuster [204], and Fernández-Zepeda *et al.* [110, 111] addressed various algorithmic scalability issues of reconfigurable models. Chapter 8 describes these topics in detail.

Cormen *et al.* [65] provided an excellent introduction to sequential algorithms and their analysis. Duato *et al.* [90], JáJá [142], Kumar *et al.* [165], and Leighton [174] provided a comprehensive discussion of parallel models, architectures, and algorithms.

Chapter 2

THE RECONFIGURABLE MESH: A PRIMER

Chapter 1 introduced the idea of reconfiguration in terms of a simple segmentable-bus model and an informal description of the R-Mesh model. In this chapter we will build on these ideas and reconstruct the R-Mesh, this time more formally (Section 2.1). Although simple, the R-Mesh is general enough to capture most ideas in dynamic reconfiguration and will be the primary medium of expression for most of this book. In Section 2.2, we describe the pseudocode convention that we employ in this book. Following this, Section 2.3 will introduce several R-Mesh algorithmic techniques through examples spanning a wide range of applications. In the process we will also develop a palette of fundamental methods that other algorithms will invoke.

2.1   The Reconfigurable Mesh

Another way of viewing the segmentable bus of Section 1.1 is as follows. Consider a linear array of processors numbered $0, 1, \cdots, N - 1$ in which, for each $0 \leq i < N$, processor i is connected to processors $i \pm 1$, if they exist (see Figure 2.1). Each processor has two ports, the East and

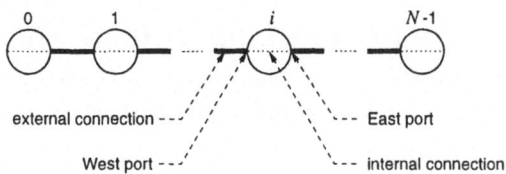

Figure 2.1.   A reconfigurable linear array.

West ports (abbreviated E and W), that connect it to its neighbors. In addition to these *external connections* between processors, each processor can internally connect its ports to form a bus that passes through the processor. Indeed, if all processors connect their E and W ports, a bus spans the entire linear array. Internally disconnecting the ports of processor i is analogous to setting switch i on the segmentable bus. As observed in Chapter 1, the model described here is very similar to the segmentable bus and is called a *one-dimensional R-Mesh* with N processors. One can view the internal connection in a processor of a one-dimensional R-Mesh as a partition[1] of the set, $\{E, W\}$, of ports of the processor. The two possible partitions here have the following meanings.

- $\{\overline{EW}\}$ indicates that the E and W ports are connected within the processor.

- $\{\overline{E}, \overline{W}\}$ indicates that the E and W ports are not connected within the processor.

In other words, the ports are connected if and only if they are in the same block of the partition.

For completeness, we state the results of Section 1.1 as the following theorems.

THEOREM 2.1 *The problem of applying an associative operation to N inputs can be solved on a one-dimensional R-Mesh with N processors in $O(\log N)$ time. Initially, each processor holds one input.*

Since finding the AND of N bits reduces to the OR problem (see Problem 1.2), we have the following theorem.

THEOREM 2.2 *The problem of finding the AND or OR of N bits can be solved on a one-dimensional R-Mesh with N processors in $O(1)$ time. Initially, each processor holds one input bit.*

Remark: Section 2.3.3 describes a technique called "neighbor localization," that generalizes the bus-splitting method used for OR.

2.1.1   The (Two-Dimensional) R-Mesh

The one-dimensional R-Mesh described above readily extends to two dimensions, where a two-dimensional mesh replaces the underlying linear

---

[1]A *partition* of a set S is a collection $\{B_1, B_2, \cdots, B_x\}$ of pairwise-disjoint, non-empty sets, whose union is the set S itself (see also Footnote 3, page 196). The sets $B_1, B_2, \cdots, B_x$ are *blocks* of the partition. We will indicate a block by grouping all its elements under a line. For example, $\{\overline{ab}, \overline{c}, \overline{def}\}$ denotes a partition with blocks $\{a, b\}$, $\{c\}$, and $\{d, e, f\}$.

array of the one-dimensional R-Mesh. An $R \times C$ *2-dimensional recon-figurable mesh* (or simply an $R \times C$ *R-Mesh*) consists of RC processors arranged in R rows and C columns as an $R \times C$ two-dimensional mesh. Figure 2.2 shows the structure of a 3×5 R-Mesh. We will usually number rows (resp., columns) $0, 1, \cdots, R-1$ (resp., $0, 1, \cdots, C-1$) with row 0 at the top (resp., column 0 at the left). For $0 \leq i < R$ and $0 \leq j < C$, call the processor in row i and column j as processor (i, j). Subsequently in this book, we will use more compact notation such as $p_{i,j}$ or $\pi_{i,j}$ to denote processor (i, j).

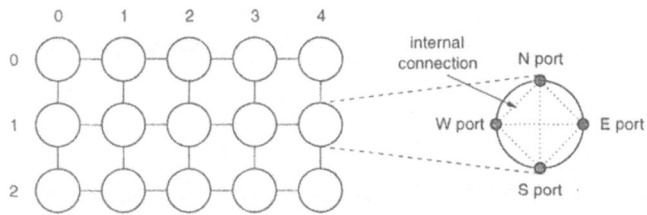

Figure 2.2. Structure of a 3×5 R-Mesh.

Each processor has four ports, N, S, E, and W, through which it connects to processors (if any) to its North, South, East, and West. Besides these *external connections*, each processor can also establish *internal connections* among its ports that correspond to partitions of the set, $\{N, S, E, W\}$, of ports. Figure 2.3 shows the 15 possible port partitions along with the corresponding internal connections. A processor can change its internal connections at each step.

The external and internal connections together connect processor ports by *buses*. The buses formed by a given set of port partitions of processors of the R-Mesh comprise a *bus configuration* of the R-Mesh. Figure 2.4(a) shows a bus configuration of a 3×5 R-Mesh with one of the buses shown in bold. We say that a port (or processor) through which a bus passes is *incident* on that bus or that the bus *traverses* the port (or processor). Any port that is incident on a bus can read from and write to that bus. For the most part we will permit at most one port to write to a bus at a time, although several ports may read from it simultaneously. Such a rule is called the Concurrent Read, Exclusive Write (CREW) rule. In Chapter 3, we introduce R-Meshes that permit concurrent writes as well.

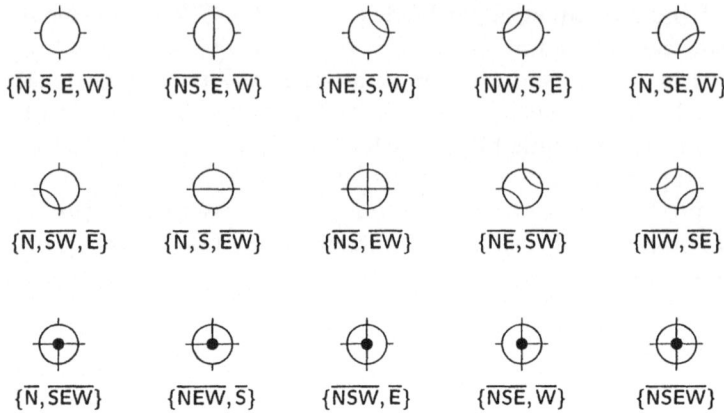

$\{\overline{N}, \overline{S}, \overline{E}, \overline{W}\}$ $\{\overline{NS}, \overline{E}, \overline{W}\}$ $\{\overline{NE}, \overline{S}, \overline{W}\}$ $\{\overline{NW}, \overline{S}, \overline{E}\}$ $\{\overline{N}, \overline{SE}, \overline{W}\}$

$\{\overline{N}, \overline{SW}, \overline{E}\}$ $\{\overline{N}, \overline{S}, \overline{EW}\}$ $\{\overline{NS}, \overline{EW}\}$ $\{\overline{NE}, \overline{SW}\}$ $\{\overline{NW}, \overline{SE}\}$

$\{\overline{N}, \overline{SEW}\}$ $\{\overline{NEW}, \overline{S}\}$ $\{\overline{NSW}, \overline{E}\}$ $\{\overline{NSE}, \overline{W}\}$ $\{\overline{NSEW}\}$

Figure 2.3. Port partitions of an R-Mesh.

Regardless of the write rule assumed, write(s) to a bus result(s) in a *bus value*[2] that all ports incident on the bus may read.

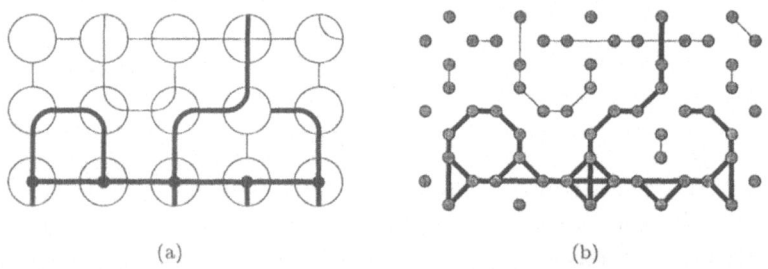

(a)   (b)

Figure 2.4. A bus configuration and its graph for a 3 × 5 R-Mesh. A bus of the configuration and the corresponding component of the graph are shown in bold.

A *configuration graph*, whose vertices are ports of the R-Mesh, offers a convenient tool to capture the structure of a bus configuration. An edge connects two vertices (ports) in the graph if an external connec-

---

[2] For the CREW rule, the value written is the bus value. Conflict resolution rules explained in Section 3.1.3 define the bus value in case of concurrent writes.

tion between neighboring processors connects these ports or an internal connection within a processor connects the ports. A bus corresponds to a connected component[3] of the configuration graph. Figure 2.4(b) shows the graph for the configuration in Figure 2.4(a). (Although the term "bus" denotes the collection of all ports in a connected component of the configuration graph, we will occasionally use the term in a more intuitive sense to denote a subset of ports in a component. For instance, we may refer to a "row bus" as one that spans an entire row of the R-Mesh, even though other parts of the same bus traverse processors outside the row. As an example, one could say that a row bus connects the processors in the bottom row of the R-Mesh of Figure 2.4(a).) Since each processor can internally partition its ports independently in one of 15 ways, the R-Mesh can create a large variety of bus configurations, connecting ports in numerous ways (see Problem 2.2). Moreover, the bus configuration can change at each step of the computation.

Each processor of the R-Mesh has its own local memory (there is no shared memory). Processors operate synchronously in a single instruction, multiple data (SIMD) environment, where each active processor executes the same instruction, usually on different data. Processors communicate with each other through the reconfigurable bus system described above. The following phases constitute a *step* of the R-Mesh.

1. Partitioning: A processor internally connects its ports in one of the 15 ways shown in Figure 2.3. The SIMD mode of operation does not restrict processors to assume the same internal port partition. This ability of processors to configure independently is called *connection autonomy*.

2. Communication: A processor writes to and reads from (possibly all) its ports. A processor may write and not read, or vice versa. A processor could write to or read from a subset of its ports. When both reads and writes occur on a bus during the same step, the value read (if any) is the consequence of a value written during the same step.

3. Computation: The processor performs an operation on local data. This local data could be from the local memory or values read in the Communication phase. The permitted operations are the commonly used arithmetic and logical operations.

---

[3]A *connected component* $\mathcal{G}'$ of a graph $\mathcal{G}$ is a maximally connected subgraph of $\mathcal{G}$. That is, $\mathcal{G}'$ is a connected subgraph of $\mathcal{G}$ and no supergraph of $\mathcal{G}'$ is a connected subgraph of $\mathcal{G}$.

At any given step, an R-Mesh processor could participate in one or more of the above phases, or simply idle. Assume each step to run in constant time. (The Partitioning phase involves selecting one of 15 port partitions and the Computation phase performs a single operation.) Crucial to running the Communication phase in constant time is the assumption that information placed on a bus is available in constant time to all ports incident on that bus; that is, the "bus delay" is a constant. This assumption is called the *unit-cost* measure of bus delay. Under this measure, the delay of a bus is independent of the number of processors it traverses. We will assume this unit-cost measure of bus delay for most of this book, as it permits us to focus on the core techniques of dynamic reconfiguration, without getting caught up in details of bus delay. Section 11.5 discusses other bus-delay models.

The idea of a (two-dimensional) R-Mesh naturally extends to higher dimensions as well. We discuss this in Chapter 3.

2.2   Expressing R-Mesh Algorithms

Before we proceed, a few words are due about the pseudocode convention for R-Mesh algorithms. Though most of the constructs used are standard, some points require elaboration. As an illustration, consider the following pseudocode for a non-recursive version of the binary tree algorithm for adding N inputs (see Illustration 1 of Section 1.1).

Algorithm 2.1   (Non-Recursive Binary Tree Addition)

Model: An N-processor, one-dimensional R-Mesh ($N = 2^n$ for integer n).

Input: For $0 \leq i < N$, processor i holds input a_i.

Output: Processor 0 holds $a_0 + a_1 + \cdots + a_{N-1}$ in variable $value(0)$.

begin

1. $value(i) \longleftarrow a_i$ /* variable $value(i)$ is local to processor i */

2. **for** $\ell \longleftarrow 0$ **to** $n - 1$ **do**

3.   **if** i is divisible by 2^ℓ **then**
          processor i configures as $\{\overline{\mathsf{E}}, \overline{\mathsf{W}}\}$

4.   **else** processor i configures as $\{\overline{\mathsf{EW}}\}$

5.   **if** i is divisible by 2^ℓ **then**

6.   **if** bit ℓ of i is 1 **then**
             processor i writes $value(i)$ on its W port
             /* bits are numbered $0, 1, \cdots, n - 1$, with 0 as the lsb */

7.   **else** processor i reads from its E port into $new\_value(i)$

8. $value(i) \longleftarrow value(i) + new\_value(i)$

        end_if_else

      end_if

    end_for

end

An algorithm will usually specify in a preamble the R-Mesh model used, input(s) and outputs(s), and their location within the R-Mesh. Comments are enclosed within "/*" and "*/" (see line 1). Variables (such as $value(i)$) that are local to a processor are usually indexed by the processor's index (i in this case).

All "enabled" processors execute a statement. Conditional statements (**if** and **if-then-else**) divide the algorithm into several (possibly nested) *conditional environments*. Each conditional environment (except possibly the outermost one) corresponds to a conditional statement. For example, line 3 constitutes a conditional environment with condition "i is divisible by 2^ℓ," whereas the conditional environment of line 7 has condition "bit ℓ of i is 0." The *enabling condition* for an environment $\mathcal{E}$ is the conjunction of conditions of all environments enclosing $\mathcal{E}$ (including itself). As an example, the enabling condition for line 7 is "(i is divisible by 2^ℓ) and (bit ℓ of i is 0)."

All processors satisfying the enabling condition of an environment execute the statements in that environment. For example, in the **if** statement of line 3, processor i is enabled if and only if i is divisible by 2^ℓ. The outermost environment (outside the scope of all conditional statements) has no enabling condition. Therefore, all N processors are enabled in the assignment of line 1.

In general, the **if** and **else** parts of each **if-then-else** statement execute in parallel. For instance in lines 3–4, the processors participate (simultaneously) in a partitioning phase. In lines 6–7, where the enabled processors carry out the communication phase, processors of line 7 read the values written by processors of line 6. We also assume that if no processor writes to a bus, then reading from that bus into a variable does not alter the contents of that variable.

2.3   Fundamental Algorithmic Techniques

In this section we present R-Mesh algorithms for problems on a wide array of topics including graphs, arithmetic, and sorting. In the process, we will identify several techniques useful for algorithm design on reconfigurable models and develop a tool box of fundamental procedures that subsequent chapters will invoke.

Section 2.3.1 deals with data movement techniques for the R-Mesh. These techniques exploit the communication flexibility of the R-Mesh and are among the most fundamental for algorithm design. In Section 2.3.2, we introduce methods for adding a set of input bits. Besides being an important member of the tool box, these methods serve to underscore the idea of "efficiency acceleration," a technique that exploits lopsided time-efficiency tradeoffs to improve algorithm efficiency without compromising speed. Section 2.3.3 uses chain sorting (whose output is a list of elements in sorted order) to introduce a rudimentary technique called "neighbor localization." Sections 2.3.4–2.3.6 use maximum finding, list ranking, and s-t connectivity to illustrate how an R-Mesh can embed various aspects of graphs. Section 2.3.7 presents an algorithm for adding N k-bit integers in constant time on the R-Mesh. In the process we develop several new ideas, including the value of using various data representations in R-Mesh algorithms. Most importantly, we introduce a technique called "function decomposition" that connects several "small R-Mesh algorithms" in tandem to solve a larger problem.

The techniques introduced in Sections 2.3.1–2.3.7 range from those that purely exploit the power of reconfiguration to general methods applicable to any model of parallel computation but that hold particular import for reconfigurable models. Other techniques that exploit the communication flexibility of the R-Mesh (and can be replicated on a network with a sufficiently dense topology) occupy a middle ground. For example, neighbor localization (Section 2.3.3), graph embedding (Sections 2.3.5 and 2.3.6), and function decomposition (Section 2.3.7) use the ability of the R-Mesh to assume a configuration suited to the particular problem instance (as in the solution to the OR problem). On the other hand, techniques for data movement (Section 2.3.1) and sub-R-Mesh generation (Section 2.3.4) exploit the communication flexibility of the R-Mesh. Efficiency acceleration (Section 2.3.2) and data representations (Section 2.3.7) are ideas applicable to all models, but carry special significance for reconfigurable models.

2.3.1   Data Movement

As in conventional interconnection topologies, R-Mesh data movement techniques hold a position of prime importance in algorithm design. In this section we describe broadcasting and permutation routing, two of the most commonly encountered data movement problems.

Broadcasting. Processors of the R-Mesh make autonomous decisions based on local data. Capturing the global picture often necessitates broadcasts[4] (on multiple buses) from a small set of processors to other processors. Indeed, the first step of many algorithms involves such a broadcast. The key to broadcasting on the R-Mesh is the fact that a bus is a constant-delay medium for sending a piece of information to all ports incident on the bus. By configuring buses suited to the specific needs of the problem, a constant number of steps can accommodate several broadcasting scenarios. The large number of bus configurations of an R-Mesh reflects the variety of constant-time broadcasts possible.

A common communication pattern is broadcasting along columns or rows of an R-Mesh. Configuring processors as $\{\overline{NS}, \overline{E}, \overline{W}\}$ sets up a bus spanning each column, as illustrated in Figure 2.5(a). Analogously, configuring as $\{\overline{N}, \overline{S}, \overline{EW}\}$ constructs row buses. Figure 2.5(b) shows a bus configuration for broadcasting along diagonals.

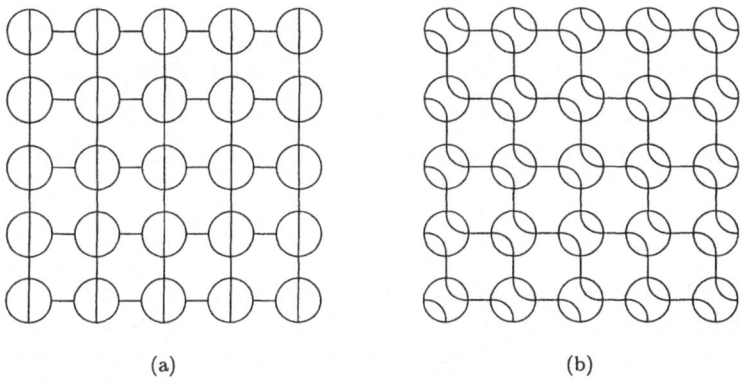

(a)   (b)

Figure 2.5.   Bus configuration for column and diagonal broadcast on a 5 × 5 R-Mesh.

Permutation Routing. Let $P = \{p_0, p_1, \cdots, p_{N-1}\}$ denote a set of processors with each processor p_i (where $0 \leq i < N$) holding some

---

[4]The term *multicasting* is often used to convey the idea of sending information to disjoint sets of processors. In the setting of models with reconfigurable buses, the term broadcasting is more common, conveying the idea of sending the same information to all processors on a bus.

data d_i. Let $\pi : \{0, 1, \cdots, N-1\} \longrightarrow \{0, 1, \cdots, N-1\}$ be a bijection[5].
Permutation routing[6] with respect to π requires each processor p_i to send
its data d_i to processor $p_{\pi(i)}$. If the set P consists of the processors in
a row of an $N \times N$ R-Mesh, then the R-Mesh can perform permutation
routing in constant time. For convenience, let π be a permutation on
the set $\{0, 1, \cdots, N-1\}$ of column indices. For $0 \le j < N$, let processor
$(0, j)$ hold data d_j and let the object be to send d_j to processor $(0, \pi(j))$.
The procedure consists of two data movement steps on columns, and one
row broadcast. Algorithm 2.2 provides details.

Algorithm 2.2   (Permutation Routing)

Model: An $N \times N$ R-Mesh.

Input: Let $\pi : \{0, 1, \cdots, N-1\} \longrightarrow \{0, 1, \cdots, N-1\}$ be a bijection.
   For $0 \le j < N$, processor $(0, j)$ holds $\pi(j)$ and data $d(j)$.

Output: For $0 \le j < N$, processor $(0, \pi(j))$ holds $d(j)$.

begin

1. Processor $(0, j)$ uses column j to send $d(j)$ and $\pi(j)$ to processor (j, j).

2. Processor (j, j) broadcasts $d(j)$ and $\pi(j)$ to all processors on row j.

3. Processor $(j, \pi(j))$ uses column $\pi(j)$ to send $d(j)$ to processor $(0, \pi(j))$.

end

Since Step 2 sends the value of $\pi(j)$ along with d_j, a processor (j, k) of
row j can ascertain whether $k = \pi(j)$. This is necessary to determine the
source of the broadcast in Step 3. Observe that since π is a bijection, no
two processors send their data to the same destination. This guarantees
that the broadcasts are without concurrent writes. Figure 2.6 illustrates
the algorithm.

THEOREM 2.3 *The permutation routing of N elements in a row of an
$N \times N$ R-Mesh can be performed in $O(1)$ time.*

Problems 2.6–2.13 at the end of this chapter address other routing
scenarios.

---

[5]A function $f : A \longrightarrow B$ is a *bijection* if and only if each $a \in A$ corresponds to a unique
$f(a) \in B$ and each $b \in B$ corresponds to a unique $a \in A$ such that $b = f(a)$.
[6]The term *one-to-one communication* also denotes the problem we describe as permutation
routing.

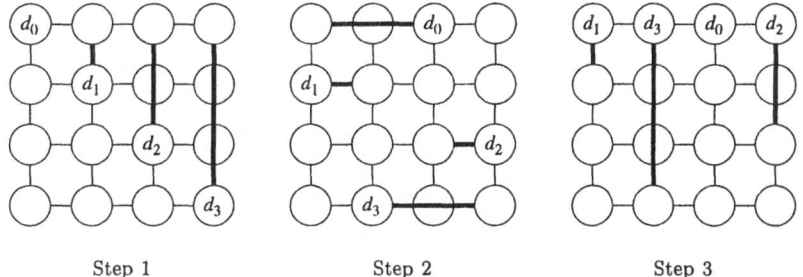

Step 1 Step 2 Step 3

Figure 2.6. An illustration of permutation routing using Algorithm 2.2 with $\pi(0) = 2, \pi(1) = 0, \pi(2) = 3, \pi(3) = 1$; data paths are shown in bold. For clarity, the figure shows the broadcast of Step 2 as a communication between processors (j, j) and $(j, \pi(j))$.

2.3.2 Efficiency Acceleration—Adding Bits

This section examines several variations on the problem of adding a set of bits. Besides being fundamental in nature with numerous applications, these problems also serve to highlight the power of reconfiguration and an important technique called efficiency acceleration. They also provide a first peek at a powerful R-Mesh algorithmic paradigm called function decomposition that Section 2.3.7 describes in detail.

Basic Counting. Consider the problem of adding N input bits, $b_0, b_1, \cdots, b_{N-1}$. One way to solve this problem is to start at the top of a flight of stairs, moving down one step for each 1 encountered in the input; if the xth step from the top is the final step reached, then the answer is x. With row i representing the ith step, an $(N + 1) \times N$ R-Mesh can implement this approach as Figure 2.7 illustrates and as Section 1.2 sketched earlier. Each input bit corresponds to a column of the R-Mesh and each row represents a possible answer to the problem. The idea is to set up a bus that starts from row 0 and moves to the next row for each 1 in the input. Specifically, the bus originating at the W port of processor $(0, 0)$ reaches the E port of processor $(x, N - 1)$, for some $0 \leq x \leq N$, if and only if the input contains x 1's. A signal written by processor $(0, 0)$ on this bus indicates the sum to processor $(x, N - 1)$. Algorithm 2.3 provides detailed pseudocode.

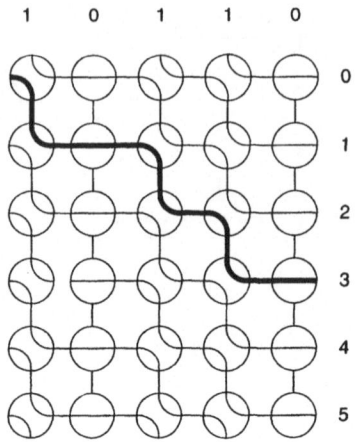

Figure 2.7.   Using a 6×5 R-Mesh to add five input bits. The bus shown in bold sets up a path from the W port of processor $(0,0)$ to the E port of processor $(3,4)$ as there are three 1's in the input.

Algorithm 2.3   (Counting Bits)

Model: An $(N+1) \times N$ R-Mesh.
Input: For $0 \le j < N$, processor $(0,j)$ holds bit b_j.
Output: For $0 \le i \le N$, processor $(i, N-1)$ sets a flag if and only if $i = b_0 + b_1 + \cdots + b_{N-1}$.

begin

1. Processor $(0,j)$ broadcasts b_j to all processors in column j.

2. **if** $b_j = 1$ **then**
       processor (i,j) configures $\{\overline{\text{NE}}, \overline{\text{SW}}\}$ /* skip to next row */
   else processor (i,j) configures $\{\overline{\text{N}}, \overline{\text{S}}, \overline{\text{EW}}\}$ /* stay in same row */

3. Processor $(0,0)$ sends a signal on its W port and processor $(i, N-1)$ reads from its E port.

4. **if** processor $(i, N-1)$ detects the signal in Step 3 **then**
       it sets a flag to indicate that $i = b_0 + b_1 + \cdots + b_{N-1}$.

end

Step 1 uses the configuration of Figure 2.5(a). Step 2 configures the bus to step down by one row for each 1 bit in the input. Observe that, if the answer is x, then in Step 3, the only processor of the last column that receives the signal in its E port is processor $(x, N-1)$. Since each step runs in constant time, the entire algorithm runs in constant time.

LEMMA 2.4 *Addition of N bits can be performed on an $(N+1) \times N$ R-Mesh in $O(1)$ time. Initially, each processor of row 0 holds an input bit.*

Modulo Addition of Bits. In Algorithm 2.3, the bus originating at the W port of processor $(0,0)$ moves to the next row for each 1 in the input. Let $m > 1$ be an integer. If, in Algorithm 2.3, each bus in row $m-1$ routes to row 0 on encountering a 1, instead of row m, then the R-Mesh can perform modulo m addition of bits. To implement this strategy on the R-Mesh, we will use $2N$ columns and an additional row to allow the bus to fold back from row $m-1$ to row 0. Figure 2.8 illustrates this method for a small example. Its generalization is left as an exercise (Problem 2.18).

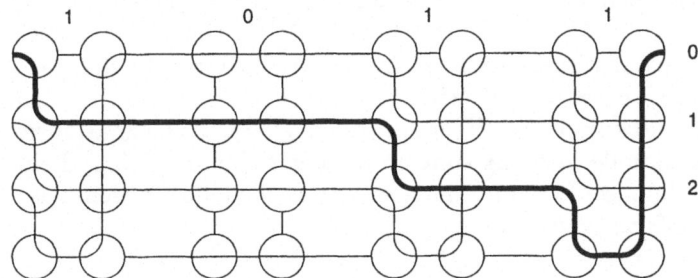

Figure 2.8. Modulo-3 addition of input bits 1,0,1,1 on a 4 × 8 R-Mesh. Columns have been paired and separated in correspondence with the inputs. The bus carrying the signal is shown in bold. Notice how the last 1 causes the bus to fold back and exit at the E port of row 0.

LEMMA 2.5 *For any $m > 1$, the modulo m addition of N bits can be performed on an $(m+1) \times 2N$ R-Mesh in $O(1)$ time. Initially, each even-indexed processor of row 0 holds an input bit.*

Since the exclusive OR (or parity) of N bits is their modulo 2 sum, we have the following result.

COROLLARY 2.6 *The exclusive OR of N bits can be computed on a $3 \times N$ R-Mesh in $O(1)$ time. Initially, each processor of row 0 holds an input bit.*

Proof: The only point requiring explanation is the use of N (rather than $2N$) columns. In one step, each adjacent pair of processors computes the exclusive OR of their inputs, leaving the results in even numbered processors and reducing the number of inputs to $\frac{N}{2}$.   ∎

Remark: A CRCW PRAM with polynomially bounded number of processors requires $\Omega\left(\frac{\log N}{\log \log N}\right)$ time to compute the exclusive OR of N bits. Corollary 2.6 shows an instance where the R-Mesh proves to be "more powerful" than a CRCW PRAM.

Prefix Sums of Bits. For $0 \leq i < N$, the ith *prefix sum* of bits $b_0, b_1, \cdots, b_{N-1}$ is $s(i) = b_0 + b_1 + \cdots + b_i$. For example, if $\langle b_0, b_1, b_2, b_3, b_4 \rangle = \langle 0, 1, 1, 0, 1 \rangle$ then $\langle s(0), s(1), s(2), s(3), s(4) \rangle = \langle 0, 1, 2, 2, 3 \rangle$. For integer $m > 1$, the ith *modulo m prefix sum* of bits $b_0, b_1, \cdots, b_{N-1}$ is $s_m(i) = (s(i)) \pmod{m}$. For the above example, $\langle s_3(0), s_3(1), s_3(2), s_3(3), s_3(4) \rangle = \langle 0, 1, 2, 2, 0 \rangle$. Algorithms presented so far in this section generalize to prefix sums of bits as well as simply adding bits. In Step 3 of Algorithm 2.3, processor (i, j) (for any $0 \leq j < N$) receives the signal at its E port if and only if the jth prefix sum $s(j) = i$. Analogous observations apply to modulo m prefix sums in the algorithm implied by Lemma 2.5. For completeness, we state these results as the following lemmas, leaving their proofs as exercises.

LEMMA 2.7 *The prefix sums of N bits can be computed on an $(N+1) \times N$ R-Mesh in $O(1)$ time. Initially, each processor of row 0 holds an input bit.*

LEMMA 2.8 *For any $m > 1$, the modulo m prefix sums of N bits can be computed on an $(m+1) \times 2N$ R-Mesh in $O(1)$ time. Initially, each even-indexed processor of row 0 holds an input bit.*

We now extend the result of Lemma 2.7 by establishing that for any $2 \leq m \leq N$, an $(m+1) \times 2N$ R-Mesh can find the prefix sums of N bits in $O\left(\frac{\log N}{\log m}\right)$ time. We first introduce some definitions. Recall that $s(i)$ and $s_m(i)$ denote the ith prefix sum and i^{th} modulo m prefix sum, respectively. For $0 \le i < N$, define $f_m(i)$ and $p_m(i)$ as follows:

$$f_m(i) \;=\; \begin{cases} 1, & \text{if } b_i = 1 \text{ and } s_m(i) = 0 \\ 0, & \text{otherwise} \end{cases} \;=\; \begin{cases} \text{flag indicating whether} \\ b_i \text{ caused the modulo} \\ m \text{ prefix sum to go} \\ \text{from } m - 1 \text{ to } 0, \end{cases}$$

$$p_m(i) \;=\; f_m(0) + f_m(1) + \cdots + f_m(i) \;=\; i^{\text{th}} \text{ prefix sum of flags } f_m.$$

Figure 2.9 illustrates these quantities.

i	0	1	2	3	4	5	6	7	8
b_i	0	1	0	1	1	0	1	1	1
$s(i)$	0	1	1	2	3	3	4	5	6
$s_2(i)$	0	1	1	0	1	1	0	1	0
$f_2(i)$	0	0	0	1	0	0	1	0	1
$p_2(i)$	0	0	0	1	1	1	2	2	3
$s_3(i)$	0	1	1	2	0	0	1	2	0
$f_3(i)$	0	0	0	0	1	0	0	0	1
$p_3(i)$	0	0	0	0	1	1	1	1	2
$s_4(i)$	0	1	1	2	3	3	0	1	2
$f_4(i)$	0	0	0	0	0	0	1	0	0
$p_4(i)$	0	0	0	0	0	0	1	1	1

Figure 2.9. Examples of s_m, f_m, and p_m for $m = 2, 3, 4$.

LEMMA 2.9 *For* $0 \le i < N,$ $\quad s(i) = p_m(i) \cdot m + s_m(i).$

Proof: Let $s(i) = qm + r$, where $q \ge 0$ and $0 \le r < m$ are integers. This implies that $s_m(i) = (s(i))(\text{mod } m) = r$. Since the input consists of bits, there must be $s(i)$ indices j (where $0 \le j < i$) such that $b_j = 1$. After each set of m 1's, f_m assumes a value of 1; that is, there are $\left\lfloor \frac{s(i)}{m} \right\rfloor = q$ values of j (again with $0 \le j < i$) such that $f_m(j) = 1$. This, in turn, implies that $p_m(i) = q = \left\lfloor \frac{s(i)}{m} \right\rfloor$. Therefore, $s(i) = qm + r = p_m(i) \cdot m + s_m(i)$. ∎

For any $1 < m < N$, Lemma 2.9 decomposes the prefix sums of N bits into terms that an $(m + 1) \times 2N$ R-Mesh can compute. First determine the modulo m prefix sums s_m using Lemma 2.8. With s_m, the processors can easily compute flags f_m. Next, recursively determine p_m, the prefix sums of the flags f_m. Compute the final prefix sums using Lemma 2.9. Algorithm 2.4 provides details.

Algorithm 2.4   (Prefix Sums of Bits)

Model: An $(m+1) \times 2N$ R-Mesh, where $1 < m < N$.

Input: For $0 \le j < N$, processor $(0, 2j)$ holds bit b_j.

Output: For $0 \le j < N$, processor $(0, 2j)$ holds the jth prefix sum $s(j) = b_0 + b_1 + \cdots + b_j$.

begin

if there is no 1 among $b_0, b_1, \cdots, b_{N-1}$ **then**
      $s(i) \longleftarrow 0$; return   /* base case for recursion */

else

1. For $0 \le j < N$, determine the modulo m prefix sums $s_m(j) = (b_0 + b_1 + \cdots + b_j)(\mathrm{mod}\ m)$. Processor $(0, 2j)$ holds $s_m(j)$.

2. Processor $(0, 2j)$ sets flag $f_m(j)$ to 1 iff $b_j = 1$ and $s_m(j) = 0$.

3. Recursively compute $p_m(j) = f_m(0) + f_m(1) + \cdots + f_m(j)$, the prefix sums of the flags, for each $0 \le j < N$. Processor $(0, 2j)$ holds $p_m(j)$.

4. Processor $(0, 2j)$ assigns $s(j) \longleftarrow p_m(j) \cdot m + s_m(j)$

end_if_else

end

Determining if there is a 1 among $b_0, b_1, \cdots, b_{N-1}$ amounts to finding the OR of N bits and can be done in constant time (Theorem 2.2). Step 1 uses the constant time algorithm of Lemma 2.8. Clearly Steps 2 and 4 run in constant time. Therefore, the recursion depth in Step 3 determines the time required for the algorithm.

For $0 \le k \le N$, let $T(k)$ denote the time needed for Algorithm 2.4 to compute the prefix sums of N bits, at most k of which are 1's. Clearly, $T(0) = 1$. For constant c and $k > 0$, we have the following recurrence.

$$T(k) = T\left(\left\lfloor \frac{k}{m} \right\rfloor\right) + c \qquad\qquad (2.1)$$

Solving this recurrence gives $T(k) = O\left(\frac{\log k}{\log m}\right)$. Since the N input bits can each be 1, the time for the algorithm is $T(N) = O\left(\frac{\log N}{\log m}\right)$.

One can improve the algorithms of Lemmas 2.5 and 2.8 to run in constant time on an $(m+1) \times N$ R-Mesh (see Problem 2.19). (A constant reduction in R-Mesh size is not possible in general without affecting the time complexity (see Section 1.3 and Chapter 8).) Minor changes to Algorithm 2.4 give the following result.

THEOREM 2.10 *For $1 < m < N$, the prefix sums of N bits can be computed on an $m \times N$ R-Mesh in $O\left(\frac{\log N}{\log m}\right)$ time. Initially, each processor of row 0 holds an input bit.*

Efficiency Acceleration. Many R-Mesh algorithms trade efficiency for running time. Often the cost of a small decrease in time is a disproportionately large increase in the size of the R-Mesh. In these situations, a small increase in time buys a much larger savings in the R-Mesh size. Here we examine situations where this saving in R-Mesh size comes without any increase in the time complexity of the algorithm. Chapter 8 describes other trade-offs between speed and processor requirements of R-Mesh algorithms. We now illustrate this efficiency acceleration technique using Theorem 2.10.

Notice that a linear decrease in m in Algorithm 2.4 incurs a time cost that is only logarithmic in m. Therefore an increase in time by a constant factor buys more than a constant decrease in size. Take the $(N+1) \times N$ R-Mesh of Algorithm 2.3 as a baseline. Setting $m = N^{\epsilon}$ for an arbitrarily small constant $\epsilon > 0$ gives a running time of $O\left(\frac{\log N}{\log m}\right) = O\left(\frac{1}{\epsilon}\right)$ for Algorithm 2.4. This time is a constant while the R-Mesh size reduces by a polynomial factor to $N^{\epsilon} \times N$.

COROLLARY 2.11 *For any constant $\epsilon > 0$, the prefix sums of N bits can be computed on an $N^{\epsilon} \times N$ R-Mesh in $O(1)$ time. Initially, each processor of row 0 holds an input bit.*

2.3.3   Neighbor Localization—Chain Sorting

This section generalizes the bus splitting technique of Illustration 2 (Section 1.1) to find the OR of N bits. This generalization, called *neighbor localization*, is fundamental to dynamic reconfiguration and has numerous applications. This section illustrates neighbor localization via one such application, chain sorting.

Neighbor Localization. Given a one-dimensional R-Mesh with each processor flagged as active or inactive, neighbor localization generates a list of active processors in the order of their position in the one-dimensional array. Consider a one-dimensional R-Mesh with N processors indexed $0, 1, \cdots, N-1$. Let processor i (where $0 \leq i < N$) hold a flag $f(i)$. If $f(i) = 1$, then processor i is termed active; otherwise, the processor is inactive. For $0 \leq i < j < N$, processor j is the *neighbor* of processor i if and only if $f(i) = f(j) = 1$ and for any index k such that $i < k < j$, flag $f(k) = 0$. That is, processor j is the nearest active processor after active processor i. It is possible for a processor to not have a neighbor. (Though we do not define neighbors for inactive processors here, it is easy to do so meaningfully as in Problem 2.24.) *Neighbor localization* determines the neighbor of each active processor i (for $0 \leq i < N$). Figure 2.10 illustrates these ideas.

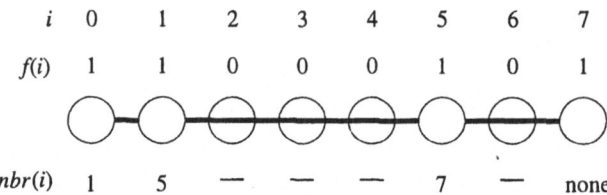

Figure 2.10. A neighbor localization example with the bus structure used for the solution. The last active processor has no neighbor. The neighbor is undefined for processors for which $f(i) = 0$; a "—" indicates this.

The method used to solve the neighbor localization problem is that of Illustration 2 (Section 1.1) to find the OR of N bits. The idea is to establish a bus between an active processor and its neighbor by fusing ports of all inactive processors between them. Figure 2.10 illustrates these buses for a small example and Algorithm 2.5 provides details.

Algorithm 2.5   (Neighbor Localization)

Model: An N-processor, one-dimensional R-Mesh.

Input: For $0 \leq i < N$, processor i holds a flag $f(i)$.

Output: For $0 \leq i < N$ and if $f(i) = 1$, then processor i holds a pointer $nbr(i)$ to its neighbor, if any. If $f(i) = 0$ or if processor i has no neighbor, then $nbr(i) = $ NIL.

begin

1. $nbr(i) \longleftarrow$ NIL

2. **if** $f(i) = 1$ **then**
   processor i configures $\{\overline{\mathsf{E}}, \overline{\mathsf{W}}\}$
   else processor i configures $\{\overline{\mathsf{EW}}\}$

3. **if** $f(i) = 1$ **then**
   processor i writes i to W port and reads from E port into $nbr(i)$

   /* Recall the assumption that reading from a bus on which no value
   has been written does not change $nbr(i)$ */

end

THEOREM 2.12 *Neighbor localization can be performed on a one-dimensional R-Mesh in $O(1)$ time.*

We have defined neighbor localization to underscore the basic theme of the technique. Most invocations of the technique in later chapters will use minor variations of the definition used in this section. Indeed, in the chain sorting algorithm presented later in this section, we require neighbor localization to identify the head of the list. Though this information is not readily available from Algorithm 2.5, the R-Mesh can easily derive it by reversing the list and identifying the only active processor without a neighbor. Also observe that Algorithm 2.5 does not use processor indices (except as data). Therefore, neighbor localization will run on any "oriented, acyclic, linear bus" where a processor can distinguish its "left" from its "right" (see Problem 2.25). Note also that the data communicated in Step 3 of Algorithm 2.5 need not be confined to processor indices. Problem 2.24 captures some such common variations of neighbor localization.

We now illustrate the use of neighbor localization in an algorithm to construct a list of input elements in sorted order.

Chain Sorting. Let $a_0, a_1, \cdots, a_{N-1}$ be N elements from a totally ordered set. The object of *chain sorting* is to string these elements in increasing (or decreasing) order in a list. The standard sorting problem outputs the information as an array of elements in the sorted order. A chain sorted list is a step shy of a sorted array: ranking a chain sorted list and relocating its elements produces a sorted array. In this section, we design an algorithm to chain sort N b-bit numbers (where $1 \leq b \leq \log N$) on a $2^b \times N$ R-Mesh. Note that each b-bit input takes a value from the set $\{0, 1, \cdots, 2^b - 1\}$. The algorithm has three stages (see Figure 2.11).

- The first stage creates a (possibly empty) list L_i for each value $0 \leq i < 2^b$. List L_i strings together all input elements (if any) of value i in the order of their indices. This guarantees a stable[7] chain sorting algorithm.

- Let $V \subseteq \{0, 1, \cdots, 2^b - 1\}$ be the set of values that appear in the inputs. The second stage constructs a list L of elements of V in ascending order.

- The third stage concatenates the lists L_i (for $i \in V$) in the order specified by L. (Note that if $i \notin V$, then L_i is empty). This concatenated list strings all the input elements in the stably sorted order.

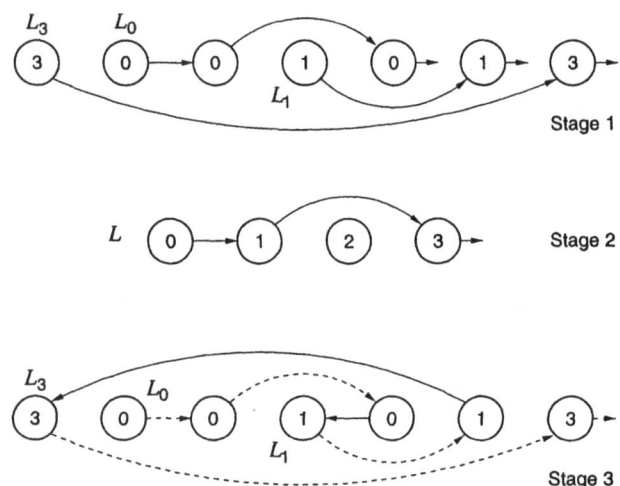

Figure 2.11. An illustration of the chain sorting algorithm with $N = 7$ and $b = 2$.

The key to the first two stages is neighbor localization. The chain sorting algorithm assumes the neighbor localization algorithm to output not just a list of neighbors, but also to flag the first element of this list; as noted in the paragraph following Theorem 2.12, this assumption is without loss of generality. Algorithm 2.6 provides details of chain sorting

---

[7] A sorting algorithm is said to be *stable* if it does not alter the relative ordering of equal-valued inputs. That is, if $a_i = a_j$ and $i < j$, then a_i appears before a_j in the final output. Stability is important in extending sorting algorithms for small-sized inputs to work for larger-sized inputs.

on the R-Mesh. In this algorithm we say that a pointer points to the "next" element of a list to mean that it points to the next element if one exists; otherwise, the pointer holds a distinguished value (such as NIL) indicating the end of the list.

Algorithm 2.6 (Chain Sorting)

Model: A $2^b \times N$ R-Mesh.

Input: For $0 \leq j < N$, processor $(0, j)$ holds a b-bit integer a_j, where $0 < b \leq \log N$.

Output: For $0 \leq j < N$, processor $(0, j)$ holds a pointer $next(j)$ linking element a_j to $a_{next(j)}$. These pointers form a list of the inputs in stably sorted order.

begin

/* In the following pseudocode, for simplicity we do not discuss boundary conditions for ends of lists or the initialization needed to ensure that lists are properly ended. */

/* Stage 1: Construct list L_i for each value i in the input */

1. Processor $(0, j)$ broadcasts a_j to all processors in column j. For Stage 1, processor (i, j) is "active" iff $a_j = i$.
2. For $0 \leq i < 2^b$, perform neighbor localization on row i to construct a list L_i of active processors in ascending order of their column indices.
3. Let $next(j)$ point to the element following a_j in list L_{a_j}. Each active processor (i, j) sends $next(j)$ to processor $(0, j)$.

/* Stage 2: Construct list L of input values in ascending order. */

1. **if** processor $(0, j)$ holds the first element of list L_{a_j} **then** use row a_j to send index j to processor $(0, a_j)$. Processor $(0, a_j)$ assigns $first(a_j) \longleftarrow j$.
2. **if** processor $(0, j)$ holds the last element of list L_{a_j} **then** use row a_j to send index j to processor $(0, a_j)$. Processor $(0, a_j)$ assigns $last(a_j) \longleftarrow j$.

    /* Processor $(0, i)$ now holds pointers to the first and last elements of list L_{a_i}, if the list exists. */
3. For Stages 2 and 3, processor $(0, i)$ is active iff it received indices in Steps 1 and 2 of Stage 2.

4. Perform neighbor localization on row 0 to construct list L of active processors in ascending order of their column indices.
   For active processor $(0, i)$, let $link(i)$ point to the next element of list L.

/* Stage 3: Concatenate non-empty lists L_i according to list L.
   If $link(i) = k$, then this stage constructs a pointer from the last element of L_i to the first element of L_k. */

1. /* This step finds the predecessor, $pred(i)$, of each element i of list L. */
   if processor $(0, i)$ is active **then**
      send index i to processor $(0, link(i))$ using row i.
      Processor $(0, link(i))$ assigns $pred(link(i)) \longleftarrow i$.

2. if processor $(0, i)$ is active **then**
      send $first(i)$ to processor $(0, pred(i))$ using row i.
      Processor $(0, pred(i))$ assigns $next\_list(pred(i)) \longleftarrow first(i)$.
   /* If $link(i) = k$, then at this point each active processor $(0, i)$ holds a pointer $next\_list(i)$ to the first element of L_k. */

3. if processor $(0, i)$ is active **then**
      send $next\_list(i)$ to processor $(0, last(i))$ using row i.
      Processor $(0, last(i))$ assigns $next(last(i)) \longleftarrow next\_list(i)$.

end

We now explain the algorithm and its correctness.

Stage 1: Step 1 flags all processors of row i that hold inputs of value i (after the broadcast). Step 2 strings these inputs together as list L_i. Notice that if two inputs a_j and $a_{j'}$ each have value i and if $j < j'$, then the definition of neighbor localization ensures that a_j precedes $a_{j'}$ in list L_i; this property of L_i will ensure that the chain sorting is stable. Step 3 of Stage 1 simply moves each list L_i to row 0.

Stage 2: At the start of this stage, processor $(0, j)$ is flagged to indicate if element a_j heads its list L_{a_j} (as a result of neighbor localization in Stage 1). Similarly, processor $(0, j)$ is also flagged to indicate if a_j is the last element of L_{a_j}. In Step 1, each processor $(0, i)$ obtains a pointer $first(i)$ to the first element of list L_i, if it exists. Similarly in Step 2, each processor $(0, i)$ obtains a pointer $last(i)$ to the last element of list L_i, if it exists. Note that since input values are drawn from the set $\{0, 1, \cdots, 2^b - 1\}$, the 2^b rows of the R-Mesh suffice for the communications in Steps 1 and 2. Step 3 flags processor $(0, i)$ as active, if list L_i exists; that is, if value i appears in the input. The neighbor localization of Step 4 now simply strings the input values (active processors) in the sorted order. Observe that since $2^b \leq N$, enough room exists for all input values.

Stage 3: Suppose that value k follows i in list L; that is, after i, the next higher value in the input is k. Here the R-Mesh concatenates list L_k to the end of list L_i. Figure 2.12 shows how Stage 3 accomplishes this. Step 1 determines the predecessor of each element of list L, so that active processor $(0, k)$ has the identity of its predecessor processor $(0, i)$ through a pointer $pred(k)$; in the original list L, processor $(0, k)$ has only a pointer $link(k)$ to its successor, if any. In Step 2, processor $(0, i)$ receives a pointer to the first element of list L_k from processor $(0, k)$, which it holds in $next\_list(i)$; recall that processor $(0, k)$ obtained a pointer to the first element of L_k in Step 1 of Stage 2. In Step 3, processor $(0, i)$ uses $next\_list(i)$ to point the last element of list L_i to the first element of list L_k; processor $(0, i)$ obtained a pointer to the last element of L_i in Step 2 of Stage 2.

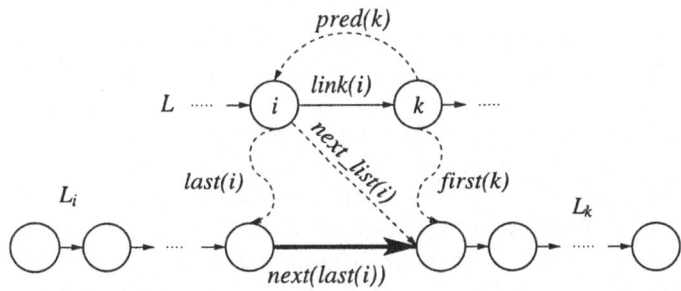

Figure 2.12. Concatenating list L_i to list L_k.

Since the neighbor localization of Stage 2 lists the values in the correct order, the output is chain sorted. Since the neighbor localizations of Stage 1 create lists in order of input indices, the sorting is stable. Since each step runs in constant time, so does the entire algorithm.

THEOREM 2.13 *For $1 \leq b \leq \log N$, a stable chain sort of N b-bit integers can be performed on a $2^b \times N$ R-Mesh in $O(1)$ time. Initially, each processor of row 0 holds an input.*

2.3.4   Sub-R-Mesh Generation—Maximum Finding

The problem of finding the largest (or smallest) element from a set of inputs is a very basic one, finding uses in applications as varied as computational geometry and manipulation of floating point numbers. In this section we present an algorithm for this problem, in the process illustrating a simple way to generate sub-R-Meshes of an R-Mesh. The mesh topology readily lends itself to a decomposition into sub-meshes. In this decomposition, neighboring processors of each sub-mesh have to be neighbors in the underlying mesh as well. An R-Mesh, however, can also decompose into sub-meshes whose neighboring processors need not be neighbors in the underlying mesh topology. This ability is crucial to the following maximum finding algorithm.

Maximum Finding.   Let $a_0, a_1, \cdots, a_{N-1}$ be N elements drawn from a totally ordered set. The *maximum finding* problem is to find the largest of the inputs. Since inputs can be distinguished by their indices, no loss of generality arises in assuming that all inputs are distinct. We first develop a fast, but inefficient, algorithm for maximum finding, which, in turn, leads to a much more efficient algorithm.

LEMMA 2.14   *The maximum of N inputs can be determined on an $N \times N$ R-Mesh in $O(1)$ time. Initially, processors of a row hold the inputs.*

<u>Proof outline:</u>   For $0 \leq j < N$, let processor $(0, j)$ hold input a_j. First broadcast a_j to all processors of column j. Next, use a row broadcast from processor (i, i) to send a_i to all processors of row i. At this point, processor (i, j) holds inputs a_i and a_j, and sets a flag $f(i, j)$ to 1 if and only if $a_i > a_j$. Input a_k is the maximum if and only if each of the flags $f(0, k), f(1, k), \cdots, f(N-1, k)$ is 0; that is, their OR is 0. By Theorem 2.2, this step runs in constant time.   ∎

Although the above algorithm runs in constant time, it uses N^2 processors. At the other extreme, the binary tree algorithm of Theorem 2.1 solves maximum finding more efficiently with N processors, albeit in $O(\log N)$ time. We now generalize these results to an $O\left(\frac{\log N}{\log m}\right)$-time algorithm running on an $m \times N$ R-Mesh, for any $1 < m \leq N$.

Let each processor in the top row of the $m \times N$ R-Mesh hold an input. The algorithm consists of the following steps: (1) Decompose the R-Mesh into $\frac{N}{m}$ square "sub-R-Meshes," each of size $m \times m$ and find the "local maxima" within these sub-R-Meshes. (2) Generate an $m \times \frac{N}{m}$ sub-R-Mesh within the R-Mesh, with the local maxima of Step 1 in the top row of this sub-R-Mesh. (3) Recursively find the maximum of $\frac{N}{m}$ elements on the $m \times \frac{N}{m}$ sub-R-Mesh. Algorithm 2.7 provides details and Figure 2.13 shows an example.

Algorithm 2.7   (Efficient Maximum Finding)

Model: For $1 < m \leq N$, an $m \times N$ R-Mesh, with $N = m^k$ for integer $k \geq 1$. (This assumption is only for convenience and is without loss of generality.)

Input: Processor $(0, j)$ holds input a_j, an element from a totally ordered set.

Output: Processor $(0, 0)$ holds $\max\{a_j \ : \ 0 \leq j < N\}$.

begin

if $k = 1$ **then**
     use Lemma 2.14 to find the maximum; return

else

1. For $0 \leq \ell < \frac{N}{m}$, divide the R-Mesh into $m \times m$ sub-R-Meshes, $\mathcal{S}_\ell$, consisting of columns $\{\ell m + y \ : \ 0 \leq y < m\}$ of the original R-Mesh. Determine $a'_\ell = \max\{a_{\ell m + y} \ : \ 0 \leq y < m\}$ within $\mathcal{S}_\ell$ (using Lemma 2.14). Let processor $(0, \ell m)$ hold a'_ℓ.

2. **if** j is not divisible by m **then**
     for each $0 \leq i < m$, processor (i, j) configures $\{\overline{N}, \overline{S}, \overline{EW}\}$

3. Recursively find the maximum of the elements $\left\{ a'_\ell \ : \ 0 \leq \ell < \frac{N}{m} \right\}$ in the $m \times \frac{N}{m}$ sub-R-Mesh formed by columns $\left\{ \ell m \ : \ 0 \leq \ell < \frac{N}{m} \right\}$ of the original R-Mesh.

end_if_else

end

As in the pseudocode, let $N = m^k$. Step 1 decomposes the R-Mesh into sub-R-Meshes. At the end of Step 1, processor $(0, \ell m)$ holds a local maximum a'_ℓ for each $0 \leq \ell < \frac{N}{m}$. The task now is to find $\max\left\{ a'_\ell \ : \ 0 \leq \ell < \frac{N}{m} \right\}$.

Step 2 establishes row buses between columns ℓm and $(\ell + 1)m$, for each $0 \leq \ell < \frac{N}{m} - 1$. By treating these buses as external connections, we have an $m \times \frac{N}{m}$ sub-R-Mesh distributed over the columns of the original

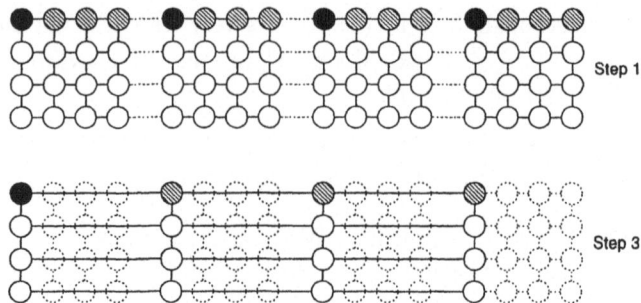

Figure 2.13. An illustration of Algorithm 2.7 with $m = 4$ and $N = 16$. Processors holding inputs to a step are hatched, while those with outputs are shaded black.

R-Mesh (see Figure 2.13). The top row of this sub-R-Mesh holds the $\frac{N}{m}$ local maxima, and Step 3 recursively finds their maximum.

Since Steps 1 and 2 run in constant time, the number of levels of recursion determines the running time of the algorithm. With $N = m^k$, let $T(k)$ denote the time to find the maximum of N elements on an $m \times N$ R-Mesh using Algorithm 2.7. From Lemma 2.14, $T(1)$ is a constant and therefore, for constant c,

$$T(k) = T(k-1) + c. \tag{2.2}$$

This recurrence has the solution $T(k) = kc = O(\log_m N) = O\left(\frac{\log N}{\log m}\right)$. We now have the following result.

THEOREM 2.15 *For any* $1 < m \leq N$, *the maximum of* N *elements can be determined on an* $m \times N$ *R-Mesh in* $O\left(\frac{\log N}{\log m}\right)$ *time. Initially, processors of a row hold the inputs.*

Sub-R-Mesh Generation. A mesh topology decomposes nicely into sub-meshes, where neighboring processors of each sub-mesh are neighbors in the underlying mesh as well. (Step 1 of Algorithm 2.7 uses such a decomposition.) By creating buses, an R-Mesh can also decompose into sub-meshes whose neighboring processors are not neighbors in the underlying mesh topology. This ability of the R-Mesh to embed a "distributed sub-R-Mesh" (Step 2) is crucial to Algorithm 2.7. With this ability, we can treat inputs as though they are in adjacent columns of the R-Mesh, a prerequisite for running the algorithm recursively. (Note also that insisting that the inputs be in actually adjacent columns necessitates moving the local minima to $\frac{N}{m}$ contiguous columns which would require $\Omega\left(\frac{N}{m^2}\right)$ time.)

Embedding a distributed sub-R-Mesh is a special case of embedding a graph in the R-Mesh, with each vertex of the graph corresponding to an R-Mesh processor and each edge to a bus between processors emulating vertices. A major drawback of this approach to embedding (mapping vertices to processors and edges to buses) is that the embedded graph must be of degree at most 4. Sections 2.3.5 and 2.3.6 illustrate various graph embeddings (including dense graph embedding) that overcome this drawback, with emphasis on aspects of graphs including distance between vertices and connectivity.

2.3.5   Graph Distance Embedding—List Ranking

As illustrated in Section 2.3.4, the ability to establish a bus between any pair of processors regardless of their distance in the underlying mesh is useful because it allows processors to act as neighbors, even though they are not physically adjacent. In this section, we use a slightly different approach that maps an entire path to a bus, snaking the bus through different sections of the R-Mesh to capture the notion of distance between points on the path. We employ this approach in an algorithm to rank a linked list.

List Ranking.   Let L be a list of N elements. The *rank* of an element of list L is the number of elements preceding it in L. (For example, the first and last elements of L have ranks 0 and $N - 1$, respectively.) *List ranking* determines the ranks of all elements of a list. It is an important procedure, useful in converting a list into an array, a much more regular structure. (Relocating the elements of a list according to their ranks transforms a list into an array with elements in the order of the original list.)

Let list L contain elements $a_0, a_1, \cdots, a_{N-1}$ (in some order). Consider list element a_i with successor a_j. Let r_i and r_j denote their ranks in the list. Our approach to list ranking hinges on the, rather obvious, observation that $r_j = r_i + 1$. That is, the rank of an element can be computed by incrementing the rank of its predecessor (if any). On the R-Mesh, this strategy takes the following form. For element a_k, assign a bundle of N row buses indexed $(k, 0), (k, 1), \cdots, (k, N-1)$, corresponding to the N possible ranks of a_k. Connect row buses (i, r_i) and $(j, r_i + 1)$ by a column bus. This configuration guarantees that a signal on bus (i, r_i) will also traverse bus (j, r_j). Since the precise value of r_i is not known *a priori*, the algorithm must be prepared to handle all possible values of r_i. In other words, the R-Mesh connects buses (i, ℓ) and $(j, \ell + 1)$, for each $0 \le \ell < N - 1$. The R-Mesh configures its buses in this manner for each element of the list and its successor (if any). Let a_f be the first element of the list; clearly its rank is 0. By configuring buses as described above and then sending a signal on bus $(f, 0)$, the R-Mesh guarantees that for any element a_i of the list, bus (i, r_i) receives the signal if and only if the rank of a_i is r_i. Figure 2.14 illustrates this strategy and Algorithm 2.8 provides details.

Observe that this method generalizes the stair step approach to adding bits in Section 2.3.2. That algorithm steps down one row for each 1 in the input. The algorithm here steps down one row from one bundle to the next for each element of the list. In both cases, a signal reaches a given row i if the count (number of 1s, list rank) is i.

Algorithm 2.8   (List Ranking)

Model: An $N^2 \times N^2$ R-Mesh with rows and columns indexed (i, j), where $0 \leq i, j < N$. Let processor (i, j, k, ℓ) be the processor in row (i, j) and column (k, ℓ).

Input: An array $a_0, a_1, \cdots, a_{N-1}$ of elements with element a_k associated with a pointer $next(k) \in \{0, 1, \cdots, N - 1\} \cup \{\text{NIL}\}$, for each $0 \leq k < N$. These pointers collectively form a list L. Pointer $next(k) = \text{NIL}$ if a_k is the last element of L; otherwise, $next(k)$ points to the successor, $a_{next(k)}$, of a_k. For $0 \leq k < N$, processor $(0, 0, k, 0)$ holds element a_k and pointer $next(k)$. Processor $(0, 0, k, 0)$ also holds a flag $first(k)$ that is set to 1 if and only if a_k is the first element of L.

Output: For $0 \leq k < N$, processor $(0, 0, k, 0)$ holds the rank of a_k in list L.

begin

1. For $0 \leq k < N$, processor $(0, 0, k, 0)$ broadcasts $next(k)$ and $first(k)$ to all processors in columns (k, ℓ), where $0 \leq \ell < N$.

2. **if** $(i = k$ and $j = \ell)$ or $(i = next(k)$ and $j = \ell + 1)$ **then**
       processor (i, j, k, ℓ) configures $\{\overline{\text{NSEW}}\}$
   else processor (i, j, k, ℓ) configures $\{\overline{\text{NS}}, \overline{\text{EW}}\}$

3. **if** $first(k) = 1$ **then** processor $(0, 0, k, 0)$ sends a signal on its S port.
   else for $0 \leq \ell < N$, processor $(0, 0, k, \ell)$ reads from its S port.

4. **if** $first(k) = 1$ **then** set the rank of a_k to 0
   else if processor $(0, 0, k, \ell)$ receives the signal in Step 3 **then**
       set the rank of a_k to ℓ.

end

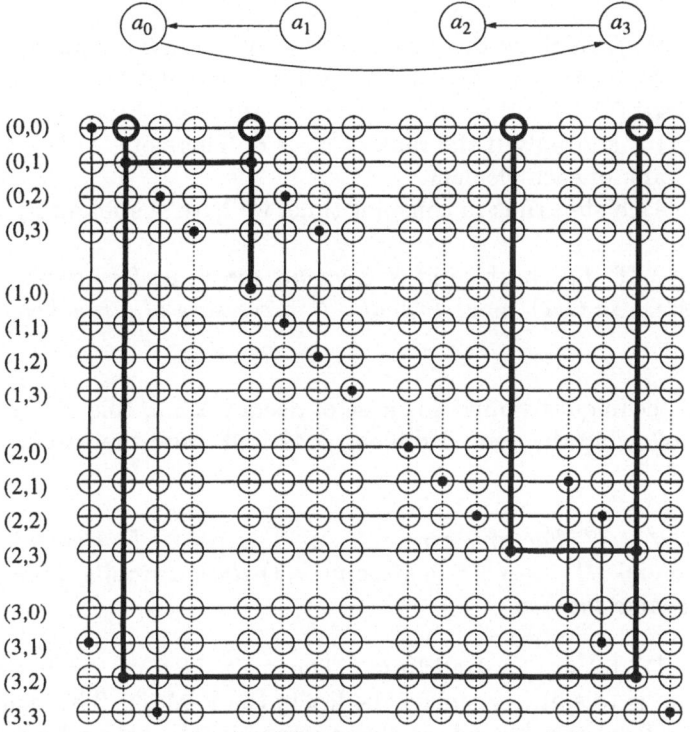

Figure 2.14. An illustration of the list ranking algorithm. The list elements at the top of the figure align with the corresponding four column bundles of the R-Mesh. For clarity, only those portions of column buses that serve to connect two row buses are shown solid; the rest of the column bus is shown dotted. The path traversed by the signal is shown in bold as are processors sending and receiving the signal.

The broadcast in Step 1 of Algorithm 2.8 allows any processor in column (k, ℓ) to treat $next(k)$ and $first(k)$ as local quantities in the remaining steps.

In Step 2, observe first that (regardless of the **if** condition) each processor connects its E-W ports and N-S ports together. This ensures that each row (resp., column) has a horizontal (resp., vertical) bus spanning its entire length. Processors satisfying the **if** condition simply connect the horizontal and vertical buses passing through them. More specifically, consider an element a_k with successor $next(k) \neq$ NIL. For each index $0 \leq \ell < N - 1$, processors (k, ℓ, k, ℓ) and $(next(k), \ell+1, k, \ell)$ satisfy the **if** condition, connecting horizontal buses (k, ℓ) and $(next(k), \ell+1)$. This configuration ensures that a signal traversing horizontal bus (k, ℓ) traverses bus $(next(k), r)$ if and only if $r = \ell + 1$.

In Step 3, the first element of the list (a_f say) sends a signal on horizontal bus $(f, 0)$. Since the rank of a_f is 0, our observation in the previous paragraph ensures that the signal reaches horizontal buses $(next(f), 1)$, $(next(next(f)), 2)$ and so on. In general, this signal reaches horizontal bus (k, ℓ) if and only if the rank of a_k is ℓ. Therefore, Step 4 finds the correct rank of each element.

Since each step runs in constant time, we have the following result.

LEMMA 2.16 *List ranking of N elements can be performed on an $N^2 \times N^2$ R-Mesh in $O(1)$ time. Initially, N processors of a row hold the list.*

With techniques similar to those of Section 2.3.2, this result extends to the following theorem. Problems 2.42–2.48 walk the reader through its proof.

THEOREM 2.17 *For any constant $\epsilon > 0$, a list of N elements can be ranked on an $N^{1+\epsilon} \times N^{1+\epsilon}$ R-Mesh in $O(1)$ time. Initially, N processors of a row hold the list.*

Graph Distance Embedding. The main idea of the list ranking algorithm is to suitably embed the list in the R-Mesh. This embedding takes the form of a bus whose shape resembles the list and whose path through the R-Mesh points to the answer (much like the algorithms of Section 2.4 for adding bits). Notice that the embedding does not break a bus at each vertex of the list, yet captures the notion of succession in the list. It does this by snaking different segments of the bus (corresponding to different vertices of the list) through different portions of the R-Mesh (each corresponding to a position in the list). This approach extends to distance-related problems in other graphs as well.

Besides the approach used in this section and earlier in Section 2.3.4, the idea of embedding information about a graph in an R-Mesh has many other applications; Section 2.3.6 illustrates one of these.

2.3.6   Graph Connectivity Embedding—*s-t* Connectivity

In Section 2.3.4 we mentioned a method for embedding graphs with vertices mapped to processors and edges to buses; this embedding captures the general topology of the embedded graph. Section 2.3.5 illustrated a method for embedding distance information in the R-Mesh. In this section, we use the R-Mesh to embed connectivity information of a graph. Moreover, unlike the previous two sections, we now place no restrictions on the graph itself. We illustrate this technique through an algorithm for *s-t* connectivity.

***s-t* Connectivity.** Given an undirected graph $\mathcal{G}$ and a pair of vertices s and t, the *s-t connectivity* problem asks the question "Does $\mathcal{G}$ have a path between s and t?" This problem is a fundamental one with applications in areas ranging from reliability to complexity theory.

Let $\mathcal{G}$ be an N-vertex graph. Our solution to *s-t* connectivity hinges on embedding $\mathcal{G}$ in an $N \times N$ R-Mesh as follows. Without loss of generality, let the vertices of $\mathcal{G}$ be $0, 1, \cdots, N - 1$. For each row (column) of the R-Mesh, construct a bus spanning the entire row (column). Let the bus in row i represent vertex i. Suppose vertex i connects by an edge to vertex j and by another edge to vertex j'. The algorithm connects row bus i to row buses j and j' using the column i bus. If $\mathcal{G}$ has a path $s, j_1, j_2, \cdots, j_k, t$, then the R-Mesh has connections from row bus s, to column bus s, to row bus j_1, to column bus j_1, to row bus j_2, $\cdots$, to column bus j_k, to row bus t. If $\mathcal{G}$ has no path from s to t, then no sequence of connections in the R-Mesh links row buses s and t.

An $N \times N$ R-Mesh can implement the above strategy in a simple manner using the $N \times N$ adjacency matrix[8] of $\mathcal{G}$. Processor (i, j) connects buses in row i and column j if and only if entry (i, j) of the adjacency matrix is 1 (that is, if and only if $\mathcal{G}$ contains an edge between vertices i and j). This connects row buses s and t (possibly via other row buses) if and only if there is a path between vertices s and t. Algorithm 2.9 provides details and Figure 2.15 shows an example of this strategy.

Algorithm 2.9 *(s-t* **Connectivity)**

Model: An $N \times N$ R-Mesh.

Input: Adjacency matrix $A_{\mathcal{G}} = [a_{i,j}]$ of an N-vertex undirected graph $\mathcal{G}$. Processor (i, j) holds bit $a_{i,j}$. Two vertices s and t are marked as the "source" and "terminal" vertices, respectively; processors (s, s) and (t, t) hold this information.

Output: Processor (t, t) sets flag *connected*(t) if and only if $\mathcal{G}$ has a path between vertices s and t.

---

[8]The *adjacency matrix* of a graph $\mathcal{G}$ of N vertices is an $N \times N$ Boolean matrix with rows (and columns) corresponding to vertices of the graph. Entry (i, j) (corresponding to vertices i and j) is a 1 if and only if $\mathcal{G}$ has an edge between vertices i and j.

begin

1. **if** $a(i,j) = 1$ or $i = j$ **then**
   processor (i,j) configures $\{\overline{\text{NSEW}}\}$
   else processor (i,j) configures $\{\overline{\text{NS}}, \overline{\text{EW}}\}$

2. Processor (s,s) writes a signal and processor (t,t) reads from any one of its ports.

3. Processor (t,t) sets flag $connected(t)$ to 1 if and only if it receives the signal in Step 2.

end

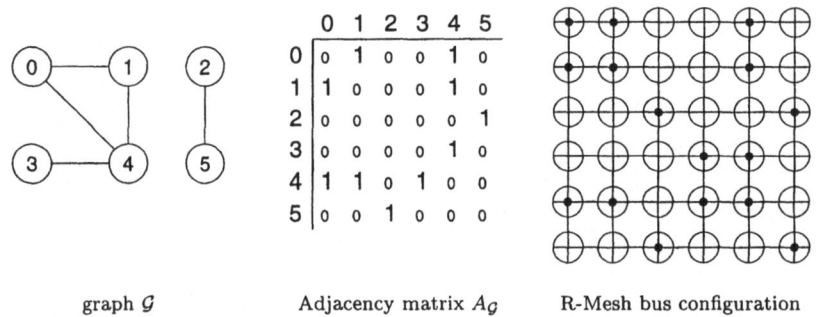

graph $\mathcal{G}$ Adjacency matrix $A_{\mathcal{G}}$ R-Mesh bus configuration

Figure 2.15. An illustration of Algorithm 2.9 for a 6-vertex graph. Notice the correspondence between the adjacency matrix and the port partitions within the R-Mesh processors.

Both port partitions used in Step 1 place the N and S ports together, thus generating buses that span entire columns. Similarly, the step places the E and W ports together, creating row buses. The **if** part of the statement causes processor (i,j) to connect buses in row i and column j. The clause $i = j$ in the condition of Step 1 ensures that buses in row i and column i are always connected. This, in turn, guarantees that if $a_{i,j} = 1$, then by connecting buses in row i and column j, processor (i,j) indeed causes row buses i and j to be connected. As noted earlier, this bus configuration connects buses in rows i and j if and only if vertices i and j have a path between them; a formal proof is left as an exercise (Problem 2.50).

In Step 2, the source indicates its presence on the bus of row s; note that since processor (s,s) has configured $\{\overline{\text{NSEW}}\}$, it could write on any port. Processor (t,t) similarly looks for the signal to arrive at any of its ports. The bus configuration guarantees that it receives the signal if and only if vertices s and t are connected in $\mathcal{G}$; accordingly, processor (t, t) sets the flag *connected*(t) in Step 3.

THEOREM 2.18 *The s-t connectivity problem for an N-vertex graph can be solved on an $N \times N$ R-Mesh in $O(1)$ time. Initially, the processors hold the corresponding bits of the adjacency matrix of the graph.*

Connectivity Embedding. Compared to the graph embedding of Section 2.3.5, the method here differs on two counts. First, the embedding captures only the connectivity of the graph's structure. That is, the embedding does not distinguish vertices connected by an edge from vertices that are distant but in the same connected component of the graph. Second, the embedding applies to arbitrary graphs (including directed graphs as explained in Chapter 3). The embedding of Section 2.3.5 focuses on the notion of distance of a vertex from the start of a path (list). It exploits the fact that the graph is a list and performs the embedding to facilitate quick computation of the rank (by establishing buses for all N possible ranks of an element). The embedding in this section simply ensures that a unique bus connects all processors corresponding to vertices in the same component of the graph.

Another noteworthy point about the method in this section is that it uses an entire row bus to represent a vertex and an entire column to connect row buses (vertices). Consequently, the bounded degree of R-Mesh processors does not curtail the degree of the embedded graph.

2.3.7 Function Decomposition—Adding N Numbers

A recurring theme in many R-Mesh algorithms is to configure a bus that carries a signal to a processor whose index holds the answer. For example, Algorithm 2.3 for adding bits creates a bus from row 0 to row x if the input contains x 1's, and a signal sent on this bus reveals the answer. This approach has obvious applications in situations where the answer to one stage of an algorithm is the input to the next—here the R-Mesh can cascade buses to carry the signal through an intermediate answer to the final answer. Conversely, if a function decomposes into several "component functions," each of which has an R-Mesh solution that works by sending a signal to the answer, then the R-Mesh can compute the function itself by cascading the solutions to its components. This "function decomposition" technique is the main focus of this section. We illustrate this technique in an algorithm for adding N b-bit numbers on an R-Mesh. In the process we will also discuss some non-standard representations for integers that lend themselves to easy manipulation in constant time.

Data Dissection and Collection.   Conventional algorithms usually treat input data as atomic words, whose actual representations are irrelevant to the algorithm. On the other hand, some algorithms exploit specific knowledge of the input elements. For instance, the problem of sorting N $O(\log N)$-bit integers (integer sorting) has an $O(N)$-time sequential solution, whereas comparison-based sorting (that makes no assumptions about the length or representation of the inputs) requires $\Omega(N \log N)$ time. Many fast algorithms on the R-Mesh exploit knowledge of the input size and/or representation.   As a result, resource bounds for R-Mesh algorithms often depend on both the number and size of the inputs. For example, the chain sorting algorithm of Section 2.3.3 uses an R-Mesh whose size depends on b, the numbers of bits in each input.

When the input to an R-Mesh algorithm is in the conventional "word" format, some algorithms dissect the input into smaller pieces (usually bits), often with new representations. Conversely, after having obtained a dissected output, the R-Mesh has to collect the pieces and reconstruct the output in the conventional word format. In this section, we illustrate some ideas on data dissection and collection; a more detailed discussion of the topic appears in Chapter 4. We will briefly discuss two integer representations commonly employed by R-Mesh algorithms, the distributed unary and distributed binary representations.   We also present some algorithms for them.

The standard unary and binary representations are well known. The b-bit unary representation of a non-negative integer x usually consists of a b-bit string with the rightmost x bits set to 1. For our discussion we will represent x with $x + 1$ ones so that the representation of each non-negative integer (including 0) has at least one 1.   More formally, for integer $b \geq 1$, the b-bit unary representation of x (for $0 \leq x < b$) is $x_{b-1}x_{b-2}\cdots x_1x_0$, where $x_i = 1$ if and only if $i \leq x$, for each $0 \leq i < b$. For example if $b = 5$, then the unary representations of $0, 1, 2, 3, 4$ are $00001, 00011, 00111, 01111, 11111$, respectively. The b-bit *binary representation* of x (for $0 \leq x < 2^b$) is $x_{b-1}x_{b-2}\cdots x_1x_0$, where $x = \sum_{i=0}^{b-1} x_i 2^i$.

In the b-bit *distributed unary* and *distributed binary* representations, the b bits are distributed over b processors. We use the term *word format* to denote the conventional (non-distributed) binary representation with all bits local to a single processor.

Algorithms for Distributed Unary Integers.   The strategy of Algorithm 2.3 for adding bits is to start a signal from the West end of row 0 of the R-Mesh (see Figure 2.7) and monitor this signal at the East end of the R-Mesh. Observe that if the signal originates instead from the West end of some row i, then it will arrive at the East end of row $i + x$, where x is the number of 1's in the input. Observe also that if separate signals originate at the West ends of rows $0, 1, \cdots, x$, and at the North ends of columns with a 1 input, then signals will arrive at the East end of rows $0, 1, \cdots, i + x$, where i is the number of 1's in the column input (see Figure 2.16). This gives a method for adding a number represented in distributed unary (x in Figure 2.16) with N 1-bit numbers (column inputs), producing the sum in distributed unary format.

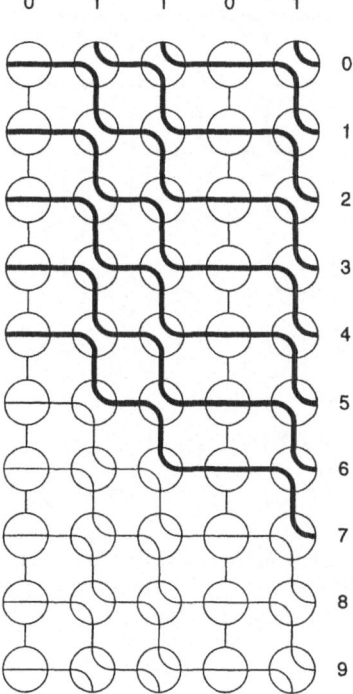

Figure 2.16.   Using an $(N + b) \times N$ R-Mesh to add a b-bit distributed unary integer x to N bits; the example uses $b = N = 5$ and adds $x = 4$ to 5 bits, three of which are 1s. The buses shown in bold carry signals originating from the West and North borders of the R-Mesh. The five signals originating at the West border correspond to the unary representation 11111 of $x = 4$. The numbers above the North border of the R-Mesh are the $N = 5$ input bits, while the numbers to the right of the West border are the row indices.

LEMMA 2.19 *For any integer $0 \le x < b$, the sum of x and N input bits can be computed on an $(N+b) \times N$ R-Mesh in $O(1)$ time, where x is in distributed unary format in the leftmost column.*

We now consider the problem of dividing an integer by 2; that is, computing $\lfloor \frac{x}{2} \rfloor$ for a given integer x. Once again, it is useful to represent x in distributed unary. Figure 2.17 shows the underlying idea of the algorithm, which generalizes quite easily.

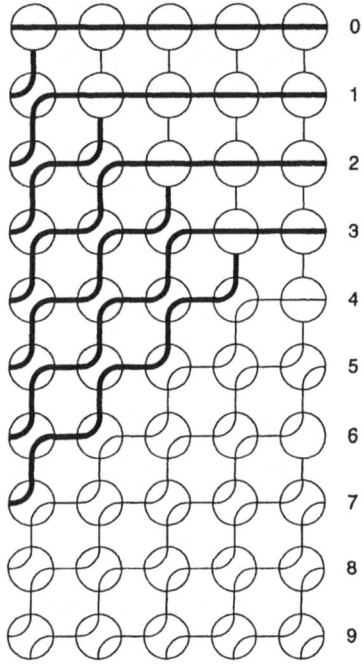

Figure 2.17. Using a $b \times \lfloor \frac{b}{2} \rfloor$ R-Mesh to divide b-bit distributed unary integer x by 2; the example uses $b = 10$ and $x = 7$. The buses shown in bold carry the signals. Number on the right of the figure are row indices.

LEMMA 2.20 *For any integer $0 \le x < b$, the quantity $\lfloor \frac{x}{2} \rfloor$ can be computed on a $b \times \lfloor \frac{b}{2} \rfloor$ R-Mesh in $O(1)$ time. Both input and output are in b-bit distributed unary format in the leftmost column of the R-Mesh.*

Collecting Distributed Binary Bits into a Word. We now present a method for collecting the information from a distributed binary representation to the usual "word" representation. Specifically, let x be a

b-bit integer in distributed binary representation. The aim here is to collect the value of x into a single processor. A simple method is to use the binary tree algorithm in Illustration 1 of Section 1.1 to solve the problem in $O(\log b)$ time. We describe a constant time method here.

THEOREM 2.21 *A b-bit distributed binary integer can be converted to the word format on a $2^b \times b$ R-Mesh in $O(1)$ time. The input is distributed over a row of the R-Mesh.*

Proof outline: Without loss of generality, let processor $(0, j)$ (where $0 \leq j < b$) hold x_j, the jth bit of the input. The idea is for processor (i, j) to compare x_j with i_j, the jth bit in the binary representation of i. If $x_j = i_j$ for all $0 \leq j < b$, then $x = i$. Checking this condition amounts to determining the AND of b bits in a row of the R-Mesh, which, by Theorem 2.2, is possible in constant time. ∎

Adding N b-bit integers. We now apply the ideas developed so far to design a constant time algorithm for adding N b-bit integers (with $b = O(\log N)$). The inputs and output are in the conventional word format.

For $0 \leq i < N$ and $0 \leq j < b$, let integer x_i have binary representation $x_{i,b-1}x_{i,b-2} \cdots x_{i,1}x_{i,0}$. (Figure 2.18 illustrates the following definitions with a running example.) Let the sum of the input integers

			6	5	4	bit j 3	2	1	0
x_0	$=$	14				1	1	1	0
x_1	$=$	2				0	0	1	0
x_2	$=$	3				0	0	1	1
x_3	$=$	15				1	1	1	1
x_4	$=$	4				0	1	0	0
x_5	$=$	0				0	0	0	0
x_6	$=$	14				1	1	1	0
x_7	$=$	7				0	1	1	1
	L_j		0	0	0	3	5	6	3
	C_j		0	1	3	4	3	1	0
$S = 59,$	s_j		0	1	1	1	0	1	1

Figure 2.18. An illustration of terms for adding N b-bit integers with $N = 8$ and $b = 4$.

be $S = \sum_{i=0}^{N-1} x_i$. Assuming $\log N$ to be an integer, S has $b + \log N$ bits. Let the binary representation of S be $s_{b+\log N-1} s_{b+\log N-2} \cdots s_1 s_0$. The algorithm must ultimately compute bits s_j, for each $0 \le j < b + \log N$. In what follows, we derive an expression for these output bits in terms of input bits $x_{i,j}$ (where $0 \le i < N$ and $0 \le j < b$). Key to this expression is a recurrence relation for the jth carry (generated by the addition of the first $j - 1$ bits of the input numbers), in terms of the $(j-1)^{\text{th}}$ carry and $x_{i,j}$, the jth bits of the inputs x_i. This leads to a method in which a sub-R-Mesh generates the jth carry, given the $(j-1)^{\text{th}}$ carry and input bits $x_{i,j}$, for $0 \le j < b$. The R-Mesh cascades these carry generators to produce all the carries needed to compute the sum bits s_j, for each $0 \le j < b + \log N$. We now detail the various parts of the algorithm.

An Expression for the Sum Bits: For $0 \le j < b + \log N$, define the local sum, L_j, as follows:

$$L_j = \begin{cases} \sum_{i=0}^{N-1} x_{i,j}, & \text{if } 0 \le j < b \\ 0, & \text{if } b \le j < b + \log N. \end{cases}$$

For $0 \le j < b + \log N$, let C_j denote the carry due to bits $0, 1, \cdots, j-1$. Clearly,

$$C_j = \begin{cases} 0, & \text{if } j = 0 \\ \left\lfloor \frac{L_{j-1}+C_{j-1}}{2} \right\rfloor, & \text{if } 0 < j < b + \log N. \end{cases}$$

Therefore the final sum bit at position j (for $0 \le j < b + \log N$) is

$$s_j = (L_j + C_j)(\text{mod } 2).$$

Key to computing the bits s_j of the sum are the quantities L_j and C_j. While L_j depends only on the jth bits of the inputs, C_j can depend on bits $0, 1, \cdots, j-1$ of the inputs. The novelty of the following solution to the problem is in the use of the bus to propagate the information from bits $0, 1, \cdots, j-1$ to construct the value of C_j.

Computing the Carry Bits: Observe first that since $L_j = 0$ for $b \le j < b + \log N$, the binary representation of C_b equals the most significant $\log N$ bits of the final sum S. Note also that $L_j \le N$ and $C_j < N$. We now explain how a $2N \times 2Nb$ R-Mesh can determine s_j for each $0 \le j < b$.

We first describe a module S_j (where $0 \leq j < b$) that generates carry C_{j+1} (in distributed unary format), given C_j (also in distributed unary format) and the jth input bits $x_{i,j}$ (for all $0 \leq i < N$). Subsequently, we will string together modules $S_0, S_1, \cdots, S_{b-1}$ to add the given N b-bit inputs.

To construct module S_j, first use Lemma 2.19 to compute $C_j + L_j = C_j + \sum_{i=0}^{N} x_{i,j}$ on a $2N \times N$ R-Mesh. Next, use Lemma 2.20 to compute $C_{j+1} = \left\lfloor \frac{L_j + C_j}{2} \right\rfloor$ on another $2N \times N$ R-Mesh. The output of the first $2N \times N$ R-Mesh produces $C_j + L_j$ in distributed unary and feeds it directly into the second $2N \times N$ R-Mesh which computes C_{j+1} as shown in Figure 2.19. Observe that a $2N \times 2N$ R-Mesh suffices to implement module S_j.

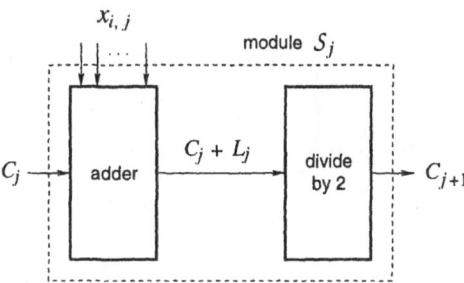

Figure 2.19. Module S_j for generating C_{j+1} from C_j and inputs $x_{i,j}$, for $0 \leq i < N$.

We now employ modules $S_0, S_1, \cdots, S_{b-1}$ to unconditionally generate all carries. For $0 \leq j < b$, partition the given $2N \times 2Nb$ R-Mesh into b sub-R-Meshes (modules) S_j, each a $2N \times 2N$ R-Mesh. Sub-R-Mesh S_j is responsible for computing C_{j+1}, using C_j and the input bits $x_{i,j}$ (for all $0 \leq i < N$) as explained above. By definition, $C_0 = 0$. For $j > 0$, S_j obtains C_j from S_{j-1} (see Figure 2.20). This carry generation scheme starts signals from the W port of processor $(0,0)$ of S_0 (as $C_0 = 0$), and from the N port of each processor $(0,i)$ of S_j that has $x_{i,j} = 1$. These signals flow seamlessly across the sub-R-Meshes, as the algorithms implied by Lemmas 2.19 and 2.20 require only one signal propagation step after the initial steps for establishing signal paths.

Generating the Sum: The input is in the word format. That is, the N inputs are initially in N different processors (typically processors

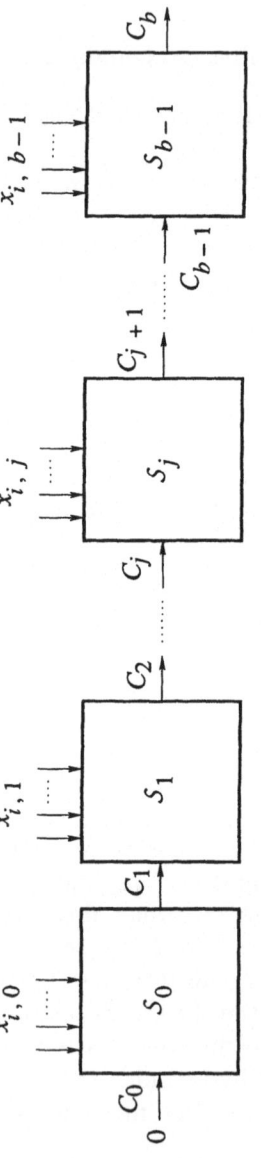

Figure 2.20. Cascading modules $S_0, S_1, \cdots, S_{b-1}$ for generating all carries from $C_0 = 0$.

$(0, i)$, for $0 \le i < N$). To make the jth bits of the inputs available to each sub-R-Mesh, broadcast all N inputs to each sub-R-Mesh $\mathcal{S}_j$ (for this, each sub-R-Mesh only requires size $N \times N$). Within sub-R-Mesh $\mathcal{S}_j$, a processor simply extracts the required bit from the input. To obtain bit s_j of the final sum for $0 \le j < b$, sub-R-Mesh $\mathcal{S}_j$ extracts $L_j + C_j$ from column N (see Figure 2.19) and computes $s_j = (L_j + C_j)(\text{mod } 2)$, which is just the least significant bit of $L_j + C_j$.

At this point, the first b bits of the final sum S are in the distributed binary format. The R-Mesh can collect these bits into a single processor using Theorem 2.21 and its extension in Problem 4.1. The available R-Mesh suffices for this conversion as $b = O(\log N)$. Let S' denote the value of the first b bits of S. The last $\log N$ bits of S (that equal C_b) are in distributed unary format; the R-Mesh can easily convert these to the word format as well. Computing $S = S' + 2^b C_b$ gives the result in word format.

THEOREM 2.22 *The sum of N $b = O(\log N)$-bit integers can be computed on a $2N \times 2Nb$ R-Mesh in $O(1)$ time. Initially, the inputs are in the first N processors of a row of the R-Mesh.*

Function Decomposition. The principal idea in the preceding result is the cascading of several small R-Mesh solutions (additions and divisons by 2, in this case) to solve a larger problem (carry propagation, in this case). Indeed, some of the algorithms discussed so far in this chapter can be expressed conveniently in terms of function decomposition. For example, consider a function $f_1 : \{0, 1, \cdots, N-1\} \longrightarrow \{1, 2, \cdots, N\}$ with $f_1(i) = i + 1$ for any $0 \le i < N$. An $(N + 1) \times 1$ column of R-Mesh processors can implement this function by establishing buses from the W port of processor i to the E port of processor $i + 1$. This, with the identity function f_0 that has $f_0(i) = i$ for each $0 \le i \le N$, is sufficient to express Algorithm 2.3 for adding bits. Simply cascade functions F_j (for $0 \le j < N$), where $F_j = f_0$ if the jth input bit is 0, and $F_j = f_1$ if the bit is 1 (see Figure 2.7).

The function decomposition technique often relies on the ability of the R-Mesh to embed a function in the form of a bus from each point in the domain to its image in the range. Functions computed by concatenating other functions can themselves serve as building blocks for more complex functions. Each such building block must, however, work in one step by providing a path to the solution, after the initial phase to configure buses.

2.4   Why an R-Mesh?

Although the literature on dynamic reconfiguration abounds with models, including variations of the R-Mesh, we will adopt the R-Mesh in most of this book for the following reasons.

Simplicity: With the popularity of the mesh as an interconnection topology, the R-Mesh is simple to describe and understand. Indeed the definition of Section 2.1 will suffice to illustrate most concepts in dynamic reconfiguration, as evidenced by the rich selection of algorithms and techniques of Section 2.3.1–2.3.7.

Wide Acceptance: Concepts and techniques in dynamic reconfiguration appear in the literature for a myriad of models. Of these, most published results use the R-Mesh (sometimes with minor variations) as the model of computation. Therefore, the R-Mesh is the natural choice to present dynamic reconfiguration ideas on a uniform platform.

Universality: Although the R-Mesh (as defined in Section 2.1) suffices for the most part, some ideas require additional abilities, such as directionality or concurrent writing ability. Chapter 3 discusses models with these abilities. For each of these extra abilities, some enhancement of the R-Mesh fits the bill.

Problems

2.1   Let $b_0, b_1, \cdots, b_{N-1}$ denote N bits. The *prefix OR problem* is determining b_0 OR b_1 OR $\cdots$ OR b_i for each $0 \leq i < N$.

Design an algorithm to determine the prefix OR of N bits on a one-dimensional R-Mesh with N processors. Assume that processor i holds input bit b_i.

2.2   Consider an $X \times Y$ R-Mesh.

(a)   How many different bus configurations can this R-Mesh have?

(b)   How many different bus configurations to within isomorphism can this R-Mesh have?

2.3   Write pseudocode for the algorithms of Theorems 2.1 and 2.2. For Theorem 2.1, use a recursive algorithm.

2.4   Prove that Algorithm 2.1 correctly adds the N inputs.

2.5   A *binary tree algorithm* for reducing $N = 2^n$ inputs to one result can be represented as an N-leaf balanced binary tree with inputs at the leaves, the result at the root, and internal vertices representing the reduction operation. Running such an algorithm on an N-processor platform involves assigning vertices of the tree to processors. Initially, each processor has an input, so leaves are labeled with distinct processors. An internal vertex labeled u with children labeled v and w requires processors v and w to send inputs/partial results to processor u (if different). Therefore, the labeling of vertices plays a vital role in determining the communication requirements of the algorithm.

Figure 2.21(a) shows an example of the tree for Algorithm 2.1. Notice

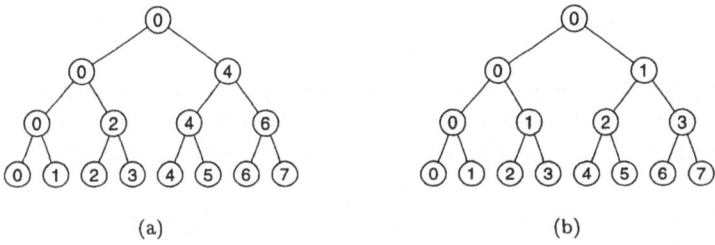

(a)   (b)

Figure 2.21.   Examples of labeled binary trees.

in this figure that if processors x and y (with $x < y$) communicate in a step, then for all $x < i < y$, processor i is not involved in a communication during that step. This permits a pair of processors to use a segment of the bus exclusively. As a result, the algorithm runs optimally in n steps.

(a)   Are there other ways of labeling vertices of the tree for which the algorithm runs optimally?

(b)   For the labeling shown in Figure 2.21(b), how many steps are needed to run an N-input binary tree algorithm on a one-dimensional R-Mesh with N processors? How many steps are needed on an $N \times N$ R-Mesh?

2.6   Algorithm 2.2 for permutation routing uses three data movement steps. Modify it to run with two data movement steps.

2.7   Is it possible to perform permutation routing of a row of a square R-Mesh with one broadcast?

2.8   Consider an $N \times N$ R-Mesh with $\sqrt{N}$ as an integer. For each $0 \le i, j < \sqrt{N}$, let processor $(i\sqrt{N}, j\sqrt{N})$ hold an element. Design a constant time algorithm to move all N elements to row 0.

2.9   Consider an $N \times N$ R-Mesh with a set P of N processors. Let $\pi : P \longrightarrow P$ be a bijection. For each of the following cases, design the fastest possible algorithm for permutation routing with respect to π.

        (a) P includes any one processor from each column.

        (b) P consists of the processors in the first $\sqrt{N}$ rows and $\sqrt{N}$ columns of the R-Mesh.

2.10   Repeat Problem 2.9 with π replaced by an injective partial function $f : P \longrightarrow P$. Here $f(p)$ need not be defined for all $p \in P$. If $f(p_1)$ and $f(p_2)$ are defined for some $p_1 \ne p_2$, then $f(p_1) \ne f(p_2)$.

2.11   Consider an $M \times N$ R-Mesh, where $1 \le M < N$. For inputs in row 0 and any permutation, prove that this R-Mesh can perform permutation routing in $O\left(\frac{N}{M}\right)$ time. Is this bound tight?

2.12   Let $m > 1$ be an integer. Consider the following partial function $f_m : \{0, 1, \cdots, N - 1\} \longrightarrow \{0, 1, \cdots, N - 1\}$, such that for all $0 \le i < N$, $f_m(i) = \frac{i}{m}$, if $\frac{i}{m}$ is an integer; otherwise, $f_m(i)$ is not defined. Consider an $N \times x$ R-Mesh in which processor $(i, 0)$ needs to communicate with processor $(f_m(i), 0)$, for each $0 \le i < N$ for which $f_m(i)$ is defined.

        Find a lower bound on (the order of) x that allows performing the data movement in constant time.

2.13   Design an optimal algorithm to perform permutation routing among all processors of an R-Mesh.

2.14 For any constant c, design a constant time algorithm to add N bits on an $\frac{N}{c} \times N$ R-Mesh.

2.15 Design a constant time R-Mesh algorithm to add N inputs a_j (for $0 \le j < N$) with $a_j \in \{x, y\}$, where x and y are any given pair of numbers.

2.16 Repeat Problem 2.15 with $a_j \in \{x, x+1, x+2\}$, where x is any given number.

2.17 A sequence of left and right parentheses is said to be *well-formed* if the number of left and right parentheses is the same and if every prefix of the sequence contains at least as many left parentheses as right parentheses. In a well-formed sequence, each left parenthesis has a matching right parenthesis, and for any two matching pairs (ℓ_1, r_1) and (ℓ_2, r_2), if ℓ_1 lies between ℓ_2 and r_2, then so does r_1.

Extend the "stepping down by a level" approach of Section 2.3.2 to a "stepping up or down by a level" constant time algorithm for an $N \times N$ R-Mesh that:

(a) Checks if an N-element parenthesis sequence is well formed.

(b) Finds each pair of matching parentheses in an N-element well-formed parenthesis sequence.

2.18 Write pseudocode for the modulo m addition algorithm of Lemma 2.5.

2.19 Improve the result of Lemma 2.5 to run in $O(1)$ time on an $(m+1) \times N$ R-Mesh. Assume that the inputs are initially in row 0.

2.20 Can a $2 \times N$ R-Mesh find the Exclusive OR of N bits in constant time? Explain.

2.21 The R-Mesh of Algorithm 2.3 can be viewed as a finite automaton where each row corresponds to a state (see Figure 2.22). Given an input sequence (input bits of the algorithm), the automaton goes to the state indicative of their sum. Conversely, running an input stream of N symbols through the automaton of Figure 2.22 can be implemented on an R-Mesh as shown in Figure 2.7.

(a) Implement the running of N input symbols through the automaton of Figure 2.23 on an R-Mesh. How does your solution relate (if at all) to the solution to Problem 2.17?

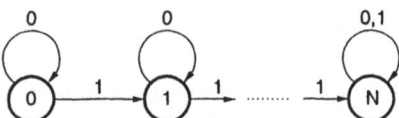

Figure 2.22.   Finite automaton for Algorithm 2.3.

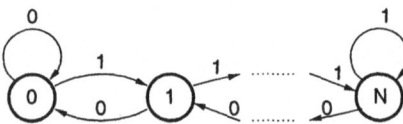

Figure 2.23.   Finite automaton for Problem 2.21(a).

(b)   Implement the running of N input symbols through any given finite automaton on an R-Mesh. Express the size of the R-Mesh in terms of the number of states, input symbols, and output symbols in the finite automaton.

(c)   Given the implementation of Part (b) and $M > N$, how would you run an input symbol stream of length M?

2.22   Prove Lemmas 2.7 and 2.8.

2.23   Extend the result of Lemma 2.8 to run on an $(m+1) \times N$ R-Mesh.

2.24   Consider a linear bus segment with processors $p_0, p_1, \cdots, p_{N-1}$. For $0 \leq i < N$, let processor p_i hold a flag $f(i)$ and a piece of data $d(i)$. The *general neighbor localization* problem requires each processor p_i (regardless of the value of $f(i)$) to obtain $left(i)$ and $right(i)$, defined below.

$$left(i) \quad = \quad d(\ell) \text{ if and only if}$$
$$0 \leq \ell < i \text{ and } f(\ell) = 1 \text{ and } \text{ for all } \ell < k < i, \; f(k) = 0$$
$$right(i) \quad = \quad d(r) \text{ if and only if}$$
$$i < r < n \text{ and } f(r) = 1 \text{ and } \text{ for all } i < k < r, \; f(k) = 0$$

In other words, $left(i)$ (resp., $right(i)$) is the data held by the nearest flagged processor (if any) to the left (resp., right) of processor p_i; for $0 \leq i < j < N$, consider processor p_i to be to the left of processor p_j.

Design a constant-time algorithm to solve the general neighbor localization problem.

2.25 A bus is *linear* if each vertex in its connected component of the configuration graph has a degree of at most 2. A linear bus is defined to be *acyclic* if its connected component in the configuration graph is acyclic. Consider an acyclic linear bus between end points L and R. This bus is *oriented* if and only if each processor on the bus knows which of the (at most) two processors adjacent to it on the bus is closer to L.

Prove that the general neighbor localization problem (see definition in Problem 2.24) can be solved on any oriented linear bus (that could snake its way through various rows and columns of the R-Mesh).

Why is it important for the linear bus to be acyclic and oriented for solving neighbor localization?

2.26 Let $\mathcal{L}$ be an $R \times C$ LR-Mesh and let $\mathcal{M}$ be a $2R \times 2C$ LR-Mesh. Prove that $\mathcal{M}$ can convert (in constant time) any bus configuration of $\mathcal{L}$ into an "equivalent" configuration of $\mathcal{M}$ in which every linear acyclic bus is oriented as well (see also Problem 2.25).

2.27 For integer $q \geq 1$, a q-neighborhood of an N element binary array $A = [a_i]$ (where $0 \leq i < N$) is another N element binary array $B = [b_i]$, where $b_i = 1$ if and only if there exists an index j such that $0 \leq i - q \leq j \leq i + q < N$ such that $a_j = 1$.

Design a constant time R-Mesh algorithm to solve the q-neighborhood problem. What sized R-Mesh would you use?

2.28 For any constant $c > 1$, design a constant time algorithm to chain sort N $\log N$-bit numbers on an $\frac{N}{c} \times N$ R-Mesh.

2.29 Algorithm 2.6 requires that $2^b \leq N$. What changes, if any, are needed to make the algorithm work for $2^b > N$. How will this change the performance of the algorithm?

2.30 Algorithm 2.6 can be trivially adapted to find the maximum of N b-bit integers. Use this observation to prove that for any constant $\epsilon > 0$ and $b = O(\log N)$, a $2^{b\epsilon} \times N$ R-Mesh can find the maximum of N b-bit integers in constant time.

2.31 Let $S = \{a_i : 0 \leq i < N\}$ consist of N elements drawn from a linearly ordered set. The *unbiased rank* of a_i (for any $0 \leq i < N$) is the number of elements $a_j \in S$ such that $a_j < a_i$.

Consider a one-dimensional R-Mesh with N processors holding a sorted N-element array. Design a constant time algorithm to determine the unbiased ranks of the array elements.

2.32   Write pseudocode for the algorithm of Lemma 2.14.

2.33   Let $a_0, a_1, \cdots, a_{N-1}$ be an array of N elements from a totally ordered set. The *prefix maxima* of this array is the sequence $b_0, b_1, \cdots, b_{N-1}$, where $b_i = \max\{a_j \; : \; 0 \leq j \leq i\}$, for $0 \leq i < N$.

Adapt the algorithm of Lemma 2.14 to determine the prefix maxima of the inputs without altering the resource bounds.

2.34   For $1 \leq m \leq N$, design an $O\left(\frac{\log N}{1 + \log m}\right)$ time algorithm on an $m \times N$ R-Mesh to determine the prefix maxima (see definition in Problem 2.33) of N inputs.

2.35   For any constant $\epsilon > 0$, prove that an $N^\epsilon \times N$ R-Mesh can find the maximum of N elements in constant time.

2.36   Given N planar points in a row of an $N \times N$ R-Mesh, design a constant time algorithm to determine their bounding rectangle (the smallest rectangle with horizontal and vertical sides that encloses all input points).

2.37   In embedding a distributed sub-R-Mesh in an R-Mesh, each external edge of the sub-R-Mesh maps to an R-Mesh bus. Define the *congestion* of the embedding as the maximum number of edges mapped to an R-Mesh bus.

Prove that a distributed sub-R-Mesh with congestion C can operate as an R-Mesh in which each broadcast on the bus requires at most C steps. What assumptions, if any, are needed about the embedding?

2.38   An $R \times C$ R-Mesh can embed several different distributed sub-R-Meshes.

(a)   One class of sub-R-Meshes includes those whose external edges are represented by only horizontal and vertical buses (as in Algorithm 2.7). Characterize sub-R-Meshes in this category.

(b)   As the previous problem implies, external edges need not be mapped to horizontal or vertical edges. Indeed, processors in the same row or column of the sub-R-Mesh may map to processors in different rows and/or columns of the R-Mesh. Without the restrictions in Part (a), how would you characterize a sub-R-Mesh that can be embedded in an $R \times C$ R-Mesh?

(c)   Would your answers to the previous parts change if the embedding is permitted to have a congestion of $C > 1$ (see Problem 2.37)?

2.39   Consider a graph $\mathcal{G}$ representing an interconnection topology. A *communication step* on this topology can be represented as a subgraph of $\mathcal{G}$ consisting only of "active" edges that represent communications in that step. Unless specified otherwise, all edges could be active in a step.

If a model $\mathcal{M}$ can run an arbitrary communication step of $\mathcal{G}$ in t steps, then $\mathcal{M}$ is said to admit a t-*step* emulation of $\mathcal{G}$.

(a)   An *embedding* of a guest graph $\mathcal{G} = (V_1, E_1)$ in a host graph $\mathcal{H} = (V_2, E_2)$ consists of (i) a mapping $f : V_1 \longrightarrow V_2$ of vertices of $\mathcal{G}$ to vertices of $\mathcal{H}$ and (ii) a mapping of each edge (u, v) of $\mathcal{G}$ to a path (possibly of length 0) between vertices $f(u)$ and $f(v)$ of $\mathcal{H}$. The *dilation* of the embedding is the length of the longest path of $\mathcal{H}$ to which an edge of $\mathcal{G}$ is mapped. The quantity $\frac{|V_2|}{|V_1|}$ is called the *expansion* of the embedding. The *congestion* of the embedding is the maximum number of edges of $\mathcal{G}$ that employ any given edge of $\mathcal{H}$ (that is, whose corresponding paths include the given edge of $\mathcal{H}$). The *load* of the embedding is the maximum number of vertices of $\mathcal{G}$ mapped to any given vertex of $\mathcal{H}$.

Prove that if a communication step of $\mathcal{G}$ has a congestion-1, load-1 embedding in an $R \times C$ mesh, then an $R \times C$ R-Mesh admits a 1-step emulation of $\mathcal{G}$. Do the dilation and expansion of the embedding affect the emulation speed?

(b)   Prove that an $O(\sqrt{N}) \times O(\sqrt{N})$ R-Mesh admits a 1-step emulation of an N-vertex balanced binary tree.

(c)   Design a 1-step emulation of an $N \times N$ mesh of trees on an R-Mesh of the smallest possible size.

(d)   How would your emulation change if the mesh of trees in Part (c) above restricts each tree to use edges from at most one level at any given communication step? Again use the smallest R-Mesh possible.

2.40   The *aspect ratio* of an $X \times Y$ R-Mesh is $\frac{\max\{X,Y\}}{\min\{X,Y\}}$. A low aspect ratio can often be advantageous as it leads to a "nearly square" layout.

Consider an $X \times Y$ R-Mesh with $X < Y$. Prove that this R-Mesh can be embedded within a constant aspect ratio $\sqrt{XY} \times \Theta\left(\sqrt{XY}\right)$ R-Mesh with the same number of processors (to within a constant).

2.41   Algorithm 2.8 for list ranking requires the first element of the list to be flagged. Modify the algorithm to determine the first element. The new algorithm must run within the same resource bounds as the original one.

2.42   For any integer m, design an algorithm to determine the modulo m ranks of elements of an N-element list. Your algorithm must run in constant time on an $Nm \times Nm$ R-Mesh.

2.43   Show how an N-element list can be embedded as a single bus in an $N \times N$ R-Mesh. View the list as an N vertex, $(N-1)$ edge, directed graph, and let the diagonal processors of the R-Mesh represent these vertices. Your embedding should generate a single bus that traverses the diagonal processors (vertices) in their order in the list. Between two diagonal processors, the bus may traverse non-diagonal processors.

2.44   Use Problem 2.43 to design a constant time, $N \times N$ R-Mesh algorithm to determine the rank of one given element x of a list of size N.

2.45   Use Problem 2.44 to rank an N-element list on an $N \times N^2$ R-Mesh.

2.46   Let L be an N element list with elements flagged as active or inactive. *Contracting* the list L creates a new list L' that strings together the active elements of L in the same relative order as in L.

Design a constant time algorithm to contract an N-element list L on an $N \times N$ R-Mesh.

2.47   Use Problems 2.42 to 2.46 and ideas from Algorithm 2.4 to design an algorithm for ranking a list of N elements in $O\left(\frac{\log N}{\log m}\right)$ time on an $Nm \times Nm$ R-Mesh, where $2 \leq m \leq N$.

In Chapter 6 we will refer to this algorithm as the *basic list ranking* algorithm.

2.48 For any constant $\epsilon > 0$, design a constant time algorithm for ranking a list of N elements on an $N^{1+\epsilon} \times N^{1+\epsilon}$ R-Mesh.

2.49 Prove that an $N \times N$ R-Mesh can rank a list of N elements in $O(\log N)$ time.

2.50 Prove Algorithm 2.9 correct.

2.51 The transitive closure of a graph $\mathcal{G} = (V, E)$ is another graph $\mathcal{G}^* = (V, E^*)$ in which two vertices are connected by an edge if and only if those vertices have a path between them in $\mathcal{G}$.

Design an R-Mesh algorithm to determine the transitive closure of an N-vertex graph. For a constant time solution, use an $N^2 \times N^2$ R-Mesh. What time can you achieve on an $N \times N$ R-Mesh? Assume that both the input graph and output transitive closure are in the form of $N \times N$ adjacency matrices.

2.52 Write pseudocode for the algorithm of Lemma 2.19.

2.53 Design a constant time algorithm to add two b-bit distributed unary integers on a b-processor, one-dimensional R-Mesh.

2.54 Write pseudocode for the algorithm of Lemma 2.20.

2.55 Generalize Lemma 2.20 by designing a constant time algorithm to compute $\lfloor \frac{x}{m} \rfloor$, for any integer $m \geq 2$. What sized R-Mesh will you use?

2.56 The unary representation used in Section 2.3.7 has $i + 1$ ones in the representation of integer $i \geq 1$. One could also consider the following "positional unary" representation with only one 1 in the representation for any integer.

For any integer $0 \leq i < b$, a b-bit *positional unary representation* has 0s in all positions except in bit i which is a 1. This naturally extends to the *distributed positional unary representation*.

Will the algorithms of Section 2.3.7 work for the distributed positional unary representation?

2.57 Express the one-dimensional R-Mesh algorithm for finding the OR of N bits in terms of the function decomposition technique.

2.58   Express the modulo m addition algorithm of Section 2.3.2 in terms of the function decomposition technique.

2.59   For integer x, let $\mathbf{Z}_x = \{0, 1, \cdots x - 1\}$. A function $f : \mathbf{Z}_x \longrightarrow \mathbf{Z}_y$ can be *embedded* in an $N \times M$ R-Mesh (where $N = \max\{x, y\}$) if for all $i \in \mathbf{Z}_x$ such that $f(i) = j$, the R-Mesh has a bus configuration that connects the W port of processor $(i, 0)$ to the E port of processor $(j, M - 1)$.

   (a)   For any integers $k, N > 1$, let function $f_k : \mathbf{Z}_N \longrightarrow \mathbf{Z}_{N+k}$ be such that for any $i \in \mathbf{Z}_N$, $f_k(i) = i + k$.
         Show that f_k can be embedded in an $(N + k) \times k$ R-Mesh.

   (b)   For $1 \leq \ell \leq L$, let $X_{\ell-1}, X_\ell, N_\ell, M_\ell$ be integers. Suppose function $f_\ell : \mathbf{Z}_{X_{\ell-1}} \longrightarrow \mathbf{Z}_{X_\ell}$ can be embedded in an $N_\ell \times M_\ell$ R-Mesh.
         Prove that the function $f = f_1 \circ f_2 \circ \cdots \circ f_L$, composed[9] of the f_ℓ's can be embedded in an $N \times M$ R-Mesh, where

$$N = \max\{N_1, N_2, \cdots, N_L\} \text{ and}$$
$$M = M_1 + M_2 + \cdots + M_L.$$

Bibliographic Notes

Ben-Asher and Schuster [21], Trahan *et al.* [314, 325], Vaidyanathan [330], Thangavel and Muthuswamy [312, 313], Bertossi and Mei [29], and El-Boghdadi *et al.* [93, 94, 96, 95], among others, studied the one-dimensional R-Mesh (segmentable bus). The two-dimensional R-Mesh model of Section 2.1 evolved from the "RMESH" model first proposed by Miller *et al.* [213, 215, 216], the polymorphic torus of Li and Maresca [179, 180], and the PARBS introduced by Wang *et al.* [348]. Miller *et al.* [213, 215, 216] proposed the unit-cost measure of bus delay. Section 11.5 describes other bus delay measures.
    Many of the techniques presented in Section 2.3 have been gleaned from a variety of sources and some modified for presentation in the

---

[9]The *composition* of functions $f : A \longrightarrow B$ and $g : B \longrightarrow C$ is the function $f \circ g : A \longrightarrow C$ where $(f \circ g)(i) = g(f(i))$, for each $i \in A$.

R-Mesh setting. Several of these techniques have been developed independently by various researchers in different contexts. Here we point to some of the sources for these techniques.

Miller *et al.* [213, 214] presented some of the earliest results in data movement on the R-Mesh. Subsequently, other results were developed for various routing scenarios [59, 135, 155, 157, 167, 191, 244, 276, 287].

Wang *et al.* [350] first proposed the basic algorithm for adding bits (Section 2.3.2) in the setting of a "triangular processor array." Subsequently, Olariu *et al.* [241, 245] developed the algorithm for modulo m addition of bits and the efficient prefix sums algorithm. In their paper on adding bits, Nakano and Wada [232] provided a chronological listing of results for this problem. In a later work, Bertossi and Mei [28] improved on the result of Corollary 2.11 for adding N bits by using a residue number system representation in $O(1)$ time on an $N \times O\left(\frac{\log^2 N}{\log \log N}\right)$ CREW bit-model LR-Mesh.

Although we presented the exclusive OR algorithm as a corollary to the modulo addition result, Wang *et al.* [348, 349] developed it independently. The $\Omega\left(\frac{\log N}{\log \log N}\right)$ PRAM lower bound for this problem is due to Beame and Hastäd [16]. The exclusive OR algorithm has also played an important part in separating the computational power of reconfigurable and conventional (non-reconfigurable) models of computation [194, 242, 325].

Vaidyanathan [330] applied neighbor localization, a generalization of the bus-splitting technique of Miller *et al.* [213, 215, 216], to reconfigurable models. The neighbor localization problem itself was first defined by Hagerup [123]. The chain sorting algorithm of Section 2.3.3 is based on integer sorting algorithms for the reconfigurable models, B-PRAM [330], and RMBM [324]. Hagerup [124] provided randomized PRAM algorithms for chain sorting. Cormen *et al.* [65, pp 168–179] discussed sequential approaches to integer sorting.

The underlying idea of the maximum finding algorithm of Section 2.3.4, namely comparing all input pairs, has been known for a long time. Miller *et al.* [213, 215, 216] first adapted this approach to the reconfigurable mesh. The more general result of Theorem 2.15 is a special case of the result of Trahan *et al.* [322] who developed maximum finding algorithms for R-Meshes of different aspect ratios.

Olariu *et al.* [241] developed the list ranking algorithms of Section 2.3.5. Similar results also exist for other reconfigurable models [306, 324]; Problems 2.47 and 2.48 are based on this body of work. Hayashi *et al.* [134] (see also Section 6.5) presented more efficient list ranking algorithms; Problems 2.43–2.45 are based on some of their work.

Other algorithms that employ the distance embedding approach can be found in Trahan *et al.* [323, 324].

The s-t connectivity problem is a useful tool that could provide answers to important questions in complexity theory. It is particularly relevant toward separating the capabilities of different R-Mesh versions. Chapter 9 explores this issue; bibliographic notes at the end of Chapter 9 provide references on this topic. Wang and Chen [346] proposed the s-t connectivity approach of Section 2.3.6 and used it to solve a variety of graph algorithms on the R-Mesh; Problem 2.51 is based on their work. Subsequently, the connectivity embedding approach has been used for other graph algorithms [4, 323, 324] and reconfigurable model simulations [17, 110, 291, 325].

Chen *et al.* [55] introduced the concept of function decomposition for reconfigurable models; some their results also appeared in an earlier paper [348]. Jang and Prasanna [148] and Bertossi and Mei [28] detailed the various number representation formats and methods to convert among them; the names of the representations used in this book are different from theirs, however. Jang and Prasanna [148] also developed the distributed unary and multiple addition algorithms of Section 2.3.7.

Schuster [291], Trahan *et al.* [325], and Vaidyanathan and Trahan [332] established that a two dimensional R-Mesh is at least as powerful as any other reconfigurable model in its class[10].

Dharmasena and Vaidyanathan [81, 82, 83] discussed binary trees and their labeling (Problem 2.5). Fernández-Zepeda *et al.* [111] and El-Boghdadi [93] described methods for orienting a linear bus (Problem 2.26). Problem 2.27 is motivated by the the image shrinking and expanding algorithms described by Jenq and Sahni [150]. Leighton [174], among others, described details of the concept of embedding one graph in another (Problems 2.37 and 2.39).

---

[10]Here we refer to reconfigurable models with bidirectional buses of the sort described in Section 2.1.1. There exist reconfigurable models called "directed models" (Section 3.1.5) and "non-monotonic models" [291] that could be more powerful than the two dimensional R-Mesh.

Chapter 3

MODELS OF RECONFIGURATION

In Chapter 2, we introduced the R-Mesh and described several algorithmic techniques for it. This model suffices for most of the discussion in this book. Enhancements to R-Meshes, however, suit some problems better, while restrictions on the R-Mesh address some practical considerations. Also, other reconfigurable models often provide a different (and sometimes equivalent) view of dynamic reconfiguration than the R-Mesh that can help in understanding dynamic reconfiguration. This chapter deals with these variations on the R-Mesh idea.

We first build on the R-Mesh model, exploring some new angles, restrictions, and extensions. Then we briefly describe other reconfigurable models, restricting our discussion to their salient features; subsequent chapters will discuss some of these models further. In Section 3.3, we compare these models, placing them in relation to each other and traditional models of parallel computation, to give the reader a better feel for the power and limitations of dynamic reconfiguration.

Although this chapter introduces the reader to several dynamically reconfigurable models, the coverage is not comprehensive. Bibliographic notes at the end of the chapter point to some of the models not discussed here and to references for further reading.

3.1   The Reconfigurable Mesh—A Second Coat

The R-Mesh introduced in Chapter 2 is the basic model used in this book. This model, however, does not address some important considerations. What is the cost of permitting the model to have buses of arbitrary shape? What is the implication of using processors of very small word size? Does any advantage arise from writing concurrently to

buses? Does an extension of the R-Mesh idea to higher dimensions add
to its computing capability? What can be gained by imparting direction to buses? These questions raise important issues that impact the
cost, power, and implementability of reconfigurable models. This section introduces these issues through enhancements and restrictions on
the R-Mesh model of Chapter 2. Specifically, we discuss five additional
facets to the reconfigurable mesh:

1. Restrictions on the structure of the bus,

2. Bit-model (constant word size) R-Mesh,

3. Concurrent and exclusive bus accesses,

4. Higher dimensional reconfigurable meshes, and

5. Directed buses.

The first two represent restrictions of the R-Mesh model of Chapter 2,
while the rest enhance the model. These considerations are, for the
most part, independent of each other; for example, it is possible to have
a reconfigurable mesh capable of concurrent writes, with or without
directed buses. Chapter 9 uses simulations to relate some of these models
and conventional models of parallel computation such as the PRAM.

3.1.1   Models with Restricted Bus Structure

The R-Mesh of Chapter 2 permits a processor to partition its ports
in fifteen different ways, enabling the model to assume numerous bus
configurations. In this section we describe derivatives of this model
that place restrictions on the structure of buses. Most of these restrictions boil down to permitting some of the fifteen port partitions of an
R-Mesh processor, though some apply a global criterion. These models,
for the most part, represent various trade-offs between "power" and implementability. Section 3.3 explains the notion of power; here we use the
term in a more intuitive sense, in that a more powerful model is capable
of solving problems faster (although not necessarily more efficiently).

Another consideration useful in selecting an R-Mesh restriction is
"algorithmic scalability," the ability of a model to run an algorithm for
a problem of fixed size on smaller-sized instances of the model. Chapter 8 deals with this concept in detail; here we informally describe the
relationship between restricted R-Meshes and algorithmic scalability. If
an algorithm for a problem of size N is designed to run in T steps
on a model with $P(N)$ processors, then for $M < P(N)$ the algorithm
runs on an M-processor instance of the model in $\Theta\left(T \cdot \frac{P(N)}{M} \cdot F(N, M)\right)$
steps, where $\frac{P(N)}{M}$ represents the slowdown factor resulting from the use

of fewer processors, and $F(N, M)$ represents an overhead. Ideally, this overhead should be a small constant; this is indeed the case for most conventional models, as fewer processors can usually be employed without loss of efficiency. All known methods for scaling arbitrary algorithms on the unrestricted R-Mesh have an overhead, $F(N, M)$, that depends on N. This is a serious disadvantage for algorithm design and development, as the "best" algorithm for a given problem could depend on the relative sizes of the available machine and the problem instance. As discussed below, restricted R-Meshes fare better in this respect.

Horizontal-Vertical R-Mesh (HVR-Mesh). An HVR-Mesh permits only the port partitions $\{\overline{NS}, \overline{EW}\}$, $\{\overline{NS}, \overline{E}, \overline{W}\}$, $\{\overline{N}, \overline{EW}, \overline{S}\}$, and $\{\overline{N}, \overline{S}, \overline{E}, \overline{W}\}$ within each processor.

This requires a bus in the HVR-Mesh to lie entirely within a row or a column, so that a bus is representable as a horizontal or vertical line (see Figure 3.1(a)). This restriction severely curtails the power of the model. The HVR-Mesh, however, has one of the simplest implementations among reconfigurable meshes (see Problem 3.1 and Section 11.5). Moreover, algorithms for it scale with optimal (constant) overhead.

Among the algorithms of Chapter 2, the binary tree algorithm (Algorithm 2.1, page 22), row/column broadcasts (Section 2.3.1), permutation routing (Algorithm 2.2, page 26), chain sorting (Algorithm 2.6, page 37), neighbor localization (Algorithm 2.5, page 34), and maximum finding (Algorithm 2.7, page 41) run on an HVR-Mesh; the binary tree algorithm and neighbor localization run on a one-dimensional sub-R-Mesh that could be restricted to a row or column of the R-Mesh, and, hence, an HVR-Mesh.

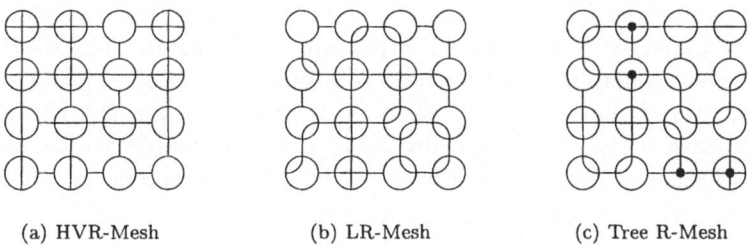

(a) HVR-Mesh   (b) LR-Mesh   (c) Tree R-Mesh

Figure 3.1. R-Meshes with restricted bus structures.

Linear R-Mesh (LR-Mesh). The LR-Mesh permits all port partitions that connect at most two ports of a processor. As a result, a bus cannot branch, and one can view it as being linear. Figure 3.1(b) shows a sample bus configuration of a 4×4 LR-Mesh. Note that the LR-Mesh allows a bus to be a simple cycle (as shown in the southeast corner of Figure 3.1(b)).

Clearly, the HVR-Mesh is a special case of the LR-Mesh. Like the HVR-Mesh, algorithms on the LR-Mesh scale with optimal (constant) overhead. Moreover, the LR-Mesh is more powerful than the HVR-Mesh. The LR-Mesh is more difficult to realize than the HVR-Mesh. Some LR-Mesh algorithms, that do not run directly on an HVR-Mesh, can be implemented efficiently, however. Section 11.5 discusses some of these issues.

Most R-Mesh algorithms run on an LR-Mesh. In fact, all algorithms of Chapter 2 except *s-t* connectivity (Algorithm 2.9, page 47) run on the LR-Mesh. As stated, the algorithm for list ranking (Algorithm 2.8, page 44) uses port partitions that are not permitted on an LR-Mesh; one can easily modify them to run on an LR-Mesh, however (see Problem 3.3).

Fusing R-Mesh (FR-Mesh). The FR-Mesh permits its processors to configure as either $\{\overline{NS}, \overline{EW}\}$ or $\{\overline{NSEW}\}$. Despite this limited repertoire of port partitions, the FR-Mesh is as powerful as the unrestricted R-Mesh. (That is, the FR-Mesh can simulate any unrestricted R-Mesh step in constant time, although with a polynomial blowup in the number of processors.) Figure 2.15(c) shows a bus configuration of an FR-Mesh. A way to view the configuration is as horizontal and vertical bus segments that span entire rows or columns, with the possibility for connecting horizontal and vertical buses.

Algorithm 2.8 (page 44) for list ranking can be modified to run in constant time on an FR-Mesh (see Problem 3.6). Algorithm 2.9 (page 47) for *s-t* connectivity runs on an FR-Mesh. Whether the LR-Mesh can solve this problem in constant time is a longstanding open problem. It is conjectured that the FR-Mesh is more powerful than the LR-Mesh. Algorithms on the FR-Mesh also scale well. Although the overhead, $F(N, M)$ is not constant, it is independent of the problem size (N) and depends only on the available machine size (M).

Tree R-Mesh. The Tree R-Mesh restricts its buses to be acyclic (Figure 3.1(c) shows an example). Unlike the restrictions described so far, no set of allowed port partitions adequately describes the Tree R-Mesh; in fact, it is possible for a Tree R-Mesh to have processors with all fifteen possible port partitions. None of the algorithms of Chapter 2 specifically uses a Tree R-Mesh, except in the sense that all LR-Mesh algorithms using only acyclic buses also run on the Tree R-Mesh. In fact, it is possible to prove that every Tree R-Mesh algorithm can run on an LR-Mesh without loss of speed or efficiency. Therefore, all Tree R-Mesh algorithms also scale optimally.

Of the restrictions described above, the HVR-Mesh has the simplest implementation (see Section 11.5). Most R-Mesh algorithms run on an LR-Mesh, while some significant applications (such as *s-t* connectivity) require an FR-Mesh. Individually, the LR-Mesh is not known to have a constant time solution to some graph problems that the FR-Mesh can solve in constant time. On the other hand, the LR-Mesh can solve (in constant time) many other problems using far fewer processors than the FR-Mesh. Between them, the LR-Mesh and FR-Mesh can run almost all known algorithms for the R-Mesh. From this point of view it is sometimes useful to think of R-Mesh restrictions as algorithmic (rather than hardware) restrictions. For instance, a "separable R-Mesh," each step of which runs on an LR-Mesh or an FR-Mesh, has good algorithmic scalability and can solve a very wide array of problems.

3.1.2 Word Size

So far we have not explicitly considered the bus width and processor word size in the R-Mesh. In fact, each processor in a N-processor R-Mesh implicitly requires a word size of $\Omega(\log N)$ to address other processors in constant time. Since many algorithms use processor addresses as data (for instance in chain sorting), it is also customary to assume the bus width to be the same as the processor word size; this ensures constant time movement of one word of data. This model is called the *word model*. We now describe a restricted version of the R-Mesh called the bit model.

The *bit model* of the R-Mesh restricts processor word size and bus width to be constants. To retain the R-Mesh's assumption of constant time local operations, the bit model also bounds the local memory in each processor to a constant. The bit model is useful in designing special purpose hardware for a small suite of applications. It has also been suggested as a basis for designing asynchronous reconfigurable circuits.

Impact on Algorithm Design. Constant word size and bus width have important implications for designing algorithms on the bit-model R-Mesh. In the following, we assume the bit model to have a non-constant number of processors.

Addressing other processors: In a bit-model R-Mesh, a processor cannot address other processors in the usual way by writing its own or another processor's index on the bus. In constant time, it can only distinguish among a constant number of sets of processors (such as those within a constant distance on the underlying mesh, or those flagged by a constant number of bits).

Self addresses: One of the most common assumptions about any model of parallel computation is for each processor to have its own address. In a word-model R-Mesh, a processor can use this information in many ways such as determining its position relative to the diagonal or R-Mesh border, or identifying itself to a neighbor in neighbor localization. Clearly, assuming knowledge of processor self-addresses is not valid for the bit model.

On the other hand, a constant amount of information that depends on the processor's index can be "hardwired" into each processor's memory. For example, if the algorithm requires all processors on the main diagonal (with indices (i, i)) to execute a step, then it can do so by checking a hardwired flag. Since a processor's local memory can accommodate a constant number of such flags, an algorithm can check a constant number of such conditions.

Algorithm form: In the word model, a non-constant time algorithm can assume a recursive or iterative form. Since a non-constant time recursive algorithm requires a stack of non-constant size, the bit model cannot specify such algorithms recursively. Iterative algorithms on the bit model must ensure that the terminating condition can be evaluated in constant time. For example, the bit model cannot use the construct "**for** $i \longleftarrow 0$ **to** N," as a bit-model processor cannot store, increment, and compare i with N in constant time. Generally, iterations have the form "**while** a flag is set **do**," for which the bit model could evaluate the terminating condition in constant time.

Global Bus Configurations: Among the data movement algorithms of Chapter 2, row and column broadcasts are clearly possible on the bit model. In fact, the bit model can perform constant time broadcasts for a fixed set of configurations (see Problem 3.9). Routing an arbitrary permutation poses a problem, however, as the index of the destination processor would be too large for the bit model. (To route a constant number of predetermined permutations, however, the bit model can use "hardwired" flags.) The binary tree algorithm (Algorithm 2.1, page 22) does not run on the bit model (even if the operation to be performed is on a constant number of bits). This is because a processor requires its address and the iteration number (both non-constant) to determine its function during the iteration.

On the other hand, the algorithm for finding the OR of N bits runs on the bit model. Indeed, the bit-model R-Mesh can run all instances of neighbor localization in which neighbors (that may be arbitrarily far apart on the underlying one-dimensional R-Mesh) communicate constant sized data (rather than processor indices). Similarly, the maximum finding algorithm implied by Lemma 2.14 (page 40) runs in constant time on the bit model, provided the inputs are of constant size. The algorithm of Theorem 2.15 (page 42), even in an iterative form, requires the identification of processors in columns with indices divisible by m^j, for each $1 \leq j \leq \log_m N$. Therefore, this algorithm is not suitable for the bit model, unless $\log_m N$ is a constant. Sections 2.3.2 and 2.3.7 represent a class of algorithms well-suited to the bit model. These algorithms use the input to configure a bus that carries a 1-bit signal to the answer. The bit model can also run Algorithm 2.9 (page 47) for s-t connectivity. Most of the remaining algorithms of Chapter 2 are for problems that cannot be defined in a straightforward manner for the bit model. (For example, chain sorting requires an output involving $\log N$-bit pointers.) For these problems, a solution may be possible if the output is represented in distributed format (see Section 2.3.7).

The Power of Bits. Despite the numerous restrictions on its operation, the bit model is surprisingly powerful. In Chapter 9, we show that an $Nb \times Nb$ bit-model R-Mesh can simulate each step of an $N \times N$, b-bit, word-model R-Mesh in constant time, assuming standard arithmetic and logical operations for processors of the word model.

Relationship to Other Restrictions. Since the word-size of an R-Mesh is independent of the restrictions in Section 3.1.1, one could have bit-models of the HVR-Mesh, LR-Mesh, FR-Mesh, and Tree R-Mesh.

3.1.3 Accessing Buses

In our discussion so far, the R-Mesh permits multiple processors to read simultaneously from a bus, while restricting the number of writers to (at most) one per bus. A model with this form of bus access is called a *Concurrent Read, Exclusive Write (CREW)* model, based on the nomenclature used for the Parallel Random Access Machine (PRAM). Other possibilities include *Exclusive Read, Exclusive Write (EREW)*, *Exclusive Read, Concurrent Write (ERCW)*, and *Concurrent Read, Concurrent Write (CRCW)*. Of these, the ERCW model has found little, if any, application in dynamic reconfiguration, so we will not consider it further.

The most restrictive bus access model requires all accesses to be exclusive—the EREW model. In most implementations of a bus, there is little advantage to restricting bus reads to be exclusive. Indeed, many algorithms on the reconfigurable mesh rely on concurrent reads to broadcast information and enable processors to make autonomous decisions in subsequent steps. All algorithms of Chapter 2, except neighbor localization and the binary tree algorithm, use concurrent reads during row/column broadcasts. From a theoretical point of view, however, restricting the model to exclusive reads can provide useful insight into the power of reconfiguration. We will not discuss the EREW model further until Chapter 9 that deals with the relative powers of different models.

The CRCW Model. In the CRCW model, there is no restriction on the number of simultaneous accesses to the bus. When several processors attempt to write simultaneously to a bus, a *write rule* defines the *bus value* that a processor reading from the bus would obtain. We will consider the following write rules, which are well known in the context of the PRAM.

COMMON: All concurrent writes on a bus must be of the same value.

COLLISION: Under this rule, any concurrent write produces a distinguished "collision symbol" as the bus value. Therefore, this rule only permits a reader to detect whether a concurrent write has occurred.

COLLISION+: This combines the COMMON and COLLISION rules. When writers are all writing the same value, then this value is the bus value; otherwise, the bus value is the collision symbol.

ARBITRARY: Of the processors/ports attempting to write concurrently to a bus, exactly one succeeds. The value written by this processor/port is the bus value. Note that an arbitrary writer could succeed (possibly changing each time the algorithm is executed). Therefore algorithms using this rule should work for any choice of writer.

PRIORITY: Of the processors/ports attempting to write concurrently to a bus, the one with the highest priority (usually the lowest index) succeeds. The value written by this processor/port is the bus value. Note that unlike the ARBITRARY rule, PRIORITY selects a fixed processor/port and is therefore a stronger rule.

The COMMON rule is simple to implement on a bus. The ARBITRARY and PRIORITY rules are not simple to implement directly on a bus. We will employ these rules, however, as algorithmic conveniences, using other write rules to simulate them on reconfigurable models.

In Section 3.1.4 we present a method for simulating the PRIORITY rule on a COMMON (or COLLISION) CRCW R-Mesh (that is, an R-Mesh that resolves concurrent writes according to the COMMON (or COLLISION) rule). This simulation translates to simulations of all other rules on a COMMON or COLLISION CRCW R-Mesh, as PRIORITY is the strongest of the rules described above, and COMMON and COLLISION are the weakest. Such simulations permit algorithm design on the R-Mesh using the most convenient write rule, without getting caught up in details of their implementation. In some situations, this approach can even speed up the resulting algorithm (see Problem 8.17).

Relationship to Other Models. The bus access model is independent of the restrictions of Section 3.1.1 and the processor word size (Section 3.1.2). That is, each restriction can access its buses exclusively or concurrently. Note that although the definition of the PRIORITY CRCW model is based on processor indices, the PRIORITY rule does not require processors to perform the priority resolution. Therefore, this rule applies to the bit model as well.

It should be noted that although each of the bus access models (EREW, CREW, and CRCW) for the R-Mesh has a PRAM counterpart, their contribution to the "power" of the two models is vastly different. For example in a reconfigurable model, the ability to perform concurrent reads can compensate for the lack of concurrent writing capability, possibly with an increase in the size of the model. This is not true for the PRAM where a CRCW PRAM can find the OR of N bits in constant time, while a lower bound of $\Omega(\log N)$ applies without concurrent writing ability, regardless of the size of the model.

3.1.4   Higher Dimensions

As indicated in Chapter 2, the idea of a two-dimensional R-Mesh readily extends to higher dimensions. For $d \geq 1$, an $N_1 \times N_2 \times \cdots \times N_d$ (d-dimensional) R-Mesh has an underlying $N_1 \times N_2 \times \cdots \times N_d$ (d-dimensional) mesh. Figure 3.2 shows a three-dimensional R-Mesh. Each processor of a d-dimensional R-Mesh creates internal connections by partitioning its set of $2d$ ports. If d is a constant, then the Partitioning, Communication, and Computation phases (see Section 2.1.1) are the same for two-dimensional and d-dimensional R-Meshes.

Universality of the Two-Dimensional R-Mesh. Notwithstanding the denser underlying topology of a d-dimensional R-Mesh (with $d > 2$), a two-dimensional R-Mesh can simulate each step of a higher

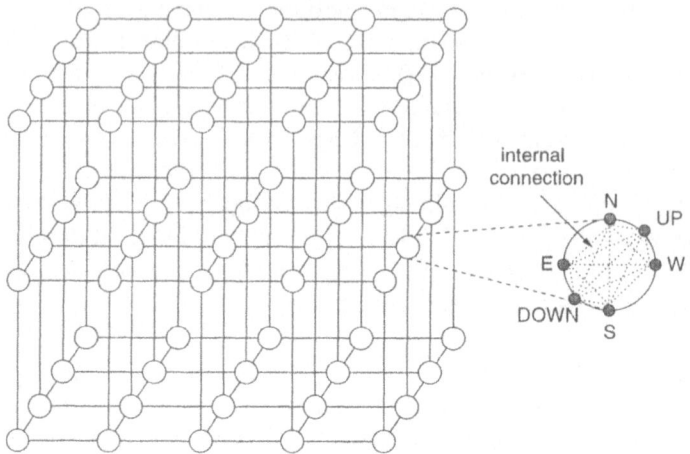

Figure 3.2. A $3 \times 5 \times 4$ R-Mesh. As in the two-dimensional R-Mesh, the ports connected by external edges in the first two dimensions are denoted by N, S, E, and W. The ports in the third dimension are denoted in this figure by UP and DOWN.

dimensional R-Mesh in constant time. (For most cases, the size of the simulating R-Mesh is optimal.) We now present a part of this result for running three-dimensional R-Mesh algorithms on a two-dimensional R-Mesh; Section 9.1.2 presents the full result.

THEOREM 3.1 *Any step of a $P_0 \times P_1 \times P_2$ R-Mesh can be simulated in $O(1)$ time on a $(7P_0 + P_0P_1) \times 6P_1P_2$ R-Mesh.*

For the most part we will use a two-dimensional R-Mesh, occasionally expressing ideas in three dimensions before converting them back to two dimensions. We now illustrate this technique in an algorithm to simulate a PRIORITY CRCW R-Mesh on a COMMON CRCW R-Mesh.

Priority Simulation. We will first construct a simulation of a two-dimensional PRIORITY CRCW R-Mesh on a three-dimensional R-Mesh with the COMMON concurrent write. Ultimately, we will want the simulating R-Mesh to be two-dimensional, however. The simulation approach makes multiple copies of the PRIORITY R-Mesh. Communication among these copies is simplest if they are stacked in a third dimension. The simulation will, then, first use a three-dimensional COMMON CRCW R-Mesh, then convert it to a two-dimensional R-Mesh using Theorem 3.1.

Simulation on a Three-Dimensional R-Mesh. Let $\mathcal{P}$ be an $N \times N$ PRIORITY CRCW R-Mesh, and let $\mathcal{C}$ be an $N \times N \times m$ COMMON CRCW R-Mesh, where $4N^2 = m^k$ for integer $k \geq 1$. The aim is to simulate an arbitrary step of $\mathcal{P}$ on $\mathcal{C}$. Since $\mathcal{C}$ has an $N \times N$ sub-R-Mesh, all aspects of the simulation, except priority resolution, are quite straightforward.

Let the $4N^2$ ports of $\mathcal{P}$ (potential writers) be indexed $0, 1, \cdots, 4N^2 - 1$. Resolving priority is tantamount to selecting the least indexed writing port for each bus of $\mathcal{Q}$. The priority resolution algorithm employs the base-m representation of the ports' indices; recall that $4N^2 = m^k$. For $0 \leq i < 4N^2$, let $x_{i,k-1}x_{i,k-2} \cdots x_{i,1}x_{i,0}$ denote the base-m representation of i, where $0 \leq x_{i,j} < m$ for each $0 \leq j < k$. In the following discussion, we will refer to $x_{i,j}$ as the jth digit of port i (rather than the jth digit of the index of port i).

We now explain the algorithm to resolve priority for ports on one bus of $\mathcal{P}$; the argument readily extends to all buses of $\mathcal{P}$. We will use the example in Figure 3.3 as an illustration. Part (a) of this figure shows a sample bus with 9 writing ports. Although the example shows only one bus with multiple writes, the underlying ideas apply independently to all such buses. We have numbered the 64 ports of the 4×4 R-Mesh from 0 to 63 in order of the row-major indices of processors and clockwise starting from N within each processor. For clarity, Figure 3.3 shows indices of only the writing ports and those at the perimeter of the R-Mesh.

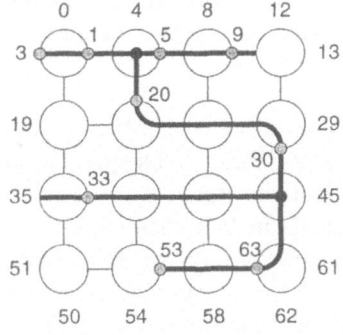

(a) A sample bus with multiple writers

writers	
decimal	base 4
1	001
3	003
5	011
9	021
20	110
30	132
33	201
53	311
63	333

(b) Writer indices

Figure 3.3. An illustration of port indices for the priority resolution algorithm with $N = m = 4$. Part (a) shows a bus on a PRIORITY CRCW R-Mesh with writing ports as shaded circles. Part (b) shows the indices of writing ports in both decimal and base m.

Initially, flag all writing ports as active. The algorithm proceeds in $k = \log_m 4N^2$ iterations (numbered $k-1, k-2, \cdots, 2, 1, 0$), progressively reducing the pool of active ports until a single (highest priority) active writing port remains. The first iteration, that is, iteration $k-1$, resolves priority based on only the most significant base-m digit, $x_{i,k-1}$, of the ports. The ports that survive this iteration further resolve priority based on their next most significant digit, $x_{i,k-2}$. Once this method iterates through all k digits (from the most significant down to the least significant), only one writing port remains active.

The Local Priority Problem. The key to this method is a solution to the "local priority problem" defined below. For $0 \leq j < k$, let S_j be a subset of the ports of $\mathcal{P}$ and let

$$y = \min \{x_{i,j} \ : \ i \in S_j\} \tag{3.1}$$

be the value of the smallest j^{th} digit of the ports in S_j. Given S_j and j, the local priority problem is to find set

$$M_j = \{i \in S_j \ : \ x_{i,j} = y\} \tag{3.2}$$

of all ports with this smallest value of the jth digit.

For the example of Figure 3.3(a), let $S = \{1, 3, 5, 9, 20, 30, 33, 53, 63\}$ denote the set of all writing ports, and let $S_1 = \{1, 3, 5, 9\} \subseteq S$. Consider the base-$m$ representations of elements of S_1 (the first four elements in Figure 3.3(b)). Given S_1 and index $j = 1$, the local priority problem is to determine set M_1. For digit $j = 1$ (the center digit), the smallest value is 0. The set of elements of S_1 with this smallest value for digit 1 is $M_1 = \{1, 3\}$.

The Role of Local Priority. We now explain the role of the local priority problem in the PRIORITY simulation algorithm. Subsequently, we will derive a solution to the local priority problem itself.

As noted above, the algorithm proceeds in k iterations, one for each digit in the base-m representation of the ports' indices. The initial set of active ports is S_{k-1} and consists of all writing ports. Iteration j (where $k > j \geq 0$) solves the local priority problem for index j and the current active set, S_j, to determine the set $M_j \subseteq S_j$. Set M_j becomes S_{j-1} and is the set of active ports for the next iteration (if any).

More specifically, the first iteration $k-1$ solves the local priority problem for index $k-1$ and set S_{k-1}, the initial set of active ports (that is, all writing ports). This iteration produces M_{k-1}, the set of all writing ports that could have the smallest index, based only on the most significant digit. Next, iteration $k-2$ uses index $k-2$ and set $S_{k-2} = M_{k-1}$

to solve the local priority problem and obtains set M_{k-2}. In general, for $k > j > 0$, iteration j uses set S_j and index j to solve the local priority problem and obtain set $M_j = S_{j-1}$. Clearly, M_j consists of those writing ports whose indices are the least on the basis of digits $k-1, k-2, \cdots, j+1, j$. At the end of all k iterations, the algorithm resolves priority by obtaining set M_0 that consists of only the least indexed writer. Since $k = O\left(\frac{\log N}{\log m}\right)$, we obtain the following result.

LEMMA 3.2 *If an $N \times N \times m$ COMMON CRCW R-Mesh can solve the local priority problem for an $N \times N$ R-Mesh in T steps, then it can simulate any step of an $N \times N$ PRIORITY CRCW R-Mesh in $O\left(\frac{T \log N}{\log m}\right)$ time.*

Solving Local Priority. We now establish that an $N \times N \times m$ R-Mesh, $\mathcal{C}$, can solve the local priority problem in constant time. Specifically, the input to the problem at hand is an index j (where $k < j \leq 0$) and a set S_j of active ports. Therefore, for a given instance of the local priority problem, j and S_j are fixed. The output of the algorithm is the set M_j described by Equations (3.1) and (3.2).

View the three-dimensional R-Mesh $\mathcal{C}$ as m two-dimensional $N \times N$ sub-R-Meshes, $\mathcal{C}_0, \mathcal{C}_1, \cdots, \mathcal{C}_{m-1}$. Each sub-R-Mesh is a copy of the emulated R-Mesh, $\mathcal{P}$, with COMMON rather than PRIORITY concurrent writing ability. We use the same symbol to refer to corresponding ports of $\mathcal{P}$ and $\mathcal{C}_\ell$ (for $0 \leq \ell < m$). The input to the local priority problem indicates membership in set S_j by an "active port" flag. Assume that each sub-R-Mesh $\mathcal{C}_0, \mathcal{C}_1, \cdots, \mathcal{C}_{m-1}$ holds all necessary information about $\mathcal{P}$, including the bus configuration and active port indices. No loss of generality arises from this assumption as R-Mesh $\mathcal{C}$ can use its third dimension to broadcast information in constant time from any sub-R-Mesh $\mathcal{C}_\ell$ to all others. This is one aspect in which using a three-dimensional simulating R-Mesh simplifies the algorithm design.

Step 1: For each $0 \leq \ell < m$, configure $\mathcal{C}_\ell$ exactly as $\mathcal{P}$.

Step 2: In each sub-R-Mesh, $\mathcal{C}_\ell$, each active port $x_i \in S_j$ writes a signal to its bus if and only if its jth digit $x_{i,j} = \ell$. The purpose of this write is to indicate the presence of at least one active port whose j^{th} digit has the value ℓ. Concurrent writes in this step use the same valued signal and pose no problem on the COMMON CRCW R-Mesh. During this step, each active port x_i of each $\mathcal{C}_\ell$ reads from its bus.

Step 3: Each active port x_i of each sub-R-Mesh $\mathcal{C}_\ell$ sets a flag $f_{i,\ell}$ to 1 if and only if it reads a signal in Step 2.

Step 4: For each active port i, use flags $f_{i,0}, f_{i,1}, \cdots, f_{i,m-1}$ and neighbor localization (see Section 2.3.3) along the third dimension of C to determine the smallest value ℓ_0 (where $0 \le \ell_0 < m$) such that $f_{i,\ell_0} = 1$. Call ℓ_0 the *minimum digit* for port i. Clearly, at least one active port i_0 (say) incident on the bus has a jth digit, $x_{i_0,j}$, equal to the minimum digit ℓ_0. For active ports, if $x_{i,j} > \ell_0$, then $i \notin M_j$; if $x_{i,j} = \ell_0$, then $i \in M_j$. By definition of the minimum digit, the case $x_{i,j} < \ell_0$ is not possible. Thus, port i flags itself as an element of M_j if and only if $x_{i,j} = \ell_0$.

Figure 3.4(b) illustrates the solution to the local priority problem for $j = 1$ and $S_1 = \{1, 3, 5, 9\}$. The four R-Meshes in the figure correspond to sub-R-Meshes C_0, C_1, C_2, C_3. Ports 1 and 3, whose first (center) digit is 0, write on C_0, while ports 5 and 9 with first digits 1 and 2, respectively, write on sub-R-Meshes C_1 and C_2; no write occurs in C_3 for the bus being considered. All active ports on all four sub-R-Meshes read from the bus. Observe that all active ports of S_1 receive the signal in sub-R-Meshes C_0, C_1, and C_2. Consequently for all $i \in S_1$, flags $f_{i,0} = f_{i,1} = f_{i,2} = 1$ and $f_{i,3} = 0$. Here the minimum digit for all ports of S_1 is 0. Since $x_{1,1} = x_{3,1} = 0$, ports 1 and 3 are members of M_1. Since $x_{5,1} = 1$ and $x_{9,1} = 2$ are both larger than the minimum digit, ports 5 and 9 are not elements of M_1. That is, $M_1 = \{1, 3\}$.

LEMMA 3.3 *The local priority problem for an $N \times N$ R-Mesh can be solved on an $N \times N \times m$* COMMON *CRCW R-Mesh in $O(1)$ time.*

Example. We now use the example of Figure 3.4 to illustrate the entire priority resolution procedure. Initially, set $S_2 = S = \{1, 3, 5, 9, 20, 30, 33, 53, 63\}$ is the active set consisting of all writers. For Iteration 2 (see Figure 3.4(a)), flag $f_{i,j} = 1$ for all $i \in S_2$ and all $0 \le j < 4$. Consequently, the minimum digit of all the active ports is 0. Therefore, Iteration 0 selects subset $M_2 = \{1, 3, 5, 9\}$, all of whose ports have a 0 as the most significant digit (digit 2). As explained earlier, Iteration 1 (see Figure 3.4(b)) starts with set $S_1 = M_2$ and whittles it down to set $M_1 = \{1, 3\}$. (The final) Iteration 0 (see Figure 3.4(c)) reduces set $S_0 = M_1$ to $M_0 = \{1\}$. Here the minimum digit is 1, the value of the least significant digit of port 1.

Putting it All Together. As noted at the start of the algorithm, we restricted our discussion to only one bus of the simulated R-Mesh $\mathcal{P}$. This restriction is without loss of generality, as we now explain. Let β denote the bus of $\mathcal{P}$ that we considered in our description of the algorithm. Let the corresponding buses of sub-R-Meshes $C_0, C_1, \cdots, C_{m-1}$

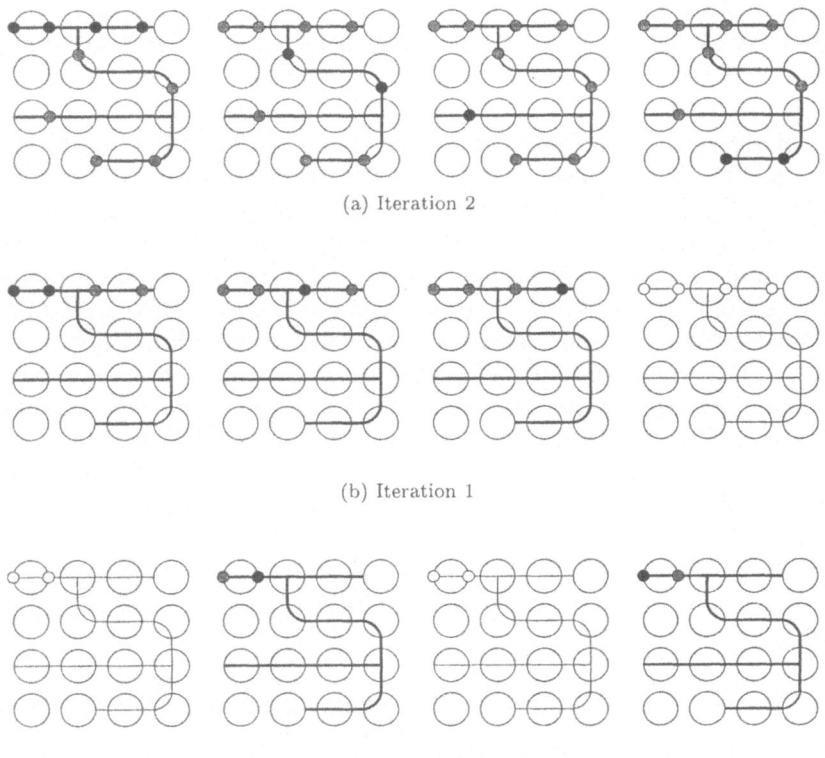

(a) Iteration 2

(b) Iteration 1

(c) Iteration 0

Figure 3.4. An illustration of the priority resolution algorithm for the bus of the PRIORITY CRCW R-Mesh shown in Figure 3.3. Parts (a)–(c) illustrate the three iterations of the algorithm. The four R-Meshes in each iteration represent the $m = 4$ slices C_0, C_1, C_2, C_3. These figures show the active ports as circles. Ports writing a signal are shaded black. Among non-writing ports, those that detect a signal are shaded grey. The remaining active ports are unshaded.

be $\beta_0, \beta_1, \cdots, \beta_{m-1}$. It is easy to verify that the algorithm uses a port of C only if it traverses one of the buses $\beta_0, \beta_1, \cdots, \beta_{m-1}$. Since the algorithm uses only the copies of β and the edges in the third dimension among them, the algorithm readily extends to all buses of the simulated R-Mesh $\mathcal{P}$. From Lemmas 3.2 and 3.3 we have the following result.

THEOREM 3.4 *Any step of an* $N \times N$ PRIORITY *CRCW R-Mesh can be simulated on an* $N \times N \times m$ COMMON *CRCW R-Mesh in* $O\left(\frac{\log N}{\log m}\right)$ *time.*

Converting to Two Dimensions. The PRIORITY simulation algorithm on a three-dimensional R-Mesh $\mathcal{C}$ uses the first two dimensions as m copies, $\mathcal{C}_0, \mathcal{C}_1, \cdots, \mathcal{C}_{m-1}$, of the simulated R-Mesh $\mathcal{P}$. For each set of m corresponding ports in the m sub-R-Meshes of $\mathcal{C}$, the algorithm employs the third dimension only to emulate a one-dimensional R-Mesh spanning this set of m ports. Thus, viewing $\mathcal{C}$ as an m-element linear array of $N \times N$ R-Meshes allows the algorithm designer to focus on important aspects of the algorithm, without being caught up in tedious (but conceptually simple) details, such as routing communication channels between sub-R-Meshes, that would arise if the sub-R-Meshes are tiled in two dimensions.

With Theorem 3.1, we can convert the three-dimensional simulating R-Mesh to two dimensions, obtaining the following result.

THEOREM 3.5 *Any step of an* $N \times N$ PRIORITY *CRCW R-Mesh can be simulated on an* $O(Nm) \times O(Nm)$ COMMON *CRCW R-Mesh in* $O\left(\frac{\log N}{\log m}\right)$ *time.*

The above results easily extend to a simulation on the COLLISION and COLLISION[+] CRCW R-Mesh (see Problem 3.17).

Relationship of R-Mesh Dimension to Other Restrictions. The dimensionality of the R-Mesh alters only the topological properties of the underlying mesh and, therefore, is independent of word size and bus access rules. The definitions of LR-Mesh, Tree R-Mesh, and the equivalents of the HVR-Mesh and FR-Mesh readily extend to dimensions larger than two.

3.1.5   One-Way Streets—The Directed R-Mesh

The R-Mesh defined in Chapter 2 uses buses on which information can flow in any direction. In other words, a write to a bus can be read from any port incident on the bus. The variant of the R-Mesh that we describe here (*Directed R-Mesh* or *DR-Mesh*) allows control of the direction of information flow in each segment of a bus. For example, in the non-directed bus of Figure 3.5(a), a value written at any point is available at all points on the bus. On a directed bus (Figure 3.5(b)), however, information written at the point indicated by a black circle is available at only those points shown as grey circles. The six unshaded circles have no directed path from the source of the information. On the other hand, some points that receive the information have multiple paths from the source. Much of the motivation for the directed model stems

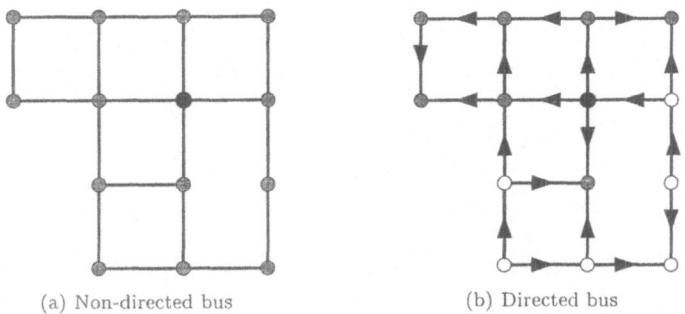

(a) Non-directed bus   (b) Directed bus

Figure 3.5. Directedness in buses. The source of the write is shown as a black circle. Points receiving the information from the write are shown as grey circles, while those not receiving this information are unshaded circles.

from the observation that, in practice, fiber-optic buses allow directional propagation of data and electronic buses with active components on them are directed. The directed model also admits elegant solutions to some problems, notably for directed graphs, and offers some theoretical insight.

To make the definition of a DR-Mesh precise, we will assign directions to the ports of processors. An *incoming port* is only permitted to bring information into a processor and an *outgoing port* takes information out of a processor. Each processor of a two-dimensional DR-Mesh has four incoming ports and four outgoing ports, with adjacent ports externally connected by directed external edges as shown in Figure 3.6(a). As in the (non-directed) R-Mesh, processors in the DR-Mesh partition their ports to form buses. Within the same block of the port partition, all incoming ports connect to all outgoing ports. With subscripts "i" and "o" denoting input and output ports, respectively, consider the port partition $\{\overline{W_i, E_o}, \overline{N_i, S_o, W_o}, \overline{E_i, S_i, N_o}\}$ of a two-dimensional DR-Mesh (see Figure 3.6(b)). The block $\{\overline{W_i, E_o}\}$ allows information written to (or entering from) port W_i to travel to port E_o, but not vice versa. In block $\{\overline{N_i, S_o, W_o}\}$, information arriving at port N_i travels out of the processor through both ports S_o and W_o. Block $\{\overline{E_i, S_i, N_o}\}$ presents a more interesting situation. If information arrives at both E_i and S_i as a result of a single write (that reaches E_i and S_i by different paths), then we treat this at port N_o as an exclusive write. This is analogous to the

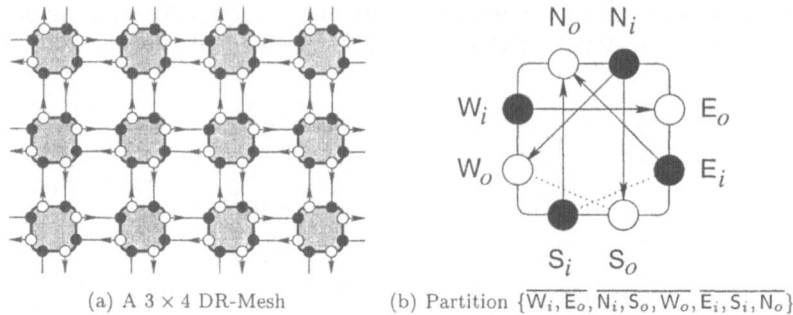

(a) A 3 × 4 DR-Mesh   (b) Partition $\{\overline{W_i, E_o}, \overline{N_i, S_o}, \overline{W_o}, \overline{E_i, S_i, N_o}\}$

Figure 3.6. The directed R-Mesh. Incoming and outgoing ports are shown as shaded and unshaded circles, respectively. In part (b), directed edges show directions of information flow, while dotted lines connect ports within the same block but with no information flow between them.

treatment given in the undirected R-Mesh. Consequently, the DR-Mesh passes this information on to all output ports in the block (N_o is the only one in our example). In the CRCW model, an additional case can arise in which port N_o could receive information from multiple sources (including a write to port N_o itself). Here, the concurrent write rule (see Section 3.1.3) determines the bus value at the port.

As an example, consider a processor in a COLLISION CRCW DR-Mesh. Suppose that this processor assumes the partition shown in Figure 3.6(b). Let the values entering ports E_i and S_i be α and β, respectively, written by different sources; no other writes performed outside the processor send values to the remaining input ports. Let the processor write values γ, δ, ρ to ports W_o, N_i, S_i, respectively, with no writes to the remaining ports. Since no value enters through port W_i and the processor does not write to ports W_i or E_o, no value leaves port E_o. Port N_i receives no value but writes δ, so the value leaving port S_o (to which there is no write) is δ. The value leaving port W_o, however, is the collision symbol resulting from the value δ entering the port and the value γ written to the port. The values entering port N_o are α and the collision symbol (resulting from values β and ρ at port S_i). Consequently, the value leaving port N_o is the collision symbol.

The value entering a port may differ from the value leaving the port if the DR-Mesh processor writes to the port. The value leaving a port is a "combination" of the values entering the port and the value written to the port. The write rule that the DR-Mesh uses to resolve concurrent writes determines this combination. It is generally assumed that the value read is the value leaving the port. Problem 3.30 deals with the case where the value read is the value entering the port.

Reachability. To give an example in which directionality of the buses plays a critical role in an algorithm, we now present a DR-Mesh algorithm solving the reachability problem, the counterpart of *s-t* connectivity for directed graphs. Let $\mathcal{G}$ be a directed graph, and let s and t be two of its vertices. Given the adjacency matrix of $\mathcal{G}$ and vertices s and t, the problem is to determine if $\mathcal{G}$ has a directed path from s to t. As in the *s-t* connectivity algorithm (Algorithm 2.9, page 47), the idea is to set up buses so that a signal originating at a processor representing vertex s arrives at a processor representing vertex t if and only if $\mathcal{G}$ has a directed path from s to t.

We will use a COMMON CRCW $N \times N$ DR-Mesh, where N is the number of vertices in $\mathcal{G}$. Without loss of generality, let the vertices of $\mathcal{G}$ be numbered $0, 1, \cdots, N - 1$. The DR-Mesh configures its processors so that each column has two buses (one in each direction) running the entire length of the column, and each row has a bus directed leftward from its diagonal element and a bus directed rightwards from its diagonal element (see Figure 3.7(b)). For each edge $\langle i, j \rangle$ (where $0 \leq i, j < N$)

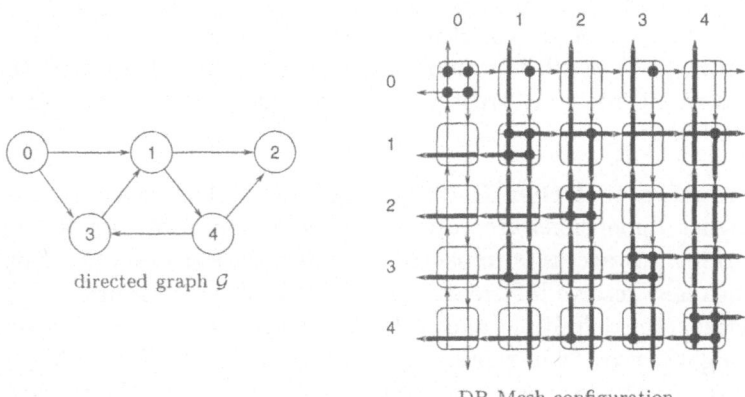

directed graph $\mathcal{G}$

DR-Mesh configuration

Figure 3.7. A 5 × 5 directed R-Mesh configured to solve the reachability problem on a directed graph (with vertex 3 as source). The figure does not show edges that are not used in the solution. Buses carrying the signal issued by processor (3,3) are shown in bold.

of $\mathcal{G}$, processor (i, j) connects its row bus directed from (i, i) to the column bus directed to (j, j). Diagonal processors also connect all their ports to fuse horizontal and vertical buses traversing the processor (see Figure 3.7). It is easy to prove the following:

> With the configuration described above, a signal sent from each outgoing port of processor (s, s) reaches at least one incoming port of processor (t, t) if and only if $\mathcal{G}$ has a directed path from vertex s to vertex t.

The reachability algorithm simply configures the DR-Mesh as described above, issues a signal from an outgoing port of processor (s, s), and checks each incoming port of processor (t, t). Vertex t is reachable from vertex s if and only if processor (t, t) receives the signal. Note that all vertices of the graph could simultaneously check their incoming ports to determine whether they are reachable from s.

THEOREM 3.6 *Given the adjacency matrix of an N-vertex directed graph, the reachability problem can be solved on an $N \times N$ DR-Mesh in $O(1)$ time.*

Figure 3.7 illustrates the algorithm. Notice that the signal issued by processor $(3, 3)$ appears on vertical buses of column j if and only if the graph contains a path from vertex 3 to j. Notice also that a (non-directed) R-Mesh would not have worked here as the signal from processors $(0, 1)$ or $(0, 3)$ would have reached vertex $(0, 0)$, and the algorithm would have incorrectly concluded that vertex 0 was reachable from vertex 3.

Relationship to Other R-Mesh Variants. The ideas of word size and higher dimensions are completely independent of directed buses. Concurrent bus access is impacted by directedness as two ports on the same bus may receive information from different sets of sources. For bus restrictions, the definitions of directed HVR-Mesh and directed LR-Mesh are straightforward, while directed counterparts for the Tree R-Mesh and FR-Mesh are a little more cumbersome to define. In fact, the reachability algorithm runs on a directed FR-Mesh.

3.2   More Ways to Reconfigure

In this section we touch upon some of the other reconfigurable models that have appeared in the literature. The coverage is far from comprehensive. On the contrary, we limit the discussion here to representatives from some important classes of reconfigurable models. The bibliographic notes at the end of this chapter point to many other models.

3.2.1 Reconfigurable Network

The *Reconfigurable Network* (*RN*) is a generalization of the R-Mesh, embodying all "graph-based" models. It consists of a set of processors connected by external edges according to some underlying connected graph. Each processor can internally partition its ports (that connect it to its neighbors in the underlying graph) to form buses as in the R-Mesh. Indeed, the R-Mesh is a special case of the RN in which the underlying graph is a mesh.

Like the R-Mesh, the RN has variants based on word size, bus shapes, bus accesses, and directedness; indeed, many of the R-Mesh variants described in Section 3.1 were first defined for the RN.

3.2.2 Reconfigurable Multiple Bus Machine

The *Reconfigurable Multiple Bus Machine* (*RMBM*), unlike models described so far, separates its processors from the reconfigurable bus system. The RMBM consists of a set of processors that communicate using multiple buses (see Figure 3.8(a)). Each processor-bus pair has a set of switches that allow the processor to locally manipulate the bus to create various bus configurations. A processor can alter its read and write connections from one bus to another (using *connect switches*), break a bus into separate bus segments (using *segment switches*), and connect buses by "fuse lines" (using *fuse switches*). Figure 3.8(b) shows these switches.

The RMBM identifies two fundamental operations on buses, segmenting and fusing, and uses the model's ability to perform these operations to define four variants. The *Basic RMBM* (*B-RMBM*) has only connect switches, the *Segmenting RMBM* (*S-RMBM*) has connect and segment switches, the *Fusing RMBM* (*F-RMBM*) has connect and fuse switches, and the *Extended RMBM* (*E-RMBM*) has all three types of switches. The S-RMBM is similar to the HVR-Mesh, which can be viewed as segmenting horizontal and vertical buses. The F-RMBM resembles the FR-Mesh, with F-RMBM buses and fuse lines corresponding to row and column buses of the FR-Mesh.

Besides providing a natural separation between the abilities to segment and fuse buses, the RMBM also distinguishes the role of processors and switches. This allows some processors in R-Mesh solutions to be replaced by switches in RMBM solutions, leading to much more efficient solutions to certain problems. For instance, a 16-processor, 16-bus F-RMBM suffices to implement the 16×16 R-Mesh list ranking example of Figure 2.14. Align 16 RMBM processors above the top row of R-Mesh processors. An RMBM bus (fuse line) replaces each row bus

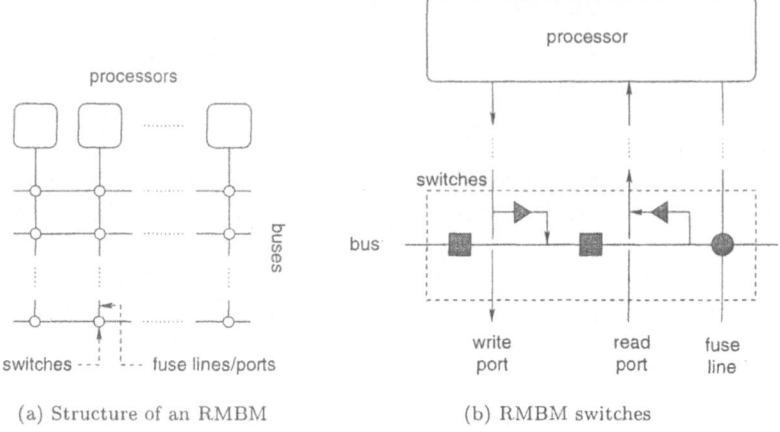

(a) Structure of an RMBM   (b) RMBM switches

Figure 3.8. The Reconfigurable Multiple Bus Machine (RMBM). Triangles, squares and circles denote connect, segment, and fuse switches, respectively.
Reprinted from the *Journal of Parallel and Distributed Computing*, vol. 46, 1997, J. L. Trahan, R. Vaidyanathan, and C. P. Subbaraman, "Constant Time Graph Algorithms on the Reconfigurable Multiple Bus Machine," pp. 1–14, © Copyright (1997) with permission from Elsevier.

(column bus) of the R-Mesh. Problems 3.34–3.37 illustrate situations where RMBM algorithms use fewer processors than their R-Mesh counterparts.

Some R-Mesh solutions, on the other hand, use all (or a large number of) processors simultaneously. Here an RMBM solution can be slower or more expensive, as an RMBM processor can set only one switch at a time. Problem 3.38 points to such examples.

Section 9.5.1 provides a detailed definition of the RMBM.

3.2.3   Optical Models

Researchers have proposed several reconfigurable models employing optical buses. A typical one-dimensional optical model has the structure shown in Figure 3.9. It consists of a linear arrangement of processors connected to a U-shaped optical bus structure comprising a data bus and buses for addressing. Information traverses this bundle of buses in one direction. Processors write to the buses at the *transmitting segment* and read from the *receiving segment*. Two features based on predictable delays in optical fibers distinguish these models from reconfigurable models discussed so far: (1) information pipelining and (2) coincident pulse addressing. We describe these features below. We employ a simplified

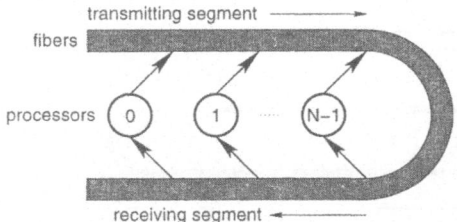

Figure 3.9. Structure of an optical reconfigurable model.

model here, aiming only to introduce the basic ideas; Chapter 10 discusses optical models in detail.

Information Pipelining. Let the optical delay on the bus between any pair of adjacent processors be the same and denote this delay by ϕ. Consider the case where processor i writes to the bus at time t. The next processor $i + 1$ can accurately ascertain that the above write will not reach its own write port until time $t + \phi$. Processor $i + 1$ can therefore write to the bus at time t (simultaneously with processor i) provided that the written signal (stream of optical pulses) is less than ϕ units in duration. Letting τ denote the time unit corresponding to one optical pulse, this means that if $\phi \geq b\tau$, then processor $i + 1$ can write a message b bits long. This idea readily extends to allow all processors to simultaneously and independently write to the bus. If each write is short enough to not overlap with the write from the previous processor, then multiple signals can travel in tandem along the bus. This ability to pipeline data endows optical models with large data movement capacity (see Figure 3.10).

Coincident Pulse Addressing. The second feature of optical models that distinguishes them from other models is coincident pulse addressing. This addressing scheme uses two buses, the reference and select buses, that carry independent pulses. When these pulses simultaneously reach a processor at its receiving segment (that is, coincide in time at the processor), then the processor reads from the data bus at that point in time.

We now illustrate the use of coincident pulse addressing through a constant time algorithm to add N bits. Before we can proceed with the algorithm, we must introduce a new feature to the optical model described so far. The model has the ability (not shown in Figure 3.9) to selectively introduce a delay between the select and reference pulses. This ability manifests as a conditional (or programmable) set of delays

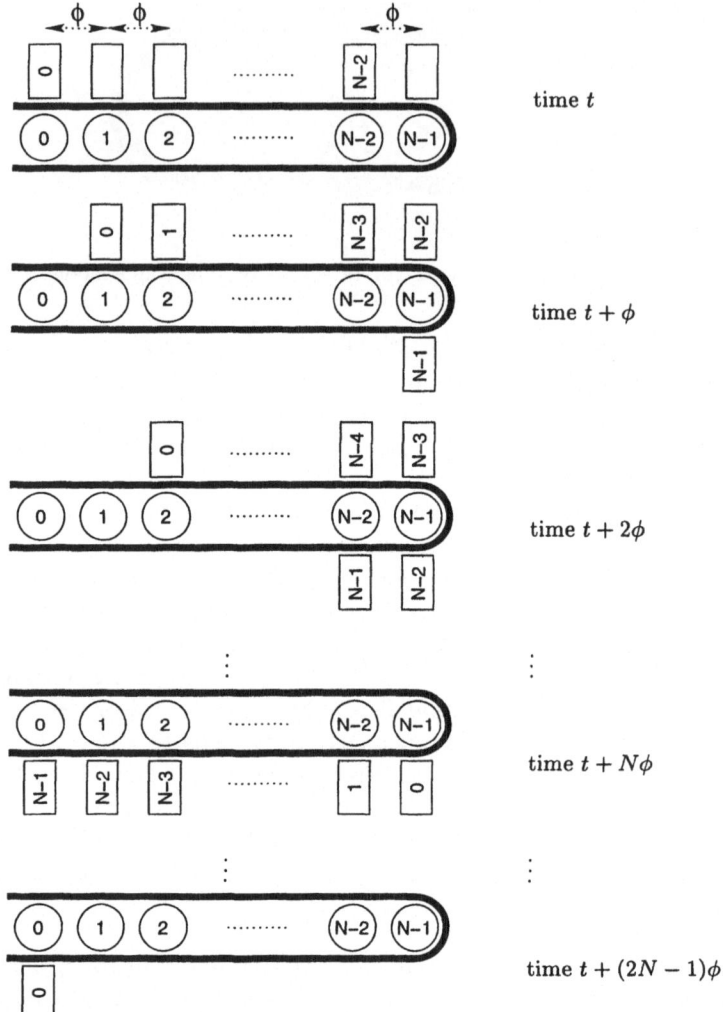

Figure 3.10. Pipelining information in an optical reconfigurable model. At time t each of the N processors writes to the data bus (each data element is shown as a rectangle with the processor's index). The data moves by one processor along the bus per each inter-processor delay ϕ until it marches off the bus after $2N\phi$ time.

on the transmitting segment of the select bus and a set of fixed delays on the receiving segments of the reference and data buses (see Figure 3.11). Each of the fixed and programmable delays is of τ duration.

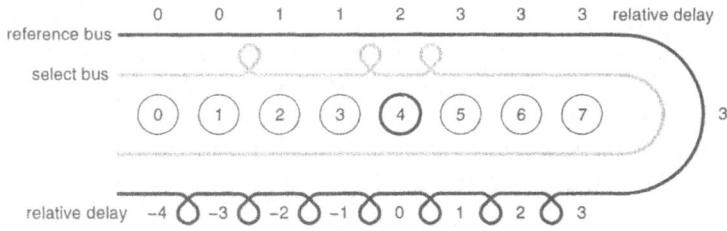

Figure 3.11. An illustration of coincident pulse addressing. Each τ units of delay is shown as a delay loop. Initially, the reference and select pulses start out simultaneously (indicated by a 0 relative delay at processor 0); the figure expresses relative delays in multiples of τ, so 2 stands for 2τ delay and so on. Then the select pulse falls τ units behind the reference pulse for each conditional (or programmable) delay loop in the transmitting segment of the select bus. In the receiving segment, the select pulse then gains on the reference pulse by τ units per processor at each fixed delay loop until it coincides with the reference pulse at processor 4. This causes processor 4 to read a signal from the data bus.

Let each processor hold an input bit; for the illustration in Figure 3.11, processors 2, 4, and 5 hold 1's and the remaining five processors hold 0's. The objective is to add the input bits. Each processor with a 1 introduces a delay in its transmitting segment of the select bus. Next, processor 0 issues a reference pulse, a select pulse, and a signal pulse on the data bus, all at the same time. Assuming $x < N$ 1's in the input, the select pulse lags behind the reference pulse by $x\tau$ units when it reaches the U-turn between the transmitting and receiving segments. In the receiving segment, the select pulse gains on the reference pulse, τ units per processor, due to the fixed delays in the reference and data buses. It coincides with the reference pulse at processor $N - x - 1$, which reads the signal issued by processor 0. Conversely, if processor j (where $0 \leq j < N$) receives the signal, then the sum of the input bits is $N - j - 1$. Figure 3.11 shows an example of this method with $N = 8$ and $x = 3$. In this example, processors 2, 4, and 5 that hold 1's introduce delays of duration τ. In the receiving segment, the select pulse coincides with the reference pulse at processor 4. This causes processor 4 to read a signal from the data bus and conclude that there are $N - 4 - 1 = 3$ ones in the input.

This method is very similar to the adding bits technique of Section 2.3.2; the analogy between stepping down rows in Algorithm 2.3 (page 28) and delays in the method here is clear.

For simplicity, our description of optical models and their features skirts several details and many possible variations that Chapter 10 explains. In general, optical models employ pipelining and the coincident pulse technique, often simultaneously, to solve many complex problems. Some models possess additional features, such as the ability to segment the bus. Higher dimensional optical models also exist. These models set local switches to configure linear, U-shaped buses that connect processors as in the one-dimensional model.

3.2.4   Reconfiguration in FPGAs

Field programmable gate arrays (*FPGAs*) have also drawn considerable interest in reconfigurable systems. Typically, these devices consist of an array of function blocks and a configurable interconnection fabric connecting them (Figure 3.12). It is possible to configure function

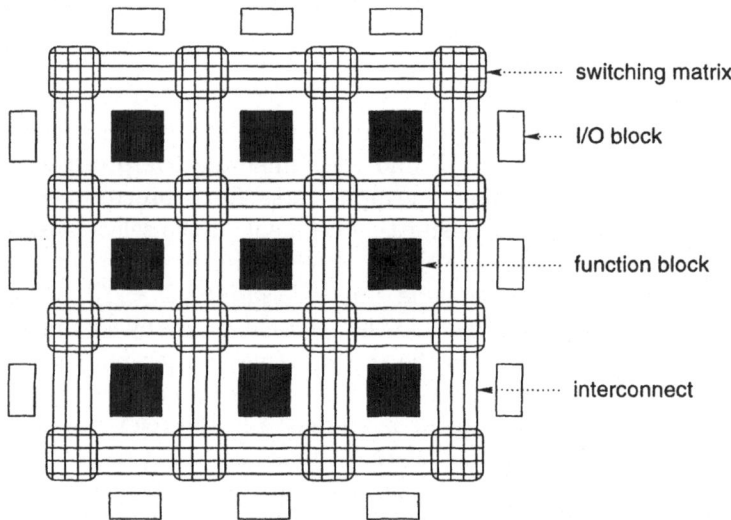

Figure 3.12.   Structure of a typical FPGA.

blocks to perform different logic functions (such as addition, multiplication, etc.) and the interconnection fabric to connect different function blocks.

Though reconfigurable models and FPGA-based systems have evolved relatively independently, there is common ground. For example, techniques for the bit-model R-Mesh can implement rudimentary arithmetic operations on FPGAs. Some RMBM techniques could prove useful in configuring FPGA interconnects. On the other hand, FPGA implementations can provide valuable clues to the direction of implementing devices with R-Mesh-type reconfiguration abilities.

A fundamental difference between FPGAs and other reconfigurable models described so far is the manner in which they obtain the reconfiguration information. In models such as the R-Mesh, a global configuration could result from a set of relatively independent, local configurations, made on the basis of local data. A typical FPGA, in contrast, requires reconfiguration information to be supplied to it from an external source. This makes the configuration speeds of FPGAs pin-limited. Unlike an R-Mesh that can (quite reasonably) assume a small constant configuration time, the configuration time for FPGAs can be quite high. Advances in FPGA technology have somewhat narrowed this divide through ideas such as partial reconfiguration (where only a small subset of the device is reconfigured) and context switching (where a small set of switch states for the entire device is preloaded into local memory to be speedily accessed when needed).

Run-time reconfiguration (RTR) is a method of computing using FPGAs (or similar reconfigurable devices) that exploits the ability of the FPGA to embed new hardware configurations. In RTR techniques, an FPGA changes configurations from phase to phase of a computation. By loading hardware specific to each phase, the FPGA can often perform the entire computation faster than with a single static configuration, even accounting for the time cost of reconfiguration in an FPGA. Partial reconfiguration and context switching are particularly useful in an RTR setting.

A more severe limitation of the FPGA type of reconfiguration is that run-time data plays a constrained role in the device's configuration because of considerations of circuit layout and loading configurations. This obstructs finely adapting hardware resources to a given problem instance. The notion of self-reconfiguration (where information needed to reconfigure the device is generated from within the device itself) allows R-Mesh-type reconfiguration in an FPGA-type setting. Self-reconfiguration is neither pin limited nor is it restricted to using only compile-time information. To make the internal generation of reconfiguration information possible, however, the granularity of the device must be higher (more complex function blocks, control mechanisms). This alters the device's level of abstraction from a circuit (for a purely FPGA solution) to that of a bit-level parallel processing environment (similar to a bit-model R-Mesh).

Chapter 11 details FPGA techniques, including notions of partial reconfiguration, context switching, and self-reconfiguration.

3.3   How Powerful Is Reconfiguration?

In this section, we briefly compare the "computational power" of reconfigurable and traditional models of computation, with the aim of giving the reader a feel for the capabilities and limitations of these models. More details appear in Chapters 8 and 9.

Before we proceed, let us understand the notion of computational power. For a problem of size N and for some constant $c > 0$, a *polynomially bounded* instance of a model has $O(N^c)$ elements (processors, wires, gates, etc.). In the following definitions, we loosely use the term model-instance $\mathcal{M}$ to refer to a polynomially bounded instance of model $\mathcal{M}$. Model $\mathcal{M}_1$ is *as powerful as* model $\mathcal{M}_2$ if, for every problem that an instance of $\mathcal{M}_2$ can solve, there is an instance of $\mathcal{M}_1$ that can solve the problem as fast as $\mathcal{M}_2$. Model $\mathcal{M}_1$ is *more powerful* (or model $\mathcal{M}_2$ is *less powerful*) if, in addition, an instance of $\mathcal{M}_1$ can solve at least one problem faster than $\mathcal{M}_2$.

Figure 3.13 illustrates the relative powers of reconfigurable and traditional models. The well known PRAM model is as powerful as (often

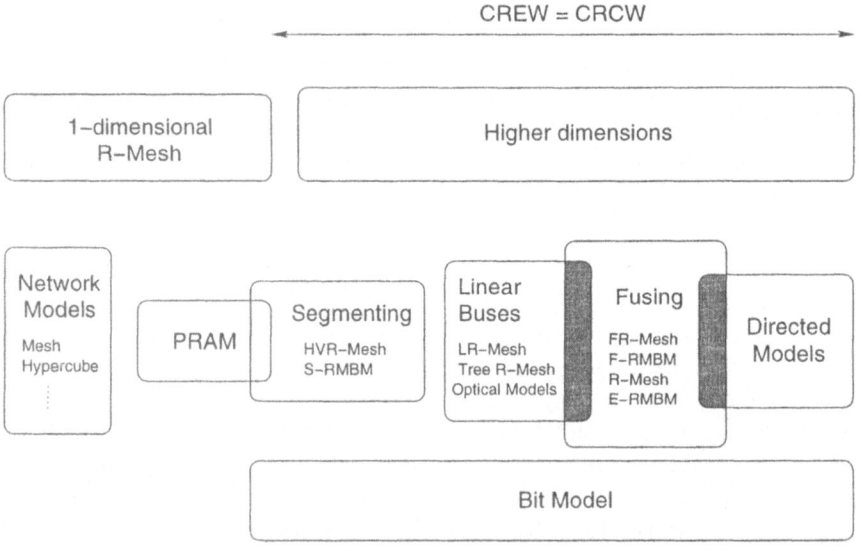

Figure 3.13. Relative powers of conventional and reconfigurable models. Model powers increase towards the right. Possible class overlaps that are yet unproven are shown shaded.

more powerful than) conventional point-to-point network models (such as meshes, hypercubes, etc.). The PRAM, in turn, occupies a place near the weakest reconfigurable models. Specifically, the EREW and CREW PRAMs are less powerful than their S-RMBM and HVR-Mesh counterparts that represent models with only bus segmenting ability. With concurrent write, the PRAM is equal in power to the S-RMBM and HVR-Mesh, but less powerful than most other reconfigurable models. Indeed, for reconfigurable models, concurrent writing ability does not add to their power. Unlike the PRAM, where concurrent writing ability adds to the power, reconfigurable models with the ability to read concurrently can emulate concurrent writing ability.

Rather surprisingly, the ability to fuse buses is more powerful than the ability to segment buses. Indeed, if the model is permitted to fuse buses, then the ability to segment adds nothing to the power. As a result, the E-RMBM, F-RMBM, FR-Mesh, and the (unrestricted) R-Mesh are all equally powerful.

The LR-Mesh that restricts its buses to be linear is provably more powerful than models with only segmenting ability. It is also as powerful as the Tree R-Mesh, of which the "cycle-free" LR-Mesh is a special case. Because of data pipelining, optical models restrict their buses to be linear and acyclic. The data pipelining itself allows for algorithms to run efficiently, but does not contribute to the power of the model. Therefore, optical models also occupy the same place as the LR-Mesh in the power hierarchy. Whether the LR-Mesh is as powerful as the unrestricted R-Mesh is an open problem, however.

Directed models occupy the next tier in the hierarchy. It is straightforward to establish that directed models are at least as powerful as their non-directed counterparts. In fact, it can be shown that the directed and non-directed LR-Meshes are of the same power. It is not known, however, whether directedness in general makes a model more powerful. It should be noted that though optical models use unidirectional buses, they are really not directed models as the buses cannot select the direction of information flow in parts of the bus.

Assuming the standard set of constant-time arithmetic and logical operations (including addition, subtraction, multiplication, division, bitwise AND, OR, NOT, Exclusive OR), the word model is only as powerful as its bit-model counterpart.

Similarly, beyond two dimensions, the dimensionality of the model does not contribute to its power. The primary limitation of the one-dimensional model is its low bisection width, making it slower for certain problems than some point-to-point topologies. On the other hand, its ability to dynamically alter connections allows one-dimensional models to solve some problems as fast as the CRCW PRAM.

Although reconfigurable models are, in general, more powerful than conventional ones, their power is not unlimited. Indeed the set of problems that any reconfigurable model can solve in polylogarithmic time is NC, the corresponding class for PRAMs.

This and the preceding chapters provide an overall view of reconfigurable models in general, their basic features and variations, algorithmic techniques, capabilities and limitations, and important issues (such scalability and bus delay models). They will give the reader a better handle on the underlying reconfiguration ideas in the remaining chapters that deal with more narrowly focused topics.

Problems

3.1   Given an implementation of a segmentable bus, how would you realize an HVR-Mesh ?

3.2   How many different buses can traverse any given processor of an $N \times N$ HVR-Mesh? Two buses are different if the corresponding components of the configuration graph (see page 20) of the HVR-Mesh are different.

3.3   Modify Algorithm 2.8 (page 44) to run on an LR-Mesh in constant time.

3.4   A linear acyclic bus is *oriented* (see also Problem 2.25) if every processor on the bus can distinguish one end of the bus from the other.

Let $\mathcal{L}_1$ (resp., $\mathcal{L}_2$) denote an $R \times C$ (resp., $2R \times 2C$) LR-Mesh. Let each processor of $\mathcal{L}_1$ correspond to a 2×2 sub-R-Mesh of $\mathcal{L}_2$. Prove that every set of linear buses of $\mathcal{L}_1$ can be converted into a set of oriented buses connecting the corresponding 2×2 sub-R-Meshes of $\mathcal{L}_2$.

3.5 Prove that an $N \times N$ LR-Mesh has $\Omega\left(2^{N^2}\right)$ different buses that traverse all N^2 processors. Two buses are different if the corresponding components of the configuration graph (see page 20) of the LR-Mesh are different.

3.6 Modify Algorithm 2.8 (page 44) to run on an FR-Mesh in constant time.

3.7 Find an example of a Tree R-Mesh configuration that uses all 15 port partitions of the R-Mesh (see Figure 2.3).

3.8 The RMESH (also called the reconfigurable mesh) was a precursor to the R-Mesh model used in this book. Figure 3.14 shows a 3×5 RMESH.

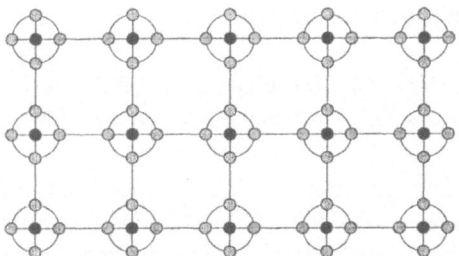

Figure 3.14. A 3×5 RMESH. The solid circle centered at each processor indicates a connection between all the ports, whereas a shaded circle at a port is a switch that could segment the bus traversing the port.

(a) Which of the 15 port partitions of the R-Mesh (see Figure 2.3) can an RMESH processor have?

(b) Design an algorithm to add N bits in constant time on the RMESH. What sized RMESH does your algorithm use? Could you use a smaller RMESH to determine the exclusive OR of N bits?

3.9   Let B be a constant-sized set of bus configurations of a non-constant sized bit-model R-Mesh. How can the bit model realize all configurations in B?

3.10 The algorithm implied by Theorem 2.21, page 53, requires a word-model R-Mesh, as it relies on the ability of processor (i,j) to pick out bit j from the binary representation of a b-bit number i.

      Design a constant time algorithm on a $2^b \times (2^b - 1)$ bit-model R-Mesh for the above problem. Your algorithm should flag processors in row i if and only if the input number has value i.

3.11 Let $\mathcal{L}$ be an $R \times C$ CRCW LR-Mesh that uses one of the ARBITRARY, COMMON, COLLISION, or COLLISION$^+$ rules and whose buses are all acyclic and oriented (see Problem 3.4). Prove that an $R \times C$ CREW LR-Mesh can simulate each step of $\mathcal{L}$ in constant time.

      Will your simulation work for the PRIORITY write rule? Explain.

3.12 Prove that an $R \times C$ CREW LR-Mesh with acyclic buses can simulate each step of an $R \times C$ CREW LR-Mesh (whose buses are not necessarily acyclic) in constant time.

3.13 Repeat Problem 3.12 for COMMON CRCW LR-Meshes. Will the simulation work for other concurrent write rules?

3.14 How many port partitions are possible for each processor of a three-, four-, or five-dimensional R-Mesh? Derive an expression for the number of port partitions of a d-dimensional R-Mesh.

3.15 Write pseudocode for the priority resolution algorithm of Theorem 3.4.

3.16 What is the maximum size of the set M_j produced by iteration j (where $k > j \geq 0$) of the priority resolution algorithm of Theorem 3.4?

3.17 Adapt the algorithm of Theorem 3.4 to run on a COLLISION or a COLLISION$^+$ CRCW R-Mesh.

3.18 Theorems 3.1 and 3.4 imply a size of $N(7 + m) \times 6Nm$ for the simulating R-Mesh of Theorem 3.5. This R-Mesh size is based on a general simulation algorithm.

Use your knowledge of the three-dimensional priority simulation algorithm to construct an $O\left(\frac{\log N}{\log m}\right)$ time priority simulation algorithm that runs on a two-dimensional R-Mesh of smaller size (smaller by a constant factor).

3.19 For any constant $\epsilon > 0$, design a constant time algorithm to simulate a step of an $N \times N$ PRIORITY CRCW R-Mesh on an $N \times N \times N^\epsilon$ three-dimensional COMMON CRCW R-Mesh or an $O(N^{1+\epsilon}) \times O(N^{1+\epsilon})$ two-dimensional COMMON CRCW R-Mesh.

3.20 Design an $O(\log N)$ time algorithm to simulate a step of an $N \times N$ PRIORITY CRCW R-Mesh on an $N \times N$ COMMON CRCW R-Mesh.

3.21 What restrictions, if any, on writing processors of a PRIORITY CRCW R-Mesh can be used to reduce the simulation time and/or size of the simulating COMMON CRCW R-Mesh in Theorems 3.4 or 3.5?

3.22 Use ideas from the priority simulation algorithm of Section 3.1.4 to design an algorithm to find the maximum of N b-bit integers on an $m \times N$ R-Mesh (where $1 \leq m \leq b$) in $O\left(\frac{\log b}{\log m}\right)$ time. Assume that the N inputs are initially in the top row of the R-Mesh.

3.23 The reachability algorithm is expressed in terms of connections between row and column buses. Determine the port partitions needed to effect these connections.

3.24 Write pseudocode for the algorithm of Theorem 3.6.

3.25 Assuming that a DR-Mesh processor can internally connect its incoming and outgoing ports without any restriction, how many port partitions can each DR-Mesh processor have? How many partitions are possible if no two incoming ports can be in the same block of the partition?

3.26 Prove the algorithm of Theorem 3.6 correct (see the assertion about the DR-Mesh bus configuration on page 89).

3.27 Adapt the algorithm of Theorem 3.6 to run on a COLLISION CRCW DR-Mesh.

3.28   For this problem suppose that the DR-Mesh is defined to have concurrent writes if and only if a port receives two or more values (from
a write to it and/or other ports in the same block of a port partition).
Under this rule, a single write arriving at a port by different paths is
considered a concurrent write.

(a)   Are multiple writing ports necessary to produce a "concurrent
write"?

(b)   Does the algorithm of Theorem 3.6 use "concurrent writes"?

(c)   What concurrent write rule does this new definition of concurrent write affect?

3.29   Will the priority resolution algorithm of Section 3.1.4 work for the
directed model?

3.30   The value entering a port of a DR-Mesh could differ from the value
leaving the port. In Section 3.1.5 we assumed the value read to be
the value leaving the port; term such a read to be *exit consistent*.
Consider a DR-Mesh in which reads are *entry consistent*; that is, a
port reads the value entering the port.

(a)   Prove that a $2R \times 2C$ DR-Mesh with exit consistent reads can
simulate each step of an $R \times C$ DR-Mesh with entry consistent
reads in constant time.

(b)   Prove that a $2R \times 2C$ DR-Mesh with entry consistent reads can
simulate each step of an $R \times C$ DR-Mesh with exit consistent
reads in constant time.

3.31   Explain why Algorithm 2.8 (page 44) did not require a directional
model, even though a list is a directed graph.

3.32   An $R \times C$ PARBS (Processor Array with a Reconfigurable Bus System) can be defined as a Reconfigurable Network (RN) in which the
underlying graph is planar for an arrangement of the vertices as an
$R \times C$ array. (An R-Mesh is a special case of a PARBS.)

Design a constant time algorithm to compute the Exclusive OR of N
bits on a $2 \times N$ PARBS. (A $2 \times N$ R-Mesh cannot solve this problem
in constant time.)

3.33   Design an N processor, 1 bus, S-RMBM algorithm for finding the
OR of N bits in constant time.

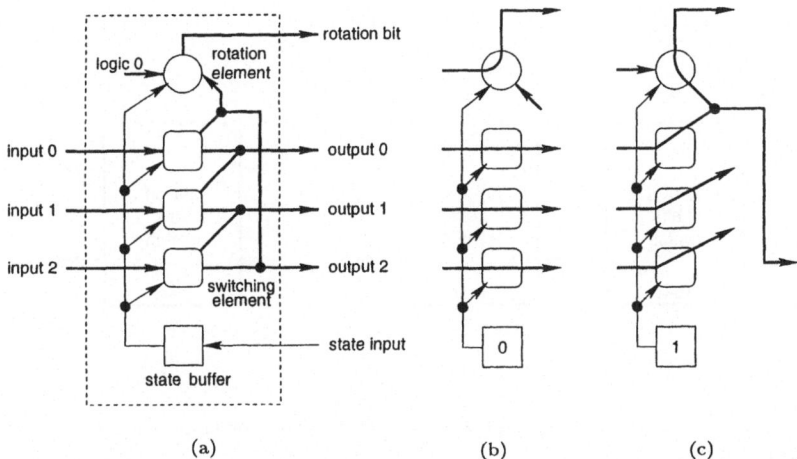

Figure 3.15. Part (a) shows the structure of 3-port shift switch. Part (b) shows the settings for the switching elements and the rotation element when the switch is in state $s = 0$. Similarly, Part (c) illustrates the settings for state $s = 1$.

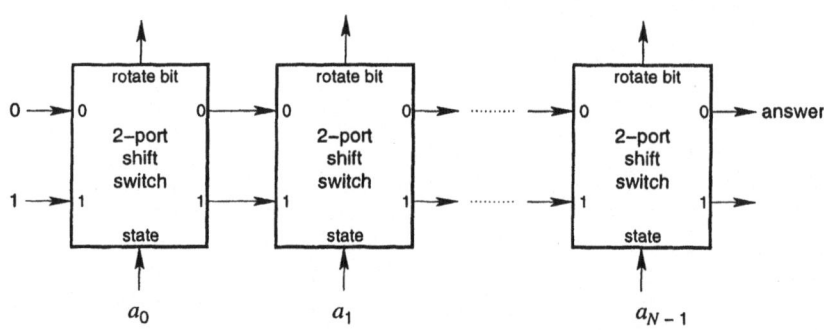

Figure 3.16. N element array of 2-port shift switches for computing the exclusive OR of input bits $a_0, a_1, \cdots, a_{N-1}$.

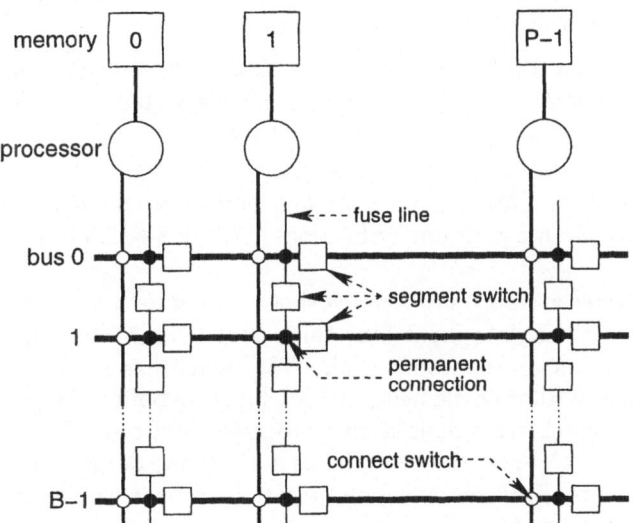

Figure 3.17. A $P \times B$ Distributed Memory Bus Computer.

3.34   Design an N processor, N bus, RMBM algorithm for constant time permutation routing. What variant of the RMBM would you use?

3.35   Prove that an N processor, 2^b bus S-RMBM (where $0 \le b < \log N$) can chain sort (see Section 2.3.3) N b-bit integers in constant time.

3.36   Prove that for any constant $\epsilon > 0$, an $N^{1+\epsilon}$ processor, $N^{1+\epsilon}$ bus F-RMBM can rank a list of N elements in constant time.

3.37   Prove that for any constant $\epsilon > 0$, an $N^{1+\epsilon}$ processor, $N^{1+\epsilon}$ bus RMBM can sort N $O(\log N)$-bit integers in constant time. What variant of the RMBM would you use?

       Hint: Use Problems 3.35 and 3.36 and the fact that for constant $c > 0$, if N $c \log N$-bit integers can be sorted stably in $O(T(N))$ time, then so can N $O(\log N)$-bit integers.

3.38   How many RMBM processors and buses are required to implement the R-Mesh algorithms of Sections 2.3.2, 2.3.4, 2.3.6, and 2.3.7?

3.39   Consider a 3-port *shift switch* shown in Figure 3.15.
       It has three data input bits, three data output bits, one state input bit, and a rotation output bit. The switch has three switching elements, a rotation element, and a 1-bit state buffer. The inputs to the shift switch are produced by a processor that controls the switch. In general, a w-port shift switch has w input and output bits and w shift elements. Each switching and rotation element can be configured to connect its input(s) to output(s) in various ways. The contents, s, of the 1-bit state buffer determine the internal configurations of the switching and rotation elements. Figure 3.15 (b) and (c) show the swich configurations in states $s = 0$ and $s = 1$, respectively. In state $s = 0$, the shift switch connects input i to output i (where $0 \le i < w$). In state $s = 1$, the switch has the effect of shifting the input by one bit. The rotation bit could be fed back to achieve a rotate.

       (a)   Prove that the N element array of 2-port shift switches shown in Figure 3.16 can compute the exclusive OR of N input bits.

       (b)   Design a method to produce the $\log(N+1)$-bit sum of N input bits using the structure of Figure 3.16. How long would your method require?

3.40 Translate the list ranking algorithm (Algorithm 2.8, page 44) to run on a two-dimensional array of N-port shift switches. Adapt your solution to m-port shift switches, where $m < N$.

3.41 The *Distributed Memory Bus Computer* (DMBC), shown in Figure 3.17, is a derivative of the RMBM (see Section 3.2.2). Like the RMBM, a $P \times B$ DMBC has P processors connected via B buses. Each processor has a connect switch on each bus through which it could write to or read from any one bus at a time. It also has a fuse line placed perpendicular to the buses. Each fuse line is permanently connected to the buses at their points of intersection, and segment switches allow segmenting of both buses and fuse lines. Thus the bus structure of the DMBC can be viewed as P horizontal segmentable buses and B vertical segmentable buses that are connected at their intersection much like the RMESH model of Problem 3.8.

As in an RMBM, a DMBC processor controls the switches associated with it, using one control signal at a time. While this allows a processor to individually address any one switch at a time, the processor can also broadcast an instruction to all the switches. Typically this instruction can be to set/reset all segment switches or only those on odd or even buses.

(a) Design a constant time algorithm to add N bits on the DMBC using as few processors and buses as possible.

(b) Design a constant time algorithm to solve the q-neighborhood problem (see Problem 2.27) on the DMBC. Use as few processors and buses as possible.

3.42 Will the algorithm for adding bits on the optical model of Section 3.2.3 work when the input has only 0's? If so, explain why, and if not, explain how you would modify it to work correctly.

3.43 Discuss features of R-Meshes that would be useful in an FPGA-type setting. What implementation details from FPGAs could benefit R-Meshes?

3.44 Based on the notion of power discussed in Section 3.3, which of the following relationships are possible between two models $\mathcal{M}_1$ and $\mathcal{M}_2$? Interpret the statement "$\mathcal{M}_1$ is not less powerful than $\mathcal{M}_2$" as "there exists a problem that $\mathcal{M}_1$ can solve faster than $\mathcal{M}_2$."

(a) $\mathcal{M}_1$ is as powerful as $\mathcal{M}_2$ and $\mathcal{M}_2$ is as powerful as $\mathcal{M}_1$.

(b) $\mathcal{M}_1$ is more powerful than $\mathcal{M}_2$ and $\mathcal{M}_2$ is more powerful than $\mathcal{M}_1$.

(c) $\mathcal{M}_1$ is not less powerful than $\mathcal{M}_2$ and $\mathcal{M}_2$ is not less powerful than $\mathcal{M}_1$.

3.45   An RN with the torus (mesh with wraparound connections) as the underlying graph that restricts its buses to be horizontal or vertical line segments (as in the HVR-Mesh) is the basis for the *polymorphic processor array* (PPA) architecture.

Prove that this RN is only as powerful as the HVR-Mesh.

3.46   Determine the relative powers of the RMBM, RMESH (Problem 3.8), an array of shift switches (Problem 3.39), and the DMBC (Problem 3.41).

3.47   Use neighbor localization to prove that a CREW one-dimensional R-Mesh is as powerful as a CRCW one-dimensional R-Mesh.

3.48   Prove that an S-RMBM and HVR-Mesh are equal in power.

3.49   Prove that an FR-Mesh and F-RMBM are equal in power.

3.50   Prove that a one-dimensional R-Mesh and a CREW PRAM are not less powerful than each other; see the definition of "not less powerful than" in Problem 3.44. (Use a bisection width argument and the fact that a CREW PRAM requires $\Omega(\log N)$ time to find the OR of N bits.)

3.51   Prove that an LR-Mesh is not less powerful than a CRCW PRAM; see the definition of "not less powerful than" in Problem 3.44. (Use the fact that a CRCW PRAM requires $\Omega\left(\frac{\log N}{\log \log N}\right)$ time to find the Exclusive OR of N bits.)

Bibliographic Notes

Bibliographic notes at the ends of Chapters 1 and 2 list many of the early reconfigurable models. Among these, Miller *et al.* [213, 215, 216] (see also Problem 3.8) proposed one of the first R-Mesh-type models (also called the reconfigurable mesh or RMESH). This model permits only some of the 15 possible port partitions of the R-Mesh model (see Figure 2.3, page 20). The polymorphic processor array [200], whose underlying topology is a torus (mesh with wraparound connections), restricts each processor to use either a segmentable row bus or a segmentable column bus at any given step. This restriction is similar to that of the HVR-Mesh, the Basic R-Mesh [231], and the Sub-Bus Mesh [62]. Ben-Asher *et al.* [19] and Schuster [291] were among the earliest to categorize reconfigurable models based on their bus structures and first introduced the HVR-Mesh, LR-Mesh, and the Tree R-Mesh. They also proposed the non-monotonic RN model in which a signal traversing a bus can invert its value. Fernández-Zepeda *et al.* [110] proposed the FR-Mesh model and presented a scaling simulation for it. Alnuweiri [5], Lai and Sheng [168], and Wang and Chen [346] are some of the sources of FR-Mesh algorithms, including *s-t* connectivity, connected components, transitive closure, and cycle detection. Ben-Asher *et al.* [17] proved that all LR-Mesh algorithms can be scaled with an optimal (constant) overhead. Fernández-Zepeda *et al.* [111] gave a method to convert any Tree R-Mesh bus configuration into an equivalent LR-Mesh bus configuration, thereby establishing that all Tree R-Mesh algorithms can be scaled with an optimal overhead. El-Boghdadi *et al.* [93, 94, 95, 96] described implementations of the HVR-Mesh and some LR-Mesh algorithms. The notion of a separable R-Mesh algorithm was introduced by Trahan and Vaidyanathan [321] in the setting of an RMBM.

Jang *et al.* [145] introduced the bit-model R-Mesh and proved that a $w \times w$ bit-model R-Mesh can perform the usual arithmetic and logic operations of a w-bit word-model processor in constant time. Ben-Asher and Schuster [23] suggested the bit model as a basis for designing asynchronous reconfigurable circuits. Ben-Asher and Stein [24] presented some fundamental algorithmic techniques for an asynchronous R-Mesh. The idea of using a constant amount of hardwired information in the bit-model R-Mesh (see also Problem 3.9) shares some similarities with the notion of context-switching (Section 11.4.2), particularly as used in the Self-Reconfigurable Gate Array (SRGA) architecture [299, 300]. Bus access rules have descended directly from the corresponding rules for memory access in PRAMs; JáJá [142] and Karp and Ramachandran [156] are good sources for more information on these PRAM rules. Wang and Chen [347], Olariu *et al.* [242], Trahan *et al.* [325], Fernández-Zepeda *et al.* [109, 110], and others discussed these rules for reconfigurable models and their impact on the models' power.

Wang *et al.* [350] used a three-dimensional reconfigurable model for sorting. Wang and Chen [346] used three-dimensional R-Meshes for many graph algorithms.

The priority resolution algorithm of Theorem 3.5 is an adaptation of the RMBM result of Trahan *et al.* [324] to the R-Mesh.

Schuster [291] and Ben-Asher *et al.* [21, 22] introduced the directed RN. Subsequently, the abilities of directed models have been used in various contexts, for example, Trahan *et al.* [323, 324] used directed RMBMs for graph problems and Ercal and Lee [107] used a directed R-Mesh for maze routing. The reachability algorithm of Theorem 3.6 is an extension of the *s-t* connectivity algorithm for undirected graphs. Wang and Chen [346] proposed this approach and used it to solve a variety of graph problems on the R-Mesh. The reachability problem itself is a useful tool that could provide answers to important questions in complexity theory; bibliographic notes at the end of Chapter 9 provide references on this topic.

Schuster [291] and Ben-Asher *et al.* [19] introduced the RN model. Besides the R-Mesh, particular cases of the RN that have received attention include the polymorphic torus [179, 180] and the PARBS (also called the PARBUS) [348]. Trahan *et al.* [325] introduced the RMBM and its versions. The optical model of Section 3.2.3 is based on the Linear Array with a Reconfigurable Pipelined Bus System (LARPBS) [185, 258]. The bibliographic notes of at the end of Chapter 10 point to the full range of optical models. Researchers have studied different structures to support partial reconfiguration [354] and context switching [37, 129, 289]. Sidhu *et al.* [299, 300] introduced the idea of self-reconfiguration in an FPGA-type setting in the form of the SRGA architecture. El-Boghdadi *et al.* [95] showed that the basic interconnection fabric of the SRGA architecture can implement the bit-model HVR-Mesh. Chapter 11 has more details on FPGAs and run-time reconfiguration and provides additional references on the subject.

The notion of power used in Section 3.3 is from Vaidyanathan *et al.* [329, 331]. Leighton [174, p. 782] provides references to the relationship between point-to-point networks and PRAMs. Trahan *et al.* [325] developed the separation between models with the ability to fuse buses (F-RMBM) and without the ability to fuse buses (S-RMBM). They also established that every RN model is at most as powerful as the F-RMBM. Several authors take up the issue of cycles in LR-Mesh buses [111, 265, 317]. Trahan *et al.* [316], Fernández-Zepeda *et al.* [111], and Bourgeois and Trahan [40] derived relationships among optical and non-optical reconfigurable models. Trahan *et al.* [317] derived relationships between the LR-Mesh and DR-Mesh; Chapter 9 provides details. Jang *et al.* [145] established that for commonly used arithmetic and logic operations, word- and bit-model R-Meshes are equal in power. Schuster [291] and Vaidyanathan and Trahan [332] established the two-dimensional R-Mesh as a universal model, capable of a constant-time simulation of higher dimensional R-Meshes. They also showed that a one-dimensional

R-Mesh does not possess the power of higher dimensional models. Ben-Asher *et al.* [18], Schuster [291], Nisan and Ta-Shma [236], and Trahan *et al.* [317] developed the relations among the various R-Mesh versions and corresponding Turing machine complexity classes.

Like the RMBM [325], other reconfigurable models exist that separate processors from the bus system. Lin and Olariu [188] introduced the shift switches of Problems 3.39 and 3.40 and used them to define the Reconfigurable Buses with Shift Switching (REBSIS) model. Sahni [287] introduced the DMBC model of Problem 3.41. The Reconfigurable Multiple Bus (RMB) network of ElGindy *et al.* [102] uses a reconfigurable interconnection network (like the RMBM, REBSIS, and the DMBC). Rosenberg *et al.* [283] proposed a reconfigurable ring of processors (RRP) with some similarities to the above models. The Crossbridge Reconfigurable Array of Processors [153, 154] has elements of the PARBS and the REBSIS.

PART II

ALGORITHMS

Chapter 4

ARITHMETIC ON THE R-MESH

The R-Mesh readily lends itself to implementing arithmetic operations. Two features apply most strongly. The first is the ability to decompose an input into its constituent bits, then manipulate the bits individually. The second is the ability to readily route and permute hordes of data from one region of the R-Mesh to another.

The operations that this chapter explores range from simple addition of a pair of numbers to sparse matrix multiplication. To begin, Section 4.1 identifies a variety of number formats and conversions among them. As many methods of performing arithmetic operations decompose and recombine numbers, choice of representation affects technique and complexity. The section also briefly examines manipulation of floating-point numbers and efficiently finding the maximum of N numbers. Section 4.2 begins with a simple linear R-Mesh algorithm to add two N-bit numbers. It then presents algorithms, whose techniques are quite involved, for adding N bits and for adding N b-bit numbers. It also details prefix sums algorithms for these cases. Finally, Section 4.3 describes algorithms first for matrix-vector multiplication, then for matrix multiplication, and then for multiplication of sparse matrices.

4.1 Starter Set

To lay the groundwork for arithmetic algorithms, this section surveys number representations that have proved useful in R-Mesh algorithms that manipulate numbers. Additionally, it covers the methods to convert from one representation to another, as this is often necessary to move from an input format to a format amenable to the algorithm, then to the output format. We also briefly examine floating-point number representation and how to adapt the integer-focused algorithms of this chapter to apply to floating-point numbers. Afterwards, we present an algorithm to efficiently compute the maximum (or minimum) of a set of numbers.

4.1.1   Conversion among Number Formats

A variety of formats exist to express the value of an integer in a distributed manner. Section 2.3.7 offered an initial look at some of these formats. We now present definitions for a full range of formats to represent an integer v in the range $[0, 2^b - 1]$. In some cases, multiple processors take part in the representation. Figure 4.1 gives an example of these representations. We use p_i to denote the ith processor in a linear array of processors.

Word: A processor holds integer v in a b-bit register.

BIN – Distributed binary: b processors hold the bits of the binary representation of v. Specifically, processor p_i holds bit i of v.

POS – Distributed positional: 2^b processors hold the representation of v. Processor p_v holds a 1, and all other processors hold 0.

1UN – Distributed unary 1: 2^b processors hold the representation of v. The first $v + 1$ processors, p_i for $0 \leq i \leq v$, hold 1, and all other processors hold 0.

2UN – Distributed unary 2: 2^b processors hold the representation of v. Each processor in a subset of v processors holds 1, and all other processors hold 0. Note that the set of processors holding 1's can be any subset of the 2^b processors, so this representation is not unique.

We now sketch some of the methods to convert between number representations. Others we leave to Problems 4.1–4.5 at the end of the chapter. One can construct the remainder by stringing together the given conversions. These conversions run in $O(1)$ time, except in one case as noted.

Word → BIN: On a $1 \times b$ R-Mesh, let p_0 hold integer value v. Processor p_0 broadcasts v to all processors. Processor p_i, for $0 \leq i < b$, tests bit i of v (by bitwise ANDing with 2^i): if the bit is 1, then p_i sets its value to 1; otherwise, p_i sets its value to 0.

BIN → Word: On a $b \times 2^b$ R-Mesh, let the leftmost column of processors initially hold the BIN representation of v. These processors broadcast their values along the rows. Each processor $p_{i,j}$, for $0 \leq i < b$ and

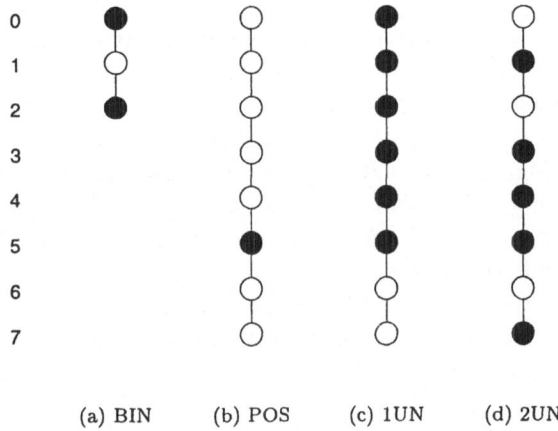

Figure 4.1. Example representations of $v = 5$ for $b = 3$.

$0 \leq j < 2^b$, compares the bit it receives at its E port with bit i of the binary representation of j, setting a flag if they are the same. Each column of processors now ANDs these flags. Column v will be the only column with an AND of 1, hence, the Word value is v.

$O(\log b)$ time BIN $\rightarrow$ Word: On a $1 \times b$ R-Mesh, let each processor hold one bit of the BIN representation of v. Each processor p_i sets a variable to 2^i if its bit is 1, and to 0 otherwise. The R-Mesh now sums these variables by a binary tree algorithm in $O(\log b)$ time (Theorem 2.1, page 18).

Word $\rightarrow$ POS: On a 1×2^b R-Mesh, the processor holding the Word form of v broadcasts this to all other processors. Processor p_v sets its value to 1, and all other processors set their values to 0.

POS $\rightarrow$ 1UN: On a 1×2^b R-Mesh, processor p_v holds a 1 and all other processors hold 0 in the POS representation of v. Processor p_v broadcasts a 1 signal to all lower indexed processors. Processor p_v and each processor reading a 1 set their values to 1, and all others set their values to 0.

2UN $\rightarrow$ 1UN: This conversion is a special case of the problem of adding N bits. Section 4.2.1.2 deals with this problem in detail.

4.1.2 Floating Point Numbers

Many R-Mesh algorithms that this chapter will cover are extremely fast because they decompose input elements into bits; therefore, the resource bounds often depend on the word size of the input elements. The use of floating point numbers can increase the utility of an R-Mesh of given size, as floating point numbers can represent values in fewer bits than required for integers. Standard floating point number representation has the form $(-1)^s \times M \times 2^E$, where s is the sign bit, the mantissa M is m bits long, and the exponent E is e bits long, so the total length of a b-bit floating point number is $b = m + e + 1$. The mantissa M is in a normalized form; that is, for nonzero numbers, the first bit after the binary point will always be 1.

Most integer manipulation algorithms in this chapter readily adapt to floating point numbers, following a general method like the one below for adding floating point numbers:

1. Find the maximum exponent $E_{\max}$ among the floating point numbers, and shift the mantissa of each input to make its exponent equal to $E_{\max}$.

2. Add the adjusted mantissas.

3. Normalize and round the result.

4.1.3   Maximum/Minimum

Finding the maximum (or minimum) among a set of elements is, of course, a common task in many algorithms. Recall that Lemma 2.14 (page 40) established that an $N \times N$ R-Mesh can find the maximum of N elements in $O(1)$ time. Building on this result, this section presents a fast algorithm using only as many processors as there are elements, then a lower bound corresponding to this fast algorithm. Finally, the section gives a more general algorithm that accommodates different aspect ratios for the R-Mesh, and that has special cases that give rise to the first two algorithms mentioned.

The constant time R-Mesh algorithm for maximum uses a larger number of processors than there are elements. At a time cost, the R-Mesh can find the maximum among N elements using only N processors by adopting a PRAM algorithm for the problem. The structure of the computation follows a "doubly logarithmic tree." Though we state results of this section for maximum, they apply to minimum finding as well.

THEOREM 4.1 *The maximum of N elements can be determined on a $\sqrt{N} \times \sqrt{N}$ R-Mesh in $O(\log \log N)$ time.*

<u>Proof:</u>   Let each processor of the R-Mesh initially hold one input element. Apply the following idea. Decompose the $N^{\frac{1}{2}} \times N^{\frac{1}{2}}$ R-Mesh into $N^{\frac{1}{2}}$ sub-R-Meshes, each of size $N^{\frac{1}{4}} \times N^{\frac{1}{4}}$. Recursively find the maximum within each sub-R-Mesh. Route these $N^{\frac{1}{2}}$ results to the top row

of the full R-Mesh (see Problem 2.8) and apply Lemma 2.14 to find the maximum.

Plainly, the algorithm spends only a constant amount of time at each level of recursion. As the algorithm recurses for $O(\log \log N)$ levels, the time complexity is $O(\log \log N)$. ∎

A lower bound exists for the maximum finding problem for the case in which the N elements are initially located one per processor in a $\sqrt{N} \times \sqrt{N}$ R-Mesh.

THEOREM 4.2 *With N input elements initially located in a $\sqrt{N} \times \sqrt{N}$ sub-R-Mesh of an $\infty \times \infty$ R-Mesh, finding the maximum element requires $\Omega(\log \log N)$ time.*

We now discuss a more general algorithm that applies to R-Meshes with various aspect ratios (that need not be square) whose size can range between the N processors of Theorem 4.1 and the N^2 processors of Lemma 2.14. It also generalizes the Nm processor, $O\left(\frac{\log N}{\log m}\right)$ time algorithm of Theorem 2.15 (page 42). The algorithm makes the assumption that the input elements for an $R \times C$ R-Mesh are given in the top $\left\lceil \frac{N}{C} \right\rceil$ rows, held one per processor.

THEOREM 4.3 *For any $1 \leq R \leq C \leq N$ such that $RC \geq N$, the maximum of N numbers can be found in $O\left(\log \log \frac{N}{C} + \frac{\log \frac{C^2}{N}}{\log R} \right)$ time on an $R \times C$ R-Mesh.*

Proof: For simplicity we do not use $\lceil\ \rceil$ and $\lfloor\ \rfloor$ with expressions such as $\frac{N}{C}$ and $\frac{C^2}{N}$ in this proof. The input is in the first $\frac{N}{C}$ rows, where $\frac{N}{C} \leq R \leq C$. Partition the first $\frac{N}{C}$ rows of the R-Mesh into sub-R-Meshes of size $\frac{N}{C} \times \frac{N}{C}$. (See Figure 4.2.) This produces $\frac{C^2}{N}$ such sub-R-Meshes,

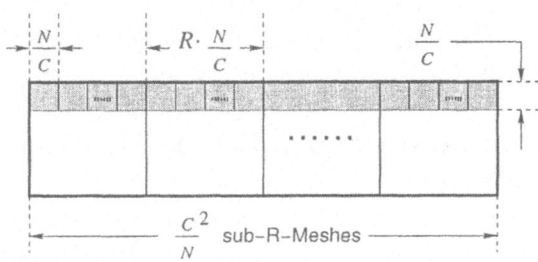

Figure 4.2. Partitioning an $R \times C$ R-Mesh for the case $R \leq C \leq N$.

each holding $\frac{N^2}{C^2}$ inputs (one per processor). By Theorem 4.1, find the maximum within each sub-R-Mesh in $O\left(\log \log \frac{N}{C}\right)$ time. At this point, the first row of the R-Mesh has $\frac{C^2}{N}$ partial results, and an $R \times \frac{C^2}{N}$ logical R-Mesh is available. By Theorem 2.15, the R-Mesh finds the maximum of these $\frac{C^2}{N}$ elements in $\Theta\left(\frac{\log \frac{C^2}{N}}{\log R}\right)$ time. Thus, the total time for the algorithm is $O\left(\log \log \frac{N}{C} + \frac{\log \frac{C^2}{N}}{\log R}\right)$.   ∎

In Theorem 4.3, the number of rows, R, was no larger than C, the number of columns. Next, we consider the case where $R \geq C$. Note, however, that the input is still distributed in the first $\left\lceil \frac{N}{C} \right\rceil$ rows of the mesh.

THEOREM 4.4 *For any* $1 \leq C \leq R \leq N$ *such that* $RC \geq N$*, the maximum of N numbers can be found in* $O\left(\log \log C + \frac{\log \frac{N}{C^2}}{\log C}\right)$ *time on an $R \times C$ R-Mesh.*

<u>Proof:</u> As before, we omit $\lceil\ \rceil$ and $\lfloor\ \rfloor$ for simplicity. For this theorem, we will use only the first $\frac{N}{C}$ rows of the R-Mesh that contain the inputs. (See Figure 4.3.) If $\frac{N}{C} \leq C$, then by Theorem 4.3, the maximum can be found in $O\left(\log \log \frac{N}{C} + \frac{\log \frac{C^2}{N}}{\log \frac{N}{C}}\right)$ time. It is possible to show that this quantity is $O\left(\log \log C + \frac{\log \frac{N}{C^2}}{\log C}\right)$; see Problem 4.7. If $C \leq \frac{N}{C}$, then view the R-Mesh as a $C \times \frac{N}{C}$ R-Mesh and once again apply Theorem 4.3 to find the maximum in $O\left(\log \log C + \frac{\log \frac{N}{C^2}}{\log C}\right)$ time.   ∎

Observe that Lemma 2.14 (page 40), Theorem 2.15 (page 42), and Theorem 4.1 are special cases of Theorems 4.3 and 4.4.

COROLLARY 4.5 *For any* $\sqrt{N} \leq S \leq N$*, the maximum of N elements can be found on an $S \times S$ R-Mesh in* $O\left(\log \log \frac{N}{S}\right)$ *time.*

4.2   The Foundation: Addition, Multiplication, and Division

This section first looks at addition, starting with the base of adding two numbers, then building to adding N bits, then to adding N b-bit numbers, then further building to computing their prefix sums. Following that, we describe a straightforward but suboptimal multiplication

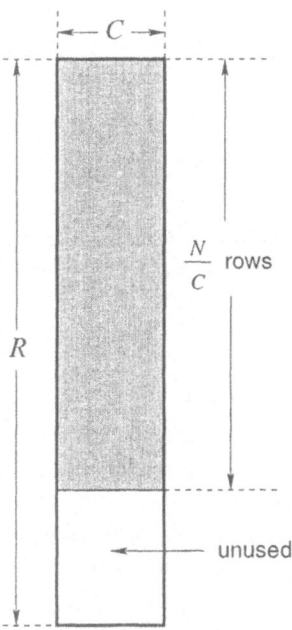

Figure 4.3. Input data arrangement in an $R \times C$ R-Mesh, for the case $C \leq R \leq N$.

algorithm, then a much more involved, and optimal, multiplication algorithm based on the Rader transform. Finally, this section describes an optimal division algorithm.

4.2.1 Addition

4.2.1.1 Adding Two N-bit Numbers

The algorithm for adding two N-bit integers on an N processor, one-dimensional R-Mesh is a simple embodiment of the potential of processors speeding up a computation by making local decisions on bus configurations and writing. The underlying idea is independent of reconfiguration, but reconfiguration permits a constant time implementation.

Let $f = f_{N-1}f_{N-2}\ldots f_0$ and $g = g_{N-1}g_{N-2}\ldots g_0$ denote the two N-bit integers to be added, and let $s = s_N s_{N-1} \ldots s_0$ denote their $(N+1)$-bit sum. Recalling basic binary arithmetic, sum bit

$$s_j = f_j \oplus g_j \oplus c_j,$$

where c_j denotes the carry-in to bit position j. Further, the following recursive expression generates the carry bits:

$$c_j = (f_{j-1} \wedge g_{j-1}) \vee [(f_{j-1} \oplus g_{j-1}) \wedge c_{j-1}],$$

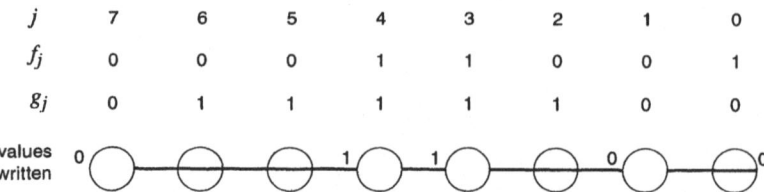

Figure 4.4. Example of R-Mesh algorithm adding two 8-bit numbers. Note that processors are numbered 0 to 7 from right to left to match the indices of bits in a binary number written in the standard way with the most significant bit to the left.

for $1 \leq j \leq N$ and where $c_0 = 0$. Given this expression for c_j, one can say that bit position $j - 1$ *generates* a carry if both f_{j-1} and g_{j-1} are 1, that bit position $j - 1$ *propagates* a carry if exactly one of f_{j-1} and g_{j-1} is 1, and that bit position $j - 1$ *kills* a carry if neither f_{j-1} nor g_{j-1} is 1.

To implement this idea on an N processor, one-dimensional R-Mesh, let each processor p_j hold input bits f_j and g_j, for $0 \leq j < N$. (To match the standard way of representing binary numbers with the least significant bit (bit 0) to the right, we will number the processors $0, 1, \cdots, N$ from the right.) If $f_j = g_j = 1$, then p_j disconnects its E and W ports and writes a 1 on its W port (towards p_{j+1}) to generate a carry (see Figure 4.4). If $f_j \neq g_j$, then p_j fuses its E and W ports to allow the carry-in value to propagate. If $f_j = g_j = 0$, then p_j disconnects its E and W ports and writes a 0 on its W port to send a 0 carry bit. (Also, p_0 writes 0 on its E port to correspond to $c_0 = 0$.) All processors read from their E ports and store the value as the carry-in to their position. (Note: Processor p_{N-1} also reads from its W port and stores that value as c_N, which is s_N.) Each processor now computes $s_j = f_j \oplus g_j \oplus c_j$.

THEOREM 4.6 *Two N-bit integers can be added in $O(1)$ time on an N processor, one-dimensional, CREW R-Mesh.*

4.2.1.2   Adding N Bits: Counting

The next addition problem that we will examine is the problem of adding N bits, or, simply, *counting* the number of 1's in a sequence of 0's and 1's. Obviously, this problem will arise later in many contexts. The staircase approach to counting that we saw earlier (Lemma 2.4, page 29) applies here. It adds N bits in $O(1)$ time on an $N \times N$ R-Mesh. Recall that we also improved this result by reducing the size of the R-Mesh to $N^\epsilon \times N$, for constant $\epsilon > 0$, while retaining constant time (Corollary 2.11, page 33). In this section, we will present a more efficient result, adding N bits on a $\sqrt{\frac{N}{\log^* N}} \times \sqrt{\frac{N}{\log^* N}}$ R-Mesh in $O(\log^* N)$ time[1].

Other notable results exist for adding N bits. We list these here, though we will not discuss their solution methods other than to note that their approach is very different from (and more difficult than) the one we will describe.

THEOREM 4.7   (*i*) *Addition of N bits can be performed on a $\sqrt{Nm} \times \sqrt{N}$ R-Mesh, where $1 \leq m \leq \log N$, in $O(\log^* N - \log^* m)$ time.*

(*ii*) *Addition of N bits can be performed on a $\sqrt{N} \log^\epsilon N \times \sqrt{N}$ R-Mesh, where $\epsilon > 0$ is a constant, in $O(1)$ time.*

An outline of the $\sqrt{\frac{N}{\log^* N}} \times \sqrt{\frac{N}{\log^* N}}$ R-Mesh algorithm now follows. This algorithm is a generalization of the doubly logarithmic tree approach of Theorem 4.1. The R-Mesh recursively decomposes itself into smaller and smaller square sub-R-Meshes until reaching constant size sub-R-Meshes after $\log^* N + 1$ levels of recursion. Each processor holds $\log^* N$ bits, which it now adds locally in $O(\log^* N)$ time, then the constant size sub-R-Meshes add their sums in constant time, returning these sums up one level in the recursion. The recursive decomposition into sub-R-Meshes is such that the decomposed R-Mesh contains rows of sub-R-Meshes (called *horizontal slices* or *h-slices*) of sufficient size to add the sums generated recursively by the sub-R-Meshes. Figure 4.5 shows sample h- and v-slices. Each square in the figure represents a sub-R-Mesh that recursively generates a partial sum. The sub-R-Meshes of an h-slice collectively add their partial sums into one value for the entire h-slice. Next, sub-R-Meshes in a v-slice use a similar method to add the values in h-slices. This process continues until the full R-Mesh has the entire sum. The algorithm runs in $O(\log^* N)$ time, running in $O(\log^* N)$ time at the bottom level, and $O(1)$ time at each of the other $\log^* N$ levels of recursion.

Implicit in the above outline is the need for an algorithm to add multiple integers more than one bit long. Odd at first, the R-Mesh must perform *multiple addition* (adding N b-bit numbers) in order to count bits. This is more natural on second thought, however, since

---

[1]For integer $k \geq 1$, let $\log^{(k)} N = \underbrace{\log \log \cdots \log N}_{k \; times}$ denote the kth iterate of the log function. The function $\log^* N$ is the smallest integer k such that $\log^{(k)} N \leq 1$. This function grows extremely slowly.

Note that $\log^{(k)} N$ is the kth iterate of the log function, while $\log^k N$ is the kth power of $\log N$, that is, $(\log N)^k$.

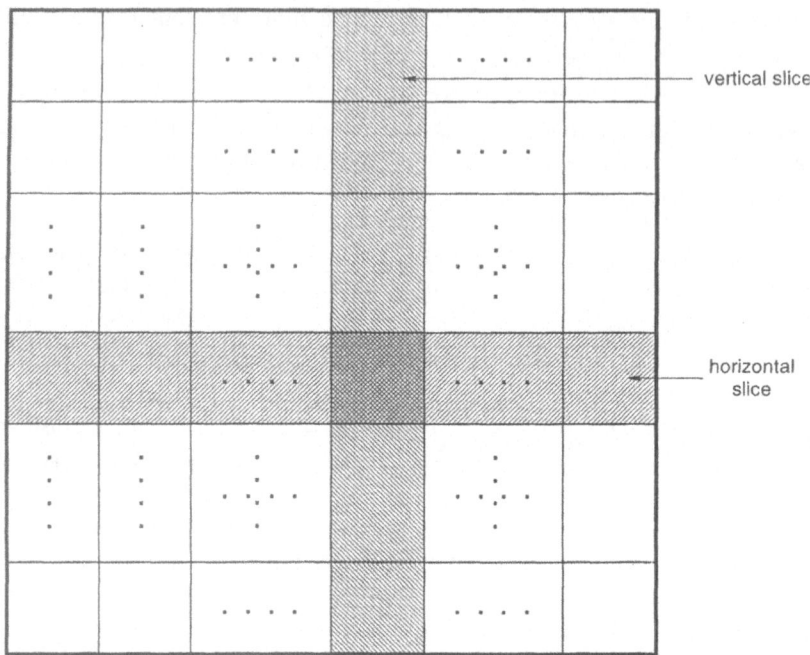

Figure 4.5.   Sample h-slice and v-slice in an R-Mesh comprised of sub-R-Meshes.

the partial sums of bits become these integers. Before describing the counting algorithm then, we will present a tool for multiple addition. (Note: Section 4.2.1.3 will present a different multiple addition algorithm that is more efficient than the one below. That algorithm will build on the algorithm for counting bits in this section.)

The algorithm of the following lemma combines the basic stair step algorithm for prefix sums of bits modulo k (Lemma 2.8, page 30) and the Chinese Remainder Theorem.

LEMMA 4.8 *Addition of N bits can be performed on a $\log^2 N \times N$ R-Mesh in $O(1)$ time.*

Theorem 2.22 (page 57) adds N b-bit integers on a $2N \times 2Nb$ R-Mesh in $O(1)$ time. One can readily remove the factors of 2 from the size (Problem 4.9). The theorem statement bounds $b = O(\log N)$, but if it is not necessary to convert the result to Word format, then the result holds for $1 \le b \le N$. We obtain the following lemma.

LEMMA 4.9 *Addition of N b-bit integers, where $1 \le b \le N$, can be performed on an $N \times Nb$ R-Mesh in $O(1)$ time. Inputs and the output are in BIN format.*

The multiple addition tool of Lemma 4.10 builds on Lemmas 4.8 and 4.9. Problem 4.11 asks to construct the algorithm.

LEMMA 4.10 **Multiple Addition Tool:** *Addition of N b-bit integers, where $b \le \sqrt{N}$, can be performed in $O(1)$ time on a $b \log^2 N \times N$ R-Mesh. If $b = O(\log N)$, then the final sum is in word format; otherwise, it is in BIN format.*

Now, we plunge into the details of the algorithm for adding N bits.

Model: A $\sqrt{\frac{N}{\log^* N}} \times \sqrt{\frac{N}{\log^* N}}$ R-Mesh.

Input: N bits held $\log^* N$ per processor.

Output: The sum of the bits held in processor $p_{0,0}$.

Recall that the algorithm proceeds in several levels of recursion. We now walk through these levels, starting from Level 1, the outermost level, moving down to Level $\log^* N + 1$, the innermost level, and finally returning to Level 1.

Level 1: The R-Mesh is of size $\sqrt{\frac{N}{\log^* N}} \times \sqrt{\frac{N}{\log^* N}}$. The h-slices and v-slice will apply the multiple addition tool (Lemma 4.10) to add results from sub-R-Meshes and h-slices, respectively. The R-Mesh will partition itself into sub-R-Meshes such that an h-slice is of sufficient size to add the partial sums that its sub-R-Meshes return from Level 2. (Actually, a constant number of h-slices together are of sufficient size.) In applying Lemma 4.10 to this proof, we adopt the notation that the algorithm adds R w-bit numbers on a $w \log^2 R \times R$ R-Mesh. To determine the size of an h-slice, we must determine the word size, w, returned by the sub-R-Meshes from Level 2 and the number of values to be added, R. (Note that R depends on w in this decomposition.) As a rough start, letting $R = N$ implies that $w \log^2 R$ will be a small polylog function of N. Therefore, each sub-R-Mesh will hold polylog N bits, so their sum will be at most $O(\log \log N) = O(\log^{(2)} N)$ bits long. To simplify the explanation, we will let word size w be up to $\log N$-bits long. Consequently, the R-Mesh will partition itself into sub-R-Meshes of size $\log^3 N \times \log^3 N$. This will give rise to h-slices of size $\log^3 N \times \sqrt{\frac{N}{\log^* N}}$. On the return to Level 1 later, we will verify that such an h-slice has sufficient size to use the multiple addition tool in constant time.

Level 2: Each sub-R-Mesh is of size $\log^3 N \times \log^3 N$. The word size of partial sums returned from Level 3 will be $O(\log^{(3)} N)$, so Level 2 permits a word size for these partial sums of $\log \log N$ bits. Therefore, each Level 2 sub-R-Mesh partitions itself into sub-R-Meshes of size $(\log \log N)^3 \times (\log \log N)^3$.

Level 3: Each sub-R-Mesh is of size $(\log \log N)^3 \times (\log \log N)^3$. The word size of partial sums returned from Level 4 will be $O(\log^{(4)} N)$, so Level 3 permits a word size for these partial sums of $\log^{(3)} N$ bits. Therefore, each Level 3 sub-R-Mesh partitions itself into sub-R-Meshes of size $(\log^{(3)} N)^3 \times (\log^{(3)} N)^3$.

Continue partitioning until reaching constant size sub-R-Meshes.

Level $\log^* N + 1$: Each sub-R-Mesh is of constant size $2^3 \times 2^3$. Each processor locally adds its input bits in $O(\log^* N)$ time, then each sub-R-Mesh adds these sums in $O(1)$ time.

The sums return up level-by-level, adding all h-slices in parallel, then adding these sums in a v-slice. (As we shall see, the R-Mesh groups a constant number of slices into a team.) The descriptions of the following levels detail the process.

Return to Level 3: Each h-slice is of size $(\log^{(3)} N)^3 \times (\log \log N)^3$ and holds $\left(\frac{\log \log N}{\log^{(3)} N}\right)^3$ values, each up to $\log^{(3)} N$ bits long. (Recall that an h-slice is a row of sub-R-Meshes each of size $(\log^{(3)} N)^3 \times (\log^{(3)} N)^3$, hence, the number of values.) Using the tool of Lemma 4.10 to perform the multiple addition, $w = \log^{(3)} N$ and $R = \left(\frac{\log \log N}{\log^{(3)} N}\right)^3$, so this calls for an R-Mesh of size

$$\log^{(3)} N \cdot \log^2 \left(\frac{\log \log N}{\log^{(3)} N}\right)^3 \times \left(\frac{\log \log N}{\log^{(3)} N}\right)^3$$

to perform the addition.

Is an h-slice of sufficient size? Checking the number of columns, $(\log \log N)^3 > \left(\frac{\log \log N}{\log^{(3)} N}\right)^3$, so it has a sufficient number of columns. Checking the number of rows, $9 \cdot (\log^{(3)} N)^3 \geq \log^{(3)} N \cdot \log^2 \left(\frac{\log \log N}{\log^{(3)} N}\right)^3$ for $N \geq 16$, so one h-slice is not high enough, but nine h-slices are. Therefore, gather h-slices into teams of nine, then run their additions in nine phases.

Return to Level 2: Each h-slice is of size $(\log \log N)^3 \times \log^3 N$ and holds $\left(\frac{\log N}{\log \log N}\right)^3$ values, each up to $\log \log N$ bits long. Using the multiple addition tool, $w = \log \log N$ and $R = \left(\frac{\log N}{\log \log N}\right)^3$, so this calls for an

R-Mesh of size

$$\log\log N \cdot \log^2 \left(\frac{\log N}{\log\log N}\right)^3 \times \left(\frac{\log N}{\log\log N}\right)^3$$

to perform the addition.

Checking the size of an h-slice, as in the return to Level 3, an h-slice has a sufficient number of columns, but we again gather h-slices into teams of nine, and run the multiple additions of h-slices in nine phases.

As a result, adding the partial sums in the h-slices runs in $O(1)$ time. Similarly, each sub-R-Mesh adds the sums from the h-slices in a team of nine v-slices in $O(1)$ time.

Return to Level 1: Each h-slice is of size $\log^3 N \times \sqrt{\frac{N}{\log^* N}}$ and holds $\sqrt{\frac{N}{\log^* N}} / \log^3 N$ values, each up to $\log N$ bits long. Using the multiple addition tool, $w = \log N$ and $R = \left(\sqrt{\frac{N}{\log^* N}}\right) / \left(\log^3 N\right)$, so this requires an R-Mesh of size

$$\log N \cdot \log^2 \left(\frac{\sqrt{\frac{N}{\log^* N}}}{\log^3 N}\right) \times \frac{\sqrt{\frac{N}{\log^* N}}}{\log^3 N}$$

to perform the addition.

Next, check whether the size of an h-slice is adequate. Checking the number of columns, $\sqrt{\frac{N}{\log^* N}} > R$. Checking the number of rows, $\log^3 N > \log N \cdot \log^2 R$. Each h-slice is large enough to add the values it holds in $O(1)$ time. Finally, a v-slice computes the overall sum from the partial sums obtained by the h-slices in $O(1)$ time.

Therefore, we have the following result.

THEOREM 4.11 *Addition of N bits can be performed in $O(\log^* N)$ time on a $\sqrt{\frac{N}{\log^* N}} \times \sqrt{\frac{N}{\log^* N}}$ R-Mesh.*

4.2.1.3 Adding N b-bit Numbers: Multiple Addition

The recursive approach of the algorithm for adding bits extends to the multiple addition problem of adding b-bit numbers. This is not surprising, since the algorithm of the previous subsection adds multiple integers in each of its levels of recursion, except for the very base. The extension must attend to certain additional details, of course. The most prominent of these arise because the word size returned from each level increases by b bits (and this b-bit increase does not change from level to level), so the sub-R-Mesh sizes must accommodate this and the recursion terminates when this b factor dominates the sub-R-Mesh size over the iterated $\log N$ factor.

Here we describe a method for adding N b-bit integers in $O(\log b + \log^* N)$ time with optimal efficiency on a $\sqrt{\frac{N}{\log b + \log^* N}} \times \sqrt{\frac{N}{\log b + \log^* N}}$ R-Mesh. Since an N-processor R-Mesh can add N elements (of any word size) in $O(\log N)$ time using the binary tree algorithm approach (Theorem 2.1, page 18), the method of this section is useful only when $\log b = o(\log N)$. Accordingly, we assume that $\log b = o(\log N)$.

Model: A $\sqrt{\frac{N}{\log b + \log^* N}} \times \sqrt{\frac{N}{\log b + \log^* N}}$ R-Mesh.

Input: N b-bit integers in Word format held $\log b + \log^* N$ per processor.

Output: The sum of the inputs held in processor $p_{0,0}$.

The algorithm follows that of Section 4.2.1.2.

Level 1: The R-Mesh is of size $\sqrt{\frac{N}{\log b + \log^* N}} \times \sqrt{\frac{N}{\log b + \log^* N}}$. It will partition itself into sub-R-Meshes such that an h-slice is of sufficient size to add the partial sums that its sub-R-Meshes return from Level 2. To use the tool of Lemma 4.10 for this addition, we must determine the word size, w, returned by these sub-R-Meshes and the number of values to be added, R. This word size will be $b + O(\log \log N)$ bits. To simplify details in the following explanation, we will let $w = b + \log N$. Consequently, the R-Mesh will partition itself into sub-R-Meshes of size $(b + \log N) \log^2 N \times (b + \log N) \log^2 N$.

Level 2: A sub-R-Mesh has size $(b + \log N) \log^2 N \times (b + \log N) \log^2 N$. The word size of partial sums returned from Level 3 will be $b + O(\log^{(3)} N)$ bits. Again, we will partition to allow a word size, $b + \log \log N$ that is slightly larger than the required size of $b + O(\log^{(3)} N)$ bits. Therefore, each Level 2 sub-R-Mesh partitions itself into sub-R-Meshes of size $(b + \log \log N)(\log \log N)^2 \times (b + \log \log N)(\log \log N)^2$.

Continue to Level k, where $k = 2 + g$ and g is the largest integer such that $b < \log^{(g)} N$. (For instance, if $\log \log N \le b < \log N$, then $g = 1$ and $k = 3$. Recall that $\log^{(g)} N$ denotes log iterated g times on N.)

Level k: Each sub-R-Mesh is of size $(b + \log^{(k-1)} N)(\log^{(k-1)} N)^2 \times (b + \log^{(k-1)} N)(\log^{(k-1)} N)^2$. Each processor locally adds its input elements in $O(\log b + \log^* N)$ time, then each sub-R-Mesh adds these local sums by a binary tree algorithm in $O(\log(b + \log^{(k-1)} N)) = O(\log b)$ time (Theorem 2.1, page 18).

As in the proof of Theorem 4.11, the sums return up level-by-level, adding all h-slices in parallel, then adding these sums in a v-slice. (The R-Mesh again groups a constant number of slices into a team.) The descriptions of the following levels detail the process.

Return to Level 2: Each h-slice is of size $(b + \log \log N)(\log \log N)^2 \times (b + \log N) \log^2 N$ and holds $\frac{(b + \log N) \log^2 N}{(b + \log \log N)(\log \log N)^2}$ values, each up to

$(b + \log \log N)$-bits long. (Recall that an h-slice is a row of Level 2 sub-R-Meshes, hence, the number of values.) Using Lemma 4.10 for multiple addition, $w = b + \log \log N$ and $R = \frac{(b+\log N)\log^2 N}{(b+\log \log N)(\log \log N)^2}$, so this calls for an R-Mesh of size $(b + \log \log N)\log^2 R \times R$ to add the numbers in constant time.

As in Section 4.2.1.2, nine h-slices suffice for the multiple addition. Therefore, gather h-slices into teams of nine, then run their additions in nine phases. Adding the partial sums in the h-slices then runs in $O(1)$ time. Similarly, each sub-R-Mesh adds the sums from the h-slices in a team of nine v-slices in $O(1)$ time.

Return to Level 1: Each h-slice is $(b + \log N)\log^2 N \times \sqrt{\frac{N}{\log b + \log^* N}}$ in size and holds $\left(\sqrt{\frac{N}{\log b + \log^* N}}\right) / \left((b + \log N)\log^2 N\right)$ values, each value up to $(b + \log N)$-bits long. Using the multiple addition tool,

$$w = b + \log N \text{ and } R = \frac{\sqrt{\frac{N}{\log b + \log^* N}}}{(b + \log N)\log^2 N},$$

so this calls for an R-Mesh of size $(b + \log N)\log^2 R \times R$ to add the numbers in constant time.

Here each h-slice is large enough to add the values it holds in $O(1)$ time. Finally, a v-slice computes the overall sum from the partial sums obtained by the h-slices in $O(1)$ time.

Therefore, we have the following result.

THEOREM 4.12 *Addition of N b-bit integers can be performed in $O(\log b + \log^* N)$ time on a $\sqrt{\frac{N}{\log b + \log^* N}} \times \sqrt{\frac{N}{\log b + \log^* N}}$ R-Mesh.*

4.2.1.4   Prefix Sums

The preceding subsections examined adding N bits and adding N b-bit integers, and now, to extend the concepts, we discuss algorithms for prefix sums.

The algorithm for prefix sums of N b-bit integers builds on a method for computing prefix sums of integers whose values are bounded by a function of N. This method, in turn, naturally builds on an algorithm for computing prefix sums of bits.

The algorithm to compute the prefix sums of N b-bit integers works in two stages. Stage 1 is a recursive procedure that computes "sampled" prefix sums. At the top level of recursion, Stage 1 returns the prefix sums of a sample of every $(N^{\frac{1}{2}})^{\text{th}}$ element of the input. The stage decomposes an $N^{\frac{1}{2}} \times N^{\frac{1}{2}}$ R-Mesh into $N^{\frac{1}{2}}$ sub-R-Meshes, each of size $N^{\frac{1}{4}} \times N^{\frac{1}{4}}$. Each sub-R-Mesh computes the sampled prefix sums of the $N^{\frac{1}{2}}$ elements it holds. Each sub-R-Mesh also sends the sum of its $N^{\frac{1}{2}}$ elements on its return from recursion and retains the remaining $N^{\frac{1}{4}}$ prefix sums for Stage 2. Stage 1 finishes by computing the prefix sums of the $N^{\frac{1}{2}}$ values received from the sub-R-Meshes using radix-$N^{\frac{1}{2}}$ notation[2] on the $N^{\frac{1}{2}} \times N^{\frac{1}{2}}$ R-Mesh. Stage 2 iteratively sends each sampled prefix sum computed at a level of Stage 1 down to the corresponding sub-R-Mesh, which broadcasts it to its processors to use to refine their prefix sums. This continues until the last level of recursion.

We now state two results critical to the algorithm and defer their proofs to a sequence of problems (Problems 4.12–4.15). The prefix sums result of Lemma 4.14 implicitly decomposes integers into radix-N notation using Lemma 4.13.

LEMMA 4.13 *Given N integers in the range $[0, N^c)$, an $N \times N$ R-Mesh can decompose them into radix-N notation in $O(c)$ time.*

LEMMA 4.14 *The prefix sums of N integers in the range $[0, N^c)$ can be computed on an $N \times N$ R-Mesh in $O(c)$ time.*

Observe that the order in which the R-Mesh holds the prefix sums results from the structure of the decomposition of the R-Mesh. Call this ordering as *nested column-major order*.

Algorithm 4.1   (Prefix Sums of N b-bit Integers)

Model: An $N^{\frac{1}{2}} \times N^{\frac{1}{2}}$ R-Mesh.

Input: N b-bit integers, $Z = \{z_0, z_1, \ldots, z_{N-1}\}$, held one per processor in nested column-major order.

Output: Prefix sums of the input values, held one per processor in nested column-major order.

begin

/* Stage 1 */

SAMPLED-PREFIX-SUMS($Z, N^{\frac{1}{2}}$)

    /* Z is the input, $N^{\frac{1}{2}}$ is the side dimension of the R-Mesh. */

---

[2]The radix-r notation of an integer i is its representation as digits $i_{x-1}i_{x-2}\ldots i_1 i_0$, where

$0 \leq i_j < r$ for each $0 \leq j < x$ and $i = \displaystyle\sum_{j=0}^{x-1} i_j \cdot r^j$.

if $N^{\frac{1}{2}} \leq 4$ **then**
> compute prefix sums directly and return overall sum in top left processor.

else

1. Decompose the $N^{\frac{1}{2}} \times N^{\frac{1}{2}}$ R-Mesh into $N^{\frac{1}{2}}$ sub-R-Meshes, M_j, each of size $N^{\frac{1}{4}} \times N^{\frac{1}{4}}$. Let Z_j denote the inputs in M_j.
2. Each sub-R-Mesh, M_j, recursively calls
   SAMPLED-PREFIX-SUMS$(Z_j, N^{\frac{1}{4}})$.
3. Route the $N^{\frac{1}{2}}$ partial sums from the sub-R-Meshes to the top row of the $N^{\frac{1}{2}} \times N^{\frac{1}{2}}$ R-Mesh.
4. Decompose each of the partial sums (in the range $[0, 2^b N^{\frac{1}{2}})$) into radix-$N^{\frac{1}{2}}$ notation.
5. Compute the prefix sums of the $N^{\frac{1}{2}}$ partial sums in radix-$N^{\frac{1}{2}}$ notation.
6. Return the sum of the $N^{\frac{1}{2}}$ partial sums.

end_if_else

/* End of Stage 1 */

/* Stage 2 */
for $i \leftarrow 1$ **to** $\log \log N$ **do**
> /* Each sub-R-Mesh at level i executes in parallel */

1. Send the $N^{\frac{1}{2^i}}$ prefix sums held on the top row down to the corresponding $N^{\frac{1}{2^i}}$ sub-R-Meshes at level $i + 1$
2. Each sub-R-Mesh at level $i + 1$ broadcasts the prefix sum to its $N^{\frac{1}{2^{i+1}}}$ processors holding their own prefix sums from Stage 1; these processors add the received prefix sum to their own prefix sums.

end_for

end

Stage 1 of the prefix sums algorithm has $\log \log N$ levels of recursion following along the lines of the algorithm of the doubly logarithmic tree algorithm of Theorem 4.1 (see also Problem 4.6). The R-Mesh can decompose into sub-R-Meshes in $O(1)$ time and route sums to its top row in $O(1)$ time. By Lemma 4.13, it can decompose each sum in $\frac{2^i b}{\log N} + 1$ time at level i of the recursion, as a sum in the range $[0, 2^b N^{\frac{1}{2^i}})$ decomposes into this number of radix-$N^{\frac{1}{2^i}}$ digits. By Lemma 4.14, computing the prefix sums in radix-$N^{\frac{1}{2^i}}$ notation at level i takes the same time. This leads to $O(b + \log \log N)$ time for Stage 1. Stage 2 runs in $O(1)$ time for each of $\log \log N$ iterations.

THEOREM 4.15 *The prefix sums of N b-bit integers can be computed in $O(b + \log \log N)$ time on an $N^{\frac{1}{2}} \times N^{\frac{1}{2}}$ R-Mesh.*

4.2.2   Multiplication

The aim of multiplying two N-bit binary integers, X and Y, is to compute their $2N$-bit product, Z. As a first approach, one can express Z as $\sum_{i=0}^{N-1} x_i \cdot 2^i \cdot Y$. Multiplying by a power of 2 is simply a shift operation, and multiplying by bit x_i results in 0 or $2^i Y$, so multiplication reduces to the multiple addition problem of adding these N $2N$-bit numbers. Using Theorem 4.7(ii) extended to multiple bit numbers (Problem 4.16), we obtain the following result.

COROLLARY 4.16 *The product of two N-bit integers can be computed in $O(1)$ time on a $\sqrt{N} \log^\epsilon N \times N\sqrt{N}$ R-Mesh, where $\epsilon > 0$ is a constant.*

A similar method with Lemma 4.9 runs on a bit-model R-Mesh. Recall that Lemma 4.9 established that an $N \times Nb$ R-Mesh can add N b-bit integers, where $1 \leq b \leq N$, in $O(1)$ time. Observe that the algorithm actually runs on a bit-model R-Mesh. Lemma 4.9 assumes that the input integers are in BIN representation and arranged such that processor $(i, 2jN)$ holds the jth bit of the ith integer. That is, the ith integer is held in row i with bits held every $2N$ processors.

COROLLARY 4.17 *The product of two N-bit integers can be computed in $O(1)$ time on an $N \times N^2$ bit-model R-Mesh.*

The approach to multiply two numbers optimally on a bit-model R-Mesh ($O(1)$ time on an $N \times N$ R-Mesh) is decidedly less simple. Rather than reducing to multiple addition, an alternative approach to solving multiplication is to reduce the problem to cyclic convolution of two integer sequences. Let A and B denote the N-bit integers to be multiplied. The algorithm consists of several stages shown in Figure 4.6. It will first construct sequence $A_0, A_1, \ldots, A_{2M-1}$ from A and sequence $B_0, B_1, \ldots, B_{2M-1}$ from B, where $M = N^{\frac{1}{4}}$ and each A_i and B_i is in the range $[0, 2^{\frac{N}{M}} - 1]$. Next the algorithm performs cyclic convolutions of these sequences as described below. Let C_i denote the cyclic convolution

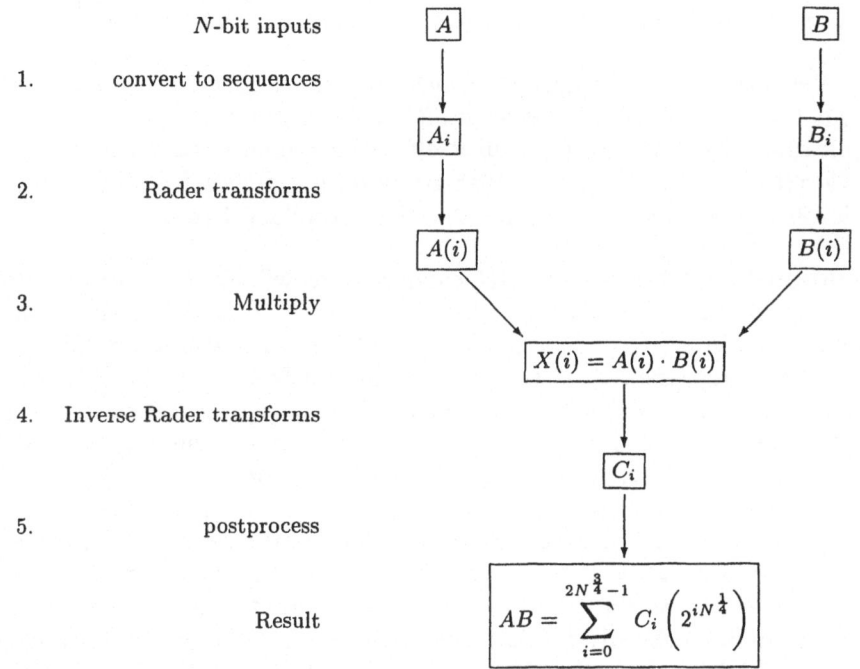

Figure 4.6. Stages of the bit-model R-Mesh multiplication algorithm. Stages 2–4 collectively perform cyclic convolutions of sequences A_i and B_i. In all cases, $0 \leq i < 2M = 2N^{\frac{3}{4}}$.

of the two sequences, where $0 \leq i < 2M$, then

$$C_i = \sum_{k=0}^{i} A_k B_{i-k}.$$

To compute the cyclic convolution, the algorithm will employ the *Rader Transform* as follows.

- Compute the Rader transform of each sequence,
- Multiply the corresponding elements of the two transformed sequences, and
- Compute the inverse Rader transform of the product sequence.

The Rader transform satisfies the cyclic convolution property. That is, the transform of the cyclic convolution of two sequences is equal to the product of the transforms of the two individual sequences. Finally, the product AB of the input numbers is the quantity $\displaystyle\sum_{i=0}^{2N^{\frac{3}{4}}-1} C_i\left(2^{iN^{\frac{1}{4}}}\right)$.

We now discuss background, including the Rader Transform (RT) and the *diminished-1 notation* useful in its computation. The multiplication algorithm uses within itself another multiplication algorithm (Corollary 4.17), though one that grows from a different multiple addition base (Lemma 4.9) than the one that Corollary 4.16 used.

Diminished-1 Notation. RT computations will involve addition and multiplication modulo $2^b + 1$, for an integer $b \geq 1$. To perform the operations in b bits, rather than the $b + 1$ bits that would normally be needed to represent $2^b + 1$, apply the diminished-1 notation. In this notation, 2^b represents value 0 and the binary representation of $i - 1$ represents value i, where $1 \leq i \leq 2^b$. Observe that value 0 is the only value with a 1 in bit position b (numbering bits from 0 to b). Due to the special cases of adding 0 or multiplying by 0, if one operand is 0, then the R-Mesh need not actually perform the addition or multiplication. It can simply handle these cases separately, writing the correct result. Consequently, the only arithmetic operations that must be performed can be done with only b bits rather than $b + 1$. The following result, whose proof is left as Problems 4.17 and 4.18, is useful in establishing Lemma 4.19.

LEMMA 4.18 *For numbers in the ring of integers modulo $2^b + 1$ represented using the diminished-1 notation, addition of two numbers or multiplication by a constant 2^k in the ring of integers modulo $2^b + 1$, where $0 \leq k < b$, can be performed in $O(1)$ time on a $b \times b$ R-Mesh.*

Rader Transform. The Rader Transform (RT) is a transform of a sequence of $G = 2^m$ elements, $x(0), x(1), \cdots, x(G-1)$ in a ring closed under addition and multiplication modulo some integer F of the form $2^{2^t} + 1$. The condition $G \leq 2\log(F-1)$ must hold. Let α be a power of 2 that is a Gth root of 1 in the ring. Given input element $x(g)$ in the ring, where $0 \leq g < G$, the G-point RT is defined as:

$$X(k) = \sum_{g=0}^{G-1} x(g)\alpha^{gk} \pmod{F}, \quad \text{for } k = 0, 1, \ldots, G-1,$$

and the inverse RT is defined as:

$$x(g) = 2^{-m} \sum_{k=0}^{G-1} X(k)\alpha^{-gk} \pmod{F}, \quad \text{for } g = 0, 1, \ldots, G-1.$$

LEMMA 4.19 *Given 2M points in BIN format in a row of the R-Mesh, the 2M-point RT (and its inverse) in the ring of integers modulo $2^b + 1$ can be computed in $O(1)$ time on an $M^2b \times Mb$ bit-model R-Mesh, where b is a multiple of M and a power of 2.*

Proof: Let α denote the $2M^{\text{th}}$ primitive root of unity, that is, $2M$ is the smallest integer such that $\alpha^{2M} \equiv 1 \pmod{2^b + 1}$. In this case, $\alpha = 2^{b/M}$. Let $\vec{x} = [x(i)]$ denote an input vector of $2M$ integers, and let $\vec{X} = [X(i)]$, also a vector of $2M$ integers, denote the $2M$-point RT of $\vec{x}$. For the following transform matrix T, $\vec{X} = T\vec{x}$ using arithmetic in the ring of integers modulo $2^b + 1$.

$$T = \begin{bmatrix} 1 & 1 & 1 & \cdots & 1 \\ 1 & \alpha & \alpha^2 & \cdots & \alpha^{2M-1} \\ 1 & \alpha^2 & \alpha^4 & \cdots & \alpha^{4M-2} \\ \vdots & & \vdots & & \vdots \\ 1 & \alpha^{2M-1} & \alpha^{4M-2} & \cdots & \alpha^{(2M-1)(2M-1)} \end{bmatrix}$$

The remainder of the proof is left as Problems 4.19 and 4.20 and falls under the following structure. For simplicity, assume that the R-Mesh is of size $4M^2b \times 2Mb$. Partition the R-Mesh into $2M$ sub-R-Meshes $RM(i)$ of size $2Mb \times 2Mb$. Each $RM(i)$ is responsible for computing

$$X(i) = \sum_{j=0}^{2M-1} \alpha^{ij} x(j) \pmod{2^b + 1}.$$

Within this, partition each $RM(i)$ into $2M$ sub-R-Meshes $SM(i,j)$ of size $2Mb \times b$. Each $SM(i,j)$ is responsible for computing $\alpha^{ij} x(j) \pmod{2^b + 1}$. ∎

The Optimal Multiplication Algorithm. Recall that we are performing multiplication by reducing the problem to computing the cyclic convolution of two sequences. Recall further that we will compute the cyclic convolution by (*i*) computing the RT of each sequence, (*ii*) multiplying corresponding elements of the two transforms, then (*iii*) computing the inverse transform of the product.

We develop the algorithm in a sequence of three results: a lemma on one-dimensional cyclic convolution, a lemma on four-dimensional cyclic convolution, then a theorem pulling the results into a multiplication algorithm.

LEMMA 4.20 *Cyclic convolution of two binary integer sequences of length 2M, where each integer is in $[0, 2^b - 1]$, can be performed in $O(1)$ time on an $M^2b \times Mb$ bit-model R-Mesh, where $M \leq b \leq M^2$ and b is a multiple of M and a power of 2.*

<u>Proof:</u> Following the outline described above, the R-Mesh performs cyclic convolution of sequences A and B by the following steps.

1. Compute the RT of each sequence: Since each element of A and B is in $[0, 2^b - 1]$, then each element of result C is in $[0, 2^{3b-1} - 1]$. By Lemma 4.19, an R-Mesh of size $3M^2b \times 3Mb$ can compute the RT in the ring of integers modulo $2^{3b} + 1$ in $O(1)$ time. (By suitably adjusting the algorithm, we can reduce the size to $M^2b \times Mb$.)

2. Multiply corresponding elements of the two transforms: The R-Mesh performs $2M$ multiplications of $3b$-bit numbers. By Corollary 4.17, each multiplication runs on a $9b^2 \times 3b$ sub-R-Mesh in $O(1)$ time. Given that $M^2 \geq b$, all the multiplications fit on the available R-Mesh.

3. Compute the inverse transform of the product: The R-Mesh executes this step in a way similar to to Step 1.   ∎

LEMMA 4.21 *Cyclic convolution of two binary integer sequences of length* $2N^{\frac{3}{4}}$, *where each integer is in* $[0, 2^{N^{\frac{1}{4}}} - 1]$, *can be performed in* $O(1)$ *time on an* $N \times N$ *bit-model R-Mesh.*

<u>Proof:</u> The algorithm uses the $2N^{\frac{3}{4}}$-point RT in the (one-dimensional) cyclic convolution, though decomposed into four-dimensional cyclic convolution. This leads to four-dimensional cyclic convolution of two four-dimensional arrays of length $(16N^{\frac{3}{4}})^{\frac{1}{4}}$ in each dimension. The $16N^{\frac{3}{4}}$ numbers arise from the original $2N^{\frac{3}{4}}$ numbers padded with 0's. The algorithm performs cyclic convolution along each dimension by $(16N^{\frac{3}{4}})^{\frac{3}{4}}$ cyclic convolutions, performing each on two sequences of $(16N^{\frac{3}{4}})^{\frac{1}{4}}$ numbers.

Let A_i and B_i denote elements of the two sequences of length $2N^{\frac{3}{4}}$. Let the R-Mesh initially hold A_i and B_i in processors $(0, iN^{\frac{3}{4}})$, for $0 \leq i < 2N^{\frac{3}{4}}$. Padding with 0's, the data array is of size $2N^{\frac{3}{16}} \times 2N^{\frac{3}{16}} \times 2N^{\frac{3}{16}} \times 2N^{\frac{3}{16}}$. This proof describes the convolution in one dimension; Problems 4.21 and 4.22 deal with data distribution and routing to perform the convolutions in the other dimensions. We describe the result for a $16N \times 16N$ R-Mesh; Problem 4.22 deals with restricting the size to $N \times N$. The R-Mesh stores the four-dimensional data arrays in lexicographic order along its top row. Partition the R-Mesh into strips (sub-R-Meshes) of size $16N \times 2N^{\frac{3}{16} + \frac{1}{4}}$. This creates $8N^{\frac{9}{16}} = (16N^{\frac{3}{4}})^{\frac{3}{4}}$ such strips, each holding $2N^{\frac{3}{16}}$ numbers. By Lemma 4.20, each strip has a sufficient number of processors to perform the cyclic convolution of $2N^{\frac{3}{16}}$ numbers in $O(1)$ time, hence, the R-Mesh performs all $(16N^{\frac{3}{4}})^{\frac{3}{4}}$

such cyclic convolutions in parallel in $O(1)$ time. The R-Mesh permutes the data and repeats the operation in each of the remaining three dimensions. ∎

THEOREM 4.22 *Multiplication of two N-bit numbers given in a row can be performed in $O(1)$ time on an $N \times N$ bit-model R-Mesh.*

<u>Proof:</u> Let $a_{N-1} \ldots a_1 a_0$ and $b_{N-1} \ldots b_1 b_0$ denote the binary representations of two numbers to be multiplied. The R-Mesh computes several terms from these inputs. Let $A_i = a_{(i+1)N^{\frac{1}{4}}-1} \cdots a_{iN^{\frac{1}{4}}+1} a_{iN^{\frac{1}{4}}}$, for $0 \le i < N^{\frac{3}{4}}$, and $A_i = 0$, for $N^{\frac{3}{4}} \le i < 2N^{\frac{3}{4}}$. Let $A(x) = \displaystyle\sum_{i=0}^{2N^{\frac{3}{4}}-1} A_i x^i$.

Define B_i, $B(x)$, and $C(x)$ similarly. Recall that $C_i = \displaystyle\sum_{k=0}^{i} A_k B_{i-k}$, where $0 \le i < 2N^{\frac{3}{4}}$. Computing $C\left(2^{N^{\frac{1}{4}}}\right)$ suffices to compute the product of the two input numbers (Problem 4.23). By Lemma 4.21, the R-Mesh computes each C_i, for $0 \le i < 2N^{\frac{3}{4}}$, in $O(1)$ time. Computing the summation for $C\left(2^{N^{\frac{1}{4}}}\right)$ follows readily. ∎

4.2.3   Division

The aim of division is to compute the most significant N bits of the quotient of $\frac{A}{B}$, where A and B are N-bit integers. (We omit the R-Mesh division algorithm, only sketching the outline.) As is common in these parts, the problem reduces to computing the inverse $\frac{1}{B}$ then multiplying it by A. Computing the inverse of B boils down to adding the first N powers of $U = 1 - B$, truncating the result to N bits. Powering efficiently draws on a PRAM algorithm involving the Chinese Remainder Theorem, DFTs, and Newton approximation. The end result is the following.

THEOREM 4.23 *Division of two N-bit numbers given in a row can be computed in $O(1)$ time on an $N \times N$ bit-model R-Mesh.*

4.3   Multiplying Matrices

A natural next step in arithmetic operations is to examine operations on matrices, particularly matrix multiplication, since they arise so frequently in many applications. This section builds on earlier results to present algorithms for matrix-vector multiplication (Section 4.3.1), matrix multiplication (Section 4.3.2), and sparse matrix multiplication (Section 4.3.3). The matrix-vector multiplication algorithm relies on efficient organization of sub-R-Meshes and compact data routing to run on a small sized R-Mesh. The matrix multiplication algorithm arranges sub-R-Meshes performing matrix-vector multiplication so as to attain AT^2 optimality. On sparse matrices, we will see two algorithms, one for a pair of uniformly sparse matrices and another for multiplying a column-sparse matrix by a row-sparse matrix.

4.3.1   Matrix-Vector Multiplication

The matrix-vector multiplication algorithm builds on the foundation of the multiple addition tool (Lemma 4.10) used in Section 4.2.1.2. Why? Because the structure of the R-Mesh involved in this algorithm and the input and output data arrangements lend themselves to placement in sub-R-Meshes in the larger algorithm. Chapter 8 will take up the algorithm again, examining a method for "scaling" the algorithm, that is, for reducing the number of processors involved at a corresponding time cost. Such time-size tradeoffs are important for using the algorithm as a component in some larger scale algorithm, and they are important in their own right.

Let $A = [a_{i,j}]$ be an $N \times N$ matrix and let $\vec{d} = [d_i]$ be an N-element vector. The problem of matrix-vector multiplication is to compute their N-element product vector $\vec{c} = [c_i]$, where $c_i = \sum_{j=0}^{N-1} a_{i,j} \cdot d_j$. As is customary for models of word size b-bits, we will assume that the elements of A, $\vec{d}$, and $\vec{c}$ are b-bits long. We refer to this problem as computing a matrix-vector multiplication of size N (with word size b). Results assume $b \leq \sqrt{N}$. If $b > \sqrt{N}$, then the simple binary tree algorithm (Theorem 2.1, page 18) has better resource bounds.

Let the kth *XY-slice* of a three-dimensional R-Mesh denote the two-dimensional sub-R-Mesh comprising processors (i, j, k), for fixed k and all i, j (see Figure 4.7). Define the ith *YZ-slice* similarly to be the two-dimensional sub-R-Mesh comprising processors (i, j, k), for fixed i and all j, k.

THEOREM 4.24 *Matrix-vector multiplication of size N (with word size b) can be performed in $O(1)$ time on an $N \times N \times b \log^2 N$ three-dimensional R-Mesh; the final result is stored in BIN format.*

Proof: Let the 0th XY-slice initially hold matrix A, where $p_{i,j,0}$ holds matrix element $a_{i,j}$, so row i of A is in row i of the XY-slice. Let the 0th row of the 0th XY-slice initially hold vector $\vec{d}$, where $p_{0,j,0}$ holds

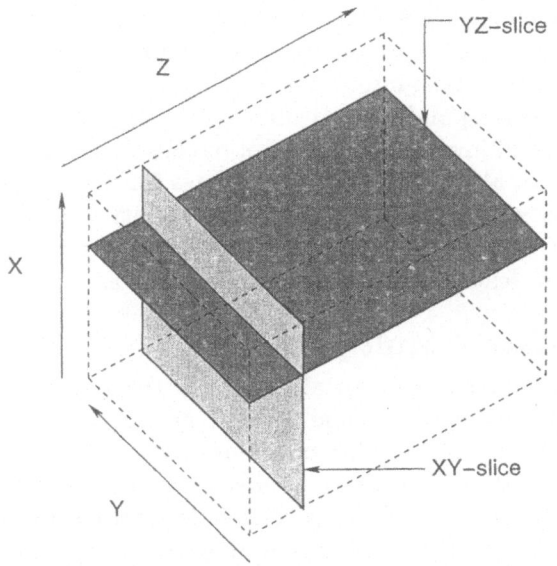

Figure 4.7. Slices of a three-dimensional R-Mesh.
Reprinted from *Parallel Computing*, vol. 29, 2003, R. Vaidyanathan, J. L. Trahan, and C.-m. Lu, "Degree of Scalability: Scalable Reconfigurable Mesh Algorithms for Multiple Addition and Matrix-Vector Multiplication," pp. 95–109, © Copyright (2003) with permission from Elsevier.

element d_j. Broadcast $\vec{d}$ down the columns of the 0th XY-slice. Each processor $p_{i,j,0}$ now holds $a_{i,j}$ and d_j, and, next, multiplies them. Each YZ-slice is an $N \times b\log^2 N$ sub-R-Mesh that holds the N b-bit products $a_{i,j} \cdot d_j$ whose sum is c_i, the ith element of the result vector. Each such sub-R-Mesh adds these values in $O(1)$ time (Lemma 4.10). The ith YZ-slice holds c_i stored in BIN format, that is, $p_{i,k,0}$ holds bit k of c_i, where $0 \leq i < N$ and $0 \leq k < b$. ∎

This three-dimensional R-Mesh readily converts to a two-dimensional R-Mesh using Theorem 3.1 (page 80), where $P_0 = N$, $P_1 = b\log^2 N$, and $P_2 = N$.

COROLLARY 4.25 *Matrix-vector multiplication of size N (with word size b) can be performed in $O(1)$ time on an $O(Nb\log^2 N) \times O(Nb\log^2 N)$ two-dimensional R-Mesh; the final result is stored in BIN format.*

Scaling the Algorithm. In Chapter 8, we will revisit the multiple
addition tool cited earlier to incorporate a time-size tradeoff that allows
the R-Mesh running the algorithm to scale down in size. This modified
algorithm can then plug into the matrix-vector multiplication algorithm
to produce a corresponding tradeoff.

Chapter 8 will investigate scaling of models in a manner that applies
to any arbitrary algorithm, so it manipulates features of the models only,
not the algorithm. The problem we take up relative to multiple addition
and matrix-vector multiplication is algorithm-specific scaling, so we will
seek to exploit features of the algorithm as well as the model.

4.3.2   Matrix Multiplication

The AT^2 complexity of an algorithm is the product of the layout
area, A, and the square of time T. The notion derives from studying
the complexity of VLSI implementations of algorithms. The measure is
relevant in the R-Mesh context as area corresponds to the number of
processors. Matrix multiplication of $N \times N$ matrices has an AT^2 lower
bound of $\Omega(N^4)$ in the word model of VLSI, in which each processor
occupies one unit of area. The matrix multiplication algorithm that
this section describes (Theorem 4.26) has optimal AT^2 complexity for
constant time. (In Chapter 8, we will see how to extend this algorithm
to preserve the AT^2 complexity over a range of T (time) from 1 to N.)

While it is eminently natural to build a matrix multiplication algorithm from a matrix-vector multiplication algorithm, the algorithm of
Section 4.3.1 does not arise here because of the $\log^2 N$ factors in size.
Instead, the algorithm implicitly uses an $N \times N^2$ size matrix-vector multiplication algorithm, which uses more processors, but the size N side
fits better. Because of the data routing necessary, the matrix multiplication algorithm uses an R-Mesh of size $N^2 \times N^2$, so the size N^2 side is
already available.

THEOREM 4.26 *For* $1 \leq b \leq \sqrt{N}$, *the multiplication of two* $N \times N$
matrices, where each element is b-bits long, can be performed by an $N^2 \times$
N^2 *R-Mesh in* $O(1)$ *time.*

Proof: Let A and D denote the $N \times N$ matrices to be multiplied. Initially, let each processor in the top row hold an element of A in row-major
order and let each processor in the leftmost column hold an element of
D in column-major order. Partition the mesh into $N \times N$ sub-R-Meshes.
Broadcast A down the columns and D across the rows, letting the diagonal elements of each sub-R-Mesh grab the elements that reach them (a
row of A and a column of D for each sub-R-Mesh). Each sub-R-Mesh
multiplies the corresponding elements of row i of A and column j of D,

then adds these N elements in $O(1)$ time to produce element $c_{i,j}$ of the product matrix C. Since each sub-R-Mesh is of size $N \times N$, which is larger than $b \log^2 N \times N$, Lemma 4.10 suffices for this addition. The R-Mesh can then easily route the product elements to the top row. ∎

4.3.3 Sparse Matrix Multiplication

A *sparse* $N \times N$ matrix is one with substantially fewer than N^2 non-zero elements. Operations on such sparse matrices can exploit this information to run more efficiently than on non-sparse matrices. Since sparse matrices arise in numerical computations such as modeling systems by large systems of linear equations, the potential for time and space savings has drawn attention to sparse matrices. One can characterize the sparseness of a matrix in different ways. We will say that a matrix is:

- *row sparse* with degree ρ if the maximum number of non-zero elements in a row is ρ,

- *column sparse* with degree κ if the maximum number of non-zero elements in a column is κ, and

- *uniformly sparse* with degree ρ if the maximum number of non-zero elements in each row and each column is ρ.

This section discusses two algorithms for multiplying $N \times N$ sparse matrices. Both algorithms use an $N \times N$ R-Mesh, rather than the $N^2 \times N^2$ R-Mesh of Theorem 4.26. The first multiplies a pair of uniformly sparse matrices with degree ρ in $O(\rho^2)$ time on an $N \times N$ R-Mesh. (Note that this time is constant if ρ is a constant.) The second multiplies a column-sparse matrix with degree κ_A by a row-sparse matrix with degree ρ_D in $O(\kappa_A \rho_D \sqrt{N})$ time on an $N \times N$ R-Mesh. (Compare this to the $\Omega(\sqrt{N})$ lower bound.) We will highlight how the algorithms take advantage of the sparseness of the matrices.

Multiplying Uniformly Sparse Matrices. Let A and D denote $N \times N$ matrices that are uniformly sparse with degree ρ. Initially, processor $p_{i,j}$ holds element $a_{i,j}$ of A and element $d_{i,j}$ of D. At the end, processor $p_{i,j}$ will hold element $c_{i,j}$ of product matrix C. For simplicity of explanation, assume that ρ divides N.

The R-Mesh first compresses each row of A to the leftmost ρ columns (Figure 4.8). It accomplishes this by moving one element at a time in $O(\rho)$ steps. It then partitions the rows into clumps of ρ rows each and swings the data in the kth clump from the leftmost ρ columns to the top ρ rows in the kth interval of columns, that is, columns $k\rho$ through

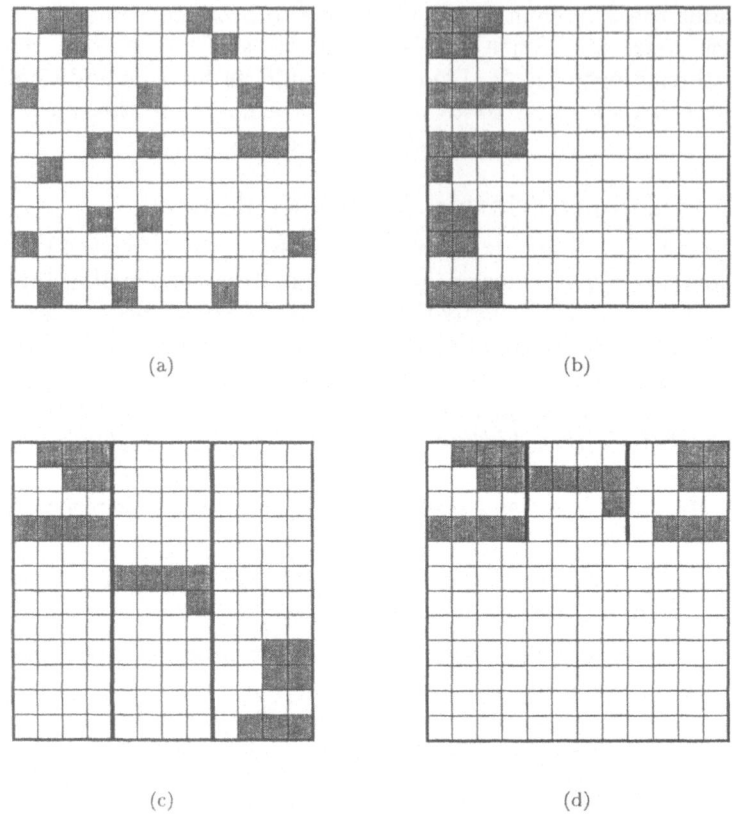

(a)   (b)

(c)   (d)

Figure 4.8. (a) A uniformly sparse matrix A with degree 4, (b) compressing rows of A, (c, d) swinging clumps of rows to the top for $\rho = 4$ on a 12×12 R-Mesh.

$(k+1)\rho - 1$. The R-Mesh moves each clump simultaneously in $O(\rho)$ time.

The R-Mesh similarly compresses each column of D to the top, then swings the kth clump of columns to the leftmost ρ columns in the kth interval of rows in $O(\rho)$ time.

Observe that row g of the R-Mesh holds the compressed contents of rows g, $g + \rho$, $\ldots, g + \left(\frac{N}{\rho} - 1\right)\rho$ of A, and column h holds the corresponding compressed columns of D. The next phase of the algorithm computes the inner product of each row of A and each column of D. This phase proceeds in an outer loop of ρ iterations, handling those rows of A held by row g of the R-Mesh in iteration g. Each processor in row g broadcasts its element of A on its column. Next, the R-Mesh executes an inner loop of ρ iterations, handling each of ρ columns of compressed D. In the hth iteration of the inner loop, each processor in column h broadcasts its element of D along its row. Now each $\rho \times \rho$ sub-R-Mesh received only elements of compressed row i of A and compressed column j of D. Processors receiving elements $a_{i,k}$ and $d_{k,j}$ multiply them. At the end of the inner loop, each sub-R-Mesh adds these products that contribute to $c_{i,j}$ by a binary tree algorithm in $O(\log \rho)$ time, storing it in the first processor of row g of the sub-R-Mesh (Problem 4.26). The nested loops computing the $c_{i,j}$ values run in $O(\rho^2)$ time. Finally, the R-Mesh routes the $c_{i,j}$ values to the final positions (Problem 4.27).

THEOREM 4.27 *The product of uniformly sparse $N \times N$ matrices with degree ρ can be computed by an $N \times N$ R-Mesh in $O(\rho^2)$ time.*

Multiplying a Column-Sparse and a Row-Sparse Matrix. Let A denote an $N \times N$ matrix that is column sparse with degree κ_A, and let D denote an $N \times N$ matrix that is row sparse with degree ρ_D. Initially, processor $p_{i,j}$ holds element $a_{i,j}$ of A and element $d_{i,j}$ of D. At the end, $p_{i,j}$ will hold element $c_{i,j}$ of the product matrix C.

Overall, the R-Mesh performs the following κ_A times (one iteration for each element in a column of A). The key observation on which the algorithm builds is that every non-zero element in column k of A is multiplied by every non-zero element in row k of D. For each column k, where $1 \leq k \leq N$, send the non-zero element with smallest row index (not handled in a previous iteration) to $p_{k,k}$, which then broadcasts this element along row k. Each processor $p_{k,j}$ that holds a non-zero element $d_{k,j}$ of D now multiplies that element with the value $a_{i,k}$ just received along the row.

Now, within this outer loop, the R-Mesh executes an inner loop ρ_D times (once for each element in a row of D). For each row k, where $1 \leq k \leq N$, let $p_{k,j}$ that just computed $a_{i,k} \cdot d_{k,j}$ be the processor with smallest column index (not handled in a previous iteration). Processor $p_{k,j}$ creates a triplet $\langle i, j, a_{i,k} \cdot d_{k,j} \rangle$ and sends it to $p_{k,0}$. The R-Mesh sorts the triplets, with first priority to the second key (column address in D), then with second priority to the first key (row address in A). The R-Mesh now adds triplets with the same i, j values; these contribute to $c_{i,j}$. The R-Mesh routes to $p_{i,j}$ results contributing to $c_{i,j}$. It splits the routing into two cases: columns to receive fewer than $\sqrt{N}$ values and those to receive more than $\sqrt{N}$ values (Problem 4.28). Each $p_{i,j}$ adds to its accumulator the value it receives.

THEOREM 4.28 *The product of a column-sparse matrix with degree κ_A and a row-sparse matrix with degree ρ_D, both of size $N \times N$, can be computed by an $N \times N$ R-Mesh in $O(\kappa_A \cdot \rho_D \sqrt{N})$ time.*

Problems

4.1   Design an algorithm to convert a b-bit integer from the BIN representation to the Word representation in $O\left(1 + \log\left(\frac{b}{\log x}\right)\right)$ time on a $b \times x$ R-Mesh, where $x \leq 2^b$.

4.2   Design an algorithm to convert a b-bit integer from the BIN representation to the Word representation on a $b \times 2^{\epsilon b}$ R-Mesh in $O\left(\frac{1}{\epsilon}\right)$ time, for constant $0 < \epsilon \leq 1$. Next, specify an input placement and algorithm to perform the conversion on an $\epsilon b \times 2^{\epsilon b}$ R-Mesh in the same time.

4.3   Design an efficient algorithm to convert a b-bit integer from the 1UN representation to the 2UN representation.

4.4   Design an efficient algorithm to convert a b-bit integer from the 1UN representation to the BIN representation.

4.5   Design an efficient algorithm to convert a b-bit integer from the POS representation to the BIN representation.

4.6   Prove that the algorithm of Theorem 4.1 recurses for $O(\log \log N)$ levels.

4.7   If $1 \leq \frac{N}{C} \leq C < N$, then prove that

$$\log \log \frac{N}{C} + \frac{\log \frac{C^2}{N}}{\log \frac{N}{C}} = O\left(\log \log C + \frac{\log \frac{N}{C^2}}{\log C}\right).$$

4.8   Prove that if an $R \times C$ R-Mesh, where $RC \geq N$, can find the maximum of N inputs in T time, then an $\frac{R}{\sqrt{T}} \times \frac{C}{\sqrt{T}}$ R-Mesh can solve the problem in $O(T)$ time.

4.9   Construct an algorithm for an $N \times Nb$ R-Mesh, where $1 \leq b \leq N$, to add N b-bit integers given in BIN format in $O(1)$ time and produce a $(b + \log N)$-bit output in BIN format. (That is, reduce the size of the R-Mesh in Theorem 2.22, page 57, from $2N \times 2Nb$ to the $N \times Nb$ size of Lemma 4.9.)

4.10 Prove that the algorithm of Problem 4.9 can be designed to run in constant time on an $N \times Nb$ LR-Mesh.

4.11 Given (1) an $O(1)$ time algorithm to add N bits on a $\log^2 N \times N$ R-Mesh (Lemma 4.8), and (2) an $O(1)$ time algorithm to add N k-bit numbers on an $N \times Nk$ R-Mesh (Lemma 4.9), construct an $O(1)$ time algorithm to add N b-bit numbers on a $b \log^2 N \times N$ R-Mesh. (That is, prove Lemma 4.10.)

4.12 To decompose an $N \times N$ R-Mesh into $\sqrt{N} \times \sqrt{N}$ sub-R-Meshes, one must compute integer division by $\sqrt{N}$ and modulo $\sqrt{N}$. Given N integers z_i in the range $[0, N)$, construct an algorithm to compute $x_i = \left\lfloor \frac{z_i}{\sqrt{N}} \right\rfloor$ and $y_i = z_i \pmod{\sqrt{N}}$ in $O(1)$ time on an $N \times N$ R-Mesh.

4.13 Prove Lemma 4.13 (decomposing integers into radix-N notation).

4.14 Give an algorithm for an $N \times M$ R-Mesh to compute the prefix sums of a sequence $z_0, z_1, \ldots, z_{M-1}$ of integers in the range $\left[0, \left(\frac{N}{M}\right)^2\right)$ in $O\left(\min\left\{\log M, \log \frac{N}{M}\right\}\right)$ time.

      Hint: Use the $N \times M$ R-Mesh algorithm to compute the prefix sums of N bits in $O\left(\frac{\log N}{\log M}\right)$ time (Theorem 2.10, page 33).

4.15 Prove Lemma 4.14 (prefix sums). Use the result of Problem 4.14, setting $M = \sqrt{N}$ within the algorithm for this proof.

4.16 Extend the algorithm of Theorem 4.7(ii) that adds N bits in $O(1)$ time on a $\sqrt{N} \log^\epsilon N \times \sqrt{N}$ R-Mesh to an algorithm for adding N b-bit numbers in $O(1)$ time on a $\sqrt{N} \log^\epsilon N \times b\sqrt{N}$ R-Mesh.

4.17 Prove the first part of Lemma 4.18: For integers X and Y in diminished-1 notation, where $0 \leq X, Y \leq 2^b$, compute $X + Y \pmod{2^b + 1}$ in $O(1)$ time on a $b \times b$ R-Mesh.

4.18   Prove the second part of Lemma 4.18: For integer X in diminished-1 notation, where $0 \leq X \leq 2^b$, and constant k, compute $X \cdot 2^k$ (mod $2^b + 1$) in $O(1)$ time on a $b \times b$ R-Mesh.

4.19   From the proof of Lemma 4.19, prove that sub-R-Mesh $SM(i,j)$ of size $2Mb \times b$ can compute $\alpha^{ij}x(j)$ (mod $2^b + 1$) in $O(1)$ time.

4.20   From the proof of Lemma 4.19, prove that sub-R-Mesh $RM(i)$ of size $2Mb \times 2Mb$ can compute $X(i) = \displaystyle\sum_{j=0}^{2M-1} \alpha^{ij}x(j)$ (mod $2^b + 1$) in $O(1)$ time, given the result of the previous problem.

4.21   Describe the layout of sequences A and B padded with 0's in the proof of Lemma 4.21 to store a $2N^{\frac{3}{16}} \times \cdots \times 2N^{\frac{3}{16}}$ array on a $16N \times 16N$ R-Mesh. Describe the data routing to rearrange elements from their positions for performing cyclic convolution in the first dimension to their positions for performing cyclic convolution in the second, third, and fourth dimensions. These must run in $O(1)$ time.

4.22   The proof of Lemma 4.21 presents a four-dimensional cyclic convolution algorithm for a $16N \times 16N$ R-Mesh. Describe modifications to the algorithm to permit it to run on an $N \times N$ R-Mesh, still in $O(1)$ time.

4.23   Given the C_i values (see the proof of Theorem 4.22) for $0 \leq i < 2N^{\frac{3}{4}}$, construct an algorithm to compute $C\left(2^{N^{\frac{1}{4}}}\right) = \displaystyle\sum_{i=0}^{2N^{\frac{3}{4}}-1} C_i\left(2^{iN^{\frac{1}{4}}}\right)$ in $O(1)$ time on an $N \times N$ R-Mesh.

4.24   Construct an R-Mesh algorithm to multiply an $N \times N$ matrix and an N-element vector, with word size $b \leq \sqrt{N}$, on an $N \times N^2$ R-Mesh in $O(1)$ time.

4.25   Prove that the matrix-vector multiplication algorithm of Theorem 4.24 and the matrix multiplication algorithm of Theorem 4.26 run on an LR-Mesh. Assume that Lemma 4.10 runs on an LR-Mesh.

4.26   For the uniformly sparse matrix multiplication of Theorem 4.27, write the details in pseudocode of the nested loops to multiply corresponding elements of compressed rows of A and compressed columns of

D. This is to run in $O(\rho^2)$ time for uniformly sparse matrices with degree ρ.

4.27 Design an efficient algorithm to route product elements in the algorithm for Theorem 4.27 from the places where they are generated in the nested loops to their final destinations.

4.28 For the algorithm of Theorem 4.28, develop an $O(\sqrt{N})$-time method to route elements contributing to $c_{i,j}$ from the locations where they are generated to $p_{i,j}$. Recall that this algorithm handles columns to receive fewer than $\sqrt{N}$ values separately from those to receive more than $\sqrt{N}$ values.

4.29 Fill in the details of the column-sparse matrix multiplication algorithm of Section 4.3.3. That is, prove Theorem 4.28.

Bibliographic Notes

Jang and Prasanna [148] and Bertossi and Mei [28] detailed the various number representation formats and methods to convert among them. Koren [161] and Trahan *et al.* [319] discussed the basics of floating point representation and R-Mesh manipulation of floating point numbers.

Miller *et al.* [216] presented the $O(\log \log N)$ time algorithm for an R-Mesh to find the maximum of N elements using a square array with N processors. Valiant [334] developed the PRAM algorithm on which Miller *et al.* based their R-Mesh algorithm. The algorithms of Lemma 2.14 (page 40) and Theorem 4.1 will run on a CREW HVR-Mesh. Nakano and Olariu [231] derived the lower bound of Theorem 4.2. They proved it for a "Basic R-Mesh," which is a restricted version of an HVR-Mesh, but the derivation holds for a general R-Mesh. Trahan *et al.* [322] developed the maximum finding algorithms for different aspect ratios in Theorems 4.3 and 4.4 and Corollary 4.5.

Wang *et al.* [349] first presented the one-dimensional R-Mesh algorithm for adding two N-bit integers. Other researchers subsequently rediscovered the algorithm independently. Cormen *et al.* [65] gave a clear derivation of the technique of finding carries using kill, propagate, and generate signals.

Nakano and Wada [232] developed the $O(\log^* N - \log^* m)$ and $O(1)$ time algorithms for adding N bits noted in Theorem 4.7. Their paper includes a useful table of the history of results on this problem. Park *et al.* [267] devised Lemma 4.8 for adding N bits, and Jang *et al.* [146] constructed Lemma 4.9 for multiple addition (adding N b-bit numbers), which were the building blocks of the multiple addition tool, Lemma 4.10. Park *et al.* [267] and Jang *et al.* [146] gave an algorithm establishing Lemma 4.10 for multiple addition for the case $b = O(\log N)$. Bertossi and Mei [28] also developed a constant time multiple addition algorithm—if $b < \log N$, then it runs on a smaller LR-Mesh of size $O\left(b\log N + \frac{\log^2 N}{\log\log N}\right) \times Nb$, but this requires an interleaved input. The algorithm of Theorem 4.11 that runs on a $\sqrt{\frac{N}{\log^* N}} \times \sqrt{\frac{N}{\log^* N}}$ R-Mesh in $O(\log^* N)$ time follows the structure of an algorithm by Jang *et al.* [146]. Their algorithm computes the histogram of an image, but a special case of this algorithm adds bits on a $\sqrt{N} \times \sqrt{N}$ R-Mesh. The algorithm in Section 4.2.1.2 improves the size by a standard technique and explicitly accounts for an increase in word size as sub-R-Meshes return sums up levels of the algorithm.

For multiple addition, Nakano and Wada [232] developed the best known results. They developed an algorithm with the same bounds as Theorem 4.12, though it works by very different techniques. They also developed algorithms for adding N b-bit integers with the following resources:

(*i*) $\sqrt{Nm} \times b\sqrt{N}$ R-Mesh in $O(\log^* N - \log^* m)$ time, where $1 \leq m \leq \log N$,

(*ii*) $\sqrt{N}(\log N)^\epsilon \times b\sqrt{N}$ R-Mesh in $O(1)$ time, for constant $\epsilon > 0$, and

(*iii*) $\sqrt{\frac{N}{\log^* N}} \times b\sqrt{\frac{N}{\log^* N}}$ in $O(\log^* N)$ time.

Fragopoulou [113] introduced the $O(b + \log\log N)$ time algorithm for prefix sums of N b-bit numbers. This algorithm builds on a sequence of results of Olariu *et al.* [243] that culminates in an algorithm for prefix sums of N numbers bounded in value by $O(N^c)$ presented in Lemma 4.14. Bertossi and Mei [28] constructed a constant time algorithm for prefix sums of N b-bit numbers on an $O\left(\frac{b^2 + \log^2 N}{\log(b + \log N)}\right) \times O(N(b + \log N))$ bit-model LR-Mesh. The best result for prefix sums of N bits runs on an $N \times m$ R-Mesh, where $1 \leq m \leq \frac{\log^2 N}{\log\log N}$, in $O\left(\frac{\log N}{\sqrt{m\log m}} + \log\log N\right)$ time, due to Nakano [227]. This algorithm is decidedly different than that in Section 4.2.1.4, following a "parallel prefix-remainders technique" that computes the prefix sums for different divisors, then obtains the prefix remainder for a larger divisor.

Jang *et al.* [147] constructed the algorithm to optimally multiply two numbers on a bit-model R-Mesh via the Rader Transform. They also derived the building block Lemma 4.9 for multiple addition and Corollary 4.17 for multiplication. Their paper also gives algorithms for the portions of the proof left as exercises.

Park *et al.* [268] constructed the division algorithm for the R-Mesh (see also Jang *et al.* [145]). The algorithm adapts a CRCW PRAM algorithm of Shankar and Ramachandran [293] to the R-Mesh.

Vaidyanathan *et al.* [333] developed the matrix-vector multiplication algorithms of Theorem 4.24 and Corollary 4.25. Savage [288] established the AT^2 complexity of matrix multiplication. Park *et al.* [267] constructed the AT^2-optimal matrix multiplication algorithm that preserves the AT^2 optimality over a range of T. They described their algorithm for $b = \Theta(\log N)$, but the extension to other values of b is straightforward. Note for $b = \Theta(\log N)$ that the algorithm preserves AT^2 values for the entire range $1 \leq T \leq N$. Park *et al.* also developed the constant time matrix-vector multiplication algorithm on an $N \times N^2$ R-Mesh cited in Problem 4.24.

Middendorf *et al.* [211] offered the row sparse, column sparse, and uniformly sparse definitions used in Section 4.3.3. They presented the $O(\rho^2)$ time algorithm for multiplying uniformly sparse matrices (Theorem 4.27). ElGindy [98] constructed the $O(\kappa_A \cdot \rho_D \sqrt{N})$ time algorithm for multiplying a column-sparse matrix and a row-sparse matrix (Theorem 4.28).

Chapter 5

SORTING AND SELECTION

Sorting is one of the most fundamental problems in computing and plays an important role in solving numerous problems, while providing insight to many others. Not surprisingly, sorting is perhaps one of the most widely researched problems in computing. This chapter deals primarily with sorting on the R-Mesh. The sorting algorithm we present is optimal over a large range of R-Mesh sizes. When the available R-Mesh is large enough, the sorting algorithm also suffices to solve other "easier" comparison-based problems such as merging and selection. To illustrate a case where a smaller R-Mesh solves an easier problem more efficiently than sorting, we also present a selection algorithm in this chapter.

The rest of this chapter has two main parts: sorting (Sections 5.1–5.3) and selection (Section 5.4) The main result for sorting N elements is an optimal $\frac{N}{T} \times \frac{N}{T}$ R-Mesh algorithm that runs in $O(T)$ steps for any $1 \leq T \leq \sqrt{N}$. This algorithm scales well over a large range of values of T, improving in efficiency as the size of the R-Mesh decreases. When $T > \sqrt{N}$, the same considerations limit sorting on an R-Mesh as on a regular (non-reconfigurable) mesh, for which several optimal sorting algorithms exist. In Section 5.2, we first develop a sub-optimal sorting algorithm that serves as a building block for the optimal algorithm (Section 5.3). In Section 5.3.3, we extend the sorting algorithm to higher dimensional R-Meshes.

In Section 5.4 we present an algorithm for selecting the kth smallest from a set of N elements. This algorithm uses a $\sqrt{N} \times \sqrt{N}$ R-Mesh and runs in $O(\log N)$ time.

5.1   Sorting on an R-Mesh

Given an array $A = (a_0, a_1, \cdots, a_{N-1})$ of elements from a totally ordered set[1], the problem of sorting is to arrange the elements of A in increasing (or decreasing) order. No assumption is made about the elements of A, except that they are pair-wise comparable. Under these circumstances, no loss of generality results in assuming that all elements of A are distinct, for one could distinguish equal valued elements on the basis of their indices, without any significant change to the notion of comparison.

Consider a $(P$ processor$)$ $\sqrt{P} \times \sqrt{P}$ R-Mesh for sorting N elements. Several factors bound the time, T, for this problem. The well known comparison lower bound requires that $T = \Omega\left(\frac{N \log N}{P}\right)$. While this bound is significant for small values of P, for R-Meshes with $\omega(\log^2 N)$ processors the following lower bound is more useful. A bisection width argument based on the fact that in one step no more than $\sqrt{P}$ (of a maximum possible N elements) can cross over from one side of the R-Mesh to the other requires that

$$T = \Omega\left(\frac{N}{\sqrt{P}}\right). \tag{5.1}$$

Since the number of processors P in a (two-dimensional) R-Mesh reflects its area A, the above bound can also be cast as the well-known

$$AT^2 = \Omega\left(N^2\right) \tag{5.2}$$

lower-bound.

In particular, sorting N elements on a $\sqrt{N} \times \sqrt{N}$ R-Mesh requires $\Omega\left(\sqrt{N}\right)$ time. Considering the fact that a $\sqrt{N} \times \sqrt{N}$ (non-reconfigurable) mesh can sort N elements optimally in $\Theta\left(\sqrt{N}\right)$ time, we will restrict our discussion to sorting N elements on a $\sqrt{P} \times \sqrt{P}$ R-Mesh, where $P \geq N$. In fact, we will show that for any $1 \leq T \leq \sqrt{N}$, an $\frac{N}{T} \times \frac{N}{T}$ R-Mesh can sort N elements in $O(T)$ time. This will admit constant-time sorting on the R-Mesh and achieve the optimal AT^2 complexity for R-Meshes ranging in size from $\sqrt{N} \times \sqrt{N}$ to $N \times N$.

---

[1]A *binary relation*, R, on a set S is a subset of $S \times S$. Element $s_1 \in S$ is related to $s_2 \in S$ (often written as $s_1 R s_2$) if and only if $\langle s_1, s_2 \rangle \in R$. A binary relation $\preceq$ on a set S is a *partial order* if and only if $\preceq$ is reflexive (for all $a \in S$, $a \preceq a$), antisymmetric (if $a \preceq b$ and $b \preceq a$, then $a = b$), and transitive (if $a \preceq b$ and $b \preceq c$, then $a \preceq c$). A set S is *totally ordered* with respect to a partial order $\preceq$ if and only if for each $a, b \in S$, $a \preceq b$ or $b \preceq a$. Here the relation $\preceq$ is called a *total order*.

5.2 A Sub-Optimal Sorting Algorithm

Consider the following three-step algorithm for sorting N elements $a_0, a_1, \cdots, a_{N-1}$. The correctness of this algorithm is obvious.

1. For each $0 \leq i, j < N$, set flag $f_{i,j}$ to 1 if and only if $a_i > a_j$.

2. Compute $rank(i) = \sum_{j=0}^{N-1} f_{i,j} =$ number of elements that are smaller than a_i.

3. Route element a_i to position $rank(i)$ in the sorted array.

An R-Mesh implementation of this algorithm hinges on the counting algorithm required for Step 2. With $m = 2N^{\frac{1}{T}}$ in Theorem 2.10 (page 33), we have the following result.

LEMMA 5.1 *For any $1 \leq T \leq \log N$, N bits can be added on a $2N^{\frac{1}{T}} \times N$ R-Mesh in $O(T)$ time. Initially, the input bits are in a row of the R-Mesh.*

We now use Lemma 5.1 in an algorithm to sort N elements in $O(T)$ steps on a $2N^{1+\frac{1}{T}} \times N$ R-Mesh. Let the N elements to be sorted be $a_0, a_1, \cdots, a_{N-1}$, and let a row of the R-Mesh initially hold these elements.

For $0 \leq j < N$, first broadcast a_j to each processor of column j. Now partition the R-Mesh into N sub-R-Meshes, $\mathcal{R}_0, \mathcal{R}_1, \cdots, \mathcal{R}_{N-1}$, each of size $2N^{\frac{1}{T}} \times N$. For $0 \leq i < N$, broadcast a_i to all processors in the first row of $\mathcal{R}_i$. Next for each $0 \leq j < N$, processor $(0, j)$ of $\mathcal{R}_i$ that holds a_i and a_j sets flag $f_{i,j}$ to 1 if and only if $a_i > a_j$ (Step 1 of the 3-step algorithm). Next $\mathcal{R}_i$ uses Lemma 5.1 to compute $rank(i) = \sum_{j=0}^{N-1} f_{i,j}$ in T steps (Step 2). Finally the R-Mesh routes a_i to the top row of column $rank(i)$ (Step 3); this is simply a case of constant-time permutation routing (see Section 2.3.1).

THEOREM 5.2 *For any $1 \leq T \leq \log N$, a $2N^{1+\frac{1}{T}} \times N$ R-Mesh can sort N elements in $O(T)$ time. Initially, the inputs are in a row of the R-Mesh.*

The following corollary expresses a special case of Theorem 5.2 that we use in the constant-time sorting algorithm of Section 5.3.1.

COROLLARY 5.3 *An $N \times N^{\frac{3}{4}}$ R-Mesh can sort $N^{\frac{3}{4}}$ numbers in constant time. Initially, the inputs are in a row of the R-Mesh.*

<u>Proof:</u>   With $T = 10$, for example, in Theorem 5.2, a $2N^{\frac{33}{40}} \times N^{\frac{3}{4}}$ R-Mesh can sort the elements in constant time. A value of $N \geq 53$ suffices to ensure that $N \geq 2N^{\frac{33}{40}} = 2N^{\frac{3}{4}(1+\frac{1}{T})}$.   ∎

5.3   An Optimal Sorting Algorithm

In this section, we use Corollary 5.3 to construct a constant-time, AT^2-optimal, $N \times N$ R-Mesh algorithm for sorting N elements. Next we extend this algorithm to an $O(T)$-time, AT^2-optimal, $\frac{N}{T} \times \frac{N}{T}$ R-Mesh algorithm, for any $1 \leq T \leq \sqrt{N}$, and to run on three-dimensional R-Meshes.

5.3.1   Constant Time Sorting

The constant time, $N \times N$ R-Mesh sorting algorithm of this section is based on a sorting technique called *columnsort*, which we first describe.

5.3.1.1   Columnsort

Consider $N = rs$ elements organized as an $r \times s$ matrix, where $r \geq 2(s-1)^2$ and $\frac{r}{s}$ is an integer. It can be shown that the following 8-step algorithm correctly sorts the N elements.

1. Independently sort each column.
2. "Transpose" the matrix by picking its elements up in column-major order and setting them down in row-major order (see Figure 5.1).

1	10	19			1	2	3
2	11	20			4	5	6
3	12	21			7	8	9
4	13	22	⟶ transpose ⟶		10	11	12
5	14	23			13	14	15
6	15	24	⟵ untranspose ⟵		16	17	18
7	16	25			19	20	21
8	17	26			22	23	24
9	18	27			25	26	27

Figure 5.1.   Transposing and untransposing for columnsort.

3. Independently sort each column.
4. "Untranspose" the matrix by applying the inverse of the permutation of Step 2 (see Figure 5.1).
5. Independently sort each column.

6. "Shift" the elements into an $r \times (s+1)$ matrix as follows. Pick up the N elements in column-major order and set them down in column-major order in an $r \times (s+1)$ matrix, starting from the $\left(\lfloor \frac{r}{2} \rfloor + 1 \right)^{\text{th}}$ position of the first column. The $\lfloor \frac{r}{2} \rfloor$ positions before the start of the string are filled with $-\infty$ and vacant positions at the end of the string with $+\infty$ (see Figure 5.2).

1	10	19		$-\infty$	6	15	24
2	11	20		$-\infty$	7	16	25
3	12	21		$-\infty$	8	17	26
4	13	22	$\longrightarrow$ shift $\longrightarrow$	$-\infty$	9	18	27
5	14	23		1	10	19	∞
6	15	24	$\longleftarrow$ unshift $\longleftarrow$	2	11	20	∞
7	16	25		3	12	21	∞
8	17	26		4	13	22	∞
9	18	27		5	14	23	∞

Figure 5.2. Shifting and unshifting for columnsort.

7. Independently sort each column of the $r \times (s+1)$ matrix.

8. "Unshift" the $r \times (s+1)$ matrix back into an $r \times s$ matrix using the inverse of the permutation in Step 6 (see Figure 5.2).

As shown in Figure 5.3, columnsort sorts N elements using only permutations (Steps 2, 4, 6, and 8) and r-element sorters (Steps 1, 3, 5, and 7). Observe in Figure 5.3 that sorting appropriate sets of elements achieves the effect of the shift and unshift permutations.

5.3.1.2   Columnsort on the R-Mesh

To implement columnsort on an $N \times N$ R-Mesh, let $r = N^{\frac{3}{4}}$ and $s = N^{\frac{1}{4}}$. For a sufficiently large value of N, the requirement that $r \geq 2(s-1)^2$ will be satisfied. Assume that the N elements to be sorted are in the leftmost column of the R-Mesh. (We deviate here from our usual assumption of placing inputs in a row only to keep the columns for columnsort in columns of the mesh.) With respect to the $r \times s$ columnsort matrix, the inputs are in column-major order so that an entire column of r elements is in adjacent processors in a column of the R-Mesh. Divide the R-Mesh into s sub-R-Meshes, each of size $r \times N$. By Corollary 5.3, each sub-R-Mesh can sort the $r = N^{\frac{3}{4}}$ elements in constant time. Thus, the $N \times N$ R-Mesh can run Steps 1, 3, and 5 of columnsort in constant time. For running Step 7, simply shift the sub-R-Mesh boundaries by $\lfloor \frac{r}{2} \rfloor$ rows as shown in Figure 5.3. The R-Mesh

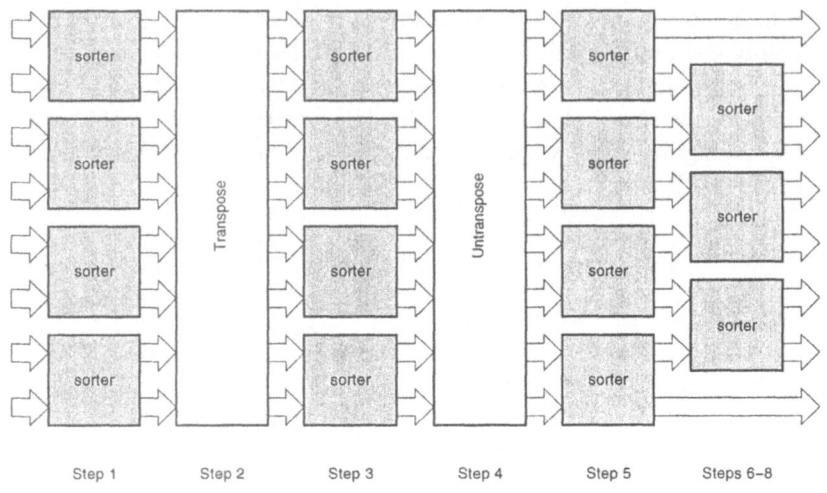

Figure 5.3. A columnsorting network; each arrow represents $\frac{r}{2}$ elements and each sorter sorts r elements.

can implement the permutations of Steps 2 and 4 in constant time (see Section 2.3.1).

THEOREM 5.4 *An $N \times N$ R-Mesh can sort N elements in $O(1)$ time. Initially, the inputs are in a column of the R-Mesh.*

5.3.2   Area-Time Tradeoffs

In this section, we extend the constant time sorting algorithm of Section 5.3.1 to run in $O(T)$ time for any $1 \le T \le \sqrt{N}$, while maintaining its AT^2 optimality. That is, we will establish that an $\frac{N}{T} \times \frac{N}{T}$ R-Mesh can sort N elements in $O(T)$ time. Scaling the algorithm for AT^2 optimality involves mapping the large problem instance onto a small R-Mesh. Due to differences in the mapping, we consider two ranges of values for T.

Sorting when $1 \le T \le N^{\frac{1}{4}}$. Consider an $\frac{N}{T} \times \frac{N}{T}$ R-Mesh with the N elements to be sorted in the first T rows. We now describe how this R-Mesh can execute columnsort in $O(T)$ time. As before, we will use $r = N^{\frac{3}{4}}$. Unlike the constant time algorithm, however, each columnsort step may take $O(T)$ time here.

Let $K = \frac{N^{\frac{1}{4}}}{T}$. Consequently, $\frac{N}{T} = KN^{\frac{3}{4}}$ and $1 \le K \le N^{\frac{1}{4}}$. For each sorting step of columnsort, divide the given R-Mesh into K sub-R-Meshes, each of size $N^{\frac{3}{4}} \times \frac{N}{T}$. Since $T \le N^{\frac{1}{4}}$, each of these sub-R-Meshes contains an $N^{\frac{3}{4}} \times N^{\frac{3}{4}} = r \times r$ sub-R-Mesh, which can sort r elements in constant time by Theorem 5.4. Each sorting step of columnsort uses at most $s = \frac{N}{r} = N^{\frac{1}{4}}$ sorters, each sorting $r = N^{\frac{3}{4}}$ elements. The $K = \frac{s}{T}$ sub-R-Meshes serve to perform these sorts in T steps. Except in Step 7, the data is in place for each of the sorting steps. As before, perform the sorting in Step 7 by simply shifting the sub-R-Mesh boundaries by $\lfloor \frac{r}{2} \rfloor$ rows.

An $\frac{N}{T} \times \frac{N}{T}$ R-Mesh can permute $\frac{N}{T}$ elements in a row in constant time (see Section 2.3.1). Therefore the R-Mesh can permute N elements in $O(T)$ steps using T rounds of $\frac{N}{T}$-element permutation routing.

LEMMA 5.5 *For any $1 \leq T \leq N^{\frac{1}{4}}$, an $\frac{N}{T} \times \frac{N}{T}$ R-Mesh can sort N elements in $O(T)$ time. Initially, the inputs are in T rows of the R-Mesh.*

Sorting when $N^{\frac{1}{4}} \leq T \leq N^{\frac{1}{2}}$. Once again consider an $\frac{N}{T} \times \frac{N}{T}$ R-Mesh, with the inputs distributed over the first T rows. Let $t = \frac{T}{N^{\frac{1}{4}}}$. This implies that $1 \leq t \leq N^{\frac{1}{4}}$ and $\frac{N^{\frac{3}{4}}}{t} = \frac{N}{T}$. One can view the entire R-Mesh as an $\frac{N^{\frac{3}{4}}}{t} \times \frac{N^{\frac{3}{4}}}{t}$ R-Mesh that can, by Lemma 5.5, sort $N^{\frac{3}{4}}$ elements in $O(t)$ steps. This implies that the given R-Mesh can implement each columnsort sorting step (which uses $s = N^{\frac{1}{4}}$ sorters, each sorting $r = N^{\frac{3}{4}}$ elements) in $O(tN^{\frac{1}{4}}) = O(T)$ steps. As in the $1 \leq T \leq N^{\frac{1}{4}}$ case, the permutation routing steps run in $O(T)$ time.

LEMMA 5.6 *For any $N^{\frac{1}{4}} \leq T \leq N^{\frac{1}{2}}$, an $\frac{N}{T} \times \frac{N}{T}$ R-Mesh can sort N elements in $O(T)$ time. Initially, the inputs are in T rows of the R-Mesh.*

From Lemmas 5.5 and 5.6, we have the following result.

THEOREM 5.7 *For any $1 \leq T \leq \sqrt{N}$, an $\frac{N}{T} \times \frac{N}{T}$ R-Mesh can sort N elements optimally in $O(T)$ time. Initially, the inputs are in T rows of the R-Mesh.*

5.3.3 Sorting on Three-Dimensional R-Meshes

In this section, we extend the ideas of Section 5.3.1 to three-dimensional R-Meshes. In particular, we show that a $\sqrt{N} \times \sqrt{N} \times \sqrt{N}$ R-Mesh can sort N elements in constant time.

Establishing the following lemma requires only proving that a three-dimensional R-Mesh can perform the sorts and permutations required for columnsort with parameters r and s (Problem 5.12).

LEMMA 5.8 *Let $N = rs$ such that $r \geq 2(s-1)^2$ and $\frac{r}{s}$ is an integer. An $r \times s \times r$ three-dimensional R-Mesh can sort N elements in $O(1)$ time. Initially, the inputs are in an $r \times s$ two-dimensional sub-R-Mesh, consisting of processors on one XY-slice[2] of the R-Mesh.*

The smallest value of r that satisfies the conditions in Lemma 5.8 gives $r = \Theta\left(N^{\frac{2}{3}}\right)$ and $s = \Theta\left(N^{\frac{1}{3}}\right)$ and results in a three-dimensional R-Mesh with sides of vastly different sizes. Since our objective is to derive an algorithm for a $\sqrt{N} \times \sqrt{N} \times \sqrt{N}$ R-Mesh, we now develop a method to reduce the aspect ratio of the R-Mesh used in Lemma 5.8.

Let m be an integer such that, with r and s as described above, $r \geq \max\{2m^3, sm^2\}$. Consider an $\frac{r}{m} \times ms \times \frac{r}{m}$ R-Mesh in which one $\frac{r}{m} \times ms$ XY-slice (the input slice) holds the N input elements (data) (see Figure 5.4(a)). The algorithm will ensure data placement in this "input slice" at the start and end of each columnsort step. To run columnsort on this R-Mesh, we only need show how to sort r elements and how to permute N elements according to the "transpose" permutation. (If the R-Mesh can transpose the elements, then it can untranspose them too.)

Assume that the r elements of a column of the $r \times s$ columnsort array correspond to a column-major enumeration of m successive columns of the input slice. To sort these r elements, divide the input slice into s two-dimensional sub-R-Meshes, each of size $\frac{r}{m} \times m$. Each such sub-R-Mesh induces a three-dimensional $\frac{r}{m} \times m \times \frac{r}{m}$ sub-R-Mesh (see Figure 5.4(b)). Since $r \geq 2m^3$, we have $\frac{r}{m} \geq 2m^2 > 2(m-1)^2$. By Lemma 5.8, the $\frac{r}{m} \times m \times \frac{r}{m}$ sub-R-Mesh can sort r elements on the input slice in constant time.

The transpose permutation takes the r elements of a columnsort column and arranges them as $\frac{r}{s}$ columnsort rows. An r-element columnsort column consists of m columns in the input slice of the R-Mesh. An s-element columnsort row maps to (non-contiguous) processors of an m-processor row on the input slice of the R-Mesh; specifically, processors holding successive elements of a columnsort row are m columns apart on the input slice. In the following we will refer to a processor on row x and column y of the zth XY-slice (where $0 \leq x, z < \frac{r}{m}$ and $0 \leq y < ms$) as processor (x, y, z). Let $z = 0$ represent the input slice. Suppose that the transpose permutation moves data $d_{x,y}$ (say) from processor $(x, y, 0)$ of the input slice to processor $(u, v, 0)$. Broadly speaking, the R-Mesh proceeds in five steps (see Figure 5.4(c)). Though these steps are described for one data element $d_{x,y}$, it should be noted that all N data elements undergo corresponding movements (along different

---

[2]See Figure 4.7 for a depiction of an XY-slice.

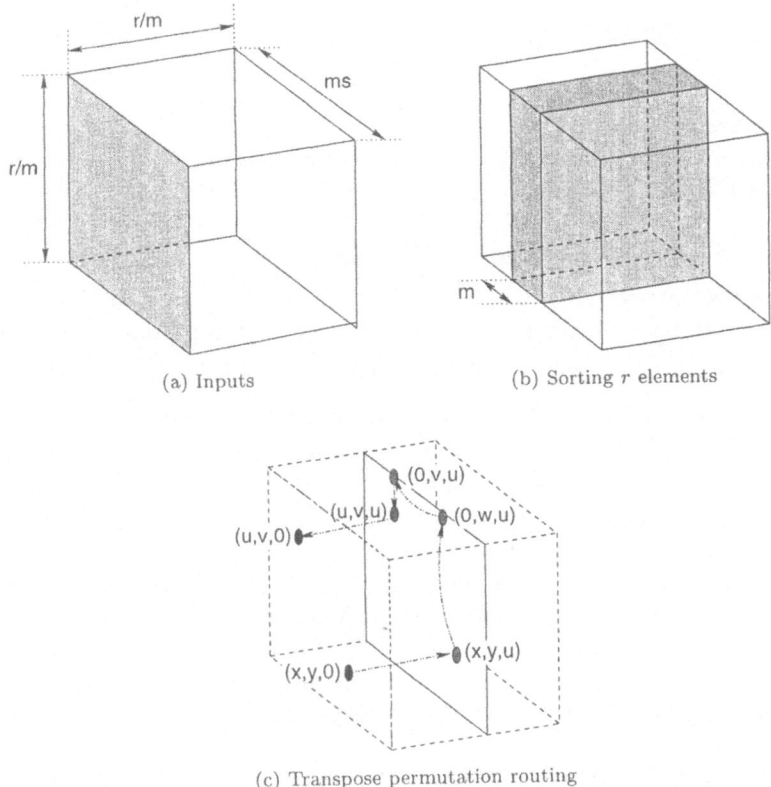

(a) Inputs   (b) Sorting r elements

(c) Transpose permutation routing

Figure 5.4. Components of columnsort on a three-dimensional R-Mesh.

paths). The first step moves $d_{x,y}$ from processor $(x, y, 0)$ of the input slice to the corresponding processor (x, y, u) of the uth slice. The next three steps move $d_{x,y}$ entirely within the uth slice. The second step moves $d_{x,y}$ from processor (x, y, u) to some processor $(0, w, u)$ in the top row of the uth slice. The third and fourth steps move $d_{x,y}$ from processor $(0, w, u)$, via processor $(0, v, u)$, to processor (u, v, u). Finally, the fifth step brings $d_{x,y}$ from processor (u, v, u) to processor $(u, v, 0)$ back in the input slice. Details are left as an exercise (Problem 5.13).

LEMMA 5.9 *Let* $N = rs$ *such that* $r \geq 2(s-1)^2$, *and let* $\frac{r}{s}$ *be an integer. Let* m *satisfy* $r \geq \max\{2m^3, sm^2\}$. *An* $\frac{r}{m} \times ms \times \frac{r}{m}$ *three-dimensional R-Mesh can sort* N *elements optimally in* $O(1)$ *time. Initially, the inputs are in an* $\frac{r}{m} \times ms$ *slice of the R-Mesh.*

With an appropriate choice of values for r, s, and m in Lemma 5.9, we have the following result.

THEOREM 5.10 *A $\sqrt{N} \times \sqrt{N} \times \sqrt{N}$ three-dimensional R-Mesh can sort N elements optimally in $O(1)$ time. Initially, the inputs are in a $\sqrt{N} \times \sqrt{N}$ slice of the R-Mesh.*

5.4   Selection on an R-Mesh

Given an array[3] $A = (a_1, a_2, \cdots, a_N)$ of elements from a totally ordered set and an integer $1 \leq k \leq N$, selection is finding the kth smallest element in A. By symmetry, one may assume that $k \leq \left\lceil \frac{N}{2} \right\rceil$. The special case when $k = \left\lceil \frac{N}{2} \right\rceil$ is called the median finding problem, which has several useful applications. Clearly, selection is trivial if array A is sorted; that is, selection is no more difficult than sorting. In fact, selection is easier than sorting—while sorting requires $\Omega(N \log N)$ comparisons, selection can be performed sequentially in $O(N)$ steps. In this section, we present an N-input selection algorithm that runs in $O(\log N)$ time on a $\sqrt{N} \times \sqrt{N}$ R-Mesh. The same sized R-Mesh requires $\Theta(\sqrt{N})$ time for sorting N elements.

Before we proceed, we review some indexing schemes for R-Mesh processors that the selection algorithm will employ.

5.4.1   Indexing Schemes

For $0 \leq i, j < \sqrt{N}$, we index the processor in row i and column j of a $\sqrt{N} \times \sqrt{N}$ R-Mesh as (i, j) and denote it by $p_{i,j}$. To solve a problem involving a totally ordered set (such as selection), it is often necessary to order the R-Mesh processors by a total order; that is, index each of the N processors by a unique index from $\{1, 2, \cdots, N\}$. In other words, the indexing simply enumerates the R-Mesh processors. There are many ways to perform this indexing. We describe two methods that the selection algorithm will employ.

Row-Major Indexing.   This indexing enumerates elements of row 0, then elements of row 1, then elements of row 2, and so on. Within each row, it enumerates elements in the order of their column indices (see Figure 5.5(a)).

---

[3]In this section, we index array elements from 1 to N (rather than from 0 to $N - 1$) to avoid confusion in defining the kth smallest element.

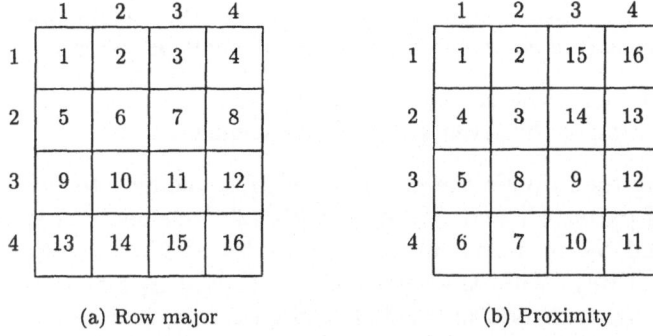

Figure 5.5. Indexing examples for R-Mesh processors.

Proximity Indexing. This indexing requires a $2^n \times 2^n$ R-Mesh, for integer $n \geq 1$. Figure 5.5(b) shows the proximity indexing for a 4×4 R-Mesh. We defer a detailed definition of proximity indexing to Problem 5.18. It suffices to observe that a proximity indexing of a $2^n \times 2^n$ R-Mesh has the following properties.

1. Processor indices are from a set of 2^{2n} consecutive integers.
2. Processors with consecutive indices are adjacent in the underlying mesh (formed by the external edges of the R-Mesh).
3. Properties 1 and 2 above hold recursively within the four quadrants of the R-Mesh.

Observe that these properties hold for the 4×4 R-Mesh of Figure 5.5(b) and each of the 2×2 sub-R-Meshes at its four quadrants.

5.4.2 An Outline of the Selection Algorithm

The R-Mesh selection algorithm is based on a sequential selection algorithm. The general idea of this sequential algorithm is to start with all N input elements as candidates and iteratively whittle down the candidate set until it is small enough to process quickly. At each iteration, the algorithm reduces the current candidate set to the next candidate set with the help of a "bandpass filter" with low and high cutoff values ℓ and h. Specifically, the next candidate set contains an element of value x from the current candidate set if and only if $\ell \leq x \leq h$. The algorithm uses a parameter s and computes the filter cutoff values ℓ and h from an s-element "sorted sample" of the current candidate set, which we define below.

Let $M = s2^i$, where $s \geq 2$ is even and $i \geq 0$. Define the *s-element sorted sample* of a set of M elements as follows.

If $i = 0$, then the sorted sample is simply a sorted array consisting of the given set of $M = s$ elements.

If $i > 0$, then divide the given set of M elements into two equal parts, M_1 and M_2, each with $s2^{i-1}$ elements. Let S_1 and S_2 be s-element sorted samples of M_1 and M_2, respectively. Thin the sorted arrays S_1 and S_2 by pruning away their odd indexed elements (that is, remove the first, third, fifth, $\cdots$ elements) to obtain sorted $\frac{s}{2}$-element sequences. Merge these sorted sequences to obtain the s-element sorted sample of the given set of $M = s2^i$ elements.

For the R-Mesh selection algorithm, $s = \log N$. Where the value of s is implicit, we will refer to an s-element sorted sample simply as a sorted sample. We will refer to the thinning and merging described above as a "sample-merge." The above definition of a sorted sample does not require the M elements to be sorted. If the M elements are sorted, however, then selecting s equally spaced elements from this sorted list constitutes a sorted sample.

Let $N = 2^{2^n}$ for integer $n \geq 1$, let $s = \log N = 2^n$, and let the number of candidates be $M = s^2 2^{2^r} = 2^{2n+2^r}$, where $r \geq 0$ is an integer. The task is to find the kth element of this candidate set. The R-Mesh selection algorithm has the overall structure described below.

1. Determine an s-element sorted sample of a candidate set C (details appear later).

2. Select elements in positions $u = \left\lceil \frac{k-1}{s2^{2^r}} \right\rceil - \log s - r$ and $v = \left\lceil \frac{k}{s2^{2^r}} \right\rceil$ of the sorted sample as the low and high filter cutoffs. Let ℓ and h, respectively, denote the values of these cutoff elements. (The sequential algorithm on which the R-Mesh algorithm is based uses a different pair of functions of k and r to determine the cutoff positions u and v.)

3. Construct the new candidate set $C' = \{x \in C : \ell \leq x \leq h\}$. (Both the sequential and the R-Mesh algorithms guarantee that the kth element of C is in C'.) If b is the number of elements of C that are less than ℓ, then the kth element of C is the $(k - b)^{\text{th}} = (k')^{\text{th}}$ element (say) of C'.

4. If C' is sufficiently small, then determine its $(k')^{\text{th}}$ element by sorting. Otherwise, go to Step 1 with C' and k' replacing C and k, respectively.

We now detail various parts of the R-Mesh selection algorithm. In Section 5.4.3 we explain the iterative part of the R-Mesh selection algorithm and in Section 5.4.4 we describe the R-Mesh algorithm to obtain a sorted sample of a candidate set. Section 5.4.5 analyzes the time complexity of the algorithms. In general, we do not delve into details of the algorithms' correctness which, for the most part, follow from the correctness of their sequential counterparts. Rather, we focus our discussion on the various R-Mesh techniques used to execute the steps of the algorithm. To keep our discussion focused on the main ideas, we relegate many details to problems at the end of the chapter.

5.4.3   The Selection Algorithm

Keeping the outline of Section 5.4.2 in mind, consider the pseudocode of Algorithm 5.1. An explanation follows the pseudocode.

Algorithm 5.1   (Selection)

Model: A $\sqrt{N} \times \sqrt{N}$ R-Mesh, where $N = 2^{2^n}$, for integer $n \geq 1$.

Input: An array $A = (a_1, a_2, \cdots, a_N)$ of elements from a totally ordered set and an integer $1 \leq k \leq \left\lceil \frac{N}{2} \right\rceil$. Each element of A is in a separate R-Mesh processor.

Output: The kth smallest element of A.

begin

1. Flag each R-Mesh processor as active and assign $M \longleftarrow N$.

    /* An "active" processor holds a candidate. Initially, each processor is active and there are $M = N$ candidates. */

2. Let $s = \log N$. Partition the R-Mesh into a $\frac{\sqrt{N}}{s} \times \frac{\sqrt{N}}{s}$ array of $s \times s$ sub-R-Meshes and sort the elements in each $s \times s$ sub-R-Mesh in row-major order.

    /* The iterative part of the algorithm begins here. */

3. Number the active processors in row-major order within each sub-R-Mesh and with proximity indexing between the sub-R-Meshes.

4. Add dummy candidates so that $M \bmod 2s^2 = 0$.

5. **if** $M = 2s^2$ **then**
    Sort the M candidates and return the kth element.

6. Construct an s-element sorted sample of the candidate set.
   /* see Algorithm 5.2   */

7. Let $M = s^2 2^{2^r}$. Set ℓ to the value of the $\left(\left\lceil\frac{k-1}{s2^{2^r}}\right\rceil - \log s - r\right)^{\text{th}}$ element and h to the value of the $\left(\left\lceil\frac{k}{s2^{2^r}}\right\rceil\right)^{\text{th}}$ element of the sorted sample.

8. Compute $b =$ number of active processors holding a value $x < \ell$, and assign $k \longleftarrow k - b$.

9. Flag a processor as active if and only if the value, x, it holds satisfies $\ell \leq x \leq h$.

10. Go to Step 3.

end

The assumption that the number of inputs $N = 2^{2^n}$ is only for convenience and is without loss of generality. The assumption that input $k \leq \left\lceil\frac{N}{2}\right\rceil$ is also without loss of generality; for a larger value of k, simply determine the $(N - k + 1)^{\text{th}}$ largest input.

Step 1 expresses the fact that initially the candidate set consists of all N inputs; M is the size of the current candidate set, and a processor holding a candidate is said to be active.

Observe that the quantity $\frac{\sqrt{N}}{s} = 2^{2^{n-1}-n}$ in Step 2 is an integer. Step 2 is a preprocessing step that ensures that candidates are "locally sorted" for the remainder of the algorithm. This step runs in $\Theta(s) = \Theta(\log N)$ time and can use one of the several optimal sorting algorithms for a mesh. Note that the algorithm executes Steps 1 and 2 only once. The iterative part of the algorithm starts from Step 3.

To determine the active processor indices for Step 3, first determine the prefix sums of the active flags in the order of the proximity indices of the entire R-Mesh. (The R-Mesh can compute the proximity indices of processors once in $O(\log N)$ time at the start of the algorithm; see Problem 5.18.) Given the proximity indices, the R-Mesh determines the prefix sums of the N active flags in $O(\log \log N)$ time along the same lines as the doubly logarithmic tree approach of Theorem 4.1 (page 120), with Lemma 4.14 (page 132) replacing Lemma 2.14 (page 40) in the proof (see Problem 5.19). Next, the R-Mesh alters the indices within each $s \times s$ sub-R-Mesh to row-major. This is easy as all candidates occupy contiguous positions in row-major indexing after the inputs have been sorted in Step 2. Moreover, altering indices within a sub-R-Mesh does not affect the proximity ordering among the sub-R-Meshes.

The procedure for generating the sorted sample in Step 6 requires that the number of candidates be an integer multiple of $2s^2$. Step 4 satisfies this requirement by adding $(M - (M \bmod 2s^2)) \pmod{2s^2}$ dummy candidates of value ∞ that are certain to be filtered off in subsequent iterations. Problem 5.20 addresses details of this step.

If the number of candidates is $M = 2s^2$, then in Step 5 the R-Mesh moves all the candidates to the top row and uses Theorem 5.4 to sort them in constant time on an $M \times M$ sub-R-Mesh and returns the kth smallest input. Details of the data movement step to move candidates to the top row are left as an exercise (Problem 5.21). We note that the most time consuming case for this data movement occurs when all $2s^2$ elements are densely packed within a constant number of $s \times s$ sub-R-Meshes, whose perimeter is $O(s)$. Even in this case $\Theta(s)$ time suffices to move all candidates to the top row.

Step 6 constructs a sorted sample of the candidate set (details appear in Section 5.4.4) and Steps 7–9 determine the new candidate set and the new value of k as explained earlier in Section 5.4.2.

5.4.4   The Sorted Sample Algorithm

We begin with a look at the sequential algorithm for generating a sorted sample of a candidate set. This algorithm first groups candidates into s-element groups and then sorts these groups individually. (For the R-Mesh algorithm, Step 2 of Algorithm 5.1 has more or less done this task.) Next, the sequential algorithm uses a sequence of sample-merges (like the binary tree pattern of conventional merges in a merge sort algorithm), in which a sample-merge of two sorted arrays each of size s results in a sorted array of size s (rather than an array of size $2s$ that results from performing a conventional merge on two arrays, each of size s). The R-Mesh algorithm implements the sample-merges in a manner similar to the sequential algorithm, but in parallel.

For M candidates, consider the $\frac{M}{s}$-leaf binary tree (henceforth called the *merge tree*; see Figure 5.6) representing these sample-merges. Each internal vertex of the merge tree represents a sample-merge. Call the s-element sorted array at the left (resp., right) child of an internal vertex the *left* (resp., *right*) *array* of the corresponding sample-merge. At the lowest level (level 1) of internal vertices of the tree, there are $\frac{M}{2s}$ sample-merges, each of two s-element sorted arrays. These sample-merges result in $\frac{M}{2s}$ s-element sorted arrays. Similarly, level 2 of the tree involves $\frac{M}{4s}$ sample-merges. In general, at level λ ($1 \leq \lambda \leq \log \frac{M}{s}$) of the tree, there are $\frac{M}{s2^\lambda}$ sample-merges that result in $\frac{M}{s2^\lambda}$ s-element sorted arrays.

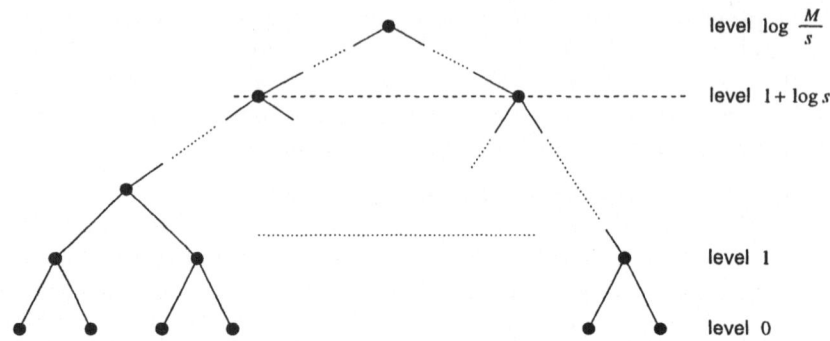

Figure 5.6. Merge tree for determining a sorted sample of M candidates. Each circle represents a sorted sample of s candidates and each internal vertex is a result of the sample merge of its two children.

We use these observations in Algorithm 5.2 which details the R-Mesh steps for constructing a sorted sample of candidates. The elaborate conditions placed on the input to Algorithm 5.2 stem from actions taken by the R-Mesh selection algorithm (Algorithm 5.1) before it invokes the sorted sample algorithm. A detailed explanation of the sorted sample algorithm follows the psuedocode below.

Algorithm 5.2   (Sorted Sample)

Model: A $\sqrt{N} \times \sqrt{N}$ R-Mesh (with $N = 2^{2^n}$, for integer $n \geq 1$) divided into a $\frac{\sqrt{N}}{s} \times \frac{\sqrt{N}}{s}$ array of $s \times s$ sub-R-Meshes, where $s = \log N$.

Input: Each processor holds a value and is flagged as active or inactive. An active processor is called a candidate. Within each $s \times s$ sub-R-Mesh, candidates are placed contiguously in row-major order and in ascending order by values. The number of candidates is M, an integer multiple of $2s^2$. Candidates are numbered in row-major order within each sub-R-Mesh and by proximity indexing among sub-R-Meshes (see Step 3 of Algorithm 5.1).

Output: An s-element sorted sample of the set of M candidates.

begin

1. Partition the candidates into groups each with s contiguous candidates. Move elements between sub-R-Meshes (if necessary) so that each group is located entirely within a sub-R-Mesh.

2. Sort each group containing elements that have moved in from another sub-R-Mesh (see Step 1).
   /* We use the term "group" to denote the s-element sorted array resulting from this step, as well as an s-element sorted array resulting from a sample-merge in Steps 3 and 4 below. */

3. Perform the first $1 + \log s$ levels of sample-merges of the $\log \frac{M}{s}$-level merge tree (see Figure 5.6).

4. Sample-merge the remaining groups of the R-Mesh.

end

First observe that after Step 5 of Algorithm 5.1, all input conditions of Algorithm 5.2 hold.

Algorithm 5.2 exploits the fact that the $s \times s$ sub-R-Meshes of the $\sqrt{N} \times \sqrt{N}$ R-Mesh are numbered by proximity indexing. Consequently, sub-R-Meshes with consecutive proximity indices are adjacent in the R-Mesh. It is useful to think of the given $\sqrt{N} \times \sqrt{N}$ R-Mesh as an $s \times \frac{N}{s}$ R-Mesh formed by a linear array of sub-R-Meshes arranged according to their proximity indices. Alternatively, one could view the R-Mesh as a one-dimensional $\frac{N}{s}$-element "R-Mesh," where each element is an $s \times s$ sub-R-Mesh with connections that are s buses wide.

For Step 1, use indices of active processors to determine group borders. The algorithm moves all elements of a group to the sub-R-Mesh that initially holds the first element of that group. It is straightforward to perform this data movement in constant time on the "linear array of sub-R-Meshes" described above. Observe that at the end of Step 1, each sub-R-Mesh has at most one group some of whose elements moved in from a different sub-R-Mesh. Consequently, Step 2 calls upon each sub-R-Mesh to sort at most s elements; the algorithm of Theorem 5.4 can accomplish this in constant time. At the end of this step we may also assume that each active processor holds its group index as well its index within its group.

At this point, each group of s candidates is in sorted order and is located entirely within a sub-R-Mesh. The remaining task is to sample-merge the $\frac{M}{s}$ groups into the final sorted sample of the candidates. Steps 3 and 4 break this task into two phases that employ different methods.

Step 3 sample-merges groups pairwise according to a binary tree structure for the first (lowest) $1 + \log s$ levels of the merge tree. Because candidates that entered their sub-R-Mesh during Step 1 or later must be treated differently in a sample-merge than candidates that were present prior to Step 1, the algorithm handles groups differently based on their constituent candidates. Assume that the result of each sample merge resides in the sub-R-Mesh that holds the left array of that sample merge.

For the purpose of the following discussion, we will use the term "group" to denote both a sorted s-element collection resulting from Step 2 of Algorithm 5.2, as well as an s-element sorted array resulting from a sample-merge in Step 3. Each group contained within a sub-R-Mesh can be categorized as follows:

- Category I: Groups such that all elements have resided in the sub-R-Mesh before the start of Step 1 of Algorithm 5.2.

- Category II: Groups containing some elements that have not resided in the sub-R-Mesh since the start of Step 1. These elements may have entered during Step 1 or as part of a right array in a sample-merge during an earlier iteration of Step 3.

We now explain how Step 3 of the algorithm performs all the sample-merges at each level of the merge tree in constant time. We consider Category I and II groups separately, as the algorithm processes them quite differently.

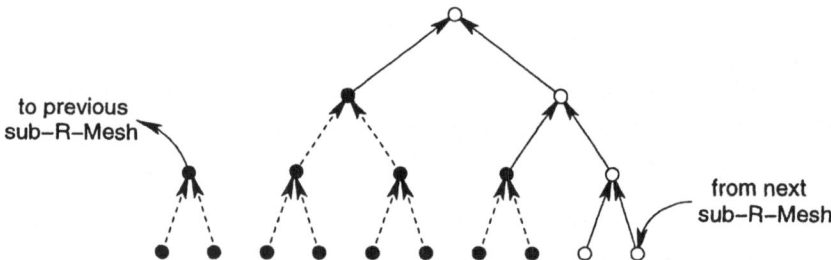

Figure 5.7. Part of the merge tree for a sub-R-Mesh of Algorithm 5.2. A dark circle indicates a Category I group, with only elements that have been in the sub-R-Mesh since the start of Step 1 of Algorithm 5.2. An unshaded circle indicates a Category II group with some elements that have not resided in the sub-R-Mesh since the start of Step 1. Of the two Category II groups at the level of the leaves, the first results from Step 1 of the algorithm. The second group moves in from the "next" sub-R-Mesh as a right array for a sample-sort. A balanced sub-tree of the merge tree containing only Category I groups has dashed edges.

Category I Groups: Consider a balanced 2^λ-leaf sub-tree of the merge tree consisting only of Category I groups of a sub-R-Mesh (such sub-trees are shown with dashed edges in Figure 5.7). By virtue of Step 2 of Algorithm 5.1 and the fact that candidates are selected using a band-pass filter, the candidates in the groups at the leaves of this subtree correspond to a list of $s2^\lambda$ contiguous processors (in row-major indexing) of the sub-R-Mesh. Moreover, the candidates in this list are sorted (across all 2^λ groups), so their sorted sample is simply every $\left(2^\lambda\right)^{\text{th}}$ element of this list. In other words, the sub-R-Mesh can compute the sorted sample of the candidates at the leaves of the subtree in constant time. Up to level $1 + \log s$ of the merge tree, there can be $O(\log s)$ such subtrees for each sub-R-Mesh; consequently, the sub-R-Mesh processes all these subtrees in $O(\log s)$ time.

Category II Groups: Consider now a sample-merge that involves at least one Category II group. Here the sub-R-Mesh performs the sample merge by first thinning the two sorted s-element groups and then merging the thinned groups by sorting the s elements using Theorem 5.4. Thus, each sample-merge involving a Category II group can be handled in constant time. At any given level of the merge tree, each sub-R-Mesh has at most one sample-merge involving groups from Category II (see Problem 5.22). Therefore, there can be at most $1 + \log s$ such sample-merges per sub-R-Mesh up to level $1 + \log s$ of the merge tree. Thus, the sub-R-Mesh processes these sample merges also in $O(\log s)$ time.

Since the communications have the form of a binary tree algorithm (see Illustration 1, page 5), they can be performed in constant time on the "one-dimensional $\frac{N}{s}$-element R-Mesh" view of the given $\sqrt{N} \times \sqrt{N}$ R-Mesh. In summary, Step 3 of Algorithm 5.2 runs in $O(\log s) = O(\log \log N)$ time.

Observe that since each sub-R-Mesh contains at most s groups at the start of Step 3, and Step 3 performs the merges up to level $1 + \log s$ of the merge tree, there are at most $\frac{M}{2s^2}$ groups at the start of Step 4, with at most one group per "odd-even" pair of sub-R-Meshes. Step 4 proceeds along the same lines as the doubly logarithmic tree approach of Theorem 4.1 (page 120), replacing the maximum of 2^λ elements by a 2^λ-way sample-merge of groups. We use the fact that a $\frac{\sqrt{M}}{s} \times \frac{\sqrt{M}}{s}$ R-Mesh can sort (hence determine the sorted sample of) $\frac{\sqrt{M}}{s}$ groups in constant time (Theorem 5.4) in the same way Theorem 4.1 uses Lemma 2.14 (page 40). Data movement and other details needed to pull this strategy off are relegated to Problem 5.23. Thus, Step 4 runs in $O(\log \log M) = O(\log \log N)$ time.

5.4.5 Complexity Analysis

We now derive the running time for the selection algorithm. Steps 1 and 2 of Algorithm 5.2 run in constant time, while Steps 3 and 4 run in

$O(\log \log N)$ time. That is, the entire sorted sample algorithm runs in $O(\log \log N)$ time.

Steps 1 and 7–10 of Algorithm 5.1 run in constant time. Steps 2 and 5, which are each executed only once during the whole algorithm, run in $O(\log N)$ time; we need not count these steps in analyzing the iterative part of Algorithm 5.1. Steps 4 and 6 each run in $O(\log \log N)$ time. Thus, each iteration of Algorithm 5.1 runs in $O(\log \log N)$ time. In other words, the time $T(N)$ needed to run the selection algorithm on N inputs is as follows:

$$T(N) = O(\log N + \alpha \log \log N), \tag{5.3}$$

where α is the number of iterations in Algorithm 5.1. We now determine α.

Recall that ℓ and h are the cutoff values for the band-pass filter. Let the elements with these values have indices u and v, respectively, in the sorted sample. As stated in Section 5.4.2, for $M = s^2 2^{2^r}$ we have the following.

$$u = \left\lceil \frac{k-1}{s 2^{2^r}} \right\rceil - \log s - r \tag{5.4}$$

and

$$v = \left\lceil \frac{k}{s 2^{2^r}} \right\rceil. \tag{5.5}$$

For any index i of the sorted sample (where $1 \leq i \leq s$), let L_i and U_i denote the least and most number, respectively, of elements from the original N-element input that can be smaller than the ith element of the sorted sample. We state the following result without proof; bibliographic notes at the end of this chapter provide references to the proof.

LEMMA 5.11 *Let the candidate set size be* $M = s^2 2^{2^r}$. *For any* $1 \leq i \leq s$, $L_i = i s 2^{2^r} - 1$ *and* $U_i \leq (i + r + \log s) s 2^{2^r}$.

We are now in a position to determine what fraction of the candidate set is filtered off at each iteration. The number of elements in the new candidate set is at least

$$
\begin{aligned}
U_v - L_u - 1 \ &\leq \ (v - u + r + \log s) s 2^{2^r} &&\text{[Lemma 5.11]} \\
&\leq \ 2(r + \log s) s 2^{2^r} + 2 &&\text{[Equations 5.4 and 5.5]} \\
&= \ 2 \left(\log \log \tfrac{M}{s^2} + \log s \right) \left(\tfrac{M}{s} \right) + 2 \\
&= \ O\!\left(\tfrac{M \log \log N}{\log N} \right) \\
&= \ O\!\left(\tfrac{M}{\sqrt{\log N}} \right)
\end{aligned}
$$

That is, at each iteration, the selection algorithm reduces the candidate set by a factor of $\Omega(\sqrt{\log N})$. It is easy to now show that the selection algorithm has $\alpha = O\left(\frac{\log N}{\log \log N}\right)$ iterations (see Problem 5.25). With Equation 5.3 we have

$$T(N) = O\left(\log N + \alpha \log \log N\right) = O(\log N).$$

THEOREM 5.12 *The problem of selecting the kth smallest of N input elements (where $1 \le k \le N$) can be solved on a $\sqrt{N} \times \sqrt{N}$ R-Mesh in $O(\log N)$ time. Initially, each R-Mesh processor holds an input.*

Problems

5.1 Prove that the AT^2 lower bound of $\Omega(N^2)$ holds for any (two dimensional) sorting hardware (not just the R-Mesh).

5.2 Why does Lemma 5.1 restrict T to be at most $\log N$?

5.3 Prove that the algorithm of Lemma 5.1 runs on an LR-Mesh.

5.4 Write pseudocode for the algorithm of Theorem 5.2.

5.5 Prove that the algorithm of Theorem 5.2 runs on an LR-Mesh.

5.6 The proof of Corollary 5.3 uses a value of $N \ge 53$. Does the corollary hold for all values of N?

5.7 The columnsort algorithm of Section 5.3.1.1 assumes that $\frac{r}{s}$ is an integer. How would you modify the algorithm if this condition is not met?

5.8 Prove that the optimal sorting algorithm of Theorem 5.4 runs on an LR-Mesh.

5.9   Is it possible to run the optimal sorting algorithm of Theorem 5.4 on a non-crossover R-Mesh (that allows all port partitions except $\{\overline{NS}, \overline{EW}\}$ (see Figure 2.3))? Explain.

5.10 Why will Lemma 5.5 not hold for $T > N^{\frac{1}{2}}$?

5.11 All the sorting algorithms considered in Section 5.3 specify the position of the initial inputs. Why is this important? Are there other input placements that will (or will not) work?

5.12 Prove Lemma 5.8.

5.13 This problem deals with the transpose permutation used in the $\frac{r}{m} \times ms \times \frac{r}{m}$ three-dimensional R-Mesh sorting algorithm of Lemma 5.9. Suppose this permutation maps processor (x, y) of the input face to processor (u, v).

   (a)   Derive expressions for u and v in terms of x, y, and the R-Mesh parameters r, s, and m.

   (b)   Derive the details of the five step routing procedure described in Section 5.3.3.

5.14 Choose appropriate values for r, s, and m in Lemma 5.9 to prove Theorem 5.10.

5.15 Modify the algorithm of Theorem 5.7 so that it runs in $O(T)$ time on a $\sqrt{\frac{N}{T}} \times \sqrt{\frac{N}{T}} \times \sqrt{\frac{N}{T}}$ three-dimensional R-Mesh.

5.16 Prove that if a three-dimensional R-Mesh with P processors can sort N elements in T time, then $P^{\frac{2}{3}}T = \Omega(N)$. If the above R-Mesh is d-dimensional, then how are P, T, and N related?

5.17 Extend the ideas of Section 5.3.3 to higher dimensional R-Meshes.

5.18 Let the *end-points* of a proximity indexing (see Section 5.4.1) of an $2^n \times 2^n$ R-Mesh be the lowest and highest indexed processors, that is, the processors with indices 1 and 2^{2n}. Assume that the end-points of a proximity indexing are located at two adjacent corners of the R-Mesh; that is, a straight line connecting these points would be one of the sides of the R-Mesh, rather than, say, its diagonal. By symmetry, any pair of adjacent corners can be end-points. Figure 5.8 gives a recursive definition of proximity indexing.

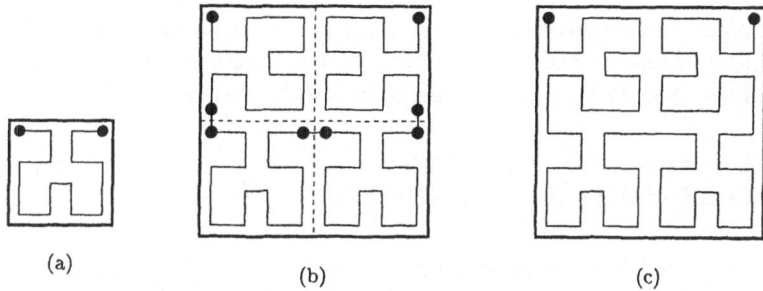

(a)   (b)   (c)

Figure 5.8. Definition of proximity indexing. Part (a) shows a proximity indexing of a $2^n \times 2^n$ R-Mesh, for integer $n \geq 1$, with end-points shown as shaded circles. Part (b) shows the construction of a proximity indexing of a $2^{n+1} \times 2^{n+1}$ R-Mesh in terms of different orientations of the indexing in (a). Part (c) shows the resulting proximity indexing of the $2^{n+1} \times 2^{n+1}$ R-Mesh, with end-points as shaded circles.

(a) Write a sequential procedure (based on the definition given above) to assign proximity indices to processors of a $2^n \times 2^n$ R-Mesh.

(b) Prove that for any $n \geq 1$, the proximity indexing (as defined above) of a $2^n \times 2^n$ R-Mesh satisfies the following two properties.

- Processors with consecutive indices are adjacent on the R-Mesh (connected by external edges)

- The above property holds recursively within the four quadrants of the R-Mesh.

(c) Prove that for any integer $n \geq 1$, if each processor of a $2^n \times 2^n$ R-Mesh holds its row and column indices, then it can compute its proximity index in $O(n)$ time.

5.19 Design an $O(\log \log N)$ time algorithm to determine the prefix sums of N bits (initially one bit per processor) on a $\sqrt{N} \times \sqrt{N}$ R-Mesh in the order imposed by proximity indexing. Assume each processor to hold its proximity index.

5.20   Design an $O(\log \log N)$ time method to add enough dummy candidates (see Step 4 of Algorithm 5.1) to make the total number of candidates divisible by $2s^2$.

Although these candidates may be placed anywhere, as far as the algorithm's correctness is concerned, your solution should bear in mind Steps 1–3 of Algorithm 5.2, whose time complexity depends on how candidates are arranged in the sub-R-Meshes.

5.21   Prove that a $\sqrt{N} \times \sqrt{N}$ R-Mesh can perform the data movement of Step 5 of Algorithm 5.1 in $O(s)$ time.

5.22   In the sorted-sample algorithm (Algorithm 5.2), prove that at any given level of the merge tree, each sub-R-Mesh has at most one sample-merge involving groups from Category II (see definition on page 170).

5.23   Prove that Step 4 of Algorithm 5.2 can be performed in $O(\log \log M)$ steps.

5.24   Use Lemma 5.11 and Equations 5.4 and 5.5 to prove that the kth element of the current candidate set of the selection algorithm is also in the next candidate set; that is, the kth element lies between the filter cutoffs ℓ and h.

5.25   Prove that if each iteration of the selection algorithm for N inputs reduces the candidate set by a factor of $\Omega(\sqrt{\log N})$, then the algorithm terminates in $O\left(\frac{\log N}{\log \log N}\right)$ iterations.

5.26   Prove that a $\sqrt{N} \times \sqrt{N}$ R-Mesh can select the kth smallest of N input elements in $O(\min\{k, (N - k) \log \log N\}$ time.

Bibliographic Notes

Leighton [172, 173] discussed sorting lower bounds. Azar and Vishkin [12] established that an $\Omega(N^2)$ lower bound on the work (or number of comparisons) for constant time sorting applies even to the parallel comparison model, which is not bisection bounded like the R-Mesh. Thompson and Kung [315] gave an algorithm for sorting N elements on a $\sqrt{N} \times \sqrt{N}$ mesh in $\Theta(\sqrt{N})$ time; several other algorithms also achieved this result [199, 233, 290]. The columnsort technique due to Leighton [173] is a generalization of Batcher's odd-even merge sort [15].

The problem of sorting on reconfigurable models, in general, and the R-Mesh, in particular, has received much attention. The optimal algorithm of Section 5.3 is due to Jang and Prasanna [148]. Although we have presented Lemma 5.1 as a special case of Theorem 2.10 (page 33), Jang and Prasanna [148] independently derived the result of Lemma 5.1. Other similar sorting results that were derived independently include those of Lin *et al.* [190], Nigam and Sahni [235], and Olariu and Schwing [239]. Sorting on multidimensional R-Meshes has been discussed by Chen and Chen [56] and Nigam and Sahni [235]. Chen and Chen [56] provide a solution to Problem 5.17.

The selection algorithm of Section 5.4 is due to Hao *et al.* [127]. This algorithm builds on a very similar R-Mesh algorithm designed by ElGindy and Węgrowicz [103]. Both algorithms are based on Munro and Paterson's sequential selection algorithm [221]. Hao *et al.* [127] provide details on the proof of Lemma 5.11 and Problems 5.23 and 5.24. They also gave an $O\left(\frac{b \max\{1, \log^* N - \log^* b\}}{\log b}\right)$ time selection algorithm for N b-bit inputs. The proximity order used to index processors for the selection algorithm is also known as the Hilbert's space-filling order [169].

Many other results for reconfigurable models exist for sorting [157, 167, 189, 229, 241, 276, 314, 330, 350], selection [89, 240, 276], and related problems [20, 50, 59, 135, 155, 160, 191, 328].

Chapter 6

GRAPH ALGORITHMS

Graphs provide a handy and natural way to model systems with applications that range from complex communication and transport systems, ecosystems, and programming language syntax to games, puzzles, and family trees. A good handle on techniques for graph problems translates to a rich tool box of fundamental methods for dealing with many other problems as well. In Chapter 2 (Sections 2.3.5, 2.3.6) and Chapter 3 (Section 3.1.5) we have seen that the R-Mesh is well suited to handle some graph problems. In this chapter we will build on these and other techniques developed so far to derive R-Mesh algorithms for a wide range of problems on graphs, both undirected and directed.

Section 6.1 describes basic conventions and graph representations used in this chapter. Section 6.2 is devoted to tree algorithms, specifically Euler tour techniques and tree reconstruction. Next in Section 6.3 we describe algorithms for undirected graphs, including minimum spanning tree and connectivity related problems. In Section 6.4, we examine directed graphs first through a general algorithmic strategy called the algebraic path problem technique, and then through algorithms for the particular class of directed acyclic graphs. Finally, Section 6.5 deals with efficient R-Mesh algorithms for list ranking.

As we noted earlier, the algorithms of this chapter build on techniques discussed in earlier chapters. For instance, the Euler tour technique (Section 6.2.1) invokes prefix sums (Section 2.3.2) and neighbor localization (Section 2.3.3). Sorting techniques (Chapter 5) play an important role in tree reconstruction (Section 6.2.3), minimum spanning tree determination (Section 6.3.1), and topological sorting (Section 6.4.2). Connectivity related algorithms (Section 6.3.2) all build on the graph connectivity embedding technique (Section 2.3.6) and employ the priority resolution algorithm of Section 3.1.4. Arithmetic computations (Chapter 4), including matrix multiplication, multiple addition, and maximum/minimum are central to the algebraic path problem (Section 6.4.1), while graph distance embedding (Section 2.3.5) plays an important role in the transitive contraction (Section 6.4.2) and list ranking (Section 6.5) algorithms.

6.1 Graph Representations

Unless mentioned otherwise, we will assume a graph $\mathcal{G} = (V, E)$, with vertex set V and edge set E, to be undirected. Also assume that $\mathcal{G}$ has N vertices and M edges. In general, we will assume vertices of $\mathcal{G}$ to be indexed 0 to $N - 1$; this will permit algorithms to order vertices when necessary. Denote an undirected edge between vertices u and v by (u, v). For a directed graph, $\langle u, v \rangle$ denotes a directed edge from u to v. In a similar manner, $(v_0, v_1, \cdots, v_\ell)$ (resp., $\langle v_0, v_1, \cdots, v_\ell \rangle$) denotes an undirected (resp., directed) path of length ℓ between vertices v_0 and v_ℓ (resp., from v_0 to v_ℓ).

Most algorithms in this chapter use the following two well known representations for (directed or undirected) graph $\mathcal{G} = (V, E)$.

Adjacency matrix: This is an $N \times N$ Boolean matrix whose rows and columns correspond to vertices of $\mathcal{G}$. The entry in row u and column v is a 1 if and only if $\mathcal{G}$ has an edge from u to v. This representation requires $\Theta(N^2)$ space and is well suited to dense graphs (with $\Theta(N^2)$ edges).

Edge set: This is the set E of edges of $\mathcal{G}$ (in no particular order). This representation requires $\Theta(M)$ space and suits sparse graphs such as trees.

In addition to these, we will also employ other representations that include a form of adjacency lists for Euler tour techniques, predecessor/successor pointers for lists, and parent pointers for trees.

6.2 Algorithms for Trees

Their simple and yet rich structure, with numerous applications, places trees in a unique position among graphs. In this section, we develop several algorithms for trees. We will start with a simple R-Mesh implementation of a well known "Euler tour" algorithm. This technique will lead to solutions for several tree problems, including rooting, traversal, and determining levels and descendants of vertices. Following that, we describe an algorithm for reconstructing a tree from its preorder and inorder enumerations.

Throughout this section we assume that $\mathcal{T} = (V, E)$ is an N vertex tree. Since a tree is a sparse graph, we will use the edge set representation. If the tree is rooted, then we assume the root to also be specified. Alternatively, the input could specify the parent of each non-root vertex. Many algorithms in this section use a $2N \times 2N$ R-Mesh, but only for clarity. One can easily modify them to run on $N \times N$ R-Meshes.

6.2.1 Euler Tour

In this section we describe an R-Mesh implementation of a very versatile technique that is well known in the context of PRAMs. This technique involves determining an "Euler tour" of a tree and is the basis for solutions to several other problems.

The given tree $\mathcal{T}$ induces a directed graph $\mathcal{T}'$ described below. The vertices of $\mathcal{T}'$ are the vertices of $\mathcal{T}$. Replace each edge (u, v) of $\mathcal{T}$ by two directed edges $\langle u, v \rangle$ and $\langle v, u \rangle$ in $\mathcal{T}'$. Thus, $\mathcal{T}'$ is a graph that replaces each undirected edge of $\mathcal{T}$ by two oppositely directed edges. An *Euler tour* of $\mathcal{T}$ is a directed cycle in $\mathcal{T}'$ that traverses each directed edge of $\mathcal{T}'$ exactly once. One can view this as a cycle of $\mathcal{T}$ that traverses each edge exactly twice, once in each direction. Since an Euler tour is a sequence (cycle) of edges, a circularly-linked list of directed edges suffices to specify it—that is, a successor pointer for each edge of $\mathcal{T}'$. Figure 6.1 illustrates these ideas.

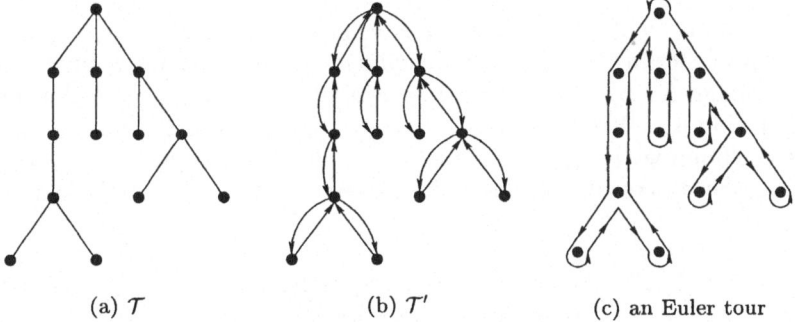

(a) $\mathcal{T}$ (b) $\mathcal{T}'$ (c) an Euler tour

Figure 6.1. An example illustrating an Euler tour of a tree.

The following method forms the basis for the Euler tour algorithm. For any vertex $v \in V$ of degree d, let $u_0, u_1, \cdots, u_{d-1}$ (enumerated in some order) be its neighbors in $\mathcal{T}$. (We assume here that the aim is to construct <u>an</u> Euler tour of the tree. Some applications are sensitive to the order in which vertices/edges are enumerated. The R-Mesh can also handle this situation (see Problem 6.3).) It is possible to prove that for each directed edge $\langle u_i, v \rangle$, selecting its successor to be

$$succ(u_i, v) = \left\langle v, u_{(i+1) \,(\text{mod } d)} \right\rangle \qquad (6.1)$$

gives an Euler tour of $\mathcal{T}$.

To implement this we will employ an $N \times 2(N-1)$ R-Mesh. Initially, the first $N-1$ processors in the top row of the R-Mesh hold the edges of $\mathcal{T}$. The algorithm has three constant-time steps.

Step 1 (Construct $\mathcal{T}'$): For $0 \le j < N-1$, let processor $(0, j)$ hold edge (u, v). To construct $\mathcal{T}'$, processor $(0, j)$ sends its edge to processor $(0, N-1+j)$ using row j. Assuming $u < v$, processor $(0, j)$ interprets its edge as $\langle u, v \rangle$, while processor $(0, N-1+j)$ interprets the received edge as $\langle v, u \rangle$. In general, a processor holding edge $\langle u, v \rangle$ also holds the identity of the processor holding edge $\langle v, u \rangle$ and vice versa.

Step 2 (Construct Circularly-Linked List of Neighbors): Use neighbor localization in row v of the R-Mesh to construct a list of all edges of the form $\langle v, x \rangle$—recall that vertices, like rows, are numbered from 0 to $N-1$. It is simple to now point the last element of this list to the first element and construct a circularly linked list, $\mathcal{C}_v$, of neighbors of vertex v.

Step 3 (Construct Euler Tour): Let v have neighbors $u_0, u_1, \cdots, u_{d-1}$ in that order in the circularly linked list $\mathcal{C}_v$. This step determines, for each edge $\langle u_i, v \rangle$, its successor $succ(u_i, v) = \langle v, u_{(i+1)\,(\text{mod } d)} \rangle$ using Equation 6.1. The processor holding $\langle u_i, v \rangle$ accesses $\mathcal{C}_v$ (via the processor holding $\langle v, u_i \rangle$) and obtains a pointer to edge $\langle v, u_{(i+1)\,(\text{mod } d)} \rangle$ (and the processor holding it, by traversing the circularly linked list $\mathcal{C}_v$).

THEOREM 6.1 *The Euler tour of an N vertex tree can be determined on an $N \times 2(N-1)$ R-Mesh in $O(1)$ time.*

6.2.2   Euler Tour Applications

The Euler tour technique described in the last section has several applications, including rooting a tree (obtaining parent pointers for all vertices, given any vertex as root), preorder/postorder/inorder enumeration of vertices, determining vertex levels, and computing the number and set of descendants of vertices. Broadly speaking, this approach starts from an Euler tour and first converts it to a list (not circularly linked) of tree edges. The next step is to assign some weights to edges of this list and compute the prefix sums of the weights (in the order imposed by the list). Finally, the algorithm derives the answer from these prefix sums. An algorithm based on this method has the following general form.

Algorithm 6.1 **(General Euler Tour Application)**

Model: A $2(N-1) \times 2(N-1)$ R-Mesh.

Input: A rooted tree $\mathcal{T}$ represented as a root and an edge set.

Output: For each vertex v, a quantity, $X(v)$. For example, this quantity can be a pointer to the parent of v if the object is to root the tree.

begin

1. Construct an Euler tour of $\mathcal{T}$.

2. Let r be the root of $\mathcal{T}$ and let its first and last neighbors be r_0 and r_x, respectively. Cut the Euler tour between the edges $\langle r_x, r \rangle$ and $\langle r, r_0 \rangle$ to construct a list $\mathcal{L}$ of edges. (We call this list the "Euler list.")

3. Relocate the edges according to their ranks in $\mathcal{L}$.

4. Assign polynomially bounded integer weights to each edge—that is, for an N vertex tree, the absolute value of the weights is $O(N^c)$ for some constant c.

5. Compute the prefix sums of edge weights. Let $pref(u,v)$ denote the prefix sum of edge $\langle u,v \rangle$.

6. Deduce $X(v)$ from $pref(u,v)$ and $pref(v,u)$.

end

Algorithm 6.1 runs in $O(T_L(N))$ time, where $T_L(N)$ is the time for ranking an N element list on an $N \times N$ R-Mesh (Problem 6.4). We describe various applications of the Euler tour technique—these applications differ only in Steps 4 and 6. They build on well known results, hence we keep our discussion brief.

Rooting. Let $\mathcal{T}$ be a tree represented as a set of edges. Given a vertex r as the root, the object is to determine for each vertex $v \neq r$ a pointer $par(v)$ to its parent in $\mathcal{T}$ with r as the root. Let $par(r)$ be NIL.

In Step 4, set the weight of each directed edge to be 1. Let v be a non-root vertex with u as its parent. The Euler list starts from the root r, subsequently traversing edge $\langle u,v \rangle$ to vertex v then the descendants of v, before returning to u via edge $\langle v,u \rangle$. That is, edge $\langle u,v \rangle$ appears before $\langle v,u \rangle$ in the Euler list, demonstrated by $pref(u,v) < pref(v,u)$. Observe that only one neighbor of v satisfies this condition. Thus, Step 6 of Algorithm 6.1 sets $par(v) \longleftarrow u$ if and only if $pref(u,v) < pref(v,u)$.

Tree Traversal. Three commonly used methods for systematically traversing the vertices (and edges) of a tree are the preorder, postorder, and inorder traversals. Let $\mathcal{T}$ be an ordered, rooted tree with root r. If r is the only vertex of $\mathcal{T}$, then its preorder, postorder, or inorder traversal consists only of the vertex r. Suppose r has $x \geq 1$ children $r_1, r_2, \cdots, r_x$ (in that order) with subtrees $\mathcal{T}_1, \mathcal{T}_2, \cdots, \mathcal{T}_x$ rooted at them.

The *preorder traversal* of $\mathcal{T}$ is the list

$$pre(\mathcal{T}) = r, pre(\mathcal{T}_1), pre(\mathcal{T}_2), \cdots, pre(\mathcal{T}_x). \tag{6.2}$$

The "commas" in Equation 6.2 denote list concatenation.

The *postorder traversal* of $\mathcal{T}$ is the list

$$post(\mathcal{T}) = post(\mathcal{T}_1), post(\mathcal{T}_2), \cdots, post(\mathcal{T}_x), r. \tag{6.3}$$

For the inorder traversal, each vertex can have at most two children. Let the subtrees (if any) rooted at the left and right children of r be $\mathcal{T}_1$ and $\mathcal{T}_2$, respectively. Note that a subtree could be empty, in which case its inorder traversal would be an empty list. The *inorder traversal* of $\mathcal{T}$ is the list

$$in(\mathcal{T}) = in(\mathcal{T}_1), r, in(\mathcal{T}_2). \tag{6.4}$$

For the tree $\mathcal{T}$ in Figure 6.2,

$pre(\mathcal{T}) = a, b, d, g, h, c, e, i, f, j, k.$
$post(\mathcal{T}) = g, h, d, b, i, e, j, k, f, c, a.$
$in(\mathcal{T}) = g, d, h, b, a, e, i, c, j, f, k.$

We describe below the adaptation of Algorithm 6.1 for preorder numbering of an N vertex tree on a $2(N-1) \times 2(N-1)$ R-Mesh. The postorder and inorder cases are left as exercises (Problems 6.5 and 6.6).

A preorder traversal starts at the root and then performs preorder traversals of the subtrees rooted at the children of the root; the order of the subtree traversals is in order of the root's children (if any). Here we assume that the order imposed by the Euler tour is consistent with the order of children of each vertex. The object is to assign to each vertex v a number, $preorder(v)$, between 0 and $N-1$ that specifies the position of v in a preorder traversal of $\mathcal{T}$.

The definition of preorder traversal requires $\mathcal{T}$ to be rooted. Without loss of generality, let r be the root and represent each edge as $\langle v, par(v) \rangle$ and $\langle par(v), v \rangle$, where $par(v)$ denotes the parent of non-root vertex v.

The Euler list starts at the root r traversing its first child, v_1, first, and then the subtree rooted at v_1 in the same manner, before similarly traversing the other children of r. Thus, $\langle par(v), v \rangle$ precedes $\langle v, par(v) \rangle$ in the Euler list. In Step 4 of Algorithm 6.1, assign a weight of 1 to each edge $\langle par(v), v \rangle$ and a weight of 0 to each edge $\langle v, par(v) \rangle$. It is easy to see that Step 6 simply sets $preorder(v)$ to $pref(par(v), v)$ and $preorder(r)$ to 0.

Vertex Levels. The level of a vertex v in a (rooted) tree is the length of the unique simple path between the root and v. Thus, the root is at level 0, its children at level 1, and so on.

As before, consider a non-root vertex v. Assign a weight of 1 to edge $\langle par(v), v \rangle$ and a weight of -1 to edge $\langle v, par(v) \rangle$. Each time the Euler list moves from a vertex to one of its children, it increments the level by 1 (by traversing a $+1$ weight edge). Each time the list moves from a vertex to its parent, it similarly decrements the level. Thus, the level of vertex v is simply $pref(par(v), v)$.

Descendants and Leaves. Here we consider the problem of computing, for each vertex v, the number of descendants of v and the number of leaves in the subtree rooted at v. Assign a weight of 1 to edge $\langle par(v), v \rangle$ and a weight of 0 to edge $\langle v, par(v) \rangle$. Since the Euler list traverses edge $\langle par(v), v \rangle$, then all edges incident on descendants of v, and then edge $\langle v, par(v) \rangle$, the number of descendants of v (not including itself) is $pref(v, par(v)) - pref(par(v), v)$.

Observe that vertex v is a leaf if and only if the successor of edge $\langle par(v), v \rangle$ in the Euler list is $\langle v, par(v) \rangle$. By assigning a weight of 1 only to edges $\langle par(v), v \rangle$ of leaves v, the algorithm for the number of descendants now computes the number of leaves in the subtree rooted at each vertex.

These ideas also apply to determining the set of descendants and leaves for each vertex (see Problem 6.7).

It is easy to show that all algorithms in this and the previous section run on an $N \times N$ R-Mesh (rather than a $2(N-1) \times 2(N-1)$ R-Mesh). The following result summarizes the ideas of this section, with Theorems 6.28 and 6.32 (derived later in Section 6.5) providing the time bounds for list ranking.

THEOREM 6.2 *An $N \times N$ R-Mesh can solve the following problems on an N vertex tree in $O(\log^* N)$ deterministic time or $\widetilde{O}(1)$ randomized time[1]:*

---

[1] A randomized algorithm for a problem of size N is said to run in $\widetilde{O}(T)$ time if the probability of the algorithm running in $O(T)$ time is at least $1 - N^{-c}$ for $c \geq 1$. Quantities $\widetilde{\Theta}(T)$, $\widetilde{\Omega}(T)$, $\widetilde{o}(T)$, and $\widetilde{\omega}(T)$ (corresponding to deterministic quantities $\Theta(T)$, $\Omega(T)$, $o(T)$, and $\omega(T)$) can be defined similarly.

(*i*) *Rooting a tree,*

(*ii*) *Preorder, postorder, and inorder traversals of a rooted tree,*

(*iii*) *Determining the levels of vertices in a rooted tree,*

(*iv*) *Determining the number of descendants of vertices in a rooted tree, and*

(*v*) *Determining the number of leaves in subtrees of a rooted tree.*

6.2.3   Tree Reconstruction

In the last section we discussed methods for obtaining the preorder, postorder, and inorder traversals of a binary tree. It is well known that the preorder and inorder traversals (or the postorder and inorder traversals) of a binary tree uniquely specify the tree. In this section we describe an R-Mesh method for reconstructing a tree from its preorder and inorder traversals. The analogous method for postorder and inorder traversals is left as an exercise (Problem 6.19).

Let $\mathcal{T}$ be an N vertex binary tree. The reconstruction algorithm proceeds in two stages. The first stage uses the preorder and inorder numbering of $\mathcal{T}$ to construct an intermediate structure called a "preorder-inorder traversal." The second stage converts the preorder-inorder traversal into the binary tree $\mathcal{T}$. We first define the preorder-inorder traversal and then describe the two stages.

Preorder-Inorder Traversal. For the definition below, we permit a binary tree to be empty, in which case it has no vertices (as in the definition of an inorder traversal in Equation 6.4). Let $\mathcal{T}$ be a binary tree rooted at vertex r. Let $\mathcal{T}_1$ and $\mathcal{T}_2$ denote the subtrees rooted at the left and right children of r (if they exist). If the left (resp., right) child of r does not exist, then binary tree $\mathcal{T}_1$ (resp., $\mathcal{T}_2$) is empty. For strings s_1 and s_2, let s_1, s_2 denote the concatenation of s_1 and s_2. The *preorder-inorder traversal* of $\mathcal{T}$ is a string, *Pre-In*$(\mathcal{T})$, of vertices of $\mathcal{T}$. If $\mathcal{T}$ is empty, then so is *Pre-In*$(\mathcal{T})$. For a non-empty tree $\mathcal{T}$, we have the following:

$$Pre\text{-}In(\mathcal{T}) = r, Pre\text{-}In(\mathcal{T}_1), r, Pre\text{-}In(\mathcal{T}_2). \qquad (6.5)$$

Figure 6.2 illustrates the idea of preorder-inorder traversal for a small tree. Clearly, a given tree has a unique preorder-inorder sequence. In fact, the converse is also true. That is, a given preorder-inorder sequence corresponds to a unique tree.

This leads us to the question of what makes a sequence of vertices a preorder-inorder sequence. The following preorder-inorder property is a useful characterization of preorder-inorder sequences (see Problem 6.9).

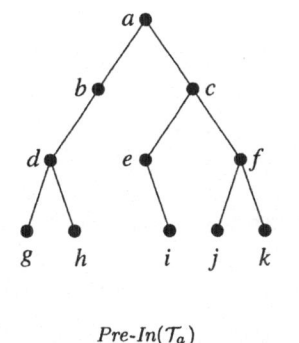

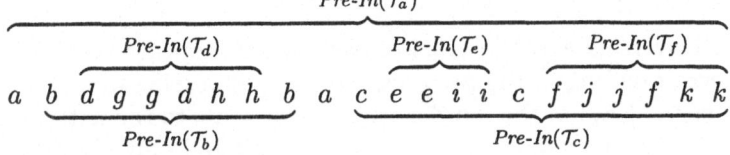

Figure 6.2. An illustration of the preorder-inorder traversal of a tree. The figure denotes the subtree rooted at vertex v by $\mathcal{T}_v$.

DEFINITION 6.3 A sequence $\langle s_0, s_1, \cdots, s_{2N-1} \rangle$ of symbols has the *preorder-inorder property* if and only if the following conditions are satisfied:

1. Each symbol in the sequence occurs exactly twice.

2. There exist no integers $0 \le i < j < k < \ell < 2N$ such that $s_i = s_k$ and $s_j = s_\ell$. ∎

Intuitively, the above property ensures a "well nested" sequence. That is, it does not permit a structure such as $\cdots a \cdots b \cdots a \cdots b \cdots$, in which neither one of the aa or the bb pairs encloses the other nor are they completely outside each other.

We now describe the two stages of the tree reconstruction algorithm.

Stage 1—Constructing the Preorder-Inorder Traversal from the Preorder and Inorder Traversals. Let $Q = \langle q_0, q_1, \cdots, q_{N-1} \rangle$ and $R = \langle r_0, r_1, \cdots, r_{N-1} \rangle$ be the preorder and inorder traversals of an N vertex tree. This procedure will be shown to be tantamount to merging two sorted lists. Clearly, each vertex of $\mathcal{T}$ appears once in each sequence Q and R. By Equation 6.5, a vertex of $\mathcal{T}$ appears twice in the preorder-inorder sequence. Figure 6.3 illustrates these ideas with the tree of Figure 6.2 as an example. Observe that the preorder-inorder sequence maintains the relative order of the elements in the preorder and

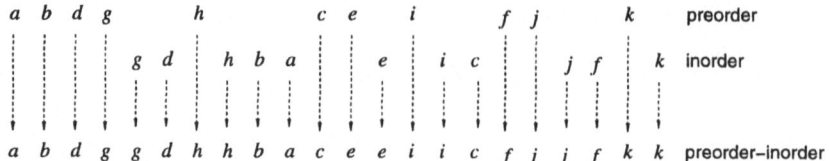

Figure 6.3. An example illustrating the merging of preorder and inorder traversals into a preorder-inorder traversal.

inorder traversals and the label of each vertex appears twice with the copy corresponding to the preorder sequence appearing first. Moreover, an element x (say) of the inorder sequence appears to the left of (or precedes) an element y of the preorder sequence if and only if x precedes y in both the preorder and inorder sequences. For example, vertex g, the first element of the inorder sequence, precedes vertex h of the preorder sequence, as g precedes h in both sequences. On the other hand, vertex g of the inorder sequence follows vertex b of the preorder sequence since g follows b in the preorder sequence (even though g precedes b in the inorder sequence). Later in this section we will formalize these observations.

We now structure the information in the preorder and inorder traversals to facilitate their merging.

For this part, index the tree vertices according to their preorder numbers. Therefore, $Q = \langle 0, 1, \cdots, N-1 \rangle$ is the preorder sequence. Let $R = \langle r_0, r_1, \cdots, r_{N-1} \rangle$ be the vertices (preorder indices) in inorder sequence. For any (preorder) index i (where $0 \le i < N$), let $\delta(i)$ be the (inorder) index such that $r_{\delta(i)} = q_i = i$. That is, the vertex at position i in the preorder sequence is the same as the vertex at position $\delta(i)$ of the inorder sequence.

Now define set X of doublets as follows:

$$X = \{\langle \delta(i), i \rangle \ : \ 0 \le i < N\}. \tag{6.6}$$

Note that i, $\delta(i)$, and $r_{\delta(i)}$ are all from the set $\{0, 1, \cdots, N-1\}$. One could view element $\langle \delta(i), i \rangle \in X$ as corresponding to vertex $i = q_i$ or vertex $r_{\delta(i)}$.

For the example of Figure 6.3, the set X is as follows. We have assumed that vertices are indexed (from 0 to 10) according to their position in the preorder traversal. That is, vertex 0 is a, vertex 1 is b, vertex 2 is d, vertex 3 is g, and so on.

$$X = \big\{ \langle 4,0 \rangle, \langle 3,1 \rangle, \langle 1,2 \rangle, \langle 0,3 \rangle, \langle 2,4 \rangle,$$
$$\langle 7,5 \rangle, \langle 5,6 \rangle, \langle 6,7 \rangle, \langle 9,8 \rangle, \langle 8,9 \rangle, \langle 10,10 \rangle \big\}$$

Element $\langle 4,0 \rangle$ of X corresponds to the 0th element, a, of the preorder traversal (as its second coordinate is 0) or the 4th element of the inorder sequence (as $a = r_4$). Similarly, entry $\langle 9,8 \rangle$ corresponds to the elements $f = q_8 = r_9$.

Now define sets X_1 and X_2 of triplets as follows:

$$\begin{aligned} X_1 &= \{ \langle 1,\beta,\gamma \rangle \ : \ \langle \beta,\gamma \rangle \in X \}, \\ X_2 &= \{ \langle 2,\beta,\gamma \rangle \ : \ \langle \beta,\gamma \rangle \in X \}. \end{aligned} \tag{6.7}$$

For each element of X, sets X_1 and X_2 each have a corresponding element. Letting $\langle \delta(i), i \rangle \in X$ represent vertex i of the preorder sequence, one can view X_1 as representing the preorder sequence. Similarly, letting $\langle \delta(i), i \rangle \in X$ represent vertex $r_{\delta(i)}$ of the inorder sequence, one can view X_2 as representing the inorder sequence.

We now show how X_1 and X_2 can be merged into the preorder-inorder sequence.

DEFINITION 6.4 Let $Z = X_1 \cup X_2$. Define a binary relation[2] $\preceq$ on Z as follows. Let $\langle \alpha_1, \beta_1, \gamma_1 \rangle$, $\langle \alpha_2, \beta_2, \gamma_2 \rangle \in Z$. If $\alpha_1 = \alpha_2$, $\beta_1 = \beta_2$, and $\gamma_1 = \gamma_2$, then $\langle \alpha_1, \beta_1, \gamma_1 \rangle = \langle \alpha_2, \beta_2, \gamma_2 \rangle$. When $\langle \alpha_1, \beta_1, \gamma_1 \rangle \neq \langle \alpha_2, \beta_2, \gamma_2 \rangle$, then $\langle \alpha_1, \beta_1, \gamma_1 \rangle \prec \langle \alpha_2, \beta_2, \gamma_2 \rangle$ if and only if one of the following conditions is satisfied:

Condition 1: $\alpha_1 = \alpha_2 = 1$ and $\gamma_1 < \gamma_2$,

Condition 2: $\alpha_1 = \alpha_2 = 2$ and $\beta_1 < \beta_2$, or

Condition 3: $\alpha_1 = 1$, $\alpha_2 = 2$, and ($\beta_1 \leq \beta_2$ or $\gamma_1 \leq \gamma_2$).

The intuition underlying the above definition is as follows. Conditions 1 and 2 maintain the relative orders of elements of the preorder and inorder sequences, respectively. Condition 3 permits an element $r_{\delta(i)}$ of the inorder sequence to be placed ahead of an element i' of the preorder sequence if and only if $\delta(i) < \delta(i')$ and $i < i'$; that is, if and only if vertex $r_{\delta(i)}$ precedes vertex $q_{i'} = i'$ in both the preorder and inorder sequences. Earlier we made the same observations for the example of Figure 6.3.

---

[2]See Footnote 1 on page 154.

It is easy to show that the relation $\preceq$ is a total order (see Footnote 1 on page 154 and Problem 6.11). We now prove that when ordered by $\preceq$, the elements of $Z = X_1 \cup X_2$ form a preorder-inorder sequence.

LEMMA 6.5 *Let X_1 and X_2 be sets of triplets derived from the preorder and inorder sequences of a tree $\mathcal{T}$. Let $Z = X_1 \cup X_2 = \{\langle \alpha_i, \beta_i, \gamma_i \rangle : 0 \leq i < 2N\}$ with $\langle \alpha_i, \beta_i, \gamma_i \rangle \prec \langle \alpha_{i+1}, \beta_{i+1}, \gamma_{i+1} \rangle$, for $0 \leq i < 2N - 1$. Then, the sequence $S = \langle \gamma_0, \gamma_1, \cdots, \gamma_{2N-1} \rangle$ is the preorder-inorder sequence of tree $\mathcal{T}$.*

<u>Proof:</u> We only need prove that S has the preorder-inorder property (Definition 6.3). From the definitions of X_1, X_2, and Z it is clear that each vertex index occurs exactly twice in S. Therefore, the proof boils down to establishing that there do not exist integers $0 \leq i < j < k < \ell < 2N$ such that $\gamma_i = \gamma_k$ and $\gamma_j = \gamma_\ell$.

Suppose such integers exist. Then the corresponding elements of Z satisfy

$$\langle \alpha_i, \beta_i, \gamma_i \rangle \prec \langle \alpha_j, \beta_j, \gamma_j \rangle \prec \langle \alpha_k, \beta_k, \gamma_k \rangle \prec \langle \alpha_\ell, \beta_\ell, \gamma_\ell \rangle. \tag{6.8}$$

Since $\gamma_i = \gamma_k$ and $\gamma_j = \gamma_\ell$, the definition of the triplets of X_1 and X_2 requires that

$$\beta_i = \beta_k \qquad \text{and} \qquad \beta_j = \beta_\ell. \tag{6.9}$$

Also since $\langle \alpha_i, \beta_i, \gamma_i \rangle \neq \langle \alpha_k, \beta_k, \gamma_k \rangle$, we have $\alpha_i \neq \alpha_k$. Similarly, $\alpha_j \neq \alpha_\ell$. Also since $\langle \alpha_i, \beta_i, \gamma_i \rangle \prec \langle \alpha_k, \beta_k, \gamma_k \rangle$ and $\gamma_i = \gamma_k$, Condition 3 in the definition requires that $\alpha_i = 1$ and $\alpha_k = 2$. Similarly, $\alpha_j = 1$ and $\alpha_\ell = 2$. That is,

$$\alpha_i = \alpha_j = 1 \qquad \text{and} \qquad \alpha_k = \alpha_\ell = 2. \tag{6.10}$$

Since $\langle \alpha_j, \beta_j, \gamma_j \rangle \prec \langle \alpha_k, \beta_k, \gamma_k \rangle$, Condition 3 in the definition of $\preceq$ implies that

$$\beta_j \leq \beta_k \qquad \text{or} \qquad \gamma_j \leq \gamma_k. \tag{6.11}$$

From Equations 6.9 and 6.11 and the fact that $\gamma_j = \gamma_\ell$, we have

$$\beta_\ell \leq \beta_k \qquad \text{or} \qquad \gamma_\ell \leq \gamma_k. \tag{6.12}$$

Since $\langle \alpha_k, \beta_k, \gamma_k \rangle \prec \langle \alpha_\ell, \beta_\ell, \gamma_\ell \rangle$ and $\langle \alpha_i, \beta_i, \gamma_i \rangle \prec \langle \alpha_j, \beta_j, \gamma_j \rangle$ by Equation 6.8, and $\alpha_k = \alpha_\ell = 2$ and $\alpha_i = \alpha_j = 1$ by Equation 6.10, then Conditions 1 and 2 of the definition of $\preceq$ imply that

$$\beta_k < \beta_\ell \qquad \text{and} \qquad \gamma_i < \gamma_j. \tag{6.13}$$

From Equation 6.13 and the assumption that $\gamma_i = \gamma_k$ and $\gamma_j = \gamma_\ell$, we have

$$\beta_k < \beta_\ell \qquad \text{and} \qquad \gamma_k < \gamma_\ell. \tag{6.14}$$

Equations 6.12 and 6.14 provide the necessary contradiction. ∎

Thus, the problem of generating the preorder-inorder traversal of tree $\mathcal{T}$ boils down to merging the N element preorder and inorder sequences. Merging is a special case of the constant time sorting algorithm of Theorem 5.4 (page 158) for an $N \times N$ R-Mesh.

LEMMA 6.6 *The preorder and inorder traversals of an N vertex tree can be converted to the tree's preorder-inorder traversal on an $N \times N$ R-Mesh in $O(1)$ time.*

Stage 2—Reconstructing the Tree from its Preorder-Inorder Traversal. Stage 1 constructs a preorder-inorder traversal of the tree. Since this traversal is unique to the given tree, it is possible to reconstruct the tree from it. That is, every sequence with the preorder-inorder property corresponds to a binary tree. Here we show how to use any such sequence to reconstruct the corresponding tree. Let sequence $\langle s_0, s_1, \cdots, s_{2N-1} \rangle$ have the preorder-inorder property. Let $\mathcal{T}$ be the corresponding binary tree. Each symbol appears exactly twice in the sequence. We will refer to the first (resp., second) occurrence of a symbol as its first (resp., second) copy. The following lemma is the basis for reconstructing the tree corresponding to the sequence. Its proof is left as an exercise (Problem 6.13).

LEMMA 6.7 *Let $S = \langle s_0, s_1, \cdots, s_{2N-1} \rangle$ be a sequence with the preorder-inorder property. Let $\mathcal{T}$ be the binary tree corresponding to S.*

(i) *Every first copy of a symbol is a vertex of $\mathcal{T}$.*

(ii) *For any $0 \leq i < 2N - 1$, if both s_i and s_{i+1} are first copies, then s_{i+1} is the left child of s_i.*

(iii) *For any $0 \leq i < 2N - 1$, if s_i is a first copy and s_{i+1} is a second copy, then s_i has no left child.*

(iv) *For any $0 \leq i < 2N - 1$, if s_i is a second copy and s_{i+1} is a first copy, then s_{i+1} is the right child of s_i.*

(v) *For any $0 \leq i < 2N - 1$, if both s_i and s_{i+1} are second copies, then s_i has no right child.*

Lemma 6.7 results in a simple constant time algorithm on an $N \times 2N$ R-Mesh for reconstructing a tree from its preorder-inorder sequence. Assume the preorder-inorder sequence to initially be in a row of the R-Mesh. By using neighbor localization on a separate row for each symbol in the sequence (vertex of the tree), the R-Mesh can pair the first and second copies of each symbol. Now the remaining task of determining the left and right children (if any) of each vertex is straightforward from of Lemma 6.7. It is easy to modify this algorithm to run on an $N \times N$ R-Mesh. Therefore, we have the following result.

LEMMA 6.8 *An N vertex tree can be reconstructed from its preorder-inorder sequence on an $N \times N$ R-Mesh in $O(1)$ time.*

From Lemmas 6.6 and 6.8, we have the following result.

THEOREM 6.9 *An N vertex tree can be reconstructed from its preorder and inorder sequences on an $N \times N$ R-Mesh in $O(1)$ time.*

6.3   Algorithms for Graphs

In this section we present R-Mesh algorithms for graphs, including spanning trees, transitive closure and contraction, and problems related to connectedness (connectivity, strong connectivity, biconnectivity, and identifying cut edges/vertices). In Section 6.4, we examine algorithms for directed graphs, with particular focus on a class of directed graphs called directed acyclic graphs (DAGs) that have a wide range of applications. For many of these problems, we describe multiple solutions (some in the context of directed graphs) that provide various tradeoffs between the speed and size of the R-Mesh used.

Section 6.3.1 deals with algorithms for spanning trees. In Section 6.3.2, we describe R-Mesh solutions to connectivity related problems. Most algorithms of this section build on the *s-t* connectivity algorithm (Algorithm 2.9, page 47) described earlier. Other, more complex problems such as biconnected components apply R-Mesh techniques to algorithms designed for other models.

In this section we will assume, in general, that a graph $\mathcal{G} = (V, E)$ is undirected and that it has N vertices and M edges. For the most part, we will represent $\mathcal{G}$ as a set of M edges. Some algorithms will employ the adjacency matrix representation, however.

6.3.1   Minimum Spanning Tree

A *spanning tree* of a connected graph $\mathcal{G}$ is a subgraph of $\mathcal{G}$ that is a tree containing all vertices of $\mathcal{G}$. If $\mathcal{G}$ has weighted edges, then a *minimum spanning tree* is one with edges of minimum total weight. The minimum spanning tree problem has several applications, including in solutions to other graph problems.

In this section we describe a constant time minimum spanning tree algorithm for the R-Mesh that uses the idea of the well known method of Kruskal. For an N vertex, M edge graph, it runs in constant time on an $M \times MN$ R-Mesh. In Section 6.4.1, we present an $O(\log N)$ time solution that runs on a smaller $N^{1+\epsilon} \times N^{1+\epsilon}$ R-Mesh.

Let $\mathcal{G}$ be an N vertex, M edge, connected, loopless, weighted graph. This implies that $N - 1 \leq M \leq \frac{N(N-1)}{2}$. If $M = N - 1$, then the graph is a tree already. Therefore, we assume that $M \geq N$. Without loss of generality, let the edge weights be distinct—this ensures a unique minimum spanning tree. Let the edges of $\mathcal{G}$ be $e_0, e_1, \cdots, e_{M-1}$, in increasing order of their weights. For $0 \leq i < M$, define graph $\mathcal{G}_i$ to be the subgraph of $\mathcal{G}$ containing all its vertices, but only edges $e_0, e_1, \cdots, e_{i-1}$. In this notation, $\mathcal{G}_0$ has no edge and $\mathcal{G}_{M-1}$ has all edges except e_{M-1}. The minimum spanning tree algorithm uses the following fact.

LEMMA 6.10 *For $0 \leq i < M$, edge e_i is part of the minimum spanning tree if and only if there is no path in $\mathcal{G}_i$ between the end points of e_i.*

Remark: Notice that if $\mathcal{G}_i$ has a path P between the end points of edge e_i, then P and e_i will form a cycle in which e_i has the largest weight.

To begin with, the R-Mesh must sort the edges of $\mathcal{G}$ by their weights. A $\sqrt{M} \times \sqrt{M} \times \sqrt{M}$ three-dimensional sub-R-Mesh (Theorem 5.10, page 162) or an $M \times M$ two-dimensional sub-R-Mesh can sort the edges in constant time (Theorem 5.4, page 158). Since s-t connectivity (see Section 2.3.6) has a constant time solution on an $N \times N$ R-Mesh, the algorithm uses Lemma 6.10 and tests each edge for membership in the minimum spanning tree. Thus, M R-Meshes, each of size $N \times N$, can test all edges for membership in parallel. Since $\sqrt{M} \leq N$, an $N \times N \times M$ three-dimensional R-Mesh can solve the problem in constant time. In two dimensions, an $M \times MN$ R-Mesh suffices; converting the $N \times N \times M$ R-Mesh to two dimensions by using Theorem 3.1 (page 80) could result in a larger two-dimensional R-Mesh. Further, it is easy to show that the algorithm runs on a "nearly square" $M\sqrt{N} \times M(2 + \sqrt{N})$ R-Mesh.

THEOREM 6.11 *The minimum spanning tree of an N vertex, M edge graph can be determined in $O(1)$ time on an $N \times N \times M$ three-dimensional R-Mesh or an $M\sqrt{N} \times M(2 + \sqrt{N})$ two-dimensional R-Mesh.*

6.3.2 Connectivity Related Problems

Many problems on graphs stem from the question of whether or not paths exist between portions of a graph. In this section we address such connectivity related problems in an R-Mesh setting. Previously, we have seen that the R-Mesh lends itself to an elegant solution to s-t connectivity (see Section 2.3.6). This solution embeds the structure of the graph in the R-Mesh in such a way that for each path in the graph, a bus exists between corresponding R-Mesh processors. In this section we build on this basic R-Mesh technique to design algorithms for connected components, transitive closure, and biconnected components. Problems 6.27–6.31 identify other applications of this technique. In Section 6.4.1, we describe a technique that can also be used for, among other things, solving some connectivity problems on directed and undirected graphs (Problems 6.45–6.48).

6.3.2.1   Connected Components

A *connected component* of a graph $\mathcal{G}$ is a maximally connected subgraph of $\mathcal{G}$. Identifying the connected components of $\mathcal{G}$ is tantamount to assigning a unique component number to each component; this is usually the lowest indexed vertex in the component.

We now look at the salient features of the *s-t* connectivity algorithm of Section 2.3.6 that play a key role in most connectivity related graph problems, including connected components.

1. Embed the graph (via its adjacency matrix) in an $N \times N$ R-Mesh. Let processor (v, v) represent vertex v. The embedding guarantees that for any pair of vertices u and v, processors (u, u) and (v, v) are connected to a common bus if and only if a path exists between vertices u and v in the graph.

2. Send a signal from processor (s, s) representing the source vertex s.

3. The target vertex t is connected to s if and only if processor (t, t) receives the signal.

Observe in the above procedure that the signal from processor (s, s) reaches processor (v, v) for every vertex v in the same connected component as s. Thus, with minor modifications, the *s-t* connectivity algorithm serves to flag all vertices in the same component as s. To identify all (potentially $\Theta(N)$) connected components of the graph, it is convenient to first use a PRIORITY CRCW R-Mesh and then convert it using Theorem 3.4 or 3.5 (page 85) to the COMMON or COLLISION model.

Consider a PRIORITY CRCW $N \times N$ R-Mesh in which the graph has been embedded as in the *s-t* connectivity algorithm. Each processor (v, v), representing vertex v, writes index v to its bus. Consequently, all processors representing vertices in the same connected component write concurrently to the same bus. The PRIORITY rule ensures that the bus value is the smallest of the indices written. Thus, processor (v, v) can now read the component number of vertex v off its bus. Since information originating from vertices in a component is confined to the bus unique to that component, separate components can proceed independently.

THEOREM 6.12 *The connected components of an N vertex graph can be determined on a* PRIORITY *CRCW N × N R-Mesh in O(1) time.*

With Theorems 3.4 and 3.5 (page 85), we have the following result.

THEOREM 6.13 *For* $1 \leq m \leq N$, *the connected components of an N vertex graph can be determined on a* COMMON, COLLISION, *or* COLLISION$^+$ *CRCW N × N × m three-dimensional R-Mesh or* $O(Nm) \times O(Nm)$ *two-dimensional R-Mesh in* $O\left(\frac{\log N}{\log m}\right)$ *time.*

With $m = \Theta(N^\epsilon)$ (where $\epsilon > 0$ is a constant) in Theorem 6.13 we have the following result.

COROLLARY 6.14 *For any constant* $\epsilon > 0$, *the connected components of an N vertex graph can be determined on a* COMMON, COLLISION, *or* COLLISION$^+$ *CRCW N × N × N$^\epsilon$ three-dimensional R-Mesh or* $N^{1+\epsilon} \times N^{1+\epsilon}$ *two-dimensional R-Mesh in O(1) time.*

6.3.2.2 Transitive Closure

The *transitive closure* of a graph $\mathcal{G} = (V, E)$ is another graph $\mathcal{G}^* = (V, E^*)$ such that (u, v) is an edge of $\mathcal{G}^*$ if and only if $\mathcal{G}$ contains a path between u and v. Transitive closure captures the idea of connectedness in a graph, connecting two vertices directly by an edge whenever one can reach the other.

Observe that entry $a^*_{u,v}$ in the adjacency matrix, A^*, of $\mathcal{G}^*$ is 1 if and only if u and v are in the same connected component of $\mathcal{G}$. Connected components can use an $N \times N$ R-Mesh to determine A^* as follows. Let processors (u, u) and (v, v) send the component numbers of vertices u and v, respectively, to processor (u, v). Entry $a^*_{u,v} = 1$ if and only if vertices u and v have the same component number.

THEOREM 6.15 *For* $1 \leq m \leq N$, *the transitive closure of an N vertex graph can be computed on a* COMMON, COLLISION, *or* COLLISION$^+$ *CRCW N × N × m three-dimensional R-Mesh or* $O(Nm) \times O(Nm)$ *two-dimensional R-Mesh in* $O\left(\frac{\log N}{\log m}\right)$ *time.*

6.3.2.3 Biconnected Components

Let $\mathcal{G} = (V, E)$ be a connected graph. Graph $\mathcal{G}$ is biconnected if and only if each pair of vertices has at least two disjoint paths between them. A maximally biconnected subgraph of $\mathcal{G}$ is a biconnected component of $\mathcal{G}$. Formally, define a relation, R, on E as follows: for any $e, e' \in E$, we have eRe' if and only if $e = e'$ or e and e' lie on a common simple cycle of $\mathcal{G}$. Clearly, R is an equivalence relation[3]. The blocks of the partition induced by R are the *biconnected components* of $\mathcal{G}$. Graph $\mathcal{G}$ is *biconnected* if and only if the above partition has only one block. Finding the biconnected components of a graph $\mathcal{G}$ involves assigning a number $biconn\_no(e)$ to each edge e of $\mathcal{G}$ such that for any $e, e' \in E$ of $\mathcal{G}$, $biconn\_no(e) = biconn\_no(e')$ if and only if e and e' are in the same biconnected component.

In this section we adapt Tarjan and Vishkin's biconnected components algorithm for the PRAM to run on the R-Mesh. It provides a good example of how many of the R-Mesh techniques studied so far apply to solve a larger and more complex problem. Tarjan and Vishkin's algorithm reduces the biconnected components problem on the given graph $\mathcal{G}$ to the connected components problem on an induced graph $\mathcal{G}'$. It consists of the following stages.

Stage 1: Find $\mathcal{T} = (V, E_t)$, a spanning tree of $\mathcal{G}$ rooted at an arbitrary vertex.

Stage 2: Compute for each vertex $v \in V$ its preorder number $pre(v)$ in $\mathcal{T}$; the root of $\mathcal{T}$ is vertex 0. Subsequent steps will assume the index of a vertex to be its preorder number.

Stage 3: For each $v \in V$, compute the following quantities:

- $par(v) =$ parent of v in $\mathcal{T}$; $par(0) =$ NIL,

- $des(v) =$ number of descendants of v in $\mathcal{T}$,

- $low(v) =$ the lowest indexed vertex that is either a descendant of v or adjacent to a descendant of v by a non-tree edge, and

- $high(v) =$ the highest indexed vertex that is either a descendant of v or adjacent to a descendant of v by a non-tree edge.

Stage 4: Construct a graph $\mathcal{G}' = (E, E')$, whose nodes are edges of $\mathcal{G}$. Two nodes e and e' of $\mathcal{G}'$ (edges of $\mathcal{G}$) are directly connected by a link in $\mathcal{G}'$ if and only if

(a) $e = (u, par(u))$ and $e' = (u, v) \notin E_t$ and $v < u$,   or

(b) $e = (u, par(u))$ and $e' = (v, par(v))$ and $(u, v) \notin E_t$ and
     $v + des(v) \leq u$,   or

---

[3] A binary relation (see also Footnote 1, page 154) R on a set S is an *equivalence relation* if and only if it is reflexive ($\forall s \in S$, sRs), symmetric ($\forall s_1, s_2 \in S$, $s_1 R s_2 \implies s_2 R s_1$), and transitive ($\forall s_1, s_2, s_3 \in S$, $(s_1 R s_2$ and $s_2 R s_3) \implies (s_1 R s_3)$). The equivalence relation R partitions the set S into disjoint blocks, $B_0, B_1, \cdots, B_x$ such that for $0 \leq i \leq x$, elements $s_1, s_2 \in B_i$ if and only if $s_1 R s_2$.

(c) $e = (u, par(u))$ and $par(u) = v > 0$ and $e' = (v, par(v))$ and $(low(u) < v$ or $high(u) \geq v + des(v))$.

Stage 5: Find the connected components of $\mathcal{G}'$ and assign to each edge e of $\mathcal{G}$ (node of $\mathcal{G}'$) its biconnected component number $biconn\_no(e)$. It can be shown that each connected component of $\mathcal{G}'$ is a biconnected component of $\mathcal{G}$.

We now explain how an $M\sqrt{N} \times M(2 + \sqrt{N})$ R-Mesh can find the biconnected components of an M edge, connected graph $\mathcal{G}$. Since $\mathcal{G}$ is connected, no loss of generality arises in eliminating the case where $\mathcal{G}$ is a tree and assuming $M \geq N$. Assume the graph to be input as M edges in the top row of the R-Mesh.

Use the minimum spanning tree algorithm of Theorem 6.11 for Stage 1. Observe that with the list ranking algorithm of Theorem 2.17 (page 46), the tree algorithms of Theorem 6.2 run in constant time on an $N^{1+\epsilon} \times N^{1+\epsilon}$ R-Mesh, where $\epsilon > 0$ is a constant. Therefore, the R-Mesh can compute the quantities $pre(v)$ in Stage 2 and $par(v)$ and $des(v)$ in Stage 3 in constant time.

Computing $low(v)$ needs some elaboration; the R-Mesh can compute $high(v)$ along the same lines. For each $v \in V$, define $L(v) = \min[\{v\} \cup \{u : (u, v) \in E - E_t\}]$. It can be shown that

$$low(v) = \min\{L(u) : u \text{ is a descendant of } v \text{ in } \mathcal{T}\}. \tag{6.15}$$

To compute $L(v)$, we employ an $N \times N$ sub-R-Mesh. Row v of this sub-R-Mesh uses neighbor localization to form a list of all vertices u such that $(u, v) \in E - E_t$. The first (least indexed) element of this list is used to compute $L(v)$. Determining $low(v)$ now boils down to finding the set of descendants of each vertex v. An $N^{1+\epsilon} \times N^{1+\epsilon}$ R-Mesh can solve this problem in constant time for an N vertex tree (see also Problem 6.7(c)). Therefore, the given R-Mesh can complete Stage 3 in constant time.

Clearly, Stage 4 runs in constant time. Before we analyze Stage 5, let us determine the size of the induced graph $\mathcal{G}'$. In the following, we use the terms "vertex" and "edge" in the context of the input graph $\mathcal{G}$. On the other hand, we reserve the terms "node" and "link" for the induced graph $\mathcal{G}'$. In this convention, the edges of $\mathcal{G}$ are nodes of $\mathcal{G}'$. The three rules of Stage 4 generate the links of $\mathcal{G}'$. It can be shown that for each link of $\mathcal{G}'$, only one of the three rules applies (Problem 6.34). We now bound the number of links in $\mathcal{G}'$.

By rule (a), each non-tree edge $(u, v) \in E - E_t$ generates at most one link (either between the nodes $(u, par(u))$ and (u, v) or between nodes

$(v, par(v))$ and (u, v)). Therefore, this rule generates at most $M - N + 1$ links in $\mathcal{G}'$. By rule (b), each non-tree edge $(u, v) \in E - E_t$ generates at most one link (between the nodes $(u, par(u))$ and $(v, par(v))$). Therefore, this rule also generates at most $M - N + 1$ links in $\mathcal{G}'$. By rule (c), each tree edge $(u, par(u))$ generates at most one link between nodes $(u, par(u))$ and $(par(u), par(par(u)))$. Therefore, rule (c) generates at most $N - 1$ links, and the number of links in $\mathcal{G}'$ is at most $2M - N + 1$. Since $\sqrt{N} = \Omega\left(M^{\frac{1}{4}}\right)$, we have $M\sqrt{N} = \Omega(M^{1+\epsilon})$, where $\epsilon = \frac{1}{4}$. Thus with Theorem 6.13, the R-Mesh can execute Stage 5 in constant time.

THEOREM 6.16 *The biconnected components of an N vertex, M edge connected graph can be determined on an $M\sqrt{N} \times M(2+\sqrt{N})$ COMMON, COLLISION, or COLLISION$^+$ CRCW R-Mesh in $O(1)$ time.*

6.4   Algorithms for Directed Graphs

So far, we have restricted our discussion to R-Mesh algorithms for undirected graphs, with the exception of lists which can be viewed as a special case. In general, directed graphs pose difficulties in both conventional and reconfigurable models. The large number of applications that can be modeled as directed graphs makes their study important, however.

This section deals with two approaches to directed graphs. The first, called the algebraic path problem approach, works on a non-directional R-Mesh, albeit somewhat slowly. We use this method to examine the all-pairs shortest distances and the minimum spanning tree problems. The second approach uses a directional R-Mesh (DR-Mesh), possibly a more powerful model than its non-directional counterpart (see Section 3.1.5), and achieves constant time. We illustrate this approach through algorithms for directed acyclic graphs (DAGs). Some of the ideas explored in previous sections also have DR-Mesh counterparts that work for directed graphs. These include strongly connected components and transitive closure (see Problems 6.45–6.47).

6.4.1   The Algebraic Path Problem Approach

The algebraic path problem approach is suitable for both directed and undirected graphs. Moreover, it works for any model of computation; here we focus on an R-Mesh implementation.

Let $\mathcal{G} = (V, E, w)$ be a weighted graph where each edge $e \in E$ has a weight $w(e)$ from a set S. Let $\oplus$ and $\odot$ be two associative binary operations[4] on set S. Let quantities $0, 1 \in S$ be such that 0 is the identity of $\oplus$ and the zero element of $\odot$; let 1 be the identity of $\odot$.

Let π denote a path that traverses edges $e_1, e_2, \cdots, e_k$. Define the weight of path π as follows:

$$w(\pi) = w(e_1) \odot w(e_2) \odot \cdots \odot w(e_k) = \bigodot_{i=1}^{k} w(e_i). \qquad (6.16)$$

Note that if $k = 0$, then the value of the product in Equation 6.16 is 1, the identity of operation $\odot$. For vertices $u, v \in V$, let $P_{u,v}$ be the set of "interesting paths" between u and v; for our applications, an interesting path is one whose length is at most $N - 1$. The *algebraic path problem* is to compute for each vertex pair $u, v \in V$ the quantity

$$d_{u,v} = \bigoplus_{\pi \in P_{u,v}} w(\pi). \qquad (6.17)$$

Note that if $P_{u,v}$ is empty, then the sum in Equation 6.17 has value 0, the identity of operation $\oplus$.

Let us now consider a special case of the algebraic path problem that suits some graph algorithms. This "restricted algebraic path problem" has the following properties.

1. The interesting paths are those of lengths between 0 and $N - 1$, and

2. Considering paths of length N or more does not affect the solution.

Let $A = [a_{u,v}]$ denote the "weighted adjacency matrix" of $\mathcal{G}$, in which the entry $a_{u,v}$ (corresponding to vertices u and v) has the following value.

$$a_{u,v} = \begin{cases} w(u, v), & \text{if } (u, v) \in E \\ 0, & \text{if } (u, v) \notin E \end{cases} \qquad (6.18)$$

Note that the symbol "0" in Equation 6.18 denotes the zero element of the operation $\odot$ and the identity of the operation $\oplus$, rather than the number 0.

Let $A^0 = I$, the identity matrix with respect to the operation $\odot$. For $k > 1$, define $A^k = A \cdot A^{k-1}$, where operation $\cdot$ denotes matrix

---

[4]A *binary operation* $\circ$ on a set S is a function $\circ : S \times S \longrightarrow S$ that combines any two elements $a, b \in S$ to element $(a \circ b) \in S$. The operation is *associative* if and only if for all $a, b, c \in S$, $(a \circ b) \circ c = a \circ (b \circ c)$. Element $i \in S$ is the *identity* of $\circ$ if and only if for all elements $a \in S$, $a \circ i = i \circ a = a$. An element $z \in S$ is called the *zero element* of $\circ$ if and only if for all elements $a \in S$, $a \circ z = z \circ a = z$.

multiplication with the conventional $+$ and $\times$ operators replaced by the generic operations $\oplus$ and $\odot$ described earlier. That is, if $A^k = [a^k_{u,v}]$, then

$$a^k_{u,v} = \bigoplus_{z \in V} a_{u,z} \odot a^{k-1}_{z,v}. \tag{6.19}$$

Also, define the addition of matrices $A = [a_{u,v}]$ and $B = [b_{u,v}]$ as

$$A + B = [a_{u,v} \oplus b_{u,v}]. \tag{6.20}$$

The following result is simple to prove.

LEMMA 6.17 *The solution to the restricted algebraic path problem is*

$$D = [d_{u,v}] = I + A + A^2 + \cdots + A^{N-1} = \sum_{\ell=0}^{N-1} A^\ell.$$

From the second property of the restricted algebraic path problem, we have the following:

$$D = \sum_{\ell=0}^{N-1} A^\ell = \sum_{\ell=0}^{\alpha} A^\ell, \text{ for any } \alpha \geq N. \tag{6.21}$$

With $\alpha = 2^{\beta+1} - 1$, where $\beta = \lceil \log_2 N \rceil$, Equation 6.21 implies

$$D = \sum_{\ell=0}^{N-1} A^\ell = \sum_{\ell=0}^{2^{\beta+1}-1} A^\ell. \tag{6.22}$$

Recasting Equation 6.22 in a form more amenable to computation,

$$D = \sum_{\ell=0}^{2^{\beta+1}-1} A^\ell = \prod_{\ell=0}^{\beta} (I + A^{2^\ell}), \tag{6.23}$$

where I is the identity matrix and $\prod$ denotes matrix product. Given I and A, it is possible to compute matrix D in β rounds, each involving matrix multiplication (including squaring) and addition. On an R-Mesh, algorithms for matrix multiplication and addition defined by Equations 6.19 and 6.20 parallel their conventional counterparts with addition $(+)$ and multiplication $(\times)$ replaced by operations $\oplus$ and $\odot$, respectively.

Suppose that for $X \geq N$ and $Y \geq 1$, an $X \times Y$ R-Mesh can compute $\bigoplus_{i=1}^{N} a_i$ for any inputs $a_1, a_2, \cdots, a_N$ in T steps. Then it is easy to show that an $N \times NY \times X$ R-Mesh can multiply two $N \times N$ matrices in $O(T)$ time, using the definition in Equation 6.19. Since matrix addition runs in constant time on an $N \times N$ R-Mesh, we have the following result.

LEMMA 6.18 *For $X \geq N$ and $Y \geq 1$, the restricted algebraic path problem of size N can be solved on an $N \times NY \times X$ three-dimensional R-Mesh in $O(T \log N)$ time, where T is the time needed by an $X \times Y$ R-Mesh to compute $\bigoplus\limits_{i=1}^{N} a_i$ for any inputs $a_1, a_2, \cdots, a_N$.*

One can express some important graph problems as instances of the restricted algebraic path problem. In this section we describe two of these—all-pairs shortest distances and minimum spanning tree. We now formulate these instances and outline an R-Mesh solution for them.

All-Pairs Shortest Distances. Here weights of edges of $\mathcal{G}$ are typically positive real numbers. (Alternatively, $\mathcal{G}$ could be a graph with no negative weight cycles.) The shortest distance between vertices u and v is the weight of the least weighted path between these vertices. If no path exists between the vertices, then their shortest distance is denoted by ∞.

It is easy to see that the shortest distance between vertices u and v is $\min\{w(\pi) : \pi \in P_{u,v}\}$. Therefore for this instance of the algebraic path problem, $\oplus$ is the minimum operation and $\odot$ is the conventional addition operation $+$. Note that the symbol 0 of Equation 6.18 denotes the identity for the minimum operation and the zero element for conventional addition, both of which in this case equal ∞.

Minimum Spanning Tree. As mentioned earlier, the algebraic path problem technique works for both directed and undirected graphs. Since a spanning tree is for undirected graphs, we consider an undirected graph, $\mathcal{G}$, here. For any edge e of $\mathcal{G}$, let $w(e)$ denote its weight (typically a real number). Assume that the edge weights are all different so that the minimum spanning tree is unique. Define the weight $w(\pi)$ of a path π to be the largest of the weights of all edges on it. That is, $\odot$ is the maximum operation, whose identity is $-\infty$ and zero element is ∞. It can be shown that an edge $e = (u, v)$ of $\mathcal{G}$ belongs to the minimum spanning tree if and only if $w(e) = \min\{w(\pi) : \pi \in P_{u,v}\}$. Thus, $\oplus$ is the minimum operation and $\odot$ is the maximum operation.

In essence, both problems have min as the operation $\oplus$. Since an $N^\epsilon \times N$ R-Mesh can determine the minimum of N quantities in constant time (see Problem 2.35), we have the following results from Lemma 6.18.

THEOREM 6.19 *Let $\mathcal{G}$ be an N vertex directed or undirected graph with non-negative edge weights. For any constant $\epsilon > 0$, the shortest distances between each pair of vertices of $\mathcal{G}$ can be computed on a three-dimensional $N \times N^{1+\epsilon} \times N$ R-Mesh or a two-dimensional $N^{1+\epsilon} \times N^{1+\epsilon}$ R-Mesh in $O(\log N)$ time.*

THEOREM 6.20 *Let $\mathcal{G}$ be an N vertex graph with distinct edge weights. For any constant $\epsilon > 0$, the minimum spanning tree of $\mathcal{G}$ can be determined on an $N \times N^{1+\epsilon} \times N$ three-dimensional R-Mesh or a two-dimensional $N^{1+\epsilon} \times N^{1+\epsilon}$ R-Mesh in $O(\log N)$ time.*

<u>Remarks:</u>   Although a general conversion from three to two dimensions incurs constant overheads, it is possible to express the above results for R-Meshes of size $N^{1+\epsilon} \times N^{1+\epsilon}$ (rather than $O(N^{1+\epsilon}) \times O(N^{1+\epsilon})$).

6.4.2   Directed Acyclic Graphs

Section 6.4.1 used the algebraic path problem technique to derive R-Mesh algorithms for graphs. This technique is general and, to a large extent, model independent. In this section we present algorithms that specifically use the ability of the R-Mesh to configure its buses to suit the problem instance. We will use the directional R-Mesh (or DR-Mesh) here, as it has the ability to capture the asymmetric nature of directed graphs.

We present these algorithms in the setting of directed acyclic graphs (DAGs), which model a large variety of applications, including partial orders, scheduling, and dependency analysis. As its name indicates, a DAG is a directed graph with no cycles.

We describe three algorithms for DAGs. The first, for transitive contraction of DAGs representing partial orders, tersely expresses DAGs using the smallest possible number of edges. The second algorithm determines the distance (number of edges in a directed path) between a fixed vertex and all other vertices. This algorithm works for all types of graphs (directed or undirected) and is not restricted to DAGs. The third algorithm uses the distances algorithm for topological sorting, which is the problem of arranging elements according to an underlying partial order. All three algorithms run on an $N^2 \times NM$ DR-Mesh for an N vertex, M edge DAG.

Transitive Contraction.   Let $\preceq$ be a partial order on a set V. This partial order induces a directed graph $\mathcal{G} = (V, E)$ that has an edge $\langle u, v \rangle$ if and only if $u \preceq v$. If we ignore self-loops at each vertex, then $\mathcal{G}$ is a directed acyclic graph. Since $\preceq$ is transitive, then by definition, $\langle u, v \rangle, \langle v, w \rangle \in E$ implies that $\langle u, w \rangle \in E$, for all $u, v, w \in V$. Thus, edge $\langle u, w \rangle$ is redundant as its existence can be inferred from $\langle u, v \rangle$ and $\langle v, w \rangle$.

The transitive contraction[5] of $\mathcal{G}$ is the smallest subgraph of $\mathcal{G}$ with all information needed to reconstruct $\mathcal{G}$. More precisely, the *transitive contraction*, $\mathcal{G}'$, is the smallest subgraph of $\mathcal{G}$ whose transitive closure equals $\mathcal{G}$. For a DAG, the transitive contraction is unique.

We start with an $N \times N \times M$ three-dimensional DR-Mesh. Let the third dimension of the R-Mesh hold the DAG, represented as a set of M edges. The first step is to convert the graph into M copies of its adjacency matrix, one per $N \times N$ sub-R-Mesh. Each of these sub-R-Meshes now checks to see if an edge $\langle u, v \rangle$ needs to be included in the transitive contraction. This it does by checking if $\mathcal{G} - \{\langle u, v \rangle\}$ has a directed path from u to v. Edge $\langle u, v \rangle$ belongs to the transitive contraction if and only if $\mathcal{G} - \{\langle u, v \rangle\}$ has no path from u to v. The reachability algorithm (Theorem 3.6, page 90) provides a simple way to perform this test. By converting the three-dimensional R-Mesh to two dimensions we have the following result; it is possible to reduce the constants incurred by the conversion and express the result for an R-Mesh of size $N^2 \times NM$ (rather than $O(N^2) \times O(NM)$).

THEOREM 6.21 *The transitive contraction of an N vertex, M edge DAG can be determined on an $N^2 \times NM$ DR-Mesh in $O(1)$ time.*

Distances. Let $\mathcal{G}$ be an N vertex, M edge graph. For any given source vertex s, the problem is to find, for each vertex v, the smallest number of edges in a path (if any) from s to v. We present a constant time, $N^2 \times M(N-1)$ DR-Mesh algorithm for this problem. This algorithm uses the distance embedding technique of Section 2.3.5.

For $0 \leq v, k < N$, $0 \leq e < M$, and $0 \leq \ell < N-1$, index the rows and columns of the DR-Mesh as (v, k) and (e, ℓ), respectively. Configure the DR-Mesh so that each row has two oppositely directed buses each spanning the entire row. The bus in row (v, k) corresponds to vertex v and a path of length k from s to v. Column (e, ℓ) corresponds to edge e and a path of length ℓ from s with e as its last edge.

The algorithm uses the following rather simple observation. Suppose $\mathcal{G}$ has an edge $e = \langle u, v \rangle$ from u to v. If u has a path of length k from s, then v has a path of length $k + 1$ from s. To capture this observation within the DR-Mesh configuration, the algorithm connects the bus in row (u, k) via a directional bus in column (e, k) to the bus

---

[5]For partial orders, an undirected, but suitably oriented, version of the transitive contraction is called the *Hasse diagram*.

in row $(v, k + 1)$, for each $0 \leq k < N - 1$. For the directed graph of Figure 6.4(a), Figure 6.4(b) (page 205) illustrates the resulting DR-Mesh configuration.

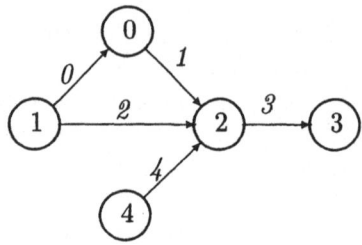

Figure 6.4. (a) Directed graph for the distances algorithm example. Edge numbers are in italics.

The following lemma holds for the above DR-Mesh configuration. Its proof is left as an exercise.

LEMMA 6.22 *With the DR-Mesh configured as explained above, a signal written to bus $(s, 0)$ traverses bus (v, k) if and only if graph $\mathcal{G}$ has a path of length k from vertex s to vertex v.*

With Lemma 6.22, a "lead" processor in row (v, k) can simply read from its bus to determine if $\mathcal{G}$ has a path of length k from the source vertex s to vertex v. Now finding the smallest distance to vertex v is simply a matter of performing neighbor localization on the lead processors of rows (v, k), for $0 \leq k < N$.

Notice that nowhere in the algorithm have we used the fact that the given graph is a DAG. Therefore, the algorithm applies to any directed graph. In fact, it also applies to undirected graphs with each edge replaced by a pair of oppositely directed edges.

THEOREM 6.23 *Let s be a given source vertex of an N vertex, M edge directed graph. The lengths of the shortest paths (if any) from s to all other vertices of the graph can be determined on an $N^2 \times M(N - 1)$ DR-Mesh in $O(1)$ time.*

Topological Sorting. Let $\mathcal{G} = (V, E)$ be an N vertex, M edge DAG. The problem of *topologically sorting* the elements of V is assigning distinct indices $0, 1, \cdots, N-1$ to the elements of V such that for any distinct vertices $u, v \in V$, if $\mathcal{G}$ has a path from u to v, then $index(u) < index(v)$.

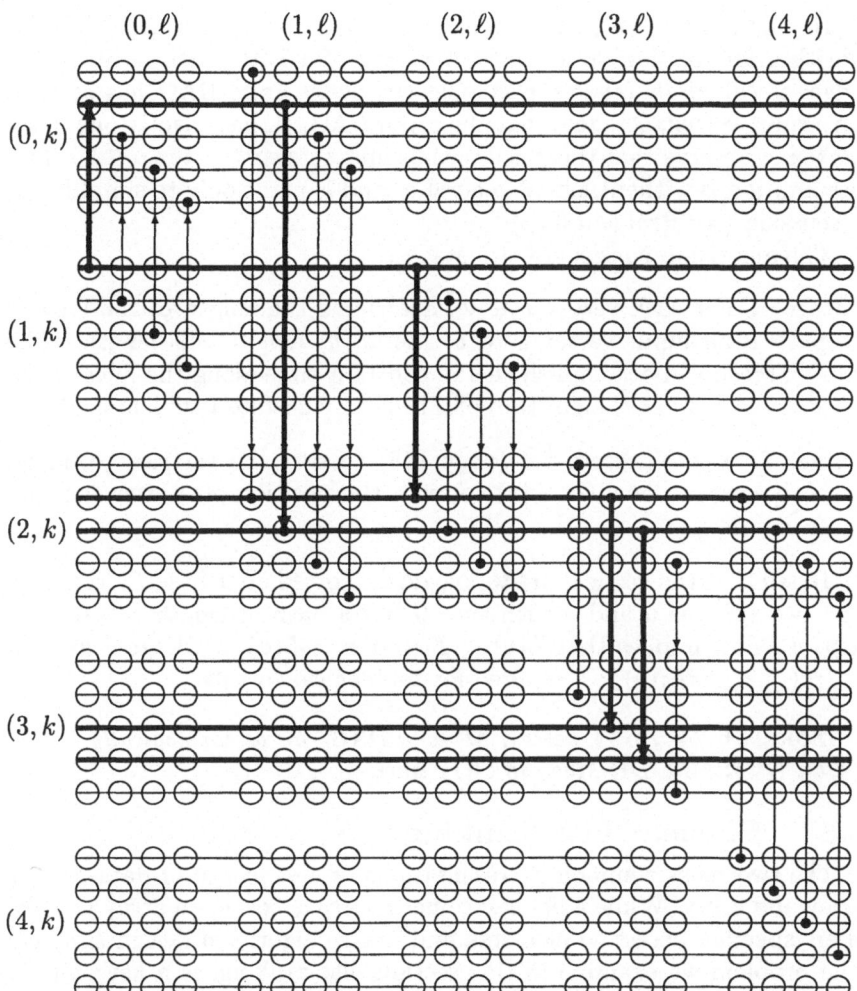

Figure 6.4 (continued)

(b) An illustration of the algorithm for finding distances from vertex 1 of the graph in Part (a). For clarity, the DR-Mesh shows only those external edges needed to show the configuration. Buses traversed by a signal written on row $(1, 0)$ are shown in bold. Observe that since there is no path from vertex 1 to vertex 4, the signal does not traverse any bus corresponding to vertex 4. Also, since vertex 3 has paths of length 2 and 3, the signal traverses buses $(3, 2)$ and $(3, 3)$.

In this section we present a constant time $N^2 \times NM$ DR-Mesh algorithm for topological sorting. A vertex of a DAG with no incoming edges is called an *input vertex*. Clearly, every finite DAG has at least one input vertex. Assume that the given DAG, $\mathcal{G}$, has exactly one input vertex s; observe that there is a path from s to every vertex $v \in V$. This assumption is without loss of generality and is made only to simplify the discussion (see Problem 6.58).

The algorithm consists of two stages.

Stage 1: For each vertex $v \in V$, determine the length of the longest path from input vertex s to v. Let $L(v)$ denote this length. The DR-Mesh can accomplish this in constant time along the lines of the shortest distances algorithm of Theorem 6.23 (see Problem 6.53).

Stage 2: Use Theorem 5.4 (page 158) to sort the vertices based on their largest distances $L(v)$. Assign the position of v after the sort to $index(v)$.

To see that the vertices are topologically sorted after Stage 2, consider any two vertices u and v such that $\mathcal{G}$ has a path of length $x > 0$ from u to v. This implies that $L(v) \geq L(u) + x > L(u)$, so Stage 2 assigns $index(u) < index(v)$, as required for topological sorting.

THEOREM 6.24 *An N vertex, M edge DAG can be topologically sorted on an $N^2 \times NM$ DR-Mesh in $O(1)$ time.*

6.5   Efficient List Ranking

The two most common representations of a sequence of data are an array and a list. While a list can sometimes save space, an array usually offers speedier access to elements and makes algorithm design simpler. The problem we examine in this section, list ranking, is a key step in converting a list into an array.

In Chapter 2, we presented an algorithm (Algorithm 2.8, page 44) for ranking an N element list that runs in constant time on an $N^2 \times N^2$ R-Mesh. This algorithm extends to one that runs in $O\left(\frac{\log N}{\log m}\right)$ time on an $Nm \times Nm$ R-Mesh, for any $1 < m \leq N$ (see Problem 2.47). On an $N \times N$ R-Mesh, this algorithm would run in $O(\log N)$ time. The key idea of performing list ranking on a smaller R-Mesh is to contract the list systematically until it is small enough for Algorithm 2.8 to rank it. It is then straightforward to translate the ranks of elements of the contracted list to those of the original list. (Typically, a list L is contracted by a factor of $m > 1$ into list L' by stringing together every m^{th} element of L in their order in L. If element α of L' has rank r, then element β of L

that is placed x elements after α has rank $rm + x$.) On an $Nm \times Nm$ R-Mesh, the list contracts by a factor of m^t at the end of iteration t.

In this section we describe two list ranking algorithms for $N \times N$ R-Meshes that run much more efficiently than those mentioned above. The first algorithm builds on the ideas of Chapter 2 and uses properties of prime numbers to contract the list extremely rapidly, achieving $O(\log^* N)$ time[6]. The second algorithm uses randomization to select a "balanced" subset of list elements to reduce the problem to a manageable size in $\tilde{O}(1)$ randomized time (that is, constant time with very high probability).

Throughout this section we will sacrifice exactness for clarity by avoiding the use of the ceiling and floor functions (usually in the context of quantities such as $\frac{x}{y}$ or $z^{\frac{a}{b}}$).

6.5.1   The Deterministic Method

The approach used in this section is an extension of the ideas of Section 2.3.5. To make this relationship clear, we construct a generic list ranking algorithm skeleton and refine techniques through increasingly efficient algorithms to obtain a "super-efficient" algorithm.

Thinning out the list to contract its size is central to these algorithms. The concept of an m-sample is pertinent here. Let L be an N element list. For integer $m \geq 2$, an *m-sample* of L, denoted by L/m, is a list of every m^{th} element of L in the same relative order as in L. For example, if $L = \langle a_0, a_1, \cdots, a_7 \rangle$ (in the order shown), then $L/2 = \langle a_0, a_2, a_4, a_6 \rangle$, $L/3 = \langle a_0, a_3, a_6 \rangle$, $L/4 = \langle a_0, a_4 \rangle$, $L/5 = \langle a_0, a_5 \rangle$, $L/6 = \langle a_0, a_6 \rangle$, $L/7 = \langle a_0, a_7 \rangle$, and $L/m = \langle a_0 \rangle$, for all $m > 7$. For integers $m_1, m_2 \geq 2$, observe that an m_1-sample of list L/m_2 is the same as $L/(m_1 m_2)$, an $(m_1 m_2)$-sample of list L. Verify in the example above that $L/6$ is a 3-sample of $L/2$.

It is straightforward to determine an m-sample of an N element list in constant time on an $Nm \times Nm$ R-Mesh (Problem 2.42). In fact, this method gives the modulo m ranks of the elements of the list. The m-sample would simply consist of all elements with rank 0 (modulo m). The R-Mesh can string these elements together as a list (Problem 2.46). Given the ranks of elements of L/m, it is now easy to determine the ranks of elements of the original list L.

Algorithm 6.2 is a generic list ranking algorithm based on the idea of contracting the list, then ranking the contracted list, and finally reconstructing the ranks of elements of the original list.

---

[6]For definition of $\log^* N$, see Footnote 1 on page 125.

Algorithm 6.2 **(Generic List Ranking)**

Model: An $Nm \times Nm$ R-Mesh, where $1 < m \leq N$.

Input: A list, L, of N elements.

Output: The rank of each element of the list.

begin

1. $x_0 \longleftarrow 1; t \longleftarrow 0$

2. **while** $\left(\frac{N}{x_t}\right)^2 > Nm$ **do**   /* while current list is too large */

   $t \longleftarrow t + 1;$

   determine L/x_t, where $1 \leq x_t \leq N$ is an integer

   end_while

   /* List is now small enough */

3. Rank contracted list with Algorithm 2.8

4. Reconstruct ranks of elements of original list

end

The most important part of the algorithm is the procedure for contracting the list by generating an x_t-sample in iteration t of Step 2. The speed of the algorithm depends on the rate at which the list contracts. In general, since the size of the list is $\frac{N}{x_t}$ at the end of iteration t, the algorithm iterates T times where T is the smallest integer such that

$$\frac{N}{x_T} \leq \sqrt{Nm}.$$

Step 3 runs in constant time. A feature of the procedure to convert L/x_{t-1} to L/x_t (Step 2) is that it determines for each element α of $L/x_{t-1} - L/x_t$, its distance from the closest element of L/x_t that precedes α in list L/x_{t-1}. Thus, Step 4 simply reverses the course of the iterative step (Step 2). Therefore, Step 2 solely determines the time complexity of the algorithm. Further, all algorithms we describe in this section execute each iteration in constant time. Thus, the number of iterations indicates the time required by the entire algorithm.

We now examine the ideas of Section 2.3.5 in this setting and develop the basis for more efficient algorithms.

Basic List Ranking. For the algorithm of Problem 2.47, the first iteration determines L/m; that is, $x_1 = m$. In the next iteration it determines the m-sample of L/m—that is, L/m^2; here $x_2 = m^2$. In general at the end of iteration t, it generates L/m^t and $x_t = m^t$. When $\frac{N}{m^T}$ becomes less than $\sqrt{Nm}$, then $T = O\left(\frac{\log N}{\log m}\right)$.

Efficient List Ranking. Make the Basic List Ranking algorithm more efficient as follows. The first iteration proceeds as before. For the second iteration, we have an $\frac{N}{m}$ element list, L/m, and an $\frac{N}{m}m^2 \times \frac{N}{m}m^2$ R-Mesh. So the second iteration can determine an m^2-sample of L/m (that is, L/m^3) in constant time; here $x_2 = m^3$. In general, in t iterations the R-Mesh can determine $L/(m^{2^t-1})$. This leads to an $O\left(\log\left(\frac{\log N}{\log m}\right)\right)$ time algorithm for ranking an N element list on an $Nm \times Nm$ R-Mesh (see Problem 6.62).

Super-Efficient List Ranking. The difference between the algorithms of Problems 2.47 (basic list ranking) and 6.62 (efficient list ranking) is in the latter's more efficient use of the R-Mesh—it uses the entire R-Mesh in every iteration. Its efficiency cannot be improved further, unless the m-sample can be determined more efficiently. This is exactly what the next technique does. It is based on properties of prime numbers. The following lemma is easy to prove.

LEMMA 6.25 *Let π and π' be relatively prime integers (that is, they have no common factor other than 1). For any integer i, if $i \pmod{\pi} = i \pmod{\pi'} = j$, then $i \pmod{\pi\pi'} = j$.*

Let π_i denote the ith prime number. That is, $\pi_1 = 2$, $\pi_2 = 3$, $\pi_3 = 5$, $\pi_4 = 7$, $\pi_5 = 11$, and so on. As discussed above, an $N\pi_i \times N\pi_i$ R-Mesh can determine the π_i-sample of an N element list L in constant time. This sample will include all elements whose ranks (modulo π_i) are 0. If an R-Mesh computes the π_i-sample of L for all $1 \le i \le k$, then by Lemma 6.25 it can obtain a $(\pi_1\pi_2\cdots\pi_k)$-sample of L in constant time. All that this requires is checking if an element of the list is in all the samples—that is, an AND operation which the R-Mesh can perform in constant time.

The following lemma captures the essence of the above observation.

LEMMA 6.26 *Let $m = \pi_1 + \pi_2 + \cdots + \pi_k$ and let $x = \pi_1\pi_2\cdots\pi_k$, then an $Nm \times Nm$ R-Mesh can compute L/x in constant time.*

Recall that in the Basic and Efficient List Ranking algorithms, an $Nm \times Nm$ R-Mesh (representing an m-factor increase in the size of the side) constructs L/m (a reduction in list size by a (linear) factor of m) in constant time. The significance of Lemma 6.26 is that an m-factor increase in the size of the side of the R-Mesh buys a a factor of x (an exponentially larger quantity) reduction in the size of the list.

The super-efficient list ranking algorithm uses the list contraction technique of Lemma 6.26 in Step 2 of the Generic List Ranking algorithm. Since at least one prime number is required for the reduction (that is, $k \geq 1$), we have $m \geq \pi_1 = 2$. We now describe the first few steps of the algorithm on a $2N \times 2N$ R-Mesh.

For the first step, $m_1 = 2 = \pi_1 = x_1$. Thus, the algorithm contracts the N element list L to $L/x_1 = L/2$. We now have an $\frac{N}{2}$ element list and a $4\frac{N}{2} \times 4\frac{N}{2}$ R-Mesh. Consequently for the second step, m_2 can be as large as 4. Since $\pi_1 + \pi_2 = 2 + 3 = 5 > 4$, we once again use $m_2 = 2 = \pi_1 = x_2$. Again the algorithm contracts the list by a factor of 2 and produces $L/4$ at the end of the second iteration. (We could also have used $m_2 = x_2 = \pi_2 = 3$ to produce $L/6$, but this will not alter the time complexity of the algorithm.) The third iteration handles an $\frac{N}{4}$ element list on an $8\frac{N}{4} \times 8\frac{N}{4}$ R-Mesh, so m_3 can be as large as 8. This implies that $m_3 = \pi_1 + \pi_2 = 2 + 3 = 5$ and $x_3 = 2 \cdot 3 = 6$. Consequently, iteration 3 produces $L/24$. In iteration 4, we could use a value for m that is at most 48. Since $2 + 3 + 5 + 7 + 11 + 13 = 41 \leq 48$, the algorithm sets $m_3 = 41$ and $x_3 = 2 \cdot 3 \cdot 5 \cdot 7 \cdot 11 \cdot 13 = 30,030$. Thus, at the end of the third iteration the algorithm produces $L/(24 \cdot 30,030) = L/720,720$. Clearly, the contraction proceeds very rapidly.

The time complexity of the algorithm depends on the reduction factor x that an $Nm \times Nm$ R-Mesh can support for an N element list. Towards this end, we now derive a relationship between m and x.

Relating m and x. Here we relate quantities m and x of Lemma 6.26. This relationship determines the rate at which the list contracts and is crucial to ascertaining the speed of the algorithm. The following is a well known result from number theory.

LEMMA 6.27 *The ith prime number π_i is $\Theta(i \log i)$.*

From this lemma, $m = \Theta\left(\sum_{i=1}^{k} i \log i\right) = O(k^2 \log k) = O(k^3)$. Put differently, $k = \Omega\left(m^{\frac{1}{3}}\right)$. Also $x = \Theta\left(\prod_{i=1}^{k} i \log i\right) = \Omega(k!) = \Omega(8^k) = \Omega(2^{3k})$

$= \Omega\left(2^{3m^{\frac{1}{3}}}\right)$. Therefore beyond a constant point,

$$x \geq 2^{3m^{\frac{1}{3}}}. \tag{6.24}$$

Analysis of the Super-Efficient Algorithm. Let us now examine the list ranking algorithm in light of the above relationship between x and m. As before, assume that the list L is of size N and an $Nm \times Nm$ R-Mesh is available. The algorithm fits the mold of the generic list ranking algorithm (Algorithm 6.2), computing L/x_i at the end of iteration i. Let the relationship in Equation 6.24 hold for any iteration $t \geq c$, where c is a constant. In the following analysis we will only count the number of steps beyond c. While this will make the time complexity analysis easier, it will not affect the result, as c is a constant.

In iteration c, the algorithm computes L/x_c, where $x_c \geq 2^{3m^{\frac{1}{3}}}$. We now have a list of size $\frac{N}{x_c}$ and an $\frac{Nm_c}{x_c} \times \frac{Nm_c}{x_c}$ R-Mesh, where $m_c = mx_c$. Iteration $c + 1$ computes L/x_{c+1}, where $x_{c+1} \geq x_c 2^{3(m_c)^{\frac{1}{3}}} \geq 2^{3(m_c)^{\frac{1}{3}}}$ and we now have a list of size $\frac{N}{x_{c+1}}$ and an $\frac{Nm_{c+1}}{x_{c+1}} \times \frac{Nm_{c+1}}{x_{c+1}}$ R-Mesh, where $m_{c+1} = mx_{c+1}$. The next iteration computes L/x_{c+2}, where $x_{c+2} \geq x_{c+1} 2^{3(m_{c+1})^{\frac{1}{3}}} \geq 2^{3(m_{c+1})^{\frac{1}{3}}}$. We now have a list of size $\frac{N}{x_{c+2}}$ and an $\frac{Nm_{c+2}}{x_{c+2}} \times \frac{Nm_{c+2}}{x_{c+2}}$ R-Mesh, where $m_{c+2} = mx_{c+2}$. In general at the end of iteration $c + t$, the R-Mesh computes L/x_{c+t}, where $x_{c+t} \geq 2^{3(m_{c+t-1})^{\frac{1}{3}}}$. The list size is $\frac{N}{x_{c+t}}$ and an $\frac{Nm_{c+t}}{x_{c+t}} \times \frac{Nm_{c+t}}{x_{c+t}}$ R-Mesh is available, where $m_{c+t} = mx_{c+t} \geq x_{c+t}$. That is,

$$m_{c+t} \geq x_{c+t} \geq 2^{3(m_{c+t-1})^{\frac{1}{3}}} \geq 2^{3(x_{c+t-1})^{\frac{1}{3}}}. \tag{6.25}$$

Given Equation 6.25 with $x_c \geq 1$ (the smallest possible value), x_{c+t} satisfies the inequality

$$\text{for integer } 1 \leq i \leq t, \quad \log^{(i)} x_{c+t} \geq (x_{c+t-i})^{\frac{1}{3}}. \tag{6.26}$$

With $i = t$, Equation 6.26 becomes $\log^{(t)} x_{c+t} \geq x_c \geq 1$, which implies that

$$m_{c+t} \geq x_{c+t} \geq \underbrace{2^{2^{2^{\cdot^{\cdot^{2}}}}}}_{t \text{ times}}. \tag{6.27}$$

If $c + t \geq \log^* N$ in Equation 6.27, then $m_{c+t} \geq N$. Thus, in $O(\log^* N)$ iterations (steps) the R-Mesh can generate L/N, a single element list.

Notice that the result is independent of the quantity m in the $Nm \times Nm$ R-Mesh used. To ensure that at least one prime number is used ($k \geq 1$), the algorithm requires $m \geq 2$. The algorithm also implicitly assumes that the R-Mesh has all the prime numbers necessary for the algorithm. Problem 6.67 addresses the case where the R-Mesh generates these prime numbers. Also this method can be shown to run on an LR-Mesh, which implies that it can be run on an $N \times N$ LR-Mesh with a constant slowdown factor (Theorem 8.4, page 284).

THEOREM 6.28 *A list of N elements can be ranked on an $N \times N$ R-Mesh in $O(\log^* N)$ time.*

6.5.2   The Randomized Approach

The randomized approach decomposes the given list, L, into a number of sub-lists. The algorithm first individually ranks the sub-lists and then combines these "local ranks" to obtain the final rank of elements of the original list, L. If the algorithm decomposes L into few, but large, sub-lists, then the sub-list ranking phase can be too slow. On the other hand, a decomposition into a large number of small sub-lists would make the local rank combination phase very slow. Clearly a balanced decomposition is essential. The algorithm implements this list decomposition by identifying a subset of elements of L at which to cut the list. Therefore key to the randomized approach is the determination of a "balanced subset" of the list, which we formally define below. Consider a list L of N elements. In the following we will abuse notation to denote both the list and the set of its elements by L.

DEFINITION 6.29 *A subset S of list L is a balanced subset if and only if $|S| \leq N^{\frac{2}{3}}$ and every element $x \in L - S$ has a path (in L) of length at most $\sqrt{N}$ to an element of S.*

A balanced subset decomposes list L into at most $N^{\frac{2}{3}}$ sublists, each of which has at most $\sqrt{N}$ elements. The effect is that the elements of a balanced subset are spaced neither too closely nor too far apart. The above definition implies that the last element of L is always included in a balanced subset.

List Ranking with a Balanced Subset. The significance of a balanced subset of a list is that it makes the task of efficiently ranking the list considerably simpler. In this section we will see that given a balanced subset of an N element list, an $N \times N$ R-Mesh can rank the list in constant time. We present a high-level algorithmic description of this method and illustrate it with an example in Figure 6.5. For technical reasons, we assume that elements of the list are ranked from 1 to N, rather than from 0 to $N - 1$ (as was the case so far). Clearly no loss of generality results from this assumption.

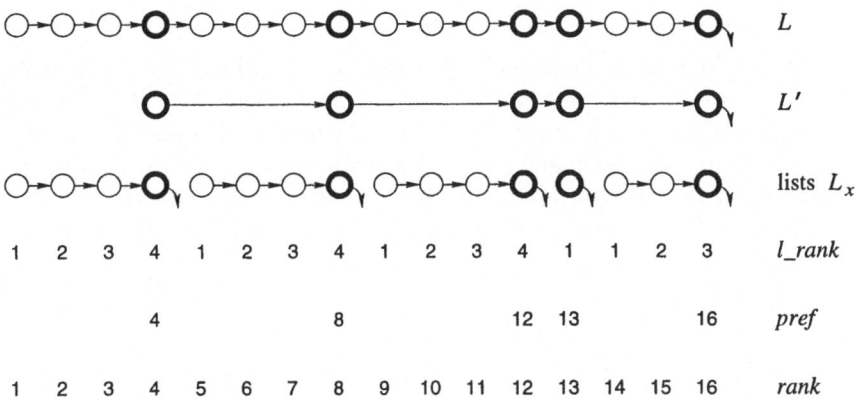

Figure 6.5. An illustration of list ranking with a balanced subset. Elements of the balanced subset are shown in bold.

Algorithm 6.3 (List Ranking with Balanced Subset)

Model: An $N \times N$ R-Mesh.
Input: A list, L, of N elements. A balanced subset S of L.
Output: The rank of each element of the list.

begin

1. Construct list L' of elements of S in the same order in which they occur in L.

2. For each $x \in S$ determine the sublist L_x consisting of all elements of L between x and its predecessor, $pred(x)$, in L'. List L_x includes x but not $pred(x)$. If x is the first element of L', then L_x starts at the first element of L.

3. For each $x \in S$, rank sublist L_x. For each element $k \in L_x$, let $l\_rank(k)$ denote its rank in list L_x. We will refer to this rank as the local rank of k.

4. Arrange the elements of S according to their ranks in L' and find the prefix sums of the local ranks of elements $x \in S$. Let $pref(x)$ denote the result of the above prefix computation corresponding to element x.

5. Determine the final rank of element $k \in L_x$ as follows:

$$rank(k) \longleftarrow l\_rank(k) + pref(pred(x)).$$

end

We now look at the details of Algorithm 6.3 and determine its complexity. Step 1 involves embedding the list in an $N \times N$ R-Mesh. Figure 6.6 shows an example for $N = 7$, where each diagonal processor represents a list element and a bus traverses these processors in the order of the list. In the following we will refer to this bus as the "embedding bus." Now generating list L' is only a matter of performing

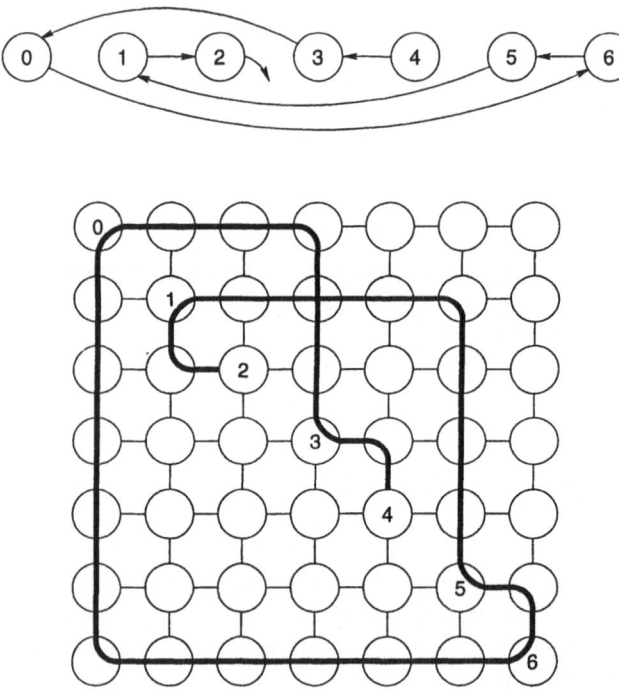

Figure 6.6. An example of list embedding in an $N \times N$ R-Mesh for $N = 7$.

neighbor localization on the elements of S using the embedding bus.

In Step 2, each diagonal processor representing an element of S cuts the embedding bus. Each of the resulting $|S|$ buses represents list L_x, corresponding to element $x \in S$. This structure also conveys the index x to all elements of L_x.

To rank list L_x (Step 3), its elements must first be aggregated to a contiguous portion of the R-Mesh. Since each element of L_x has the value of x, this will serve as the basis for sorting and relocating elements to columns of the R-Mesh (Theorem 5.4, page 158) so that elements of any one list L_x are in adjacent columns. If $|L_x| = N_x$, then list L_x has an $N \times N_x$ R-Mesh available to it. The definition of a balanced subset guarantees that $N_x \leq \sqrt{N}$. Thus, with Problem 2.45, the algorithm ranks list L_x, for each $x \in S$, in constant time.

Algorithm 6.3 uses Theorem 2.17 (page 46) to rank L' (Step 4) in constant time. Observe that since $|L'| \leq N^{\frac{2}{3}}$, the available R-Mesh size is at least $(|L'|)^{\frac{3}{2}} \times (|L'|)^{\frac{3}{2}}$. Now, in constant time, relocate the elements of L' in the order of their ranks, and compute the prefix sums using Lemma 4.14 (page 132). Clearly Step 5 now runs in constant time.

LEMMA 6.30 *Given a balanced subset, a list of N elements can be ranked on an $N \times N$ R-Mesh in $O(1)$ time.*

Observe that the algorithm is, to this point, deterministic. The remainder of this section deals with constructing a balanced subset of a given list.

Randomized Balanced Subset Determination. Consider the following algorithm for generating a balanced subset of an N element list on an $N \times N$ R-Mesh.

Algorithm 6.4 (Randomized Balanced Subset Generation)

Model: An $N \times N$ R-Mesh.

Input: A list, L, of N elements, one element per processor of a row of the R-Mesh.

Output: A balanced subset S of L.

begin

  repeat

    1. For all i, diagonal processor (i, i) selects vertex i as an element of set S with probability $N^{-\frac{5}{12}}$.

    2. Check if S is a balanced subset.

  until S is a balanced subset

end

Clearly, Step 1 runs in constant time. It is not difficult to show that Step 2 also runs in constant time (Problem 6.72). Thus, each iteration of the algorithm runs in constant time. We will show below that, with high probability, the algorithm will find a balanced subset within a constant number of iterations.

For the purpose of the analysis, cut list L into sublists L_i ($1 \leq i \leq 2\sqrt{N}$), each consisting of $\frac{\sqrt{N}}{2}$ contiguous elements of L. (These lists L_i are not to be confused with the lists L_x of Algorithm 6.3.) If Algorithm 6.4 selects at least 1 and at most $\frac{N^{\frac{1}{6}}}{2}$ elements from each sublist L_i, then it selects a balanced subset (Problem 6.73). Thus, the problem boils down to determining the probability[7] of selecting between 1 and $\frac{N^{\frac{1}{6}}}{2}$ elements from each sublist L_i.

Consider a fixed sublist L_i. Let X_j be a random binary variable that is 1 if and only if the jth element of L_i is selected. As is clear from Step 1 of Algorithm 6.4, $\mathbf{Pr}\,[X_j = 1] = N^{-\frac{5}{12}}$. Since each X_j is an independent Bernoulli trial[8] with probability $p = N^{-\frac{5}{12}}$, the size of a random variable $X = X_1 + X_2 + \cdots + X_{\frac{\sqrt{N}}{2}}$ can be bounded by the Chernoff bound[9], with $n = \frac{\sqrt{N}}{2}$, $p = N^{-\frac{5}{12}}$, $\mu = \frac{1}{2}N^{\frac{1}{12}}$, and $\delta = N^{\frac{1}{12}} - 1$ as

$$\mathbf{Pr}\left[X > \frac{1}{2}\left(N^{\frac{1}{6}}\right)\right] \; < \; \left(\frac{e^{\left(N^{\frac{1}{12}}-1\right)}}{N^{\frac{1}{12}}\left(N^{\frac{1}{12}}\right)}\right)^{\frac{1}{2}N^{\frac{1}{12}}}. \tag{6.28}$$

Beyond a constant value for N, Equation 6.28 simplifies to

$$\mathbf{Pr}\left[X > \frac{1}{2}\left(N^{\frac{1}{6}}\right)\right] \; < \; e^{-\frac{1}{24}\left(N^{\frac{1}{6}}\right)}. \tag{6.29}$$

---

[7]The probability of an event $\mathcal{E}$ occurring will be denoted by $\mathbf{Pr}\,[\mathcal{E}]$.

[8]A *Bernoulli trial* is an experiment (such as a coin toss) with only two outcomes, 0 and 1. The probability of outcome 1 (resp., 0) is denoted by p (resp., $1 - p$).

[9]Let $X_1, X_2, \cdots, X_n$ be independent Bernoulli trials with $\mathbf{Pr}\,[X_j = 1] = p$, $\mathbf{Pr}\,[X_j = 0] = 1 - p$ and $0 < p < 1$ (for each $1 \leq j \leq n$). If $X = X_1 + X_2 + \cdots + X_n$ and $\mu = np$, then for any $\delta > 0$,

$$\mathbf{Pr}\,[X > (1 + \delta)\mu] \; < \; \left(\frac{e^{\delta}}{(1 + \delta)^{1+\delta}}\right)^{\mu}.$$

The above probability bound is called the *Chernoff bound*.

Also, $\mathbf{Pr}\,[X = 0] = (1-p)^n = \left(1 - N^{-\frac{5}{12}}\right)^{\frac{\sqrt{N}}{2}}$. Using the fact that for all real x, $\left(1 + \frac{x}{n}\right)^n \leq e^x$, we have

$$\mathbf{Pr}\,[X = 0] \leq e^{-\frac{1}{2}\left(N^{\frac{1}{12}}\right)}. \tag{6.30}$$

Therefore (beyond a constant value for N), the probability of selecting at least one element (Equation 6.30) and at most $\frac{1}{2}\left(N^{\frac{1}{6}}\right)$ elements (Equation 6.29) from any one sublist L_i is

$$\mathbf{Pr}\left[1 \leq X \leq \tfrac{1}{2}\left(N^{\frac{1}{6}}\right)\right] \;>\; 1 - \left(e^{-\frac{1}{24}\left(N^{\frac{1}{6}}\right)} + e^{-\frac{1}{2}\left(N^{\frac{1}{12}}\right)}\right)$$

$$>\; 1 - e^{-\frac{1}{4}\left(N^{\frac{1}{12}}\right)}.$$

This implies that the probability of selecting a balanced subset (by selecting between 1 and $\frac{1}{2}\left(N^{\frac{1}{6}}\right)$ elements from each of the $2\sqrt{N}$ sublists is at least

$$\left(1 - e^{-\frac{1}{4}\left(N^{\frac{1}{12}}\right)}\right)^{2\sqrt{N}} \;\geq\; 1 - 2\sqrt{N}\left(e^{-\frac{1}{4}\left(N^{\frac{1}{12}}\right)}\right).$$

The above simplification is due to Bernoulli's inequality[10]. Thus, the probability of Algorithm 6.4 finding a balanced subset in one iteration is

$$1 - 2\sqrt{N}\left(e^{-\frac{1}{4}\left(N^{\frac{1}{12}}\right)}\right) \;=\; 1 - 2N^{-\left(\frac{N^{\frac{1}{12}}}{4\ln N} - \frac{1}{2}\right)} \;>\; 1 - N^{-c},$$

for sufficiently large N and constant $c \geq 1$. Thus, we have the following lemma.

LEMMA 6.31 *A balanced subset of an N element list can be determined on an $N \times N$ R-Mesh in $\widetilde{O}(1)$ randomized time.*

From Lemmas 6.30 and 6.31, we have the following.

THEOREM 6.32 *A list of N elements can be ranked in an $N \times N$ R-Mesh in $\widetilde{O}(1)$ randomized time.*

---

[10]Bernoulli's Inequality: For real $x > -1$ and integer $x \geq 1$, $(1+x)^n \geq 1 + nx$.

Problems

6.1   Design R-Mesh algorithms to convert between the adjacency matrix
      and edge set of a graph.

6.2   Design an R-Mesh algorithm to determine the degree of each vertex
      of a graph. If the graph has degree bounded by a quantity x (not
      necessarily a constant), then improve your algorithm so that the size
      of the R-Mesh it uses depends on x.

6.3   Consider an "ordered tree" whose edge set is specified in the following
      form. Each edge is represented as $\langle (u, v), (r_u, r_v) \rangle$, where u and v are
      the terminal vertices of the edge. If u has degree d, then the quantity
      $0 \leq r_u < d$ is the rank (or position) of vertex v in an (ordered)
      enumeration of neighbors of u. Two neighbors of u can have the
      same rank only if their relative order is unimportant. Similarly, the
      quantity r_v is the rank of u in the list of neighbors of v.

      Modify the Euler tour algorithm (without altering its performance) to
      create the tour consistent with the ordering of neighbors in ordered
      trees.

6.4   Prove that Algorithm 6.1 runs in $O(T_L(N))$ time, where $T_L(N)$ is
      the time to rank an N element list on an $N \times N$ R-Mesh.

6.5   Adapt Algorithm 6.1 for numbering an N vertex tree in postorder.

6.6   Adapt Algorithm 6.1 for numbering an N vertex binary tree in inorder.

6.7   Design an $N \times N$ R-Mesh algorithm to determine the following sets
      for each vertex v of a rooted, N vertex tree. What is the running
      time of your algorithm? Represent each set as a sequence of N bits
      that indicate membership.

      (a)   The set of descendants of v.

      (b)   The set of leaves in the subtree rooted at v.

      (c)   If previous parts are to be done in constant time, then what
            sized R-Mesh would you use?

6.8   The *lowest common ancestor* of two vertices u and v in a rooted tree is an ancestor w of u and v such that no descendant of w is an ancestor of both u and v.

Construct an R-Mesh algorithm using the Euler tour technique to determine the lowest common ancestor of a given pair of vertices.

6.9   Prove that a sequence $\langle s_0, s_1, \cdots, s_{2N-1} \rangle$ is a preorder-inorder traversal of an N vertex tree if and only if it has the preorder-inorder property.

6.10 Prove that the following sets are the same as the set X defined in Equation 6.6.

(a) $\{\langle \delta(i), q_i \rangle \ : \ 0 \leq i < N\}$

(b) $\{\langle q_i, r_i \rangle \ : \ 0 \leq i < N\}$

6.11 Prove that the relation $\preceq$ of Definition 6.4 is a total order.

6.12 Let X_1 and X_2 be sets of triplets corresponding to the preorder and inorder traversals of a tree. Let $\preceq$ be the total order defined on $X_1 \cup X_2$ (see Problem 6.11). Prove that the preorder and inorder sequences are sorted with respect to $\preceq$.

6.13 Prove Lemma 6.7.

6.14 Write pseudocode to detail the algorithm of Lemma 6.7.

6.15 Section 6.2.1 treats an Euler path of a rooted tree as a list of directed edges of the tree. This problem expresses the Euler path as a list of vertices. Let $\mathcal{T}$ be a rooted binary tree. For each vertex v of the tree, make three copies v_1, v_2, v_3. Create a list L of copies of vertices as described below.

- If v has no left child, then v_2 follows v_1 in list L.
- If v has no right child, then v_3 follows v_2 in list L.
- If u is the left child of v, then u_1 follows v_1 and v_2 follows u_3 in list L.
- If u is the right child of v, then u_1 follows v_2 and v_3 follows u_3 in list L.

Figure 6.7 illustrates this list for a 7 vertex tree.

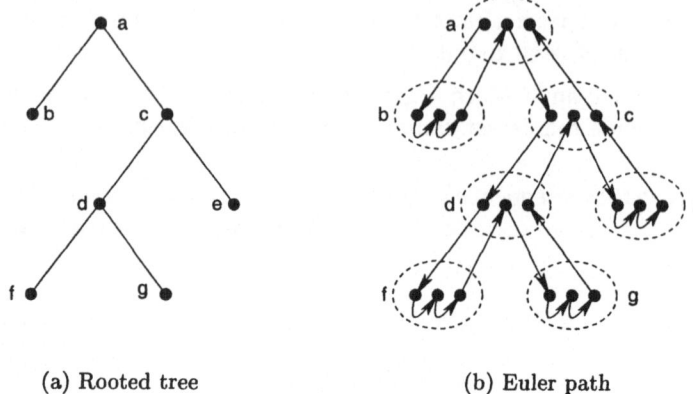

(a) Rooted tree   (b) Euler path

Figure 6.7. An Euler path as a list of vertex copies. The copies v_1, v_2, v_3 of vertex v are shown in part (b) from left to right. For clarity, the copies have not been separately labeled. For this example the list is $\langle a_1, b_1, b_2, b_3, a_2, c_1, d_1, f_1, f_2, f_3, d_2, g_1, g_2, g_3, d_3, c_2, e_1, e_2, e_3, c_3, a_3 \rangle$.

(a)   Prove that list L generates an Euler path of the tree.

(b)   Prove that the sublist of L consisting only of the first copy v_1 of each vertex v is the preorder traversal of the tree.

(c)   Prove that the sublist of L consisting only of the second copy v_2 of each vertex v is the inorder traversal of the tree.

(d)   Prove that the sublist of L consisting only of the third copy v_3 of each vertex v is the postorder traversal of the tree.

(e)   Prove that the sublist of L consisting only of the first and second copies v_1, v_2 of each vertex v is the preorder-inorder traversal of the tree.

6.16   Let Q and R be lists of vertices representing the preorder and inorder traversals of a tree $\mathcal{T}$. Let S be a list of elements of Q and R. Prove that S is a preorder-inorder traversal of $\mathcal{T}$ if and only if it satisfies the following four conditions.

• S maintains the relative order of elements of Q.

• S maintains the relative order of elements of R.

• In list S, each element of Q precedes the corresponding element of R.

- No element of S that satisfies the above three conditions can be placed earlier in the list.

6.17 The tree reconstruction algorithm based on Lemma 6.7 uses an $N \times 2N$ R-Mesh (see page 191). Without using the fact that this algorithm runs on an LR-Mesh (on which algorithms scale optimally; see Theorem 8.4, page 284), prove that an $N \times N$ LR-Mesh suffices for the algorithm as stated in Lemma 6.8.

6.18 The algorithm of Lemma 6.8 specifies the tree in terms of left and right children of a vertex. How would you convert it to a set of pointers to parents of non-root vertices?

6.19 Given the postorder and inorder numbering of an N vertex, binary tree, design a constant time $N \times N$ R-Mesh algorithm to reconstruct the tree.

6.20 An ordered forest, $\mathcal{F}$, is a sequence, $\langle \mathcal{T}_1, \mathcal{T}_2, \cdots, \mathcal{T}_k \rangle$, of rooted trees $\mathcal{T}_i$, for $1 \leq i \leq k$. Let $\mathcal{T}_1$ have root r. If r has $x \geq 1$ children, then let the subtrees rooted at these children be $\mathcal{T}_{1,i}$, for $1 \leq i \leq x$. Denote by $\mathcal{F}'$ and $\mathcal{F}''$ the ordered forests $\langle \mathcal{T}_{1,1}, \mathcal{T}_{1,2}, \cdots, \mathcal{T}_{1,x} \rangle$ and $\langle \mathcal{T}_2, \mathcal{T}_3, \cdots, \mathcal{T}_k \rangle$, respectively.
Recursively define a binary tree $\mathcal{B}(\mathcal{F})$ as follows.

- The root of $\mathcal{B}(\mathcal{F})$ is r.
- The left subtree of $\mathcal{B}(\mathcal{F})$ is $\mathcal{B}(\mathcal{F}')$.
- The right subtree of $\mathcal{B}(\mathcal{F})$ is $\mathcal{B}(\mathcal{F}'')$.

(a) If the preorder enumeration of $\mathcal{F}$ enumerates the vertices of the constituent trees in the given order, then prove that $\mathcal{F}$ and $\mathcal{B}(\mathcal{F})$ have the same preorder sequence.

(b) Prove that the postorder sequence of $\mathcal{F}$ is the inorder enumeration of $\mathcal{B}(\mathcal{F})$.

(c) Prove that given the preorder and postorder enumerations of an ordered forest, an R-Mesh can reconstruct the forest in constant time. What is the size of the R-Mesh for your algorithm?

6.21 Prove Lemma 6.10.

6.22 Explain how the minimum spanning tree algorithm of Section 6.3.1 runs on an $M \times MN$ R-Mesh. (Using Theorem 3.1, page 80, to translate the three-dimensional $N \times M \times M$ R-Mesh to two dimensions could result in a larger R-Mesh.) Is an $N \times MN$ R-Mesh sufficient? How would you run it in constant time on an $M\sqrt{N} \times M(2 + \sqrt{N})$ R-Mesh?

6.23   Modify the minimum spanning tree algorithm of Section 6.3.1 to determine a minimum spanning forest of a (not necessarily connected) graph. What are the resource bounds of your algorithm?

6.24   Design a constant time $N \times N$ CREW R-Mesh algorithm to determine the connected components of an N vertex graph with a constant number of connected components.

6.25   Design a constant time connected components algorithm for an N vertex graph on a CREW three-dimensional $N \times N \times N$ R-Mesh.

6.26   Show that the connected components algorithm of Theorem 6.12 runs in constant time on a separable R-Mesh (see page 75). That is, prove that each step of the algorithm runs in constant time on either an LR-Mesh or an FR-Mesh.

6.27   Design a constant time $N \times N$ R-Mesh algorithm to determine whether an N vertex graph is connected.

6.28   A *cut vertex* of a graph is one whose removal increases the number of components of a graph.

       Design a constant time R-Mesh algorithm to determine all cut vertices of a graph.

6.29   A *bridge* of a graph is an edge whose removal increases the number of components of a graph.

       Design a constant time R-Mesh algorithm to determine all bridges of a graph.

6.30   A *bipartite graph* is one whose vertices can be partitioned into sets V_1 and V_2 in such a way that the graph has no edge between two vertices of V_1 or two vertices of V_2. Put differently, a bipartite graph is one with no odd-length cycles.

    (a)   If A is the adjacency matrix of an N vertex bipartite graph and if I is an $N \times N$ identity matrix, then define

$$B = (A - I) \times (A - I) + I.$$

Prove that B has a 1 in row u and column v if and only if $u = v$ or there is a path of even length between u and v.

(b) Design an R-Mesh algorithm to determine whether a given graph is bipartite.

6.31 In Section 6.3.2.2 we outlined a method to convert the connected components of an N vertex graph into its transitive closure in constant time on an $N \times N$ R-Mesh. Use the same R-Mesh to convert the transitive closure (input as the adjacency matrix A^*) into the connected components in constant time.

6.32 Many algorithms of Section 6.3 assume a graph to be represented as an adjacency matrix. Modify each of these algorithms to accept an edge list as input. Each modified algorithm must run in the same time as the original algorithm, and use no more processors than the original algorithm. Whenever possible, try to reduce the number of processors further.

6.33 Prove that the relation R defined in Section 6.3.2.3 is an equivalence relation.

6.34 Consider Rules (a), (b), and (c) for links of the graph $\mathcal{G}'$ in Stage 4 of the biconnected components algorithm of Section 6.3.2.3. Prove for each link of $\mathcal{G}'$ that only one of the three rules applies.

6.35 Design a constant time algorithm to determine whether a given graph is biconnected. Your algorithm must use fewer processors than the algorithm for determining the biconnected components of the graph (Theorem 6.16).

6.36 Prove Equation 6.15.

6.37 The biconnected components algorithm of Section 6.3.2.3 requires the graph to be connected. Modify the algorithm to work for graphs with more than one connected component. What are the resource bounds for your algorithm?

6.38 Prove Lemma 6.17.

6.39 Prove Equation 6.23.

6.40 Let $\oplus$ be an associative binary operation. Suppose that, for $X \geq N$, an $X \times Y$ R-Mesh can compute in T steps the quantity $a_1 \oplus a_2 \oplus \cdots \oplus a_N$, given inputs $a_1, a_2, \cdots, a_N$ in N contiguous elements of a row of the R-Mesh.

Let A and B be two $N \times N$ matrices whose product is as defined in Equation 6.19. Prove that an $N \times NY \times X$ R-Mesh can multiply A and B in $O(T)$ time.

6.41 The minimum spanning tree algorithm of Theorem 6.20 assumes edge weights to be distinct. Modify the algorithm to adapt to graphs whose edge weights need not be distinct.

6.42 Prove that for any $1 < m \leq N$, an $N \times Nm \times N$ R-Mesh can find the all-pairs shortest distances of an N vertex graph in $O\left(\frac{\log^2 N}{\log m}\right)$ time.

6.43 Prove that for any $1 < m \leq N$, an $N \times Nm \times N$ R-Mesh can find the minimum spanning tree of an N vertex weighted graph in $O\left(\frac{\log^2 N}{\log m}\right)$ time.

6.44 Prove that an $N \times N \times N$ R-Mesh can solve any N-sized instance of the restricted algebraic path problem in $O(\log^2 N)$ time.

6.45 Extend the reachability algorithm of Section 3.1.5 to a CRCW DR-Mesh algorithm that finds the transitive closure of a directed graph in constant time.

6.46 A directed graph is *strongly connected* if for every pair u, v of vertices, u is reachable from v and v is reachable from u.

Use the reachability algorithm of Section 3.1.5 to determine if a graph is strongly connected.

6.47 A *strongly connected component* of a directed graph $\mathcal{G}$ is a maximally strongly connected subgraph $\mathcal{G}'$ of $\mathcal{G}$; that is, any new vertex added to $\mathcal{G}'$ cannot reach or will not be reachable from all other vertices.

Design an algorithm to determine the strongly connected components of a directed graph in constant time. What are the type and size of R-Mesh used for your algorithm?

6.48 Use the algebraic path problem technique to determine the transitive closure of a directed N vertex graph in $O(\log N)$ time. Use a (non-directed) R-Mesh without concurrent writing ability for your algorithm.

Extend your algorithm to find the strongly connected components (see Problem 6.47) of the graph in $O(\log N)$ time.

6.49 Write pseudocode for the $N \times N \times M$ DR-Mesh algorithm for transitive contraction.

6.50 Since a DR-Mesh is not known to be scalable, translating an $N \times N \times M$ three-dimensional DR-Mesh algorithm to two dimensions using Theorem 3.1 (page 80) results in a $(7N + N^2) \times (6MN)$ DR-Mesh.

Explain how the algorithm of Theorem 6.21 works in constant time on an $N^2 \times NM$ DR-Mesh.

6.51 Describe the port partitions needed in the DR-Mesh to achieve the configuration for the distances algorithm of Section 6.4.2.

6.52 Prove Lemma 6.22.

6.53 Design an algorithm to determine the maximum distance from a source vertex s to each other vertex of a DAG.

Will your algorithm work for a directed graph with cycles? Explain.

6.54 Adapt the algorithm of Theorem 6.23 to work for undirected graphs. Explain why the modified algorithm will or will not run on a non-directed R-Mesh.

6.55 Use the distances algorithm with source s to find a spanning tree of a graph rooted at vertex s.

6.56 The *diameter* of a graph is the largest of the shortest distances between all vertex pairs.

If a graph is given to have diameter d, then use this fact to improve the resource bounds of the distances algorithm of Theorem 6.23.

6.57 Let $\preceq$ be a partial order on a set S (see Footnote 1 on page 154). Element x is a *minimal element* of the partial order if no other element is "smaller" than x. That is, there is no $y \in S$ such that $y \preceq x$.

Design a constant time DR-Mesh algorithm to determine all minimal elements of a partial order (represented as a DAG).

6.58   The topological sorting algorithm of Section 6.4.2 assumes the graph to have only one input vertex (that has no incoming edges). How would you modify the algorithm for a DAG with multiple input vertices?

6.59   The topological sorting algorithm of Section 6.4.2 assumed the DAG to have a least element. Modify the algorithm to run within the same resource bounds if the DAG has no least element; that is, if it has multiple minimal elements (see Problem 6.57).

6.60   Let $\preceq$ be a partial order on a set S (see Footnote 1 on page 154). For any $x, y \in S$, an element $z \in S$ is an *upper bound* for the pair x and y if and only if $x, y \preceq z$. Element z is the *least upper bound* (or lub) if for all upper bounds w of x, y, $z \preceq w$. A pair of elements may not have an lub. In an analogous manner define the *lower bound* and the *greatest lower bound* (glb) for any pair of elements of S.

Design a constant time DR-Mesh algorithm to determine the lubs and glbs (if they exist) of all vertex pairs of a partial order (represented as a DAG).

6.61   Let $\preceq$ be a partial order on a set S (see Footnote 1 on page 154). An element ℓ is the *least element* if and only if for every $x \in S$, $\ell \preceq x$. In an analogous manner, the *greatest element* g satisfies $x \preceq g$ for every $x \in S$.

Let the partial order have least element ℓ and greatest element g. Also let each pair of elements $x, y \in S$ have an lub and a glb (see Problem 6.60).

An element x is said to be a *complement* of element y if and only if the lub of x and y is g and their glb is ℓ.

Design a constant time DR-Mesh algorithm to determine all complements (if any) of each element of the partially ordered set S.

6.62   Without using Theorem 6.28, prove that for $m > 1$, an $Nm \times Nm$ R-Mesh can rank a list of N elements in $O\left(\log\left(\frac{\log N}{\log m}\right)\right)$ time.

6.63   Prove that the algorithm of Problem 6.62 can run on an LR-Mesh (see Section 3.1.1).

6.64 Without using Theorem 6.28, prove that a $2N \times 2N$ R-Mesh can rank a list of N elements in $O(\log \log N)$ time.
Note: It is possible to design the algorithm to run on an LR-Mesh (see Problem 6.62) and so an $N \times N$ LR-Mesh suffices (see Theorem 8.4, page 284).

6.65 The "Basic List Ranking" algorithm (see page 209) has similarities with the prefix sums algorithm (Algorithm 2.4, page 32) and the priority simulation algorithm of Theorem 3.5 (page 86). Is it possible to redesign the above prefix sums and priority simulation algorithms as in Problem 6.62 so that they run on an $Nm \times Nm$ R-Mesh in $O\left(\log\left(\frac{\log N}{\log m}\right)\right)$ time? Explain your answer.

6.66 Prove Lemma 6.25.

6.67 The $O(\log^* N)$ deterministic time list ranking algorithm uses the first k prime numbers, $\pi_1, \pi_2, \cdots, \pi_k$, for some integer $k \geq 1$. The number of prime numbers it can use in an iteration depends on the size of the list during that iteration relative to the available R-Mesh size. Assuming a $2N \times 2N$ R-Mesh to be available, what is the largest number of prime numbers (largest value of k) that the algorithm can employ in any given iteration? How will the R-Mesh generate these k prime numbers in $O(\log^* N)$ time?

6.68 Write a detailed algorithmic description of the super-efficient deterministic list ranking method of Theorem 6.28.

6.69 Show that the algorithm of Theorem 6.28 runs on an LR-Mesh (see Section 3.1.1). This allows a $2N \times 2N$ LR-Mesh algorithm to run without asymptotic loss of speed on an $N \times N$ LR-Mesh.

6.70 Let L be an N element list. *Deterministic coin tossing* is a technique that uses N processors to generate a 3-*ruling set* $S \subseteq L$ such that the following conditions hold.

- Each processor holds one element of L and pointers to its successor and predecessor in the list.
- The algorithm runs in $O(\log^* N)$ time.
- No two elements of S are adjacent in L.

- Let $s_1, s_2, \cdots, s_k$ be the elements of S in their order within L. Then before s_1, and after s_k and between any s_i, s_{i+1} (where $1 \leq i < k$), list L has at most 3 elements.

Use deterministic coin tossing to rank an N-element list in $O(\log^* N)$ time on an $N \times N$ R-Mesh, without using the algorithm described in Section 6.5.1.

6.71 Step 4 of Algorithm 6.3 requires relocation of the list. Explain how you would maintain the pointers through this relocation.

Prove that given such a general balanced subset of a list, an $N \times N$ R-Mesh can rank an N element list in constant time.

6.72 Given a subset S of an N element list, design a constant time algorithm to check whether S is a balanced subset on an $N \times N$ R-Mesh.

6.73 Let L be an N element list, and let L_i (where $1 \leq i \leq 2\sqrt{N}$) be sublists, each consisting of $\frac{\sqrt{N}}{2}$ contiguous elements of L. If S contains N_i elements (where $1 \leq N_i \leq \frac{N^{\frac{1}{6}}}{2}$) from each list L_i, then prove that S is a balanced subset of L.

6.74 Let $Prob(1) \geq 1 - 2\sqrt{N}\left(e^{-\frac{1}{4}\left(N^{\frac{1}{12}}\right)}\right)$ denote the probability that Algorithm 6.4 generates a balanced subset in one iteration.

 (a) For $t \geq 1$, determine $Prob(t)$, the probability of Algorithm 6.4 terminating in exactly t iterations.

 (b) Prove that the expected number of iterations for Algorithm 6.4 is $\frac{1}{Prob(1)}$.

6.75 The definition of a balanced subset S of an N element list L requires S to have at most $N^{\frac{2}{3}}$ elements with at most $\sqrt{N}$ list elements between successive elements of S. Consider a more general definition of a balanced subset S that has at most N^{ϵ_1} elements and at most N^{ϵ_2} list elements between successive elements of S, for some constants $\epsilon_1, \epsilon_2 > 0$ such that $\frac{\epsilon_1}{2} < 1 - \epsilon_2 < \epsilon_1$.

Will Algorithm 6.3 run in constant time for this new definition of a balanced set? For Algorithm 6.4, will the probability of running in constant time be any higher?

Bibliographic Notes

Cormen *et al.* [65] presented a good collection of sequential graph algorithms. A variety of sources exist for parallel graph algorithms on various traditional parallel models [142, 165, 174, 279].

The Euler tour technique and its application to tree problems is due to Tarjan and Vishkin [309]. Its adaptation to the R-Mesh is a modification of Trahan, Vaidyanathan, and Subbaraman's tree algorithms for the RMBM [324]. Lin [187] also independently developed an Euler tour algorithm with the same resource bounds.

The tree reconstruction algorithm is based on a PRAM solution for the problem due to Olariu *et al.* [238]. Here the authors reduced the problem of generating a preorder-inorder sequence to that of merging two sorted arrays, an easier problem than sorting on the PRAM. On the R-Mesh, however, both sorting and merging run in constant time. Chen *et al.* [53] described its adaptation to the R-Mesh.

Most of the algorithms of Section 6.3 are based on Wang and Chen's PARBS algorithms [346] and Trahan, Vaidyanathan, and Subbaraman's RMBM algorithms [324]. The minimum spanning tree algorithm is based on Kruskal's algorithm [164]. The sorting algorithms of Theorems 5.4 and 5.10 allow a better size bound than the original MST algorithm of Wang and Chen. Pan and Lin [249] developed an $N \times N \times M$ R-Mesh algorithm without sorting by using Lemma 6.10 where graph $\mathcal{G}_i$ contains all edges with weights less than the weight of edge e_i. Observe that this does not require sorting edges by weight. Pan and Lin also developed algorithms for MST verification, construction of a spanning tree, and spanning tree verification.

The biconnected components algorithm was first designed by Tarjan and Vishkin [309] for the PRAM. Wang and Chen [346] pointed to an alternative algorithm that works on a smaller R-Mesh for dense graphs. The techniques for biconnected components are also useful to translate the ear decomposition algorithm of Maon *et al.* [198] and Miller and Ramachandran [212] to the R-Mesh. Jájá [142] provided a detailed treatment of these PRAM algorithms.

The algebraic path problem approach has been studied in various contexts [171, 178, 237, 280, 284, 308]. Maggs and Plotkin [195] expressed the minimum spanning tree problem as an instance of the algebraic path problem. The R-Mesh implementation of this technique is due to Chen *et al.* [54]. The results for DAGs are adaptations of Trahan, Vaidyanathan, and Subbaraman's algorithms for the RMBM [323].

The list ranking algorithms of Section 6.5 are based on the work of Hayashi *et al.* [134]. They used the term "good ruling set" instead of "balanced subset" (see Definition 6.29). The result of Lemma 6.27 is often called the prime number theorem; several sources [78, 128, 141, 171, 292] provide additional discussion of this topic. Motwani and Raghavan [220] described randomized algorithms and discussed Chernoff bounds in detail. Mitrinović [217] included a comprehensive discussion of inequalities, including the Bernoulli inequality and the inequality used for Equation 6.30.

Problem 6.8 is based on Lin [187]. The solutions to Problems 6.27–6.31 can be found in Wang and Chen [346]. Cole and Vishkin [60] proposed the concept of deterministic coin tossing (Problem 6.70) for the PRAM model.

Other graph problems have been addressed in the context of various reconfigurable models [4, 5, 14, 153, 201].

Chapter 7

COMPUTATIONAL GEOMETRY & IMAGE PROCESSING

We now turn to two application areas that have been sources of many problems to which the R-Mesh has been fruitfully applied: computational geometry and image processing. Both areas deal with relations among a large number of points. Both have problems that benefit from the R-Mesh's ability to configure its buses to conform to input data and the body of arithmetic algorithms for the R-Mesh. For image processing problems, the mesh structure naturally matches the arrangement of an array of pixels comprising an image.

For these reasons, and also because several computational geometry problems find application in image processing, we treat these topics in the same chapter. Many of the R-Mesh techniques used here arose in earlier chapters. (Researchers developed some techniques, however, in the original setting of image processing problems, such as an efficient algorithm for multiple addition developed for solving a histogram problem.) We will first deal with computational geometry, then image processing. Under computational geometry, we will study algorithms for finding the convex hull of a set of planar points, several problems related to convex polygons, identifying the nearest neighbors of a set of points, constructing a Voronoi diagram (or tessellation of the plane) for a set of planar points, constructing the Euclidean minimum spanning tree, and triangulation. Under image processing, the problems we will investigate include labeling connected components in an image, constructing a histogram, template matching, constructing a quadtree representation of an image, computing moments of an image, and computing transforms of an image.

7.1   Computational Geometry

The field of computational geometry deals, essentially, with developing algorithms to solve geometric problems on a computer. Most of the topics with which it works are discrete and combinatorial. It finds applications in many areas including pattern recognition, motion planning in robotics, image processing, VLSI design, statistics, database search, and computer graphics. This section describes R-Mesh algorithms for a number of computational geometry problems, starting with convex hull.

7.1.1   Convex Hull

A *convex polygon* is a polygon for which a line segment between any two points on the boundary or in the interior of the polygon lies on or within the boundary of the polygon. The *convex hull* of a set of N points in the plane is the convex polygon with smallest area enclosing the points. The *upper hull* (*lower hull*) is the upper (lower) portion of the convex hull between the point with minimum x-coordinate and the point with maximum x-coordinate. Figure 7.1 shows an example. An *upper*

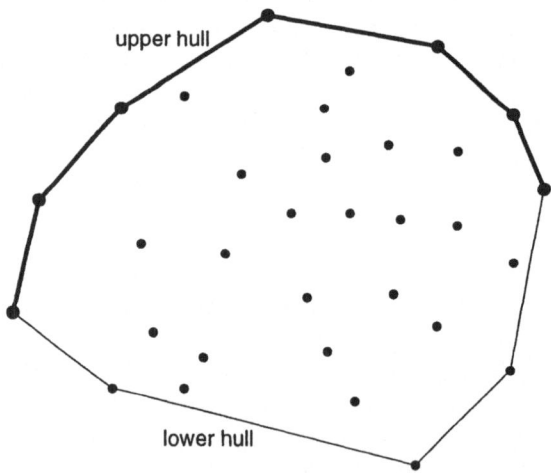

Figure 7.1.   Convex hull of a set of planar points, with the upper hull shown in bold.

supporting line (or an *upper common tangent*) for two sets of points S and T is a line through one point in S and one point in T such that all other points in S and T are below the line; see Figure 7.2. A *lower supporting line* (or a *lower common tangent*) is defined analogously.

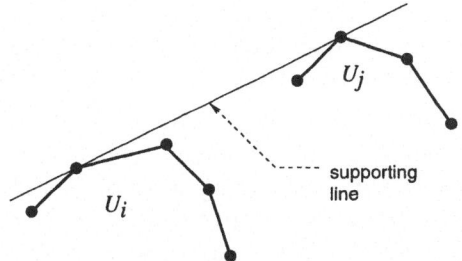

Figure 7.2. Example of supporting line for two convex hulls U_i and U_j.

The convex hull problem has received extensive attention from both sequential and parallel algorithm designers as it is a basic problem with wide applications. Since sorting N elements reduces to the problem of finding the convex hull of a set of N points, all sorting lower bounds apply to convex hull as well (see Problem 7.1). Consequently, the convex hull problem requires $\Omega(N \log N)$ sequential time (or work) and has $\Omega(N^2)$ AT^2 complexity. If the points are initially sorted (say, by x-coordinate), then sequential algorithms exist to solve the convex hull problem optimally in $\Theta(N)$ time.

We begin with an AT^2 optimal, constant time algorithm on an $N \times N$ R-Mesh that sorts the points, then partitions the problem into subproblems and merges their solutions. Following that, we describe an algorithm that finds the convex hull of a set of pre-sorted points with optimal work in $O(\log \log^2 N)$ time[1] using only $\frac{\sqrt{N}}{\log \log N} \times \frac{\sqrt{N}}{\log \log N}$ processors.

7.1.1.1 A Constant Time Algorithm

Let $S = \{s_0, s_1, \ldots, s_{N-1}\}$ be a set of N points in the plane, with each point s_i represented by its coordinates, (x_i, y_i). To simplify the algorithm description, assume that no three points are collinear and that no two points share the same x or y coordinate. (One can modify the algorithm to work with these assumptions removed; see Problem 7.2.) We will construct an algorithm for an $N \times N$ R-Mesh $\mathcal{R}$ that will determine the convex hull of S in $O(1)$ time. The general idea is to compute the upper hulls of clusters of points from S, then draw the supporting line for each pair of these upper hulls. This determines which points in the upper hulls will be in the overall upper hull of S. The algorithm then does the same thing for lower hulls. In the following discussion, we will treat only the upper hull, as steps for the lower hull follow on the same lines.

---

[1]Let $\log \log^2 N$ denote $(\log \log N)^2$.

R-Mesh $\mathcal{R}$ first sorts the points in S according to ascending order of x-coordinate in constant time (Theorem 5.4, page 158). Next, partition $\mathcal{R}$ into $\sqrt{N}$ sub-R-Meshes $\mathcal{R}_0, \mathcal{R}_1, \ldots, \mathcal{R}_{\sqrt{N}-1}$ (from left to right), each of size $N \times \sqrt{N}$. Each $\mathcal{R}_j$ holds $\sqrt{N}$ sorted points of S; denote these as S_j. Observe that this partitioning of points among sub-R-Meshes partitions S into $\sqrt{N}$ non-overlapping slices of $\sqrt{N}$ points each.

Each $\mathcal{R}_j$ now determines the upper hull U_j for its set of points S_j in $O(1)$ time (by an algorithm specified below—Lemma 7.4). Let the top row of $\mathcal{R}_j$ hold the points of U_j.

Partition $\mathcal{R}$ into N sub-R-Meshes of size $\sqrt{N} \times \sqrt{N}$, denoted $\mathcal{M}_{i,j}$, for $0 \le i, j < \sqrt{N}$. (Equivalently, partition each $\mathcal{R}_j$, for $0 \le j < \sqrt{N}$, into $\sqrt{N}$ sub-R-Meshes of size $\sqrt{N} \times \sqrt{N}$, $\mathcal{M}_{i,j}$, for $0 \le i < \sqrt{N}$.) The top row of $\mathcal{M}_{0,j}$ holds the points of the upper hull U_j, for each j. Broadcast the points of U_j to each $\mathcal{M}_{i,j}$, then $\mathcal{M}_{j,j}$ broadcasts the points of U_j to each $\mathcal{M}_{j,k}$, for $0 \le k < \sqrt{N}$. Each $\mathcal{M}_{i,j}$ now holds U_i and U_j.

Each $\mathcal{M}_{i,j}$, for $i \le j$, now determines the supporting line for U_i and U_j; see Figure 7.2. $\mathcal{M}_{i,j}$ does this in constant time.

We leave the proof of the following lemma as Problem 7.3.

LEMMA 7.1 *Let U_1 and U_2 each be upper hulls such that all points in U_1 are to the left of all points in U_2. A $\sqrt{N} \times \sqrt{N}$ R-Mesh can compute the supporting line of U_1 and U_2 in $O(1)$ time.*

At this point, the $N \times N$ R-Mesh $\mathcal{R}$ holds supporting lines for each pair of upper hulls U_i and U_j and must determine which points on supporting lines and which points in the upper hulls of subsets of points S_j will be in the overall convex hull of S. To do so, $\mathcal{R}$ must check for each supporting line whether all the points of S are on or below the line. R-Mesh $\mathcal{R}$ broadcasts the points in each U_j down the columns. Each row then holds all the points in the upper hulls of the slices. Each sub-R-Mesh $\mathcal{M}_{i,j}$, for $i \le j$, then broadcasts the two points defining its supporting line on row j of its $\sqrt{N}$ rows. Each processor in the row checks whether the point it holds is on or below the line, then $\mathcal{R}$ ANDs the results on each row. If the result is true, then $\mathcal{R}$ can eliminate all the points between (in the x-direction) the two points defining the supporting line as they will not be part of the convex hull. Finally, $\mathcal{R}$ can compact the remaining convex hull points to the first row.

THEOREM 7.2 *The convex hull of N points in the plane can be computed on an $N \times N$ R-Mesh in $O(1)$ time.*

Now, to fully establish the above result, we must describe the less efficient convex hull algorithm that it uses as a tool. This algorithm computes the convex hull of $\sqrt{N}$ sorted points $Q = \left(q_0, \ldots, q_{\sqrt{N}-1}\right)$ on an $N \times \sqrt{N}$ R-Mesh, $\mathcal{Z}$. (Note how the algorithm of Theorem 7.2, by sorting and partitioning, is able to determine the convex hull of N points on an $N \times N$ R-Mesh by using a tool that needs an $N^2 \times N$ R-Mesh to compute the convex hull of N points.)

Identify the points with maximum and minimum x-coordinate and maximum and minimum y-coordinate (Lemma 2.14, page 40). Denote these points as q_E, q_W, q_N, and q_S, respectively. Using these four extreme points, partition Q into five subsets Q_{NE}, Q_{NW}, Q_{SW}, Q_{SE}, and Q_{other} as follows. Let (x_E, y_E) and (x_N, y_N) denote the x, y-coordinates of q_E and q_N, respectively. Then $Q_{NE} = \{q_j \;:\; x_N \leq x_j \leq x_E \text{ and } y_E \leq y_j \leq y_N\}$. Define Q_{NW}, Q_{SW}, and Q_{SE} correspondingly using q_N and q_W, q_S and q_W, and q_S and q_E, respectively. Set Q_{other} comprises the remaining points in Q. (See Figure 7.3.) The upper hull of Q is the concatenation

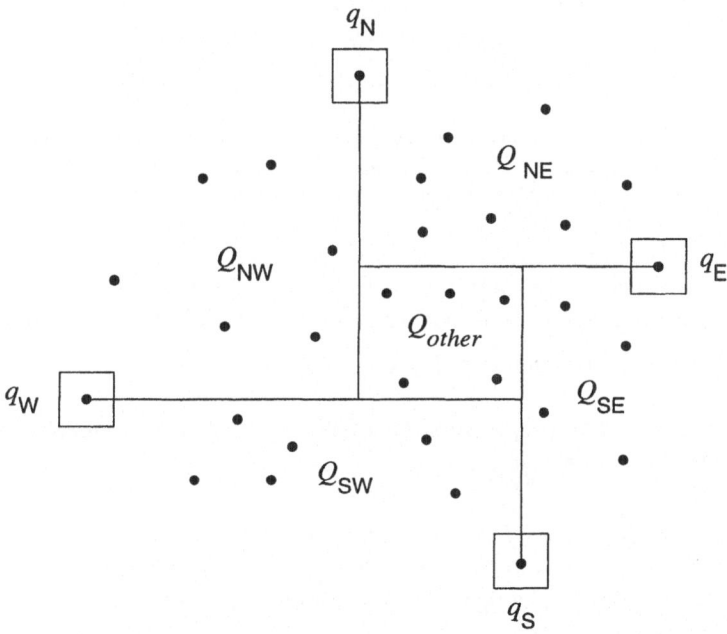

Figure 7.3. Partitioning a set Q of points using the four extreme points.

of the upper hulls of Q_{NE} and Q_{NW}, and the lower hull of Q is the concatenation of the lower hulls of Q_{SW} and Q_{SE}. From here on, we will

describe the steps only to compute the upper hull of Q_{NE} as the others
follow similarly.

Sort points in Q_{NE} by increasing y-coordinate (Theorem 5.4, page 158).
Denote this sequence by $D = \langle d_0 = q_E, d_1, d_2, \ldots, d_t = q_N \rangle$. For each d_j,
for $0 \le j \le t$, find the point $d_{f(j)}$ such that $j < f(j) \le t$ and the angle
formed by the line through points $d_{f(j)}$, d_j, and the negative direction
of the x-axis is maximum. (See Figure 7.4.)

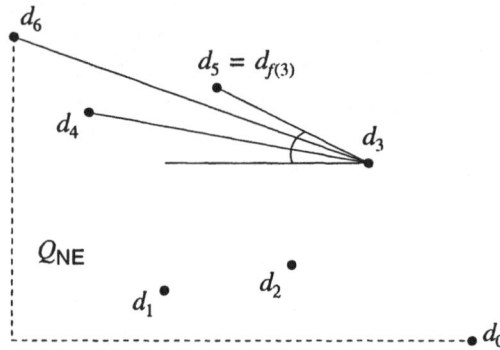

Figure 7.4. For a given point d_3 in Q_{NE}, $\mathcal{R}$ finds the angles formed by d_3, to each
other point with higher y-coordinate in Q_{NE}, and the negative direction of the x-axis.
Point $d_5 = d_{f(3)}$ is the point with the largest such angle.

Now, find the prefix maxima of the $f(j)$ values for all j using Theorem 7.3 stated below (see also Problem 2.33). That is, compute $g(j)$
$= \max_{0 \le k < j} \{f(k)\}$, for each $0 \le j \le t$.

THEOREM 7.3 *The prefix maxima of N values can be computed by an
$m \times N$ R-Mesh in $O\left(\frac{\log N}{\log m}\right)$ time.*

Figure 7.5 illustrates f and g values showing lines from each point d_j
to $d_{f(j)}$. Delete each point d_j such that $f(j) \le g(j)$ (except for extreme
points $d_0 = q_E$ and $d_t = q_N$). After the deletions, the remaining points
in D form the upper hull of Q_{NE}.

LEMMA 7.4 *The convex hull of $\sqrt{N}$ points in the plane can be computed
on an $N \times \sqrt{N}$ R-Mesh in $O(1)$ time.*

Note that the only step of the above algorithm using more than a
$\sqrt{N} \times \sqrt{N}$ R-Mesh is the step computing the $f(j)$ values.

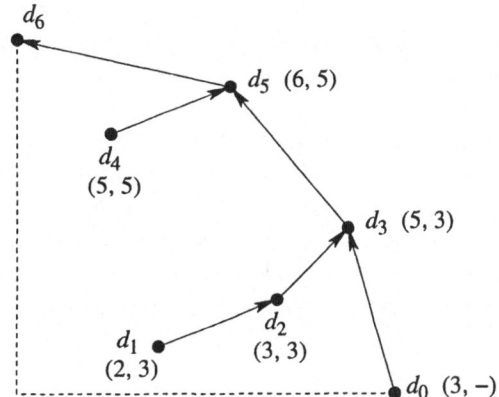

Figure 7.5. Points d_j in Q_{NE} labeled with $(f(j), g(j))$ and with a line between each d_j and $d_{f(j)}$.

7.1.1.2 An $O(\log \log^2 N)$-Time Algorithm

The next algorithm for computing the convex hull of N sorted points is work-optimal, with a processor-time product of $O(N)$. (Recall that if the points are not sorted, then the lower bound is $\Omega(N \log N)$, but presorting points allows a reduction.) The pivotal idea in this algorithm is a deterministic sampling technique. The R-Mesh computes the convex hull of a sample of points, allowing it to use proportionally more processors on fewer points. This hull of the sample is guaranteed to be inside or on the convex hull of the entire set of points. The R-Mesh adds points to the sample to refine its approximation and iterates.

The constant time algorithm of Section 7.1.1.1 and the $O(\log \log^2 N)$-time algorithm of this section both find ways to decrease the number of points relative to the available R-Mesh size. The constant time algorithm partitions the sorted points permitting use as a tool an algorithm to compute the convex hull of N points on an $N^2 \times N$ R-Mesh. The $O(\log \log^2 N)$-time algorithm works on a selected subset (or sample) of points. This permits it to use the constant time algorithm as a tool.

Before we describe the algorithm, we will first introduce some terminology. Let $D_0, D_1, \ldots, D_{m-1}$ denote disjoint upper hulls such that, for all j, all points of D_j are to the left of all points of D_{j+1}. For each j, label the points of D_j as $d(j,0), d(j,1), \ldots$. Let $D = D_0 \cup D_1 \cup \ldots \cup D_{m-1}$. If the upper hull, $U(D)$, of D intersects D_j, then the intersection will be an interval of consecutive points in D_j. Call the two extreme points of this interval, $d(j, lcon_j)$ and $d(j, rcon_j)$, as the *left and right contact points* of D_j with respect to $U(D)$. Each D_j may have two, one, or no contact points. Where there is no danger of ambiguity, we will denote points such as $d(j, lcon_j)$ and $d(j, rcon_j)$ simply as $d(lcon_j)$ and $d(rcon_j)$, respectively.

The line segment from $d(rcon_i)$ to $d(lcon_k)$ for $i < k$ is an *upper hull tangent* of $U(D)$ if, for every $i < j < k$, all points in D_j lie below the line segment. For such a D_j, call a point in D_j closest to the upper hull tangent as a *pseudocontact point* of D_j with respect to $U(D)$. See Figure 7.6. Since we have assumed that no three input points are collinear, there could be at most two pseudocontact points in D_j.

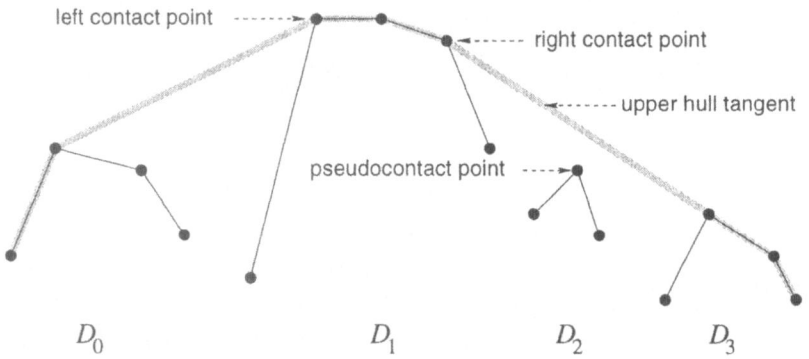

Figure 7.6. Illustration of contact points and upper hull tangent. The shaded line indicates $U(D)$.

A *sample* of a set is just a subset of that set. For $0 \leq j < m$, let $S[D_j]$ denote a sample of D_j, and let

$$S[D] = \bigcup_{j=0}^{m-1} S[D_j].$$

Let C_1 and C_2 denote two convex polygonal chains[2] such that the left endpoint of C_1 is the same as or to the right of that of C_2 and the right endpoint of C_1 is the same as or to the left of that of C_2. Chain C_2 is an *upper envelope* for C_1 if, on every vertical line intersecting C_1 and C_2, the intersection point with C_2 is the same as or above the intersection point with C_1. We leave the proof of the following lemma as Problem 7.7.

---

[2]A *convex polygonal chain* is a sequence of vertices and edges such that joining the two extreme vertices by an edge would create a convex polygon.

LEMMA 7.5 *For every choice of samples* $S[D_j]$, *for* $0 \leq j < m$, $U(D)$ *is an upper envelope of* $U(S[D])$.

This lemma is key to the algorithm. It initially finds an upper hull of a sample of points as an approximation to an upper hull, then refines that approximation by appropriately adding points to the sample. The algorithm is also recursive, partitioning a set of points, finding the upper hulls of the subsets, then using those to find the overall upper hull.

This algorithm will work with points in sorted order. The R-Mesh holds the input points in *proximity order*, an order that weaves itself through the R-Mesh so that, when decomposing the R-Mesh into sub-R-Meshes, the sub-R-Meshes will hold consecutive points. (See Figure 7.7. See also Section 5.4.1 and Problem 5.18.)

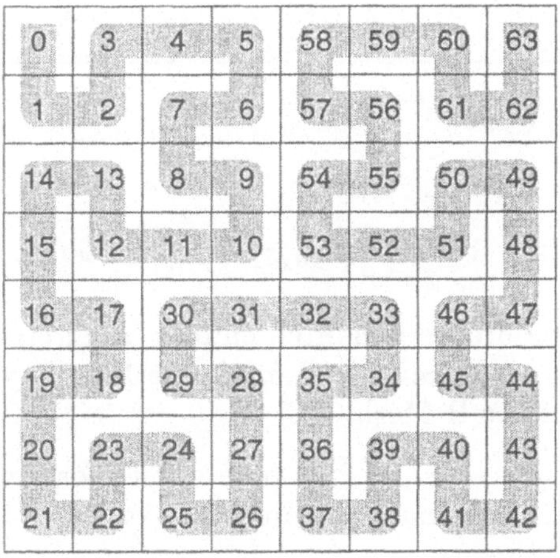

0	3	4	5	58	59	60	63
1	2	7	6	57	56	61	62
14	13	8	9	54	55	50	49
15	12	11	10	53	52	51	48
16	17	30	31	32	33	46	47
19	18	29	28	35	34	45	44
20	23	24	27	36	39	40	43
21	22	25	26	37	38	41	42

Figure 7.7. Proximity order for an 8 × 8 array.

We now describe the algorithm. Let $\mathcal{R}$ denote a $2^h \times 2^h$ R-Mesh, where $N = 2^{2h}$. Let $D = \{d_0, \ldots, d_{N-1}\}$ denote a set of N points in the plane, sorted and arranged in $\mathcal{R}$ in proximity order. We will describe an algorithm to construct the upper hull of D on $\mathcal{R}$ in $O(\log \log^2 N)$ time; the lower hull construction, of course, follows along the same lines. R-Mesh $\mathcal{R}$ is of size $\sqrt{N} \times \sqrt{N}$; we will later explain how to adapt the algorithm to run on a smaller R-Mesh of size $\frac{\sqrt{N}}{\log \log N} \times \frac{\sqrt{N}}{\log \log N}$.

For $s \geq 0$, recursively define the quantity h_s as follows.

$$\left. \begin{aligned} h_0 &= \left\lceil \frac{2h}{3} \right\rceil, \\ h_s &= \max\left\{ \left\lceil h_{s-1} - \frac{h}{8} \right\rceil, \left\lceil \frac{h_{s-1}}{2} \right\rceil \right\}, \quad \text{for all } s \geq 1 \end{aligned} \right\} \quad (7.1)$$

Let T denote the smallest integer for which $h_T = 1$. Observe that $T = O(\log h) = O(\log \log N)$.

Partition D into $2^{2(h-h_0)}$ subsets $D(0)$, $D(1)$, $\ldots, D(2^{2(h-h_0)} - 1)$ such that each $D(j_0)$ (where $0 \le j_0 < 2^{2(h-h_0)}$) includes 2^{2h_0} points consecutive in proximity order held in a sub-R-Mesh $\mathcal{R}(j_0)$ of size $2^{h_0} \times 2^{h_0}$. Next, partition each subset $D(j_0)$ into $2^{2(h_0-h_1)}$ subsets $D(j_0, 0)$, $D(j_0, 1)$, $\ldots, D(j_0, 2^{2(h_0-h_1)} - 1)$ such that each $D(j_0, j_1)$ (for $0 \le j_1 < 2^{2(h_0-h_1)}$) includes 2^{2h_1} points consecutive in proximity order held in a sub-R-Mesh $\mathcal{R}(j_0, j_1)$ of size $2^{h_1} \times 2^{h_1}$. Continue partitioning T times, partitioning $D(j_0, j_1, \ldots, j_s)$, for $0 \le s < T$, which includes 2^{2h_s} points on mesh $\mathcal{R}(j_0, j_1, \ldots, j_s)$ of size $2^{h_s} \times 2^{h_s}$ into $2^{2(h_s-h_{s+1})}$ subsets $D(j_0, j_1, \ldots, j_s, i)$, for $0 \le i < 2^{2(h_s-h_{s+1})}$.

Now for the algorithm proper. Algorithm 7.1 provides a pseudocode description.

Algorithm 7.1   (Upper Hull)

Procedure UPPER_HULL($\mathcal{R}_s, h_s, h, T$)

Model: A $2^{h_s} \times 2^{h_s}$ R-Mesh $\mathcal{R}(j_0, j_1, \cdots, j_s)$. Let $\mathcal{R}_s$ also denote this R-Mesh.
 /* In this procedure we will often employ an alternative concise notation for an object; for example, both $\mathcal{R}(j_0, j_1, \cdots, j_s)$ and $\mathcal{R}_s$ denote the same R-Mesh. */

Input: Set $D(j_0, j_1, \cdots, j_s)$ of 2^{2h_s} points (one per processor) arranged by increasing x-coordinates in proximity order in the R-Mesh. Let D_s also denote this set.

Output: Upper hull of points in D_s.

begin

if $h_s = 1$ **then**
        find the upper hull of D_s sequentially and **return**

else

1. **if** $h_s = h$ **then**
        $h_{s+1} \longleftarrow \left\lceil \frac{2h}{3} \right\rceil$
        Determine the smallest value of T such that $h_T = 1$.
       else $h_{s+1} \longleftarrow \max \left\{ \left\lceil h_s - \frac{h}{8} \right\rceil, \left\lceil \frac{h_s}{2} \right\rceil \right\}$
2. Partition R-Mesh $\mathcal{R}_s$ into $m = 2^{2(h_s-h_{s+1})}$ sub-R-Meshes, $\mathcal{R}_s(i) = \mathcal{R}(j_0, j_1, \cdots, j_s, i)$, where $0 \le i < m$. Each $\mathcal{R}_s(i)$ is a $2^{h_{s+1}} \times 2^{h_{s+1}}$

R-Mesh, consisting of adjacent processors of $\mathcal{R}_s$. Let sub-R-Mesh $\mathcal{R}_s(i)$ hold input points $D(j_0, j_1, \cdots, j_s, i)$. Denote this set of points by $D_s(i)$.

3. Recursively call Procedure UPPER_HULL$(\mathcal{R}_s(i), h_{s+1}, h, T)$, for each $0 \leq i < m$.
   /* These calls run in parallel on the $\mathcal{R}_s(i)$'s. */
   Let $U(D_s(i))$ denote the upper hull of $D_s(i)$, and let $d(\ell_i)$ and $d(r_i)$ denote the leftmost and rightmost points, respectively, in $U(D_s(i))$.

4. For each $0 \leq i < m$, assign
   $$S[D_s(i)] \longleftarrow \{d(\ell_i), d(r_i)\}$$

   $$S[D_s] \longleftarrow \bigcup_{i=0}^{m-1} S[D_s(i)]$$
   /* $S[D_s(i)]$ and $S[D_s]$ are initial samples of sets $D_s(i)$ and D_s, respectively. */

for $t \longleftarrow 0$ **to** $2T - 1$ **do**

5. Compute the upper hull, $U(S[D_s])$, of points in $S[D_s]$.

6. For $0 \leq i < m$, identify contact points of $S[D_s(i)]$ with respect to $U(S[D_s])$ as follows:
   $d(lcon_i) \longleftarrow$ left contact point
           (or pseudocontact point if no contact point exists)
   $d(rcon_i) \longleftarrow$ right contact point
           (or pseudocontact point if no contact point exists)

7. For $0 \leq i < m$, identify additional points as follows:
   $d(ln(lcon_i)) \longleftarrow$ left neighbor of $d(lcon_i)$
   $d(rn(lcon_i)) \longleftarrow$ right neighbor of $d(lcon_i)$
   $d(ln(rcon_i)) \longleftarrow$ left neighbor of $d(rcon_i)$
   $d(rn(rcon_i)) \longleftarrow$ right neighbor of $d(rcon_i)$

8. For $0 \leq i < m$, generate the following sets using procedure ADD_POINTS (Algorithm 7.2).
   $$A_i \longleftarrow \text{ADD\_POINTS}\left(D_s(i), S[D_s(i)], d(lcon_i), d(ln(lcon_i))\right)$$

   $$B_i \longleftarrow \text{ADD\_POINTS}\left(D_s(i), S[D_s(i)], d(lcon_i), d(rn(lcon_i))\right)$$

   $$C_i \longleftarrow \text{ADD\_POINTS}\left(D_s(i), S[D_s(i)], d(rcon_i), d(ln(rcon_i))\right)$$

   $$D_i \longleftarrow \text{ADD\_POINTS}\left(D_s(i), S[D_s(i)], d(rcon_i), d(rn(rcon_i))\right)$$

9. For $0 \leq i < m$, assign
$$S[D_s(i)] \longleftarrow S[D_s(i)] \cup A_i \cup B_i \cup C_i \cup D_i$$

10. Move elements of $S[D_s(i)]$ to the top row of $\mathcal{R}_s$.

end_for

12. Compute the upper hull, $U(S[D_s])$, of set $S[D_s] = \bigcup_{i=0}^{m-1} S[D_s(i)]$.

13. Identify contact points $d(lcon_i)$ and $d(rcon_i)$ with respect to $U(S[D_s])$ as in Step 6.

14. Compute the upper hull of D_s as follows:
$$U(D_s) \longleftarrow \bigcup_{i=0}^{m-1} \left\{ d(j) \ : \ lcon_i \leq j \leq rcon_i \right\}$$

end

We now explain the steps of the algorithm. We refer the reader to Hayashi *et al.* [134] for the geometric details of the correctness proof. We will highlight here the use of R-Mesh-specific features in the algorithm. Initially, the convex hull algorithm invokes the procedure UPPER_HULL($\mathcal{R}, h, h, T$), where $\mathcal{R}$ is a $\sqrt{N} \times \sqrt{N}$ R-Mesh, $N = 2^{2h}$, and T is as yet undefined. If the problem is small enough ($h_s = 1$), then the R-Mesh solves it sequentially. Otherwise, Step 1 computes h_0 and T. This step requires $O(\log \log N)$ time, but only for the first invocation of UPPER_HULL; for other recursive calls, Step 1 runs in constant time. We describe the remainder of the procedure for the first invocation of UPPER_HULL, replacing symbols such as h_s, D_s, and $\mathcal{R}_s$, by h, D, and $\mathcal{R}$, respectively.

Steps 2 and 3 partition the given R-Mesh and recursively compute the upper hull $U(D(i))$ of the points $D(i)$ in sub-R-Mesh $\mathcal{R}(i)$, where $0 \leq i < 2^{2(h-h_0)} = m$. In each sub-R-Mesh $\mathcal{R}(i)$, select a sample $S[D(i)]$ as comprising the leftmost and rightmost points of $U(D(i))$ (Step 4). Let $S[D]$ denote the union of these samples. Since an element's membership in a set is indicated by a flag, the assignments of Step 4 run in constant time. Move the points in $S[D]$ into the top row of $\mathcal{R}$.

Next, the algorithm repeats Steps 5–10 $2T$ times. Using the $O(1)$ time convex hull algorithm developed earlier (Theorem 7.2), compute $U(S[D])$ and the left and right contact points, $d(lcon_i)$ and $d(rcon_i)$, if any, of $S[D(i)]$ with respect to $U(S[D])$ for each $0 \leq i < m$. If $S[D(i)]$ does not have any contact point, then use the pseudocontact point(s) of $S[D(i)]$ with respect to $U(S[D])$ as if they were contact points. Now add points to the sample (Steps 8 and 9) using the procedure ADD_POINTS (see Algorithm 7.2). Let $d(ln(lcon_i))$ and $d(rn(lcon_i))$ denote the left and right neighbors, respectively, of $d(lcon_i)$ in $S[D(i)]$. If $d(ln(lcon_i))$ and $d(lcon_i)$ are in the same 2×2 sub-R-Mesh $\mathcal{R}(j_0, j_1, \ldots, j_{T-1})$, then add the other two points in this sub-R-Mesh to $S[D(i)]$. Otherwise, let $\mathcal{R}(j_0, j_1, \ldots, j_{s'})$, where $s' < T$, denote the smallest sub-R-Mesh containing both $d(ln(lcon_i))$ and $d(lcon_i)$. Add to $S[D(i)]$ the leftmost marked point in each sub-R-Mesh $\mathcal{R}(j_0, j_1, \ldots, j_{s'}, k)$, for $0 \leq k < 2^{2(h_{s'} - h_{s'+1})}$. Repeat this for the three pairs of points $d(lcon_i)$ and $d(rn(lcon_i))$, $d(ln(rcon_i))$ and $d(rcon_i)$, and $d(rcon_i)$ and $d(rn(rcon_i))$. Move all the newly selected sample points to the top row of $\mathcal{R}$.

Before proceeding to Step 12, we give the pseudocode for the procedure ADD_POINTS invoked by procedure UPPER_HULL in Step 8.

Algorithm 7.2 (Add Sample Points)

Procedure ADD_POINTS$(D, S[D], d_1, d_2)$

Model: A $2^{h_s} \times 2^{h_s}$ R-Mesh $\mathcal{R}(j_0, j_1, \cdots, j_s)$. Let $\mathcal{R}_s$ also denote this R-Mesh.

Input: Set $D = D(j_0, j_1, \cdots, j_s)$ of 2^{2h_s} points (one per processor), a sample $S[D] \subseteq D$, and points $d_1, d_2 \in D$.

Output: A set $Y \subseteq D$

begin

For some $s' \geq s$, let $\mathcal{R}(j_0, j_1, \cdots, j_{s'})$ be the smallest sub-R-Mesh containing both points d_1 and d_2. Let $\mathcal{R}'$ also denote this sub-R-Mesh, which has size $2^{h_{s'}} \times 2^{h_{s'}}$.

if $h_{s'} = 1$ **then**
  $Y \longleftarrow$ the two points in $\mathcal{R}'$ other than d_1 and d_2

else

  Let $m' = 2^{2(h_{s'} - h_{s'+1})}$ and let $\mathcal{R}(j_0, j_1, \cdots, j_{s'}, i) = \mathcal{R}'(i)$, for $0 \leq i < m'$. Assign
  $$Y \longleftarrow \bigcup_{i=0}^{m'-1} \text{leftmost point of } S[D] \text{ in } \mathcal{R}'(i)$$

  return Y

end

Coming back to Step 12, the algorithm uses the constant time convex hull algorithm of Theorem 7.2 to compute the upper hull $U(S[D])$ of $S[D]$ and determine the left and right contact points $d(lcon_i)$ and $d(rcon_i)$ of $S[D(i)]$ with respect to $U(S[D])$. It keeps all the points in $D(i)$ between $d(lcon_i)$ and $d(rcon_i)$ as upper hull points of D.

The running time of the algorithm is $O(\log \log^2 N)$. This arises from $O(T)$ time for the step that iteratively computes the convex hull and adds sample points and a depth of recursion of T, where $T = O(\log \log N)$. The R-Mesh techniques involved are data movement, neighbor localization, prefix sums of bits, minimum computation, and the techniques used in $O(1)$ time computation of the convex hull. The quick communication abilities of the R-Mesh enable efficient identification and distribution of sample elements as the samples were refined over the course of the algorithm.

To reduce the R-Mesh size from $\sqrt{N} \times \sqrt{N}$ to the work-optimal $\frac{\sqrt{N}}{\log \log N} \times \frac{\sqrt{N}}{\log \log N}$, start with arranging the input points in proximity order, held $\log \log^2 N$ per processor. Each processor locally computes the upper hull of its points in $O(\log \log^2 N)$ time. Observe that the union of these local hulls contains the points in the overall upper hull, so the idea is to merge these local hulls as was done above. Note that any points in a local hull that remain in the overall hull will be consecutive.

THEOREM 7.6 *The convex hull of N sorted points in the plane can be computed on a $\frac{\sqrt{N}}{\log \log N} \times \frac{\sqrt{N}}{\log \log N}$ R-Mesh in $O(\log \log^2 N)$ time.*

7.1.2   Convex Polygon Problems

Continuing with convexity, we next examine R-Mesh algorithms for several problems dealing with convex polygons, including testing an arbitrary polygon for convexity, point location, and testing whether two convex polygons intersect. For these problems, a $\sqrt{N} \times \sqrt{N}$ R-Mesh holds the N vertices of a polygon (or two polygons for some problems) one vertex per processor and the algorithms run in $O(1)$ time.

7.1.2.1   One-Polygon Problems

Assume that an input polygon is expressed in the following *standard form*. The vertices of an input polygon $D = \langle d_0, d_1, \ldots, d_{N-1} \rangle$ satisfy the following conditions: Vertex d_0 is the rightmost vertex with least y-coordinate, all vertices are distinct, the vertices are ordered counterclockwise, and no three consecutive vertices are collinear. Let us define the problems involving one polygon for which we will sketch R-Mesh algorithms.

CONVEXITY: Given an N vertex polygon, determine whether it is convex.

INCLUSION: Given an N vertex convex polygon D and a query point q, ascertain whether q belong to the interior of D.

SUPPORTING LINES: Given an N vertex convex polygon D and a query point q that lies outside of D, determine the supporting lines from q to D.

STABBING: Given an N vertex convex polygon D and a query line λ, ascertain whether λ intersects D.

For these problems, we state the following result, to be followed by algorithms and sketches of algorithms. The R-Mesh holds the vertices of the polygon in row-major order.

THEOREM 7.7 *For an N vertex (convex) polygon in standard form, a $\sqrt{N} \times \sqrt{N}$ R-Mesh can solve the following problems in $O(1)$ time:* CONVEXITY, INCLUSION, SUPPORTING LINES, *and* STABBING.

For the CONVEXITY problem, the following lemma provides the basis for the algorithm.

LEMMA 7.8 *A polygon in standard form is convex if and only if the sequence of angles formed by the sides of the polygon and the positive direction of the x-axis is monotonic.*

Given this lemma, the algorithm is straightforward. The R-Mesh holds the vertices of the polygon in row-major order. Each processor $p_{i,j}$ holds a vertex d_k, where $0 \le i, j < \sqrt{N}$ and $0 \le k < N$. Each processor determines the angle formed by the line through points $d_k, d_{k+1 \pmod{N}}$ and the positive direction of the x-axis, then checks the angles of its neighbors. The R-Mesh then ANDs the results with a processor reporting 0 if its angle is a local maximum or minimum and reporting 1 otherwise.

The INCLUSION algorithm is similarly straightforward. Let the processors of the R-Mesh hold the vertices of polygon D and let processor $p_{0,0}$ hold query point q. Processor $p_{0,0}$ broadcasts q to all other processors. Each processor $p_{i,j}$ holding vertex d_k then determines whether points q and $d_{k+2 \pmod{N}}$ are both on the same side of the line through $d_k, d_{k+1 \pmod{N}}$. If so, then the processor reports 1; otherwise, 0. (Since the polygon is convex, $d_{k+2 \pmod{N}}$ is on the "interior" side of the line through points $d_k, d_{k+1 \pmod{N}}$). The R-Mesh then ANDs these results.

We leave the algorithms for the SUPPORT LINES and STABBING problems as exercises at the end of the chapter.

7.1.2.2   Two-Polygon Problems

Assume that the vertices of two N vertex, convex polygons D and F are given in standard form (except vertices are in clockwise order) and initially stored in row-major order on a $\sqrt{N} \times \sqrt{N}$ R-Mesh, $\mathcal{R}$. We now define problems involving two polygons.

COMMON TANGENT: Given two convex polygons, compute their common tangents. See Figure 7.8.

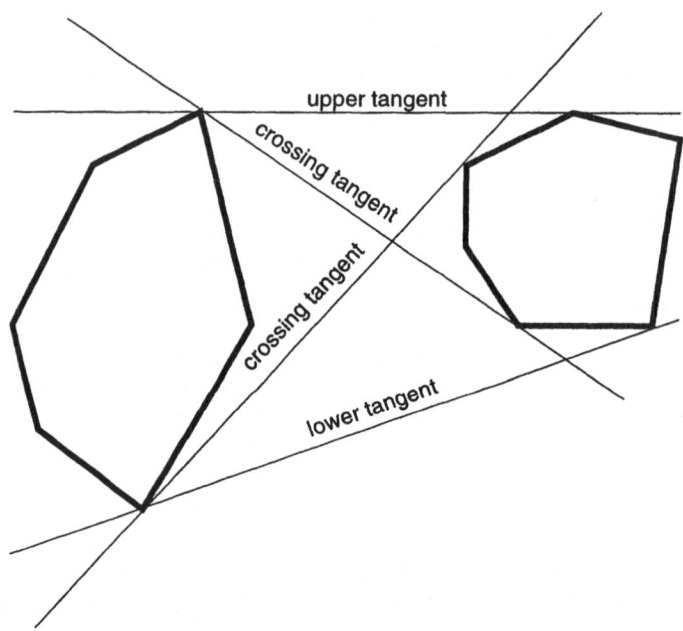

Figure 7.8. Upper, lower, and crossing common tangents of two polygons.

INTERSECTION: Given two convex polygons, determine whether they intersect.

PRIVATE POINT: Given two convex polygons, identify a point in the plane that belongs to only one of them.

MINIMUM DISTANCE: Given two nonintersecting convex polygons, compute the smallest Euclidean distance between them.

THEOREM 7.9 *For two N vertex, convex polygons in standard form, a $\sqrt{N} \times \sqrt{N}$ R-Mesh can solve the following problems in $O(1)$ time:* COMMON TANGENT, INTERSECTION, PRIVATE POINT, *and* MINIMUM DISTANCE.

A key method of these algorithms is the selection of a sample of $\sqrt{N}$ vertices of the input polygon, solving the problem for the resulting $\sqrt{N}$ vertex polygon, then refining this approximate solution. Recall from Section 7.1.1 that such sampling enabled a $\frac{\sqrt{N}}{\log\log N} \times \frac{\sqrt{N}}{\log\log N}$ R-Mesh to compute the convex hull of N points using as a tool an algorithm for an $N \times N$ R-Mesh.

We will describe the algorithm for the COMMON TANGENT problem; similar techniques work for the others (Problems 7.11–7.13). Let D and F be two N-vertex convex polygons held by R-Mesh $\mathcal{R}$. R-Mesh $\mathcal{R}$ begins by selecting a sample of $\sqrt{N}$ vertices of each of D and F by simply taking the vertices held in its rightmost column. Let $DS = \langle ds_0, ds_1, \ldots, ds_{\sqrt{N}-1} \rangle$ (resp., $FS = \langle fs_0, fs_1, \ldots, fs_{\sqrt{N}-1} \rangle$) denote the $\sqrt{N}$ vertex, convex polygon formed by the sample of vertices from D (resp., F). By Lemma 7.1, $\mathcal{R}$ computes a supporting line (upper or lower common tangent) for DS and FS in $O(1)$ time.

Observe that the sample of vertices from D partitions D into $\sqrt{N}$ chunks $DC_0, \ldots, DC_{\sqrt{N}-1}$ such that DC_j includes the vertices in D from ds_j up to ds_{j+1} (including ds_j but not ds_{j+1}). Similarly, the sample of vertices from F partitions F into $\sqrt{N}$ chunks $FC_0, \ldots, FC_{\sqrt{N}-1}$. Let d_u and f_v denote the vertices defining the supporting line of D and F, and let ds_i and fs_j denote the vertices defining the supporting line of DS and FS. (See Figure 7.9.)

At least one of the following is true:

(a) $d_u \in DC_{i-1}$,

(b) $d_u \in DC_i$,

(c) $f_v \in FC_{j-1}$,

(d) $f_v \in FC_j$.

R-Mesh $\mathcal{R}$ next determines which of these conditions holds. For example, to test condition (b), $\mathcal{R}$ computes supporting line λ_i from ds_i to F and supporting line λ_{i+1} from ds_{i+1} to F (Theorem 7.7). Vertex $d_u \in DC_i$ if and only if the right neighbor of ds_i is above λ_i and the left neighbor of ds_{i+1} is above λ_{i+1}.

Suppose condition (b) holds. R-Mesh $\mathcal{R}$ then determines a supporting line between DC_i and FS (Lemma 7.1). If that is not a supporting line for D and F, then $\mathcal{R}$ identifies a chunk FC_g of F such that the supporting

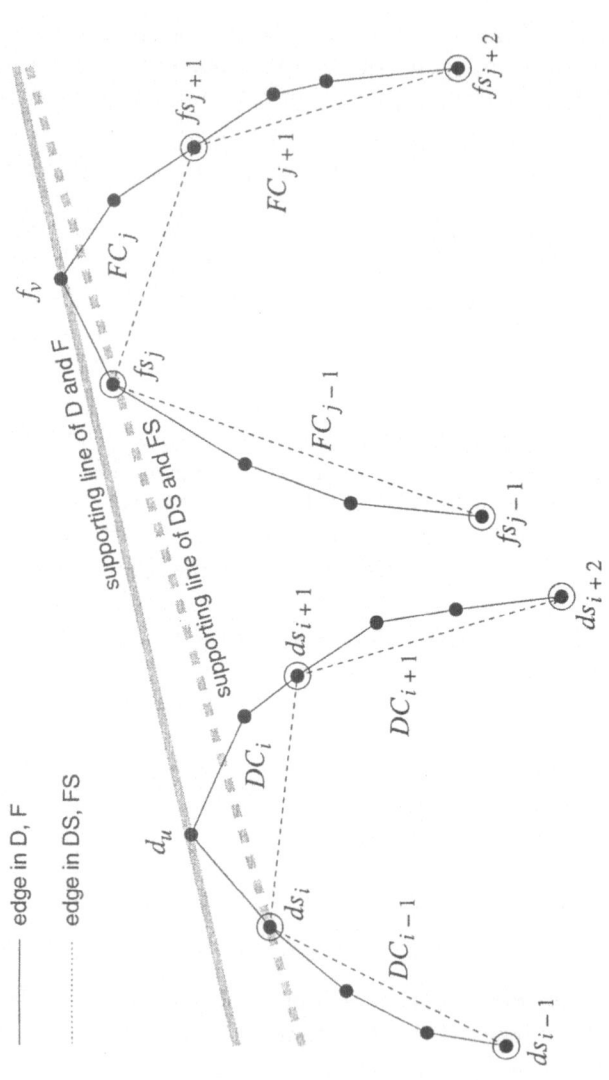

Figure 7.9. Supporting line for polygons *D* and *F* and supporting line for polygons from samples *DS* and *FS*.

line of DC_i and FC_g is a supporting line of D and F. This completes the algorithm for COMMON TANGENTS.

Observe how sampling vertices enabled the algorithm to work with smaller polygons of $\sqrt{N}$ vertices and also with chunks of $\sqrt{N}$ vertices. This enables the use of Lemma 7.1, which computed a supporting line of hulls of only $\sqrt{N}$ vertices on a $\sqrt{N} \times \sqrt{N}$ R-Mesh, as a tool to do the same for polygons of N vertices on the same size R-Mesh.

7.1.3   Nearest Neighbors

Given a set D of N points, the problem of finding all nearest neighbors is to find, for each point $d \in D$, the nearest point $f \in D$ such that $f \neq d$. It has applications in pattern recognition, image processing, computer graphics, geography, and solid-state physics.

We will give an algorithm to solve this problem in $O(1)$ time on an $N \times N$ R-Mesh, $\mathcal{R}$. The key R-Mesh techniques and results involved are data routing, multicasting, sorting, and maximum. To simplify the explanation, assume that no two points share the same x-coordinate or y-coordinate.

R-Mesh $\mathcal{R}$ begins by sorting the points by x-coordinate (Theorem 5.4, page 158). Partition the sorted points into $N^{\frac{1}{4}}$ sets, X_g, of $N^{\frac{3}{4}}$ consecutive points such that the x-coordinate of each point in X_g is greater than those of all points of X_{g-1}. Let $\mathcal{R}_g$ denote the $N \times N^{\frac{3}{4}}$ sub-R-Mesh holding X_g.

Each $\mathcal{R}_g$ solves the all-pairs nearest neighbor problem of X_g as follows. Broadcast the $N^{\frac{3}{4}}$ points in X_g down the columns of $\mathcal{R}_g$. Partition $\mathcal{R}_g$ into $N^{\frac{3}{4}}$ sub-R-Meshes, $\mathcal{R}_{g,h}$, of size $N^{\frac{1}{4}} \times N^{\frac{3}{4}}$. Let $X_g(h)$ denote the hth point in X_g. $\mathcal{R}_{g,h}$ computes the distances from $X_g(h)$ to each other point in X_g, then finds the minimum in $O(1)$ time (Theorem 2.15, page 42). For each $X_g(h)$, $\mathcal{R}_{g,h}$ then sends the distance and the identity of the point at minimum distance to the top row of $\mathcal{R}_g$.

Next, $\mathcal{R}$ sorts the points by y-coordinate, partitions them into $N^{\frac{1}{4}}$ sets, Y_f, then solves the all-pairs nearest neighbor problem for each Y_f as was done above for each X_g.

Let $0 \leq f, g < N^{\frac{1}{4}}$. For each point $d \in X_g \cap Y_f$, identify its nearest neighbor and distance in $X_g \cup Y_f$ by comparing its nearest neighbor distance in X_g and Y_f as explained below.

Partition $\mathcal{R}$ into sub-R-Meshes $\mathcal{R}_{g,f}$ of size $N^{\frac{3}{4}} \times N^{\frac{3}{4}}$. Send $X_g \cap Y_f$ to $\mathcal{R}_{g,f}$. Let x_g (resp., y_f) denote the smallest x (resp., y) coordinate of the points in X_g (resp., Y_f). Broadcast x_g, x_{g+1}, y_f, and y_{f+1} in $\mathcal{R}_{g,f}$ to all points in $X_g \cap Y_f$. For each point, compare its current distance to

the distances to (x_g, y_f), (x_g, y_{f+1}), (x_{g+1}, y_f), and (x_{g+1}, y_{f+1}). Flag a
point if the distance to any of those four points is less than its current
minimum distance. Let $Flag(g, f)$ denote this set of flagged points. At
most eight points in $X_g \cap Y_f$ will not find their nearest neighbors in
$X_g \cup Y_f$. These points are the ones flagged above, so $|Flag(g, f)| \leq 8$.

Now partition $\mathcal{R}$ into sub-R-Meshes of size $\sqrt{N} \times N$. Route $Flag(g, f)$
to the $(g \cdot N^{\frac{1}{4}} + f)^{\text{th}}$ such sub-R-Mesh. Compute the distances between
each flagged point and each other point in D. Then find the minimum
distance for each in $O(1)$ time (Theorem 2.15).

Overall, $\mathcal{R}$ finds the nearest neighbor for each of the N points in D
in $O(1)$ time.

THEOREM 7.10 *The nearest neighbor for each point of a set of N points
in the plane can be found by an $N \times N$ R-Mesh in $O(1)$ time.*

This algorithm works for points in two dimensions. Researchers have
developed an algorithm to handle points in d-dimensions, for constant d,
in the same time and size, as well as to solve the angle-restricted version
of the problem that seeks the nearest neighbor for each point within the
angle specified by two given directions.

7.1.4   Voronoi Diagrams

Given a set $D = \{d_0, d_1, \ldots, d_{N-1}\}$ of points in the plane, a *Voronoi
diagram* is a partition of the plane into N regions such that region j is
the collection of points closer to d_j than to any other point in D. For an
example, see Figure 7.10. As with the computational geometry problems
we examined earlier, the Voronoi diagram problem is a basic, widely
studied problem with a number of other applications in computational
geometry.

As is clear from Figure 7.10, one can specify the regions by the vertices and edges bordering the regions. Each edge between points d_i and
d_j is on a *bisector line* equidistant between d_i and d_j. Call such an edge
as a *V-edge* (for Voronoi edge). Some bisectors will contribute edges and
some will not; call a bisector that contributes an edge as a *V-bisector*. A
V-vertex is a vertex that is an endpoint of a V-edge separating two regions. V-edges may be bounded or unbounded. For an unbounded edge,
we can consider it to have one vertex at infinity. A *provisional vertex*
is the intersection of two bisector lines. All V-vertices are provisional
vertices, but not necessarily vice versa.

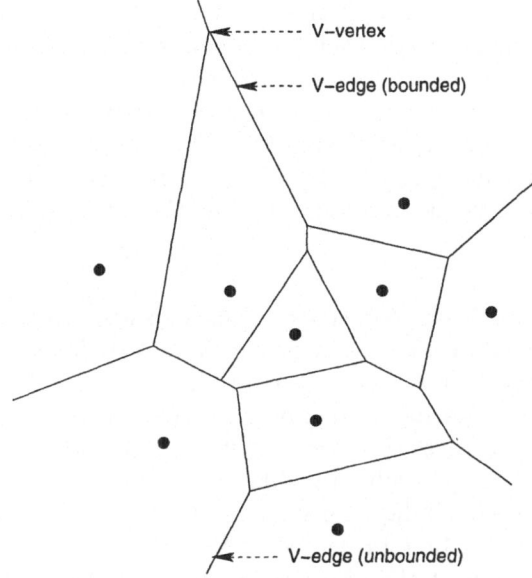

Figure 7.10. Example Voronoi diagram.

The two basic subroutines in an $N \times N$ R-Mesh algorithm are (1) probing along a ray[3] from an input vertex to find the nearest intersection with a bisector line and (2) computing the set of provisional vertices. The algorithm uses probing to identify V-edges in bisector lines and to identify V-vertices from among provisional vertices. We now outline the significant parts of the algorithm.

Probe Algorithm. The overall algorithm will run a probe on different numbers of columns at different times, so we describe the algorithm here on an $N \times M$ R-Mesh, where $M \leq N$. The idea is to start at an input point d_i and extend a ray r through a provisional vertex $vpro_{i,j,k}$, then find the closest bisector intersecting r. (The indices on $vpro_{i,j,k}$ indicate that it arises because of an intersection between the bisector of d_i and d_j and the bisector of d_i and d_k.) Initially, each processor in row j holds d_j. Broadcast the two vertices d_i and $vpro_{i,j,k}$ defining ray r to all processors. Each processor $p_{j,0}$ calculates a bisector for d_i and d_j, then the intersection, if any, of that bisector and r. Compute the minimum

---

[3]A *ray* from point u through point v is a half-line starting at u and continuing through v.

distance to an intersection (Theorem 2.15, page 42). If the intersection is closer than $vpro_{i,j,k}$ to d_i, then the intersection bisector is a V-bisector for that region. Otherwise, $vpro_{i,j,k}$ is a V-vertex. Note that establishing $vpro_{i,j,k}$ as a V-vertex also establishes two other provisional vertices, $vpro_{j,s1,i}$ and $vpro_{k,i,s2}$, as V-vertices. The first (second) is the other endpoint besides $vpro_{i,j,k}$ on the V-edge along the bisector between d_i and d_j (d_k). Due to the minimum finding, this probe algorithm runs in $O\left(\frac{\log N}{\log M}\right)$ time.

Compute Provisional Vertices. The algorithm to compute the set *PV* of provisional vertices runs on an $N \times N$ R-Mesh in $O(1)$ time. After probing, each column of the R-Mesh may hold a V-edge (held as edge $e_{i,j}$ and as edge $e_{j,i}$ belonging to regions of input points d_i and d_j, respectively) or three V-vertices. Represent V-vertex $vpro_{i,j,k}$ as two edges $e_{i,j,0,1}$ and $e_{i,k,1,0}$, where in the notation $e_{g,h,\alpha,\beta}$, $\alpha = 1$ ($\beta = 1$) means that the left (right) endpoint of the edge is known. Thus, all information can now be represented as V-edges.

Collect and compact the edges on the top row of the R-Mesh (Problem 7.14). Sort the edges using region index as the primary key and the angle of the edge as the secondary key (Theorem 5.4, page 158). Connect processors holding cyclically adjacent edges using buses on two R-Mesh rows. Eliminate duplicate edges and distribute known V-vertices one to a processor. Each processor holding a known V-vertex then informs its neighbors of its edge and vertex. If a vertex has not been identified as a V-vertex, then processors compute the intersections of cyclically adjacent bisectors as provisional vertices. (Some processors may have to generate two provisional vertices, with one at infinity.) Collect and compact the provisional vertices on the top row of the R-Mesh.

Overall Algorithm. Given the probe algorithm and the provisional vertex generation algorithm, the overall algorithm is fairly simple. To understand it, we make two observations. First, N input points will have $O(N^2)$ bisectors, but one can prove that the number of V-edges is at most $3N - 6$ and the number of V-vertices is at most $2N - 4$. Second, after probing north and south from each input point, the R-Mesh will identify at least N V-edges.

The algorithm begins by probing north and south from each input point, then computes the set *PV* of provisional vertices. While *PV* is not empty, do the following. Probe each provisional vertex in *PV* to find a new edge or identify three V-vertices. Compute *PV* again.

As the number of provisional vertices in *PV* decreases, the number of columns assigned to each increases, so the probe executes faster.

Overall, the time complexity of the Voronoi diagram algorithm becomes $O(\log N \log \log N)$.

THEOREM 7.11 *The Voronoi diagram for N points can be computed by an $N \times N$ R-Mesh in $O(\log N \log \log N)$ time.*

7.1.5   Euclidean Minimum Spanning Tree

The *Euclidean Minimum Spanning Tree* (EMST) of a set of N points is the minimum spanning tree of the complete graph with N vertices (points in a plane) in which the weight of the edge between vertices i and j is the Euclidean distance between points i and j. The EMST problem has applications in VLSI layout design, clustering, networking, and pattern recognition. In this section, we will describe a constant time algorithm to compute the EMST of points in the plane on an $N^{\frac{3}{2}} \times N^{\frac{3}{2}}$ R-Mesh.

Let $D = \{d_0, d_1, \ldots, d_{N-1}\}$ denote a set of N points in the plane. Let $dist(d_i, d_j)$ denote the Euclidean distance between d_i and d_j. Let $\mathcal{G} = (V, E, w)$ denote the corresponding complete graph with N vertices v_0, $\ldots, v_{N-1}$, and $w(v_i, v_j) = dist(d_i, d_j)$. The EMST of D is the minimum spanning tree (MST) of $\mathcal{G}$. Observe that graph $\mathcal{G}$ has $\Theta(N^2)$ edges. With the algorithm of Theorem 6.11 (page 193), a $\Theta(N^{\frac{5}{2}}) \times \Theta(N^{\frac{5}{2}})$ R-Mesh is needed to achieve constant time. To make the algorithm more efficient, the method here takes advantage of the fact that the MST of $\mathcal{G}$ (that is, the EMST of D) is a subgraph of the *relative neighborhood graph* (RNG) of D, which has at most $3N - 6$ edges.

DEFINITION 7.12 *The relative neighborhood graph $\mathcal{R}(D) = (U, F, w)$ of D comprises a set $U = \{u_0, u_1, \ldots, u_{N-1}\}$ of N vertices, set F of edges, and weight function w. An edge exists in F between u_i and u_j if and only if no point $d_k \in D$ exists such that $dist(d_k, d_i)$ and $dist(d_k, d_j)$ are both less than $dist(d_i, d_j)$. The weight $w(u_i, u_j)$ of edge (u_i, u_j) is $dist(d_i, d_j)$.*

The idea of the algorithm is to construct the RNG of D, then apply Theorem 6.11 to compute the MST of the RNG.

To construct the RNG of D, the $N^{\frac{3}{2}} \times N^{\frac{3}{2}}$ R-Mesh partitions itself into N^2 sub-R-Meshes of N processors each, for instance in sub-R-Meshes of size $N \times 1$. Let $SR_{i,j}$ denote one of these sub-R-Meshes and let $sr_{i,j}(k)$ denote its kth processor, for $0 \leq i, j, k < N$. $SR_{i,j}$ will determine whether (u_i, u_j) is an edge in the RNG of D. Each $sr_{i,j}(k)$ tests whether $dist(d_k, d_i)$ and $dist(d_k, d_j)$ are both less than $dist(d_i, d_j)$. If so, then it sets a flag to 0; otherwise, it sets a flag to 1. Sub-R-Mesh $SR_{i,j}$ then ANDs the flags; if the result is 1, then (u_i, u_j) is an edge in the RNG.

Next, the R-Mesh will compute the MST of the resulting RNG in $O(1)$ time using the algorithm of Theorem 6.11. The MST of the RNG is the EMST of the input set D of points.

THEOREM 7.13 *The Euclidean minimum spanning tree of a set of N points in the plane can be computed by an $N^{\frac{3}{2}} \times N^{\frac{3}{2}}$ R-Mesh in $O(1)$ time.*

7.1.6   Triangulation

The *triangulation* problem for a set D of N planar points is to partition the convex hull of D into triangular subregions by edges between points of D. It often arises as a building block for solving higher-level problems because the partitioning of a region into simple triangular subregions allows solutions of the higher-level problems in these subregions before combining them into an overall solution. The problem has applications in robotics, VLSI design, CAD, and manufacturing.

In this section, we will sketch an algorithm for triangulating a set of N points on an $N \times N$ R-Mesh in $O(1)$ time by a divide-and-conquer approach. The outer-level structure of the algorithm is the same as that of the constant-time convex hull algorithm of Theorem 7.2: sort the N points by their x-coordinates; partition them into $\sqrt{N}$ slices of $\sqrt{N}$ points each; assign each slice of points to an $N \times \sqrt{N}$ sub-R-Mesh that solves the triangulation problem on those points; then, finally, merge these solutions.

To triangulate $\sqrt{N}$ points on an $N \times \sqrt{N}$ R-Mesh, the basic idea is to divide the convex hull into $\sqrt{N} - 2$ polygons (each formed by a point j and the convex hull of points $j + 1, \ldots, \sqrt{N} - 1$, for $0 \le j \le \sqrt{N} - 3$), then triangulate these polygons in parallel. To merge the solutions, triangulate the regions between the convex hull of D and the convex hulls of the $\sqrt{N}$ slices of points.

THEOREM 7.14 *Triangulation of a set of N planar points can be performed on an $N \times N$ R-Mesh in $O(1)$ time.*

Observe that the straight line dual of a Voronoi diagram is also a triangulation called a Delauney triangulation.

7.2   Image Processing

The R-Mesh lends itself toward solving image processing problems in two basic ways. First, the mesh structure and buses permit embedding image features (such as objects and boundaries) into bus configurations. Second, many image processing algorithms revolve around arithmetic operations on an entire image or regions of an image, and the R-Mesh has a well-stocked arithmetic arsenal.

This section begins with some basic tasks that demonstrate these solution methods. Following that, we will take up evaluating the histogram of an image, computing a quadtree representation of an image, extracting moments of an image, and results for performing various transforms on an image.

7.2.1 Basics

An $N \times N$ *binary image* comprises an $N \times N$ array of pixels in which each pixel is either black or white. An $N \times N$ *gray-level image* contains pixels each with a value from $\{0, 1, \dots, g - 1\}$, representing a gray level between black and white, where g is usually a constant.

Given an $N \times N$ binary image, one basic operation is to label the connected components, that is, to assign a unique label to each contiguous region of black pixels. A straightforward approach to solve this problem on an $N \times N$ PRIORITY CRCW R-Mesh is as follows. Each processor holds the pixel corresponding to its position. Form buses connecting neighboring black pixels. For example, if a pixel is black and has neighbors to the South, East, and West that are also black, then its processor configures its buses as $\{\overline{N}, \overline{SEW}\}$. Processors holding white pixels do not fuse any bus ports. This creates a bus connecting each component in $O(1)$ time (Figure 7.11). In constant time, the processors can then

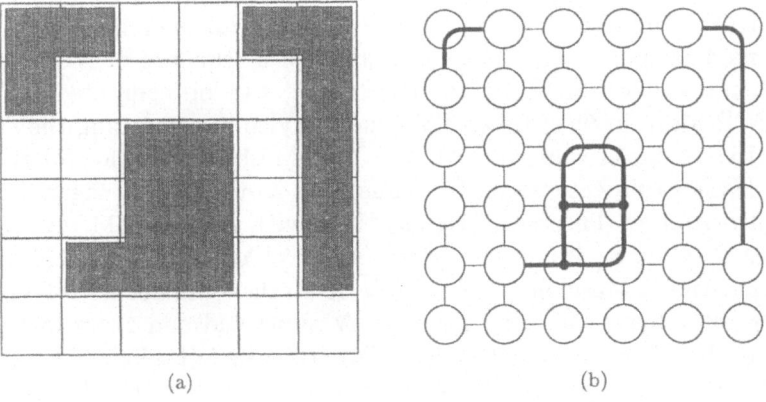

(a) (b)

Figure 7.11. (a) Image with three connected components, (b) corresponding R-Mesh buses.

select the highest priority index as the image label.

With Theorem 3.4 (page 85), setting $m = N^\epsilon$, to convert the PRI-
ORITY CRCW R-Mesh to a COMMON CRCW R-Mesh, we have the
following result.

THEOREM 7.15 *The connected components of an $N \times N$ binary image
can be labeled by a* COMMON *CRCW $N \times N \times N^\epsilon$ R-Mesh in* $O\left(\frac{1}{\epsilon}\right)$ *time,
for $\frac{1}{\log N} \leq \epsilon \leq 1$.*

Observe that the algorithm above relies on embedding an image into
an R-Mesh in the same way as we embedded a graph in an R-Mesh
configuration (see Sections 2.3.6 and 6.3.2). Exclusive writes can suffice
for the algorithm if one connects a linear bus along the boundary of
each component and omits the interior connections. Note that a two-
dimensional COMMON CRCW $N \times N$ R-Mesh can label the connected
components in $O(\log N)$ time.

As an example of harnessing the arithmetic abilities of the R-Mesh for
image processing, we will examine the *median row problem*. For a gray-
scale image, let S denote the sum of all pixel values, and let $rowsum_i$
denote the sum of the pixel values in row i, for $0 \leq i < N$. The
median row of an image is the row m such that $\sum_{i=0}^{m} rowsum_i \leq \frac{S}{2}$ and
$\sum_{i=0}^{m+1} rowsum_i > \frac{S}{2}$. The median row problem is to identify the median
row m.

As a first tool toward solving this problem, recall the following result
(Lemma 4.14, page 132): The prefix sums of a sequence of N integers
in the range 0 through N^c, for constant c, can be computed by an
$N \times N$ R-Mesh in $O(1)$ time. This finds service in computing the sum
of all the N^2 pixel values on an $N \times N$ R-Mesh in $O(\log \log N)$ time.
The idea is to proceed along the same lines as the doubly logarithmic
tree algorithm of Theorem 4.1 (page 120) with Lemma 4.14 replacing
Lemma 2.14 (page 40) in the proof (see Problem 5.19). Specifically,
partition the R-Mesh into $\sqrt{N} \times \sqrt{N}$ R-Meshes and recursively sum
their pixel values. Take the resulting N sums and add them in $O(1)$
time by the algorithm cited above. This runs in $O(\log \log N)$ time as
the algorithm has $\log \log N$ levels of recursion and spends $O(1)$ time at
each level.

LEMMA 7.16 *The sum of pixel values of an $N \times N$ gray-level image can
be computed by an $N \times N$ R-Mesh in* $O(\log \log N)$ *time.*

In the R-Mesh above partitioned into $\sqrt{N} \times \sqrt{N}$ sub-R-Meshes, let a *layer* of the R-Mesh be a row of these sub-R-Meshes, that is, a $\sqrt{N} \times N$ sub-R-Mesh. By taking the sums at the top level of recursion (that is, the sums of the $\sqrt{N} \times \sqrt{N}$ sub-R-Meshes) and ordering them according to row-major order, then computing their prefix sums, the R-Mesh can determine the prefix sums for layers of pixel values. It then identifies the layer containing the median row and recursively identifies which row in the selected layer is the overall median row. Consequently, we have the following result, which exploits the array structure of the R-Mesh matching the array structure of the image plus fast arithmetic algorithms on the R-Mesh.

THEOREM 7.17 *The median row of an $N \times N$ gray-level image can be computed by an $N \times N$ R-Mesh in $O(\log \log N)$ time.*

Consider a binary image containing a single object. Let the *area* of the object be the number of black pixels it contains, and let the *perimeter* of the object be the number of black pixels on its periphery. One can readily apply the algorithm for adding pixel values to compute the area and perimeter of a single object in a binary image.

THEOREM 7.18 *The area and perimeter of an object in an $N \times N$ binary image can be computed by an $N \times N$ R-Mesh in $O(\log \log N)$ time.*

7.2.2 Histogram

For a gray-level image with g gray-level values, a *histogram* of the image contains the number of pixels with each gray-level value. Computing the histogram is another basic image processing operation, useful for determining various image properties. One way to compute the histogram is to apply Theorem 4.11 (page 129) g times to count the number of pixels at each of the g gray levels, resulting in an $O(g \log^* N)$ time algorithm.

A faster R-Mesh algorithm exists. It exploits these results presented in earlier chapters:

- adding N b-bit numbers on an $N \times Nb$ R-Mesh in $O(1)$ time (Lemma 4.9, page 126),

- computing prefix sums modulo k of N bits on a $(k+1) \times 2N$ R-Mesh in $O(1)$ time (Lemma 2.8, page 30),

- converting between unary number representations 2UN and 1UN (Section 4.1.1), and

- adding N b-bit numbers on a $b \log^2 N \times N$ R-Mesh in $O(1)$ time (Lemma 4.10, page 127).

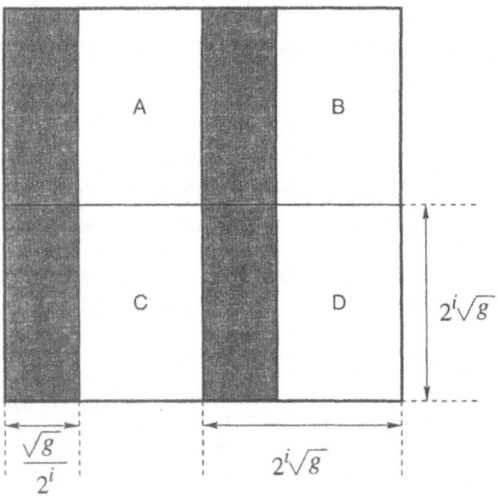

Figure 7.12.   Arrangement of four sub-R-Meshes and the gray values they hold before a merge.

We will first present a base building block, then extend it, then further extend to the final result.

LEMMA 7.19 *For any $g \geq 2$, the histogram of a $g \times g$ gray-level image with g gray levels can be computed on a $g \times g$ R-Mesh in $O(\sqrt{g})$ time.*

<u>Proof:</u> Partition the R-Mesh into $\sqrt{g} \times \sqrt{g}$ size sub-R-Meshes. Within each sub-R-Mesh, sort the elements in snakelike order by a standard, non-reconfigurable mesh algorithm in $O(\sqrt{g})$ time. Observe that all pixels with the same gray level in a sub-R-Mesh will be contiguous after this sort. By setting a bus in each run of the same value, determine the number of pixels with each gray value in $O(1)$ time. (This result is the histogram for a sub-R-Mesh.) By the same sorting algorithm, compact these numbers so that the jth processor in row-major order of each sub-R-Mesh holds the number of pixels with gray value j in that sub-R-Mesh.

Next, the R-Mesh adds the numbers of pixels at each gray level by iteratively merging values in sub-R-Meshes, merging results on four $2^i \sqrt{g} \times 2^i \sqrt{g}$ sub-R-Meshes into a $2^{i+1} \sqrt{g} \times 2^{i+1} \sqrt{g}$ sub-R-Mesh at the ith iteration step, for $O(\log g)$ iterations. At the start of iteration i, each $2^i \sqrt{g} \times 2^i \sqrt{g}$ sub-R-Mesh holds its g values in the leftmost $\frac{\sqrt{g}}{2^i}$ columns. See Figure 7.12. Add the corresponding values from block B to those in block A and from block D to block C in $O\left(\frac{\sqrt{g}}{2^i}\right)$ time. Then add the corresponding values from block C to block A in $O\left(\frac{\sqrt{g}}{2^i}\right)$ time. Now, block A holds the histogram counts for all four blocks. It keeps those in the leftmost $\frac{\sqrt{g}}{2^{i+1}}$ columns and sends those in the next $\frac{\sqrt{g}}{2^{i+1}}$ columns to the leftmost $\frac{\sqrt{g}}{2^{i+1}}$ columns of block C in $O\left(\frac{\sqrt{g}}{2^i}\right)$ time to complete a merge step.

Each merge step takes half the time of its predecessor. Overall, it is possible to show that the algorithm runs in $O(\sqrt{g})$ time. ∎

At the end of the above algorithm, the $g \times g$ R-Mesh holds the g gray-level counts in the leftmost column. One can merge from such $g \times g$ blocks in $O(1)$ time. Iterating this merge $O(\log g)$ times, one can merge the gray-level counts on a $g^4 \times g^4$ R-Mesh.

LEMMA 7.20 *The histogram of a $g^4 \times g^4$ gray-level image with g gray levels can be computed on a $g^4 \times g^4$ R-Mesh in $O(\sqrt{g})$ time.*

Now we turn to constructing a histogram algorithm using the lemma above as a tool.

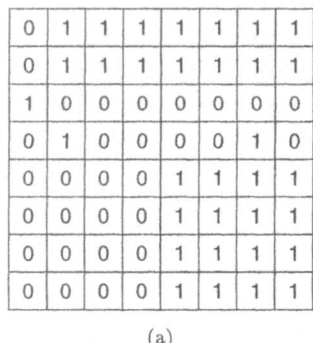

(a)

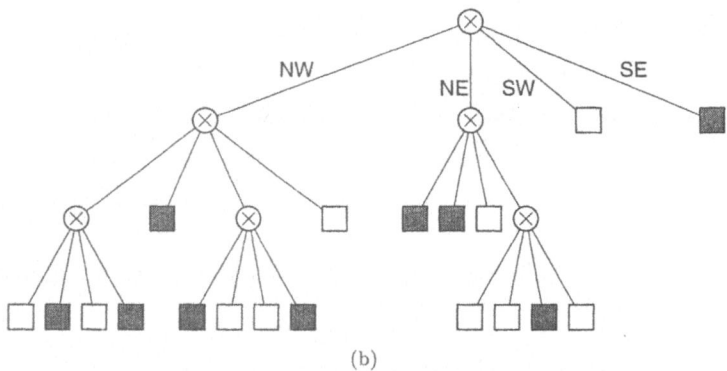

(b)

Figure 7.13.   (a) 8 × 8 binary image and (b) its quadtree representation, where a black (white) square denotes an all black (all white) quadrant.

THEOREM 7.21 *The histogram of an $N \times N$ gray-level image with g gray levels can be computed on an $N \times N$ R-Mesh in $O\left(\sqrt{g} + \log^*\left(\frac{N}{g}\right)\right)$ time.*

Proof: Partition the R-Mesh into sub-R-Meshes of size $g^4 \times g^4$ and compute each of their histograms in $O(\sqrt{g})$ time by Lemma 7.20. Next, merge these $g^4 \times g^4$ blocks into a $2^g \times 2^g$ block as follows. Collect rows of blocks into $g^4 \times 2^g$ (horizontal) strips. Slice these into $g^3 \times 2^g$ thin strips, one for each gray level. Each thin strip j adds the $\frac{2^g}{g^4}$ counts of gray level j in the strip in $O(1)$ time using Lemma 4.10, for word-size $b = \log N$. Next, add the resulting counts in the same way using a (vertical) strip of size $2^g \times g^4$ in $O(1)$ time. Repeat this merge step $\log^*\left(\frac{N}{g^4}\right)$ times to produce the overall histogram. ∎

7.2.3 Quadtree

A *quadtree* is a hierarchical data structure that serves to represent a binary image. A quadtree is a tree of degree four. The root represents the entire image, each of its four children represents a quadrant of the image in the order northwest, northeast, southwest, and southeast. If a quadrant contains all black (or all white) pixels, then the corresponding vertex in the quadtree is a leaf labeled as black (or white, respectively). Otherwise, recursively apply this decomposition to the subquadrants. Figure 7.13 provides an example.

In this section, we will describe a constant time algorithm for extracting the quadtree representation of an $N \times N$ binary image using an $N \times N$ R-Mesh. The key to the algorithm is ordering the pixels according to the proximity order as shown in Figure 7.7. This ordering traverses each quadrant (or subquadrant) fully before moving on to the next quadrant (or subquadrant). Setting up R-Mesh buses according to this order and pixel values enables the R-Mesh to capture the quadtree structure. For this section we will denote the processors of the $N \times N$ R-Mesh by p_j ($0 \le j < N^2$) in proximity order; that is, p_j is the jth processor in proximity order.

We now describe the underlying idea of the algorithm, leaving the details and the proof of correctness as exercises at the end of the chapter (Problems 7.17–7.20). As we describe the algorithm, we will use a running example to illustrate key ideas. For this example consider the 16 elements in Figure 7.14(a).

The algorithm has two main phases:

1. Determine block size for each processor.
2. Mark active processors.

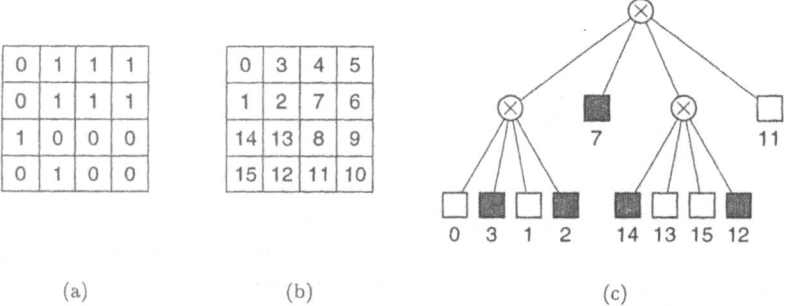

(a)   (b)   (c)

Figure 7.14. An example illustrating the quadtree construction algorithm. Part (a) shows a 4 × 4 binary image, and part (b) shows the proximity ordering of its pixels. Part (c) shows the quadtree representation of this image. Each leaf of the quadtree is labeled by the processor that holds information about the leaf.

j (dec.)	j (bin.)	$lowzero(j)$	$max\_block(j)$	$begin(j)$	$numpix(j)$ (dec.)	$numpix(j)$ (bin.)	$X(j) = numpix(j) \wedge pattern$	$highone(X(j))$	$s(j)$	block size $2^{s(j)}$
0	0000	0	1	0	1	0001	0001	0	0	1
1	0001	1	2	0	2	0010	0000	0	0	1
2	0010	0	1	2	1	0001	0001	0	0	1
3	0011	2	4	2	2	0010	0000	0	0	1
4	0100	0	1	2	3	0011	0001	0	0	1
5	0101	1	2	2	4	0100	0100	2	2	4
6	0110	0	1	2	5	0101	0101	2	2	4
7	0111	3	8	2	6	0110	0100	2	2	4
8	1000	0	1	8	1	0001	0001	0	0	1
9	1001	1	2	8	2	0010	0000	0	0	1
10	1010	0	1	8	3	0011	0001	0	0	1
11	1011	2	4	8	4	0100	0100	2	2	4
12	1100	0	1	12	1	0001	0001	0	0	1
13	1101	1	2	13	1	0001	0001	0	0	1
14	1110	0	1	14	1	0001	0001	0	0	1
15	1111	4	16	15	1	0001	0001	0	0	1

Figure 7.15. Quantities used in determining the block size of processors in the R-Mesh (image) of Figure 7.14(a).

Determine Block Size. Consider an $N \times N$ binary image, with $N = 2^n$ for integer $n \geq 0$. Each leaf of the quadtree of the image corresponds to a square subimage, all of whose pixels have the same value. This subimage is called a *block* of the image. For example, the rightmost child of the root of the quadtree of Figure 7.14(c) corresponds to the subimage (of all 0 pixels) in the southeast quadrant of the image of Figure 7.14(a). Assuming the root of the quadtree to be at level 0, a leaf at level ℓ (where $0 \leq \ell \leq n$) corresponds to a $2^{n-\ell} \times 2^{n-\ell}$ subimage. Since there is a one-to-one correspondence between R-Mesh processors and image pixels, each processor belongs to a block of the image.

In this phase, each processor p_j (where $0 \leq j < N^2$) uses the pixel values of processors p_i (where $0 \leq i < j$) to determine the size of the block to which p_j belongs.

Define $lowzero(j)$ to be the position of the least significant zero in the binary representation of j. Figure 7.15 shows $lowzero(j)$ (and other quantities) for the processors in the R-Mesh (image) of Figure 7.14(a). Let $max\_block(j)$ denote the size of the largest possible block of any $N \times N$ image whose last pixel has index j in proximity ordering. One could obtain $max\_block(j)$ by the following equation

$$max\_block(j) = \begin{cases} 2^{lowzero(j)-1}, & \text{if } lowzero(j) \text{ is odd} \\ 2^{lowzero(j)}, & \text{if } lowzero(j) \text{ is even.} \end{cases} \tag{7.2}$$

Each processor p_j locally computes $max\_block(j)$ in constant time.

A sequence $\langle p_i, p_{i+1}, p_{i+2}, \cdots, p_{k-1}, p_k \rangle$ of processors is a *run* if and only if all the processors hold the same pixel value v, and processors p_{i-1} and p_{k+1} (if they exist) hold a pixel value different from v. For example, processor sequence $\langle p_2, p_3, p_4, p_5, p_6, p_7 \rangle$ of Figure 7.14 forms a run. Clearly, each processor p_j belongs to some run. Let $begin(j)$ denote the proximity index of the first processor of the run corresponding to processor p_j. That is, if $\langle p_i, p_{i+1}, p_{i+2}, \cdots, p_{k-1}, p_k \rangle$ is a run such that $i \leq j \leq k$, then $begin(j) = i$. Figure 7.15 shows the values of $begin(j)$ for the running example.

To compute $begin(j)$, each processor p_j compares its pixel value with that in p_{j-1} (if it exists) to determine whether a run begins at p_j. Next, the R-Mesh establishes a bus connecting all its processors in proximity order. Then it breaks this bus at each processor that begins a run. These processors now broadcast their indices to other processors in the run. Clearly, this index is $begin(j)$ for all processors p_j in the run.

Let $numpix(j)$ denote the number of pixels from the start of the run of p_j up to (and including) processor p_j. Clearly,

$$numpix(j) = j - begin(j) + 1.$$

Let $pattern = 0101 \cdots 01$ be a string of $2 \log N$ repeated 01's; for the running example, $pattern = 0101$. Let $X(j)$ be the bitwise AND of $pattern$ and the binary representation of $numpix(j)$; see Figure 7.15. For any positive integer z, define $highone(z)$ to be the position of the highest order 1 in the binary representation of z. Define $highone(0)$ to be 0. Clearly, $highone$ can also be defined for a binary sequence rather than an integer. The algorithm at hand uses the quantity $highone(X(j))$ (see Figure 7.15). It can be shown that the size of the image block ending at pixel j is $2^{s(j)}$, for $s(j)$ given by the following equation.

$$s(j) = \min \left\{ \log(max\_block(j)), highone\left(X(j)\right) \right\} \qquad (7.3)$$

Clearly, each processor p_j computes $2^{s(j)}$ locally in constant time.

For the running example, observe that processors p_7 and p_{11} each end blocks of size 4, while the remaining processors end blocks of size 1. The block with processor p_7 also includes processors p_4, p_5, and p_6. Note that since a block must be square, processors p_4 and p_5 cannot form a block; consequently, the size of the block ending at p_5 is 1.

Mark Active Processors. At this point, the algorithm has determined the block size for each processor. Clearly, some processors (such as p_4, p_5, and p_6 in the running example) could be members of a larger block (the block of p_7 in the example). Such processors are said to be *covered* by the larger block (or the last processor of that block). The purpose of this phase of the algorithm is to mark all covered processors as inactive (and identify the remaining active processors).

This part of the algorithm exploits a special ability added to those of the standard R-Mesh: the ability to selectively write on individual lines (bits) of a bus. (For example, on a 3-bit bus connecting p_0 through p_3, p_0 can write a 1 to bit 2 and p_3 can write a 1 to bit 1, then processors will read 110 from the bus. A bus with no writes to it is assumed to carry a 0.)

The algorithm for this phase has the following steps.

1. For each run, the R-Mesh configures a separate bus to connect all processors in that run. Each processor p_j with $s(j) > 0$ writes 1 on bit $\frac{s(j)}{2}$ of the bus through the port in the direction of p_{j-1} (if it exists); it is possible to prove that $\frac{s(j)}{2}$ is an integer (see Problem 7.19). Each processor p_j with $s(j) > 0$ reads from the bus from the port in the direction of p_{j+1}. Call the data read by p_j as $merge(j)$. Figure 7.16(a) illustrates this for the running example.

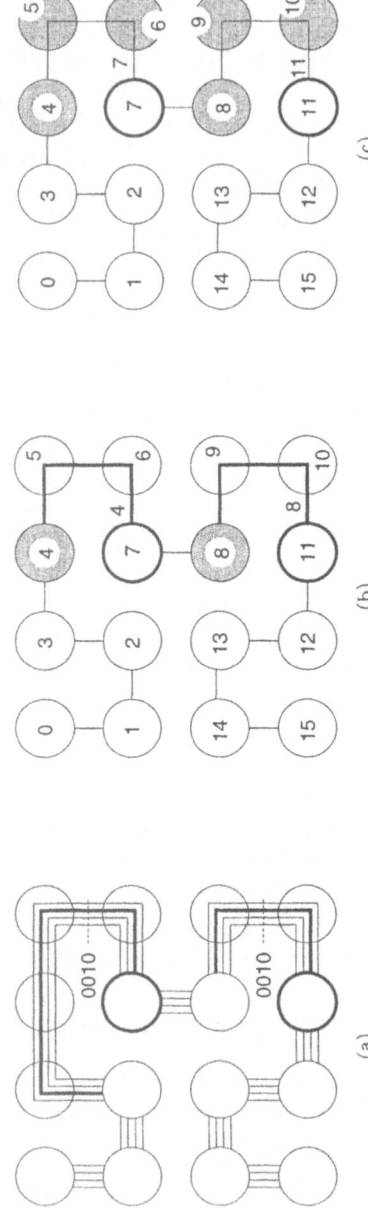

Figure 7.16. Steps in marking active processors that hold quadtree vertices for the example of Figure 7.14. Writing processors are in bold and a value next to a bold bus shows the value that a processor writes to the bus. In part (a), buses are broken into their individual bits with the bus receiving writes shown in bold. In part (b), shaded processors are those that disconnect their buses at the end of Step 3. In part (c), shaded processors are those marked inactive.

Note that this is the only step of the algorithm that requires processors to selectively write to some bits of a bus.

2. If $highone(merge(j)) \leq s(j)/2$, then $p(j)$ disconnects its ports. For the running example, processors p_7 and p_{11} disconnect their ports, though they were already disconnected because p_7 and p_{11} end runs. Thus, Figure 7.16(a) shows the situation after Step 2 as well.

3. Processors p_j that disconnected their ports in Step 2 write $j - 2^{s(j)} + 1$ to the bus on the port towards p_{j-1}. Each processor p_j reads from the bus from the port facing p_{j+1}, and if the data read equals its (proximity order) index, then it disconnects its ports.

    For the running example, processors p_7 and p_{11} write 4 and 8, respectively, causing processors 4 and 8 to disconnect their buses (see Figure 7.16(b)).

    At this point, each bus spans only a block (rather than extending across an entire run).

4. Each processor p_j with $s(j) > 0$ that disconnected its port in Step 2 writes its index j to the bus; for any processor p_k, if index k is less than the value it receives, then it marks itself as inactive. The remaining active processors hold data for the quadtree vertices.

    For the running example (see Figure 7.16(c)), processors p_7 and p_{11} write their indices causing the remaining processors in their block p_4, p_5, p_6 and p_8, p_9, p_{10} to be marked as inactive. The active processors correspond to leaves of the quadtree (see Figure 7.14(c)).

Clearly, each step runs in constant time.

THEOREM 7.22 *The quadtree of an $N \times N$ binary image can be constructed in $O(1)$ time by an $N \times N$ R-Mesh enhanced with the ability to selectively write on individual bus lines.*

7.2.4   Moments

The moments of a digital image are useful in many areas of image recognition and analysis. They find application in edge detection, aircraft recognition, character recognition, scene matching, shape analysis, robotics, and other areas. For an $N \times N$ image D and nonnegative integers p and q, define the *moment* of order $(p + q)$ as:

$$m_{pq} = \sum_{i=1}^{N} \sum_{j=1}^{N} i^p j^q D(i,j),$$

where $D(i,j)$ denotes the value of the pixel in position (i,j).

For a binary image containing one horizontally and vertically convex object (at most one contiguous sequence of black pixels on each row and each column), simpler expressions exist for many moments. For this special case, moment expressions become summations of powers of a sequence of consecutive integers. Let δ_i^r, for $1 \leq i \leq N$, denote the number of (contiguous) black pixels in row i. Let δ_j^c denote the same for column j. Let π_i^r denote the column coordinate of the leftmost black pixel in row i; let π_j^c denote the row coordinate of the bottommost black pixel in column j. For example,

$$m_{00} = \sum_{i=1}^{N} \delta_i^r = \sum_{j=1}^{N} \delta_j^c,$$

$$m_{10} = \sum_{i=1}^{N} i \cdot \delta_i^r,$$

$$m_{20} = \sum_{i=1}^{N} i^2 \cdot \delta_i^r, \text{ and}$$

$$m_{30} = \sum_{i=1}^{N} i^3 \cdot \delta_i^r.$$

Other moments m_{pq} for $0 \leq p, q \leq 3$ can be constructed using δ_i^r, δ_j^c, π_i^r, and π_j^c. For example,

$$m_{11} = \sum_{i=1}^{N} \mu_i,$$

where $\mu_i = \delta_i^r \cdot i \cdot \left(\pi_i^r + \frac{\delta_i^r - 1}{2}\right)$. Also,

$$m_{32} = \sum_{i=1}^{N} \nu_i,$$

where $\nu_i = i^3 \left(\delta_i^r \cdot (\pi_i^r)^2 + \frac{(\delta_i^r - 1) \cdot \delta_i^r \cdot (2\delta_i^r - 1)}{6} + 2\pi_i^r \cdot \frac{(\delta_i^r - 1) \cdot \delta_i^r}{2}\right)$.

For this problem, the structure of an R-Mesh matching the structure of an image and the fast arithmetic ability of the R-Mesh offer themselves for exploitation. For an $N \times N$ R-Mesh and an $N \times N$ binary image, determining δ_i^r, π_i^r, δ_j^c, and π_j^c is trivial. Local processors compute the terms to be added for the expressions above. Finally, the R-Mesh can compute each sum using the $O(1)$ time algorithm for adding N numbers with value polynomial in N (Lemma 4.14, page 132).

THEOREM 7.23 *For $p, q \in \{0, 1, 2, 3\}$, each moment m_{pq} of an $N \times N$ horizontally and vertically convex binary image can be computed by an $N \times N$ R-Mesh in $O(1)$ time.*

7.2.5 Image Transforms

Many image transforms exist with the intent of manipulating an image into a form more amenable to further calculation, such as line detection, object recognition, motion planning, etc. For the same reasons as for other image processing problems, the R-Mesh has capabilities that lend themselves to performing image transforms quickly. As the R-Mesh techniques involved are the same as those used earlier (including broadcast, bus segmenting, prefix sums, and multiple addition), we will only cite results in this section, rather than detailing algorithms.

For an $N \times N$ image, R-Mesh algorithms exist for performing the following image transforms:

- Hough Transform — $n \times n$ parameter space, $n \log^2 N \times N \times N$ R-Mesh in $O(1)$ time.

- Radon Transform — $n \times n$ parameter space, $n \log^3 N \times N \times N$ R-Mesh in $O(1)$ time.

- City Block Distance Transform — $N \times N$ R-Mesh in $O(\log^2 N)$ time.

- Euclidean Distance Transform — $N \times N \times N$ LR-Mesh in $O(1)$ time.

- Medial Axis Transform — $N \times N \times N$ R-Mesh in $O(1)$ time.

- Continuous Wavelet Transform — (m, k) integer grid and b-bit word size — $m \times k \times N$ R-Mesh in $O\left(\frac{\sqrt{N}(\log b + \log^* N)}{m}\right)$ time; $m \times kb \log^2 N \times N$ R-Mesh in $O(1)$ time.

Problems

7.1 Let the solution to the convex hull of points $D = \{d_0, d_1, \ldots, d_{N-1}\}$ be an enumeration of hull points in clockwise order. Prove that if the convex hull of N points can be computed in T steps, then sorting of N elements can be performed in $O(T)$ steps.

7.2   The constant time convex hull algorithm of Section 7.1.1 assumes that no three points are collinear and no two points share the same x or y coordinate. Describe the necessary modifications to the algorithm to work with these assumptions removed.

7.3   Let $\mathcal{M}$ be a $\sqrt{N} \times \sqrt{N}$ R-Mesh holding the up to $\sqrt{N}$ points in upper hull U_1 in its top row and the up to $\sqrt{N}$ points in upper hull U_2 in its leftmost column. All points in U_1 are to the left of all points in U_2. Design an algorithm for $\mathcal{M}$ to find the supporting line of U_1 and U_2 in $O(1)$ time. (That is, prove Lemma 7.1.)

7.4   Using the partitioning of set Q with N points into sets Q_{NE}, Q_{NW}, etc. as described in Section 7.1.1, prove that the concatenation of the upper hulls of Q_{NE} and Q_{NW} is the upper hull of Q.

7.5   Prove that the algorithm for Lemma 7.4 returns the convex hull of Q.

7.6   Describe the R-Mesh steps in detail for the convex hull algorithm of Lemma 7.4 to implement the step computing the $f(j)$ values for all points d_j.

7.7   Prove Lemma 7.5.

7.8   If T is the smallest value of s such that $h_s = 1$ (see Equation 7.1), then prove that $T = O(\log N)$.

7.9   Construct an $O(1)$ time algorithm on a $\sqrt{N} \times \sqrt{N}$ R-Mesh for the SUPPORTING LINES problem involving an N vertex polygon D and a query point q.

7.10 Use the algorithms for INCLUSION and SUPPORTING LINES as subroutines to construct an $O(1)$ time algorithm on a $\sqrt{N} \times \sqrt{N}$ R-Mesh for the STABBING problem involving an N vertex polygon D and a query line λ.

7.11 Construct an algorithm to solve the INTERSECTION problem in $O(1)$ time on a $\sqrt{N} \times \sqrt{N}$ R-Mesh.

7.12 Construct an algorithm to solve the PRIVATE POINT problem in $O(1)$ time on a $\sqrt{N} \times \sqrt{N}$ R-Mesh.

7.13 Construct an algorithm to solve the MINIMUM DISTANCE problem in $O(1)$ time on a $\sqrt{N} \times \sqrt{N}$ R-Mesh.

7.14 Given M data items in an $N \times N$ R-Mesh, where $M \leq N$, and no more than one item per column, construct an $O(1)$ time algorithm to store these in the leftmost M columns of the top row of the R-Mesh.

7.15 Let an $N \times N$ binary image $\mathcal{I}$ contain one object. Construct an $N \times N$ R-Mesh algorithm to compute the area of the object in $\mathcal{I}$ and the perimeter of the object in $\mathcal{I}$ in $O(\log \log N)$ time.

7.16 Prove in detail that the algorithm of Lemma 7.19 runs in $O(\sqrt{g})$ time.

7.17 Detail the R-Mesh steps needed for the quadtree algorithm of Section 7.2.3.

7.18 Prove Equation 7.2.

7.19 Prove that the quantity $s(j)$ defined in Equation 7.3 is always even.

7.20 Prove that Equation 7.3 correctly specifies the block sizes for the quadtree algorithm of Section 7.2.3.

7.21 Extend the quadtree algorithm of Section 7.2.3 so that the output is an ordered tree. Each vertex of this tree is in an R-Mesh processor (with no more than two vertices per processor). The processor holding a vertex also has pointers to its parent and children (if any), its rank among its siblings, and the ranks of its children.

7.22 Theorem 7.22 describes a constant time method to construct the quadtree of an $N \times N$ binary image on an $N \times N$ R-Mesh enhanced with the ability to selectively write on individual bus lines. Design an efficient constant time algorithm to construct the quadtree on an R-Mesh without this extra ability.

7.23 (a) Create expressions for the moments m_{12} and m_{13} analogous to those given in Section 7.2.4 for m_{11} and m_{32}.

   (b) Construct an $O(1)$ time algorithm for an $N \times N$ R-Mesh to compute the moments m_{10}, m_{11}, m_{12}, and m_{13} of an $N \times N$ horizontally and vertically convex, binary image.

7.24   The *city block distance transform* for an $N \times N$ binary image computes for each pixel the "city block distance" (also known as the L_1
metric) to the nearest black pixel. For a pixel at location (i, j) with a
nearest black pixel at location (g, h), this distance is $|i - g| + |j - h|$.
Construct an $O(\log^2 N)$ time algorithm for an $N \times N$ R-Mesh to calculate the city block distance transform of an $N \times N$ binary image.

7.25   The *Euclidean distance transform* for an $N \times N$ binary image computes for each pixel the Euclidean distance (also known as the L_2
metric) to the nearest black pixel.

(a)   Construct an $O(\log^2 N)$ time algorithm for an $N \times N$ R-Mesh to
calculate the Euclidean distance transform of an $N \times N$ binary
image.

(b)   Construct an $O(\log N)$ time algorithm for an $N \times N \times N$ R-
Mesh to calculate the Euclidean distance transform of an $N \times N$
binary image.

(c)   Construct an $O(1)$ time algorithm for an $N \times N \times N \times N$ R-
Mesh to calculate the Euclidean distance transform of an $N \times N$
binary image.

Bibliographic Notes

Several textbooks give good   riptions of sequential and parallel
algorithms for computational geometry, going far beyond the focused
coverage in this chapter. These include Preparata and Shamos [270],
O'Rourke [248], and Akl and Lyons [1].

Jang *et al.* [144] and Olariu *et al.* [247] presented constant time
algorithms for the convex hull of N points on an $N \times N$ R-Mesh, and
Hayashi *et al.* [133] gave the work-optimal $O(\log \log^2 N)$-time algorithm
for sorted points. The proximity order used to index processors in this
algorithm (and in the quadtree algorithm of Section 7.2.3) is also known
as the Hilbert's space-filling order [169]. For sorted points, Nakano [228]
gave an $O(1)$ time algorithm on an $N \times N^\epsilon$ R-Mesh, for constant $\epsilon > 0$.
The result on prefix maxima (Theorem 7.3) used in the algorithm for
Lemma 7.4 is due to Olariu *et al.* [244]. This result extends that of
Theorem 2.15 (page 42) from finding a single maximum to finding prefix
maxima.

Bokka *et al.* [31] developed the set of $O(1)$ time R-Mesh algorithms for problems on convex polygons presented in Section 7.1.2.

Jang *et al.* [144] constructed the $O(1)$ time algorithm for computing all nearest neighbors of a set of N points in the plane on an $N \times N$ R-Mesh. Lai and Sheng [168] extended the algorithm and supporting geometric machinery to work for a set of d-dimensional points in the same time and size. Nakano and Olariu [230] devised an R-Mesh algorithm of the same time and size to solve the angle-restricted all nearest neighbors problem, in which the R-Mesh finds for each point its nearest point within two given directions.

The Voronoi diagram algorithm of Section 7.1.4 for the L_2 (or Euclidean) distance metric was constructed by ElGindy and Wetherall [105]. The same authors also devised a Voronoi diagram algorithm for the L_1 (or Manhattan) distance metric [104].

Lai and Sheng [168] developed the Euclidean minimum spanning tree (EMST) algorithm of Section 7.1.5 for points in two dimensions. They also extended the algorithm to work in the same time and on the same size R-Mesh for points in any constant number of dimensions. Nakano and Olariu [230] developed an EMST algorithm for points in the plane that runs in $O(1)$ time on an $N \times N^2$ R-Mesh as an application of their angle-restricted all nearest neighbors algorithm. It also utilizes the relative neighborhood graph.

The triangulation algorithm of Section 7.1.6 is due to Jang *et al.* [144]. Bokka *et al.* [32] developed $O(1)$ time R-Mesh algorithms for triangulation of regions with holes.

Additional R-Mesh algorithms for computational geometry problems include the following: Kim and Cho [158] on point visibility; Jang *et al.* [144] on 3D maxima, two-set dominance counting, and smallest enclosing box; Ercal and Lee [107] on maze routing; and Murshed and Brent [223] on contour of maximal elements.

The algorithms for image component labeling are due to Miller *et al.* [216] and Alnuweiri [4]. Olariu *et al.* [243] devised the median row algorithm and the $O(g \log \log N)$ time histogram algorithm, while Jang *et al.* [146] constructed the histogram algorithm of Theorem 7.21. Lee *et al.* [169] constructed the algorithm for extracting the quadtree representation of an image on an R-Mesh with the enhanced ability to write selected bits. Kim and Jang [159] constructed an algorithm along different lines, but needing more processors. Chung [57] developed the R-Mesh algorithm for computing moments of a horizontally and vertically convex binary image.

Pan [253] devised the Hough and Radon Transform algorithms, Pan *et al.* [260] constructed the City Block Distance Transform algorithm.

Datta and Soundaralakshmi [76] designed the Euclidean Distance Transform algorithm; Pan *et al.* [256] presented a slower, but more efficient, Euclidean Distance Transform algorithm that runs on an $N \times N$ R-Mesh in $O(\log^2 N)$ time. Datta [72] framed the Medial Axis Transform algorithm, and Pan *et al.* [257] shaped the Continuous Wavelet Transform algorithm.

Other R-Mesh algorithms for image processing problems not covered in this chapter include Chung [58] for template matching and Tsai *et al.* [326] for hierarchical clustering.

PART III

SIMULATIONS AND COMPLEXITY

Chapter 8

MODEL AND ALGORITHMIC SCALABILITY

This chapter examines running an algorithm designed for a model of a particular size on a different-sized instance of that model or of a different model. In a general setting, this introduces the problem of *scaling simulations* or *self-simulations*, in which an instance of a model simulates a differently-sized instance of the same model. Here, we wish to show the flexibility of an implementation of a model in a given size. An algorithm may demand the number of processors to depend on the problem size. For instance, numerous algorithms in earlier chapters claimed N processors or N^2 processors to solve a problem of size N. An R-Mesh implementation, however, cannot vary its number of processors as the sizes of its problems vary. If a model is *scalable*, then it can scale down the number of processors that an algorithm specifies to fit an available R-Mesh, at the cost of a corresponding increase in time, while maintaining the same efficiency. This problem is trivial on many models, such as a PRAM or a standard mesh, but is not so for a reconfigurable model.

This chapter will mostly, by far, deal with cases in which a smaller model simulates a larger one, at a time cost. We will, however, also consider using a larger reconfigurable model to simulate a smaller one with the aim of speeding up a computation. These two directions of simulation fall within a framework of time-size tradeoffs: employing more time to save processors or employing more processors to save time. We want to examine the required costs in either direction to obtain a desired savings.

Apart from general scaling simulations of models, we also look at individual algorithms. Even if a model does not admit an optimal scaling simulation (or if none is yet known), it may be possible to optimally scale the number of processors down for many specific algorithms. The scaling of models discussed to this point has the aim of preserving efficiency. For particular algorithms, we may do even better. Many reconfigurable algorithms are quite inefficient, lavishly spending processors to reach the coveted goal of constant time. Scaling such algorithms simply preserves the inefficiency, while losing the merit of a constant time solution. Some algorithms permit us to increase efficiency as the number of processors scales down. Such a viewpoint has existed previously in the VLSI context in the form of AT^2 optimality, where A denotes area and T denotes time. We generalize this to AT^α-scalability, for constant α, terming the maximum value of α for a problem as the *degree of scalability*.

Section 8.1 presents self-simulations for the HVR-Mesh, LR-Mesh, FR-Mesh, and R-Mesh. Each requires different simulation techniques to accommodate the different possible bus configurations. Section 8.2 sketches results for speeding up the computation of a smaller reconfigurable model by simulating it on a larger model. Section 8.3 introduces the concept of degree of scalability, then gives a pair of examples of algorithms that increase in efficiency as the number of processors decreases.

8.1　Scaling Simulation on a Smaller Model Instance

This section deals with the ability of versions of the R-Mesh to adapt any algorithm calling for a reconfigurable mesh of an arbitrary size to run on a given smaller model instance without significant loss of efficiency. A scaling simulation achieves this adaptation, and the *simulation overhead* expresses the efficiency of the simulation. Such scaling simulations extend numerous R-Mesh algorithms in directions of greater practical use and provide a rich palette of fundamental procedures for designing algorithms that scale with low overhead on the R-Mesh.

Scaling Simulation. Let $\mathcal{M}(N)$ denote an N-processor instance of a model, $\mathcal{M}$, of parallel computation. A *scaling simulation* for $\mathcal{M}$ is an algorithm that simulates an arbitrary step of $\mathcal{M}(N)$ on a smaller instance $\mathcal{M}(P)$, for any $P < N$. In general, this simulation runs in $\Theta\left(\frac{N}{P} \cdot f(N, P)\right)$ steps. Clearly, the work of N processors on P processors takes $\Omega\left(\frac{N}{P}\right)$ steps, therefore, $f(N, P)$, a non-decreasing function, is the *simulation overhead*. (The scaling simulation serves to establish that any algorithm designed to run in T steps on $\mathcal{M}(N)$ can run in $O\left(\frac{N}{P} \cdot f(N, P) \cdot T\right)$ steps on $\mathcal{M}(P)$.)

DEFINITION 8.1 For any $P < N$, let $\mathcal{M}(P)$ simulate a step of $\mathcal{M}(N)$ in $\Theta\left(\frac{N}{P} \cdot f(N, P)\right)$ time.

(*i*) Model $\mathcal{M}$ has an *optimal scaling simulation* if and only if $f(N,P) = O(1)$.

(*ii*) Model $\mathcal{M}$ has a *strong scaling simulation* if and only if $f(N,P)$ is independent of N and $f(N,P) = o(P)$.

(*iii*) Model $\mathcal{M}$ has a *weak scaling simulation* if and only if it does not have an optimal or strong scaling simulation and $f(N,P) = o(P)$.

<u>Remark:</u> For all three definitions above, $f(N,P) = o(P)$. This ensures that the scaling simulation runs in $o(N)$ time, that is, in less time than that required for a sequential simulation of $\mathcal{M}(N)$.

If a model possesses an optimal scaling simulation, then an algorithm designer or programmer has no need for concern about the size of the actual machine that will implement the algorithm. The same algorithm retains its efficiency for all sizes up to the size for which the algorithm was designed. If a model possesses a strong scaling simulation, then the simulation overhead depends only on P, not on N. Therefore, one algorithm suffices for all sizes again. A compiler tuned to simulating model size P can perform the processor mapping according to the scaling simulation. If a model possesses a weak scaling simulation, then the algorithm fastest for one combination of problem size and machine size may not be fastest for a different combination. The programmer may need to tweak the algorithm or replace it altogether. One may need a collection of algorithms for a given problem to match different problem size-model size combinations.

In a conventional, non-reconfigurable model such as a mesh or a PRAM, an optimal scaling simulation proceeds along straightforward lines. Simply let each processor of $\mathcal{M}(P)$ simulate $\frac{N}{P}$ processors of $\mathcal{M}(N)$ in an obvious manner. The situation is different for reconfigurable models because of the different way they perform operations. For example, suppose a problem has N different answers and the R-Mesh algorithm provides for N different processors such that whichever processor receives a signal indicates the corresponding answer. If an R-Mesh has only $P < N$ destination processors, however, this solution approach will not work.

We will present scaling simulations for four variants of the R-Mesh: optimal scaling simulations of the HVR-Mesh and LR-Mesh, a strong scaling simulation of the FR-Mesh, and the currently best-known (weak) scaling simulation of the general R-Mesh. The latter three are quite involved, so we principally sketch the flow of the algorithms, and omit some intricate (though necessary) technical details. They share a common high level structure. It is an open problem whether the general R-Mesh permits an optimal scaling simulation.

Processor Mappings. Some processor mappings recur in the scaling simulations, so we define the primary ones here. Let Q denote the simulated $N \times N$ reconfigurable mesh, and let $\mathcal{R}$ denote the simulating $P \times P$ reconfigurable mesh, where $P < N$. Without loss of generality, assume that $\frac{N}{P}$ is an integer. Each processor of $\mathcal{R}$ will simulate $\frac{N^2}{P^2}$ processors of Q. (Note that Q and $\mathcal{R}$ have N^2 and P^2 processors, respectively, rather than N and P processors, as was the case for the pair of models earlier in this chapter.) In the *contraction mapping*, each processor of $\mathcal{R}$ simulates an $\frac{N}{P} \times \frac{N}{P}$ sub-R-Mesh of Q. One can view the mapping as contracting each sub-R-Mesh to a single processor (Figure 8.1(a)). We will also consider a *windows mapping* (Figure 8.1(b)) and a *folds*

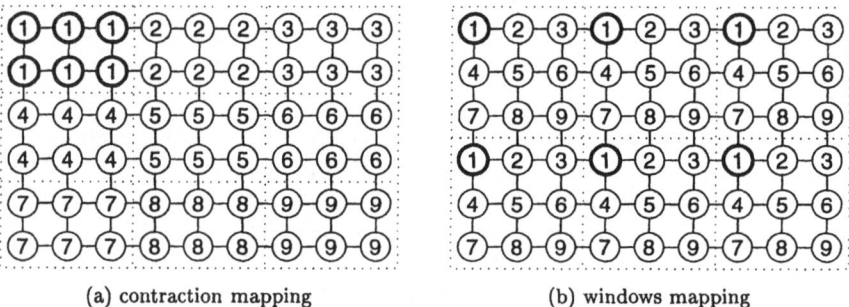

(a) contraction mapping   (b) windows mapping

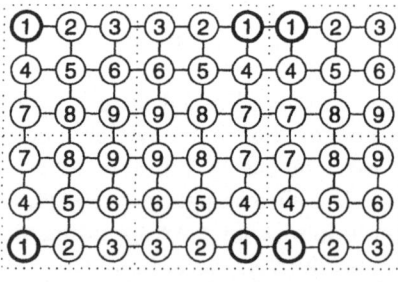

(c) folds mapping

Figure 8.1. Mappings of 6×9 R-Mesh to 3×3 R-Mesh, where numbers indicate processors of the 3×3 R-Mesh in row-major order: (a) contraction mapping, (b) windows mapping, and (c) folds mapping. The bold 1's in the figure denote the processors of 6×9 R-Mesh Q that processor 1 of 3×3 R-Mesh $\mathcal{R}$ simulates in each mapping.

Reprinted with permission from the *IEEE Transactions on Parallel and Distributed Systems*, vol. 9, no. 9, J. A. Fernández-Zepeda, R. Vaidyanathan, and J. L. Trahan, "Scaling Simulation of the Fusing-Restricted Reconfigurable Mesh," pp. 861–871, September 1998 (© 2003 IEEE).

mapping (Figure 8.1(c)), both of which partition simulating machine Q into *windows*, where each window is a $P \times P$ sub-R-Mesh. In the folds mapping, picture the larger $N \times N$ mesh folded over and over to form a stack of area $P \times P$ and $\frac{N^2}{P^2}$ layers high. Each processor of R simulates the $\frac{N^2}{P^2}$ processors stacked on top of each other. In the windows mapping, a processor of R simulates the processor in the same position in each window of Q. One can view this mapping as placing the $P \times P$ mesh R over each window of Q.

Simulation Structure. Before we proceed with the details of the individual scaling simulations, we present an overall structure that is common to all these scaling simulations. Each simulation comprises two stages.

Component determination—Partition the ports of the simulated R-Mesh into blocks, such that ports in the same block are incident on the same bus. Some simulations explicitly compute a component number for each block, analogously to numbering connected components of a graph. Other simulations implicitly use component information.

Data delivery and homogenization—Handle writes to buses so that simulating ports read the same data as in the simulated model. This requires making a uniform decision on data written at the same time in the simulated model, but at different times in the simulating model. In the simulations, this stage follows along the same structure as the component determination stage, so we generally omit its description.

8.1.1 Scaling the HVR-Mesh

The HVR-Mesh (see also Section 3.1.1) is a restriction of the R-Mesh that permits only horizontal and vertical buses. That is, a processor may fuse its N and S ports or leave them disconnected and may fuse its E and W ports or leave them disconnected. The HVR-Mesh has an optimal scaling simulation.

Let Q denote the simulated $N \times N$ HVR-Mesh. We will construct a $P \times P$ HVR-Mesh, R, that will simulate Q step-by-step. This simulation assumes that both the simulated and simulating HVR-Meshes have the same concurrent write rule, one of COMMON, COLLISION, COLLISION$^+$, ARBITRARY, or PRIORITY (see also Section 3.1.3). If the write rule is PRIORITY, then the scaling simulation also assumes that the priority is consistent with a row-major or column-major ordering of processors.

Use the the contraction mapping to map processors from $N \times N$ HVR-Mesh Q to $P \times P$ HVR-Mesh R. The simulation of Q by R proceeds in three phases. First, each processor of R resolves the writes in its $\frac{N}{P} \times \frac{N}{P}$ sub-HVR-Mesh to determine which values exit on buses at the boundary of the sub-R-Mesh. Second, processors of $\mathcal{R}$ connect their buses according to the configuration of $\mathcal{Q}$ to convey writes along rows and columns across sub-R-Mesh borders. Third, processors convey values received to readers within their simulated sub-R-Mesh.

Phase 1 — Local: The HVR-Mesh can only support independent row and column buses. Each processor of $\mathcal{R}$ locally sweeps along each row and each column of the simulated sub-R-Mesh of $\mathcal{Q}$ to determine which values are written to the bus, to resolve write conflicts according to the concurrent write rule, and to deliver data to the simulated boundary processors. Each row has $\frac{N}{P}$ processors, as does each column, and there are $\frac{N}{P}$ such rows and $\frac{N}{P}$ such columns local to each processor, so this phase runs in $O\left(\frac{N^2}{P^2}\right)$ time.

If a bus does not exit a sub-R-Mesh, then the processor can deliver the data to the readers that it simulates on this bus during this phase. If a bus exits a sub-R-Mesh, then values written on the same row or column of $\mathcal{Q}$ in a different sub-R-Mesh may affect the value read, so the next two phases identify the value appearing on the bus and convey it to readers.

Phase 2 — Global: Processors in the same row of $\mathcal{R}$ simulate processors in the same $\frac{N}{P}$ rows of $\mathcal{Q}$. To handle border-crossing writes (on buses of $\mathcal{Q}$ spanning two or more processors of $\mathcal{R}$), these processors simulate writes on each of these rows in turn. ($\mathcal{R}$ handles columns similarly.) When simulating row i, if a horizontal bus spans the sub-R-Mesh simulated by processor $p_{j,k}$ of $\mathcal{R}$, then $p_{j,k}$ fuses its W and E ports; otherwise, $p_{j,k}$ leaves its W and E ports disconnected. Next, each processor writes on its W and E ports the values conveyed out of the corresponding ports of its border processors on row i. HVR-Mesh $\mathcal{R}$ resolves concurrent writes here according to the same rule used by $\mathcal{Q}$. Each processor reads the values received on its W and E ports. These values correspond to the values received by processors on sub-R-Mesh boundaries of $\mathcal{Q}$.

Handling writes on each row (and each column) takes $O(1)$ time, so this phase runs in $O\left(\frac{N}{P}\right)$ time.

Phase 3 — Local: Each processor now delivers the values received at its simulated boundary processors in Phase 2 to interior processors. Much like Phase 1, this phase runs in $O\left(\frac{N^2}{P^2}\right)$ time.   ∎

THEOREM 8.2 *For any $P < N$, a step of an $N \times N$ CRCW HVR-Mesh can be optimally simulated by a $P \times P$ CRCW HVR-Mesh in $O\left(\frac{N^2}{P^2}\right)$ time. Hence, the HVR-Mesh possesses an optimal scaling simulation.*

<u>Remark:</u> If the simulated HVR-Mesh $\mathcal{Q}$ is CREW, then so is the simulating HVR-Mesh $\mathcal{R}$.

8.1.2   Scaling the LR-Mesh

The LR-Mesh is very similar to the HVR-Mesh in that both permit only linear buses with no branching. The added flexibility of allowing buses to bend and twist, however, endows the LR-Mesh with the potential to solve problems in ways and in times not possible for the HVR-Mesh (for instance, solving parity in constant time). It also requires a different approach to a scaling simulation. A contraction mapping fails to admit an optimal scaling simulation.

THEOREM 8.3 *A $P \times P$ LR-Mesh using the contraction mapping requires $\Omega(N)$ steps to simulate each step of an $N \times N$ LR-Mesh, for any $P < N$.*

<u>Proof:</u> The example in Figure 8.2 illustrates the idea behind Theorem 8.3 for $P = \frac{N}{2}$. Circles denote processors of the $N \times N$ LR-Mesh $\mathcal{Q}$;

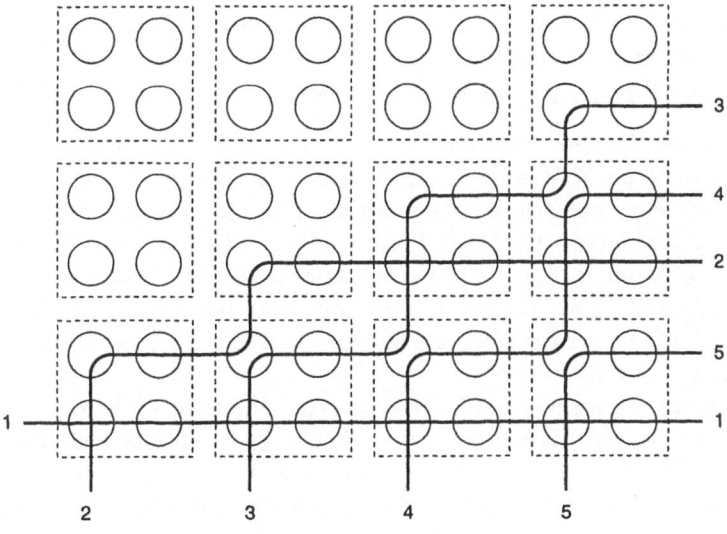

Figure 8.2. Case establishing lower bound using contraction mapping. (Dashed boxes correspond to simulating processors.)

boxes denote processors of the $\frac{N}{2} \times \frac{N}{2}$ LR-Mesh $\mathcal{R}$, where each processor simulates a 2×2 sub-R-Mesh of Q. Bus 1 is straight; bus j, for $j > 1$, has j "stair steps" except for buses toward the right side of the R-Mesh. Observe in the bottom left simulating processor of $\mathcal{R}$ that bus 1 exits from the E port of one of its simulated processors and bus 2 exits from the E port of another. Since this processor of $\mathcal{R}$ simulates both of those ports of Q with its own (one) E port, the simulating machine $\mathcal{R}$ must simulate buses 1 and 2 in separate steps. (That is, $\mathcal{R}$ must use separate steps if it is to simulate each bus in its entirety in a single step. We simplify the argument by making this assumption; it is not necessary.) Observe now for bus 3 that, in one processor of $\mathcal{R}$, it exits the E port of one simulated processor, while bus 1 exits the E port of another— sharing the E port of a processor of $\mathcal{R}$. In a different processor of $\mathcal{R}$, bus 3 exits the E port of one simulated processor, while bus 2 exits the E port of another. Consequently, buses 1, 2, and 3 must be simulated in separate steps. Continuing, Q may possess $\frac{N}{2} + 1$ such buses such that bus j shares an E port of a processor of $\mathcal{R}$ with each lower indexed bus. This establishes the lower bound.   ∎

The folds mapping, however, does permit an optimal scaling simulation of an LR-Mesh, though the simulation becomes considerably more complicated than that of the HVR-Mesh. The following theorem states the result we will now prove.

THEOREM 8.4 *For any $P < N$, each step of an $N \times N$ CRCW LR-Mesh can be optimally simulated by a $P \times P$ CRCW LR-Mesh in $O\left(\frac{N^2}{P^2}\right)$ time. Hence, the LR-Mesh possesses an optimal scaling simulation.*

Let Q denote the simulated $N \times N$ LR-Mesh. We will construct a $P \times P$ LR-Mesh, $\mathcal{R}$, that will simulate Q step-by-step. ($\mathcal{R}$ is actually of size $4P \times 4P$ to perform a connected components computation. Mostly, though, it emulates a $P \times P$ LR-Mesh readily.) Without loss of generality, assume $\frac{N}{P}$ is an integer. Map processors of Q to $\mathcal{R}$ according to the folds mapping. This simulation assumes that both Q and $\mathcal{R}$ have the same concurrent write rules, one of COMMON, COLLISION, COLLISION$^+$, ARBITRARY, or PRIORITY.

The simulation proceeds in two sweeps. The first, or forward, sweep progresses window-by-window in snakelike order across the simulated LR-Mesh Q. For each linear bus, it maintains the value appearing on the bus among those written to it in the windows scanned thus far, a bus ID, and two current endpoints. The second, or reverse, sweep progresses in the opposite order over the windows, delivering final data to each reader processor. (Within the general structure of scaling simulations sketched on page 281, the first sweep performs component determination mixed with the beginning of data delivery, while the second sweep completes data delivery.)

Some terminology will help to explain the forward sweep. The current window of Q has at most four neighboring windows, some of which may have been previously scanned. Some bus segments may enter the window from previously scanned windows. If such a segment is from the immediately preceding window, then call it an "entering segment;" otherwise, it is an "awakening segment." Some bus segments may leave the window to windows not yet scanned. If such a segment is going to the immediate successor window (or "next window"), then call it a "leaving segment;" otherwise, call it a "going-to-sleep segment."

Buses entirely contained within a window can be simulated by $\mathcal{R}$ exactly as in Q during the forward sweep; therefore, we will no longer concern ourselves with them and, instead, will focus solely on buses that cross window boundaries. Observe, with the folds mapping, that the columns (or rows) of processors on each side of a window boundary in Q are simulated by the same column (or row) of processors in $\mathcal{R}$. (See Figure 8.1.) Consequently, when moving from one window to the next, those processors of $\mathcal{R}$ already automatically hold the information that must cross window boundaries: bus data, bus ID, and current endpoints.

The vital fact that allows this simulation to work is that, for an LR-Mesh, each (acyclic) bus has exactly two endpoints. Therefore, maintaining the identity of the two current endpoints (current with respect to the sweep) and permitting the processors that simulate those endpoints to access current bus data allows an optimal scaling simulation.

Observe that window boundaries chop a linear bus that spans several windows into multiple segments. Boundaries may even create multiple segments within the same window for a single bus, as the bus may weave in and out of the window and its neighbors. Figure 8.3 shows a single linear bus with three disjoint segments within the same window. Assume $\mathcal{R}$ has previously scanned windows W_1, W_2, W_3, and W_4. In this example, reaching window W_5 simulated by $\mathcal{R}$, processors would receive as input that an awakening bus enters at A, that a bus enters at B and C, and that a bus enters at D and E—from information outside W_5, these appear to be three distinct buses. The window simulation of W_5 must determine that these are the same bus, assign a single bus ID, combine data written to these buses, and cull the endpoints to two: the endpoint prior to A and a current endpoint at F. We now proceed to describe a window simulation during the forward sweep.

1. If an entering segment has an awakening partner (the other end of the same bus with the same ID—see Figure 8.4), then it conveys bus

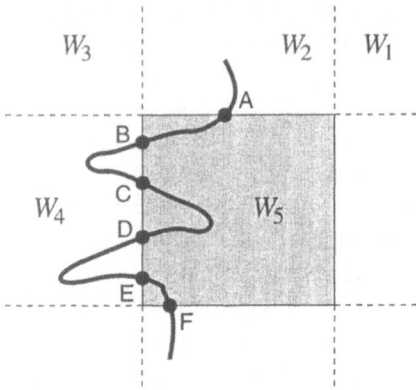

Figure 8.3.   Multiple disjoint segments of the same linear bus in the same window.

ID, data, and endpoint information that may have changed since the partner went to sleep.

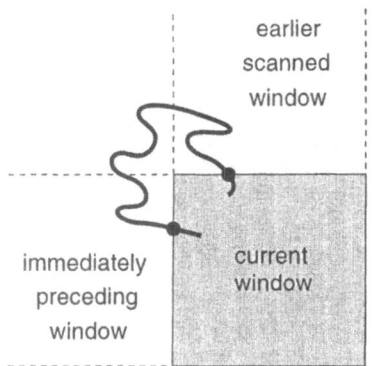

Figure 8.4.   Example of entering segment with an awakening partner.

2. If an awakening segment does not have an entering partner, then the "column stack" (in which a column of processors holds information to be extracted in later windows) conveys current information on its bus.

3. Configure processors of $\mathcal{R}$ according to the configurations of processors of the current window of $\mathcal{Q}$. Actually, use 2×2 blocks of processors of $\mathcal{R}$ for each processor of $\mathcal{Q}$ and set up a dual bus structure with two copies of each bus. (For an example, see Figure 8.5.)

Call the processor at a window boundary at the end of a bus segment

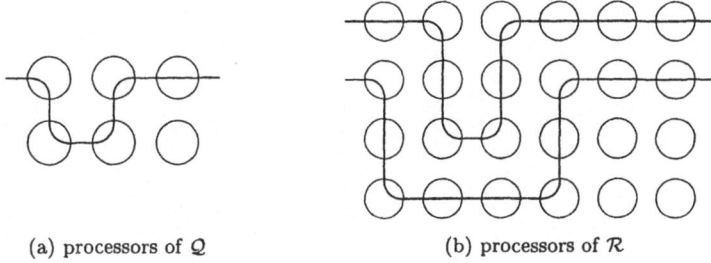

(a) processors of $\mathcal{Q}$ (b) processors of $\mathcal{R}$

Figure 8.5. Dual bus structure of $\mathcal{R}$ mimicking that of $\mathcal{Q}$.

as a boss processor for that segment. Each boss processor conveys its bus information along one of the dual buses to the processor at the opposite end of the segment.

4. Each boss processor may hold bus information from (a) no other boss processors (if the bus terminates within the window), (b) from one other boss processor (via a bus segment inside the window or a bus segment outside the window), or (c) from two other boss processors (one via a bus segment inside the window and the other via a bus segment outside the window). Each boss processor copies its information to the top row of $\mathcal{R}$ acting as a $2P \times 2P$ LR-Mesh and to the leftmost column of $\mathcal{R}$. (See Figure 8.6.)

5. Generate an adjacency matrix according to the connections described in Steps 3 and 4. Processors configure their connections such that a processor holding a 1 has a connection to the other processor holding a 1 in its column (and its row), if such a processor exists. (See Figure 8.6.) Using a dual bus structure, the processors at either end of each linear bus created from the adjacency matrix exchange bus IDs and select the minimum as the new bus ID.

6. The final step of a window simulation in the forward pass is for each boss processor to convey bus information to the opposite endpoint. If that endpoint is in the current window, then it already holds bus information from Step 5. If that endpoint is in a previous window and is not dormant (that is, it is an actual endpoint of the bus in a previous window, not a tentative endpoint created by a window boundary), then do nothing now, the reverse sweep will convey bus information. Lastly, if that endpoint is dormant, then if the bus

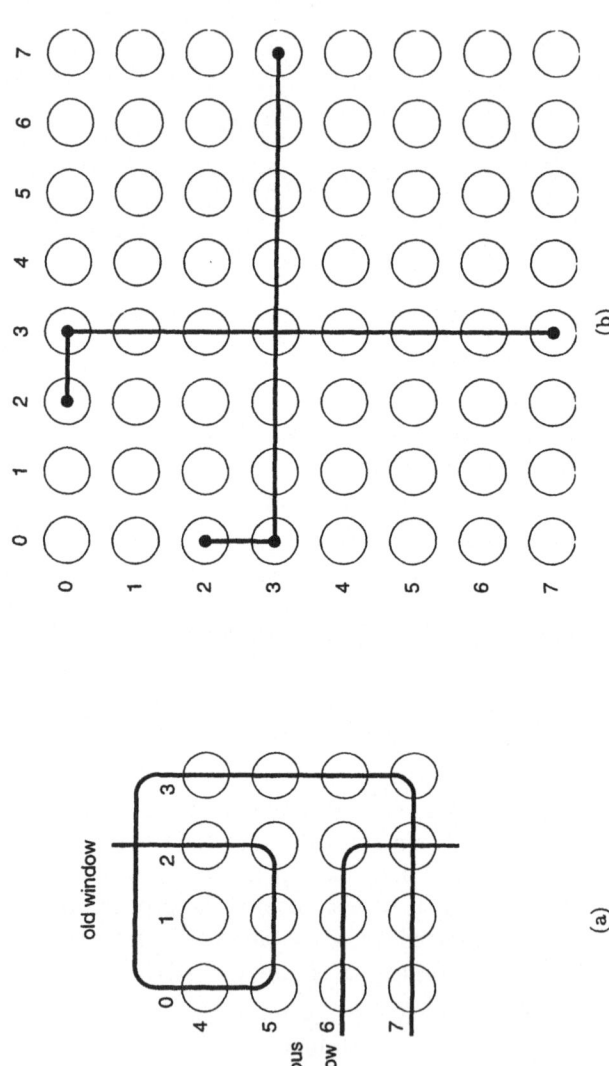

Figure 8.6. Linear connected components (LCC) example. Observe in (b) that processor (0, 2) holds a 1 because of the bus between processors 0 and 2 in (a); similarly, processor (0, 3) holds a 1 because of a connection from a previously seen (old) window. The LR-Mesh in (b) connects them because they are two ones in the same row.

segment continues to the next window, then it is not necessary to update the dormant endpoint, however, if the bus segment is going-to-sleep, then update it via the column stack.

At the end of the forward sweep, at least one endpoint (the last end-point seen in the sweep) holds final bus information—bus data, bus ID, and identity of the other endpoint. The reverse sweep simply uses this information and configuration information from the forward sweep to convey the bus data to all reader processors on the bus.

Observe that each window simulation runs in $O(1)$ time, and that each of the forward and reverse sweeps comprises $O\left(\frac{N^2}{P^2}\right)$ such simulations. Consequently, $\mathcal{R}$ simulates each step of $\mathcal{Q}$ in $O\left(\frac{N^2}{P^2}\right)$ time, and the LR-Mesh possesses an optimal scaling simulation.

8.1.3 Scaling the FR-Mesh

The FR-Mesh, or Fusing Restricted R-Mesh, allows only two of the 15 internal configurations possible on the R-Mesh, the "crossover" con-nection, joining the N port with the S port and the E port with the W port, and a "fusing" connection, joining all four ports. Nevertheless, the FR-Mesh is as "powerful" as the (unrestricted) R-Mesh (see Chapter 9 for more details). Further, the FR-Mesh admits constant time algo-rithms for fundamental problems (such as *s-t* connectivity, connected components, transitive closure, and cycle detection) that are not known to be solvable in constant time on the LR-Mesh[1]; many such problems are fundamental to algorithm development in general.

First, look at the local picture resulting from FR-Mesh internal con-figuration restrictions. Because of the FR-Mesh connections, assume without loss of generality that each processor in an FR-Mesh has only two ports, a *vertical port* (N and S ports) and a *horizontal port* (E and W ports). Second, the global picture is that the FR-Mesh has *horizon-tal* (row) *buses* and *vertical* (column) *buses* such that each intersection of a row bus and a column bus can be fused or left disconnected. A *component* is a maximally connected set of buses, connected by fusing connections in the FR-Mesh.

We now sketch a strong scaling simulation for the FR-Mesh. Specifi-cally, we simulate each step of $N \times N$ FR-Mesh, $\mathcal{Q}$, on $P \times P$ FR-Mesh,

---

[1]The class of languages accepted by an LR-Mesh (resp., R-Mesh) in constant time with poly-nomial number of processors is equivalent to the class L (resp., SL) of languages accepted in logarithmic space (resp., symmetric logarithmic space) on a Turing machine. Many prob-lems such as *s-t* connectivity are in class SL, but are not known to be in class L, and it is a longstanding conjecture that SL properly contains L.

$\mathcal{R}$, in $O\!\left(\frac{N^2}{P^2}\log P\right)$ time. This simulation maps processors of $\mathcal{Q}$ to those of $\mathcal{R}$ according to the windows mapping (Figure 8.1(b)). The structure of the simulation resembles that of the LR-Mesh (Section 8.1.2) in that it also involves a window-by-window simulation and two phases: one to determine components and the second to deliver data. (Each phase involves two sweeps across $\mathcal{Q}$.) During the component determination phase, $\mathcal{R}$ labels buses of $\mathcal{Q}$ with component numbers. By this method, $\mathcal{R}$ can recognize that ports with the same component number share a common bus, whether or not they are connected in $\mathcal{R}$. Via the use of windows, $\mathcal{R}$ can embed the same connections as a window of $\mathcal{Q}$, as in the LR-Mesh scaling simulation. The similarity ends here, however. The LR-Mesh simulation accounted for bus segments outside a window by utilizing a linear connected components algorithm, embedding the adjacency matrix. The FR-Mesh simulation actually embeds within the window the effects of the relevant connections outside the window by a process termed *prefix assimilation*. It takes advantage of the fact that, due to internal processor configurations, the FR-Mesh contains contiguous row buses and column buses (hence, the scaling simulation does not extend to the general R-Mesh).

We invoke two types of prefix assimilation: horizontal prefix assimilation and vertical prefix assimilation. A key aspect of prefix assimilation is a *leader election* procedure that selects a leader (or component number) for each component of the slice scanned so far. Without a PRIORITY concurrent write, this procedure runs in $O(\log P)$ time and is the only source of the $O(\log P)$ simulation overhead.

Define a *slice* of $\mathcal{Q}$ to be an $N \times P$ sub-FR-Mesh. Denote slice v by $\mathcal{S}_v$, where $0 \le v < \frac{N}{P}$. Each slice contains $\frac{N}{P}$ windows, each a $P \times P$ sub-FR-Mesh. Denote window u of slice $\mathcal{S}_v$ by $\mathcal{W}_{u,v}$, where $0 \le u, v < \frac{N}{P}$. (See Figure 8.7.)

FR-Mesh $\mathcal{R}$ gradually discovers the bus configurations of $\mathcal{Q}$ by a slice-by-slice horizontal sweep across $\mathcal{Q}$ (then back). Within the processing of each slice, $\mathcal{R}$ performs a window-by-window vertical sweep down (then back up) each slice of $\mathcal{Q}$. The first vertical sweeps of the first horizontal sweep traverse the windows of $\mathcal{Q}$ in column-major order (considering $\mathcal{Q}$ to be an $\frac{N}{P} \times \frac{N}{P}$ array of windows).

Algorithm 8.1 gives a pseudocode description of the component determination phase.

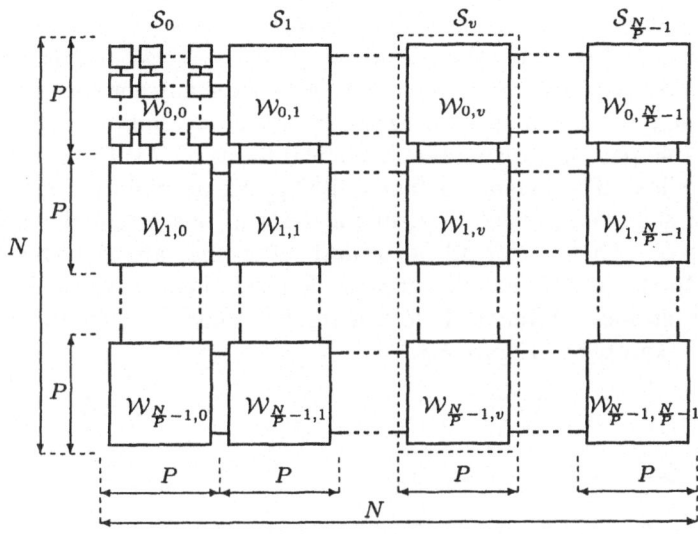

Figure 8.7. Decomposition of the simulated FR-Mesh $\mathcal{Q}$ into slices and windows. Reprinted with permission from the *IEEE Transactions on Parallel and Distributed Systems*, vol. 9, no. 9, J. A. Fernández-Zepeda, R. Vaidyanathan, and J. L. Trahan, "Scaling Simulation of the Fusing-Restricted Reconfigurable Mesh," pp. 861–871, September 1998 (© 2003 IEEE).

Algorithm 8.1 (FR-Mesh Component Determination)

Model: A $P \times P$ FR-Mesh, $\mathcal{R}$.
Input: Configuration of an $N \times N$ FR-Mesh, $\mathcal{Q}$, where $N > P$.
Output: Component numbers for each bus of the configuration of $\mathcal{R}$.

begin
    for $v \leftarrow 0$ **to** $\frac{N}{P} - 1$ **do** for slice $\mathcal{S}_v$ in $\mathcal{Q}$
        horizontal prefix assimilation
        for $u \leftarrow 0$ **to** $\frac{N}{P} - 1$ **do** for window $\mathcal{W}_{u,v}$

            vertical prefix assimilation
            component numbering

        end

        second vertical component sweep
    end
    second horizontal component sweep
end

Each iteration of the horizontal sweep consists of horizontal prefix assimilation, then two vertical sweeps, which we now briefly describe. Horizontal prefix assimilation embeds within the current slice the effects of bus configurations in preceding slices. Let C be a component such that at least one pair of horizontal and vertical buses of C is fused within the current slice. The essence of horizontal prefix assimilation is to select for each such component C a unique vertical bus b to link horizontal buses in C. That is, for all horizontal buses that are in C because of fusings to the left of the current slice, $\mathcal{R}$ fuses them to vertical bus b in the current slice. Afterward, $\mathcal{R}$ can treat the current slice in isolation. (See the example in Figure 8.8.)

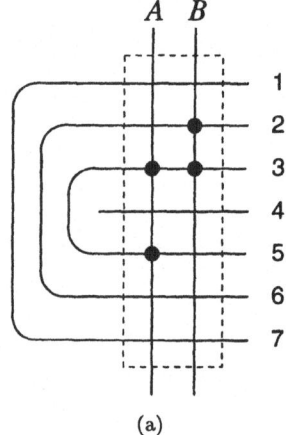 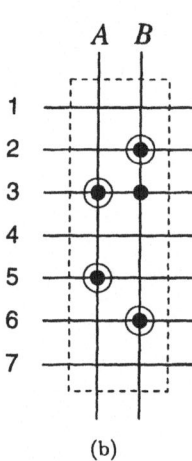

(a)   (b)

Figure 8.8. An illustration of horizontal prefix assimilation: (a) components and fusing connections in a slice before horizontal prefix assimilation, (b) slice after horizontal prefix assimilation, where added fusing connection are circled.

Reprinted with permission from the *IEEE Transactions on Parallel and Distributed Systems*, vol. 9, no. 9, J. A. Fernández-Zepeda, R. Vaidyanathan, and J. L. Trahan, "Scaling Simulation of the Fusing-Restricted Reconfigurable Mesh," pp. 861–871, September 1998 (© 2003 IEEE).

In the first vertical sweep, $\mathcal{R}$ performs vertical prefix assimilation at each window when sweeping down each slice. It is effectively a special case of horizontal prefix assimilation on a window rather than a slice. Also at each window, $\mathcal{R}$ assigns component numbers to ports in the current window. It uses leader election to select the vertical bus with the largest index, and a processor on that bus provides its component number. A $\log P$ factor overhead arises from leader election as $\mathcal{R}$ must select one of $O(P)$ candidate values. (Note that this additional overhead vanishes if simulating FR-Mesh $\mathcal{R}$ uses PRIORITY concurrent write.)

The second vertical sweep propagates component numbers assigned by the bottom window of the slice to the upper windows since fusings in lower windows may change component numbers. The second horizontal sweep serves an analogous purpose across slices.

The data delivery phase of the scaling simulation delivers the appropriate data to each port. It comprises sweeps like those of the component determination phase. *Data homogenization* refers to the work of Q to ensure that all ports in the same component receive the same data. Window homogenization performs data homogenization in a window by combining data written within the window and data entering the window through its borders, according to the concurrent write rule. The main step of window homogenization is to physically connect, within the window, all buses in the same component. Slice homogenization handles potential inconsistencies arising at a larger scale (such as two buses in the same component without a connection within a particular slice). Algorithm 8.2 gives a pseudocode description of the data delivery phase.

Algorithm 8.2 (FR-Mesh Data Delivery)

Model: A $P \times P$ FR-Mesh, $\mathcal{R}$.

Input: Port component numbers and values written for an $N \times N$ FR-Mesh, Q, where $N > P$.

Output: bus value for each port of $\mathcal{R}$.

begin
    for $v \leftarrow 0$ **to** $\frac{N}{P} - 1$ **do** for slice $\mathcal{S}_v$ in Q
        for $u \leftarrow 0$ **to** $\frac{N}{P} - 1$ **do** for window $\mathcal{W}_{u,v}$ in $\mathcal{S}_v$

           window homogenization

        end

        second vertical data sweep

        slice homogenization
    end
    second horizontal data sweep
end

THEOREM 8.5 *For any $P < N$, each step of an $N \times N$ COMMON, COLLISION, COLLISION$^+$, or PRIORITY CRCW FR-Mesh can be simulated on a $P \times P$ COMMON, COLLISION, or COLLISION$^+$ CRCW FR-Mesh in $O\left(\frac{N^2}{P^2} \log P\right)$ time. Hence, the FR-Mesh has a strong scaling simulation.*

294 *DYNAMIC RECONFIGURATION*

As observed earlier, the $O(\log P)$ simulation overhead stems from a leader election procedure. If the simulating FR-Mesh resolves concurrent writes by the PRIORITY rule, though, leader election runs in constant time and an optimal scaling simulation results.

THEOREM 8.6 *For any $P < N$, each step of an $N \times N$ COMMON, COLLISION, COLLISION$^+$, or PRIORITY CRCW FR-Mesh can be simulated on a $P \times P$ PRIORITY CRCW FR-Mesh in $O\left(\frac{N^2}{P^2}\right)$ time. Hence the PRIORITY CRCW FR-Mesh possesses an optimal scaling simulation.* ∎

8.1.4 Scaling the R-Mesh

The best known deterministic and randomized scaling simulations of the general R-Mesh, oddly enough, both scale the R-Mesh down to run on a (weaker) LR-Mesh, yet by very different techniques. Both are very involved, so we distill them to their key ideas.

8.1.4.1 The Randomized Simulations

The randomized [2] simulations have $\tilde{O}(1)$ simulation overhead for ARBITRARY concurrent write and $\tilde{O}(\log P)$ simulation overhead for COLLISION concurrent write. The key to the simulations is, naturally, component determination, which the simulating LR-Mesh performs via simulation of a PRAM executing a connected components algorithm.

THEOREM 8.7 *For any $P < N$, each step of an $N \times N$ COMMON, COLLISION, COLLISION$^+$, or ARBITRARY CRCW R-Mesh can be simulated on:*

(*i*) *a $P \times P$ ARBITRARY CRCW LR-Mesh in $\tilde{O}\left(\log N + \frac{N^2}{P^2}\right)$ randomized time, and*

(*ii*) *a $P \times P$ COLLISION CRCW LR-Mesh in $\tilde{O}\left(\log N \log \log \log P + \frac{N^2}{P^2} \log P\right)$ randomized time.*

8.1.4.2 The Deterministic Simulation

The deterministic simulation has $O(\log N)$ simulation overhead. In this simulation, the LR-Mesh constructs a spanning tree of each component, then configures itself according to an Euler tour of that tree to perform data delivery. The overhead arises from iterations of grafting segments together to form the spanning trees. One interesting aspect is

---

[2]See Footnote 1, page 185.

that the simulating LR-Mesh needs only exclusive writes, not concurrent writes, as a processor can segment a bus and write to one side without conflict.

THEOREM 8.8 *For any $P < N$, each step of an $N \times N$ COMMON, COLLISION, COLLISION^{+}, or* PRIORITY *CRCW R-Mesh can be simulated on a $P \times P$ CREW LR-Mesh in $O\left(\frac{N^2}{P^2} \log N\right)$ time.*

The deterministic scaling simulation has three levels:

Level 1: Simulation of an $N \times N$ CRCW R-Mesh on a $2N \times 2N$ CRCW LR-Mesh,

Level 2: Simulation of a $2N \times 2N$ CRCW LR-Mesh on a $\frac{P}{2} \times \frac{P}{2}$ CRCW LR-Mesh, and

Level 3: Simulation of a $\frac{P}{2} \times \frac{P}{2}$ CRCW LR-Mesh on a $P \times P$ CREW LR-Mesh.

Level 1 uses the Euler tour technique sketched above to eliminate non-linear buses in $O(\log N)$ time. We call this technique as *bus linearization* and describe it in more detail below. Level 2 is the optimal LR-Mesh scaling simulation of Theorem 8.4. Because the scaling simulation uses concurrent writes, Level 3 uses a double-bus structure to eliminate those concurrent writes with constant overhead (Problem 8.18).

To describe the bus linearization technique, consider the simulation of an $N \times N$ COMMON CRCW R-Mesh, $\mathcal{Q}$, on a $2N \times 2N$ COMMON CRCW LR-Mesh, $\mathcal{R}$. (One can adapt the simulation to accommodate other concurrent write rules.) LR-Mesh $\mathcal{R}$ uses a 2×2 sub-LR-Mesh, called a *squad*, to simulate each processor of $\mathcal{Q}$. Each squad in $\mathcal{R}$ holds the processor index, port configuration, data to be written, and computation to be performed by the processor of $\mathcal{Q}$ it simulates.

We model the configuration of $\mathcal{Q}$ as a graph. For each processor, create a vertex for each block in its port partition. Call a vertex as *terminal* if its block contains only one port, as *linear* if its block contains two ports, and as *non-linear* if its block contains three or four ports. Create an edge between vertices u and v if $\mathcal{Q}$ contains a direct link between ports corresponding to u and v.

Step 1—Identify bus types: Categorize each bus of $\mathcal{Q}$ as non-linear, cyclic linear, or acyclic linear. Each squad handling a linear vertex now configures itself after the pattern in Figure 8.9. Each squad handling a non-linear or terminal vertex leaves its ports disconnected.

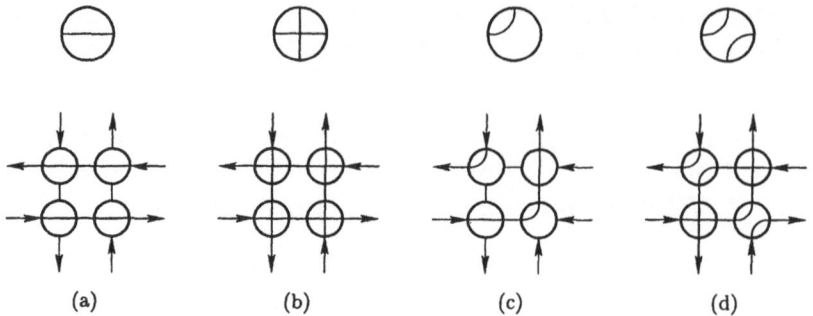

Figure 8.9. Representative linear configurations of an R-Mesh processor and corresponding LR-Mesh squad configurations.

Reprinted from the *Journal of Parallel and Distributed Computing*, vol. 62, 2002, J. A. Fernández-Zepeda, R. Vaidyanathan, and J. L. Trahan, "Using Bus Linearization to Scale the Reconfigurable Mesh," pp. 495–516, © Copyright (2002) with permission from Elsevier.

Writes by squads with non-linear vertices and with terminal vertices now identify bus types.

Step 2—Break cyclic linear buses: In each cyclic bus, elect a leader squad and cut the bus at the leader (Problem 8.19). LR-Mesh $\mathcal{R}$ can now write on all linear buses. Figure 8.10(b) illustrates this point in the algorithm for the configuration of Figure 8.10(a).

The remaining steps handle non-linear buses.

Step 3—Rake and distill the graph/configuration: Remove each terminal vertex and the chain of linear vertices connecting it to a non-linear vertex. This "rakes" leaves of the graph (Figure 8.10(c)). Next, distill the graph (and configuration) by flagging maximal chains of linear vertices as edges (Figure 8.10(d)). Call a squad representing a vertex in the raked and distilled graph as an *active squad*.

Step 4—Initiate construction of Euler tour: Each active squad selects its neighboring active squad with smallest index (if lower than its own index) as its *parent*. LR-Mesh $\mathcal{R}$ flags the edge to the selected parent as belonging to the spanning tree. Each active squad incident with a selected edge and with smaller index than its neighboring active vertices identifies itself as a *root*. Each active squad now configures itself after the pattern of Figure 8.9 for linear vertices or Figure 8.11 for non-linear and terminal vertices, except each root

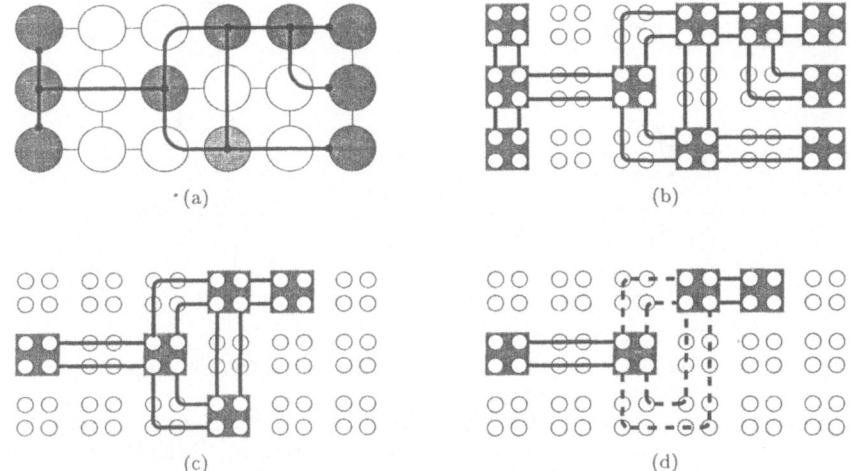

Figure 8.10. LR-Mesh simulating an R-Mesh (Steps 1–3): (a) R-Mesh configuration graph; (b) LR-Mesh simulation of edges of the graph; (c) raked graph configuration; (d) distilled graph configuration.
Reprinted from the *Journal of Parallel and Distributed Computing*, vol. 62, 2002, J. A. Fernández-Zepeda, R. Vaidyanathan, and J. L. Trahan, "Using Bus Linearization to Scale the Reconfigurable Mesh," pp. 495–516, © Copyright (2002) with permission from Elsevier.

squad removes one internal port connection. The resulting bus configuration contains a Euler tour of each tree of selected edges. The root broadcasts its index as the *label* of its tree.

Repeat the following step $2(\log N + 1)$ times.

Step 5—Graft trees: Merge trees by a graft operation as follows. Each active squad searches for a potential new parent. This parent must be in a different tree, connected by an unselected edge, and have a smaller label. The root squad of a tree selects one potential parent (if one exists) and initiates the merging of the Euler tours of the trees. After this, if a tree does not graft into another tree and is not grafted into by another tree, then it grafts into some neighboring tree.

After $2(\log N + 1)$ iterations of Step 5, $\mathcal{R}$ possesses an Euler tour of each connected component of the raked and distilled graph.

Step 6—Write data: LR-Mesh $\mathcal{R}$ now writes on unselected edges, then on Euler tours, then on raked linear chains.

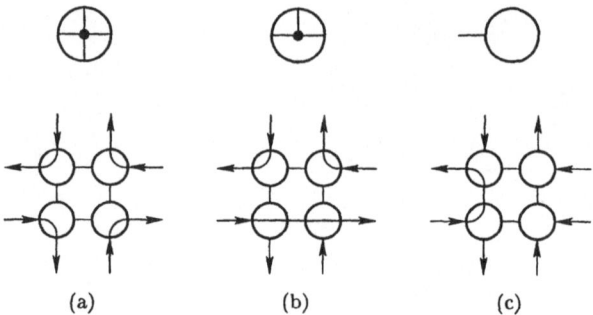

Figure 8.11. Non-linear and terminal configurations of an R-Mesh processor and corresponding LR-Mesh squad configurations.

Reprinted from the *Journal of Parallel and Distributed Computing*, vol. 62, 2002, J. A. Fernández-Zepeda, R. Vaidyanathan, and J. L. Trahan, "Using Bus Linearization to Scale the Reconfigurable Mesh," pp. 495–516, © Copyright (2002) with permission from Elsevier.

This completes the bus linearization procedure.

Whether an optimal scaling simulation is possible for the general R-Mesh is an open question. None exists, yet no lower bound proof establishing its impossibility exists either.

8.2 Self-Simulation on a Larger Model Instance

The previous section concerned itself with scaling down an arbitrary step of a model to run on a smaller version of the same model. At the expense of time, it allowed a saving in size. Its practical impetus was to permit algorithm design to assume any size model, while a compiler could map the algorithm to run on a given size machine, ideally maintaining the same efficiency. One can journey in the other direction of time-size tradeoff as well. We will state without proof self-simulations that can speed up any R-Mesh computation by any factor, at the expense of a (large) cost in size. The theoretical impact of these results is establishing that an R-Mesh can attain any speed-up of any algorithm. A potential practical motivation is to be able to construct asynchronous circuit implementations of some R-Mesh algorithms.

THEOREM 8.9 *A T step computation of an $N \times N$ bit-model DR-Mesh (directed R-Mesh) can be simulated in <u>one step</u> by an $O(N^{8^T}) \times O(N^{8^T})$ bit-model DR-Mesh.*

The simulation underlying Theorem 8.9 proceeds via composition of nondeterministic branching programs.

THEOREM 8.10 *A T step computation of an $N \times N$ bit-model R-Mesh (undirected) can be simulated in <u>one step</u> by an $N^{O(T)} \times N^{O(T)}$ bit-model R-Mesh.*

<u>Remark:</u> In particular, one side of the R-Mesh of Theorem 8.10 has size $640^{2(T-1)} \cdot N^{12T-8}$.

The simulations extend to word-model CRCW processors, though their original derivations applied to bit-model CREW processors. The size cost in both simulations is admittedly huge, yet, in both simulations, if T is a constant, as it is for many R-Mesh algorithms, then the size increase is polynomial in N. This remains within the complexity class bounds described in Chapter 9 that establish complexity classes of problems that can be solved by R-Mesh models to within a constant factor of the same time with a polynomial number of processors.

8.3   Scaling Algorithms

The preceding sections dealt with scaling an arbitrary step of a reconfigurable model, without concern about which algorithm the model was executing. This is the most general viewpoint, and holds importance for reasons stated previously. Two motivations exist, nevertheless, for examining the scalability of specific algorithms. The first motivation is that the reconfigurable model may not have a known optimal scaling algorithm in general. For specific algorithms, it may be possible to reach an optimal scaling overhead on such a model, even if such overhead is not known or even not possible for the model in general. The second motivation is that, even if the reconfigurable model does admit an optimal scaling simulation, many algorithms sacrifice efficiency to attain constant execution time. The best a standard scaling simulation can hope to accomplish is to retain the same (in-)efficiency. The irony is that the efficiency is forsaken to allow speed, yet scaling gives up speed to run on a smaller size, still burdened with inefficiency. Some algorithms can accelerate their efficiency as the number of processors decreases. The AT^2-optimal sorting algorithm of Theorem 5.7 (page 159) is an example. In this section, we briefly consider the former motivation, giving a handful of typical results, then we erect a general framework to quantify improvements in efficiency with respect to the latter motivation.

Scaling of algorithms reflects indirectly on the scaling of models, corresponding to a scaling simulation of a restricted version of the model, one restricted to those operations and patterns of communication used in the algorithms. For fundamental algorithms that admit such scaling, the corresponding restricted scalable model may still be quite general and powerful. Chapter 10 contains one such example—in developing the algorithm for routing h-relations on an LARPBS (a pipelined optical reconfigurable model for which no scaling simulation is known), it describes an optimal scaling simulation for permutation routing. This algorithm routes a permutation of N elements on P processors in $O\left(\frac{N}{P}\right)$ time. (By the way, we are adapting simulation overhead and scaling terminology from the context of model scaling simulations to the context of scaling algorithms.) A number of other scalable algorithms exist for reconfigurable optical pipelined models including prefix sums, maximum, matrix operations, selection, and singular value decomposition. Strangely, researchers have paid less attention to this topic for other reconfigurable models. The reason is probably that many R-Mesh algorithms actually run on the LR-Mesh, which possesses an optimal scaling simulation.

8.3.1   Degree of Scalability

The model scaling simulations earlier in this chapter aimed to preserve the processor-time product over a range of model sizes. In other words, an optimal scaling simulation maintains the efficiency of an algorithm as it scales. In this general setting, this is the best result possible. Many constant time R-Mesh algorithms, however, are inefficient, spending processors to save time. Blindly scaling an inefficient algorithm to run on fewer processors loses the time advantage without a compensating gain in efficiency. For specific algorithms, it is possible to accelerate the efficiency while scaling the algorithm to run on a smaller model instance. Consequently, we are interested in extending the notion of scalability to reflect the ability (or inability) of a specific algorithm to become more efficient with fewer processors (that is, for larger running times).

One such metric is AT^2 complexity, where A denotes the area occupied by the hardware used to run an algorithm and T denotes the running time. In the context of a two-dimensional R-Mesh, the area reflects the number of processors. For example, consider an R-Mesh algorithm whose AT^2 complexity does not change over a range of values for A. Let N_1 and N_0 be two values in this range with $N_1 > N_0$. If an R-Mesh with N_1 processors runs the algorithm in T_1 time, then an R-Mesh with N_0 processors can run the algorithm in $T_0 = T_1\sqrt{\frac{N_1}{N_0}}$ time. Comparing the work done with N_0 and N_1 processors, $T_0 N_0 = T_1\sqrt{N_1 N_0} < T_1 N_1$; that is, the algorithm is $\sqrt{\frac{N_1}{N_0}}$ times more efficient when run with fewer processors. Another metric is the AT complexity, which for the R-Mesh is the processor-time product. If the AT complexity does not change over a range of values for A, then the efficiency remains the same in that range. This is indeed desirable for algorithms that are efficient at the start (before they are scaled). In general, we will measure the scalability of an algorithm by its "degree of scalability," which we now define.

DEFINITION 8.11 The *degree of scalability* of an R-Mesh algorithm over a range $[T_0, T_1]$ of time is a quantity α such that for any value T such that $T_0 \leq T \leq T_1$, PT^α is the same to within a constant, where P is the number of processors needed to run the algorithm on an R-Mesh in T time.

Remark: In this section we will express results in the form: "For $T_0 \leq T \leq T_1$, an instance of size N of the problem in question can be solved on an R-Mesh with $P(N, T)$ processors in $O(T)$ time." Here $P(N, T)$ reflects the fact that the resources depend both on N and T. In this case, the degree of scalability of the algorithm is α if $\left(P(N, T) \cdot T^\alpha \right)$ is independent of T.

Notice that an algorithm with degree of scalability 1 maintains its efficiency throughout the range $[T_0, T_1]$. If an algorithm has degree of scalability $\alpha > 1$, then the algorithm increases its efficiency at lower speeds (higher values of T); by using $N_0 < N_1$ processors, the efficiency increases by a factor of $\left(\frac{N_1}{N_0} \right)^{1 - \frac{1}{\alpha}}$. Naturally, the more that an unscaled algorithm is inefficient, the more that it is likely to have a high degree of scalability. In this section, T_0 represents the highest speed that the algorithm can achieve and T_1 indicates the lowest speed that has the same degree of scalability. In general, an algorithm could exhibit different degrees of scalability over different ranges of time.

To demonstrate some examples, we will start with a multiple addition algorithm (for the problem of adding N b-bit numbers), then apply that in a matrix multiplication algorithm with degree of scalability 2. Following that, we modify the same multiple addition algorithm then apply it in a matrix-vector multiplication algorithm with degree of scalability ≥ 3.

As in Section 4.3.1, we will assume that b-bit arithmetic algorithms have inputs and outputs, each of which can be represented in b bits (in the word or distributed formats—see Section 4.1.1).

8.3.2 Matrix Multiplication with Degree of Scalability 2

The matrix multiplication algorithm uses the following multiple addition result, which was presented earlier as Lemma 4.10 (page 127). Section 8.3.3 scales it, then adapts it in a matrix-vector multiplication result with a better degree of scalability.

LEMMA 8.12 *Addition of N b-bit binary integers, where $1 \leq b \leq \sqrt{N}$, can be performed by a $b\log^2 N \times N$ R-Mesh in $O(1)$ time.*

THEOREM 8.13 *For $1 \leq T \leq N$ and $1 \leq b \leq \sqrt{N}$, the multiplication of two $N \times N$ matrices, where each element is b-bits long, can be performed by an $\frac{N^2}{T} \times \frac{N^2}{T}$ R-Mesh in $O(T)$ time.*

Proof: Let A and B denote the $N \times N$ matrices to be multiplied. For simplicity of explanation, assume N is divisible by T. Initially, let each processor in the top row hold T elements of A in row-major order and let each processor in the leftmost column hold T elements of B in column-major order. If $\log N \leq T \leq N$, then perform the algorithm of Preparata and Vuillemin [271]. Otherwise, do the following.

Partition the R-Mesh into N^2 sub-R-Meshes of size $\frac{N}{T} \times \frac{N}{T}$. In T iterations, broadcast the elements of A down each column and the elements of B across each row. Each sub-R-Mesh grabs in its diagonal processors the N elements of A that reach it in the column broadcast (a row i of A) and the N elements of B that reach it in the row broadcast (a column j of B). It multiplies the corresponding elements of row i of A and column j of B, and each diagonal processor locally adds the $\frac{N}{T}$ products it generates. Using Lemma 8.12, each sub-R-Mesh now adds these $\frac{N}{T}$ elements in constant time to produce element $c_{i,j}$ of product matrix $\hat{C}$. Substituting $\frac{N}{T}$ for N in Lemma 8.12, the sub-R-Mesh must have size $b\log^2 \frac{N}{T} \times \frac{N}{T}$, which it does, since $1 \leq T \leq \log N$ and $1 \leq b \leq \sqrt{N}$.

The R-Mesh can then route the product elements $c_{i,j}$ to the topmost row, completing the multiplication of matrices A and B. ∎

To establish the degree of scalability of the above result, recall that we can characterize the degree of scalability as α if $A \cdot T^{\alpha}$ is independent of T, where A is the area, equivalent to the number of processors, and T is the running time. For the matrix multiplication algorithm of Theorem 8.13, $A \cdot T^{\alpha} = \frac{T^{\alpha}}{T^2} \cdot N^4$, hence, the degree of scalability is 2 for $1 \leq T \leq N$.

Other R-Mesh algorithms with degree of scalability 2 exist for sorting and for computing the contour of maximal elements of a set of planar points.

8.3.3 Matrix-Vector Multiplication with Degree of Scalability 3

Before we look at matrix-vector multiplication, we first look at scaling the multiple addition algorithm cited in Lemma 8.12.

A first, tiny, step toward scaling this algorithm is the standard technique of packing more than one input to a processor and performing part of the computation sequentially. This technique generally balances the sequential portion of the computation with the remaining parallel portion. The contrasting method of the following algorithm, called *orthogonal scaling*, processes all N inputs in parallel (as in the original algorithm), but proceeds sequentially through "chunks" of bits of the input. Thus, this approach of grouping chunks of input elements is in a direction that is orthogonal to the standard method of grouping sets of entire words. Note, however, that an algorithm can utilize both scaling techniques.

THEOREM 8.14 *For any* $1 \leq T \leq \min\{b, N\}$ *and* $\frac{b}{T} \leq \sqrt{N}$, *addition of N b-bit integers can be performed in $O(T)$ time on a $\frac{b}{T}\log^2 \frac{N}{T} \times \max\{b, \frac{N}{T}\}$ R-Mesh. If $T = \Omega\left(\min\left\{\frac{b}{\log \frac{N}{T}}, \log b\right\}\right)$, then the sum is in Word format; otherwise, it is in BIN format.*

Proof: For convenience, assume that $\frac{b}{T}$ and $\frac{N}{T}$ are integers. Initially, let the first row of the R-Mesh hold the N input elements x_i, stored T per processor.

By the standard scaling method, each processor holding T input elements adds them in $O(T)$ time. Let y_j denote the intermediate sum held by processor $p_{0,j}$, where $0 \leq j < \frac{N}{T}$. The R-Mesh breaks each b-bit value y_j into T chunks of $\frac{b}{T}$ bits each. (As noted earlier, we assume for this discussion that all the sums are b-bits long. One can readily accommodate sums up to $(b + \log N)$-bits long with appropriate adjustments.)

The structure of orthogonal scaling as applied to this problem is as follows. In each of the T iterations, the R-Mesh adds corresponding chunks of the $\frac{N}{T}$ numbers using Lemma 8.12, then shifts to correct for the weights of the bits and adds this result to the partial sum from the preceding iteration.

Now, the details. Carve each b-bit intermediate sum y_j into T chunks, $g_{j,k}$, each $\frac{b}{T}$ bits long, where $0 \leq k < T$. The algorithm executes in T iterations, operating on each chunk (of all intermediate sums) in succession. Let $sum(k)$, for $0 \leq k \leq T$, denote the partial sum before iteration k (or after iteration $k - 1$), which row 0 holds in BIN format. Initially, $sum(0) = 0$.

In iteration k, for $0 \leq k < T$, the R-Mesh adds the kth chunks of the y values (intermediate sums) in constant time (Lemma 8.12). Let h_k denote this sum stored in BIN format in the first row. Observe that the weight within y_j of the kth chunk of y_j depends on k and $\frac{b}{T}$, and observe that the sum of the correspondingly weighted chunks equals y_j. That

$$\begin{matrix}
& & & & T \text{ chunks,} \\
& & & & \text{each } \tfrac{w}{T} = 3 \text{ bits long}
\end{matrix}$$

$$\frac{N}{T} = 5 \left\{ \begin{matrix}
x_0 & = & 249 \\
x_1 & = & 25 \\
x_2 & = & 88 \\
x_3 & = & 17 \\
x_4 & = & 64
\end{matrix} \right.$$

partial sums

3	7	1
0	3	1
1	3	0
0	2	1
1	0	0

$$\text{sum} = 443$$

$$h_2 = 5 \quad h_1 = 15 \quad h_0 = 3$$

$$\underbrace{}$$

sums within chunk

(a)

iteration 0	0 0 0 0 0 0 0 0 0	$sum(0) = 0$
	0 0 0 0 0 0 0 1 1	$h_0 = 3$
iteration 1	0 0 0 0 0 0 0 1 1	$sum(1) = sum(0) + h_0 = 3$
	0 0 1 1 1 1 0 0 0	$2^3 h_1 = 120$
iteration 2	0 0 1 1 1 1 0 1 1	$sum(2) = sum(1) + 2^3 h_1 = 123$
	1 0 1 0 0 0 0 0 0	$2^6 h_2 = 320$
	1 1 0 1 1 1 0 1 1	$sum(3) = sum(2) + 2^6 h_2 = 443$

(b)

Figure 8.12. An illustration of the orthogonal scaling multiple addition algorithm. Reprinted from *Parallel Computing*, vol. 29, 2003, R. Vaidyanathan, J. L. Trahan, and C.-m. Lu, "Degree of Scalability: Scalable Reconfigurable Mesh Algorithms for Multiple Addition and Matrix-Vector Multiplication," pp. 95–109, © Copyright (2003) with permission from Elsevier.

is, $y_j = \sum_{k=0}^{T-1} g_{j,k} 2^{\frac{kb}{T}}$. Consequently, the sum of correspondingly weighted h_k values equals the sum of the y_j's, that is, $\sum_{j=0}^{N/T-1} y_j = \sum_{k=0}^{T-1} h_k 2^{\frac{kb}{T}}$. The R-Mesh in iteration k then shifts h_k to weight it properly and adds the result to $sum(k-1)$ in row 0 (Theorem 4.6, page 124) to generate $sum(k)$ in constant time. Figure 8.12 gives an example.

After T iterations, the R-Mesh holds the final sum, $sum(T)$, in BIN format in row 0. If $T = \Omega\left(\min\left\{ \frac{b}{\log \frac{N}{T}}, \log b \right\} \right)$, then the R-Mesh can convert the sum to Word format as follows. If $T = \Omega(\log b)$, then by the result stated in Problem 4.1, the R-Mesh converts the sum to Word format in $O(T)$ time. If $T = \Omega\left(\frac{b}{\log N}\right)$ instead, then, in each of T phases, pivot the $\frac{b}{T} = O(\log N)$ bits to the first column and convert them to Word format, using the same conversion as before, in $O(1)$ time. Next, an R-Mesh processor weights the resulting pieces of the sum and adds them sequentially in $O(T)$ time. ∎

For the multiple addition algorithm of Theorem 8.14 and $b \leq \frac{N}{T}$, $A \cdot T^\alpha = \frac{T^\alpha}{T^2} \cdot Nb \log^2 \frac{N}{T}$. The degree of scalability, hence, is ≥ 2 for the range $1 \leq T \leq b$. (Note that AT^2 actually decreases as T increases within this range because of the $\log^2 \frac{N}{T}$ term.)

Now, given the time-size tradeoff for multiple addition offered by Theorem 8.14, we want to plug this into matrix-vector multiplication to obtain a corresponding tradeoff.

Let $A = [a_{i,j}]$ be an $N \times N$ matrix and let $\vec{d} = [d_i]$ be an N-element vector. Recall that the problem of matrix-vector multiplication is to compute their N-element product vector $\vec{c} = [c_i]$, where $c_i = \sum_{j=0}^{N-1} a_{i,j} d_j$.

We refer to this problem as a matrix-vector multiplication of size N. As before, assume the elements of A, $\vec{d}$, and $\vec{c}$ to be b-bits long.

Let the kth *XY-slice* of a three-dimensional R-Mesh denote the two-dimensional sub-R-Mesh comprising processors (i, j, k), for fixed k and all i, j (see Figure 8.13). Similarly, define the ith *YZ-slice* to be the two-dimensional sub-R-Mesh comprising processors (i, j, k), for fixed i and all j, k.

THEOREM 8.15 *For any $1 \leq T \leq \min\{b, N\}$ and $\frac{b}{T} \leq \sqrt{N}$, matrix-vector multiplication of size N (with b-bit integers) can be performed in $O(T)$ time on:*

(i) *an $N \times \frac{N}{T} \times \frac{b}{T} \log^2 \frac{N}{T}$ three-dimensional R-Mesh, or*

(ii) *an $\frac{Nb}{T} \log^2 \frac{N}{T} \times \frac{Nb}{T^2} \log^2 \frac{N}{T}$ two-dimensional R-Mesh.*

If $T = \Omega\left(\min\left\{\frac{b}{\log \frac{N}{T}}, \log b\right\}\right)$, then the result is in Word format; otherwise, it is in BIN format.

<u>Proof:</u> This algorithm follows the organization of the algorithm for Theorem 4.24 (page 140) with changes as noted to accommodate scaling. To start, assume the R-Mesh is three-dimensional, of size $N \times \frac{N}{T} \times \frac{b}{T} \log^2 \frac{N}{T}$. The same processors hold values as in Theorem 4.24, except

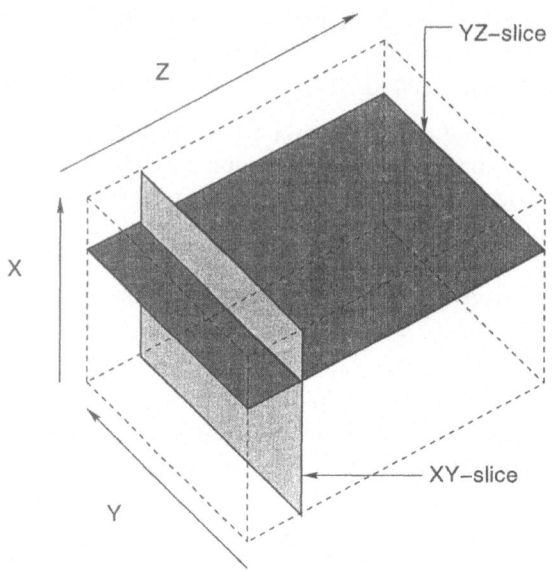

Figure 8.13.   Slices of a three-dimensional R-Mesh.
Reprinted from *Parallel Computing*, vol. 29, 2003, R. Vaidyanathan, J. L. Trahan,
and C.-m. Lu, "Degree of Scalability: Scalable Reconfigurable Mesh Algorithms
for Multiple Addition and Matrix-Vector Multiplication," pp. 95–109, © Copyright
(2003) with permission from Elsevier.

T values each this time. That is, row i of the 0th XY-slice holds row
i of matrix A and row 0 of the 0th XY-slice holds vector $\vec{d}$. The exact
mapping of elements of a row of A or vector $\vec{d}$ to processors is unim-
portant, as long as all rows and the vector are mapped in the same
manner. Broadcast $\vec{d}$ down the "columns" of the 0th XY-slice in T
phases so that, afterwards, each $p_{i,j,0}$ holds T elements of row i of A
and the corresponding T elements of $\vec{d}$, and $p_{i,j,0}$ then multiplies the
elements pairwise. Next, YZ-slices add the values comprising c_i using
Theorem 8.14. Converting the result from BIN to Word format follows
as in the proof of Theorem 8.14. Converting the R-Mesh from three
dimensions to two follows by Corollary 9.5 (page 318), noting that this
algorithm runs on an LR-Mesh.   ∎

To establish the degree of scalability of the matrix-vector multiplica-
tion algorithm of Theorem 8.15, observe that $AT^\alpha = \frac{T^\alpha}{T^3} N^2 b^2 \log^4 \frac{N}{T}$, for
$1 \leq T \leq b$. The degree of scalability, hence, is ≥ 3 for this range. That
is, an increase in time by a factor c induces a decrease in size by a factor
of at least $\Theta(c^3)$.

Problems

8.1 Construct a scaling simulation for a standard, non-reconfigurable mesh using the contraction mapping. When simulating an $N \times N$ mesh on a $P \times P$ mesh, where $P < N$, what is the simulation overhead?

8.2 Repeat Problem 8.1, except use the windows mapping.

8.3 Verify the remark after Theorem 8.2 that if the simulated HVR-Mesh $\mathcal{Q}$ is CREW, then so is the simulating HVR-Mesh $\mathcal{R}$.

8.4 Design an efficient scaling simulation of an HVR-Mesh using the windows mapping, rather than the contraction mapping used in the proof of Theorem 8.2. What is the simulation overhead of your simulation?

8.5 Theorem 8.3 established an $\Omega(N)$ step lower bound for a $P \times P$ LR-Mesh using the contraction mapping to simulate a step of an $N \times N$ LR-Mesh, for any $P < N$. Prove that the same lower bound holds under the contraction mapping for a scaling simulation of an FR-Mesh.

8.6 An LR-Mesh can create a bus that forms a cycle. The description of the algorithm for Theorem 8.4 deals explicitly only with acyclic buses. Explain what changes are needed (if any) and why they are needed (or not needed) to handle a bus that forms a cycle.

8.7 Figure 8.14 shows one bus of a $P \times 3P$ LR-Mesh to be simulated by a $P \times P$ LR-Mesh. Trace through the window-by-window forward

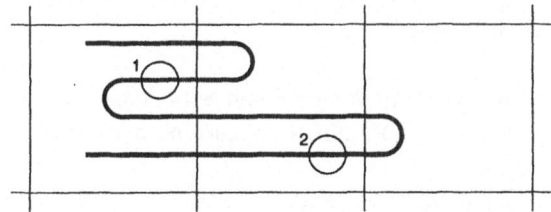

Figure 8.14. Example LR-Mesh bus configuration for Problem 8.7.

and reverse sweeps of the algorithm in Section 8.1.2 assuming that processor 1 writes 1, processor 2 writes 2, and no other processor writes to the bus. Identify for each bus segment in each window its bus ID, data, and identity of currently known endpoints. Assume that both LR-Meshes use the COLLISION concurrent write rule.

8.8   Describe the local operations of a 2×2 block of processors in setting up a dual bus structure as described in Step 3 of the LR-Mesh scaling simulation of Section 8.1.2.

8.9   Prove that, in general, an LR-Mesh can always implement the connections established in Step 5 of the LR-Mesh scaling simulation of Section 8.1.2. (Figure 8.6(b) shows an example.)

8.10 Construct a constant time FR-Mesh algorithm to compute the transitive closure of an undirected graph.

8.11 Construct a constant time FR-Mesh algorithm to detect whether adding a new edge to an undirected graph creates a cycle.

8.12 Design an $O\left(\frac{N}{P}\log P\right)$ time algorithm for a $P \times P$ FR-Mesh $\mathcal{R}$ to perform horizontal prefix assimilation for an $N \times P$ slice of an $N \times N$ FR-Mesh $\mathcal{Q}$ that $\mathcal{R}$ is simulating.

8.13 Design an $O(\log P)$ time algorithm for a $P \times P$ FR-Mesh $\mathcal{R}$ to perform vertical prefix assimilation for a $P \times P$ window of an $N \times N$ FR-Mesh $\mathcal{Q}$ that $\mathcal{R}$ is simulating.

8.14 Construct an algorithm to perform the data delivery phase of the scaling simulation of an $N \times N$ FR-Mesh on a $P \times P$ FR-Mesh in $O\left(\frac{N^2}{P^2}\log P\right)$ time. Assume that both FR-Meshes use the COMMON concurrent write rule.

8.15 Construct an algorithm for Problem 8.14 except assume that both FR-Meshes use the COLLISION concurrent write rule.

8.16 Prove that a PRIORITY CRCW FR-Mesh is optimally scalable.

8.17 Let $\mathcal{G}$ be an N-vertex graph and let $P < N$. Use Theorem 6.12 (page 194) and Problem 6.26 for parts (a) and (b).

      (a) For any $2 \le m \le N$, first use Theorem 3.5 (page 86) to convert the connected components algorithm of Theorem 6.12 for $\mathcal{G}$

to run on an $O(mN) \times O(mN)$ COMMON CRCW separable R-Mesh. Next, scale the CRCW R-Mesh algorithm to run on a $P \times P$ COMMON CRCW R-Mesh.

What is the time complexity of the $P \times P$ R-Mesh algorithm?

(b) For any $2 \leq m \leq \sqrt{P}$, first scale the connected components algorithm of Theorem 6.12 for $\mathcal{G}$ to run on an $O\left(\frac{P}{m}\right) \times O\left(\frac{P}{m}\right)$ PRIORITY CRCW R-Mesh. Next use Theorem 3.5 to convert the scaled algorithm to run on a $P \times P$ COMMON CRCW R-Mesh.

What is the time complexity of the $P \times P$ R-Mesh algorithm?

(c) Which of the two approaches in parts (a) and (b) runs faster and for what relative values of N, P, and m?

8.18 Construct a constant time simulation of each step of a $\frac{P}{2} \times \frac{P}{2}$ COMMON CRCW LR-Mesh on a $P \times P$ CREW LR-Mesh.
(Hint: Use a double-bus structure in which two undirected buses replace a single bus, and use segmenting to mimic two oppositely directed buses.)

8.19 Given a $2N \times 2N$ CREW LR-Mesh with a cyclic bus with X squads embedded in the double-bus structure of Theorem 8.8, elect a leader (that is, mark a unique squad such that this squad holds itself as marked and all other squads hold themselves as unmarked) in $O(\log X)$ time.

8.20 The scaling simulations of this chapter simulate a step of an $N \times N$ instance of a model on a $P \times P$ instance, where $P \leq N$. Do these methods extend to simulated model instances of size $N_1 \times N_2$, where $P \leq N_1, N_2$? Explain.

8.21 Give a detailed R-Mesh algorithm for the multiple addition method of Theorem 8.14.

8.22 Consider algorithms $\mathcal{A}_1, \mathcal{A}_2, \cdots, \mathcal{A}_k$, all for the same problem $\mathcal{P}$. For $1 \leq i \leq k$, let algorithm $\mathcal{A}_i$ run in time T with degree of scalability $\alpha_i(T)$.

(a) Prove that if k is a constant, then there exists an algorithm for problem $\mathcal{P}$ that runs in time T with degree of scalability $\max\{\alpha_i(T) : 1 \leq i \leq k\}$.

(b)   Prove that if k is a constant, then there exists an algorithm for problem $\mathcal{P}$ that runs in time T with degree of scalability $\min\{\alpha_i(T) \ : \ 1 \leq i \leq k\}$.

(c)   How will the observations in the above parts of this problem help in selecting the "best" algorithm for a given application?

(d)   Will the observations in the first two parts hold for non-constant k? Explain.

8.23   Can you use the degrees of scalability of two algorithms for the same problem to pick the "better" algorithm? Explain.

Bibliographic Notes

Fernández-Zepeda *et al.* [110] introduced the optimal, strong, and weak scaling simulation terminology used in this chapter. Ben-Asher *et al.* [17] constructed the optimal scaling simulation for the HVR-Mesh (Theorem 8.2). Ben-Asher *et al.* [17] established the lower bound that a $P \times P$ LR-Mesh requires $\Omega(N)$ steps to simulate each step of an $N \times N$ LR-Mesh under a contraction mapping, for any $P < N$. Maresca *et al.* [13, 200] asserted by a similar argument that the R-Mesh does not permit an optimal scaling simulation. This is mistaken, however, as evidenced by Theorem 8.4, since the argument applies only to the contraction mapping. Ben-Asher *et al.* [17] constructed the optimal scaling simulation for the LR-Mesh (Theorem 8.4). Maresca [200] developed a scaling simulation that implies an optimal scaling simulation for an HVR-Mesh. Matsumae and Tokura [205] constructed a simulation of an $N \times N$ R-Mesh on a $P \times P$ HVR-Mesh in $O\left(\left(\frac{N}{P}\right)^2 \log N \log P\right)$ time.

Fernández-Zepeda *et al.* [110] devised the strong scaling simulation for the FR-Mesh and the optimal scaling simulation using the PRIORITY concurrent write rule (Theorems 8.5 and 8.6).

Matias and Schuster [204] constructed the randomized scaling simulations for the R-Mesh cited in Theorem 8.7, and Fernández-Zepeda *et al.* [111] developed the deterministic scaling simulation in Theorem 8.8.

Ben-Asher and Schuster [22, 23] devised the self-simulations of the R-Mesh and DR-Mesh that speed up a computation from T steps to one step, increasing the model size.

The sources for scalable algorithms on reconfigurable optical models appear at the end of Chapter 10.

Vaidyanathan *et al.* [333] introduced the concept of degree of scalability. Jang *et al.* [146] and Park *et al.* [267] presented the multiple addition result cited in Lemma 8.12 (which was Lemma 4.10, page 127) for the case $b = O(\log N)$. Vaidyanathan *et al.* [333] developed the multiple addition algorithm demonstrating orthogonal scaling (Theorem 8.14).

Savage [288] is a source for AT^2 complexity the word model of VLSI. Park *et al.* [267] designed the AT^2-optimal matrix multiplication algorithm of Theorem 8.13.

Murshed and Brent [224] presented R-Mesh algorithms with degree of scalability 2 for sorting and for computing the contour of maximal elements of a set of planar points.

Vaidyanathan *et al.* [333] developed the matrix-vector multiplication algorithm with degree of scalability 3 presented in Theorem 8.15.

Chapter 9

COMPUTATIONAL COMPLEXITY OF RECONFIGURATION

Theoretical investigations of models of computation frequently concern themselves with how models relate to each other—what can Model $\mathcal{A}$ do with certain resources that Model $\mathcal{B}$ cannot, or how much of a certain resource does Model $\mathcal{B}$ use to simulate a given computation of Model $\mathcal{A}$. Such relations exist for a range of models of computation—including Turing machines (TMs), circuits, parallel random access machines (PRAMs), and a myriad of variants—and many possible resources —typically related to time, hardware, or space (memory). Because such an extensive body of work exists, because deep understanding has been attained about many of these models, and because the computational requirements of many problems have been precisely located with respect to these models, relating a new model of computation to a standard model of computation can quickly reveal limits and possibilities that would otherwise be grasped only after years of arduous research. For example, showing the equivalence, on the one hand, of a class of LR-Mesh computations and a certain TM space class, and, on the other hand, of a class of R-Mesh computations and a different TM space class, says little directly of interest because no one is going to build a TM. It does, however, say much about a possible separation in power between the LR-Mesh and the R-Mesh because of long-studied relations between the corresponding TM space classes. The connections to the TM provide leverage to shift a substantial body of knowledge from the TM context to the dynamic reconfiguration context.

In a different direction, direct investigation of relations among reconfigurable models is important. Many reconfigurable models exist, with different groups of researchers working on their favorites. Translation of results from one model to another is no trivial task when they have

features that may seem to be incomparable, that may give either an edge
on any given problem. The simulation of one reconfigurable model $\mathcal{A}$ on
another model $\mathcal{B}$ serves two closely related purposes. First, it allows us
to translate resource requirements for any problem solved on Model $\mathcal{A}$
into the corresponding resource requirements, and, indeed, an algorithm
on Model $\mathcal{B}$. This may not be the best possible algorithm on Model $\mathcal{B}$,
but it is an easily obtained start. Second, it defines limits on how much
more powerful Model $\mathcal{A}$ may be than Model $\mathcal{B}$ in terms of quantifiable
resource requirements.

This chapter examines relations among models. It accomplishes this
examination primarily by simulations of one model by another. We
first consider relations among R-Mesh models with different features.
Section 9.1 evaluates the resources required to map a higher dimensional
R-Mesh to a two-dimensional R-Mesh, in essence, showing that, within
a constant factor of time, a two-dimensional R-Mesh can do anything
that a higher dimensional R-Mesh can do. Section 9.2 derives relations
between the bit model and the word model by constructing a simulation
of a word-model R-Mesh on a bit-model R-Mesh.

Section 9.3 then investigates relations to the parallel random access
machine (PRAM), one of the most extensively studied models of parallel computation. This will help to more precisely locate the abilities
of reconfigurable models in terms of parallel complexity theory developed over the past decades. Section 9.4 shifts the focus to complexity
classes—particularly those defined by reconfigurable models with a polynomial number of processors and constant, logarithmic, or polylogarithmic time. We place these classes relative to each other for a variety of
reconfigurable models and relative to PRAM classes (Section 9.5), then
relative to conventional circuit and Turing machine classes (Section 9.6).

9.1 Not Just Two Dimensions Anymore: Mapping Higher-Dimensional R-Meshes to Two-Dimensional R-Meshes

A two-dimensional R-Mesh is the R-Mesh discussed for the most part
in this book. A d-dimensional R-Mesh just generalizes these ideas to
a higher number of dimensions (see Section 3.1.4). In this section, we
give a simulation of a d-dimensional R-Mesh, where d is a constant, by
a two-dimensional R-Mesh that uses an optimal number of processors
(optimal area) to within a constant factor. This simulation runs on the
two-dimensional R-Mesh within a constant factor of the time needed for
the simulated d-dimensional R-Mesh computation. We also show that a

one-dimensional R-Mesh cannot simulate a d-dimensional R-Mesh (for $d > 1$) to within a constant factor of time. Therefore, two is the smallest number of dimensions for an R-Mesh that can simulate a d-dimensional R-Mesh (for any $d \geq 1$) to within a constant factor of time.

9.1.1 Lower Bound on Mapping

As a first step, a lower bound on the area required to lay out a d-dimensional mesh creates a lower bound on the area (or number of processors) to lay out a two-dimensional R-Mesh that simulates a d-dimensional R-Mesh with constant time overhead. In this section, we derive a lower bound on the area to lay out a d-dimensional mesh. The next section shows that a two-dimensional R-Mesh can achieve the area lower bound (to within a constant factor) in simulating a d-dimensional R-Mesh, for any constant d.

The *bisection width* of a graph is the least number of edges that must be removed from it to disconnect the graph into two components with identical (within one) number of vertices. That the bisection width of an $N \times N \times \cdots \times N$ d-dimensional mesh is at least N^{d-1} is a well-known fact. Generalizing this result, the bisection width of a $P_0 \times P_1 \times \cdots \times P_{d-1}$ mesh is at least $\prod_{i=0}^{d-2} P_i$, where $P_{d-1} \geq P_0, P_1, \cdots, P_{d-2}$.

A network with bisection width B requires $\Omega(B^2)$ layout area. In other words, the area needed to lay out a $P_0 \times P_1 \times \cdots \times P_{d-1}$ mesh is $\Omega\left(\prod_{i=0}^{d-2} P_i^2\right)$, where $P_{d-1} \geq P_0, P_1, \cdots, P_{d-2}$. Therefore we have the following.

THEOREM 9.1 *For any constant $d \geq 2$, a $P_0 \times P_1 \times \cdots \times P_{d-1}$ mesh requires $\Omega\left(\prod_{i=0}^{d-2} P_i^2\right)$ layout area, where $P_{d-1} \geq P_0, P_1, \cdots, P_{d-2}$.*

COROLLARY 9.2 *Any two-dimensional R-Mesh that simulates each step of a $P_0 \times P_1 \times \cdots \times P_{d-1}$ d-dimensional R-Mesh in constant time has $\Omega\left(\prod_{i=0}^{d-2} P_i^2\right)$ processors, where d is a constant and $P_{d-1} \geq P_0, P_1, \cdots, P_{d-2}$.*

9.1.2 Mapping d Dimensions to Two Dimensions

To simulate a d-dimensional R-Mesh by a two-dimensional R-Mesh, we must show that the two-dimensional R-Mesh can simulate (i) the external connections and (*ii*) the internal connections for each processor of a *d*-dimensional R-Mesh.

External Connections. We detail the layout of a three-dimensional R-Mesh on a two-dimensional R-Mesh, placing each processor of the three-dimensional R-Mesh in a "block" of two-dimensional R-Mesh processors and routing connections between blocks using the two-dimensional R-Mesh buses. This touches on all the important observations needed to prove the more general result of Theorem 9.3. Note that simulating all 2*d* ports of a *d*-dimensional R-Mesh processor requires multiple two-dimensional R-Mesh processors, so each block is a constant-sized sub-R-Mesh. Temporarily, we leave the size of a block undefined (until examining internal connections). Call a layout on a two-dimensional R-Mesh that has height H (number of rows) and width W (number of columns) as an $H \times W$ layout of blocks. The placement of a three-dimensional R-Mesh on a two-dimensional R-Mesh decomposes a $P_0 \times P_1 \times P_2$ R-Mesh into P_2 R-Meshes, each of size $P_1 \times P_0$ with the corresponding processors connected in a linear array. Figure 9.1 shows a $5 \times 3 \times 4$ R-Mesh and its layout in blocks. Observe that Figure 9.1(b) arranges the three-dimensional R-Mesh as four 3×5 R-Meshes of blocks, each shown connected by bold lines. Figure 9.1(b) shows linear array connections between corresponding blocks in different sub-R-Meshes by thin lines. Each row of the layout has five (P_0) blocks simulating three-dimensional R-Mesh processors and the communication channel for each simulated column of processors is three (P_1) columns wide. Therefore, a $P_0 \times P_1 \times P_2$ R-Mesh has a $(P_1 P_2) \times (P_0 + P_0 P_1)$ layout of blocks. The following theorem generalizes the above ideas; we leave its proof to Problem 9.1.

THEOREM 9.3 *For any constant $d \geq 2$, a $P_0 \times P_1 \times \cdots \times P_{d-1}$ R-Mesh has a $\left(\prod_{i=1}^{d-1} P_i \right) \times \left(\sum_{i=0}^{d-2} \prod_{j=0}^{i} P_j \right)$ layout of blocks, with each row (resp., column) having P_0 (resp., $\prod_{i=1}^{d-1} P_i$) blocks.*

For all constant $d \geq 2$, block size will be constant (see below), so observe that a $P_0 \times P_1 \times \cdots \times P_{d-1}$ R-Mesh has an $O\left(P_0 P_{d-1} \prod_{i=1}^{d-2} P_i^2 \right)$ area layout. If P_0 and P_{d-1} are the largest two dimensions of a $P_0 \times P_1 \times \cdots \times P_{d-1}$ R-Mesh and $P_0 = \Theta(P_{d-1})$, then the above layout is within a constant factor of optimal.

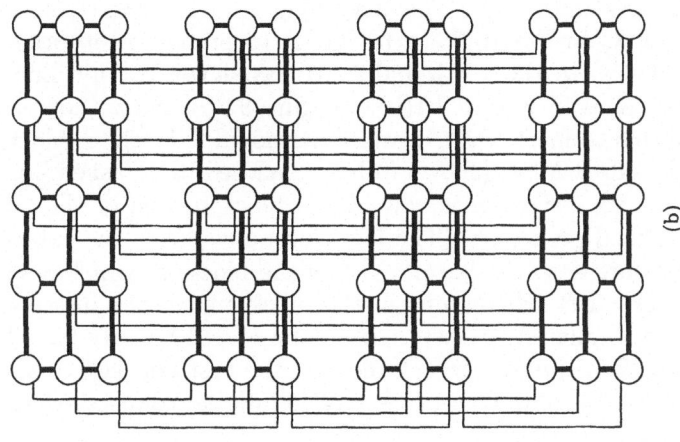

(b)

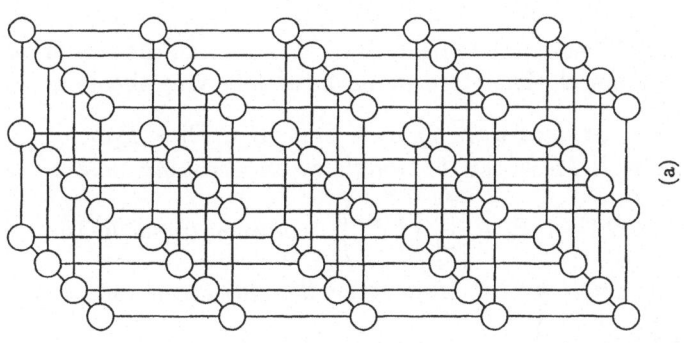

(a)

Figure 9.1. A layout for a 5 × 3 × 4 R-Mesh.
Reprinted from *Information Processing Letters*, vol. 47, 1993, R. Vaidyanathan, and J. L. Trahan, "Optimal Simulation of Multidimensional Reconfigurable Meshes by Two Dimensional Reconfigurable Meshes," pp. 267–273, © Copyright (1993) with permission from Elsevier.

Internal Connections. Now we describe how to establish any partition of ports within a simulated processor, given the above block layout for external connections. (Observe that a block requires $\Omega(d)$ perimeter to concurrently implement $2d$ ports.) In this layout, Figure 9.2(a) shows generic block connections. Ports D and H connect to neighboring blocks in its row to the west and east. The remaining $2d - 2$ ports (labeled A, B, C and E, F, G in Figure 9.2(a)) connect to processors in other sub-R-Meshes (blocks) to the north and south (as shown by thin lines and vertical thick lines in Figure 9.1(b)). Figure 9.2(b) shows how to realize these external connections in a two-dimensional R-Mesh. A block is a $2d \times (2d + 1)$ sub-R-Mesh (shown in bold enclosed in a dashed box in Figure 9.2(b)) and assigns each row of the block to one of the $2d$ ports of the simulated processor. (The last column connects the external connection of port H to the bottom row of the block, to which port H is assigned.) The first $2d$ columns in the block embed the internal connections of the simulated processor. Fuse the N and S ports for all processors in these $2d$ columns (except those in the first and last rows) to form $2d$ buses numbered $0, 1, \cdots, 2d - 1$. The internal connections of the simulated processor partition its ports into subsets, assigning each subset of the partition an index from $\{0, 1, \cdots, 2d - 1\}$. If a port x is in a subset indexed y, then connect the row for port x to the bus in column y. This fuses all ports that are in the same subset by connections to a common bus. This does not fuse ports in different subsets because the $2d$ column buses are disjoint. For d a constant, a block can fashion all local connections in constant time. If the simulated R-Mesh is an LR-Mesh, then so is the simulating R-Mesh. As the LR-Mesh is completely scalable (Theorem 8.4, page 284), constants in the size of an LR-Mesh may be ignored. Therefore we have the following theorem.

THEOREM 9.4 *For constant $d > 2$, each step of a $P_0 \times P_1 \times \cdots \times P_{d-1}$ d-dimensional R-Mesh can be simulated in constant time by a*
$$\left(2d \prod_{i=1}^{d-1} P_i\right) \times \left((2d + 1)P_0 + \sum_{i=1}^{d-2} \prod_{j=0}^{i} P_j\right) \text{ two-dimensional R-Mesh.}$$
If the simulated model is an LR-Mesh, then the simulating model is a
$$\left(\prod_{i=1}^{d-1} P_i\right) \times \left(\sum_{i=1}^{d-2} \prod_{j=0}^{i} P_j\right) \text{ two-dimensional LR-Mesh.}$$

Applying the general method for simulating a d-dimensional R-Mesh on a two-dimensional R-Mesh to $d = 3$, each step of a $P_0 \times P_1 \times P_2$ three-dimensional R-Mesh can be simulated in $O(1)$ time on a $(6P_1P_2) \times (7P_0 + P_0P_1)$ two-dimensional R-Mesh.

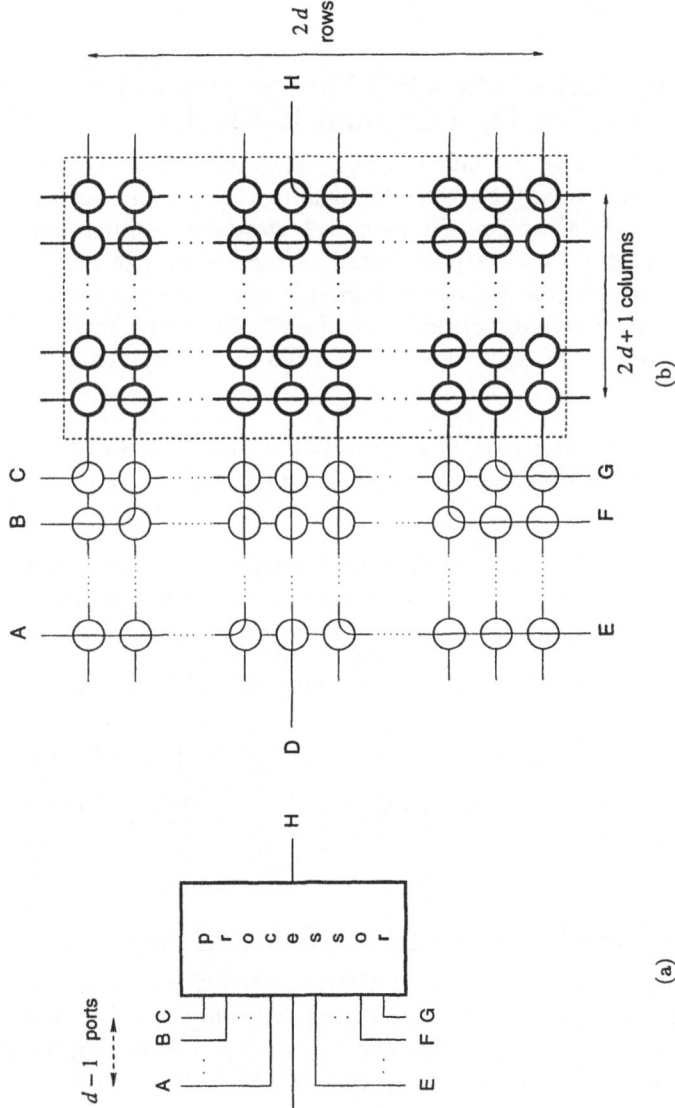

(a)

(b)

Figure 9.2. A block that simulates a processor of a *d*-dimensional R-Mesh: (a) external connections to other blocks, (b) detailed internal view.

Reprinted from *Information Processing Letters*, vol. 47, 1993, R. Vaidyanathan, and J. L. Trahan, "Optimal Simulation of Multidimensional Reconfigurable Meshes by Two Dimensional Reconfigurable Meshes," pp. 267–273, © Copyright (1993) with permission from Elsevier.

COROLLARY 9.5 *Each step of a $P_0 \times P_1 \times P_2$ three-dimensional R-Mesh can be simulated in $O(1)$ time on an $O(P_0 P_1) \times O(P_1 P_2)$ two-dimensional R-Mesh. If the simulated model is an LR-Mesh, then the simulating model is a $P_0 P_1 \times P_1 P_2$ LR-Mesh.* ∎

9.1.3 Separation of the One-Dimensional R-Mesh from Higher Dimensional R-Meshes

So far, we have considered only the simulation of a d-dimensional R-Mesh by a two-dimensional R-Mesh, establishing that for any constant d, a two-dimensional R-Mesh can simulate each step of a d-dimensional R-Mesh in constant time with a polynomial factor increase in number of processors. Is it possible to accomplish this on a one-dimensional R-Mesh rather than a two-dimensional R-Mesh? No. The following theorem (whose proof is left as Problem 9.4) leads to the explanation of this answer.

THEOREM 9.6 *A PRIORITY CRCW PRAM with P^2 processors can simulate each step of a one-dimensional R-Mesh with P processors in constant time.*

COROLLARY 9.7 *An arbitrary step of a d-dimensional R-Mesh (where $d > 1$) cannot be simulated in constant time by a one-dimensional R-Mesh with polynomially bounded number of processors.*

Proof: A two-dimensional R-Mesh can find the parity of N bits in constant time (Corollary 2.6, page 29). Since a CRCW PRAM with polynomially bounded number of processors requires $\Omega\left(\frac{\log N}{\log \log N}\right)$ time for this problem, the one-dimensional R-Mesh also requires $\Omega\left(\frac{\log N}{\log \log N}\right)$ time (by Theorem 9.6). ∎

9.2 Simulations between Bit and Word Models

As seen in many algorithms so far, R-Mesh computations frequently manipulate buses over which processors communicate only by single bits. Questions naturally arise as to whether such algorithms can run on bit-wide buses instead of word-wide buses, then whether they could run on bit-size processors, then finally as to the power of such a bit-model R-Mesh. The first two questions are algorithm-specific. We take up the last question in this section.

The R-Mesh model considered for the most part so far is the word-model R-Mesh. Its processors and buses are assumed to have some reasonable word-size. Data movement and internal operations are performed by a processor for an entire word at a time. Beyond this, the model completely abstracts away from the processor word-size. In contrast, in a bit-model R-Mesh, originally defined in Section 3.1.2, each bus can only carry a single bit of data at a time. Each processor contains only a constant number of constant size registers. Aside from the obviously limited storage and communication width, a more subtle limitation is that a processor cannot send out a unique address to identify itself to another processor over a bus, nor can a processor even hold its own address. Processors may, however, be preprogrammed with up to a constant number of bits of data that they can use distinctively in a computation. Each processor can operate on the data it stores and data it receives from others. Given the restrictions on a bit-model R-Mesh, these operations may usefully be seen as Boolean operations. Each processor can assume any of the 15 internal configurations of its ports available to a word-model processor (see Figure 2.3). If concurrent writes are assumed, then we generally restrict these rules to COMMON, COLLISION, or COLLISION$^+$.

A b-bit word-model processor would have a VLSI layout area of $O(b^2)$, so an $N \times N$ mesh of such processors would have an area of $O(N^2b^2)$. Each bit-model processor would have $O(1)$ layout area. Ideally, an $Nb \times Nb$ bit-model R-Mesh should simulate each step of an $N \times N$ word-model R-Mesh in $O(1)$ time.

To construct an optimal simulation of an $N \times N$ word-model R-Mesh by an $Nb \times Nb$ bit-model R-Mesh, letting a $b \times b$ bit-model sub-R-Mesh simulate each word-model processor, four obstacles arise. The first, and most difficult, is for the $b \times b$ bit-model sub-R-Mesh to perform all of the arithmetic operations of the word-model processor in $O(1)$ time; a word-model processor is assumed to be capable of performing the usual arithmetic and logical operations in constant time. The second, and one that is more clear how to solve, is to create buses tracking the word-model buses. The third is to generate self-addresses, and the last is to resolve concurrent writes exactly as the word-model R-Mesh does. We explain these facets below.

Arithmetic Operations. Chapter 4 presents bit-model algorithms for addition (Theorem 4.6, page 124), multiplication (Theorem 4.22, page 139), and division (Theorem 4.23, page 139).

Logical Operations. Piece of cake.

External Connections. Straightforward.

Internal Connections. An R-Mesh processor can assume 15 different internal configurations. Since this is a constant number, then each bit-model processor in the $b \times b$ sub-R-Mesh can pre-store the configuration it is to implement for each word-model processor's internal configuration.

Addressing. The $b \times b$ sub-R-Mesh that simulates word-model processor $p_{i,j}$ can have the bits of an index (such as i and j) pre-stored, say, in the top row of processors of the sub-R-Mesh. Therefore, if a step requires the word-model processor to write its index, then the bit-model sub-R-Mesh can do the same. Observe that $b = \Omega(\log N)$ for the word model, so the bit-model sub-R-Mesh has sufficient processors to hold the bits of an index in a single row.

Resolving Concurrent Writes. Each b-bit bus β of the word-model R-Mesh corresponds to a band $\beta_0, \beta_1, \cdots, \beta_{b-1}$ of b 1-bit buses in the bit-model R-Mesh. A concurrent write to bus β corresponds to concurrent writes to each of the buses $\beta_0, \beta_1, \cdots, \beta_{b-1}$. As we noted earlier, we will assume the COMMON, COLLISION, or COLLISION$^+$ rules to resolve concurrent writes.

Under the COMMON rule, each of the bit-model buses $\beta_0, \beta_1, \cdots, \beta_{b-1}$ also has concurrent writes of equal value. If a collision occurs under the COLLISION or COLLISION$^+$ rules, then at least one of the buses $\beta_0, \beta_1, \cdots, \beta_{b-1}$ has a collision. Performing a logical OR across buses $\beta_0, \beta_1, \cdots, \beta_{b-1}$ suffices to convey this information on all b buses.

THEOREM 9.8 *Each step of an $N \times N$ word-model R-Mesh with word size b that can perform standard arithmetic and logical operations can be simulated in $O(1)$ time by an $Nb \times Nb$ bit-model R-Mesh.*

Remark: Since a COMMON, COLLISION, or COLLISION$^+$ CRCW R-Mesh can simulate other write rules in constant time and with a polynomial blowup in size (see Section 9.4), so can a bit-model R-Mesh.

9.3   Relations to the PRAM

A *Parallel Random Access Machine* (PRAM) comprises a collection of processors and a shared memory. Each processor possesses its own local memory and executes the same program in a single instruction, multiple data (SIMD) environment. As in access to buses by an R-Mesh, access to cells of the shared memory by a PRAM may be exclusive or concurrent. Indeed, the notions of exclusive and concurrent accesses were defined originally for the PRAM.

- An *exclusive read* rule requires all reads from shared memory in the same step to be from different cells.

- A *concurrent read* rule allows multiple processors to simultaneously read from the same memory cell.

- An *exclusive write* rule requires all writes to shared memory in the same step to be to different cells.

- A *concurrent write* rule allows multiple processors to simultaneously write to the same cell. As for reconfigurable models, one must specify a rule to resolve write conflicts, such as COMMON, COLLISION, COLLISION$^+$, ARBITRARY, or PRIORITY. (Section 3.1.3 defines these rules.)

Via the shared memory, a PRAM abstracts away communication obstacles due to an interconnection network. It allows extracting the maximum amount of parallelism available to attack a problem. Its utility as a theoretical tool has been significant and continuing.

Because so many algorithms exist for the PRAM and because its relations to so many other (sequential and parallel) models are well-understood, we undertake to place the R-Mesh and its variants with respect to the PRAM. This can help to identify abstract computational classes (for example, just what can an R-Mesh compute—or not compute—in constant time?) and to, at least, establish bounds on the resources needed for an R-Mesh to execute any algorithm extant for the PRAM.

Previous chapters have described a number of constant time R-Mesh algorithms, yet such a creature is rare for the PRAM. Is it possible that reconfigurable models are, in some sense, more "powerful" than the PRAM? For some models, the answer is yes. For example, the parity problem separates the LR-Mesh and PRAM: an R-Mesh can compute the parity of N bits in $O(1)$ time with $3N$ processors, while a PRAM must spend $\Omega\left(\frac{\log N}{\log \log N}\right)$ time with a polynomial number of processors.

Does this mean that an R-Mesh can speed up any PRAM algorithm to run in constant time? or speed up by a log or loglog factor? Well, no. It can, however, simulate an arbitrary step of a PRAM efficiently. Numerous simulations of PRAMs (under various restrictions) exist for R-Meshes (under various restrictions). We present a pair: one straightforward, the other more involved, yet conveying the character of many PRAM simulations by fixed-degree networks.

In a T step computation of P processors, a PRAM may access up to PT shared memory cells. Usually, these have addresses up to $O(PT)$. (Using indirect addressing, however, a PRAM may access cells scattered about memory and with much larger addresses. For most such algorithms, however, these can be compressed into a much smaller region of memory.)

A Deterministic PRAM Simulation. The first PRAM simulation that we will describe is deterministic. It allots a column of HVR-Mesh processors to each PRAM processor and a row of HVR-Mesh processors to each shared-memory cell. For this simulation, shared memory size S means the cells have addresses 0 to $S - 1$.

THEOREM 9.9 *Each step of a CRCW PRAM that uses N processors and shared memory of size S can be simulated by an $S \times N$ CREW HVR-Mesh in $O(1)$ time.*

Proof: Let Q denote a PRIORITY CRCW PRAM that uses N processors and S shared memory cells (with addresses $0, \ldots, S - 1$). Let c_i denote the contents of shared memory cell i. We construct a CREW HVR-Mesh $\mathcal{R}$ that will simulate each step of Q in $O(1)$ time. Processor $p_{0,j}$ of $\mathcal{R}$ will simulate processor j of Q, for $0 \le j < N$, and processor $p_{i,0}$ of $\mathcal{R}$ will simulate shared memory cell i of Q, for $0 \le i < S$. For a PRIORITY write conflict resolution rule in which the lowest indexed processor has priority, note that processors $p_{0,j}$ of $\mathcal{R}$ are in order of decreasing priority from left to right.

Let each step of a PRAM comprise three phases:

   (i) read from a shared memory cell,

   (ii) local computation, and

   (iii) write to a shared memory cell.

To simulate a read by PRAM processor j from shared memory cell i, first, each $p_{i,0}$ broadcasts its value c_i along its row, for $0 \le i < S$. All $p_{i,j}$ read c_i, for $0 \le j < N$. Next, processor $p_{0,j}$ sends a request to $p_{i,j}$ down column j, then $p_{i,j}$ forwards c_i up the column to $p_{0,j}$.

Processor $p_{0,j}$ readily performs the same local computation as the corresponding PRAM processor j.

To simulate a write of value v_j by PRAM processor j to shared memory cell i, $p_{0,j}$ sends v_j to $p_{i,j}$ down column j. Writing processors use neighbor localization (see Section 2.3.3) to select the leftmost (lowest indexed) writer of row i to write to the memory location that processor $p_{i,0}$ represents. Specifically, all processors fuse their W and E ports, except those processors $p_{i,j}$ that have received a value to write, which leave their W and E ports disconnected. Processor $p_{i,j}$ now writes v_j on its W port, attempting to send it to $p_{i,0}$. Processor $p_{i,0}$ will receive the value written on its row from the nearest (lowest indexed) processor, which has highest priority in the event of a write conflict. Note that multiple processors may write on the same row, but to disjoint bus segments, so all writes on the HVR-Mesh are exclusive.

If the PRAM uses the COMMON or ARBITRARY concurrent write rules, then the same simulation works. If the PRAM uses the COLLISION or the COLLISION$^+$ rule, then each row of HVR-Mesh $\mathcal{R}$ again proceeds in a way similar to neighbor localization. For the COLLISION rule, row i of the HVR-Mesh configures as for the PRIORITY rule, all writers write to their W ports and read from their E ports. A processor of row i sets a flag to 1 if and only if it is a writer and reads a value at its E port (signifying at least one writer besides itself). The logical OR of these flags indicates a collision. For the COLLISION$^+$ rule, repeat the same method except that a processor sets its flag if and only if it is a writer and it reads a value (at its E port) that is differenmt from the value it wrote (to its W port).

The above steps clearly work in constant time.   ∎

Randomized PRAM Simulations. The simulations we outline here are randomized[1]. In an effort to retain the PRAM's algorithm design advantages while overcoming the obstacles to its implementation, many researchers have developed simulations of the shared-memory PRAM on various distributed memory models. The simulations here continue in this tradition. A common scheme in these simulations is to make multiple copies of each shared-memory cell, then map them to the distributed memory modules using a constant number of hashing functions chosen at random. A shared memory access then consists of accessing a majority of the copies of the desired cell. Randomization enters the simulations in the form of a random selection of a hash function and can also arise in such operations as semisorting. This approach holds an advantage of permitting any size shared memory as the R-Mesh size is independent of the PRAM memory size.

We state the following results without proof.

THEOREM 9.10 *Each step of an* ARBITRARY *CRCW PRAM that uses N processors can be simulated by:*

(i) *an $N \times N$* ARBITRARY *CRCW LR-Mesh in $\tilde{O}(1)$ randomized time, and*

(ii) *an $\frac{N}{\log\log\log N} \times \frac{N}{\log\log\log N}$* COLLISION *CRCW LR-Mesh in $\tilde{O}(\log\log\log N)$ randomized time.*

---

[1] See Footnote 1 on page 185

9.4   Loosen Up—Polynomially Bounded Models

The simulations examined so far in this chapter have closely tracked the number of processors and memory (for PRAMs). For the purposes of translating algorithms from one model to another, using one to simulate another, and understanding which features can be deleted and at what cost, it is important to know how the models relate at such a detailed level. For scaling self-simulations (Chapter 8), of course, a limited number of processors is the driving motivation. We can, however, obtain more general knowledge of the abilities of models and how they relate if we (substantially) loosen the strictures on the number of processors (and related resources) allowed. How substantially? By up to a polynomial in the problem size or model size. Why so much? What can we learn that is useful by allowing, say, N^{100} processors instead of a more reasonable N^2? By bounding the time available for the computation and allowing any reasonable number of processors (N^2, N^3, and even unreasonable N^{100}), we can classify problems according to the time used to solve them on an R-Mesh. Allowing any polynomial number of processors gives robust definitions for classes and avoids an artificial cut-off point of, for example, N^2 processors but not N^3, or N^3 but not N^4 or even $N^{3.01}$. This is also consistent with definitions used for complexity classes for other models of computation, such as PRAMs, circuits, and Turing machines.

To be more specific, we will define classes of languages that can be accepted by R-Meshes with polynomial processors and bounded time, and the time increments between classes will be a logarithmic factor. We will have a class for $O(1)$ time, for $O(\log N)$ time, for $O(\log^2 N)$ time, and so on. We relate these reconfigurable model and PRAM classes to each other and to well-known complexity classes defined in terms of Turing machine space and in terms of circuit size and depth. These relations serve to explain which problems can be solved with what resources on which reconfigurable models. They also serve to quantify the "power" of the models, offering evidence that some models can solve certain problems with bounded resources that other models cannot or are very unlikely to be able to solve. These relations also tie questions of separating the power of these models to questions of separating long-studied complexity classes.

9.5   Segmenting and Fusing Buses

Based on the abilities to segment and/or fuse buses, and concurrent reading and writing capabilities, this section derives a hierarchy of relative "powers" of the PRAM and reconfigurable models. Two fundamental abilities of a reconfigurable bus-based model stand out:

(i) its ability to segment a bus into two or more bus segments, and

(ii) its ability to fuse together two or more buses or bus segments.

Segmenting and fusing are natural operations on multiple buses. They also capture distinct operations in the context of reconfigurable bus-based models. Intuitively, segmenting creates more buses, but of smaller scope, by breaking an existing bus. On the other hand, fusing reduces the number of buses, but gives larger scope, by joining existing buses. These operations provide ways of manipulating the pattern of communication, the central feature of reconfigurable bus-based computation.

Section 3.2.2 briefly touched upon the RMBM model. Here we detail this model and use its ability to readily separate the functions of bus segmenting and bus fusing as the instrument to relate the powers of various models.

In particular, we establish in this section that

- the ability of a reconfigurable model to fuse buses is more powerful than the ability to segment buses, and

- concurrent writing ability does not contribute to the power of reconfigurable models.

9.5.1 The Reconfigurable Multiple Bus Machine

The *Reconfigurable Multiple Bus Machine* (RMBM) consists of a set of processors that communicate using multiple buses. A processor can break buses into separate bus segments, can connect (not necessarily adjacent) buses by "fuse lines," and has read and write connections that it can move from one bus to another. These abilities allow it to reconfigure the overall communication pattern.

Formally, an RMBM comprises P processors (indexed $0, 1, \cdots, P-1$), B buses (indexed $0, 1, \cdots, B-1$), P "fuse lines," and PB sets of switches, $Q_{i,j} = \{c_{i,j,0}, c_{i,j,1}, s_{i,j,0}, s_{i,j,1}, f_{i,j}\}$, where $0 \le i < P$ and $0 \le j < B$. Figure 9.3(a) illustrates the structure of the RMBM, and Figure 9.3(b) details the switches associated with processor i. A fuse line is adjacent to each processor and located perpendicular to the buses. Each processor has a write port (port 0) and a read port (port 1). Only processor i controls the switches in the set $\bigcup_{j=0}^{B-1} Q_{i,j}$. For all $0 \le i < P$, $0 \le j < B$, and $0 \le k < 2$, switches in $Q_{i,j}$ operate as follows.

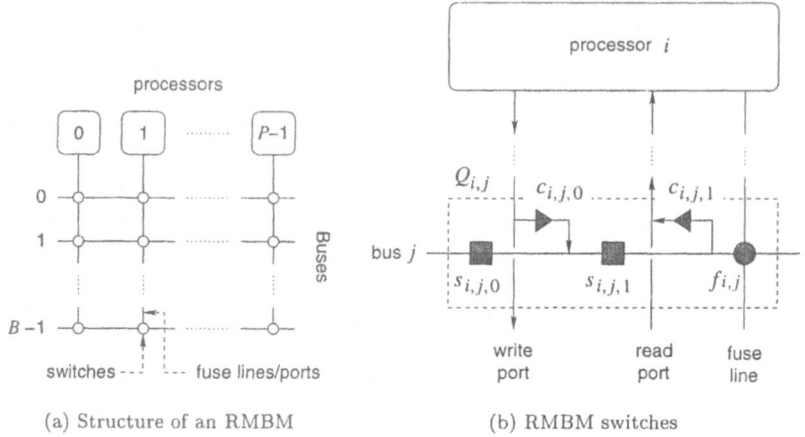

Figure 9.3. The structure of the RMBM. Triangles, squares, and circles denote connect, segment, and fuse switches, respectively.
Reprinted from the *Journal of Parallel and Distributed Computing*, vol. 46, 1997, J. L. Trahan, R. Vaidyanathan, and C. P. Subbaraman, "Constant Time Graph Algorithms on the Reconfigurable Multiple Bus Machine," pp. 1–14, © Copyright (1997) with permission from Elsevier.

- *Connect switch*: Switch $c_{i,j,k}$ performs the function of connecting port k of processor i to bus j.

- *Segment switch*: Switch $s_{i,j,k}$ performs the function of segmenting (disconnecting) bus j at the point where it is located. Switches $s_{i,j,0}$ and $s_{i,j,1}$ are located on bus j to the left of $c_{i,j,0}$ and between $c_{i,j,0}$ and $c_{i,j,1}$, respectively (see Figure 9.3(b)). When set, $s_{i,j,k}$ segments (disconnects) bus j at the point where it is located.

- *Fuse switch*: Switch $f_{i,j}$ performs the function of connecting the fuse line of processor i to bus j. If processor i has set multiple fuse switches $f_{i,j_1}, f_{i,j_2}, \cdots, f_{i,j_m}$, then this fuses buses $j_1, j_2, \cdots, j_m$ together. Switch $f_{i,j}$ is located at the intersection of the fuse line of processor i and bus j.

Assume that all switches in the RMBM are initially in the reset position. A processor can set or reset one switch in each step. A processor may connect its read and write ports to different buses; each port, however, connects to at most one bus at any point in time.

Based on the ability to segment and/or fuse buses, four versions of the RMBM exist, described below.

- The *Extended RMBM* (*E-RMBM*) is the version described so far in this section with connect, segment, and fuse switches; it is the most "powerful" of all versions of the RMBM.

- The *Fusing RMBM* (*F-RMBM*) has only connect and fuse switches; that is, it can fuse buses but not segment them.

- The *Segmenting RMBM* (*S-RMBM*) has only connect and segment switches; that is, it can segment buses but not fuse them.

- The *Basic RMBM* (*B-RMBM*) has only connect switches; that is, it cannot segment or fuse buses.

The F-RMBM has horizontal buses and vertical fuse lines that cannot be cut. In this way, it resembles the HVR-Mesh. One can use the S-RMBM as a collection of segmentable buses (Section 1.1) or one-dimensional R-Meshes, so, for instance, an S-RMBM can perform neighbor localization in constant time. The B-RMBM is not "truly reconfigurable" as it cannot manipulate the communication medium. In fact, the B-RMBM requires processors to identify a common bus to communicate with each other in constant time. This is analogous to a PRAM in which processors must identify a common memory location to communicate with each other.

For any X,Y $\in$ {C,E} (for Concurrent and Exclusive) and for any Z $\in$ {E, F, S, B} (for Extended, Fusing, Segmenting and Basic), let XRYW Z-RMBM[P, B] denote an XRYW Z-RMBM with P processors and B buses.

9.5.2 Relative Power of Polynomially Bounded Models

A model of computation $\mathcal{M}$ is *polynomially bounded* if and only if for problem size N and some constants c, c_1, c_2, and c_3, model $\mathcal{M}$ satisfies the following conditions.

(*i*) The model's size (number of processors) is $O(N^c)$,

(*ii*) Each processor has $O(N^{c_1})$ local memory,

(*iii*) The model has $O(N^{c_2})$ locations of shared memory, if any, and

(*iv*) The model has $O(N^{c_3})$ switches, if any.

This section assumes all models to be polynomially bounded (in the problem size N). The processor word-size and bus-width of all models is $\Omega(\log N)$ bits. (All simulations in this section need only word sizes of $\Theta(\log N)$ bits.)

Let *Models* $= \big\{$ B-RMBM, S-RMBM, F-RMBM, E-RMBM, R-Mesh, HVR-Mesh, PRAM $\big\}$. Let N denote the input size. For $\mathcal{M} \in$ *Models* and $j \geq 0$, let M^j denote the class of languages accepted by polynomially-bounded model $\mathcal{M}$ in $O(\log^j N)$ time. This section (Section 9.5) deals with constant time complexity classes (or, rather, relations among models to within a constant factor of time), so we will deal with classes such as S-RMBM^0 and (CREW S-RMBM)^0 where the read and write rules are important. Section 9.6 deals with polylogarithmic time classes.

Let $T(\Pi, \mathcal{M})$ denote the time needed to solve a computational problem Π on a model $\mathcal{M}$.

DEFINITION 9.11 Let $\mathcal{M}_1$ and $\mathcal{M}_2$ be (polynomially bounded) models.
  (*i*) $\mathcal{M}_1 \sqsubseteq \mathcal{M}_2$ if and only if $T(\Pi, \mathcal{M}_2) = O(T(\Pi, \mathcal{M}_1))$, for every problem Π.
  (*ii*) $\mathcal{M}_1 \; \boxed{\mathtt{c}} \; \mathcal{M}_2$ if and only if there is at least one problem Π such that $T(\Pi, \mathcal{M}_2) = o(T(\Pi, \mathcal{M}_1))$.
  (*iii*) $\mathcal{M}_1 \sqsubset \mathcal{M}_2$ if and only if $\mathcal{M}_1 \sqsubseteq \mathcal{M}_2$ and $\mathcal{M}_1 \; \boxed{\mathtt{c}} \; \mathcal{M}_2$.
  (*iv*) $\mathcal{M}_1 = \mathcal{M}_2$ if and only if $\mathcal{M}_1 \sqsubseteq \mathcal{M}_2$ and $\mathcal{M}_2 \sqsubseteq \mathcal{M}_1$.

<u>Remarks:</u> We will use the term "power" to describe relations among models according to these definitions. Model $\mathcal{M}_1$ is *at most as powerful* as $\mathcal{M}_2$ if they satisfy part (*i*). That is, a (polynomially bounded) $\mathcal{M}_2$ can simulate each step of $\mathcal{M}_1$ in constant time. Model $\mathcal{M}_1$ is *not more powerful* than $\mathcal{M}_2$ (or $\mathcal{M}_2$ is *not less powerful* than $\mathcal{M}_1$) if they satisfy part (*ii*). Specifically, by part (*ii*), $\mathcal{M}_2$ is faster than $\mathcal{M}_1$ on at least one problem. This does not, however, preclude the existence of another problem for which $\mathcal{M}_1$ is faster than $\mathcal{M}_2$, but does guarantee that $\mathcal{M}_1$ is not as fast as or faster than $\mathcal{M}_2$ for <u>all</u> problems. Model $\mathcal{M}_1$ is *strictly less powerful* than $\mathcal{M}_2$ if they satisfy part (*iii*). Models $\mathcal{M}_1$ and $\mathcal{M}_2$ have the *same power* if they satisfy part (*iv*).

Note that we can express $\mathcal{M}_1 \sqsubseteq \mathcal{M}_2$ as $\mathsf{M}_1{}^0 \subseteq \mathsf{M}_2{}^0$. Similarly, we can express $\mathcal{M}_1 \sqsubset \mathcal{M}_2$ as $\mathsf{M}_1{}^0 \subset \mathsf{M}_2{}^0$ and express $\mathcal{M}_1 = \mathcal{M}_2$ as $\mathsf{M}_1{}^0 = \mathsf{M}_2{}^0$.

Figure 9.4 summarizes the hierarchy of relationships among RMBM versions, R-Mesh, HVR-Mesh, and PRAM. In particular, it displays

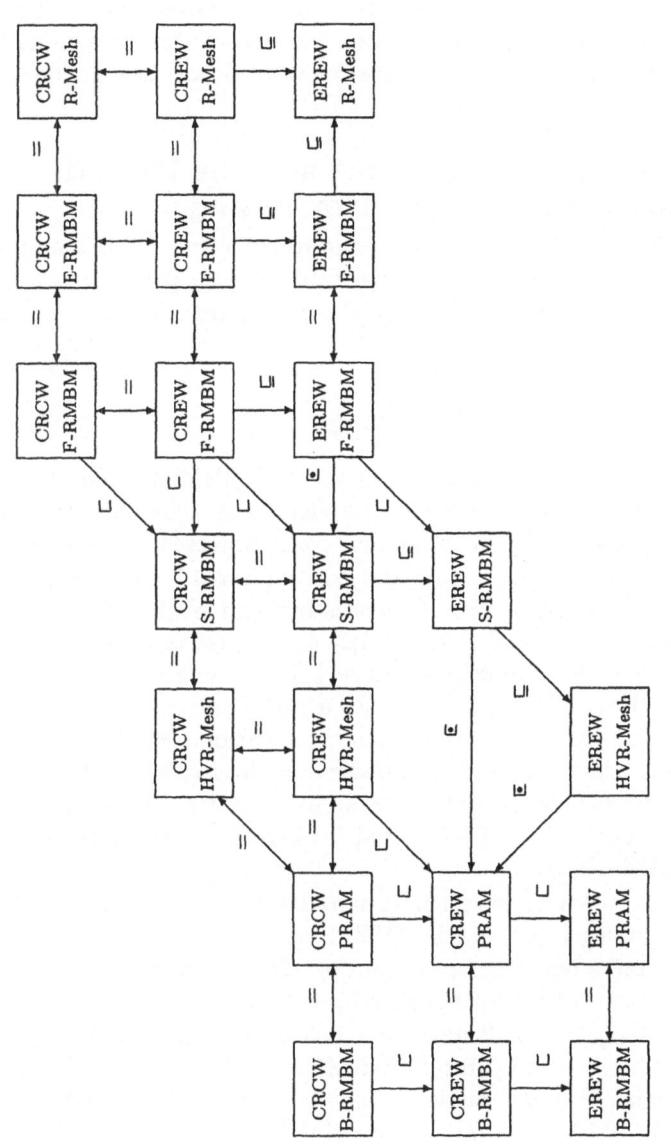

Figure 9.4. The relative powers of the PRAM, RMBM, and R-Mesh.
Reprinted from the *Journal of Parallel and Distributed Computing*, vol. 34, 1996, J. L. Trahan, R. Vaidyanathan, and R. K. Thiruchelvan, "On the Power of Segmenting and Fusing Buses," pp. 82–94, © Copyright (1996) with permission from Elsevier.

that the ability of a model to fuse buses (F-RMBM, E-RMBM, R-Mesh) is more powerful than its ability to segment buses (S-RMBM, HVR-Mesh). Additionally, for models with the ability to segment and/or fuse buses, the concurrent write ability does not add power over that obtained by concurrent read. We will now derive a portion of these relations in this section. The remaining relations are deferred to exercises at the end of this chapter (see Problem 9.17).

9.5.3   Relating the B-RMBM and the PRAM: Neither Segmenting Nor Fusing

The B-RMBM and the PRAM are equally powerful. This result is not surprising, as both are non-reconfigurable and as processors communicate via buses or shared memory cells in similar fashion.

THEOREM 9.12 *For* $X, Y \in \{C, E\}$,
$(\text{XRYW PRAM})^0 = (\text{XRYW B-RMBM})^0$.

Proof: In these simulations, a bus b_i of the B-RMBM will simulate a shared memory cell $c(i)$ of the PRAM and vice versa. The only catch is that a memory location holds a value until some processor writes a new value to it, while a bus holds a value only during a read/write cycle.

Given an XRYW PRAM with P processors and S shared memory cells, we construct an XRYW B-RMBM$[P + S, S]$ (that is, an XRYW B-RMBM with $P+S$ processors and S buses) that simulates each PRAM step in constant time. The B-RMBM uses a processor to simulate each processor of the PRAM. To simulate memory location $c(i)$ of a PRAM, let the B-RMBM use a bus b_i and a dedicated processor p_i. To let b_i convey $c(i)$'s contents that persist across steps, p_i writes its contents on b_i during the read cycle of the PRAM and reads from b_i during the write cycle of the PRAM.

The PRAM also uses a processor to simulate each processor of the B-RMBM. To simulate bus b_i of a B-RMBM, let the PRAM use a shared memory cell $c(i)$ and a dedicated processor p_i. To indicate whether some processor has written to $c(i)$ (or the simulated bus b_i) in the current cycle, p_i initializes $c(i)$ to an illegal value before each read/write cycle of the B-RMBM. Given an XRYW B-RMBM$[P, B]$, we construct an XRYW PRAM with $P + B$ processors and B shared memory cells that simulates each B-RMBM step in constant time.   ∎

Note the simplifying assumption that the number of shared memory cells accessed is known initially. Theorem 9.10 points to randomized PRAM simulations without this assumption.

9.5.4   Relating the S-RMBM, HVR-Mesh, and PRAM: Only Segmenting

We now show that a CRYW S-RMBM and a CRYW HVR-Mesh are equally powerful.

LEMMA 9.13 *For $X, Y \in \{C, E\}$, a step of an $H \times W$ XRYW HVR-Mesh can be simulated by an XRYW S-RMBM$[4HW, H + W + 4]$ in $O(1)$ time.*

Proof: Each processor of the $H \times W$ HVR-Mesh has four ports, so let a team of four adjacent RMBM processors simulate each HVR-Mesh processor. Arrange these teams according to a row-major ordering of HVR-Mesh processors. Given the limited port fusing configurations of an HVR-Mesh processor, each HVR-Mesh bus is a segment of one of the H horizontal buses (each spanning an entire row) or W vertical buses (each spanning an entire column). The S-RMBM uses a bus for each of these buses, matching the relative ordering of HVR-Mesh processors with the ordering of its processors simulating corresponding ports. Therefore, the buses preserve the relative ordering of ports in any row or column of the HVR-Mesh, and the S-RMBM processors can segment them appropriately. The S-RMBM uses the remaining four buses for communication among processors in a team. ∎

LEMMA 9.14 *For $X, Y \in \{C, E\}$, a step of an XRYW S-RMBM$[P, B]$ can be simulated by a $B \times 2P$ CRYW HVR-Mesh in $O(1)$ time.*

Proof: Let p_i and b_j denote a processor and bus, respectively, of the S-RMBM, where $0 \le i < P$ and $0 \le j < B$. Let $\pi_{g,h}$ denote a processor of the simulating HVR-Mesh, where $0 \le g < B$ and $0 \le h < 2P$. Each row of the HVR-Mesh simulates a bus of the S-RMBM. For any $0 \le i < P$, column $2i$ simulates the left segment switch and write port of processor p_i of the S-RMBM; column $2i + 1$ simulates the right segment switch and read port of p_i. Processor $\pi_{0,2i}$ of the topmost row simulates p_i. Figure 9.5 shows an example.

To simulate the action of p_i setting its left segment switch on b_j, configure the HVR-Mesh so that a vertical bus connects all processors in each column. Processor $\pi_{0,2i}$ writes j on its vertical bus, and all processors $\pi_{g,2i}$, for $0 \le g < B$, read from this bus. In subsequent reading and writing steps, until changed, $\pi_{j,2i}$ will segment the horizontal bus at its W port to correspond to the set segment switch in the S-RMBM.

To simulate a read by p_i from b_j, again, configure vertical buses and let $\pi_{0,2i+1}$ write j on this bus. During the writing and reading phase,

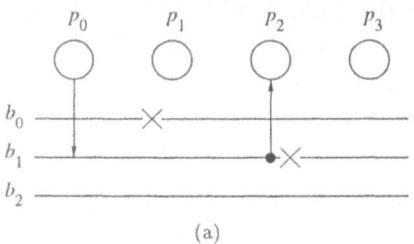

(a)

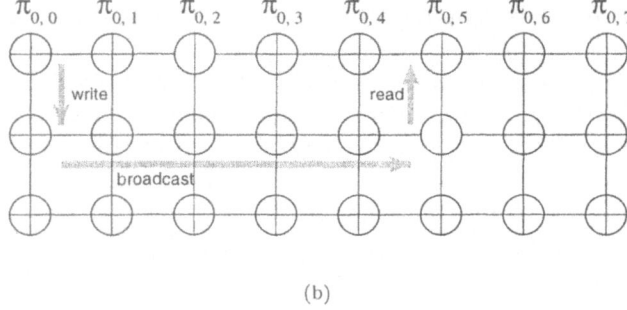

(b)

Figure 9.5. Example simulation of S-RMBM by HVR-Mesh: (a) S-RMBM[4, 3] with p_0 writing on b_1 and p_2 reading from b_1. (b) Simulating 3×8 HVR-Mesh with a three step write, broadcast, then read simulating the write and read of the S-RMBM in (a).

processors only fuse their E and W ports together, unless they are handling a set segment switch. Processor $\pi_{j,2i+1}$ reads during the writing and reading phase. Next, columns again form vertical buses, and $\pi_{j,2i+1}$ sends the value read to the top row. Handle writes similarly. ∎

We next show that a CREW S-RMBM is also equal in power to a CRCW PRAM.

LEMMA 9.15 *Each step of a* PRIORITY *CRCW PRAM with P processors and S shared memory cells can be simulated in $O(1)$ time on a CREW S-RMBM$[P + S, S]$.*

Proof: The S-RMBM can simulate each step of the CRCW PRAM, except resolution of concurrent writes, in $O(1)$ time as the B-RMBM did in the proof of Theorem 9.12 where a bus b_i in the RMBM simulates shared memory cell $c(i)$ of the PRAM. Use neighbor localization as in the proof of Theorem 9.9 to resolve concurrent writes. ∎

For a PRAM simulation of an S-RMBM, the target is to let a shared memory cell correspond to each bus segment on which a read or write occurs. The obstacle is to identify a unique memory cell for each bus segment, given the pattern of set segment switches. The following simulation maps each piece of a bus between two segment switches (call this piece an *atomic segment*) to a shared memory cell, then selects the rightmost atomic segment before a set segment switch as the *representative*. (View the right end of each bus as a dummy segment switch that is always set.) Recall that each bus b_i of an S-RMBM$[P, B]$ has $2P$ segment switches (two per processor). For ease of explanation, denote these segment switches on b_i by $s_{i,j}$ (where $0 \le j < 2P$). To index each atomic segment, assign it the index of the segment switch on its right border.

LEMMA 9.16 *Each step of a CRCW S-RMBM$[P, B]$ can be simulated in $O(1)$ time on a* PRIORITY *CRCW PRAM with $O(P^2 B)$ processors and $O(PB)$ shared memory cells.*

Proof: For each atomic segment $a_{i,j}$ of S-RMBM bus b_i on which some RMBM processor performs a read (or write), if the PRAM can determine a unique representative $r_{i,j}$ for atomic segment $a_{i,j}$, then it can perform the read (or write) on a memory cell $c(r_{i,j})$ associated with $r_{i,j}$. We now explain how the PRAM can determine $r_{i,j}$ for each atomic segment $a_{i,j}$.

For any given atomic segment $a_{i,j}$, $2P - j$ segment switches lie to its right on b_i. The RMBM employs $2P - j$ PRAM processors $p_{i,j,g}$ (where $j < g \le 2P$), one for each possible representative atomic segment. For each segment switch $s_{i,g}$, if $s_{i,g}$ is set, then PRAM processor $p_{i,j,g}$ writes g to shared memory cell $c(i, j)$. By priority write resolution, $c(i, j)$ holds $\min\{g : j < g \le 2P \text{ and } s_{i,g} \text{ is set}\}$, and hence $r_{i,j}$, as a result of this write. It is straightforward to verify that $O(P^2 B)$ processors and $O(PB)$ shared memory space suffice (Problem 9.15). ∎

The following theorem is a direct consequence of Lemmas 9.13, 9.14, 9.15, and 9.16.

THEOREM 9.17 (CRCW PRAM)^0 = (CREW S-RMBM)^0 = (CRCW S-RMBM)^0 = (CREW HVR-Mesh)^0 = (CRCW HVR-Mesh)^0.

9.5.5   Relating the F-RMBM, E-RMBM, and R-Mesh: Only Fusing

We now prove that polynomially-bounded F-RMBMs and R-Meshes have the same power by constructing an F-RMBM that can simulate each step of an R-Mesh in constant time and by constructing an R-Mesh that can simulate each step of an F-RMBM in constant time.

LEMMA 9.18 *For $X, Y \in \{C, E\}$, each step of a $\sqrt{P} \times \sqrt{P}$ XRYW R-Mesh can be simulated on an XRYW F-RMBM$[4P, 5P]$ in $O(1)$ time.*

Proof: To simplify the description below, let p_i denote a processor of the simulated R-Mesh, for $0 \leq i < P$. Divide the processors of the simulating RMBM into P teams, $T(i)$, each with four processors $\pi_{i,N}$, $\pi_{i,S}$, $\pi_{i,E}$, and $\pi_{i,W}$, for $0 \leq i < P$. The processors of $T(i)$ simulate the ports of R-Mesh processor p_i.

The first $2P$ buses of the RMBM simulate external processor-to-processor connections in the R-Mesh; let $\alpha_{i,j}$ denote the bus assigned to the connection between p_i and p_j, where $0 \leq i, j < P$. (Also let $\alpha_{j,i}$ denote the same bus.) The next $2P$ buses provide fusing locations to form internal connections—each processor can have at most two sets of internally fused connections (that is, its port partition can have at most two blocks with more than one port). Let $\beta_{i,0}$ and $\beta_{i,1}$ denote the buses belonging to team $T(i)$. The last P buses provide channels for communication among processors on the same team; let γ_i denote the bus assigned to team $T(i)$.

For an R-Mesh processor p_i, let its four neighbors be $p_{N(i)}$, $p_{S(i)}$, $p_{E(i)}$, and $p_{W(i)}$. To establish the internal connections of p_i, team $T(i)$ will fuse the α buses corresponding to fused ports of p_i to one of its β buses. For example, if p_i internally fuses its N, S, and W ports (that is, it has port partition $\{\overline{NSW}, \overline{E}\}$), then team $T(i)$ can fuse buses $\alpha_{i,N(i)}$, $\alpha_{i,S(i)}$, and $\alpha_{i,W(i)}$ to bus $\beta_{i,0}$ and fuse bus $\alpha_{i,E(i)}$ to bus $\beta_{i,1}$.

In each team $T(i)$, processor $\pi_{i,N}$ holds all information (regarding changes in the port partition, reads and/or writes, and internal computation to be performed) about simulated R-Mesh processor p_i. If p_i changes its internal port configuration, then $\pi_{i,N}$ informs its team members via bus γ_i of the new port configuration and of which β bus to use for each fusing, then they establish the corresponding fusing connections. Up to this point all reads and writes are exclusive. Concurrent writes (if any) are resolved by the RMBM in the same manner as the simulated R-Mesh. Processor $\pi_{i,N}$ now has all the necessary information to perform any internal computation of p_i in the simulated step.   ∎

LEMMA 9.19 *For $X, Y \in \{C, E\}$, a step of an XRYW F-RMBM$[P, B]$ can be simulated on a $(B + 1) \times 3P$ CRYW R-Mesh in $O(1)$ time.*

<u>Proof:</u> Let p_i and b_j denote the processors and buses, respectively, of the F-RMBM, where $0 \le i < P$ and $0 \le j < B$. Here the simulating R-Mesh is of size $(B + 1) \times 3P$. Denote the processors of the R-Mesh by $\pi_{k,g}$, where $0 \le k < B + 1$ and $0 \le g < 3P$. Rows $1, 2, \cdots, B$ of the R-Mesh simulate the B buses of the RMBM. For any $0 \le i < P$, columns $3i$, $3i + 1$, and $3i + 2$ simulate the write port, read port, and fuse line of processor p_i of the RMBM (see Figure 9.6).

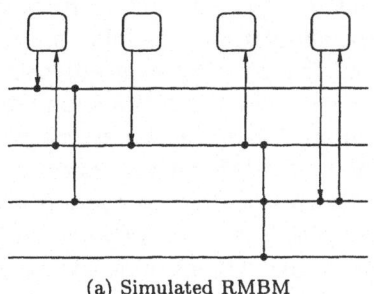

(a) Simulated RMBM

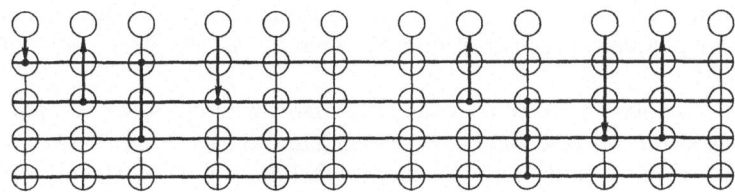

(b) Simulating R-Mesh

Figure 9.6. An illustration of the simulation of an F-RMBM on an R-Mesh.

Let processor p_i of the F-RMBM write on bus b_j in the simulated step. Configure the R-Mesh so that a vertical bus connects all processors in each column. Processor $\pi_{0,3i}$ writes $j + 1$ on its vertical bus and all processors $\pi_{g,3i}$ (for $1 \le g < B + 1$) read from this bus. Processor $\pi_{j+1,3i}$ establishes the required path for $\pi_{0,3i}$ to perform the write. Columns $3i + 1$ and $3i + 2$ handle reading and fusing similarly. The details of the simulation are straightforward (see Figure 9.6). ∎

The fact that $(\text{XRYW F-RMBM})^0 \subseteq (\text{XRYW E-RMBM})^0$ holds for any $X, Y \in \{C, E\}$ follows from the fact that the F-RMBM's abilities belong to the E-RMBM as well. Next, we show that an E-RMBM is only as powerful as the F-RMBM.

LEMMA 9.20 *For $X, Y \in \{C, E\}$, a step of an XRYW E-RMBM$[P, B]$ can be simulated in $O(1)$ time on an XRYW F-RMBM$[P + 2PB, 4PB]$.*

Proof: An E-RMBM can segment its buses and an F-RMBM cannot, but otherwise an F-RMBM can do everything that an E-RMBM can. Since an F-RMBM$[P + 2PB, 4PB]$ has more processors and buses than an E-RMBM$[P, B]$, we focus only on how the F-RMBM can simulate bus segmenting without using concurrent reads or writes.

The basic idea of the simulation is as follows. (Recall that an atomic segment is the portion of a bus between adjacent segment switches.) Each of PB *primary buses* of the F-RMBM simulates an atomic segment of the E-RMBM. Each of P *primary processors* of the F-RMBM simulates a processor of the E-RMBM, setting its connect and fuse switches on the primary buses corresponding to appropriate atomic segments. Each primary processor leads a team of *segment processors* at either end of the buses. To mimic setting or resetting a segment switch of the E-RMBM, a primary processor instructs the appropriate segment processor (over a dedicated *secondary bus*) to fuse or disconnect the appropriate pair of primary buses. (See Figure 9.7.) Within this structure, the primary processors operate exactly as the processors of the E-RMBM.

Let p_i denote a processor of the E-RMBM, where $0 \leq i < P$. For ease of explanation, we describe the processors and buses to simulate one bus; generalization to multiple buses is straightforward. Here the simulating F-RMBM has $3P$ processors and $4P$ buses. Call the first P (resp., last P) processors of the F-RMBM as *left* (resp., *right*) *segment processors* and denote them by σ_i^L (resp., σ_i^R), where $0 \leq i < P$. Call the middle P processors of the F-RMBM as *primary processors* and denote them by π_i, for $0 \leq i < P$. Each primary processor π_i simulates all actions of processor p_i of the E-RMBM, except manipulating segment switches. Segment processors σ_i^L and σ_i^R simulate the two segment switches of p_i on the E-RMBM.

Call the last $2P$ buses of the F-RMBM as *secondary buses* and denote them by $\beta_{i,j}$, where $0 \leq i < P$ and $j \in \{L, R\}$. Primary processor π_i uses secondary bus $\beta_{i,j}$ to communicate with segment processor σ_i^j, so all reads and writes are exclusive.

Call the first $2P$ buses as *primary buses*; they represent the atomic segments of the E-RMBM bus. Figure 9.7 shows one way that the segment

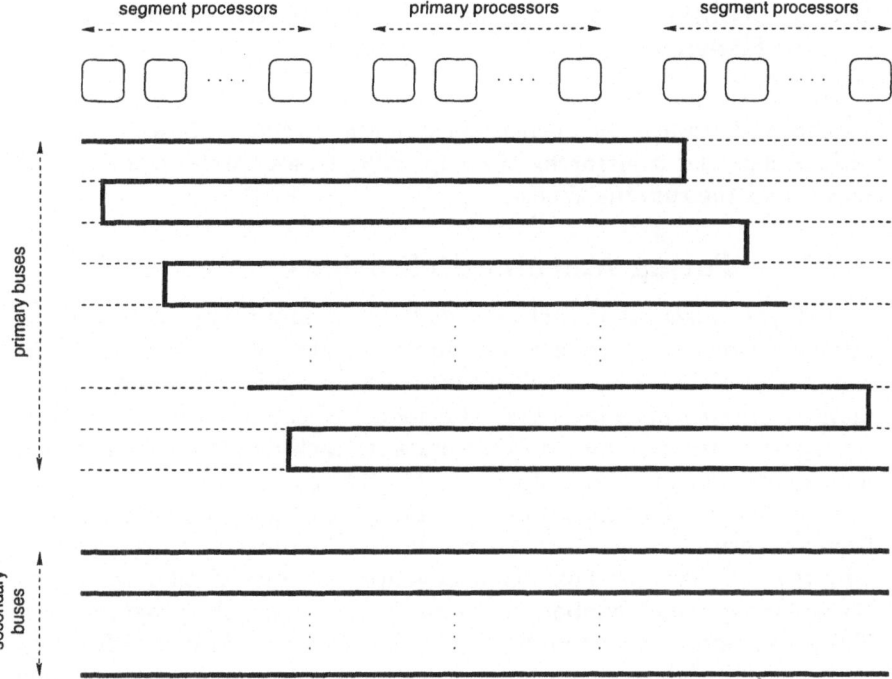

Figure 9.7. Simulation of the atomic segments of a single E-RMBM bus by an F-RMBM.

Reprinted from the *Journal of Parallel and Distributed Computing*, vol. 34, 1996, J. L. Trahan, R. Vaidyanathan, and R. K. Thiruchelvan, "On the Power of Segmenting and Fusing Buses," pp. 82–94, © Copyright (1996) with permission from Elsevier.

processors can fuse these atomic segments (if the segment switches between them are not set). This fused bus that snakes across the primary processors simulates the bus of the E-RMBM. Clearly, each primary processor can access each atomic segment of the bus. ∎

From Lemmas 9.18, 9.19, and 9.20, we have the following theorem.

THEOREM 9.21 *For $Y \in \{C, E\}$,*

(i) $(\text{CRYW R-Mesh})^0 = (\text{CRYW F-RMBM})^0 = (\text{CRYW E-RMBM})^0$,

(ii) $(\text{ERYW R-Mesh})^0 \subseteq (\text{ERYW F-RMBM})^0 = (\text{ERYW E-RMBM})^0$.

9.6 Relations to Turing Machines and Circuits: Hierarchy

In this section, we present relations between various reconfigurable models and traditional Turing machine and circuit models. These relations engender a hierarchy of complexity classes based on the type of model and the running time.

9.6.1 Turing Machine Definitions

A Turing machine is a classic model of computation. Although its structure and operation are not similar to any current computer, its complexity classes erect a widely known framework of relations. Informally, a *Turing machine* (TM) is a model of computation comprising a program, an input tape and a worktape, each divided into cells that hold symbols from a finite alphabet. The TM has a read-only tape head that reads one cell of the input tape, and a worktape head that can read from and write to one cell of the worktape. The program corresponds to a finite-state machine. For each combination of state, symbol read from the input tape, and symbol read from the worktape, the program specifies a next state, a symbol to be written to the worktape, a direction (left one cell, right one cell, remain stationary) to move the input tape head, and a direction to move the worktape head. The TM accepts an input by halting in a specially designated accepting state.

The *space* used by a TM computation is the number of worktape cells accessed during the computation. A TM may access a cell repeatedly, but the cell counts only once towards the space bound.

A *deterministic* TM (DTM) is one in which, for a given state, input symbol, and worktape symbol, the program specifies at most one transition to next state, symbol to write to worktape, and pair of directions to move tape heads. A *nondeterministic* TM (NTM) is one in which the program can specify multiple possible transitions for a given state, input symbol, and worktape symbol. An NTM accepts its input if any of the possible computation paths leads to an accepting state. A *symmetric* TM is a special case of an NTM in which each transition may be executed in both forward and backward directions.

9.6.2 Circuit Definitions

A *circuit* is a directed acyclic graph, with each vertex (gate) labeled as follows. A vertex with in-degree 0 is an *input* labeled from the set $\{0, 1, x_0, x_1, \ldots, x_{N-1}, \overline{x_0}, \overline{x_1}, \ldots, \overline{x_{N-1}}\}$, where x_i is an *input variable* and $\overline{x_i}$ is its complement. All other vertices have in-degree at least

2 and are labeled either AND or OR. Vertices with out-degree 0 are *outputs*.

A circuit has *bounded fan-in* if the number of inputs to each gate (in-degree of each vertex) is restricted to a constant, *unbounded fan-in* if the number of inputs is unrestricted, and *semi-unbounded fan-in* if the number of inputs to OR gates is unrestricted, while that of AND gates is restricted to a constant. (Note that while circuits receive complements of the input bits, they do not have any NOT gates. This is important for semi-unbounded fan-in circuits, but makes no difference for bounded and unbounded fan-in circuits.) The *size* of a circuit is the number of wires (edges) it contains. The *depth* of a circuit is the length of the longest finite path from any input to any output. A *circuit family* C is a set $\{C_1, C_2, \ldots\}$ of circuits, where C_N has N input variables. A circuit family C in which C_N is of size $Z(N)$ is *logspace uniform* if, given an input of size N, a Turing machine with $O(\log Z(N))$ work space can construct a description of circuit C_N.

9.6.3 Complexity Classes

Let N denote the input size. For $\mathcal{M} \in$ {LR-Mesh, R-Mesh, DR-Mesh, CRCW PRAM}, let M^j denote the class of languages accepted by poly-nomially-bounded model $\mathcal{M}$ in $O(\log^j N)$ time. Recall (page 329) that this implies that the number of processors and the size of the local memory in each processor in an instance of $\mathcal{M}$ will be polynomially bounded in the problem size.

Class NC^j (resp., SAC^j and AC^j) is the class of languages accepted by logspace-uniform, bounded fan-in (resp., semi-unbounded fan-in and unbounded fan-in) circuits of size polynomial in N and depth $O(\log^j N)$. Define classes NC, SAC, and AC as follows:

$$\mathsf{NC} = \bigcup_{j=0}^{\infty} \mathsf{NC}^j, \qquad \mathsf{SAC} = \bigcup_{j=0}^{\infty} \mathsf{SAC}^j, \quad \text{and} \quad \mathsf{AC} = \bigcup_{j=0}^{\infty} \mathsf{AC}^j.$$

These classes relate to each other as follows. For all $j \geq 0$,

$$\mathsf{NC}^j \subseteq \mathsf{SAC}^j \subseteq \mathsf{AC}^j = (\mathsf{CRCW\ PRAM})^j \subseteq \mathsf{NC}^{j+1}.$$

Therefore,

$$\mathsf{NC} = \mathsf{SAC} = \mathsf{AC}.$$

Class L (resp., SL and NL) is the class of languages accepted by deterministic Turing machines (resp., symmetric and nondeterministic Turing machines) with work space bounded by $\log N$. The notations L, SL, and NL stand for logspace, symmetric logspace, and nondeterministic logspace, respectively. Class P is the class of languages accepted by deterministic Turing machines in time polynomial in N. Notation P stands for polynomial time. These classes relate to each other as follows:

$$L \subseteq SL \subseteq NL \subseteq P.$$

It is a longstanding open problem as to whether these containments are proper.

At the level of constant time and polynomial processors, each of the LR-Mesh, R-Mesh, and DR-Mesh is equivalent to a corresponding Turing machine (TM) space class (see Figure 9.8 and Section 9.6.4). We

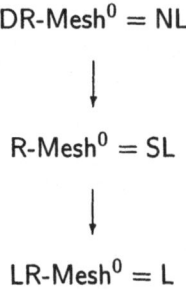

$$\text{DR-Mesh}^0 = \text{NL}$$

$$\downarrow$$

$$\text{R-Mesh}^0 = \text{SL}$$

$$\downarrow$$

$$\text{LR-Mesh}^0 = \text{L}$$

Figure 9.8.   Relations of reconfigurable model classes to TM space classes. (An arrow from A to B denotes B $\subseteq$ A.)

will discuss and establish each of these constant time relationships below. Considering greater amounts of time, $O(\log^j N)$ for $j = 0, 1, 2, \ldots$, spawns a hierarchy of classes (Figure 9.9). Section 9.6.5 will establish the two containments of Figure 9.9 that are not automatic or previously known from circuits and PRAMs: DR-Mesh$^j \subseteq$ SAC^{j+1} and NC$^{j+1} \subseteq$ LR-Mesh^j. Relating new complexity classes to the standard classes taps into a large body of knowledge about the standard classes.

9.6.4   Relations to Turing Machines

This section discusses the relations of R-Mesh classes to Turing machine classes L, SL, NL, and P. For each simulation, we sketch the key ideas without delving excessively into TM details.

THEOREM 9.22 LR-Mesh$^0 = $ L.

Proof outline: To simulate an LR-Mesh $\mathcal{R}$ that runs for $O(1)$ time using polynomial in N processors, construct a DTM $\mathcal{T}$ that uses $O(\log N)$

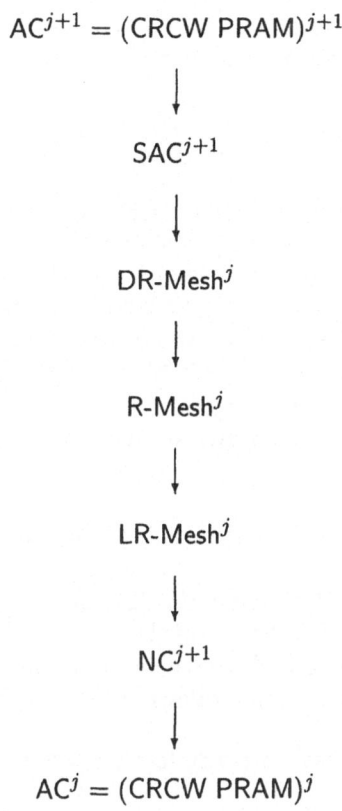

$$AC^{j+1} = (\text{CRCW PRAM})^{j+1}$$

$$\downarrow$$

$$SAC^{j+1}$$

$$\downarrow$$

$$\text{DR-Mesh}^{j}$$

$$\downarrow$$

$$\text{R-Mesh}^{j}$$

$$\downarrow$$

$$\text{LR-Mesh}^{j}$$

$$\downarrow$$

$$NC^{j+1}$$

$$\downarrow$$

$$AC^{j} = (\text{CRCW PRAM})^{j}$$

Figure 9.9. Hierarchy of reconfigurable model classes and circuit classes.

space. At a high level, $\mathcal{T}$ will simulate $\mathcal{R}$ step-by-step and, at the end of the computation, output the value held by each processor of $\mathcal{R}$. To simulate a given processor p in a given step t, $\mathcal{T}$ must determine the change to the switch configuration in p, any value read from a bus by p, and any change to the memory of p. DTM $\mathcal{T}$ determines the value read by simulating every processor $q \neq p$, determining whether q writes a value, and whether that value reaches p for the given switch configurations. (The fact that all buses are linear is critical in enabling the logspace DTM to determine whether a value reaches p.) To determine switch configurations and memory values, $\mathcal{T}$ recursively simulates $\mathcal{R}$ to determine the switch configuration of processor p at time t based on switch configurations, memory contents, and values written at time $t-1$. (Recall that workspace can be used repeatedly.)

The simulation of a logspace DTM by an LR-Mesh develops indirectly. Define the problem CYCLE as follows:

> Given a directed graph of out-degree 1 and in-degree 1 with designated vertices u and v (that is, a permutation on N vertices), output 1 if u and v are on the same cycle, and output 0 otherwise.

CYCLE is complete[2] for L with respect to NC^1 reductions. For a problem Π in L, an LR-Mesh can solve an instance of Π as follows: simulate the NC^1 circuit that maps the input instance of Π to an instance of CYCLE (Theorem 9.28), then embed the graph edges of the resulting instance of CYCLE into the LR-Mesh, and let the processors corresponding to u and v write, solving the instance of CYCLE, thereby of Π. (Note that the constraints on the degree of the graph in the CYCLE problem permit an embedding in an LR-Mesh, while an arbitrary degree graph could not be embedded.)   ∎

The above simulation of a logspace DTM by an LR-Mesh extends to a simulation by a cycle-free LR-Mesh, that is, an LR-Mesh in which every bus is acyclic (see also Problem 2.25). The simulation of the NC^1 circuit works without cycles. Further, a cycle-free LR-Mesh can solve CYCLE in $O(1)$ time with polynomial processors (Problem 9.22).

Consequently, we obtain the following.

THEOREM 9.23 $\text{LR-Mesh}^0 = (\text{cycle-free LR-Mesh})^0 = \text{L}$.

THEOREM 9.24 $\text{R-Mesh}^0 = \text{SL}$.

<u>Proof outline:</u>   The s-t CONNECTIVITY problem (a.k.a. UGAP – UNDIRECTED GRAPH ACCESSIBILITY PROBLEM; see Section 2.3.6) plays an important role in both simulations. Given an undirected graph G with two distinguished vertices s and t, the problem is to determine whether a path exists in G between s and t. The s-t CONNECTIVITY problem is complete for SL with respect to NC^1 reductions.

The simulation of an R-Mesh by a symmetric TM proceeds much as does the simulation of an LR-Mesh by a DTM. The difference arises in determining whether a value written by a processor q reaches a processor p given switch configurations. For the LR-Mesh, this was a matter of tracing a linear bus. For the R-Mesh, this is an instance of s-t CONNECTIVITY (p-q CONNECTIVITY here), which can be computed by a

---

[2] A problem Π is *complete* for a complexity class C with respect to a type of reduction if Π belongs to C and if every problem in C can be reduced to Π using the resources available in the reduction.

symmetric TM in logarithmic space, but is not known to be computable by a DTM in logarithmic space.

The simulation of a logspace symmetric TM by an R-Mesh likewise resembles the simulation of a DTM. The R-Mesh simulates the NC^1 circuit that maps the input problem instance to an instance of *s-t* CON-NECTIVITY, then embeds the graph edges of the resulting instance of *s-t* CONNECTIVITY into the R-Mesh, and lets the processors corresponding to *s* and *t* write. ∎

THEOREM 9.25 DR-Mesh^0 = NL.

Proof outline: The REACHABILITY problem for directed graphs (a.k.a. GAP – GRAPH ACCESSIBILITY PROBLEM; see Section 3.1.5) is the following problem: given a directed graph G and two distinguished vertices s and t, determine whether G contains a path from s to t. REACHABILITY is complete for NL with respect to NC^1 reductions.

The simulation of the DR-Mesh by a logspace NTM is much like the simulation of the LR-Mesh by a logspace DTM. The primary difference is that the NTM solves REACHABILITY to determine whether a value written by a processor q reaches a processor p, traveling over the directed network.

Let a *configuration* of a TM include its state, tape head positions, and worktape contents. A logspace TM has polynomially many distinct configurations. The simulation of a logspace NTM by a DR-Mesh has as a basic structure allocating a processor to each configuration, then creating a connection from a processor representing configuration X to a processor representing configuration Y if a TM in configuration X can reach configuration Y in one step. The processor representing the initial configuration writes a 1. The DR-Mesh accepts the input if any processor representing an accepting configuration (configuration with an accepting state) receives this 1. ∎

The *Non-Monotonic R-Mesh* (*NMR-Mesh*) is the same as the directional R-Mesh, but a port possesses an additional "inversion" ability, that is, a port can complement a bit passing through it. This ability further enhances the power of the model.

THEOREM 9.26 NMR-Mesh^0 = P.

Proof outline: The LEXICOGRAPHICALLY FIRST MAXIMAL INDEPEN-DENT SET problem (LEX-MIS) is the following. Given a graph, an *independent set* (of vertices) is one in which no two vertices are connected by an edge in the graph. For a set of vertices $\{v_1, v_2, \ldots, v_k\}$ where

$v_1 < v_2 < \cdots < v_k$, representing the set by the word $v_1 v_2 \ldots v_k$ induces a lexicographical ordering on sets of vertices. The LEX-MIS problem is to identify the maximal independent set that is lexicographically first among all maximal independent sets. This problem is complete for P with respect to logspace reductions. To solve the LEX-MIS problem, the NMR-Mesh embeds connections dependent on the graph structure including port connections that work as NOT-gates and OR-gates. The ability to simulate any polynomial time DTM algorithm follows.

For a polynomial time DTM to simulate a constant time (in fact, a polynomial time) NMR-Mesh of polynomial size, the DTM produces a network description and simulates each switch to convey written data and update the configuration for each step in turn.   ∎

9.6.5   Relations to Circuits

We now present relations between the DR-Mesh, LR-Mesh, and circuits shown in the hierarchy of classes in Figure 9.9.

THEOREM 9.27 DR-Mesh$^j \subseteq$ SAC^{j+1}.

Proof: Let $\mathcal{D}$ denote a polynomially bounded DR-Mesh running in time $O(\log^j N)$ for an input of size N. We construct a family of uniform, semi-unbounded fan-in circuits, $\mathcal{C}$, of size polynomial in N and depth $O(\log^{j+1} N)$ that simulates $\mathcal{D}$.

A polynomial size, log depth family of bounded fan-in circuits can simulate each step of a CRCW PRAM with polynomial number of processors. We adapt this circuit family to simulate a DR-Mesh. PRAM processors communicate via shared memory accesses, while the DR-Mesh processors communicate over directed buses. To handle communication between processors in the DR-Mesh in the circuit, view the port connections as a directed graph and compute reachability information to handle bus communications. Repeatedly squaring ($\log N$ times) the Boolean adjacency matrix of the graph will compute its transitive closure (see also Section 6.4.1). A semi-unbounded fan-in circuit of polynomial size can compute each product element of Boolean matrix multiplication in constant depth by $c_{i,j} = \bigvee\limits_{k=0}^{N-1} (a_{i,k} \wedge b_{k,j})$, and compute the transitive closure in logarithmic depth.

Putting these together, we obtain the family $\mathcal{C}$ of circuits that simulates each step of $\mathcal{D}$ in $O(\log N)$ depth, hence the entire computation of $\mathcal{D}$ in $O(\log^{j+1} N)$ depth.   ∎

THEOREM 9.28 $NC^{j+1} \subseteq$ LR-Mesh^j.

Proof: Let $\mathcal{C}$ be a family of logspace-uniform, bounded fan-in circuits of size $O(N^c)$, for constant $c \geq 1$, and depth $O(\log^{j+1} N)$ for inputs of size N. Construct a family of "layered" circuits $\mathcal{B}$ from $\mathcal{C}$ such that each gate receives its inputs only from the preceding layer; this entails only a constant factor increase in size. Circuit family $\mathcal{B}$ is also logspace-uniform and bounded fan-in. We construct an LR-Mesh $\mathcal{R}$ that simulates $\mathcal{C}_N$ via $\mathcal{B}_N$ with $O(N^{2c+1})$ processors and in time $O(\log^j N)$.

Given log-space constructibility[3] of the programs of the LR-Mesh processors, $\mathcal{R}$ can construct a description of $\mathcal{B}_N$ in $O(1)$ time that will identify, for each gate g, its type and inputs. LR-Mesh $\mathcal{R}$ will next determine for each gate the layer to which it belongs. Next, $\mathcal{R}$ constructs a directed forest such that the distance of a vertex v_g from a root is the depth of the corresponding gate g. For each gate g, the corresponding processor p_g selects one of its inputs from some gate f at the previous layer and creates a pointer from f to g. This creates a forest of trees rooted at each circuit input and containing a vertex for each gate g. Because $\mathcal{B}_N$ is layered, each path back from gate g to a circuit input is of the same length. Run a list ranking algorithm (Theorem 2.17, page 46) on the forest to identify the layer to which each gate belongs. (Note: The list ranking algorithm will run on this forest in the same way as though the paths from roots to leaves were separate lists.) Since the maximum depth of the circuit is $O(\log^{j+1} N)$, $\mathcal{R}$ uses $O(N^{2c} \log^{(j+1)} N)$ processors for the list ranking.

LR-Mesh $\mathcal{R}$ next carves $\mathcal{B}_N$ into slices of depth $\log N$ such that the output of one slice becomes the input to the next slice. Using $O(N^2)$ processors, $\mathcal{R}$ simulates these $O(\log^j N)$ slices in turn, each in $O(1)$ time. Consequently, $\mathcal{R}$ simulates $\mathcal{C}_N$ via $\mathcal{B}_N$ in $O(\log^j N)$ time using polynomial in N processors. ∎

Extending the results in this section to polylogarithmic time generates the following set of equalities: LR-Mesh^{polylog} = R-Mesh^{polylog} = DR-Mesh^{polylog} = NC = AC = (CRCW PRAM)^{polylog}.

Most algorithms for reconfigurable models use only concurrent-read, exclusive-write (CREW) access to buses rather than CRCW access. Since the CREW and CRCW R-Mesh (CREW and CRCW LR-Mesh, respectively) are equivalent to within a constant in time and polynomial

---

[3]An entity is *log-space constructible* if a Turing machine can create it given the input size N using $O(\log N)$ work space.

factor in processors, then many results in this section apply to CREW versions as well.

Problems

9.1   Use induction to prove Theorem 9.3 generalizing the two-dimensional block layout of a three-dimensional R-Mesh to a two-dimensional block layout of a d-dimensional R-Mesh.

9.2   Prove that the simulation of a d-dimensional LR-Mesh (see Theorem 9.4) runs on a two-dimensional LR-Mesh.

9.3   Design an algorithm to simulate each step of a d-dimensional R-Mesh in constant time on a two-dimensional R-Mesh for the case in which d is not a constant. Assume that port partitions change only incrementally by adding or deleting at most one port at each step. (This would extend Theorem 9.4 from constant values of d to non-constant.)

9.4   Prove Theorem 9.6 simulating a one-dimensional R-Mesh on a PRIORITY CRCW PRAM.

9.5   Does the method of Section 9.1.2 to simulate a d-dimensional R-Mesh on a two-dimensional R-Mesh apply to directed R-Meshes? Justify your answer.

9.6   Design a simulation of an N processor CRCW PRAM by a one-dimensional R-Mesh. How many processors does your simulation use? How much time to simulate each PRAM step?

9.7   Design a simulation of an N processor CRCW PRAM by a two-dimensional R-Mesh. How many processors does your simulation use? How much time to simulate each PRAM step?

9.8   Design an algorithm for finding the parity of N bits stored one per column on a $2 \times N$ R-Mesh. What is the time complexity of your algorithm?

9.9 Design an algorithm for finding the parity of N bits stored one per column on a $k \times N$ R-Mesh that does not allow processors to take the "crossover" connection, that is, port partition $\{\overline{NS}, \overline{EW}\}$. What is the time complexity of your algorithm?

9.10 Design an algorithm for a $b \times b$ sub-R-Mesh of bit-model processors to configure its buses to match the internal configurations of a word-model processor with word-size (bus-size) b. Recall that each bit-model processor has only $O(1)$ size memory.

9.11 Solve Problem 9.10, except assume that both the bit-model R-Mesh and word-model R-Mesh have directed buses.

9.12 Design algorithms for an $N \times N$ CRCW R-Mesh with one concurrent write rule to simulate an $N \times N$ CRCW R-Mesh with a different concurrent write rule, as follows:

(a) COMMON simulating COLLISION

(b) COMMON simulating COLLISION$^+$

(c) COMMON simulating ARBITRARY

(d) COMMON simulating PRIORITY

(e) COLLISION simulating COMMON

(f) COLLISION simulating COLLISION$^+$

(g) COLLISION simulating ARBITRARY

(h) COLLISION simulating PRIORITY

(i) COLLISION$^+$ simulating COMMON

(j) COLLISION$^+$ simulating COLLISION

(k) COLLISION$^+$ simulating ARBITRARY

(l) COLLISION$^+$ simulating PRIORITY

(m) ARBITRARY simulating COMMON

(n) ARBITRARY simulating COLLISION

(o) ARBITRARY simulating COLLISION$^+$

(p) ARBITRARY simulating PRIORITY

(q) PRIORITY simulating COMMON

(r)   PRIORITY simulating COLLISION

(s)   PRIORITY simulating COLLISION$^+$

(t)   PRIORITY simulating ARBITRARY

(Note: Some of these algorithms should run in $O(1)$ time, some will not.)

9.13   Design constant time algorithms for an R-Mesh with one concurrent write rule to simulate an R-Mesh with a different concurrent write rule as in Problem 9.12 except allow the simulating R-Mesh to use any polynomial in N number of processors.

9.14   Prove that an EREW S-RMBM can perform left and right neighbor localization in $O(1)$ time with P processors each holding an integer in the range from 0 to $m - 1$.

9.15   The proof of Lemma 9.16 asserts that a PRIORITY CRCW PRAM can find a representative $r_{i,j}$ for each atomic segment of the simulated S-RMBM$[P, B]$ in $O(1)$ time. Design an algorithm to do this using $O(P^2 B)$ processors and $O(PB)$ shared memory space.

9.16   Specify the steps performed in the F-RMBM simulation of an R-Mesh (Lemma 9.18) by team $T(i)$ of the F-RMBM simulating (a) a write by processor p_i of the R-Mesh to its S port, and (b) a read by p_i from its S port.

9.17   Establish the following relationships.

(a)   (CREW PRAM)^0 ⊑ (EREW HVR-Mesh)^0

(b)   (EREW HVR-Mesh)^0 ⊑ (EREW S-RMBM)^0

(c)   (EREW S-RMBM)^0 ⊏ (EREW F-RMBM)^0

(d)   (CREW S-RMBM)^0 ⊑ (EREW F-RMBM)^0

9.18   Generalize Lemma 9.18 to a simulation of a general reconfigurable network (RN) with P processors and E edges with an arbitrary structure. (See Section 3.2.1 for details of an RN.)

Assume that an RN processor can only change its port partition incrementally. Specifically, if π_1 and π_2 are port partitions of a processor in successive steps, then π_1 can be converted to π_2 by moving <u>one</u>

element from a block of π_1 to a different (possibly newly created) block.

9.19 Simulate each step of a $\sqrt{P} \times \sqrt{P}$ R-Mesh in $O(1)$ time using an E-RMBM with only $O(\sqrt{P})$ buses, rather than the $O(P)$ buses used by the F-RMBM in Lemma 9.18.

9.20 The proof of Lemma 9.19 describes (in part) a simulation of an EREW F-RMBM$[P, B]$ on a CREW R-Mesh. Construct a simulation that also runs in $O(1)$ time on an EREW reconfigurable network, which can have a general graph structure. (See Section 3.2.1 for details of a reconfigurable network.) How many processors and edges does this simulation use? What are the obstacles preventing this simulation from running on an EREW R-Mesh?

9.21 Given that the CREW versions of the F-RMBM, E-RMBM, and R-Mesh are equivalent and that the CRCW versions of these models are equivalent, prove that the CREW versions are equivalent to the CRCW versions.

9.22 Construct an algorithm for a cycle-free LR-Mesh to solve the problem CYCLE in $O(1)$ time with polynomial in N processors, where N is the number of vertices. CYCLE is the following problem: given a directed graph of out-degree 1 and in-degree 1 with designated vertices u and v (that is, a permutation on N vertices), output 1 if u and v are on the same cycle, and output 0 otherwise.

9.23 Theorem 9.24, establishing that R-Mesh^0 = SL, assumes COLLISION CRCW for the simulating R-Mesh. Prove that the simulation works for a CREW R-Mesh.

Bibliographic Notes

Vaidyanathan and Trahan [332] developed the material in Section 9.1 on mapping higher dimensional R-Meshes to two-dimensional R-Meshes. Leighton [174, pages 223–226] presented the bisection width bound on a d-dimensional mesh. Thompson [172, page 67] presented the lower bound on layout area in terms of bisection width. Beame and Hastad [16] established the $\Omega\left(\frac{\log N}{\log\log N}\right)$ lower bound on the time for a CRCW PRAM to compute parity.

Jang et al. [145] developed the simulation of a word-model R-Mesh by a bit-model R-Mesh.

Karp and Ramachandran [156] provided a good source on Parallel Random Access Machines (PRAMs) with essential information on complexity and algorithms. Olariu et al. [242] established a separation between the LR-Mesh and PRAM using the parity problem. Wang and Chen [346] constructed the straightforward PRAM simulation of Theorem 9.9. Czumaj et al. [67] and Matias and Schuster [204] developed the randomized PRAM simulations of Theorem 9.10 that use hashing functions to distribute multiple copies of each shared memory cell.

Trahan et al. [325] devised the relations among RMBMs, PRAMs, and R-Meshes presented in Section 9.5. They presented their R-Mesh-related results for the reconfigurable network, based on an arbitrary graph, rather than the mesh-structured R-Mesh (see also Problem 9.18). The notation in Section 9.5.2 relating polynomially bounded models has its origins in Vaidyanathan et al. [329, 331].

The circuit definitions in Section 9.6.2 are drawn from Venkateswaran [338]. For further Turing machine details, see Hopcroft et al. [136].

The complexity class definitions in Section 9.6.3 are drawn from Johnson [151] and Karp and Ramachandran [156]. Nisan and Ta-Shma [236] established relevant results for the complexity class SL. For additional information on complexity classes and reductions, see also Allender et al. [2, 3].

Ben-Asher et al. [18, 291] developed the relations among the various R-Mesh versions and the corresponding TM classes presented in Section 9.6.4. For the relations to a symmetric TM, Ben-Asher et al. [18] actually established an equivalence relation with SLH, the symmetric logspace oracle hierarchy, but subsequently, Nisan and Ta-Shma [236] established SLH = SL.

Trahan et al. [317] constructed the simulations of Theorems 9.27 and 9.28, relating the DR-Mesh, LR-Mesh, and circuit classes. Stockmeyer and Vishkin [304] designed a polynomial size, constant depth family of unbounded fan-in circuits simulating each step of a CRCW PRAM with polynomial number of processors, which the proof of Theorem 9.27 converts to a log depth family of bounded fan-in circuits. Trahan et al. [318] described how to convert a circuit to a "layered" circuit with a constant factor increase in size.

Olariu et al. [245] developed the list ranking algorithm cited in the proof of Theorem 9.28. Trahan et al. [324] extended list ranking algorithms to rank paths in forests. Ben-Asher *et al.* [18] constructed the circuit simulation used to simulate slices.

Trahan *et al.* [325] established the equivalence between CREW and CRCW versions of the R-Mesh and of the LR-Mesh.

PART IV

OTHER RECONFIGURABLE ARCHITECTURES

Chapter 10

OPTICAL RECONFIGURABLE MODELS

Advances in optoelectronic technologies have catapulted optical interconnects and optical computing to the forefront, opening possibilities not previously considered in conventional electrical and electronic interconnection environments. A pipelined optical bus is a prime example. It differs from an electronic bus in that it employs optical fibers to transmit information. Optical signal transmission possesses two advantageous properties: unidirectional propagation and predictable propagation delay per unit length. These two properties allow synchronized concurrent access to an optical bus, creating a pipeline of messages. Processors can also broadcast and multicast on such a bus, so this architecture suits many communication-intensive applications. Researchers have proposed several models based on pipelined optical buses as parallel computing platforms. Many parallel algorithms exist for these, indicating that such systems can be very efficient for parallel computation due to the high bandwidth that comes with pipelining messages.

Optical reconfigurable models take advantage of predictable delays in two ways. First, they can place multiple messages in transit simultaneously (pipelined in sequence) on the same optical bus. The time delay between the furthest processors is just the end-to-end propagation delay of light on the fiber. This admits the potential of significantly reducing the number of buses, hence processors, required to implement an algorithm. For example, a one-dimensional pipelined bus can route any permutation in one step. (This is impossible on one-dimensional arrays without pipelining.) Second, they can introduce limited delays, such as the duration of one optical pulse carrying one bit of data, in a way that affects addressing of messages. The immediate, and so far most useful, beneficiary of this technique has been the computation of binary prefix sums in a constant number of steps on a one-dimensional pipelined bus (see Section 10.2.2).

There are several similar models that feature "optically pipelined buses." One-dimensional models include the *Linear Array with a Reconfigurable Pipelined Bus System* (LARPBS), the *Pipelined Optical Bus* (POB), the *Linear Pipelined Bus* (LPB), and the *Linear Array with Pipelined Optical Buses* (LAPOB). Two-dimensional models include the *Array with Synchronous Optical Switches* (ASOS), the *Reconfigurable Array with Spanning Optical Buses* (RASOB), the *Array Processors with Pipelined Buses* (APPB), the *Array Processors with Pipelined Buses using Switches* (APPBS), the *Array with Reconfigurable Optical Buses* (AROB), and the *Pipelined Reconfigurable Mesh* (PR-Mesh). For the most part, the two-dimensional models allow only row and column bus connections or the same set of connections as the LR-Mesh. Consequently, they tend to be extensions to two dimensions of the one-dimensional models.

The basic similarity among these models is, of course, that they all pipeline messages on a unidirectional communication path. Most also allow processors downstream of a write to affect the destination of the stream of messages passing by them.

Differences among the models arise in particular features allowed. In some cases, the models are equivalent despite the difference in features; in others, the features appear to allow additional abilities to certain models over others. These features include the number and placement of switchable delay loops, the ability to reconfigure or segment bus connections, the presence or absence of extra buses for addressing purposes, and the ability to sample from multiple messages in a single step.

Section 10.1 gives an overview of these models. It selects one model as typical, explaining it in detail, then describes others in relation to this base. Section 10.2 presents basic techniques exploited by these models that are not available to the R-Mesh. Section 10.3 describes a range of algorithms that build upon these basic techniques and R-Mesh techniques. The main areas covered are sorting and selection, basic arithmetic, matrix multiplication, and routing h-relations. Section 10.4 addresses relations among models and their corresponding complexity classes.

10.1   Models, Models Everywhere

As noted above, many optical reconfigurable models exist. To provide a basis from which to understand the models, their features, and their algorithms, we first describe a particular one-dimensional model, the LARPBS, in detail (see Figure 10.1). We explore its essential elements, mechanisms for transmitting and receiving messages, and means of reconfiguring (segmenting) its bus. Following this, Section 10.1.2 describes a further selection of one-dimensional and two-dimensional optical models that have been conducive to algorithm development.

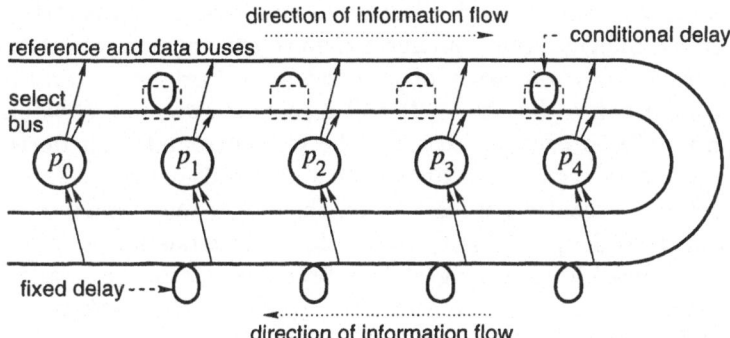

Figure 10.1. Structure of an LARPBS. For clarity, some features, discussed later, are not shown in this figure.

Reprinted with permission from the *International Journal of Foundations of Computer Science*, vol. 11, no. 4, A. G. Bourgeois, and J. L. Trahan, "Relating Two-Dimensional Reconfigurable Meshes with Optically Pipelined Buses," 2000, pp. 553–571 (© World Scientific Publishing Company).

The following framework is common to the models considered in this chapter. The models organize information to be transmitted by a processor on the bus into fixed-length *frames*, each comprising a train of pulses or *slots* (bits). The length f of a frame is the number of slots in it. (Typically, $f = N$, where N is the number of processors on the bus. Since b, the word size of each processor, is generally assumed to be $\leq N$, we have $f \geq b$ and a frame can accommodate a word of data.) Let τ denote the pulse duration. Define a unit pulse-length Δ to be the spatial length of a single pulse; that is, if c is the speed of light in the fiber, then $\Delta = c\tau$. The bus has the same length of fiber between consecutive processors, so propagation delays between consecutive processors are the same. The length of fiber between consecutive processors is at least $\Delta \cdot f$. This ensures sufficient length to enable message pipelining, as a message can be in transit between each pair of processors without overlapping with adjacent messages. Let a *bus cycle* be the end-to-end propagation delay on the bus. We will specify time complexity in terms of a step comprising one bus cycle and one local computation.

10.1.1   The LARPBS Model

Structure.   The optical bus of the Linear Array with a Reconfigurable Pipelined Bus System (LARPBS) is composed of three waveguides, one for carrying data (the *data bus*) and the other two (the *reference* and *select buses*) for addressing purposes (see Figure 10.1). Each processor connects to the bus through directional couplers for transmitting and for receiving information. The buses themselves are arranged to make a U-turn around a linear array of processors, and present a *transmitting segment* (top half of Figure 10.2) and a *receiving segment* (bottom half of Figure 10.2) to each processor. The reference and data buses each contain an extra segment of fiber of one unit pulse-length, Δ, between each pair of consecutive processors on their receiving segments (shown as a fixed delay loop in Figure 10.1). The select bus has a switch and conditional delay loop of length Δ between processors p_{i-1} and p_i on the transmitting segment, for each $1 \leq i \leq N - 1$. Processor p_i controls this switch: setting it to cross (resp., straight) introduces one unit of delay (resp., no delay). In Figure 10.1, processors p_1 and p_4 have introduced delays by setting their conditional delay switches to cross, while processors p_2 and p_3 have set their switches straight.

In addition to the features shown in Figure 10.2, the LARPBS has the ability to segment into separate subarrays, each a smaller LARPBS. For this, the LARPBS has switches on the transmitting and receiving segments of each bus for each processor. Let *segment(i)* denote this set of switches on the transmitting and receiving segments on the three buses between processors p_i and p_{i+1}. (See Figure 10.2.) With all segment switches set to *straight*, the bus system operates as the LARPBS shown in Figure 10.1. Setting *segment(i)* to *cross* segments the whole bus system into two separate LARPBSs, one consisting of processors $p_0, p_1, \cdots, p_i$ and the other consisting of $p_{i+1}, p_{i+2}, \cdots, p_{N-1}$. In Figure 10.2, processor p_3 has set *segment(3)* to cross, thus partitioning the LARPBS into two separate systems: $p_0, \ldots, p_3$ and p_4 and p_5.

Addressing Techniques.   Several addressing techniques offer themselves to the LARPBS. Common to all is an arrangement of N *frames* for writing data and address information for N processors. We describe three techniques here. The first two use only the data bus, whereas the third uses the select and reference buses as well, together with conditional delays to provide for a powerful addressing mechanism.

The first two methods assign one data frame to each processor. In the first method, processor i (where $0 \leq i < N$) always writes in data frame i, and a processor wishing to read from processor i will read from

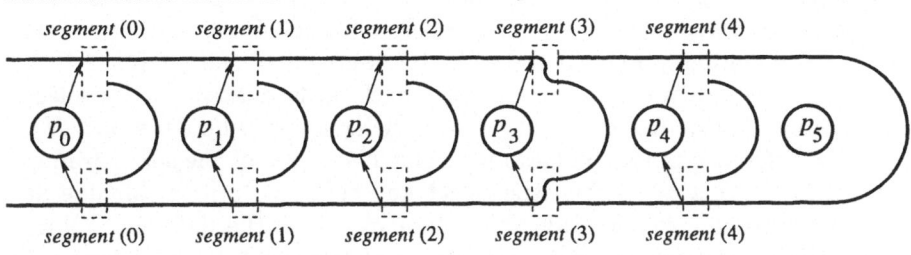

Figure 10.2. A six processor LARPBS with two subarrays. (For clarity, the figure shows only one bus and omits conditional and fixed delay loops.)
Reprinted with permission from the *International Journal of Foundations of Computer Science*, vol. 11, no. 4, A. G. Bourgeois, and J. L. Trahan, "Relating Two-Dimensional Reconfigurable Meshes with Optically Pipelined Buses," 2000, pp. 553–571 (© World Scientific Publishing Company).

frame i. While this scheme is writer-centric, the second is reader-centric. That is, processor i (where $0 \leq i < N$) always reads from frame i, and a processor wishing to send data to processor i will write to frame i.

These techniques do not require the data frame size f to exceed b, the processor word size. They also rely on the predictable delay of optical fibers to allow processors to read from and write to the data bus at the correct points in time. The third technique, called coincident pulse addressing, is more robust, relying only on processors to write at the correct times and using signal coincidence to trigger reads.

This *coincident pulse technique* is the most flexible and most commonly used LARPBS addressing technique. The LARPBS uses the coincident pulse technique to route messages to a desired receiver by manipulating the relative time delay of *select* and *reference* pulses on their separate buses. When these pulses coincide at a receiver (at any slot of a frame), that processor reads the corresponding data (which could occupy as many as b slots of the frame). More specifically, let processor p_i (where $0 \leq i < N$) inject a pulse at the rightmost slot (slot $N-1$) of the reference frame and data in the rightmost b slots of the data frame. These two frames move hand in hand through the transmitting and receiving segments. Suppose that processor p_i injects a pulse in slot j (where $0 \leq j < N$) of the select frame. We now examine what happens to these pulses under different, not necessarily disjoint, scenarios.

Without Conditional Delays: Here we assume that all conditional delays on the transmitting segment of the select bus are set to straight (introducing no delays). Then at the U-turn, the reference pulse still coincides with slot $N - 1$ of the select frame. With each traversal of a fixed delay loop in the receiving segment of the reference bus, the reference pulse moves one slot backwards relative to the select frame. Thus, after traversing x fixed delay loops (where $0 \leq x < N$), the reference pulse coincides with slot $N - 1 - x$ of the select frame. If $N - 1 - x = j$, then the select and reference pulses coincide at processor p_j, which reads the b data bits from the data bus. Note that the stream of b data bits starts at the point of coincidence of the reference and select pulses.

Without conditional delays, therefore, processor p_i sends data to processor p_j as explained above. Since p_i injects its select pulse at slot j, we will call j (or processor p_j) as the selected destination of processor p_i. As we will now demonstrate, a processor could select several destinations (for a broadcast or multicast), and the selected destination need not be the *actual destination* at which the pulses will actually coincide.

With Conditional Delays: As before, let processor p_i inject pulses in slots $N - 1$ and j of the reference and select frames, respectively. Unlike the the previous case, however, let $\alpha(i)$ (where $0 \leq \alpha(i) \leq j < N$) of the $N - i$ conditional delays downstream of processor p_i be set to cross (each introducing τ delay). Then at the U-turn, the select frame has been delayed by $\tau \cdot \alpha(i)$ time and the select pulse falls within slot $j - \alpha(i)$ of the reference frame. This situation after the U-turn is the same as the "No Conditional Delays" case with j replaced by $j - \alpha(i)$. As explained earlier, the reference and select pulses now coincide at processor $p_{j-\alpha(i)}$ which reads the data frame from the data bus.

The fixed delays on the reference bus, the delay between the reference and select pulses at the writer ($N - 1 - j$ here), and the number of conditional delays set to cross by processors downstream of the writer ($\alpha(i)$ here), all conspire to determine the actual destination (processor $p_{j-\alpha(i)}$ here). Observe that while selecting processor p_j as its selected destination, processor p_i may be oblivious to the states of the conditional delays downstream and so oblivious to the actual destination of its message.

Multiple Destinations: Observe that the ideas explained above for a single select pulse readily extend to multiple pulses in the select frame. If processor p_i issues pulses into slots j and j' of the select frame, then with the same notation as before, these pulses will coincide with the reference pulse at processors $p_{j-\alpha(i)}$ and $p_{j'-\alpha(i)}$, respectively, assuming $\alpha(i) \leq j, j'$.

Thus by injecting pulses in any subset of the N slots in its select frame, processor p_i can select any subset of processors as destinations for a multicast or broadcast of data.

Multiple Sources: Clearly, it is possible for more than one processor to select the same destination. This makes it possible for the same processor to be the actual destination of multiple writers during a bus cycle. If multiple messages arrive at the same processor in the same bus cycle, then it receives only the first message and disregards subsequent messages that have coinciding pulses at the processor. (This corresponds to PRIORITY concurrent write. An example of its use is the LARPBS algorithm in the proof of Theorem 10.2 (page 374).)

We now illustrate these ideas with an example.

Example: Figure 10.3 shows the select and reference frames transmitted by p_1. Let the conditional switch settings be those of Figure 10.1,

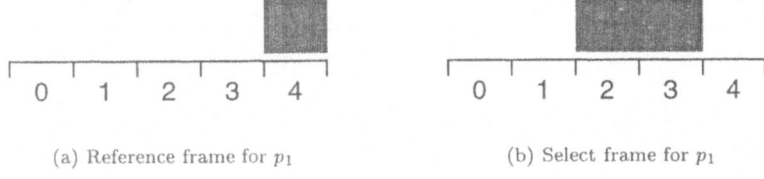

(a) Reference frame for p_1 (b) Select frame for p_1

Figure 10.3.   Select and reference frames for LARPBS example.

that is, conditional delay switches between p_0 and p_1 and between p_3 and p_4 are set to cross (set by p_1 and by p_4 respectively) and others are set straight. Let the segment switches not be set. Processor p_1 is multicasting its message to selected destinations p_2 and p_3, since slots 2 and 3 of its select frame contain pulses. The actual destinations are p_1 and p_2, since p_4 has set its conditional delay switch to cross. If p_4 also sent a message to p_2, then p_2 would receive only p_4's message (because it would arrive first) and would ignore p_1's message.

As mentioned earlier, the *selected destination* of a message is a processor whose index matches the number of a slot holding a pulse in the message's select frame (assuming the reference pulse is in slot $N-1$). The *actual destination* is the processor that detects coinciding reference and select pulses. (Actual and selected destinations may be different due to conditional delay loops and segmenting.) The *normal state of operation* is when the actual destinations of messages are the selected destinations. For the LARPBS, this is when all conditional delay switches are set to straight.

10.1.2   Other Models

In this section, we briefly describe other optical models, separating the discussion between one- and two-dimensional models.

10.1.2.1   One-Dimensional Models

APPB. The one-dimensional *Array Processors with Pipelined Buses* (APPB) is an earlier, simpler model than the LARPBS. In its most basic form, it features a single folded bus with one side dedicated to transmitting and the other to receiving (Figure 10.4). In such a model,

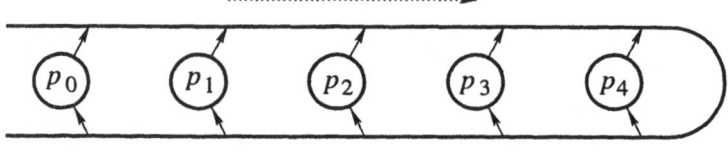

Figure 10.4. Linear Array Processors with Pipelined Buses – APPB.

addressing can take one of the first two addressing techniques (reader- and writer-centric) introduced for the LARPBS: either writing processors write to fixed slots and readers select the slot (processor) from which they wish to read, or processors read from fixed slots and writers select the slot (processor) to which they wish to write. One can enhance this with multiple buses and coincident pulse addressing.

LPB. The *Linear Pipelined Bus* (LPB) is identical to the LARPBS except that it does not have any segment switches.

POB. The *Pipelined Optical Bus* (POB) is also similar. Like the LARPBS, the POB has three buses. The POB contains no fixed delay loops. Its conditional delay switches, however, are positioned on the receiving segments of the reference and data buses, rather than on the transmitting segment of the select bus as in the LARPBS (see Figure 10.5). Section 10.4.2 will show that the presence of conditional delay switches is important for these models, but their location can be flexible. The POB contains no segment switches, so segmenting is not possible.

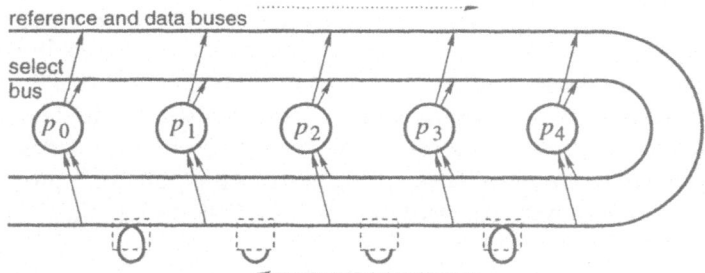

Figure 10.5. Structure of a POB.

The POB also uses the coincident pulse technique to route messages. Conditional delay switches on the POB delay the reference pulse relative to the select frame, so the POB is also able to perform one-to-one addressing, multicasting, and broadcasting. The location of the conditional delay switches on the receiving end enables the POB to multicast and broadcast without having to set multiple select pulses in a select frame, although it could set multiple select pulses as in the LARPBS and LPB. Consider the case when processor p_i is the actual destination of a message, the delay switch between p_i and p_{i-1} is straight, and all remaining delay switches are set to cross. The select and reference pulses will coincide at p_i and again at p_{i-1}, therefore both processors receive the message with only one select pulse.

Example: Consider the conditional switch settings of Figure 10.5. Figure 10.6 shows the select and reference frames transmitted by p_4. On

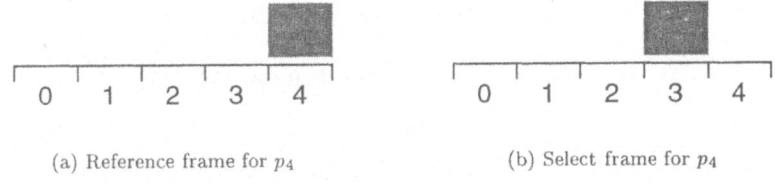

(a) Reference frame for p_4 (b) Select frame for p_4

Figure 10.6. Select and reference frames for POB example.

the receiving side, the select and reference pulses are in different slots at p_4, then the reference pulse is delayed, so they coincide at p_3, again at p_2, and again at p_1. The reference pulse is then delayed, so they are in different slots at p_0. Consequently, because of conditional delay switch settings, a single select pulse conveys the message to p_1, p_2, and p_3.

The LARPBS, LPB, and POB are equivalent in the sense that each model can simulate a step of either of the two other models in constant time, using the same number of processors. (See Section 10.4.2 for more on the equivalence of these models.) Consequently, an implementation can omit segment switches (using the LPB) or omit fixed delay loops (using the POB) and achieve the same results. For our purposes in this chapter, however, we stick to the LARPBS to simplify algorithm description.

LAROB. The *Linear Array with Reconfigurable Optical Buses* (LAROB) possesses a number of features not found in other models. Processors have conditional delay switches on the receiving segment of the select bus (rather than the transmitting segment). Each conditional delay switch allows a processor to introduce up to N unit delays, rather than only one unit delay as in the LARPBS. (See Figure 10.7.) A processor has a

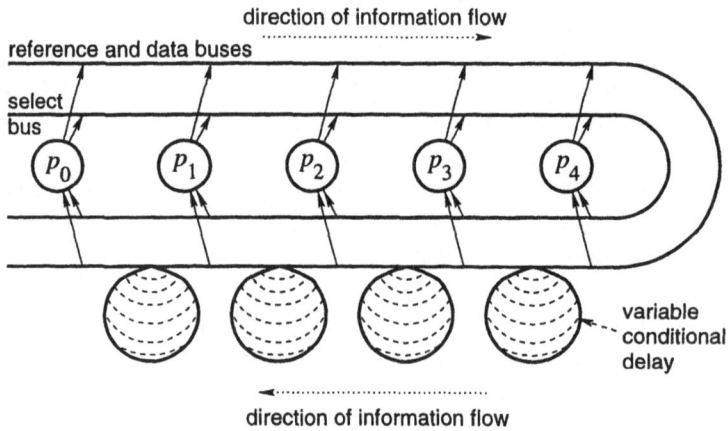

Figure 10.7.   Structure of an LAROB.

relative delay counter to determine the time between successive pulses; it also has an internal timing circuit such that a pulse can trigger this circuit to cause the processor to output a pulse after a predetermined delay (or delay determined by a value held by the processor). A processor can perform a *bit polling* operation in which it reads the values of the kth pulses of all (or a subset) of the messages in a bus cycle. It uses an optical rotate-shift register to store these bits as they are extracted. Further, a processor has a counter that can count the number of such pulses that are 1 in a given cycle. For example, if five messages sent during a bus cycle have contents 101, 001, 011, 011, and 111, and if p_4

reads bit 1 (the middle bit) of each message, then it will extract 00111 and its counter will produce 3 as its result. Aside from coincident pulse addressing, the LAROB permits the addressing technique in which each writing processor p_i writes to an assigned frame i and any processor seeking to read a message from p_i will read from frame i. The *extended* version of the LAROB allows switch settings to change on a bus during a bus cycle, triggered by detection of a pulse.

These features seem to allow the LAROB more "power" than the other models, that is, the ability to solve some problems in a constant number of steps that the others cannot. This is, however, still an open question, though the corresponding two-dimensional models are strongly related (see Section 10.4.4).

10.1.2.2   Two-Dimensional Models

Comparing a one-dimensional R-Mesh and the one-dimensional LAR-PBS, we find that communication limitations from bisection width of the R-Mesh do not carry over to the LARPBS, as all processors can communicate in pipelined fashion on the one optical bus. Moving from one dimension to two or more dimensions in the R-Mesh significantly enhanced the power of the model. In the setting of pipelined optical buses, the move from one to two or more dimensions does not increase the volume of communication possible, but it does introduce new capabilities from possible bus configurations.

PR-Mesh. The *Pipelined Reconfigurable Mesh* (PR-Mesh) is a two-dimensional extension of the LARPBS. Each processor may fuse its ports as in an LR-Mesh, that is, it may fuse pairs of ports. The resulting buses are linear, and each operates as an individual LARPBS. Observe that each processor must possess the necessary channels and hardware for making the connections. Due to the nature of the optical bus used, the processor at each end of a bus must play its role such that one connects the transmitting side to the receiving side (to make the U-turn connection as in the LARPBS) and the other leaves the ends disconnected. Observe that a bus forming a cycle is admissible in an LR-Mesh, but is to be avoided in the PR-Mesh. A PR-Mesh algorithm must attend to these special constraints, but they do not pose substantial difficulties (see Section 10.4.3). Another algorithm design issue is that addressing by the coincident pulse technique depends on a processor's position on the created bus, not on its index. One can overcome this challenge by using a round of binary prefix sums computation to identify positions (Problem 10.7). This aspect may offer opportunities for algorithm design, however.

The PR-Mesh bears a superficial appearance of being a directed network, as both the transmitting segment and receiving segment are directed. A message written by any processor, however, passes all other processors on the receiving segment, regardless of position. Hence, messages move in one direction (indeed, this is a distinguishing feature of optical buses), yet can reach all processors on a bus. Theorem 10.36 will, in fact, equate PR-Mesh and LR-Mesh (not DR-Mesh) complexity classes.

AROB. The *Array with Reconfigurable Optical Buses* (AROB) extends the LAROB to two dimensions. It too may only fuse its ports as in an LR-Mesh. It relates to the PR-Mesh as the LAROB does to the LARPBS: mostly the same, but with some added features. More details on the AROB appear on page 407.

Other Models. Other two-dimensional models exist, including the two-dimensional APPB, the *Array structure with Synchronous Optical Switches* (ASOS), and the *Array Processors with (optical) Pipelined Buses using Switches* (APPBS). In the two-dimensional APPB, each row and column is essentially a one-dimensional APPB. The other two models also have such row and column buses, but give different mechanisms to connect row and column buses. The ASOS permits switches to connect rows to columns. The APPBS contains an optical switch at each intersection of a row and column bus, which permits a subset of the LR-Mesh connections, although it allows switch setting to change during a bus cycle. Section 10.4.4 describes the APPBS in more detail.

10.2   Basic Algorithmic Techniques

This section describes basic computational techniques that are unique to optical buses because of the pipelining. These permit certain operations to execute in constant time on a linear optical model, whereas two dimensions would be required to attain constant time with non-pipelined buses. We present these techniques in the context of solving the permutation routing and binary prefix sums problems. Observe, nevertheless, that the two-dimensional PR-Mesh and AROB can form the same connections (except for cycles) and execute the same operations as the LR-Mesh, essentially by forming the same buses and broadcasting (see Section 10.4). These models can then carry out the same techniques as the LR-Mesh, but with a potential size savings by pipelining information on a single bus instead of multiple buses.

10.2.1 Permutation Routing

Message routing according to a permutation (see Section 2.3.1) in which each processor is the source of one message and the destination of one message is trivial on a pipelined optical bus. In the coincident pulse addressing technique, each processor sets a pulse in the select frame slot corresponding to its destination. Each processor writes at the same time in its own frame, and, since each processor is the destination of only one message, no conflicts arise and all processors receive their messages. In the writer-centric addressing scheme, each frame belongs to a particular destination processor. To route a permutation, each processor writes in the frame belonging to the desired destination of its message. Again, no conflicts arise and the communication takes place on a single bus in one bus cycle. Routing a permutation in the reader-centric scheme operates similarly.

THEOREM 10.1 *A permutation on N elements can be routed by an N processor LARPBS in one step.*

By a simple bisection width argument, a one-dimensional R-Mesh with N processors connected by an electronic bus would require $\Omega(N)$ steps, and a two-dimensional R-Mesh with at least N columns would require $\Omega(N)$ rows to route an arbitrary permutation among processors of a row in $O(1)$ steps. Consequently, a pipelined optical bus implements this basic communication step very efficiently, taking full advantage of the capabilities of pipelining. This is where models with such buses may attain significant size savings over a conventional R-Mesh.

10.2.2 Binary Prefix Sums

Given N bits, $v_0, v_1, \ldots, v_{N-1}$, the *binary prefix sums* problem is to compute $psum_i = \sum_{j=0}^{i} v_j$, for each $0 \leq i < N$. We will present three solutions to this problem on linear models with N processors. The solutions to this problem display, from one vantage point, a range of possible approaches available to solve a basic problem.

LARPBS Prefix Sums. Here the solution takes advantage of conditional delay switches and the segmentation ability. Initially, each processor p_i holds a bit v_i. Let the ith "reverse prefix sum" be $rpsum_i = \sum_{j=i+1}^{N-1} v_j$, for each $0 \leq i \leq N-2$, and let $rpsum_{N-1} = 0$. Each processor p_i sets its conditional delay switch to straight if $v_i = 0$ and to cross if

$v_i = 1$ (see Figure 10.8). The switch settings introduce a delay on the select line corresponding to each 1 bit. Thus the number of conditional delays $\alpha(i)$ set downstream of processor p_i is $rpsum_i$. Next, each processor injects a reference and a select pulse at slot $N-1$ and sends its own ID as data. The effect is that all processors attempt to send their ID to p_{N-1}; that is, each processor sets p_{N-1} as the selected destination. From the discussion on page 362, the actual destination of processor p_i is processor $p_{N-1-\alpha(i)} = p_{N-1-rpsum(i)}$. Multiple messages may pass the same number of crossed conditional delay switches and arrive at the same destination. Recall that the reading processor will read the contents (ID of the sending processor) of the first of these messages to arrive and ignore the rest. Some processor receives the message originating from p_i if and only if either $v_{i+1} = 1$ or $i = N-1$. Note that if a processor's message is ignored, then all processors between it and the closest processor, p_j, to its right whose message is accepted pass through the same number of conditional delays and arrive at the same destination; all these processors contain a value of 0. Also, $rpsum_i = rpsum_j$ because adding the zeros from the processors between p_i and p_j to the summation does not alter the result. (See Figure 10.8 and Figure 10.9 for an example.)

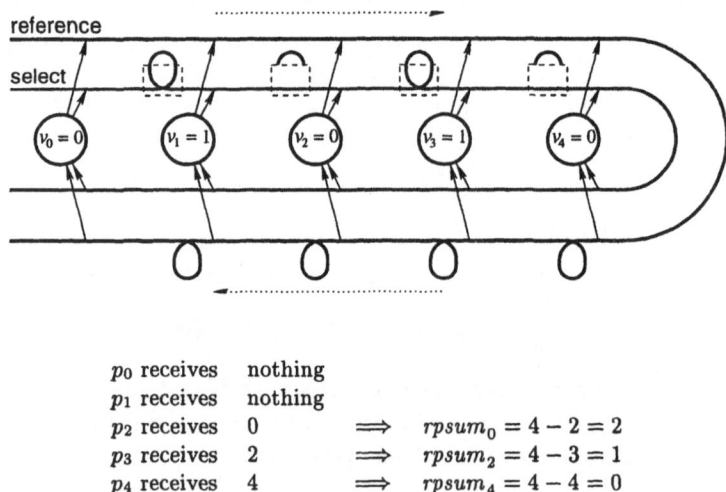

p_0 receives   nothing
p_1 receives   nothing
p_2 receives   0 $\implies$ $rpsum_0 = 4 - 2 = 2$
p_3 receives   2 $\implies$ $rpsum_2 = 4 - 3 = 1$
p_4 receives   4 $\implies$ $rpsum_4 = 4 - 4 = 0$

Figure 10.8. Example of first phase of LARPBS prefix sums algorithm.

Next, each processor that received a message sends its own address to the original sender, p_i, which calculates $rpsum_i$ from the address. If

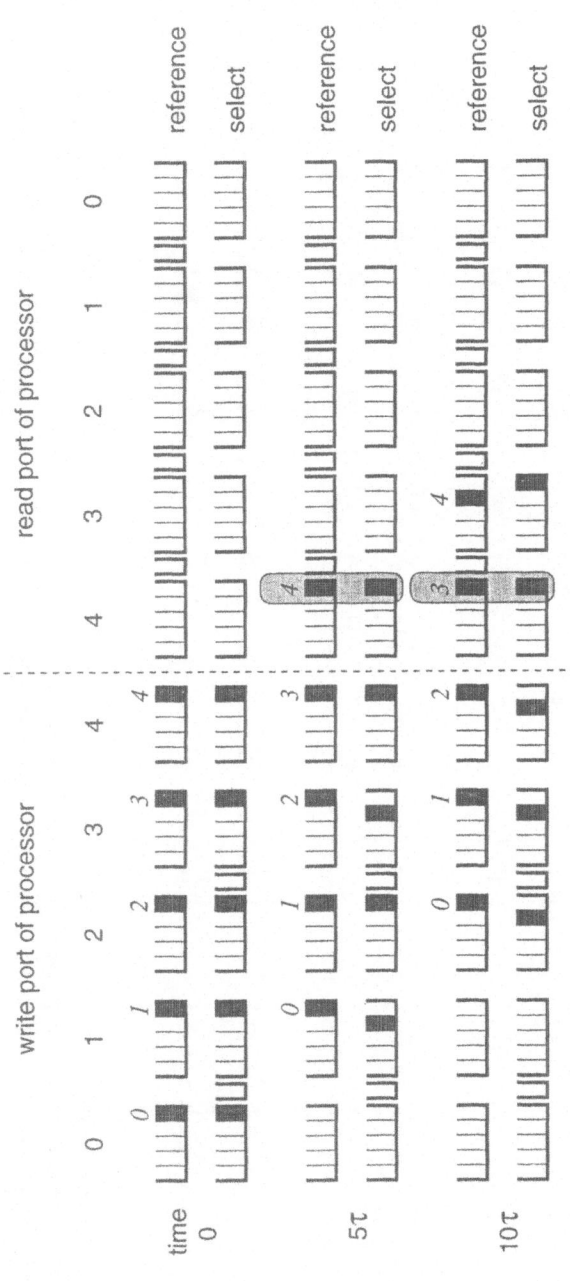

Figure 10.9. Reference and select frames after passing each processor during the example of the first phase of the LARPBS prefix sums algorithm. For clarity, the figure unfolds the U-shaped buses so transmitting and receiving segments are to the left and right, respectively, of the figure. A dotted line separates these segments. The two extra slots between frames on the write segment correspond to delays from set conditional delay switches. The extra slots between frames on the read segment correspond to delays from fixed delay loops. The figure shows the initial state of the frames and snapshots at only those points in time when reference and select pulses coincide at some processor; these are enclosed in an oval. Notice that pulses originating from processors 4 and 3 both coincide at processor 4 at times 5τ and 10τ, respectively. Since the frame from processor 4 arrives first, its message is the only one retained by processor 4.

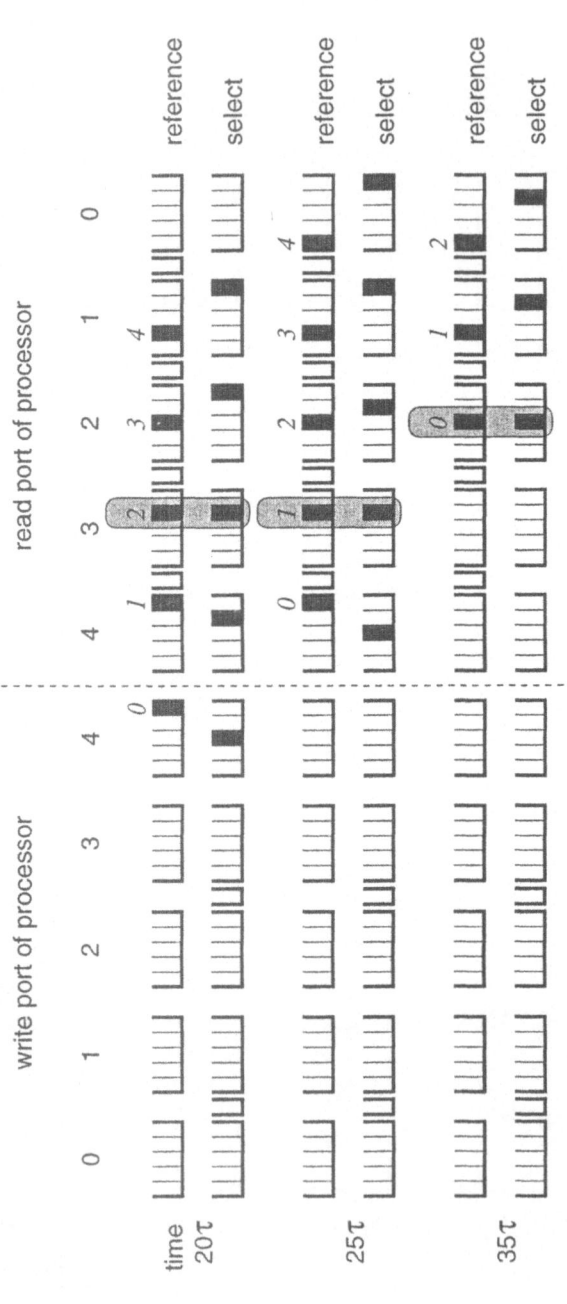

Figure 10.9 (continued)
Processor 3 receives coincident pulses in the frames from processors 2 and 1. Since the frame from processor 2 arrives first, processor 3 discards the message from processor 1. Processor 2 receives coincident pulses from processor 0, while processors 1 and 0 receive no coincident pulses.

this address is $N - 1 - k$, then the select pulse was delayed by k slots, so $rpsum_i = k$.

Since some messages in the first phase may have been ignored, the corresponding processors would not have received an $rpsum$ message in the previous step. Let S_r denote the set of processors that received an $rpsum$ message. For each $p_i \in S_r$, we want to send $rpsum_i$ to the sequence of processors preceding it that did not receive an $rpsum$ message and have the same $rpsum$ as p_i, that is, send $rpsum_i$ to $p_h, p_{h+1}, \ldots, p_{i-1}$ such that $v_{h+1} = v_{h+2} = \ldots = v_i = 0$, as $rpsum_i$ is equal to their $rpsum$ values. To accomplish this, simply segment the bus at p_i, then let p_i broadcast $rpsum_i$ (see Problem 10.6). Processors $p_h, p_{h+1}, \ldots, p_i$ will receive $rpsum_i$. Each processor p_i now has $rpsum_i = v_{i+1} + v_{i+2} + \ldots + v_{N-1}$. The total sum is $v_0 + rpsum_0$, which p_0 broadcasts to all processors. Each processor p_i now calculates its prefix sum $psum_i = totalsum - rpsum_i = v_0 + v_1 + \ldots + v_i$.

Each phase of the algorithm runs in a constant number of steps. Based on this algorithm, computing the binary prefix sums of N bits on an LARPBS can be performed in $O(1)$ steps.

LPB Prefix Sums. The LPB algorithm employs the multicasting ability of the model to avoid segmenting. It follows the structure of the previous algorithm up to the point at which each $p_i \in S_r$ is to send $rpsum_i$ to $p_h, p_{h+1}, \ldots, p_{i-1}$ for which $v_{h+1} = v_{h+2} = \ldots = v_i = 0$. The LPB algorithm now exploits the feature that a processor receives the first of multiple messages sent to it. Reverse the order of the processors, letting p_{N-1-i} substitute for p_i. For each $p_i \in S_r$, p_{N-1-i} now multicasts $rpsum_i$ to processors $p_{N-1-i}, p_{N-i}, \ldots, p_{N-1}$. Each p_k, where $0 \le k < N$, will read the first message sent to it and store it as $rpsum_{N-1-k}$. If $p_{N-1-k} \in S_r$, then the message accepted will be from itself; otherwise, the message originated from the closest processor p_{N-1-g} to its left such that $p_{N-1-g} \in S_r$. Now, for all i, processor p_{N-1-i} sends $rpsum_i$ to p_i to reverse the order of the values back to the original order. Each processor p_i now has $rpsum_i$. Then p_0 broadcasts the total sum and each processor computes $psum_i$. Again, the algorithm runs in $O(1)$ steps.

LAROB Prefix Sums. The LAROB algorithm for binary prefix sums relies on a counter to detect the relative delay between two pulses at each processor. Processors have conditional delay switches on the receiving segment of the select bus (rather than the transmitting segment). Processor p_i sets its switch to straight if $v_i = 0$ and to cross (introducing a delay) if $v_i = 1$. Processor p_{N-1} then simultaneously writes pulses on the select and reference buses. The time delay between these pulses increments by one at each processor holding a 1 bit. If p_i detects that the select pulse arrives k time units later than the reference pulse, then $rpsum_i = k$. As before, using the total sum and $rpsum_i$, each processor computes $psum_i$. Again, the algorithm runs in $O(1)$ steps.

THEOREM 10.2 *The prefix sums of N bits can be computed by an N processor LARPBS, POB, or LAROB in $O(1)$ steps.*

To examine the role of the various model features in the algorithms, all algorithms took advantage of conditional delay loops in the same way. The conditional delays here play a role analogous to the "stairstep" buses of the R-Mesh bit counting algorithm (Algorithm 2.3, page 28). In both cases, a 1 bit induces a one step (one processor on the LARPBS, one row on the R-Mesh) change in destination. The first two optical algorithms used the identity of a destination processor to evaluate the reverse prefix sum, while the third used a delay counter. The first two algorithms had the further work of delivering results to processors that did not get them in the first round. One took advantage of segmentation, while the other took advantage of multicasting and the handling of concurrent writes.

10.3   Algorithms for Optical Models

Optical models employ the basic techniques and features described above to run algorithms that improve on their R-Mesh counterparts. Typically, the improvement arises as a savings in the number of processors elicited by combining the actions of multiple electrical buses into a single pipelined optical bus. This section first presents some basic results on maximum finding and compaction, then algorithms in the areas of sorting and selection, basic arithmetic, and matrix multiplication. It finally tackles the problem of routing h-relations, in which each processor is the source of at most h messages and the destination of at most h messages.

10.3.1   Basic Results

In this section, we describe some fundamental algorithms that will be used in subsequent sections.

Compression.   The *compression* (or *compaction*) operation is to take marked elements scattered over an array and compress them to contiguous processors, keeping the relative order of marked elements unchanged. For a linear optical model, this is straightforward: compute the prefix sums of the marked elements, then using the prefix sum as the index of the destination processor, route them to these compressed locations in $O(1)$ steps.

For the *two-dimensional compression* problem, the goal is to move k marked elements on a $\sqrt{N} \times \sqrt{N}$ array to the first $\left\lceil \frac{k}{\sqrt{N}} \right\rceil$ rows of the array. The PR-Mesh solves this problem using prefix sums of binary values (Theorem 10.2) and of integers. First, it computes binary prefix sums along each row independently. Let s_i denote the sum in row i, stored in the rightmost processor. Next, compute prefix sums of the s_i values in $O(1)$ steps (emulate the R-Mesh algorithm of Lemma 4.14, page 132). Combining its prefix sum along its row and the row's prefix sum of s_i's, each marked processor determines its destination processor. Observe that all marked processors in the same row have destinations in different columns, so use permutation routing with rows to place each marked element in the correct column, then apply permutation routing on a column to send elements to their final destinations.

THEOREM 10.3 *The compression problem on N elements can be solved:*

 (i) *by an N processor LARPBS in $O(1)$ steps, and*

 (ii) *by a $\sqrt{N} \times \sqrt{N}$ PR-Mesh in $O(1)$ steps.*

Remark: Due to bisection bounds, an R-Mesh of the same size cannot achieve these results (Problem 10.8).

Maximum. An LARPBS can find the maximum of N elements by various algorithms, differing in the time and number of processors. For instance, with N^2 processors, it can trivially find the maximum in $O(1)$ steps—compare each element with all others, compute the AND of the results in each subarray of N processors, then segment the bus to the right and send the result to p_0. (This is analogous to Lemma 2.14, page 40, for the R-Mesh.)

LEMMA 10.4 *The maximum of N elements can be found by an LARPBS with N^2 processors in $O(1)$ steps.*

Using the preceding algorithm as a subroutine, an LARPBS can find the maximum value in $O(\log \log N)$ steps with only N processors, in a manner similar to the R-Mesh algorithm of Theorem 4.1 (page 120) that uses a doubly logarithmic tree. Problem 10.9 asks to prove the lemma.

LEMMA 10.5 *The maximum of N elements can be found by an LARPBS with N processors in $O(\log \log N)$ steps.*

Remarks: A two-dimensional R-Mesh with $\sqrt{N} \times \sqrt{N}$ processors can execute essentially the same procedure in $O(\log \log N)$ steps (Theorem 4.1, page 120). The LARPBS performs the same work, but needs only one dimension. Also the algorithm easily adapts to run optimally on $\frac{N}{\log \log N}$ processors in the same number of steps.

The number of participating processors to compute maximum on an LARPBS in $O(1)$ steps can reduce further, to $N^{1+\epsilon}$ processors, for constant $\epsilon > 0$. This technique again uses Lemma 10.4 as a subroutine. To explain, we sketch a two phase algorithm for $N^{\frac{3}{2}}$ processors. In the first phase, partition the N inputs into $N^{\frac{1}{2}}$ chunks, each of $N^{\frac{1}{2}}$ elements. Assign each chunk to a subarray of N processors, which find the maximum element of the chunk in $O(1)$ steps by Lemma 10.4. This uses all $N^{\frac{3}{2}}$ processors. In the second phase, find the overall maximum of the $N^{\frac{1}{2}}$ candidates for maximum; this needs N processors in $O(1)$ steps by Lemma 10.4. Following the same idea, one can design a $\left(\frac{1}{\epsilon}\right)$-phase algorithm on an $N^{1+\epsilon}$ processor LARPBS, running in $O\left(\frac{1}{\epsilon}\right) = O(1)$ steps, for constant $\epsilon > 0$. (This technique is analogous to those used by the R-Mesh in Theorem 2.15, page 42 and Problem 2.35.)

THEOREM 10.6 *For constant $\epsilon > 0$, the maximum of N elements can be found by an LARPBS with $N^{1+\epsilon}$ processors in $O(1)$ steps.*

A fourth algorithm for maximum finding uses randomization to attain expected $O(1)$ steps using N processors. Let q denote the number of "candidates" for the maximum at the start of an iteration; initially, $q = N$. For each candidate, randomly choose for it to remain in the candidate set S with probability $\frac{1}{c\sqrt{q}}$, for constant c. Compress the remaining candidates to the left side of the array; let $s = |S|$. If $s > \sqrt{N}$, then find the maximum by the $O(\log \log N)$ step algorithm (Lemma 10.5). Otherwise, sort S in $O(1)$ steps (see Theorem 10.8 below) and extract the maximum value m. Broadcast m to all processors; each processor drops its element x_i from future consideration if $x_i < m$. Compress the remaining candidates and determine the new value of q. If $q \leq \sqrt{N}$, then sort the candidates and extract the maximum; otherwise, perform another iteration. The only operation using a nonconstant number of steps is the $O(\log \log N)$ step maximum finding, and it can be shown that the probability of executing this is very small and that the number of iterations is a constant with high probability.

THEOREM 10.7 *The maximum of N elements can be found on an N processor LARPBS in $O(1)$ steps with a randomized algorithm in $\widetilde{O}(1)$ steps[1].*

---

[1] For details on the $\widetilde{O}(t)$ notation, see Footnote 1, page 185.

10.3.2   Sorting and Selection

As for the R-Mesh, and, indeed, nearly any other model of computation, sorting is a fundamental problem for models with pipelined optical buses. Sorting, of course, is a rich computational problem in its own right, as well as finding extraordinary application in other algorithms. Correspondingly, it has received a great deal of attention on one- and two-dimensional models with both deterministic and randomized algorithms. In this section, we will concentrate on these sorting algorithms and also examine algorithms for integer sorting and selection.

10.3.2.1   Two-Dimensional, Deterministic Sorting

An $N^\epsilon \times N$ PR-Mesh, where ϵ is a constant, can sort N values in $O(1)$ steps. This number of processors is optimal for constant time sorting by comparisons. The algorithm follows Leighton's columnsort algorithm, which views elements as arranged in a matrix and mostly comprises a constant number of sorts of columns and matrix transpose operations (Section 5.3.1.1). Here the N-element columnsort matrix has $N^{\frac{2}{3}}$ rows and $N^{\frac{1}{3}}$ columns. The PR-Mesh implementation takes advantage of its ability to mimic LR-Mesh algorithms and its agility at permutation routing.

To implement this algorithm on an $N^\epsilon \times N$ PR-Mesh, let the top row of processors initially hold the input elements, one per processor. The PR-Mesh can route the permutation stages and the odd-even transposition sort in $O(1)$ steps. The remaining stages each sort elements by column, which we now describe.

View each column of $N^{\frac{2}{3}}$ elements as held by consecutive processors in the top row. (If not, then a permutation routing easily arranges this.) First, we let $\epsilon = \frac{2}{3}$, then will later extend the algorithm to arbitrary $\epsilon > 0$. A subarray of $N^{\frac{2}{3}} \times N^{\frac{2}{3}}$, then, is available to sort each column of $N^{\frac{2}{3}}$ elements. By directly implementing the LR-Mesh algorithm of Theorem 5.4 (page 158, see also Problem 5.8) that sorts N elements on an $N \times N$ LR-Mesh in $O(1)$ time (by columnsort), each subarray sorts its elements in $O(1)$ steps. Consequently, the entire algorithm runs in $O(1)$ steps on an $N^{\frac{2}{3}} \times N$ PR-Mesh.

To extend the algorithm to an arbitrary ϵ (where $0 < \epsilon < 1$), recursively apply the above sorting algorithm when sorting columns. For instance, for $\epsilon = \frac{4}{9}$, a subarray of $N^{\frac{4}{9}} \times N^{\frac{2}{3}}$ is available to sort each column, so by running the $N^{\frac{2}{3}} \times N$ PR-Mesh sorting algorithm in each subarray, the column sort completes in $O(1)$ steps. Hence, the entire sort completes in $O(-\log \epsilon) = O(1)$ levels of recursion, each running in a constant number of steps.

THEOREM 10.8 *Sorting N elements can be performed by an $N^\epsilon \times N$ PR-Mesh in $O(1)$ steps, for constant $\epsilon > 0$.*

10.3.2.2   One-Dimensional, Deterministic Sorting

An LARPBS with N processors can sort N elements by a deterministic algorithm in $O(\log N \log \log N)$ steps. (Actually, the algorithm runs on a more restricted model without reconfiguring switches known as the Linear Array with Pipelined Optical Bus, LAPOB.) The overall strategy is a two-way merge sort that performs $O(\log N)$ iterations of merges. The key then is merging two sorted sequences of $\frac{N}{2}$ elements each in $O(\log \log N)$ steps. The merge strategy is a multi-way divide-and-conquer. Let processors $p_0, \dots, p_{\frac{N}{2}-1}$ hold sorted sequence $Left = \left\{ a_0, a_1, \cdots, a_{\frac{N}{2}-1} \right\}$ and processors $p_{\frac{N}{2}}, \dots, p_{N-1}$ hold sorted sequence $Right = \left\{ b_0, b_1, \cdots, b_{\frac{N}{2}-1} \right\}$, one element per processor. Without loss of generality, let the input elements be distinct.

Identify a $\sqrt{N}$-element subsequence A of $Left$ that partitions $Left$ into subsequences of almost equal lengths and a corresponding $\sqrt{N}$-element subsequence B of $Right$ as follows. Let $A = \left\{ a_{i\sqrt{N}} \ : \ 0 \le i < \frac{\sqrt{N}}{2} \right\}$ be a $\sqrt{N}$-element subsequence of $Left$. For each $a_j \in A$, define the *corresponding element* in $Right$ to be $b_{k(j)}$ if and only if $b_{k(j)-1} < a_j < b_{k(j)}$; assume that $b_{-1} = -\infty$ and $b_{\frac{N}{2}} = \infty$. Define set $B = \left\{ b_{k(j)} \ : \ a_j \in A \right\}$.

For any element x and set Y, the *rank* of x in Y is the number of elements of Y that are smaller than x. The LARPBS computes the ranks of elements of B in A by multicasting elements of A and B making $\sqrt{N}$ contiguous copies of each element of B and a copy of each element of A for each element of B. Then it finds the rank of each element of B using prefix sums (Theorem 10.2).

Next, identify pairs of subsequences in $Left$ and $Right$ to be merged. Define sorted sequences $A_i = \left\{ a_{i\sqrt{N}}, a_{i\sqrt{N}+1}, \cdots, a_{(i+1)\sqrt{N}-1} \right\}$ and $B_i = \left\{ b_{k(i)}, b_{k(i)+1}, \cdots, b_{k(i+1)-1} \right\}$, where $0 \le i < \frac{\sqrt{N}}{2}$. Each A_i has at most $\sqrt{N}$ elements and each B_i could have anything between 0 and $\frac{N}{2}$ elements. Divide each B_i into subsequences of length at most $\sqrt{N}$ (just as we sliced up $Left$ earlier) and use these subsequences to slice up A_i (just as we used A to to slice up $Right$). This results in pairs of subsequences of $Left$ and $Right$, each with at most $\sqrt{N}$ elements and each of which can now be merged separately. Route these pairs to consecutive locations, then recursively merge these pairs of sorted subsequences.

The algorithm can recurse to a depth of $O(\log \log N)$, and each level of recursion executes in a constant number of steps, leading to $O(\log \log N)$ steps to merge two sorted sequences of $\frac{N}{2}$ elements each, and overall to $O(\log N \log \log N)$ steps for sorting.

THEOREM 10.9 *Sorting N elements can be performed by an N processor LARPBS in $O(\log N \log \log N)$ steps.*

10.3.2.3   One-Dimensional, Randomized Sorting

An N processor LARPBS can execute a randomized sorting algorithm that runs in $\tilde{O}(\log N)$ steps. A component of the algorithm is a straightforward method to sort a small number of elements. To sort $\sqrt{N}$ elements on an N processor LARPBS in $O(1)$ steps, compare all pairs of elements, as in the earlier R-Mesh algorithm (Theorem 5.4, page 158). First, multicast elements as in the previous algorithm, making $\sqrt{N}$ contiguous copies of each element and $\sqrt{N}$ additional copies of each element such that a subarray (contiguous block) for an element has a copy of each other element. Next, compare all pairs and use prefix sums in each subarray (Theorem 10.2) to identify the rank of each element. Finally, route each element with rank j to processor j, a simple permutation routing.

LEMMA 10.10 *Sorting $\sqrt{N}$ elements can be performed by an N processor LARPBS in $O(1)$ steps.*

The overall sorting algorithm builds on the notion of judiciously selecting a splitter element, using the value of that element to partition the set of elements to be sorted into two disjoint sets, then recursively sorting these sets. To find a splitter, select a random sample of small size, sort it in $O(1)$ steps with the available processors, then select the median as the splitter. A more detailed description of the recursive algorithm follows.

If the subproblem size is constant, then sort the elements sequentially in constant time. Otherwise, proceed as follows. First, each processor includes its element in the sample S with probability $N^{-\frac{3}{4}}$. By Chernoff bounds (see Footnote 9 on page 216), the size of S is $\tilde{\Theta}(N^{1/4})$. Second, count the number of elements in S by prefix sums (Theorem 10.2). Repeat these two steps until $|S| \leq \sqrt{N}$. Next compress the elements of S to the first $|S|$ processors (Theorem 10.3). Now sort S by Lemma 10.10, then identify and broadcast the value of the median element of S as the splitter. Compress all elements with values less than or equal to the splitter to the left side of the array, and compress all elements with values greater than the splitter to the right side of the array. Now, recursively sort each subproblem. The algorithm runs in $\widetilde{O}(\log N)$ steps, as each level of recursion runs in $\widetilde{O}(1)$ steps and the recursion has depth $\widetilde{O}(\log N)$.

THEOREM 10.11 *Sorting N elements can be performed by an N processor LARPBS using randomization in $\widetilde{O}(\log N)$ steps.*

10.3.2.4   Integer Sorting

The problem of sorting N b-bit integers (where $b = O(\log N)$) is called *integer sorting*. Unlike comparison based sorting that requires $\Omega(N \log N)$ work, integer sorting has a $\Theta(N)$-time sequential solution. For integer sorting, one-dimensional optical models can implement radix sorting of elements with b bits in $O(b)$ steps using compression.

THEOREM 10.12 *Sorting N b-bit elements can be performed by an N-processor LARPBS in $O(b)$ steps.*

We now detail a faster algorithm for the LAROB. The LAROB can perform integer sorting in $O\left(\frac{b}{\log \log N}\right)$ steps. Its algorithm builds on the following $O(1)$ step algorithm for stably[2] sorting $O(\log \log N)$-bit integers (with values up to $\log^{O(1)} N$). Recall the bit polling ability of the LAROB (see page 366).

Let each processor of an N processor LAROB hold a value v_i that is represented with $\log \log N$ bits, so that $0 \leq v_i < \log N$.

1. Each processor p_k writes value 2^{v_k}, for all $0 \leq k < N$, and, on the receiving side, each processor p_k performs bit polling on the v_k^{th} bit of data starting from the frame belonging to p_{N-1}, continuing through the frame belonging to p_{k+1}. Processor p_k stores the resulting count as $count_k$, which is the number of processors p_i such that $v_i = v_k$ and $i > k$. (Observe that this step uses $2^{\log \log N} = \log N$ bit quantities that determine the allowable word size.)

2. Each processor p_k again writes 2^{v_k}, for all $0 \leq k < N$, and, on the receiving side, each processor p_j polls bit j, for all $0 \leq j < \log N$. Processor p_j stores the count as a_j, which is the number of processors with value j, for all $0 \leq j < \log N$.

3. Using the integer prefix sums algorithm for the LAROB (much like binary prefix sums, but where a processor can introduce a delay of a_j

---

[2]A *stable sort* outputs equal valued elements in the same order that they appear in the input.

slots instead of only one slot), compute $psum(j) = a_0 + a_1 + \ldots + a_{j-1}$, where $psum(0) = 0$, for all $0 \leq j < \log N$.

4. Each processor p_k now obtains $psum(v_k)$ and a_{v_k} from processor p_{v_k} and computes $ps_k = psum(v_k) + a_{v_k} - count_k - 1$. (Recall that in addition to coincident pulse addressing, the LAROB permits an addressing technique in which writing processors write to assigned frames and reading processors select the frame from which to read. In this case, processor p_j, for all $0 \leq j < \log N$, writes in slot j, and processor p_k chooses the slot from which to read based on v_k. For coincident pulse addressing, the writer would have to set the select frame according to the set of readers, but these are unknown to p_j, so use of the alternative addressing technique appears necessary in this case.)

5. Route each element v_k to processor ps_k by a permutation routing.

By this algorithm, an N processor LAROB stably sorts N integers, with value $0 \leq v_k < \log N$, in $O(1)$ steps. One can extend the range of integer values up to $O(\log N)$ by standard techniques (Problem 10.13).

Now, we wish to apply this algorithm to sort longer integers, for instance, those with values up to $N^{O(1)}$, hence, represented with $O(\log N)$ bits, and use the same techniques to extend the range of values. Partition the bits of each element into $\frac{b}{\log \log N}$ "digits," each of $\log \log N$ bits. The LAROB now performs a radix sort in $\frac{b}{\log \log N}$ iterations. During the ith iteration, it stably sorts values with respect to the ith least significant digit. Each iteration takes $O(1)$ steps as described above.

THEOREM 10.13 *Sorting N b-bit elements can be performed by an N processor LAROB in* $O\left(\frac{b}{\log \log N}\right)$ *steps.*

10.3.2.5 Selection

The goal of *selection* is to select the kth smallest element out of a set of N elements. We will first sketch a deterministic LARPBS algorithm that runs in $O(\log N)$ steps. Faster randomized algorithms exist: we will next see an LARPBS algorithm that runs in $\widetilde{O}(1)$ steps.

The deterministic algorithm is recursive, based on identifying the median of a set of medians of subsets of elements as a splitter, then partitioning the remaining elements with respect to this splitter. The procedure operates as follows for m remaining elements on the leftmost m processors.

In the base case, where $m \leq 5$, simply write all elements to one processor that selects the kth smallest. Otherwise, do the following.

Partition the processors into blocks of five contiguous processors each. The leftmost processor in each block identifies the median of the five elements. Compress these medians to the $\lceil \frac{m}{5} \rceil$ leftmost processors and recursively call the select procedure to select the median of these $\lceil \frac{m}{5} \rceil$ elements. Let m denote this median-of-medians. Next, after a broadcast and binary prefix sum, count the number s of elements with value less than or equal to m. If $s = k$, then return m. If $s > k$, then compress the elements with values less than or equal to m and recursively call the select procedure to find the kth smallest of the s elements. If $s < k$, then compress the elements with values greater than m and recursively call the select procedure to find the $(k-s)^{\text{th}}$ smallest of the $m-s$ elements. Letting $m = N$ initially, this procedure runs in $O(\log N)$ steps.

THEOREM 10.14 *Selection of the kth smallest out of N elements can be performed by an N processor LARPBS in $O(\log N)$ steps.*

Random sampling can quickly reduce the number m of candidate elements and identify the kth smallest in $\widetilde{O}(1)$ iterations. Initially, $m = N$. Let the m leftmost processors of the LARPBS hold the m candidates. The algorithm iteratively executes the following steps until it selects the kth smallest element.

If $m \le \sqrt{N}$, then sort the candidates using Lemma 10.10 and select the kth smallest element. Otherwise, perform the following. Each processor holding a candidate includes it in sample S with probability $m^{-\frac{3}{4}}$. Repeat this step until $c_1 m^{\frac{1}{4}} \le |S| \le c_2 m^{\frac{1}{4}}$, where $0 < c_1 < 1$ and $c_2 > 1$ are any constants. (By Chernoff bounds (see Footnote 9 on page 216), the size of S is $\widetilde{\Theta}(m^{\frac{1}{4}})$. Consequently, a suitable sample set will be generated quickly.) Compress and sort S using Lemma 10.10. Let g_1 and g_2 be the elements of S with ranks $\lceil \frac{k|S|}{m} \rceil - d\sqrt{|S| \log m}$ and $\lceil \frac{k|S|}{m} \rceil + d\sqrt{|S| \log m}$, respectively, where d is a suitably selected constant. Let m' denote the number of elements with values less than g_1 and m'' denote the number of elements with values less than or equal to g_2. Next, remove elements from the candidate set with values outside the interval $[g_1, g_2]$. If $m' < k \le m''$, then set $k = k - m'$, $m = m'' - m'$, and proceed to the next iteration; otherwise, execute this iteration again. It is possible to prove that g_1 and g_2 bracket the kth smallest element with high probability. Therefore, the likelihood of repeating an iteration is small.

The number of candidates remaining at the end of an iteration is $O\left(m^{\frac{7}{8}} \sqrt{\log m}\right) = O\left(m^{\frac{9}{10}}\right)$ leading to a constant number of iterations in the algorithm, each running in $\widetilde{O}(1)$ steps. (Notice that reducing the problem size to $\sqrt{N}$ suffices to achieve a constant number of iterations.)

THEOREM 10.15 *Selection of the kth smallest out of N elements can be performed by an N processor LARPBS using randomization in $\widetilde{O}(1)$ steps.*

10.3.3 Multiple Addition

The problem of *multiple addition*, adding N b-bit numbers, is a natural generalization of adding bits, as well as a frequent building block in algorithms, particularly matrix multiplication. Of course, optical models can implement LR-Mesh multiple addition algorithms. For instance, an LARPBS with N processors can perform multiple addition in $O(\log N)$ steps by a standard binary tree algorithm (Theorem 2.1, page 18). By following an LR-Mesh algorithm (Theorem 4.12, page 131), a $\sqrt{N} \times \sqrt{N}$ PR-Mesh can add N b-bit numbers in $O(\log b + \log^* N)$ steps.

A PR-Mesh can implement another LR-Mesh algorithm, but exploit pipelining of messages to save processors, while running in the same number of steps. An $N \times Nb$ LR-Mesh can perform multiple addition in constant time (Lemma 4.9, page 126, and Problem 4.10). The following $b \times N$ PR-Mesh algorithm saves a factor of N on processors, for $1 \leq b \leq \frac{N}{\log N}$. Initially, let each processor $p_{0,j}$ on the top row hold an input element a_j, where $0 \leq j < N$. These processors broadcast their values down their columns, and each $p_{i,j}$ grabs bit i of a_j, where $0 \leq i < b$ and $0 \leq j < N$. Next, processors along each row compute the binary sum of the bits they hold. Let the processors $p_{i,0}$ of the leftmost column hold the resulting $\log N$-bit sums. Now, a $b \times b \log N$ subarray of the PR-Mesh runs an LR-Mesh algorithm (Lemma 4.9, page 126) to add these $b \log N$-bit integers. (This is where the upper limit on b arises.) All of these operations run in $O(1)$ steps, leading to the following result.

THEOREM 10.16 *For $1 \leq b \leq \frac{N}{\log N}$, the addition of N b-bit numbers can be performed by a $b \times N$ PR-Mesh in $O(1)$ steps.*

10.3.4 Matrix Multiplication

Matrix multiplication is a fundamental operation that arises in numerous engineering and scientific applications and plays key roles in many algorithms, such as many graph algorithms. To multiply $N \times N$ matrices, the standard row-by-column matrix multiplication algorithm runs in $O(N^3)$ time on a sequential model, while the best known sequential algorithm runs in $O(N^{2.376})$ time. An $N^2 \times N^2$ R-Mesh can perform matrix multiplication in $O(1)$ time (Theorem 4.26, page 142).

In this section, we present a selection of matrix multiplication algorithms. The first algorithm is a simple one, building on the multiple addition algorithm of the previous section. The next algorithms adapt known sequential techniques to the LARPBS, further demonstrating the potential of pipelining. Finally, we describe one of a number of algorithms for sparse matrix multiplication.

10.3.4.1   A Straightforward Algorithm

The first technique implements the standard matrix multiplication algorithm, using a method for multiple addition to evaluate the inner product between row vectors of one matrix and column vectors of the other. This algorithm runs on an $N \times N \times Nb$ PR-Mesh in $O(1)$ steps to multiply a pair of $N \times N$ matrices, A and D, with b-bit elements. It computes product matrix C by the straightforward method of computing

$$c_{i,j} = \sum_{r=0}^{N-1} a_{i,r} \cdot d_{r,j}.$$

In a three-dimensional R-Mesh, let the kth *XY-slice* denote the two-dimensional sub-R-Mesh comprising processors (i, j, k), for fixed k and all i, j (see Figure 10.10). Initially, $p_{i,j,0}$ holds $a_{i,j}$ and $d_{i,j}$, for $0 \leq i, j < N$. (This is XY-slice 0.) By multicasting and rearranging data, the PR-Mesh sends elements $a_{i,r}$ and $d_{r,j}$ to each $p_{i,r,jb}$, where $0 \leq i, j, r < N$. That is, the PR-Mesh copies $a_{i,j}$ to each $p_{i,j,rb}$ and $d_{i,j}$ to each $p_{r,i,jb}$, for all $0 \leq r < N$. Each processor multiplies its pair of elements. By the data distribution, this implies that the products $a_{i,r} \cdot d_{r,j}$ that will contribute to $c_{i,j}$ are held in processors $p_{i,*,jb}$ or row i of XY-slice jb. Perform multiple addition along each such row (Theorem 10.16) using the $N \times b$ subarray along that row and up in the third dimension (part of a YZ-slice). After this, $p_{i,0,jb}$ holds $c_{i,j}$. Finally, route each product element $c_{i,j}$ to $p_{i,j,0}$.

THEOREM 10.17 *The product of two $N \times N$ matrices, whose elements are b bits long, for $1 \leq b \leq \frac{N}{\log N}$, can be computed by an $N \times N \times Nb$ PR-Mesh in $O(1)$ steps.*

10.3.4.2   One Dimension—Time-Processor Tradeoffs

We now describe an algorithm for the LARPBS and cite others that offer different choices for time-processor tradeoffs.

Parallel Version of Strassen's Algorithm. Strassen's algorithm is a recursive method of matrix multiplication and applies to elements in an arbitrary ring. The algorithm decomposes $N \times N$ matrices into

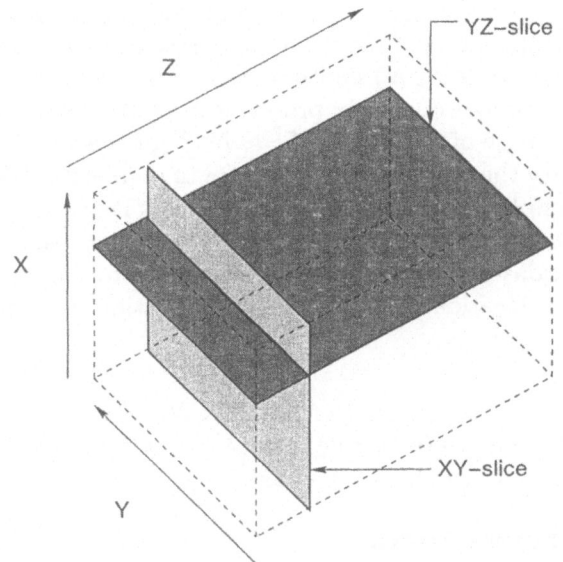

Figure 10.10. Slices of a three-dimensional R-Mesh.
Reprinted from *Parallel Computing*, vol. 29, 2003, R. Vaidyanathan, J. L. Trahan, and C.-m. Lu, "Degree of Scalability: Scalable Reconfigurable Mesh Algorithms for Multiple Addition and Matrix-Vector Multiplication," pp. 95–109, © Copyright (2003) with permission from Elsevier.

quadrants of size $\frac{N}{2} \times \frac{N}{2}$, as shown below for matrix A.

$$A = \begin{bmatrix} A_{11} & A_{12} \\ A_{21} & A_{22} \end{bmatrix}$$

The algorithm expresses the final product in terms of products of quadrants and their sums and differences. For input matrices A and B decomposed into quadrants as shown above, the quadrants of the output matrix C are as follows.

$$
\begin{aligned}
P &= (A_{11} + A_{22}) \cdot (B_{11} + B_{22}) \\
Q &= (A_{21} + A_{22}) \cdot B_{11} \\
R &= A_{11} \cdot (B_{12} - B_{22}) \\
S &= A_{22} \cdot (B_{21} - B_{11}) \\
T &= (A_{11} + A_{12}) \cdot B_{22} \\
U &= (A_{21} - A_{11}) \cdot (B_{11} + B_{12}) \\
V &= (A_{12} - A_{22}) \cdot (B_{21} + B_{22})
\end{aligned}
$$

$$
\begin{aligned}
C_{11} &= P + S - T + V \\
C_{12} &= R + T \\
C_{21} &= Q + S \\
C_{22} &= P + R - Q + U
\end{aligned}
$$

The LARPBS performs the matrix addition and subtraction directly, while the multiplication of the $\frac{N}{2} \times \frac{N}{2}$ matrices proceeds recursively until $N = 2$, leading to $O(\log N)$ depth of recursion. Each level of recursion increases the number of matrix products to be computed by a factor of 7, leading to usage of $7^{\log N} = N^{\log 7} \approx N^{2.81}$ processors.

Observe how the ability of the LARPBS to segment into separate sub-arrays can simplify attacking such a problem as it decomposes into sub-problems. Each level of recursion executes in $O(1)$ steps. The communication operations involved are multicasting data to a limited number of predetermined locations such that each destination receives exactly one datum.

THEOREM 10.18 *The product of two $N \times N$ matrices, whose elements are drawn from an arbitrary ring, can be computed by an $N^{\log 7} \approx N^{2.81}$ processor LARPBS in $O(\log N)$ steps.*

10.3.4.3   Sparse Matrices

The sparseness of a matrix may be characterized according to different limits on the number of nonzero elements: over the entire matrix, in each row, or in each column. A *row-sparse* matrix with degree ρ is one with at most ρ nonzero elements in any row; we define *column sparse* analogously.

Let A be a row-sparse matrix and D a column sparse matrix, both with degree ρ. Below we give an algorithm to multiply A and D on an $N \times N \times x$ PR-Mesh, where $1 \le x \le \rho$, in $O(\frac{\rho}{x} \log x)$ steps. At the extreme of $x = \rho$, this runs in $O(\log \rho)$ steps, and at the other extreme of $x = 1$, hence, a two-dimensional PR-Mesh, this runs in $O(\rho)$ steps.

Initially, let $p_{i,j,0}$ hold $a_{i,j}$ and $d_{i,j}$. (This algorithm assumes all elements, nonzero and zero, of the matrices are initially present.) Compress nonzero elements of each row of A into the leftmost ρ columns. Assume that elements hold information about their original positions. Swing each row of up to ρ compressed elements to a stack of x processors in the third dimension in the leftmost column such that each processor holds at most $\frac{\rho}{x}$ elements. Next, broadcast along the row so that each stack of processors in row i holds a copy of the compressed elements from row i of A. Likewise, compress nonzero elements of each column of D into the top ρ rows. Swing these up and broadcast along the column so that each stack of processors in column j holds a copy of the compressed elements from column j of D. All of this data movement takes $O(\frac{\rho}{x})$ steps.

The stack in row i and column j holds the elements of row i of A and column j of D in sorted order of their indices. Sequentially merge (according to their original positions in the row) the $\frac{\rho}{x}$ elements from A and the $\frac{\rho}{x}$ elements from D in each processor in $O\left(\frac{\rho}{x}\right)$ steps. Now each stack holds x sorted sequences of up to $\frac{2\rho}{x}$ elements each. Merge these in parallel in $\log x$ iterations (following a binary tree structure) in $O\left(\frac{\rho}{x}\right)$ steps per iteration. Pairs of elements to be multiplied will arrive in adjacent locations. After multiplying the proper pairs of elements, add the products locally in $O\left(\frac{\rho}{x}\right)$ steps then add these partial sums in a stack by a standard binary tree algorithm in $O(\log x)$ steps. Processor $p_{i,j,0}$ holds product element $c_{i,j}$.

THEOREM 10.19 *The product of a row-sparse matrix and a column-sparse matrix, both with degree ρ and of size $N \times N$, can be performed by an $N \times N \times x$ PR-Mesh in $O\left(\frac{\rho}{x}\log x\right)$ steps, where $1 \leq x \leq \rho$.*

10.3.5 h-Relations

The permutation routing algorithm is a basic one for pipelined optical models and one that the preceding algorithms have vigorously exploited. The problem of routing h-relations extends permutation routing from a 1-to-1 case to an h-to-h case, that is, it is the problem of routing messages among processors such that each processor is the source of at most h messages and the destination of at most h messages. Aside from being a fundamental communication operation, an optimal solution to this problem holds importance toward the question of whether pipelined optical models allow an optimal scaling simulation, that is, whether a P processor model can simulate an arbitrary step of an N processor model, where $P < N$, in $O\left(\frac{N}{P}\right)$ steps. Such questions are trivial for many parallel models, but not so for reconfigurable models (see Chapter 8).

Three optimal algorithms exist for routing an h-relation in $O(h)$ steps on one-dimensional pipelined optical models: a randomized algorithm that runs on an LARPBS (in $\widetilde{O}(h)$ steps); an algorithm for the extended LAROB, utilizing its capabilities such as bit polling and changing switch settings during a bus cycle; and an optimal deterministic algorithm for the LARPBS. We describe this last one as it is deterministic rather than randomized and works without the added features of the LAROB.

Let us approach the problem first as one of permuting N pieces of information on a P processor LARPBS, for any $P \leq N$ (that is, as routing an $\frac{N}{P}$-relation), then extend the algorithm to work optimally in $O(h)$ steps to route an h-relation on a P processor LARPBS.

As a way of scaling permutation routing from N to P processors, we will simulate a permutation routing step by an N processor LARPBS, $\mathcal{Q}$, on a P processor LARPBS, $\mathcal{R}$. Each processor of $\mathcal{Q}$ (and the simulating processor of $\mathcal{R}$) holds its selected destination for the permutation routing. This destination may not be the actual destination. This is because the segment switches and conditional delays of the LARPBS Q may be set arbitrarily. Assume that all routing is possible (within the appropriate segment), but individual processors do not know the extent of their segments. Let q_i denote the ith processor of Q, and let r_j denote the jth processor of R. The main challenge to the simulation is to avoid message conflicts in which multiple processors of R attempt to simultaneously send messages to simulated destination processors of Q that are all handled by the same processor of R. Mapping of processors of Q to processors of R then requires some attention.

Two obvious schemes exist to map N elements to P processors. The first, *cyclic mapping*, maps element x to processor x (mod P). The second, *block mapping*, partitions an N element array into P contiguous chunks of $\frac{N}{P}$ elements each and maps the ith chunk to the ith processor. (Observe that cyclic mapping is a one-dimensional version of window mapping and block mapping is a one-dimensional version of contraction mapping; see page 280.)

The following result is easy to prove (Problem 10.23).

LEMMA 10.20 *Conversion between cyclic and block mappings of N elements can be performed by a P processor LARPBS, LPB, or POB in $O\!\left(\frac{N}{P}\right)$ steps.*

To simulate Q on R, map $\frac{N}{P}$ processors from Q to each processor of R using the block mapping.

We present two simulations to cover different relative values of P and N. For the case $P \leq \sqrt{N}$, the first simulation builds on key steps of an algorithm originally developed on the Bulk-Synchronous Parallel model for routing an h-relation: sort the messages according to their destinations, then route them in phases without further contention, using information from the sorting. For the case $P > \sqrt{N}$, the second simulation adapts a scaling simulation of the Passive Optical Star model to the LARPBS. As a consequence of these simulations, permutation routing scales with optimal overhead on the LARPBS, that is, a P processor LARPBS can perform a permutation routing of N elements in $O\!\left(\frac{N}{P}\right)$ steps. We extend each simulation to routing h-relations in $O(h)$ steps for appropriate values of P relative to h.

10.3.5.1   Permutation Routing: Case $P \leq \sqrt{N}$

The strategy for the case of small P is to assign colors to processors, then sort messages by color of actual destination such that each processor receives one message of each color, then send all messages with the same color to their destinations at the same time, hence, without conflict. Assume that each processor of $\mathcal{R}$ initially holds the selected destination of the message to be sent by each of the $\frac{N}{P}$ processors it simulates.

LARPBS $\mathcal{R}$ first determines the actual destination of each message. Recall that the actual destination processor is the processor of $\mathcal{Q}$ at which a select pulse actually coincides with the reference pulse. The following lemma holds for any value of P such that $1 \le P \le N$.

LEMMA 10.21 *A P processor LARPBS can determine the actual destination processor for each message in the simulated N processor LARPBS in $O\left(\frac{N}{P}\right)$ steps.*

Proof: First, each processor r_j identifies the nearest segment switch in $\mathcal{Q}$ that is set to the right of each of the $\frac{N}{P}$ processors that it simulates. (This is analogous to neighbor localization, Section 2.3.3). Next, each processor r_j determines the number of set conditional delay switches between each processor that it simulates and the nearest set segment switch in $\mathcal{Q}$ to the right. If r_j simulates a processor of $\mathcal{Q}$ with a set segment switch, then r_j sets its segment switch. Each subarray of $\mathcal{R}$ computes binary prefix sums (Theorem 10.2). Each r_j determines the number of conditional delays in $\mathcal{Q}$ to the right of its simulated processors in their subarray. Then, based on the presence of conditional delays in its own simulated processors, it refines each of the prefix sums. Finally, based on the prefix sum at the nearest processor of $\mathcal{Q}$ to the right with a set segment switch, r_j further refines the number of conditional delays to the right of each of its simulated processors.

Combining the location of the select pulse within the select frame, the information on set segment switches, and the number of set conditional delay switches, r_j determines the actual destination processor for each message sent by its simulated processors of $\mathcal{Q}$ in $O\left(\frac{N}{P}\right)$ steps. ∎

Assign to each processor of $\mathcal{Q}$ one of $\frac{N}{P}$ *colors* so that each processor of $\mathcal{R}$ simulates one processor of $\mathcal{Q}$ of each color. For example, assign color $i \pmod{\frac{N}{P}}$ to processor q_i, for $0 \le i < N$, because of the block mapping of processors of $\mathcal{Q}$ to processors of $\mathcal{R}$. Assign to each message the color of its actual destination. Observe for any r_j that no prior constraints exist on the collection of colors of messages sent by processors of $\mathcal{Q}$ that it simulates. The colors of messages received by r_j, however, will all be distinct.

The next step is to sort messages by color. We adapt a mesh sorting algorithm that sorts mn elements on an $m \times n$ mesh in a constant number of phases, where each phase is a row or a column sort. Viewing the N

elements on P processors as a $P \times \frac{N}{P}$ array, each processor holds one row of the array. A processor can locally perform a row integer sort in $O\left(\frac{N}{P}\right)$ steps, as there are $\frac{N}{P}$ elements, each in the range $0, \ldots, \frac{N}{P} - 1$. To perform a column sort, transpose the array (Lemma 10.20), sort multiple columns locally in each processor, then transpose back into place, all in $O\left(\frac{N}{P}\right)$ steps. Since the algorithm comprises a constant number of row and column sorts, the LARPBS $\mathcal{R}$ sorts messages by color in $O\left(\frac{N}{P}\right)$ steps. At this point, messages to be sent are in row-major order, so $\mathcal{R}$ transposes them to give each processor at most one message of each color.

Each processor of $\mathcal{R}$ now holds at most one message of each color and simulates exactly one processor of $\mathcal{Q}$ of each color. Now, in $\frac{N}{P}$ rounds, processors write all messages with the same color in the same round. All messages reach their destinations without conflict in $O\left(\frac{N}{P}\right)$ steps.

LEMMA 10.22 *If $P \leq \sqrt{N}$, a permutation routing step of an N processor LARPBS scales with optimal overhead to a P processor LARPBS in $O\left(\frac{N}{P}\right)$ steps.*

Remark: The reason for the limit $P \leq \sqrt{N}$ in this lemma arises within the sorting of columns. If $P \leq \sqrt{N}$, then $P \leq \frac{N}{P}$, so an entire column fits within a single processor and the number of steps to sort that column by integer sorting of P elements with values in the range $0, \ldots, \frac{N}{P} - 1$ is $O\left(\frac{N}{P}\right)$. If $P > \sqrt{N}$, then $P > \frac{N}{P}$, and each column resides on multiple processors with the sorting time becoming $O(P)$. The bound on P for this lemma can, however, be raised to $P \leq N^{\frac{k}{k+1}}$ for constant $k \geq 1$. In this case, sorting by columns results in a "column" held by multiple processors, and so we apply the sorting algorithm recursively for k levels of recursion. (See Problem 10.24.)

10.3.5.2   *h*-Relations: Case $P \leq h$

We can generalize the above simulation to apply to routing an h-relation, for $P \leq h$. (In this case, h is analogous to $\frac{N}{P}$ above, so the case $P \leq \sqrt{N}$ corresponds to $P \leq h$.) In this situation, each processor of a P processor LARPBS is the source of at most h messages and the destination of at most h messages. For simplicity of explanation and without loss of generality, assume that each processor is the source and destination of exactly h messages. Let the color of a message be the index of its actual destination. Sort messages as described above so that processor r_j receives messages with the jth color, for which it is the actual destination. Since there are $P \leq h$ colors, the sorting executes in $O(h)$ steps.

LEMMA 10.23 *For* $P \leq h$, *an* h-*relation can be optimally routed by a* P *processor LARPBS in* $O(h)$ *steps.*

10.3.5.3 Permutation Routing: Case $P > \sqrt{N}$

For the case $P > \sqrt{N}$, the second simulation adapts to the LARPBS a scaling simulation of the Passive Optical Star (POS) model. The simulation works in the following phases.

1. Balance writers: As above, assign colors to messages. Initially, the message colors are unbalanced on the original writers, that is, the collection of colors of messages to be sent by a particular processor of $\mathcal{R}$ is arbitrary. Arrange messages across $\mathcal{R}$ to "balance" the colors at each processor, that is, so that each processor holds at most a constant number of messages of each color. Refer to these processors as (balanced) *intermediate writers*.

2. Route to final destination: Transmit messages from intermediate writers to their final destinations. Because both the intermediate writers and the receivers are balanced, this phase easily runs in $O\left(\frac{N}{P}\right)$ steps.

Balance Writers Phase. The initial steps here are the same as for the case $P \leq \sqrt{N}$. As above, assign to each processor of $\mathcal{Q}$ one of $\frac{N}{P}$ colors so that each processor of $\mathcal{R}$ simulates one processor of $\mathcal{Q}$ of each color. Assume that each processor of $\mathcal{R}$ initially holds the selected destination of the message to be sent by each of the $\frac{N}{P}$ processors it simulates. LARPBS $\mathcal{R}$ first determines the actual destination of each message in $O\left(\frac{N}{P}\right)$ steps (Lemma 10.21). Assign to each message the color of its actual destination.

Message handling now diverges from the previous case of $P \leq \sqrt{N}$. Each processor creates a *token* for each message that it holds containing the identity of the writing processor in $\mathcal{Q}$, the identity of the actual destination processor in $\mathcal{Q}$, the color (of the destination), and the message. Overall, $\mathcal{R}$ holds up to N tokens (one for each message) colored by $\frac{N}{P}$ colors, with each of its P processors holding up to $\frac{N}{P}$ tokens.

Example: Consider an example as shown in Figure 10.11, where $\frac{N}{P} = 4$ and the colors are numbered as 0, 1, 2, and 3. We will refer to this example in the following steps.

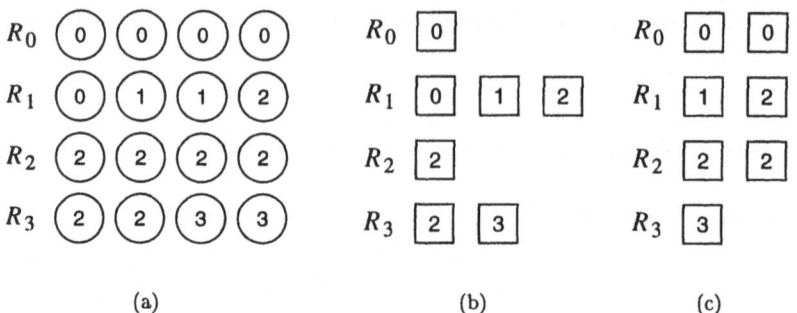

Figure 10.11.   Balancing writers phase for $\frac{N}{P} = 4$: (a) sorting in small groups; (b) packing supertokens; (c) balance within groups.

Sorting in Small Groups: Collect the processors into small groups each containing $\frac{N}{P}$ consecutive processors. Within each group, the processors will sort tokens according to color. Each group holds $\left(\frac{N}{P}\right)^2$ tokens, with color values in the range from 0 to $\frac{N}{P} - 1$. Within each group, sort tokens by color in $O\left(\frac{N}{P}\right)$ steps, adapting the mesh sorting algorithm as in Section 10.3.5.1. After sorting, each processor may hold tokens of the same color or it could hold tokens of multiple colors.

Example: Figure 10.11(a) shows the colors in sorted order at the end of this step.

Packing Supertokens: Each processor of $\mathcal{R}$ now creates a *supertoken* representing all its tokens of the same color, for each color it holds in $O\left(\frac{N}{P}\right)$ steps. A supertoken represents up to $\frac{N}{P}$ tokens, and contains their color and the identity of the processor of $\mathcal{R}$ that created it. Though a single processor may hold up to $\frac{N}{P}$ supertokens, each group of processors creates at most $\frac{2N}{P}$ supertokens, so $\mathcal{R}$ creates at most $2P$ supertokens overall.

Example: Figure 10.11(b) collapses tokens of the same color in Figure 10.11(a) into supertokens.

Balance within Groups: Each group balances the supertokens such that each processor holds at most two.

Example: Figure 10.11(c) balances the number of supertokens across the processors.

Sort Supertokens: Sort the supertokens by color using radix sort via compression on each bit position of the colors in $O(\log \frac{N}{P})$ steps (Theorem 10.12).

Send Location: LARPBS $\mathcal{R}$ sends back the location of each supertoken (after the sort) to the creator of the supertoken.

Unpacking: For each supertoken, $\mathcal{R}$ sends its component tokens from the processor that created the supertoken to the holder of the supertoken after the sort.

Transpose: Each processor of $\mathcal{R}$ now holds all tokens corresponding to (up to) two supertokens. To allow each supertoken to correspond to $\frac{N}{P}$ tokens, each processor now creates "dummy" tokens to fill empty spaces. For each color held by a group, the group can have at most two "light" supertokens representing fewer than $\frac{N}{P}$ messages of that color. Consequently, processors create up to $\frac{N}{P} - 1$ dummy tokens for each light supertoken. LARPBS $\mathcal{R}$ comprises $\frac{P^2}{N}$ small groups, so $\mathcal{R}$ creates at most $\frac{P^2}{N} \cdot 2 \cdot \left(\frac{N}{P} - 1 \right) < 2P$ dummy tokens for each color.

All tokens of the same color are in consecutive locations in consecutive processors (from P to $3P$ real and dummy tokens). LARPBS $\mathcal{R}$ now "transposes" all tokens from a block to a cyclic mapping in $O\left(\frac{N}{P}\right)$ steps (Lemma 10.20). For simplicity of explanation, assume that all processors were sending and all receiving a message (that is, a full permutation). Now, each processor holds at most three tokens (real or dummy) of each color, so the tokens are balanced.

Route to Final Destination Phase. Recall that each processor of $\mathcal{R}$ simulates one processor of $\mathcal{Q}$ of each color. Therefore, when writing information, if all writes are of the same color, then no conflict occurs because each write must be destined to a different processor of $\mathcal{Q}$, which must be simulated by different processors of $\mathcal{R}$ because they are the same color.

The intermediate writers of $\mathcal{R}$ hold at most three real tokens of each color after the previous phase. They now send messages to their final destinations as follows. For each color in turn, write (in up to three steps) all real tokens (actually, just the messages) of the current color. As described above, no conflicts occur. LARPBS $\mathcal{R}$ does this in $O\left(\frac{N}{P}\right)$ steps.

LEMMA 10.24 *If $P > \sqrt{N}$, a permutation routing step of an N processor LARPBS scales with optimal overhead to a P processor LARPBS in $O\left(\frac{N}{P}\right)$ steps.*

10.3.5.4 h-Relations: Case $P > h$

We next generalize the above simulation to apply to routing an h-relation, for $P > h$. Recall that each processor of a P processor LARPBS is the source of at most h messages and the destination of at most h messages. Each processor colors its h messages in some (arbitrary) way so that each has a distinct color from 0 to $h - 1$. (As a result, writing processors are balanced.) In the simulation of a permutation routing step, $\mathcal{R}$ found intermediate writers that are balanced and that the original (unbalanced) writers can reach efficiently. For h-relations, $\mathcal{R}$ similarly finds intermediate receivers that are balanced and that can reach the final (unbalanced) receivers efficiently. The same time analysis holds, replacing $\frac{N}{P}$ by h.

LEMMA 10.25 *For $P > h$, an h-relation can be optimally routed by a P processor LARPBS in $O(h)$ steps.*

10.3.5.5 Results

With the results in the previous subsections, we obtain the following.

THEOREM 10.26 *An h-relation can be optimally routed by a P processor LARPBS in $O(h)$ steps.*

COROLLARY 10.27 *Permutation routing on an N processor LARPBS scales with optimal overhead to a P processor LARPBS in $O\left(\frac{N}{P}\right)$ steps.*

10.4 Complexity of Optical Models

In this section, we place the computational power of reconfigurable pipelined optical models in relation to PRAMs (via simulations) and other standard models of computation (via their relations to PRAMs). We also relate one-dimensional pipelined models to each other, and discuss relations between the two-dimensional PR-Mesh and the LR-Mesh. These relations can help our understanding of the capabilities and limitations of reconfigurable pipelined optical models; they can throw light on the utility of certain features in the models; they can aid translating algorithms from one model to another, enriching the body of algorithms available for optical models.

10.4.1 Simulating PRAMs

Several simulations of PRAMs exist, differing in strategy depending on whether the simulated PRAM is EREW or CRCW and on the amount of shared memory used. We will briefly sketch two such results that tackle the more powerful CRCW PRAMs without constraints on the amount of shared memory used.

The first simulation is randomized and runs on a one-dimensional optical model.

THEOREM 10.28 *Each step of an N processor CRCW PRAM can be simulated by an N processor LARPBS using randomization in $\tilde{O}(\log N)$ steps.*

Proof outline: As in the R-Mesh simulation of a PRAM (Theorem 9.10, page 325), this one employs a random hash function to randomize the locations to which the simulating model maps shared memory cells. Again, the motivation is to reduce the likelihood of large conflicts in which many processors wish to access cells mapped to the same processor. Unlike the earlier simulation, which makes multiple copies of memory cells and uses multiple hash functions, this simulation uses only one copy and one hash function.

Both reading and writing follow a similar scheme. Compute the hash function for each read request, then sort these hashed requests. Partition the read requests into groups according to their hash function values, then into clusters of requests directed to the same processor. The processors representing requests in each cluster order the requests, then issue them in that order. ∎

The second simulation attains the same time with the same number of processors, but on a two-dimensional APPB, with its row and column buses.

THEOREM 10.29 *Each step of an N processor CRCW PRAM can be simulated by a $\sqrt{N} \times \sqrt{N}$ APPB using randomization in $\tilde{O}(\log N)$ steps.*

Proof outline: The heart of the simulation is the same as for Theorem 10.28, but the path to it differs. A butterfly network, a fixed-degree network, can simulate the PRAM, again using a random hash function. The APPB simulates this butterfly network, handling elements in the same stage of the butterfly in the same row, then using its permutation routing ability to handle communication between stages. ∎

10.4.2   Equivalence of One-Dimensional Models

In this section, we prove that the LARPBS, LPB, and POB are equivalent in the sense that each model can simulate a step of either of the other two models in constant time, using the same number of processors. (For a more detailed description on the equivalence of models see Chapter 9.) Section 10.1.2.1 defined these models. The LPB does not have segment switches, so the obstacle to equivalence for an LPB is to emulate segmentation. The POB places its conditional delay switches on receiving segments of the reference and data buses rather than on the transmitting segment of the select bus as in the LARPBS. This permits a POB to multicast with one select pulse, so emulating different manipulations of coincident pulse addressing is the obstacle to equivalence between the POB and the other models. The effect of this equivalence is that all results in preceding sections for the LARPBS translate seamlessly to the LPB or the POB.

We construct a cycle of simulations to prove the equivalence of the three optical models. Each simulation comprises three phases:

(i)   determine parameters to identify the actual destinations for all messages,

(ii)   create select frames, and

(iii)   send messages.

Throughout this section r_i, ℓ_i, and b_i refer to the ith processor of an LARPBS, LPB, and POB, respectively.

LEMMA 10.30 *Each step of an N processor LARPBS can be simulated by an N processor LPB in $O(1)$ steps.*

Proof: *Find parameters for actual destinations:* To adjust the select frame to match actual destinations for a message rather than selected destinations, each processor of the LPB will determine its location relative to the nearest set segment switch to either side and the number of set conditional delay switches ahead of it in its subarray. First, each processor ℓ_i of the LPB that simulates a processor with a set segment switch multicasts $i + 1$ to $\ell_{i+1}, \ell_{i+2}, \ldots, \ell_{N-1}$. Each processor ℓ_j stores the value it receives as *left$_j$*, the nearest segment switch that is set in the LARPBS to the left of its position. If multiple messages coincide at ℓ_j, then the first one received identifies the lowest indexed processor that is in the same subarray. If a processor did not receive a message, then it identifies ℓ_0 as the lowest indexed processor within its subarray. To identify the nearest set segment switch to the right, reverse the order of the processors and proceed as before. Each ℓ_j stores the index of the rightmost processor in its subarray as $right_j$.

Next, the LPB computes the binary prefix sums of the number of set switches (Theorem 10.2). Each processor ℓ_j then refines its prefix sum based upon the prefix sum of processor $right_j$ and stores it as $psum_j$, the number of set conditional delay switches to the right of processor r_j of the LARPBS in its subarray.

Create select frames: By combining the location of the select pulses within the select frame (selected destinations), $left_j$, $right_j$, and $psum_j$, ℓ_j determines the actual destination processors for its message. Each processor ℓ_j adjusts its select frame to reflect the alterations due to set segment and conditional delay switches by shifting the select frame by $right_j - N + 1 - psum_j$. Value $psum_j$ accounts for the shifting due to conditional delay switches and $right_j$ accounts for the segmenting. Each ℓ_j uses $left_j$ to mask off the portion of the select frame corresponding to processors that are not within its subarray.

Send messages: Processors set all delay switches to straight and transmit their messages. If r_i in the LARPBS was to receive a message, then ℓ_i in the LPB successfully receives that message. The simulation properly handles any concurrent-read or concurrent-write step of the LARPBS. ∎

Neither the LPB nor the POB can segment its buses, but the simulation of an LPB on a POB faces obstacles due to differences in the location of conditional delay switches, normal state of operation, and methods of multicasting. For instance, if processor ℓ_j of the LPB sets its conditional delay switch to cross to introduce a delay, then messages *originating from* ℓ_i, $0 \le i \le j$, will be shifted. If processor b_j of the POB sets its delay switch to straight, however, then messages *destined for* b_i, $0 \le i \le j$, will be shifted. The proof of the lemma below addresses these issues.

LEMMA 10.31 *Each step of an N processor LPB can be simulated by an N processor POB in $O(1)$ steps.*

Proof: *Find parameters for actual destinations:* The POB first determines the number of conditional delay switches set to cross to the right of each processor on the LPB using binary prefix sums (Theorem 10.2). Each processor b_i stores the prefix sum it calculated as $psum_i$. If ℓ_j is a selected destination for the message sent by ℓ_i, then the message will arrive at actual destination with index $j - psum_i$ on the LPB.

Create select frames: Based on the prefix sum values, each processor can shift and mask its select frame, as in the proof of Lemma 10.30, placing select pulses according to the actual destinations.

Send messages: After adjusting the select frame, the POB sets all delay switches to cross (normal state of operation) and sends the messages. If ℓ_i in the LPB was to receive a message, then b_i in the POB successfully receives that message. This simulation properly handles any concurrent-read or concurrent-write step.   ∎

For an LARPBS to simulate a POB, the differences mentioned before the previous lemma pose difficulties, even though the LARPBS can segment its buses and the POB cannot. In addition, one select pulse in the LARPBS can address only one processor, while the POB (due to the location of the conditional delay switches) can address multiple processors with one select pulse by setting successive conditional delay switches to straight. The following lemma establishes that these differences do not affect their computational power.

LEMMA 10.32 *Each step of an N processor POB can be simulated by an N processor LARPBS in $O(1)$ steps.*

Proof: *Find parameters for actual destinations:* Each processor r_i of the LARPBS calculates the binary prefix sum, $psum_i$, based on the number of straight switches, to provide information for the actual destinations of the messages, where $d(i) = psum_{N-1} - psum_i$. If a message was to be sent to selected destination b_i on the POB, then it would actually arrive at b_k, such that $k + d(k) = i$. Also, if the computed value $k + d(k)$ is the same for multiple processors, then these processors would receive the same message.

Create select frames and send messages: Send messages in the normal state on the LARPBS without altering the select frames. Next, r_k sends a message containing its ID k to processor $r_{k+d(k)}$ requesting the data that $r_{k+d(k)}$ originally received in the "find parameters" step. Processor $r_{k+d(k)}$ then sends this data to processor r_k whose request it received in the previous step. Processor $r_{k+d(k)}$ might be the destination of multiple requests for data, corresponding to multiple contiguous processors that should receive copies of the message it holds. The LARPBS next breaks itself into subarrays of these processors that should receive the same message. Each LARPBS processor r_i then sets its segment switch if processor b_{i+1} has its delay switch set to cross in the simulated model because the processor after that delay will receive a different message than the processor before the delay. The head of each subarray now broadcasts the data it received in the last step. Each LARPBS processor r_i now has the same message as b_i would in the POB. Also, the LARPBS properly handles any concurrent read/write step of the POB.   ∎

The cycle of simulations described by the preceding lemmas establishes the equivalence of these models.

THEOREM 10.33 *The LARPBS, LPB, and POB are equivalent models. Each one can simulate any step of one of the other models in $O(1)$ steps with the same number of processors.*

10.4.3 Relating the PR-Mesh and the LR-Mesh

The PR-Mesh can form linear buses, so this suggests a natural correspondence with the LR-Mesh and a natural setting in which to try to pin down the contributions of pipelining. We now present simulations in both directions.

Simulation of LR-Mesh by PR-Mesh. The simulation of an LR-Mesh by a PR-Mesh is almost trivial, except for one obstacle—cycles. Let a *cycle-free LR-Mesh* be an LR-Mesh in which no bus forms a cycle. (Note that this is a global constraint, not one arising from restrictions placed solely on individual local configurations.) An $N \times N$ PR-Mesh can simulate each step of an $N \times N$ cycle-free CRCW LR-Mesh in constant time as follows. Scale the LR-Mesh down to an $\frac{N}{2} \times \frac{N}{2}$ LR-Mesh. If the simulated LR-Mesh has no cycles, then neither does the simulating LR-Mesh in the scaling simulation. Using a 2×2 block of processors on the PR-Mesh to simulate each LR-Mesh processor, create a double bus structure replicating the LR-Mesh connections in duplicate. This will create two PR-Mesh buses, treated as if oppositely directed, in the place of each LR-Mesh bus. Within this structure, decide which of the two end-processors of each bus connects the transmitting and receiving segments. Finally, use one of these two buses to broadcast the written value.

Cycles are an obstacle to a PR-Mesh here because the transmitting segment would form a cycle, with no connection to the receiving segment. It is possible to break these cycles in constant time for the exclusive write model, and for concurrent write models using the COMMON, COLLISION, and the COLLISION$^+$ rules (see Problems 3.12 and 3.13). Currently, no known deterministic method exists to break these cycles in $o(\log N)$ steps for concurrent writes with other write rule.

LEMMA 10.34 *Each step of an $N \times N$ cycle-free CRCW LR-Mesh can be simulated by an $N \times N$ PR-Mesh in $O(1)$ steps.*

Simulation of PR-Mesh by LR-Mesh. The following lemma simulates an LARPBS by an LR-Mesh. Recall that an LARPBS is a one-dimensional PR-Mesh and recall that each (linear) bus of a PR-Mesh is essentially an LARPBS. The simulation of a PR-Mesh by an LR-Mesh will decompose into the simulations of individual buses, using this lemma.

LEMMA 10.35 *Each step of an N processor LARPBS can be simulated in $O(1)$ time by an $N \times N$ LR-Mesh.*

Proof: The key to this simulation is to determine actual destinations of messages. Let $\pi_{i,j}$ (p_j), where $0 \le i, j < N$, denote a processor of the LR-Mesh (LARPBS). Let $\pi_{0,j}$ of the LR-Mesh hold the message, select frame, and switch setting for processor p_j of the LARPBS. Processor $\pi_{0,j}$ will need to determine its location within its subarray (that is, distance from nearest set segment switches or end of LARPBS) and the number of set conditional delay switches between itself and the U-turn in its subarray. First, each $\pi_{0,j}$ simulating a p_j with a set segment switch disconnects its W and E ports and broadcasts its ID to lower indexed processors out of its W port, then it broadcasts its ID out of its E port to higher indexed processors. It also broadcasts the ID to its column out of its S port. Let $left_j$ ($right_j$) denote the index of the nearest set segment switch to the left (right) of p_j. The LR-Mesh partitions itself into sub-LR-Meshes corresponding to contiguous sections of the LARPBS between set segment switches. Within each sub-LR-Mesh, compute prefix sums of the number of set conditional delay switches beyond each processor p_j of the LARPBS. Let processor $\pi_{0,j}$ of the LR-Mesh save the prefix sum for p_j as d_j, for $0 \le j < N$. Each processor $\pi_{0,j}$ sends d_j, $left_j$, $right_j$, and the select frame for p_j down column j. Each processor $\pi_{i,j}$ for which $i > left_j$ tests bit $i + d_j + (N - 1 - right_j)$ of the select frame. A nonzero result indicates that reference and select pulses coincide at processor p_i of the LARPBS. To determine priority, each processor $\pi_{i,j}$ that detected coinciding pulses disconnects its ports and writes the message on its E port, along row j, while the remaining processors configure their ports as $\{\overline{N}, \overline{S}, \overline{EW}\}$. Thus, the processor in the rightmost column of row j receives the message destined for p_j that originated from the highest priority processor in $O(1)$ time and passes this information along to $\pi_{0,j}$ in the top row.   ∎

Recall the notation introduced in Section 9.5.2: M^j is the class of languages accepted by a polynomially-bounded model $\mathcal{M}$ in $O(\log^j N)$ time.

THEOREM 10.36 PR-Mesh^j = cycle-free-LR-Mesh^j = LR-Mesh^j.

Proof: We will show that the PR-Mesh and the cycle-free LR-Mesh can simulate each other within constant time and with at most a polynomial factor increase in processors. Combining this with the result cycle-free-LR-Mesh^0 = LR-Mesh^0 established in Theorem 9.23 (page 344) completes the result.

By Lemma 10.34, a PR-Mesh can simulate each step of a cycle-free LR-Mesh in constant time using the same number of processors. Therefore, cycle-free-LR-Mesh$^j \subseteq$ PR-Mesh^j.

Now we consider the simulation in the reverse direction. Let $\mathcal{P}$ be an $N \times N$ PR-Mesh and let $p_{i,j}$ denote a processor of $\mathcal{P}$. We construct an $O(N^3) \times O(N^3)$ LR-Mesh $\mathcal{Z}$ that simulates each step of $\mathcal{P}$ in constant time. This simulation will identify each (linear) bus of the simulated PR-Mesh, move each bus to the top row of its own square sub-LR-Mesh, execute the simulation of an LARPBS given in Lemma 10.35 on each such bus, then route the results back to the original simulating processors.

To use Lemma 10.35 will require a $W \times W$ sub-LR-Mesh to simulate a bus W processors long. In PR-Mesh $\mathcal{P}$, the longest possible bus is N^2 processors long, so $\mathcal{Z}$ will use an $O(N^2) \times O(N^2)$ block for each possible bus. Each of the $4N^2$ ports of $\mathcal{P}$ is a possible head of a bus, so $\mathcal{Z}$ will use one block for each processor of $\mathcal{P}$. Consequently, $\mathcal{Z}$ partitions into an array of $N \times N$ blocks, one for each processor of $\mathcal{P}$. In the first phase of simulating a step, each block $B_{i,j}$ simulates one processor $p_{i,j}$ of $\mathcal{P}$. In the second phase, for each processor $p_{i,j}$ that is the head of a bus, $B_{i,j}$ will simulate the bus according to Lemma 10.35.

Phase 1: Partition each $O(N^2) \times O(N^2)$ block $B_{i,j}$ into nine sub-blocks of size $O(N^2) \times O(N^2)$ as shown in Figure 10.12. The center sub-block will configure itself according to the internal configuration of $p_{i,j}$, as shown in Figure 10.12. "North" and "South" sub-blocks configure their ports as $\{\overline{\text{NS}}, \overline{\text{E}}, \overline{\text{W}}\}$; "East" and "West" sub-blocks configure their ports as $\{\overline{\text{N}}, \overline{\text{S}}, \overline{\text{EW}}\}$. This configuration will form multiple copies ($O(N^2)$, in fact) of the PR-Mesh buses.

Next, $\mathcal{Z}$ will determine the head of each bus, label each bus, and rank processors along each bus. Each center sub-block designates processors as incoming or outgoing so that each linear bus in the PR-Mesh corresponds to two "directed" linear buses in the LR-Mesh. (These buses are not actually directed, just labeled as such.) The outgoing processor at the head of each bus writes its processor and port number as a bus ID to label all ports on the bus. Each center sub-block corresponding to an incoming port in which a message arrives adjusts its connections for prefix sums. Identify the positions of the blocks along each bus in constant time by using prefix sums along each bus (Lemma 2.7, page 30).

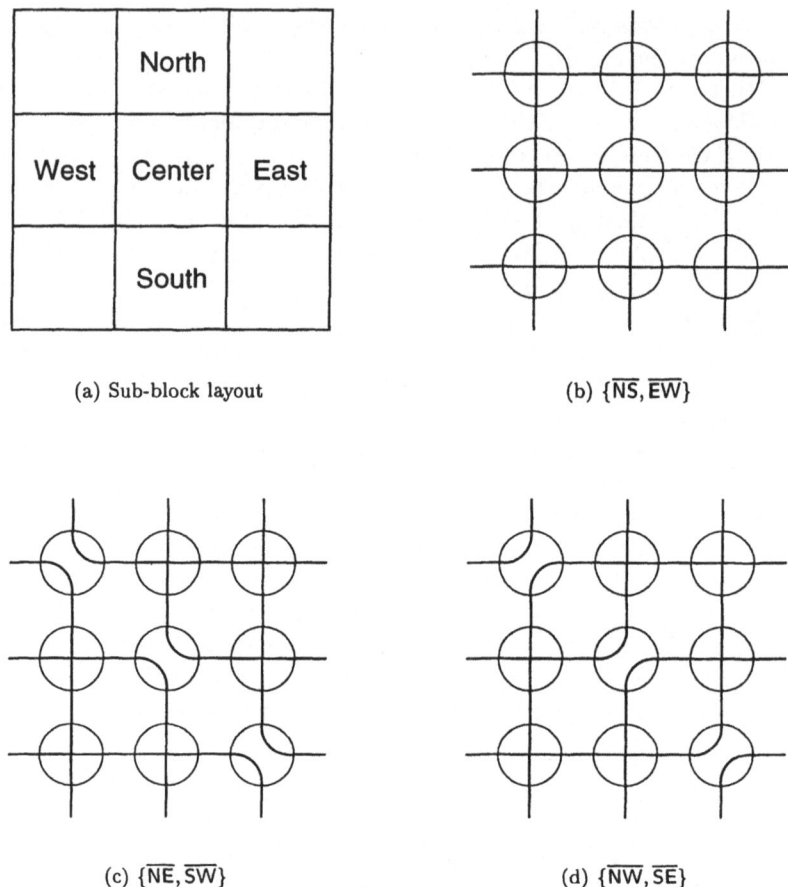

(a) Sub-block layout   (b) $\{\overline{\text{NS}}, \overline{\text{EW}}\}$

(c) $\{\overline{\text{NE}}, \overline{\text{SW}}\}$ (d) $\{\overline{\text{NW}}, \overline{\text{SE}}\}$

Figure 10.12. Block configurations for an LR-Mesh simulation of a PR-Mesh: (a) arrangement of sub-blocks; (b)-(d) center sub-block configurations for stated LR-Mesh processor configuration.

Reprinted with permission from *Parallel Processing Letters*, vol. 8, no. 3, 1998, J. L. Trahan, A. G. Bourgeois, and R. Vaidyanathan, "Tighter and Broader Complexity Results for Reconfigurable Models," pp. 271–282 (© World Scientific Publishing Company).

Phase 2: This phase will copy each bus to the block corresponding to its head, then simulate as an LARPBS. Using the separate copies of the PR-Mesh bus, each block $B_{i,j}$ passes the information for $p_{i,j}$ (bus rank, select and message frames) to the center sub-block that simulates the head of its bus. This sub-block arranges this information in ranked order along its top row. Now, each linear bus of the PR-Mesh is isolated in the top row of its own $O(N^2) \times O(N^2)$ sub-block. Simulate one step of each such bus in $O(1)$ time (Lemma 10.35) and then route results back to the proper blocks. Therefore, an LR-Mesh of $O(N^3) \times O(N^3)$ size can simulate each step of an $N \times N$ PR-Mesh in $O(1)$ time, so PR-Mesh$^j \subseteq$ cycle-free-LR-Mesh^j.

Thus, PR-Mesh$^j =$ cycle-free-LR-Mesh^j. ∎

Because PR-Mesh$^0 =$ LR-Mesh$^0 =$ L, the PR-Mesh possesses the same limitations as the LR-Mesh in solving graph problems, such as s-t connectivity, that are in SL but not known to be in L.

10.4.4 Relating Two-Dimensional Optical Models

In the one-dimensional case, the equivalence of the LARPBS, LPB, and POB (Theorem 10.33) is helpful for the development of algorithms, since an algorithm can adapt to run on any of these with no more than constant overhead. It also helps to identify which features are critical and which optional. This section examines two-dimensional models: the PR-Mesh, APPBS, and AROB. Unfortunately, these models are not known to be equivalent to within constant factors of time and processors. Yet if we stand back to view their complexity classes (allowing a polynomial factor increase in processors), then PR-Mesh$^j =$ APPBS$^j =$ AROB^j.

To establish this result, this section will flesh out the model definition then relate the model to the PR-Mesh, first for the APPBS and second for the AROB.

10.4.4.1 The APPBS and the PR-Mesh

The *Array Processors with Pipelined Buses using Switches* (APPBS) has directed optical buses along the rows and columns, and each processor has four switches at its corners to connect the buses (Figure 10.13). With the limited switch configurations available, a bus cannot stop at a processor in the interior, but only at the APPBS border. Let a *petit cycle* be the delay between one processor and the next on a bus. The APPBS permits a processor to change its switch configurations between bus cycles, as usual, and also once or twice at any petit cycle(s) within a bus cycle. Therefore, an APPBS can assume many different configurations during a single bus cycle, unlike the reconfigurable models observed previously. A closer look from the viewpoint of an individual message reveals that the message follows a linear path, regardless of switch changes, and the preceding and succeeding messages on a bus may follow different paths than the individual message.

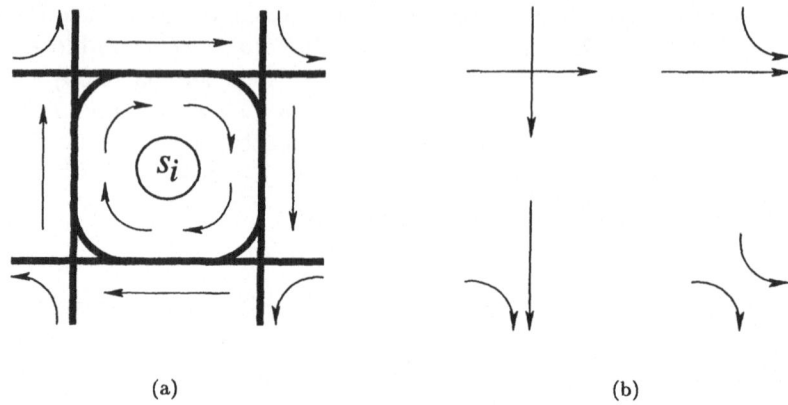

(a)   (b)

Figure 10.13. APPBS processor with switches: (a) switch connections at each APPBS processor; (b) switch configurations of top right switch at each APPBS processor.

Reprinted with permission from the *International Journal of Foundations of Computer Science*, vol. 11, no. 4, A. G. Bourgeois, and J. L. Trahan, "Relating Two-Dimensional Reconfigurable Meshes with Optically Pipelined Buses," 2000, pp. 553–571 (© World Scientific Publishing Company).

To control the destination of a message, the APPBS can use the coincident pulse technique or use functions $send(i,j)$ and $wait(k,m)$. These functions specify the number of petit cycles from the start of a bus cycle that processor (i,j) is to wait before sending a message and processor (k,m) is to wait before reading a message.

LEMMA 10.37 APPBS^j ⊆ PR-Mesh^j.

Proof: To compensate for the ability to change switch configurations within a bus cycle and the explosion of bus configurations this permits within a bus cycle, the PR-Mesh will increase the number of processors to build the linear path followed by each message separately. Let S denote an $N \times N$ APPBS, and let $s_{i,j}$ denote a processor of S. We construct a PR-Mesh $\mathcal{P}$, with N^2 sub-PR-Meshes of size $O(N) \times O(N) \times O(N^2)$, that simulates each step of S in $O(1)$ steps. PR-Mesh $\mathcal{P}$ will allocate one sub-PR-Mesh to each possible message of S. Each sub-PR-Mesh comprises N^2 layers of size $O(N) \times O(N)$. Within each layer, a 4×4 block of processors $block_{i,j}$ simulates each APPBS processor $s_{i,j}$. Layer ℓ of $\mathcal{P}$ will capture the APPBS configuration during petit cycle ℓ, for $0 \le \ell < N^2$. Figure 10.14 depicts an example APPBS processor configuration and the corresponding block configuration. To connect between layers, the bus steps up to the next layer at "out" processors. For example, in

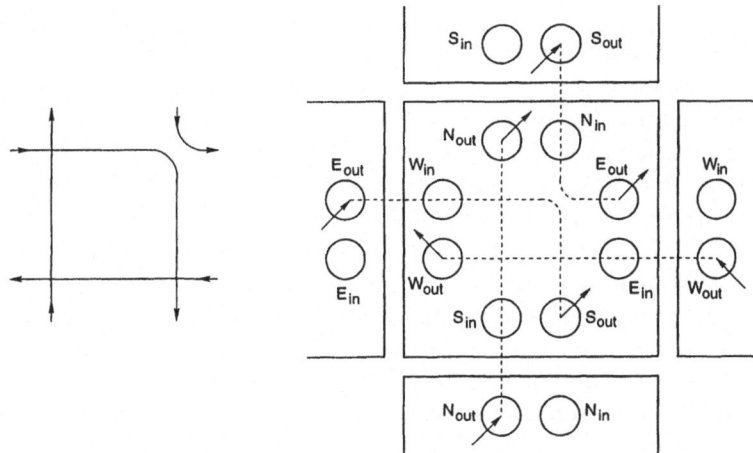

(a) Example APPBS processor configuration

(b) Corresponding PR-Mesh block configuration

Figure 10.14. Block of PR-Mesh processors to simulate an APPBS processor: (a) example configuration of an APPBS processor; (b) corresponding configuration of PR-Mesh block.

Figure 10.14, an APPBS bus enters at the northwest corner and exits at the southeast corner. In the PR-Mesh, the corresponding bus reaches the current layer ℓ from layer $\ell-1$ in the E_{out} processor of the block to the left, enters the block at W_{in} and passes to S_{out} all in layer ℓ, then steps up to layer $\ell+1$ at processor S_{out} of the same block. (Connections in the figure shown as dashed lines are all within the same layer. Connections shown as solid lines run either to the layer above or from the layer below. The "in" ports are in the XY-plane and the "out" ports are in the Z direction.)

Observe from Figure 10.13(b) that some APPBS switch configurations form linear buses, while others are "merging" configurations. The structure of a bus with merging configurations will be a binary fan-in tree. We determine switch settings in PR-Mesh $\mathcal{P}$ to match the linear path of a message in this structure as follows. For a switch with a linear connection in petit cycle ℓ, the corresponding PR-Mesh block will set its configuration as described above. For a switch with a merging connection in petit cycle ℓ, the corresponding PR-Mesh block will set its configuration to form an Euler tour of the fan-in tree structure. Generate an inorder number of tree vertices (Problem 10.31). Consider a message through a leaf with inorder number j. Tree vertices with inorder number $i < j$ (resp., $i > j$) set their switches to route a message from the right (resp., left) up the tree. Now each sub-PR-Mesh has a linear bus for its message. (Note: If the APPBS does not use merging switch configurations, then one $O(N) \times O(N) \times O(N^2)$ sub-PR-Mesh would suffice for the whole simulation.)

Let the blocks in layer 0 be the leaders of their tower of blocks. Each $block_{i,j}$ in layer 0 sends to all copies of $block_{i,j}$ its message to write and the values $send(i,j)$ and $wait(i,j)$ stating at which petit cycle processor $s_{i,j}$ is to write and read. The copy of $block_{i,j}$ in layer $send(i,j)$ writes its message to the appropriate "out" port. The copy of $block_{i,j}$ in layer $wait(i,j)$ reads from the appropriate "in" port, then relays the message read to $block_{i,j}$ in layer 0. Therefore, $\text{APPBS}^j \subseteq \text{PR-Mesh}^j$.   ∎

LEMMA 10.38 $\text{PR-Mesh}^j \subseteq \text{APPBS}^j$.

Proof: To simplify the presentation of a simulation of a PR-Mesh, the APPBS will simulate a cycle-free LR-Mesh, which can then in turn simulate a PR-Mesh. The primary obstacle to simulating an LR-Mesh is that an LR-Mesh bus can end at any port, while an APPBS bus ends only at the mesh boundary. The APPBS will create alleyways to shunt messages aside when a bus is supposed to end.

Let $\mathcal{R}$ denote an $N \times N$ cycle-free LR-Mesh, and let $r_{i,j}$ denote a processor of $\mathcal{R}$. We construct an $O(N) \times O(N)$ APPBS $\mathcal{S}$ that simulates each step of $\mathcal{R}$ in a constant number of steps.

The APPBS $\mathcal{S}$ uses a 3×3 block of processors to simulate each processor $r_{i,j}$ of $\mathcal{R}$, as shown in Figure 10.15. The center processor of a block, $sc_{i,j}$, sets its switches according to the configuration of the simulated $r_{i,j}$. The other processors set their switches straight to connect center processors and create alleyways, unless a bus is to end at the corresponding port. In that case, the corresponding port processor ($sn_{i,j}$, $ss_{i,j}$, $se_{i,j}$, or $sw_{i,j}$) sets its switches as shown in Figure 10.15(b) to divert a bus to an alleyway. To simulate a step, center processors write and read, except for the case of a bus termination, in which the corresponding port processor reads then forwards the value to the center processor.

Combined with the cycle-free LR-Mesh simulation of a PR-Mesh (Theorem 10.36), we have $\text{PR-Mesh}^j \subseteq \text{APPBS}^j$.   ∎

With Lemmas 10.37 and 10.38 we have the following result.

LEMMA 10.39 $\text{PR-Mesh}^j = \text{APPBS}^j$.

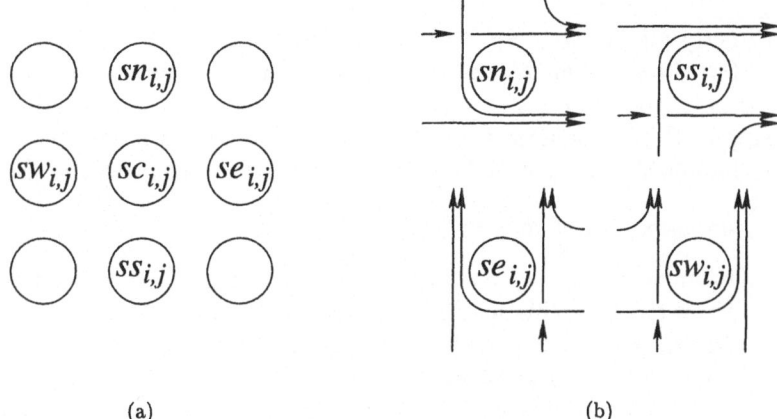

(a)   (b)

Figure 10.15. Configuration of APPBS processors to simulate an LR-Mesh processor: (a) 3 × 3 block of APPBS processors for each LR-Mesh processor; (b) configuration of port processors for a bus ending at a port of $r_{i,j}$.

Reprinted with permission from the *International Journal of Foundations of Computer Science*, vol. 11, no. 4, A. G. Bourgeois, and J. L. Trahan, "Relating Two-Dimensional Reconfigurable Meshes with Optically Pipelined Buses," 2000, pp. 553–571 (© World Scientific Publishing Company).

10.4.4.2   The AROB and the PR-Mesh

The *Array with Reconfigurable Optical Buses* (AROB) has the same capabilities as the PR-Mesh with extra hardware features. Recall that each processor of an N processor AROB:

- has an internal timing circuit that can count an arbitrary number of petit cycles between receiving a signal and sending out a new one within a bus cycle,

- can add up to N unit delays to shift the select frame relative to the reference pulse, and

- can perform bit polling (extract the kth bit of each of N messages in a bus cycle and count the number of those bits set to 1).

An *extended AROB* permits on-line changes to switch settings during a bus cycle and transmission of up to N messages.

Despite these extra features, given a polynomial increase in processors, a PR-Mesh can simulate each step of an extended AROB in constant time.

LEMMA 10.40 PR-Mesh^j = AROB^j = (extended AROB)^j.

Proof: Because the AROB features augment those of a PR-Mesh, it directly follows that PR-Mesh^j $\subseteq$ AROB^j.

Let $\mathcal{B}$ denote an $N \times N$ AROB, and let $b_{i,j}$ denote a processor of $\mathcal{B}$. We construct an $O(N) \times O(N) \times O(N^2)$ PR-Mesh $\mathcal{P}$ that simulates each step of $\mathcal{B}$ in a constant number of steps. We will explain separately how to handle the extra AROB features; combined, this gives the simulation.

Timing circuit: Problem 10.32.

Arbitrary number of unit delays: Since the buses are linear, consider the setting for this section as a simulation of this feature of an N processor, one-dimensional AROB on an N^2 processor LARPBS. Each interval of N processors of the LARPBS handles each processor of the AROB, setting k of N variables to 1 if the delay is to be by k unit delays. Using prefix sums, processors determine the number of delays ahead of a message and can move the select frame accordingly.

Bit polling: Apply the idea of layers of the PR-Mesh handling separate petit cycles as in the simulation of an APPBS by a PR-Mesh in Lemma 10.39 (Problem 10.33).

On-line switching: Again, apply ideas from the simulation of an APPBS (Problem 10.34).

Consequently, (extended AROB)^j $\subseteq$ PR-Mesh^j, so
$$\text{AROB}^j = (\text{extended AROB})^j = \text{PR-Mesh}^j. \qquad \blacksquare$$

Combining the APPBS and AROB simulations gives the following.

THEOREM 10.41 PR-Mesh^j = APPBS^j = AROB^j = (extended AROB)^j.

Problems

10.1   In a ten processor LARPBS (processors $r_0, \ldots, r_9$), suppose r_3 transmits a message along with a select frame with slots 1, 4, 5, and 9 containing pulses, and suppose r_1, r_5, and r_6 have set their conditional delay switches to cross, while other processors have left their switches straight.

    (a)   What are the selected destinations for the message r_3 transmits? What are the actual destinations?

    (b)   How should r_7 set its select frame to transmit a message to r_6 and r_8?

    (c)   For the 5-element POB with switch settings shown in Figure 10.5, design the reference and select frames needed for processor p_2 to multicast data to processors p_0, p_1, p_4, and p_5. Processor p_3 must not receive the data, and your solution must use as few select pulses as possible.

10.2   The "With Conditional Delays" case of the coincident pulse technique (see page 362) assumes that $\alpha(i) \leq j$. Discuss what might happen if $\alpha(i) > j$.

10.3   Design an N processor LARPBS algorithm to perform the bit polling operations of an N processor LAROB. What is the time complexity of your algorithm?

10.4   Let $\pi : \{0, 1, \ldots, N-1\} \rightarrow \{0, 1, \ldots, N-1\}$ be a permutation. Derive the reference and select pulse details needed to route data in a constant number of steps from each processor p_i $(0 \leq i < N)$ to processor $p_{\pi(i)}$ of an N processor LARPBS.

10.5   Let $f : \{0, 1, \ldots, N-1\} \rightarrow P(\{0, 1, \ldots, N-1\})$ such that, for all i and j, $f(i) \cap f(j) = \emptyset$. (Note: $P(S)$ denotes the power set of set S.) Design the reference and select pulse details for an N processor LARPBS to multicast in one step from each p_i to all processors in $f(i)$.

10.6   Design an N processor LARPBS algorithm to broadcast from any processor to all other processors. Specify reference and select pulse details.

10.7   Given that an N processor LARPBS can compute the prefix sums of N bits in $O(1)$ time (Theorem 10.2), construct an algorithm for each processor in an $N \times N$ PR-Mesh to discover its position in its bus and the number of processors in its bus in $O(1)$ time.

10.8   Derive lower bounds on solving the compression problem (page 374) on one- and two-dimensional R-Meshes. (Theorem 10.3 gives upper bounds for the optical models LARPBS and PR-Mesh.)

10.9   Prove Lemma 10.5: An LARPBS with N processors can find the maximum of N elements in $O(\log \log N)$ steps. Further, prove that an LARPBS with $\frac{N}{\log \log N}$ processors can also find the maximum of N elements in $O(\log \log N)$ steps.

10.10   Describe in detail the three phase algorithm to find the maximum of N elements with an $N^{\frac{4}{3}}$ processor LARPBS according to Theorem 10.6.

10.11   An $N^\epsilon \times N$ R-Mesh can find the maximum of N elements in $O(1)$ steps, for constant $\epsilon > 0$, by fixing $R = N^\epsilon$ and $C = N$ in Theorem 4.3 (page 121). This is the same number of processors as Theorem 10.6 for the LARPBS. Can Theorem 4.3 (page 121) be adapted to run on RC processors of an LARPBS in the same number of steps for $1 \leq R \leq C \leq N$ and $RC \geq N$? If so, how? If not, why not?

10.12   Prove Theorem 10.12: Sorting N b-bit elements can be performed by an N processor LARPBS in $O(b)$ steps.

10.13   Design an algorithm to stably sort N integers, with value $0 \leq v_k < c \log N$ for constant $c \geq 1$, on an N processor LAROB in $O(1)$ steps.

10.14   Prove that the selection algorithm of Theorem 10.14 runs in $O(\log N)$ steps.

10.15   Detail the LARPBS steps for the randomized selection algorithm of Theorem 10.15.

10.16   Prove that the algorithm of Theorem 10.15 for selecting the kth smallest out of N elements on an N processor LARPBS using randomization achieves constant time with probability at least $1 - N^{-c}$ for $c \geq 1$.

10.17   Construct an implementation of quicksort for N elements on an N processor LARPBS that runs in expected $O(\log N)$ steps.

10.18   Construct an implementation of radix sort of N b-bit elements on an N processor LARPBS that runs in $O(b)$ steps.

10.19   Construct an algorithm to add N b-bit numbers efficiently on a PR-Mesh, where $b = \omega\left(\frac{N}{\log N}\right)$.

10.20 Verify the correctness of Theorem 10.16 for the case $b = O(1)$.

10.21 Describe in detail the data distribution portion of the algorithm for Theorem 10.17 (matrix multiplication). That is, for an $N \times N \times Nb$ PR-Mesh where $p_{i,j,0}$ holds $a_{i,j}$ and $d_{i,j}$, for each $0 \le i, j < N$, send copies of elements $a_{i,r}$ and $d_{r,j}$ to $p_{i,r,jb}$, for each $0 \le i, j, r < N$, in $O(1)$ steps.

10.22 A naive algorithm for routing an h-relation would assign a fixed order to the messages, then write all first messages during the first communication step, write all second messages during the second communication step, and so on. Construct a 3-relation example on a 5 processor LARPBS for which the naive algorithm causes conflicts.

10.23 Prove Lemma 10.20 (conversion between cyclic and block mappings).

10.24 Prove that the bound on P in Lemma 10.22 can be raised from $P \le \sqrt{N}$ to $P \le N^{\frac{k}{k+1}}$ for constant $k \ge 1$.

10.25 The proof of Lemma 10.23 (routing an h-relation on a P processor LARPBS for $P \le h$) is described for the case that each processor is the source and destination of exactly h messages. Generalize the algorithm to the case in which each processor is the source of at most h messages and the destination of at most h messages.

10.26 For the algorithm for Lemma 10.24 (scaling permutation routing on an LARPBS for $P > \sqrt{N}$), describe in detail the implementations of the following stages such that each runs within $O\left(\frac{N}{P}\right)$ steps.

   (a) Balance within groups
   (b) Send location
   (c) Unpacking

10.27 For the algorithm for Lemma 10.24, describe in detail the generalization of the Transpose stage without the assumption that all processors are sending and all receiving a message.

10.28 Prove that the simulation of an LARPBS by an LPB (Lemma 10.30) properly handles the concurrent read and concurrent write steps of the LARPBS.

10.29   Prove that the simulation of an LPB by a POB (Lemma 10.31) prop-
        erly handles the concurrent read and concurrent write steps of the
        LPB.

10.30   Prove that the simulation of a POB by an LARPBS (Lemma 10.32)
        properly handles the concurrent read and concurrent write steps of
        the POB.

10.31   The simulation of an APPBS by a PR-Mesh (Lemma 10.39) sets con-
        nections in blocks of PR-Mesh processors corresponding to APPBS
        processors so as to construct an Euler tour in the PR-Mesh of each
        fan-in communication tree of the APPBS. Specify block connections
        in the PR-Mesh processors and construct an algorithm to calculate
        the inorder number of each tree vertex in its fan-in tree in $O(1)$ steps.

10.32   On an $O(N) \times O(N) \times O(N^2)$ PR-Mesh, simulate in $O(1)$ steps the
        internal timing circuit feature of each processor of an $N \times N$ AROB
        that can count an arbitrary number of petit cycles between receiving
        a signal and sending out a new one within a bus cycle.

10.33   On an $O(N) \times O(N) \times O(N^2)$ PR-Mesh, simulate in $O(1)$ steps the
        bit polling feature of an $N \times N$ AROB.

10.34   On an $O(N) \times O(N) \times O(N^2)$ PR-Mesh, simulate in $O(1)$ steps
        the ability to change switch settings on-line during a bus cycle of an
        $N \times N$ AROB.

Bibliographic Notes

Melhem *et al.* [207], Guo *et al.* [120], Qiao *et al.* [274], and Qiao
and Melhem [273] introduced the work on pipelining messages on optical buses that provides the basis for most of the developments reported
in this chapter. The following papers contain a range of optical models introduced [120, 177, 207, 251, 265, 273, 274] and a selection of the
algorithms developed for them [118, 125, 183, 184, 251, 252, 254, 259].
One-dimensional optical models include the Linear Array with a Re-

configurable Pipelined Bus System (LARPBS) [185, 258], the Pipelined Optical Bus (POB) [186, 368], the Linear Pipelined Bus (LPB) [252], the Linear Array with Reconfigurable Optical Buses (LAROB) [262, 264, 266], the linear Array Processors with Pipelined Buses (APPB) [120, 207], and the Linear Array with Pipelined Optical Buses (LAPOB) [99]. Two-dimensional models include the Array with Synchronous Optical Switches (ASOS) [273], the Reconfigurable Array with Spanning Optical Buses (RASOB) [272], the Array Processors with Pipelined Buses (APPB) [120, 210], the Array Processors with Pipelined Buses using Switches (APPBS) [119], the Array with Reconfigurable Optical Buses (AROB) [265, 266], and the Pipelined Reconfigurable Mesh (PR-Mesh) [317]. Pavel and Akl [265] extensively considered comparisons between some of these models and the AROB.

Qiao and Melhem [273] built the framework of grouping data into frames and equating the length of fiber between processors. Guo *et al.* [120] and Pan and Li [258] took up the time complexity issue for pipelined optical models.

Pan and Li [258] introduced the LARPBS. Qiao and Melhem [273] introduced the coincident pulse addressing technique.

Pan and Li [258] designed the LARPBS binary prefix sums algorithm, while Trahan *et al.* [316] developed the one for the LPB and Pavel and Akl [265] for the LAROB.

Pavel and Akl [265] developed the PR-Mesh algorithm (originally on AROB) for prefix sums of integers used to solve the two-dimensional compression problem (Theorem 10.3); Olariu *et al.* [246] designed the R-Mesh algorithm used to compute prefix sums of the row sums. The $O(\log \log N)$ step maximum algorithm for the LARPBS (Lemma 10.5) has as its basis algorithms of Valiant [334] and Miller *et al.* [216]. Pan *et al.* [259] developed Theorems 10.6 and 10.7.

Rajasekaran and Sahni [277] designed the $O(1)$ step algorithm to sort N values on a PR-Mesh (actually on a restricted version of the AROB) with $N^{\epsilon} \times N$ processors (Theorem 10.8), following Leighton's columnsort algorithm [173]. Azar and Vishkin [12] established the result that this number of processors is optimal for constant time sorting by comparisons. On one-dimensional models, ElGindy [99] and Datta *et al.* [74, 77] presented an $O(\log N \log \log N)$ step deterministic algorithm (Theorem 10.9); this algorithm has its roots in the work of Valiant [334] and Kruskal [163]. Pan and Hamdi [255] implemented quicksort in expected $O(\log N)$ steps, and ElGindy and Rajasekaran [101] constructed a randomized algorithm that runs in $\widetilde{O}(\log N)$ steps (Theorem 10.11). This last algorithm was presented for the LAROB, but runs on the

LARPBS. All these algorithms use N processors. For a description of multi-way divide-and-conquer used in the first algorithm, see JáJá [142].

Pan and Li [258] and Rajasekaran and Sahni [277] gave $O(b)$ step implementations of radix sort on one-dimensional pipelined optical models. Pavel and Akl [266] constructed the $O\left(\frac{b}{\log\log N}\right)$ step integer sorting algorithm of Theorem 10.13. The presentation in Section 10.3.2 is a modification of their original algorithm. The algorithm for stably sorting $\log\log N$-bit integers has its roots in a similar method for the PRAM [60].

The deterministic LARPBS selection algorithm of Theorem 10.14 that runs in $O(\log N)$ steps is due to Li *et al.* [186]. The algorithm adapts the sequential algorithm of Blum *et al.* [30]. Han *et al.* [126] improved the time for selection on an LARPBS to $O\left(\frac{(\log\log N)^2}{\log\log\log N}\right)$. Rajasekaran and Sahni [277] designed an algorithm that runs on a $\sqrt{N}\times\sqrt{N}$ PR-Mesh in $\tilde{O}(1)$ steps. (It was initially described for an AROB.) ElGindy and Rajasekaran [101] built on the same ideas to construct the N processor LARPBS algorithm of Theorem 10.15 that also runs in $\tilde{O}(1)$ steps; we presented the latter algorithm due to the greater constraints imposed by the linear model and because the two-dimensional model can implement it.

On multiple addition, Middendorf and ElGindy [210] implemented the algorithm to add N b-bit integers in $O(\log b + \log^* N)$ steps on an APPB with row and column buses without switched connections. Pavel and Akl [264] developed the multiple addition algorithm of Theorem 10.16 for the case $b = \log N$.

Coppersmith and Winograd [64] presented the current best sequential algorithm for matrix multiplication at $O(N^{2.376})$ time. See Pan and Reif [250] for an efficient, $O(\log N)$ time, CREW PRAM algorithm.

Pavel and Akl [264] developed the matrix multiplication algorithm on an $N\times N\times Nb$ PR-Mesh in $O(1)$ steps (Theorem 10.17). Li *et al.* [183] obtained similar bounds to the three-dimensional PR-Mesh of Theorem 10.17 by the same technique on a one-dimensional LARPBS: matrix multiplication with $\frac{N^3 b}{\log b}$ processors in $O(\log b)$ steps. Cormen *et al.* [65] presented Strassen's algorithm well.

Li *et al.* [183] combined two basic matrix multiplication algorithms for the LARPBS (one on N^2 processors in $O(N)$ steps, the other on $\frac{N^3 b}{\log b}$ processors in $O(\log b)$ steps) with a parameter that guides their combination and tunes the relation between time and processors. We cite the results below.

- Matrix multiplication (on an arbitrary ring) with $O(N^{2+0.81\epsilon})$ processors in $O(\log N + N^{1-\epsilon})$ steps, where $0 \le \epsilon \le 1$.

- Matrix multiplication on b-bit elements with $O\left(\frac{N^3}{1.1428^{(\log N)^\delta}} \cdot \frac{b}{\log b}\right)$ processors in $O\left((\log N)^\delta + \log b\right)$ steps, where $0 \le \delta \le 1$.

Pavel and Akl [264] developed the algorithms of Theorem 10.19 to multiply a row-sparse and a column-sparse matrix. Middendorf and ElGindy [210] designed an algorithm to multiply a dense matrix A and a sparse matrix D such that D contains at most kN nonzero elements, where $1 \le k \le N$ and elements can be represented in b bits. A three-dimensional $N \times N \times q$ APPB can compute the product of these matrices in $\frac{k}{q} + \max\{\log b, \log \log N\}$ steps.

Valiant [335, 336] described h-relations as a fundamental communication operation in the setting of the Bulk-Synchronous Parallel model. He is also the source of the base of the first of the h-relation algorithms of Section 10.3.5. Three optimal algorithms exist for routing an h-relation on one-dimensional pipelined optical models. Rajasekaran and Sahni [277] gave a randomized algorithm that runs on an LARPBS in $\tilde{O}(h)$ steps. Pavel and Akl [266] gave an $O(h)$ step algorithm for the extended LAROB, utilizing its capabilities such as bit polling and changing switch configurations during a bus cycle. Finally, Trahan *et al.* [316] gave an optimal deterministic algorithm for the LARPBS. Berthomé *et al.* [25] designed the scaling simulation of the Passive Optical Star that structures the second h-relations algorithm of Section 10.3.5. Marberg and Gafni [199] constructed the mesh sorting algorithm that plays a role in both h-relation routing algorithms.

The randomized PRAM simulation of Theorem 10.28 is due to Li *et al.* [185]. Pavel and Akl [265] devised the randomized APPB simulation of a PRAM in Theorem 10.29. Ranade [278] developed the simulation of a PRAM on a butterfly network used in the APPB simulation.

Trahan *et al.* [316] established the equivalence of the LARPBS, LPB, and the POB described in Theorem 10.33. Some few authors take up the issue of cycles in LR-Mesh buses when considering simulations [111, 265, 317]. Lemma 10.34 simulates a cycle-free LR-Mesh by a PR-Mesh, and Theorem 10.36 only indirectly relates the LR-Mesh (with cycles) and the PR-Mesh. Fernández-Zepeda *et al.* [111] established an $O(\log N)$ time simulation of an LR-Mesh (with cycles) by a PR-Mesh. El-Boghdadi [93] discussed ways of removing cyclic buses from LR-Mesh configurations. Bourgeois and Trahan [40] established the relations among the PR-Mesh, cycle-free LR-Mesh, LR-Mesh, APPBS, and AROB.

Some additional algorithms for reconfigurable optical models include fault tolerant algorithms [41], graph algorithms [73], Euclidean distance transform [75], and scalable matrix operations [182] for the LARPBS and computer vision algorithms [361], image filtering [359], parallel hierarchical clustering [360], and Euclidean distance transform [351] for the AROB.

Chapter 11

RUN-TIME RECONFIGURATION

The R-Mesh is a theoretical model that permits us to study reconfiguration as an integral tool for computation. By various limitations, enhancements, and alternatives, one can isolate the contributions of different aspects of reconfiguration. Nevertheless, one feature of the R-Mesh that cannot currently be realized is a constant delay bus of arbitrary length, spanning an almost arbitrary subset of processors. Reconfiguration is feasible, however, in a way that can lead to smaller, faster, and cheaper solutions for many problems and in a way impossible without reconfiguration.

Reconfigurable hardware may arise in the form of reconfigurable logic used as a co-processor, built on the same chip as the processor, or integrated with memory. Most often, though not always, this reconfigurable logic is in the form of a *field-programmable gate array* (FPGA). Recent years have seen faster reconfiguration times for FPGAs as well as partially reconfigurable FPGAs that can reconfigure part of their logic while the remainder continues to operate. This has permitted reconfiguration to play an active role in computations performed on FPGAs. The time scale for changes in configurations can vary from every few months, to one application to the next, and even to run-time within a single computation.

Run-time reconfiguration (RTR) refers to the fastest level, changing configurations at run time. Developing RTR is difficult because of the need for both software and hardware expertise to determine how best to partition a computation into sections to implement in hardware, how to sequence these circuit sections, and how to tie them together to produce an efficient computation. RTR offers faster overall computation on smaller circuits due to the ability to tailor circuits to specific problem inputs at run time and the ability to reuse the same logic resources in different configurations from one phase of a computation to the next. These abilities reflect the essence of the reconfiguration abilities of the R-Mesh.

One obvious advantage of RTR is that it can use less hardware than non-reconfiguring approaches (as the same physical piece of hardware can assume different roles at different times in the computation). A second key advantage of RTR is that a system can tailor itself to the problem instance at hand. This may allow it, for example, to treat certain problem parameters as fixed rather than arbitrary, leading to a smaller circuit size.

Researchers have developed RTR solutions to problems in numerous areas, including image and video processing, cryptography, object tracking, digital signal processing, and networking. This work has confirmed the merits of RTR and established a range of specific applications.

This chapter takes up RTR, its basic techniques, example applications, and current and future research directions, with a focus on the role of dynamic reconfiguration. Section 11.1 provides an overview of the basics of FPGA architecture and reconfigurable logic. This establishes the setting for understanding RTR implementations in contrast to the R-Mesh framework.

Section 11.2 details techniques and example RTR solutions in three parts. First, it discusses basic RTR techniques that can take advantage of specific inputs as opposed to fixed, general purpose circuitry. Second, it examines approaches to solving selected specific problems: an adaptive filter, neural networks, a motion estimator, and searching a database. These show the benefits that can be attained by targeting reconfiguration from phase to phase and reconfiguring for given inputs to particular problems. Third, it describes more general RTR approaches aimed at certain types of problems, but not a single narrow problem. These include approaches for handling loops and graph problems.

Section 11.3 steps further back to view reconfigurable logic as a shared computing resource. The examples in the previous section assumed the application had the entire reconfigurable logic to itself. Here, multiple tasks share the reconfigurable logic and the need arises for a type of hardware operating system to control and allocate usage of this shared resource. We examine initial approaches, some of which constrain placement of tasks, and raise some of the open research questions in this area.

Though most RTR work utilizes commercially available FPGAs, researchers are also exploring other implementations of reconfigurable logic. FPGAs can serve a wide array of purposes, such as logic prototyping;

in contrast, these alternative implementations seek hardware most beneficial to RTR. A constraint that remains foremost in RTR design is time to reconfigure, in stark contrast to the R-Mesh. At its slowest, to change configurations, an FPGA must stop, load an entire new configuration, then resume computing. To speed this process, some FPGAs are partially reconfigurable, needing only to load new configurations for the portions of the circuit that change. Time to reconfigure limits the minimum problem size that can benefit from RTR in a number of applications.

Section 11.4 reviews some attempts to speed reconfiguration and provide an alternative to FPGAs as a base for RTR. Among the most promising are context-switching FPGAs that can store multiple configurations and rapidly switch among them and self-reconfiguring logic where local controllers determine local configurations, much as in the R-Mesh where local processors determine local bus configurations. We discuss the self-reconfiguring gate array and generalize its bus structure to an R-Mesh setting with the bends-cost time measure.

A key difference between traditional FPGAs and self-reconfigurable platforms is that, unlike the former, the latter generate reconfiguration information from within the device (much like the R-Mesh model). Consequently, their reconfiguration speeds are not pin-limited like those of traditional FPGAs. Section 11.5 builds on the idea of self-reconfiguration to present an approach to implementing an R-Mesh-type platform. In this section we outline a methodology for algorithm design that translates the ideas of preceding chapters in directions of greater implementability.

11.1 FPGA Background

In this section, we present the basic components of FPGA architecture relevant to RTR. We include only an overview here necessary for understanding the examples and alternatives later in the chapter; the bibliographic notes contain pointers to references with much more detail, as well as a wider variety of FPGA styles.

11.1.1 FPGA Structure

An FPGA consists of an array of function blocks, interconnects, and I/O connects (see Figure 11.1). All of these elements are reconfigurable. A user programs the function of an FPGA by configuring its function blocks (as specific hardware), interconnects (to connect function blocks as needed), and I/O connects (to link with components external to the chip). Configuring the FPGA is tantamount to setting up data and

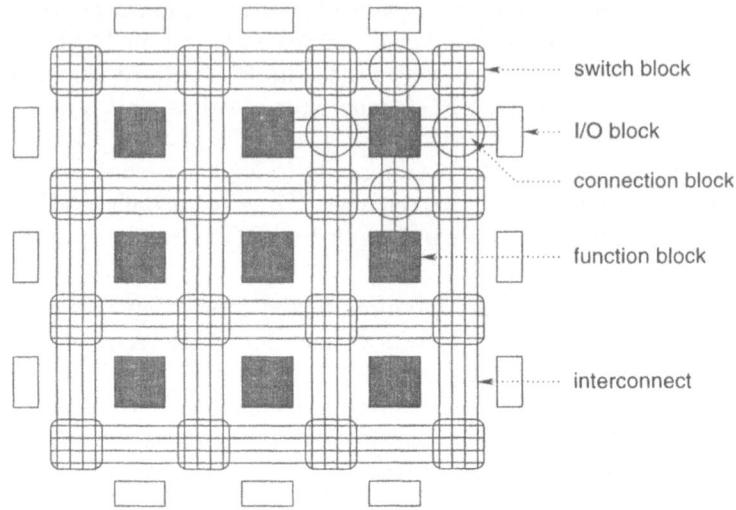

Figure 11.1. Generic structure of an FPGA. For clarity, the figure shows the connection blocks in the neighborhood of only one function block.

control paths within and between function blocks and connecting these paths to the inputs and outputs outside the chip.

Typically, each function block is fine grained, manipulating individual bits of input and producing individual bits of output. These blocks can be coarse grained, however, manipulating larger size words. The interconnection structure normally comprises horizontal and vertical routing channels along the rows and columns of function blocks. A routing channel often contains a hierarchy of connections with switches at different distances. An I/O block provides a point to connect the interconnect fabric to outside the chip. Many FPGAs also contain separate memory blocks and specialized hardware (such as look-up tables and carry logic).

An FPGA design results from tradeoffs in a range of possibilities for the amount and arrangement of routing, computation, on-chip memory, and I/O.

The FPGAs used for RTR configure many static random access memory (SRAM) bits whose states control switches. One can view the *configuration* of an FPGA as the set of values of these *configuration bits*. Many FPGAs employ other switching technologies, such as antifuses, but since these lack the fast reprogrammability needed for RTR, we do not cover them here. One establishes a configuration in an FPGA by a bitstream that sets the logical functions computed in each function block and sets the routing among function blocks by determining switch settings in the interconnections.

The interconnections on an FPGA typically start with horizontal and vertical channels of wire segments. Each segment is of fixed length, with programmable switches to connect function blocks to segments and programmable switches that enable connections between segments. A *connection block* comprises switches connecting input and output lines of a function block to the wire segments in channels. A *switch block* comprises switches connecting horizontal and vertical wire segments. A channel will contain a variety of segment lengths: nearest neighbor connections, segments that span the width or height of the FPGA, and lengths in between. A signal from one function block to another will pass through switches, and the number of switches depends on the segments used. Performance depends on the selection of segments to carry out this routing.

To make this sketch a bit more concrete, we overview the architecture of the widely used Xilinx Virtex family of FPGAs. Each function block, termed a configurable logic block (CLB), is based on look-up tables (LUTs), multiplexers, and flip-flops. Each CLB comprises four logic cells (LCs), organized in two slices; Figure 11.2 shows one logic cell. An LC contains a four-input LUT. A K-input LUT acts as a one bit

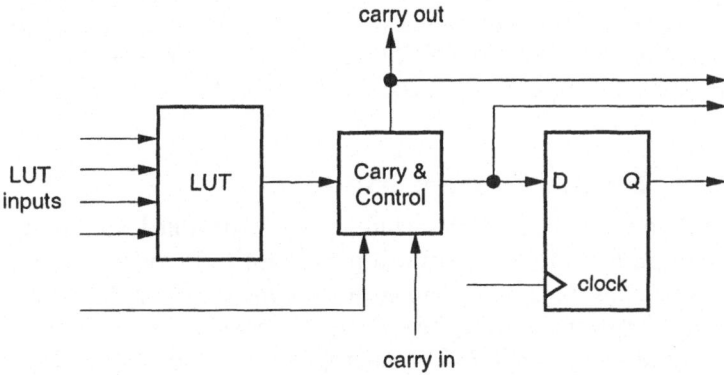

Figure 11.2. A logic cell in the Xilinx Virtex family of FPGAs.

wide, $2^K \times 1$ memory array. By properly initializing its contents, one can realize any K-input Boolean function. Given the presence of LUTs in CLBs, a CLB can serve as a logical element, as a memory element, or as a combination. The FPGA contains fast-carry logic for implementing arithmetic efficiently. The family of chips ranges from 1700 to 27,000 logic cells, with arrays of CLBs up to 64×96 in size. Each Virtex chip also contains a number of blocks of on-chip RAM. Each block contains 4096 bits of RAM, and Virtex FPGAs have from 8 to 32 blocks. (The Virtex-E and Virtex-II families have still larger chips with more and larger RAM blocks.) Routing channels provide a selection of lines: single, double, quad, and longlines. The single-length lines enter a switch block at each CLB, double-length lines enter a switch block at every two CLBs, and so on. Longlines run the entire length or width of the CLB array.

An FPGA's *configuration* is the set of states of all its configurable entities (including switches and LUTs). An FPGA can be fully or partially reconfigurable. A *fully reconfigurable* FPGA is one for which a change in configuration entails loading an entire configuration (specifying the states of all configurable entities in the FPGA), while a *partially reconfigurable* FPGA is one that permits a user to change a portion of the configuration, while leaving the remainder intact and operating. (The Virtex described above is partially reconfigurable by column slices. That is, it is possible to select a subset of columns (including a single column) and reconfigure only that subset.) Partial reconfiguration can drastically reduce configuration time. Some have noted a reduction in the number of reconfiguration bits by factors ranging from 3 to 60 compared to full reconfiguration. Another advantage of partial reconfiguration is that a portion of the FPGA not being reconfigured can operate during the reconfiguration. This can be used, for example, to save system state information for the portion being reconfigured. Partially reconfigurable FPGAs include the Atmel AT40K and AT6000 families and the Xilinx Virtex, Virtex-E, and Virtex-II families (configurable at the column level).

11.1.2   FPGA System Model

To create a view of a system including reconfigurable logic, probably in the form of an FPGA, we describe a parameterized model that basically contains reconfigurable logic connected to a microprocessor. This model is the *Hybrid System Architecture Model* (HySAM). The model includes a configurable logic unit (CLU), a microprocessor, a configuration cache, and data buffers connected via an interconnection network (Figure 11.3).

The parameters of the HySAM are as follows.

- F - set of functions $F_1, \ldots, F_n$ that can be performed in the configurable logic
- C - set of configurations $C_1, \ldots, C_m$ of the CLU
- t_{ij} - execution time of function F_i in configuration C_j

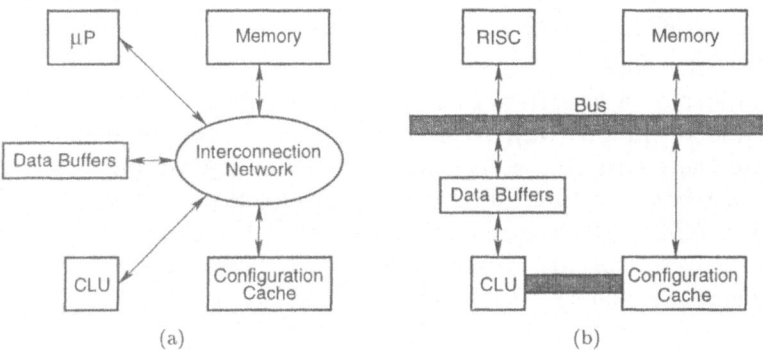

Figure 11.3. (a) The Hybrid System Architecture Model (HySAM); (b) example system with a particular interconnection network.
Reprinted with permission from the *Proceedings of the 8th International Workshop on Field-Programmable Logic and Applications, Springer-Verlag Lecture Notes in Computer Science vol. 1482,* "Mapping Loops onto Reconfigurable Architectures," K. Bondalapati and V. K. Prasanna, pp. 268–277, Figure 1, 1998 (© Springer Verlag, Berlin-Heidelberg 1998).

- R_{ij} - reconfiguration cost to change from C_i to C_j
- N_c - number of different configurations (also known as contexts) that the configuration cache can store
- k, K - reconfiguration time to configure the CLU from the cache and external memory, respectively
- W, D - width and depth of the CLU; these determine the amount of reconfigurable logic available
- w - width of a function block; this specifies the granularity of the CLU
- S - schedule of configurations to execute the input tasks; the schedule is stored in the memory and is analogous to a program specifying the sequence of configurations that the CLU assumes.
- E - execution time of a sequence of tasks, including computation time and reconfiguration time

The parameters of HySAM enable it to model a wide range of configurable system structures and sizes.

11.2   Run-Time Reconfiguration Concepts and Examples

RTR provides most benefit to applications that perform the same operations on a large set of data before changing phase to a new set of operations. In this way, reduced computation time over many inputs due to the realization of special purpose circuitry can pay for the time cost of reconfiguration. In this section, we will present key techniques used in RTR, then example RTR solutions. We group these examples into two sets: specific problems (Section 11.2.2) and general classes of problems (Section 11.2.3).

11.2.1   Basic Concepts

To introduce the methods used in many RTR solutions, we now discuss the concepts behind basic techniques, namely, tailoring the circuit design to the problem inputs, distributed arithmetic, and reconfiguring part of the circuit while computation continues on the remainder. These form the building blocks for the examples we will see later in this section. Some examples rely on only one of these, while others exploit more.

11.2.1.1   Tailoring Circuits to Inputs

The ability to change circuit configurations at run-time opens possibilities not present with fixed circuits and fixed connections. One of these is to specialize the design of portions of the circuit to match the actual input numbers. The advantage of this specialization is that the resulting circuit can be both smaller and faster than a general circuit designed to work with any arbitrary input values. This method is sometimes known as constant propagation or partial evaluation. The catch is that you have to use that specialized configuration enough times to make the time savings in operation pay for the time cost of reconfiguration.

How can circuits be specialized to input data? Routing connections may depend on the data. For example, an input value may determine which lines connect to which others or determine a shift distance or select a permutation. In the DES encryption algorithm, for example, fixed connections based on the encryption key can replace several permutations and a significant amount of routing resources. Or, in a hash function that utilizes several rotations, one can simply connect wires in an FPGA to accomplish the specific rotations desired rather than realizing a circuit block capable of performing general rotations.

Another common specialization is a *constant coefficient multiplier*, abbreviated KCM because the constant is often denoted as k. In contrast to a standard multiplier that returns the product of two inputs (arbitrary numbers), a KCM returns the product of one input and a constant, k. If, for instance, a circuit is to repeatedly multiply different values by 56, then implementing this multiplier as a KCM with $k = 56$ may be worthwhile. A KCM can be 3 to 4 times smaller than a general multiplier while affording comparable performance. In fact, to attain speed comparable to a KCM, a general multiplier would be at the larger end of its size range.

Look-up tables (LUTs) are the primary building blocks of KCMs. For instance, a 4-input LUT can store $0, k, 2k, \cdots, 15k$, so four input bits select an entry of the LUT—input 1001 produces output $9k$. By combining LUTs and additional circuitry, one can design larger KCMs, as shown in Figure 11.4 for an 8-bit value of k and an 8-bit multiplier.

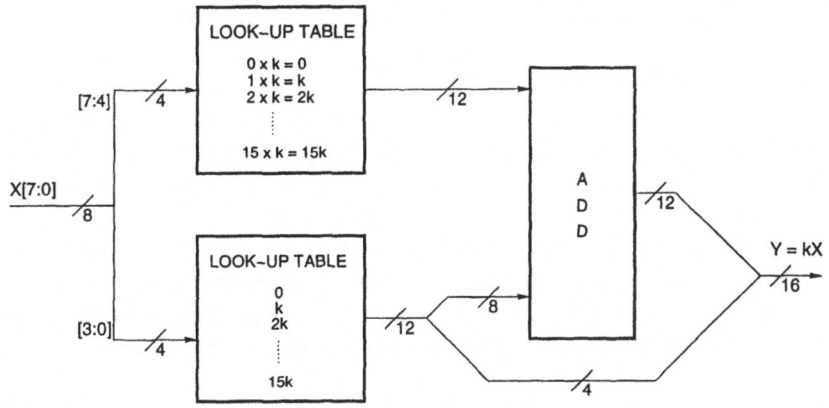

Figure 11.4. A KCM for multiplying 8-bit inputs using 4-bit LUTs.
© Copyright 1996 Xilinx, Inc.; all rights reserved; Application Note-XAPP 054.

To make this specific, suppose we wanted to build a KCM to multiply 8-bit numbers with $k = 56$ (= 38 hex). Initialize the 16 entries in each of the two LUTs as shown in Figure 11.5. Then, to multiply input 93 hex by the constant 38 hex, the 9 is input as the address to the upper LUT and the 3 is input as the address to the lower LUT of Figure 11.4. These return 1F8 (= $9 \cdot 38$ hex) and 0A8 (= $3 \cdot 38$ hex), respectively, Aligning correspondingly weighted bits and adding returns the product 2028 hex.

As LUTs are key components of function blocks of SRAM-based FPGAs, a collection of function blocks can realize the tables for multiplication. The above example used 16 entry, 12-bit wide tables. In the

Address (hex)		Data (hex)
0	× 38 =	000
1	× 38 =	038
2	× 38 =	070
3	× 38 =	0A8
⋮	⋮	⋮
9	× 38 =	1F8
⋮	⋮	⋮
F	× 38 =	348

Figure 11.5. LUT entries in a KCM with 4-input LUTs for $k = 56$ ($= 38$ hex).

Xilinx XC4000 family of FPGAs, for example, one function block can implement a 16-entry, 2-bit wide LUT, so six such function blocks can together implement one of the LUTs needed for the 8-bit KCM above.

11.2.1.2   Distributed Arithmetic

Distributed arithmetic realizes arithmetic operations in a circuit in a distributed fashion, rather than in a compact unit. The KCM was presented as an example of tailoring a circuit to problem inputs, but it is also a prime example of distributed arithmetic. A KCM distributes the multiplication operation over look-up tables and adders, in contrast to a conventional multiplier design. A multiply-accumulate operation, so useful for computing an inner product of two vectors, is another operation frequently realized in distributed fashion, by slight changes to a KCM.

11.2.1.3   Reconfiguring While Computing

The third building block used in many RTR approaches is to overlap reconfiguration of one part of a circuit with computation on another part of the circuit. This helps to reduce or eliminate the time overhead of reconfiguration. This technique is useful in partially reconfigurable FPGAs, in systems using multiple fully reconfigurable FPGAs, and in context-swapping systems (which initially load several full configurations, then can quickly switch among them).

In its simplest form, this method uses two regions of reconfigurable logic with the ability to switch from one to the other. These could be separate fully reconfigurable chips or separate regions of the same partially reconfigurable chip. One can execute Phase 1 of a computation on Region 1 while configuring Region 2 for Phase 2. On the completion of Phase 1 and the configuration of Region 2, switch to execute Phase 2 on Region 2 and begin reconfiguring Region 1 for Phase 3 (Figure 11.6).

Continue alternating through the remaining phases. If we can run each phase for a sufficient amount of time (say for a sufficiently large problem or over a sufficient number of iterations) so that the execution time matches or exceeds the reconfiguration time, then the reconfiguration time will be completely hidden.

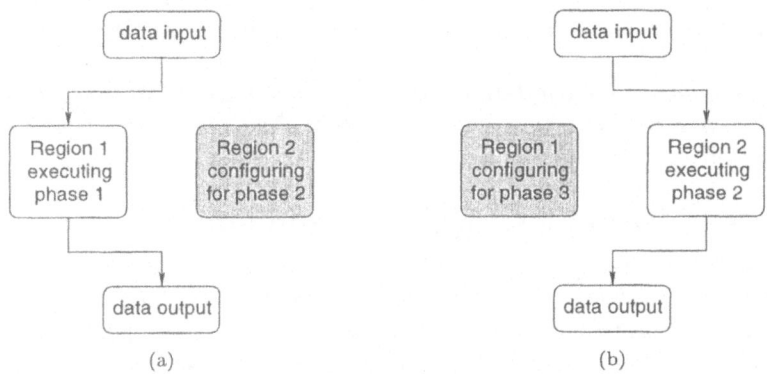

Figure 11.6. Example of reconfiguring part of a circuit while executing on another part.

A more sophisticated application of the same technique is *pipeline morphing*. This technique works on a computation that is organized into pipelined stages that are too large to all fit in the reconfigurable logic simultaneously. As a stage completes, reconfigure it to its replacement. Figure 11.7 depicts an example morphing three stage pipeline A into three stage pipeline B. This example assumes that reconfiguration time

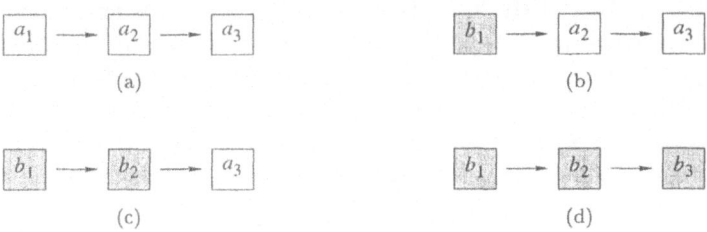

Figure 11.7. Morphing Pipeline *A* into Pipeline *B*.

is less than or equal to the time spent in each stage. If the reconfiguration time is greater, then the pipeline will need to control the data flow to slow down the data rate while reconfiguration is taking place. One can adapt this morphing from one pipeline to another into a mapping of a larger pipeline into a small space. For instance, suppose we wanted to implement a six-stage pipeline, but had only space to implement three stages at a time. In Figure 11.7, add a feedback loop and memory to store outputs that will be fed back as inputs between the third stage output and first stage input, and replace b_1 by a_4, b_2 by a_5, and b_3 by a_6.

These methods of overlapping reconfiguration are most effective when the time in a configuration meets or exceeds the time spent reconfiguring the region.

11.2.2   Examples: Specific Problems

Researchers have applied RTR to a number of different problems. Most of these problems involve performing a set of operations, some data-dependent, to large amounts of data. Many of these problems have been in the areas of signal and image processing and cryptography. This section presents RTR solutions for some particular problems, while the next section examines applying RTR to general classes of problems. This section deals with filtering, neural networks, motion estimation, and database search.

11.2.2.1   Adaptive FIR Filtering

A finite impulse response (FIR) filter computes the inner product of a coefficient vector and a finite series of time samples. An adaptive FIR filter is one in which the coefficients can change over time. The length of the coefficient vector is called the number of *taps* in the filter. Time samples stream through the filter. In each step, a t-tap FIR filter computes the inner product of the coefficient vector and t time samples, then the time samples shift by one (Figure 11.8).

A (nonadaptive) FIR filter lends itself to an implementation using KCMs. Because the coefficients are fixed, each of the multipliers in Figure 11.8 has one constant input—a natural candidate for a KCM. Further, the fan-in addition can be pipelined, either as levels of adders or as a Wallace tree of 4-2 adders or 3-2 adders (carry-save adders) before a final stage of a regular adder. Figure 11.9 shows the resulting circuit with a KCM for each coefficient.

In an adaptive FIR filter, the coefficient vector changes over time. Here, one can consider using this same circuit and reconfiguring a KCM when its coefficient changes. This approach is suitable if the coefficients

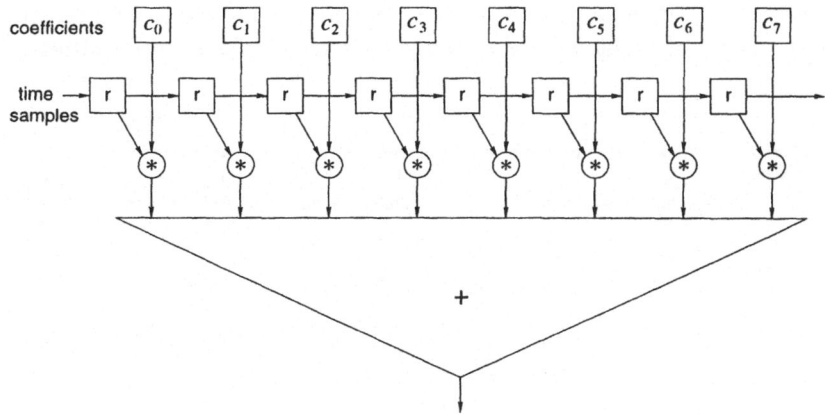

Figure 11.8. Basic flow of data in an FIR filter ("r" denotes a register).

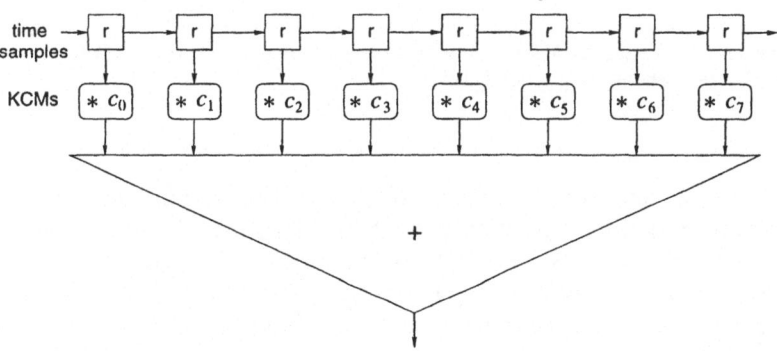

Figure 11.9. Using KCMs for fixed filter coefficients in a nonadaptive FIR filter.

change infrequently enough so that the gain of using a KCM is worthwhile over using a general multiplier. Reconfiguration overhead can be an obstacle, however, if the time between coefficient changes is too short. Nevertheless, by turning the process on its head and letting the samples be the constants for the multipliers rather than the coefficients, we can effectively handle coefficients that can change at every step. This has regularity advantages as well. For t taps, each data input sample is multiplied by a coefficient in t consecutive steps. We can configure a KCM with a sample as its constant value, know that it will be used exactly t times, then reconfigure it for another sample.

Figure 11.10 displays the basic structure for an 8-tap adaptive FIR filter. Each of eight KCMs is configured for a time sample input. At

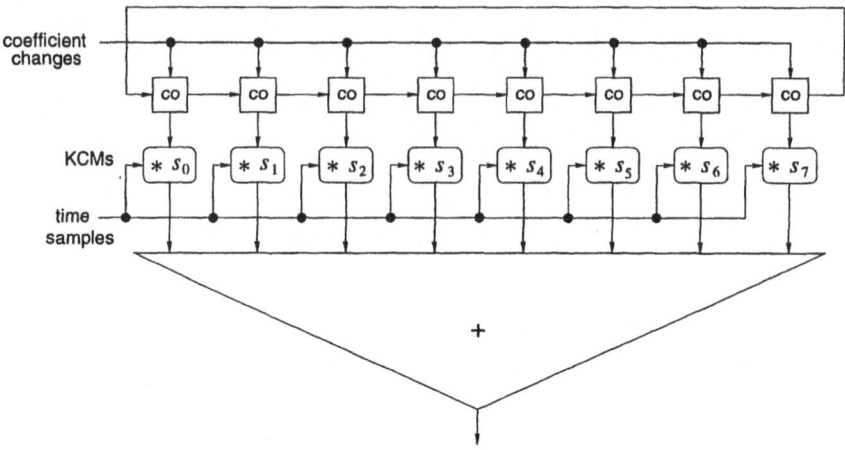

Figure 11.10. Using KCMs for time sample data in an adaptive FIR filter. ("co" denotes a register holding a coefficient.)

each step, a new sample arrives and one of the KCMs has finished its final multiplication. Reconfigure that KCM with the new sample as its constant multiplier. Since the time samples are fixed in place at their KCMs, the coefficients rotate, in contrast to Figure 11.8. Changes to coefficient values simply replace an old coefficient.

What Figure 11.10 does not show is the second reconfiguration context to allow this scheme of reconfiguring part of the circuit while the remainder continues to operate. In this case, a KCM must reconfigure in the same or less time than the duration of its use with a fixed value (eight multiplication steps in this example). Let s_1 denote one time sample value and s_1' denote its replacement (eight steps later). At the time the KCM in Context 1 is configured for s_1 and begins multiplying, the matching KCM in Context 2 is free. Begin to configure that KCM for s_1'. By the time the KCM in Context 1 with s_1 is finished, the KCM in Context 2 with s_1' is ready and can switch into place.

This RTR adaptive FIR filter hides the reconfiguration time cost and uses less area (fewer CLBs), even with two reconfiguration contexts, than an approach that uses general multipliers. This RTR solution uses the basic RTR techniques outlined in Section 11.2.1. It tailors the circuit structure to the problem inputs (via the KCMs), uses distributed arithmetic (again via the KCMs), and reconfigures part of the circuit while the remainder continues to run.

11.2.2.2 Neural Networks

The adaptive FIR filter operated in one phase of continual reconfiguration of circuit elements. The Run-Time Reconfigurable Artificial Neural Network (RRANN) is an example of reconfiguring between phases of a computation.

RRANN implements the backpropagation algorithm for training a feedforward neural network. Backpropagation repeatedly applies three phases to pairs of source inputs and target outputs: feed inputs forward, propagate errors backward, and update weights. RRANN runs a phase, reconfigures for the next phase, then runs the next phase, and so on.

Let us first sketch the backpropagation algorithm. Figure 11.11 shows a sample network with three inputs and two layers of processing elements (PEs or neurons). Each layer is completely connected to the following

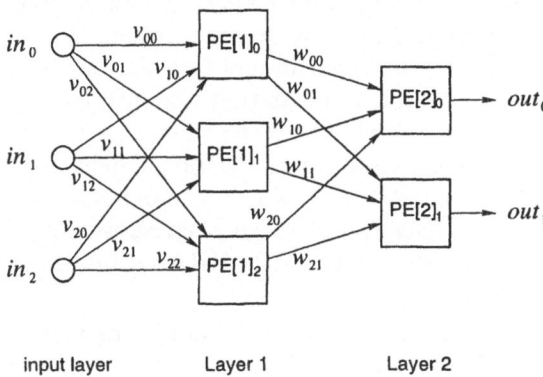

Figure 11.11. Feedforward neural network for backpropagation.

layer. Each connection has a weight.

The first phase feeds inputs forward through the network. Moving layer by layer, each PE in a layer computes the sum of its weighted inputs, then applies an *activation function* to that sum to produce its outputs. In the example in Figure 11.11, the three PEs in layer 1 would compute their outputs. In particular, $PE[1]_0$ determines $s[1]_0 = \sum_{i=0}^{2} in_i \cdot v_{i0}$ and then computes its output $f[1]_0(s[1]_0)$, where $f[1]_0$ is the activation function for $PE[1]_0$. The outputs of layer 1 are multiplied by weights w_{ij}, where $0 \leq i \leq 2$ and $0 \leq j \leq 1$, and serve as weighted inputs to layer 2. The two PEs in layer 2 would then compute their outputs, out_0 and out_1.

The second phase propagates errors backwards through the network, effectively reversing the direction of the connections. The error terms are based on the differences between the target outputs and the actual outputs produced at each output layer PE. Specifically, $PE[2]_0$ produces an error term $e[2]_0$ that it sends to the PEs in layer 1. For "hidden" layers before the output layer, the error is a function of the sum of the weighted errors from the next layer. In particular, to determine its own error term, $PE[1]_0$ calculates $e[1]_0 = \sum_{j=0}^{1} e[2]_j \cdot w_{0j}$.

The final phase uses the error term of each PE to adjust the weights feeding into it from the preceding layer.

RRANN assigns an FPGA as a global controller and other FPGAs to handle the PEs. The use of reconfiguration reduces the FPGA area needed per PE, so six PEs fit on an FPGA (Xilinx XC3090) as opposed to only one PE per FPGA without reconfiguration. To handle layer-to-layer communication in the "feed inputs forward" stage, RRANN uses a bus rather than all-to-all, point-to-point connections. This compels PEs to write one at a time, which has the advantage that each PE needs only one multiplier to multiply the connection weight by the value read from the bus. (It handles layer-to-layer communication differently in the "propagate errors backwards" stage because weights will be at the writing PE rather than the reading PE.) RRANN implements activation functions using LUTs.

Experimental results showed that for 138 PEs or more per layer, the RTR approach of RRANN outperformed a static FPGA approach. (This performance is in terms of work, which is the time-area product, also viewed as its inverse, called functional density.) The reason for the fairly large neural network size as a performance break-even point is the reconfiguration time cost. This lead to an investigation reducing that time cost by using partially reconfigurable FPGAs in RRANN2. To exploit partial reconfiguration, it is necessary to minimize the amount of reconfiguration from one phase to the next by maximizing the amount of common (and, therefore, unchanging) circuitry from one phase to the next. Examination of RRANN revealed static blocks of circuitry such as adders, multipliers, and storage locations. Retaining storage locations had other benefits by retaining data from one phase to the next without the time or wiring requirements of rewriting or transmitting the data. RRANN also contained some mostly static blocks with few changes between phases, for example, bit multipliers of different bit-widths that can be realized for the larger word-size needed and sections disconnected as needed. Also, some blocks, such as counters, differed only in terms of a constant value loaded to them. RRANN2 displayed a 25% reduction in configuration time and a 50% increase in PE density over RRANN.

11.2.2.3 Motion Estimator

The next example concerns a time-constrained application in which the object is to exploit the area savings of RTR to perform the computation with minimum reconfigurable logic while still satisfying a time constraint. Too little reconfiguration leads to too large an area; too much reconfiguration takes too much time and exceeds the time limit.

The application is an apparent-motion estimator in a log-polar image sequence, which estimates the normal optical flow. Primary components of the algorithms are Gaussian and averaging filters, temporal and spatial derivatives, and an arithmetic divider. Images arrive at a rate of 25 per second, allowing 40 ms to process each 512×512 pixel image. The algorithm proceeds in phases of computation with reconfiguration between successive phases. This implies that the sum of the computing time in each phase and the reconfiguring time between each pair of consecutive phases (including from the last stage to the first) must not exceed 40 ms.

The aim of minimum logic pushes in the direction of many phases, each reusing a small amount of logic, while the time constraint pushes in the direction of few phases, to lessen the amount of time spent reconfiguring. A preferred solution in this case will be as many phases as possible (hence, as little logic as possible) while still satisfying the 40 ms constraint.

The proposed method uses Atmel AT40K FPGAs that allow partial reconfiguration and help reduce reconfiguration time. Analysis of reconfiguration time and component size leads to a partition into four phases:

(i) Gaussian filter,

(ii) averaging filter and hardware for temporal and spatial derivatives,

(iii) first half of divider, and

(iv) second half of divider.

Figure 11.12 shows the size and time results. Summing the reconfiguration and computing times of the phases indicates 34.77 ms per image, within the 40 ms limit. In summary, this RTR motion estimator reuses

Phase	Number of logic blocks	Reconfiguration time (ms)	Computing time (ms)
Gaussian filter	106	0.08	7.10
Average and derivatives	103	0.08	6.95
Divider-pt. 1	354	0.26	10.14
Divider-pt. 2	336	0.25	9.91

Figure 11.12.   Sizes and times for phases of RTR motion estimator.

logic resources and exploits partial reconfiguration while carefully accounting for reconfiguration time.

11.2.2.4   Database Search

One candidate for a reduced circuit size from specializing to a constant is a shifter. Rather than layers of gates and multiplexers for a general shifter, a fixed-distance shifter is simply a collection of wires. Fixed-distance shifting is one of the methods employed in the following database search example.

A method of performing a database search that favors FPGA implementation is to map a word by a hash function to a pseudo-random value that indexes a look-up table to indicate whether the input word is in the user dictionary. Hash function sizes and bit-level operations that are irregular in general but fixed for given constant values can be exploited in an RTR implementation. The hash function computes the XOR or XNOR (according to a hash function mask) of each input bit with the current hash value, then it performs a rotate. To reduce the probability of a false match, one can cascade independent hash functions.

Irregular masking and rotating is the entry point for FPGA use; cascading hash functions is the entry point for RTR. Furthermore, one can take advantage of partial reconfiguration. A change in a mask bit results in an XOR instead of an XNOR, or vice versa. Changing a multiplexer selection bit can accomplish this. Changing a rotation distance from, say, 7 bits to 5 bits requires only changing a small number of routing connections (proportional to the word size). In addition, by careful layout, these changes can be placed in a small number of columns, to take advantage of FPGAs that favor partial reconfiguration by columns (such as the Xilinx Virtex chips).

11.2.3   Examples: Generic Problems

After seeing the applications of RTR to specific problems in the previous section, we now look at applying RTR techniques to general classes of problems. Essentially, we will employ the same basic methods, but with a more generic use of them. We will first consider loops, then graph problems. These efforts take steps toward expanding RTR applications and placing RTR solutions within reach of more designers.

11.2.3.1 Mapping Loops

Matching RTR techniques to problems that call for the same set of operations on large amounts of data generates the best results. The problems of the previous section (image filtering, neural networks, etc.) were of this type. Loops in general programs also fit the bill.

A first approach to the problem is, given a set of instructions (tasks) in a loop and a set of corresponding configurations (some tasks may have multiple possible configurations), identify a sequence of configurations that minimizes the sum of the computing and reconfiguring time. Assume a linear order of dependence among the tasks. Observe some restrictions here from the most general problem: tasks are to be performed in a fixed sequence, so ordering the tasks is not an issue, and one task at a time uses the reconfigurable logic, so coordinating requests from multiple tasks is not an issue.

Assume that we precompute reconfiguration costs to change from each configuration C_i to each configuration C_j. For a fully reconfigurable system, this is the same for all i and j (and the problem is simple). For a partially reconfigurable system, this cost can differ for each i, j pair as the cost will depend on how much overlap exists (that is, how much of the circuitry can remain unchanged) between C_i and C_j.

A greedy approach falters because fixing a greedy choice to reconfigure from C_i to C_j has an impact on the choices to reconfigure from C_j for the following task. Instead, use dynamic programming to identify an optimal sequence. For one execution of r tasks, let E_{kj} denote the cost of executing up to task T_k ending in configuration C_j. Using dynamic programming, we can determine an optimal sequence for r tasks and m configurations in $O(rm^2)$ time.

Since the loop will execute multiple times, we must also account for the transition from the configuration of the last task to the configuration of the first. To do so, unrolling the loop m times suffices. (Note that this is m, the number of configurations, which is independent of the number of iterations.) Following the same approach, this finds an optimal sequence in $O(rm^3)$ time.

To generalize the problem a step further, let dependences among tasks be described by a directed acyclic graph and let multiple task configurations fit on the reconfigurable logic simultaneously. In the previous problem, we executed only one iteration at a time; here we will now allow the system to execute multiple iterations in the same configuration. The new problem restricts a loop to have no dependencies between different iterations of the loop.

The aim here is to decompose a loop into multiple segments and execute a fixed number of iterations of each segment in sequence. Each segment comprises multiple pipeline stages. After each segment, reconfigure the logic, storing in memory the results to pass to the next segment. Memory size and the amount of information to pass between segments determine the number of iterations to execute at a time. Again, the aim is to minimize the time to complete the loop, accounting for computation and reconfiguration time.

Because the scheduling problem is NP-complete, use a heuristic approach. Partition the task graph so that each partition fits into the available reconfigurable logic but uses a large amount of the logic while communicating a small amount of information among partitions. The heuristic here is to add to a partition the largest possible task configuration whose inputs have already been computed, with the least communication to other partitions. Next, to arrange pipeline stages within a segment, observe that some tasks are independent and so can be scheduled in any order. For such tasks, use the heuristic of matching the corresponding stages of different pipeline segments to reduce the amount of reconfiguring between segments.

11.2.3.2　Graph Problems

Graph problems have wide applicability. For solving these problems on FPGAs, configuration time rises as one obstacle and so do synthesis and compilation time. In previous examples, either given operations determined circuit modules or run-time constants made predictable changes (such as new LUT contents for a KCM), so the synthesis and compilation, mapping the algorithm to an FPGA, could be computed in advance. For a graph whose description arrives at run-time, compiling the graph embedding in advance is clearly not possible. The idea is to employ a skeleton, a general parameterized structure (Figure 11.13). The synthesis phase can handle routing and I/O resources for the skeleton in advance. When a graph arrives, the system can make suitable adjustments to the skeleton to incorporate the graph. The resulting graph embedding will not necessarily be as good in size or delay as a circuit specifically designed for that graph, but the time to embed the graph, given a skeleton, is vastly improved (by several orders of magnitude).

The skeleton includes high-level modules that correspond to graph vertices. The circuitry in a module depends on the algorithm. The skeleton connects vertex modules in a regular manner that is independent of a particular graph instance, but sufficiently rich to accommodate

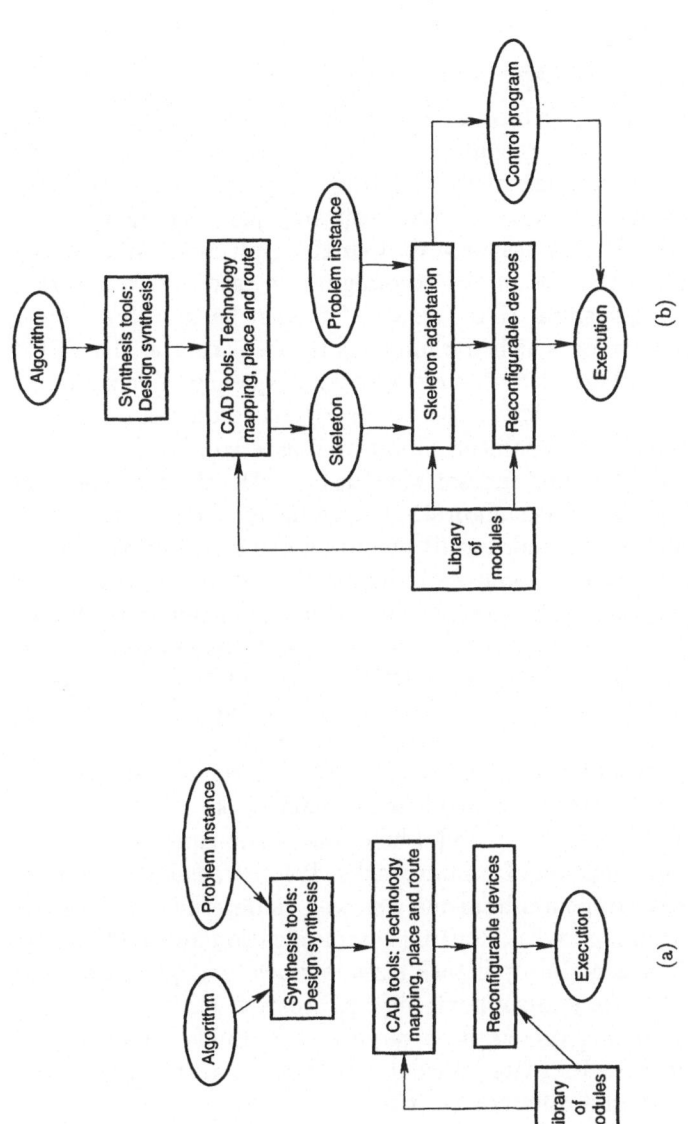

Figure 11.13. Conventional mapping approach (a) contrasted with domain-specific mapping approach (b). Reprinted with permission from the *Proceedings of the 6th Reconfigurable Architectures Workshop, Springer-Verlag Lecture Notes in Computer Science vol. 1586*, "Domain Specific Mapping for Solving Graph Problems on Reconfigurable Devices," A. Dandalis, A. Mei, and V. K. Prasanna, pp. 652–660, Figure 1, 1999 (© Springer Verlag, Berlin-Heidelberg 1999).

many different graphs. At run time, the system adapts the skeleton to an input graph. The idea of a predefined skeleton for a particular algorithm or problem domain can apply to other classes of problems as well.

11.3   Hardware Operating System

So far in this chapter, we took a problem-specific view of RTR, seeking a proper tradeoff between reconfiguration time and computation time. To move toward common use of reconfigurable logic as a resource shared by multiple applications, however, we must step past the viewpoint of tailoring the entire FPGA resource to a single application and develop methods to control the use of the reconfigurable resource in a sort of hardware operating system. Here, we stand further back with a view of handling many tasks for which the modules to be placed on the FPGA are known. This setting also assumes greater frequency of reconfiguration and has a target of efficient sharing of FPGA resources.

Currently, creating RTR solutions requires mastery of low-level device details as well as algorithm and software design. Developing operating system-style support for reconfiguration can relieve a user from a myriad of operational details and permit including reconfigurable logic in a pool of shared computing resources. The aim is very much like that of a traditional operating system—simplifying the use of shared resources, supporting multitasking, enacting a high-level view, dynamically assigning resources to tasks to minimize waiting time while still executing correctly. A hardware operating system for reconfigurable logic would permit a user to take a high level, abstract view of the hardware, and the operating system would handle low-level details. It would also enable a virtual view of the hardware as dedicated to each task.

Key issues include allocating and scheduling tasks, run-time routing, and supporting pre-emption of running tasks. It must be able to manage multiple tasks executing simultaneously as well as determine where and when to place incoming tasks. Routing communication and I/O lines to a task may be handled simply if task sizes, shapes, and placement are constrained, or they may allow flexibility within device interconnection constraints. Supporting pre-emption requires the ability to suspend a running task and save its state and data so that it can be resumed in the future, possibly in a different location.

The size of the module to assign to an incoming task is also an issue. Should the size be fixed or variable? A fixed size has advantages of simplified space management, easier task swapping, and more uniform routing. It has disadvantages of the difficulty of fitting variable-size tasks to fixed-size modules, internal fragmentation (wasting unused space in a fixed-size module), and the difficulty of arranging communication among multiple modules assigned to the same task. Variable-size modules reverse the advantages and disadvantages.

This section first looks at the DISC system that constrains tasks to span the width of the reconfigurable resource, then the RAGE system, and a configuration controller that handles more general tasks. Finally, we examine task compaction—moving currently running tasks to new locations to free up space for an incoming task.

11.3.1 Dynamic Instruction Set Computer

The Dynamic Instruction Set Computer (DISC), by constraining module shapes, uses a one-dimensional space in which to place and swap task modules. DISC pairs a core processor with reconfigurable hardware (a partially reconfigurable FPGA). For a given application, such as object thinning in an image, the user creates FPGA circuit modules for functions specific to the application. In essence, these modules are custom instructions. Before running the application on DISC, the user stores these modules in off-chip memory, where the system can load them onto the reconfigurable logic (called the instruction space) as needed.

The core processor is responsible for managing the reconfigurable logic space, loading circuit modules, initiating execution of custom instructions, and managing I/O between the FPGA and the core processor. The reconfigurable hardware includes a global controller and wires for control, address, and data that span the height of the FPGA (Figure 11.14). I/O connections are constrained to the top and bottom.

DISC requires each circuit module for a custom instruction to span the width of the array, though they can vary in height. Coupled with the communication lines that span the height of the array, this permits modules to be relocatable. That is, a circuit module can be stacked anywhere (vertically) in the array. In fact, a module can be placed in one location for one run, then removed and later replaced in a different location for a second run. It will have the same access to communication lines and I/O in any position.

While executing an application, when a request for a custom instruction arrives, the global controller checks if the corresponding module is already loaded on the reconfigurable hardware. If not, then the core processor searches for sufficient free space (that is, at least as many contiguous free rows as the height of the module). If the free space exists, then the core processor loads the module. If sufficient free space does not exist, then the core processor replaces currently loaded modules according to a least recently used policy. So the system pages instruction modules into the hardware on demand.

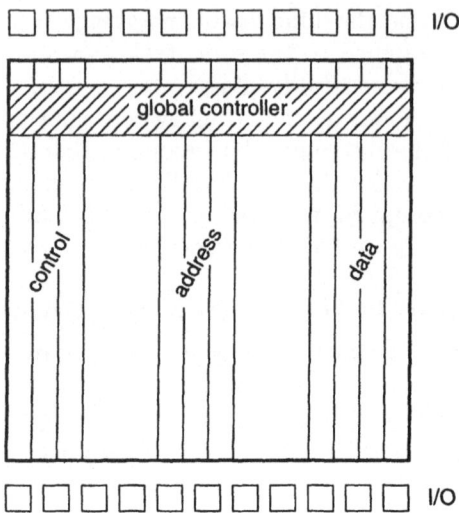

Figure 11.14.   Structure of the reconfigurable hardware of DISC.

The first implementation of DISC resided on two FPGAs, one for the core processor and one for the instruction space. The second implementation, DISC-II, resided on three FPGAs with the third FPGA for bus interface and configuration control.

11.3.2   RAGE

The RAGE system is a run-time system for managing reconfiguration of FPGAs that incorporates services after the style of a conventional operating system. It aims to satisfy the following requirements: the ability to reconfigure an FPGA; the ability to reserve a portion of the FPGA (to allow multitasking); the ability to rotate and move circuit modules; a high-level symbolic representation of circuits; and an architecturally correct representation of the FPGA. The RAGE system contains four primary components to meet these requirements—a virtual hardware manager, a configuration manager, a transformation manager, and a device driver (Figure 11.15).

The device driver presents a low-level foundation for the system by presenting an abstract view of the FPGA and hiding the programming interface of the FPGA. The configuration manager is a higher abstraction layer between the device driver and the virtual hardware manager, giving the virtual hardware manager a device-independent view of the FPGA. The transformation manager rotates and slides modules from

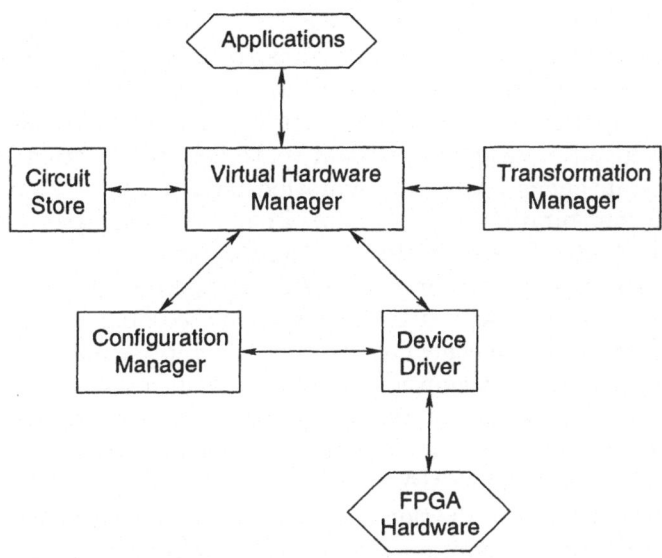

Figure 11.15. Relations among system components in RAGE.

their default orientations and positions by performing bounded run-time place-and-route to accommodate these changes. The circuit store holds circuit descriptions that have been submitted by the application then converted by the virtual hardware manager. Finally, the virtual hardware manager coordinates the other components and is the main interface with the application.

RAGE exploits the feature of the Xilinx XC6200 family of FPGAs that permits reads and writes directly to FPGA cells configured as registers. This relieves the need to route the inputs from I/O pads and improves the ability to relocate modules.

Establishing the levels of abstraction of the FPGA is important to the RAGE design. Higher level control, such as the virtual hardware manager finding a location for a module, is difficult enough with a high-level view. The structure of RAGE allows isolation of higher level problems by the use of lower level components that progressively manipulate modules to finally reach device-level details.

11.3.3 Configuration Controllers

We next view a generic model of a configuration controller for an RTR system. This model can be customized by parameterization and user-defined blocks. It faces three basic requirements: recognizing reconfiguration conditions, retrieving configuration data, and using this data to configure the device. It further aims to support priority levels for tasks and perform transformations of task layout at run-time.

The key blocks of this controller are (in order) the reconfiguration condition monitor, scheduler, central controller, pre-emption interface, memory management unit, configuration data decoder, layout transform, and configuration port interface. In operation, the reconfiguration condition monitor detects conditions requiring activation or deactivation of a task and places them in queues for the appropriate priority level. The scheduler selects tasks from these queues according to their priority and sends them to the central controller, which pre-empts other tasks, if required, via the pre-emption interface. The memory management unit fetches configuration data, which the configuration data decoder and layout transform process as needed. Finally, the configuration port interface configures the FPGA.

As noted in the introduction to this section, pre-empting a running task requires the pre-emption interface to be able to save and restore the state of a pre-empted task. The intention of the configuration data decoder is to handle compressed or encrypted configuration information. The intention of the layout transform block is to change the placement of an incoming task from its default placement. Resizing a task at run-time remains a research goal.

This controller is essentially just a framework. Some aspects are dependent on the particular FPGA(s) used, such as the configuration port interface. Others are more open research areas, such as the pre-emption interface and the layout transform.

11.3.4 Task Compaction

Allocation of tasks on an FPGA poses challenging problems. The DISC system (Section 11.3.1) handled this problem in a one-dimensional space. Moving to a two-dimensional space offers more opportunities, but at a greater computation cost to select among the opportunities. Generally, an external controller performs task allocation.

Managing the space of an array of reconfigurable logic as tasks arrive and complete is a primary problem in task allocation. Fragmentation of this space can arise even when tasks are regular in shape (rectangular) and initially tightly compacted. For example, Figure 11.16(a) shows an initial placement of six tasks on a 6×10 FPGA. Suppose tasks 2 and 5 finish, while tasks 1, 3, 4, and 6 continue. Figure 11.16(b) shows the fragmentation of the resulting space. If a request for a 6×3 task arrives, then the FPGA contains a sufficient number of free blocks to place the task, but these are not available in a contiguous 6×3 region.

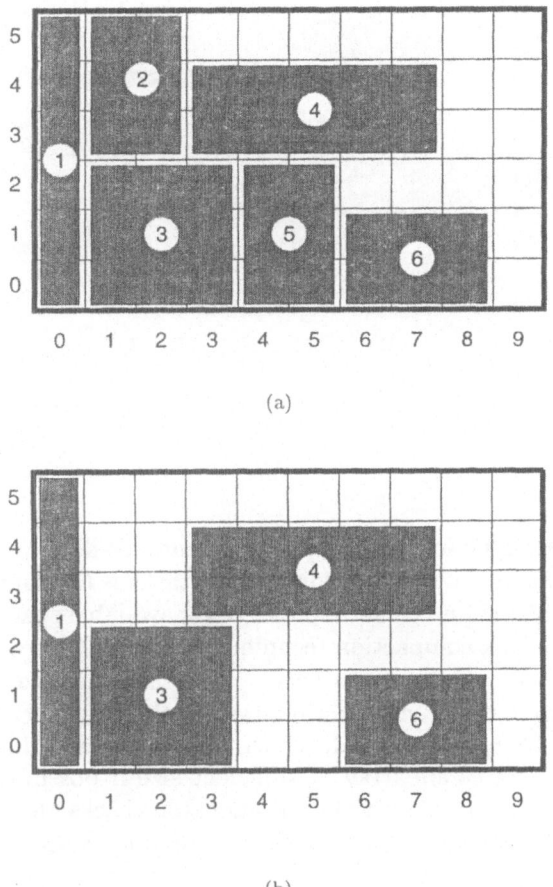

Figure 11.16. (a) Initial placement of six tasks on an FPGA, (b) placement of remaining four tasks after two tasks have completed, showing fragmentation.

Task compaction can help here. *One-dimensional, order-preserving task compaction* slides tasks in one direction as far as possible without rearranging the order of the tasks. Figure 11.17 shows tasks 1, 3, 4, and 6 compacted to the right as far as possible without overlapping or changing their order. As is clear in the figure, one can now place a 6×3 task in the region freed up by compacting the other tasks.

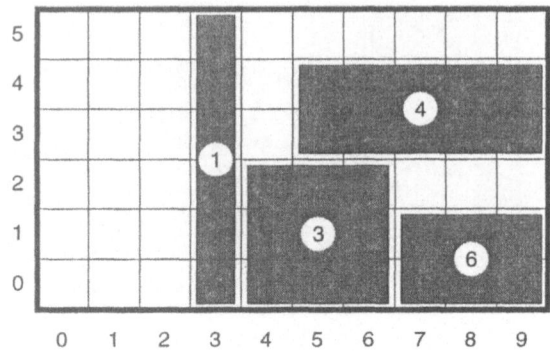

Figure 11.17. Tasks after a one-dimensional, order-preserving compaction to the right.

This task compaction heuristic is not guaranteed to be optimal, but since the problem of optimally compacting tasks is NP-complete, it provides a quickly computed method of freeing available space.

Overall, the task compaction technique works as follows. As the tasks arrive, a task allocator queues them. The task allocator attempts to find a subarray for the next pending task in the queue according to the *Bottom Left Allocation* method, which assigns an incoming task to the bottom leftmost free subarray of sufficient size if possible. If a subarray cannot be found, then the task allocator checks the possibility of compacting the currently active tasks as explained below.

DEFINITION 11.1 For active task T_k and incoming task T, the *top cell interval* extends in the row immediately above T_k from the right edge of T_k to the left for a distance one less than the sum of the widths of T_k and T; the *right cell interval* extends in the column immediately to the right of T_k from the top edge of T_k down for a distance one less than the sum of the heights of T_k and T.

To avoid searching all cells as possible base locations after a compaction, the task allocator examines cells in the intersection of top cell intervals and right cell intervals. This heuristic aims to minimize the cost of moving tasks in compaction. Call the bottom left cell assigned to a task as the *base* of the task. Placing the base of task T in the top (or right) cell interval of an active task T_k places T as close to T_k as possible without having to compact T_k.

To identify candidate cells to serve as the base of a new task, use a directed graph called the *visibility graph* having active tasks as its vertices. A task S *dominates* a task T if they occupy a common row and S is to the left of T. Task S *directly dominates* T if no task R exists such that S dominates R and R dominates T. The visibility graph has an edge from vertex S to vertex T if S directly dominates T. Assign to the edge from S to T the distance (minimum gap) from task S to dominated task T. (For example, see Figure 11.18.) Sum the edge distances in a

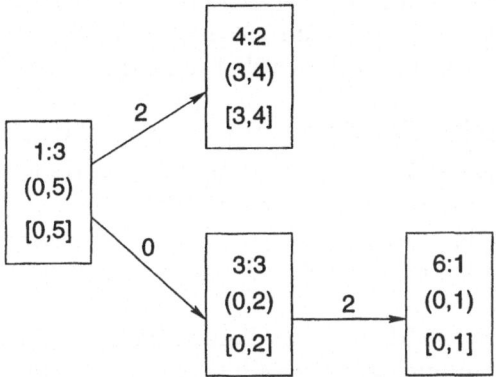

Figure 11.18. Visibility graph for Figure 11.16(b). A vertex labeled $\alpha : \beta$; (γ, δ); $[\rho, \eta]$ uses the following interpretation: α = task, β =compaction distance, which is the maximum distance that the task can move to the right when tasks are compacted, γ, δ =rows covered by task, and ρ, η =rows covered by subgraph.

bottom-up fashion to compute the maximum distance a task can move to the right in a compaction. For every potential base b from the set B of candidate bases (intersection of top cell intervals and right cell intervals), search those subgraphs whose covered rows intersect the allocation site based at b. Choose the allocation site with minimum cost of freeing its site of active tasks and then compact the necessary tasks to the right.

11.4   Alternative Implementations

Thus far in this chapter, the RTR systems have been implicitly or explicitly based on commercial FPGAs. This has advantages—a well-defined foundation and potential for adoption by existing FPGA users. Drawbacks exist, however. FPGA structures typically lend themselves to logic emulation, as that was their initial purpose. They attain flexibility at the cost of large compilation times and reconfiguration times that can be large in an RTR setting. Over the past decade, researchers have developed specialized systems tuned to RTR. We review some early implementations (Section 11.4.1) and then more recent ones (Section 11.4.2). We will emphasize three research directions: coarse-grained logic blocks, context-switching, and self-reconfiguration. Coarse-grained blocks attempt to realize a small (4-bit or 8-bit) ALU in each logic block to simplify RTR design for arithmetic and to reduce the number of configuration bits. A context-switching FPGA can store multiple configurations and switch between an active and a stored configuration quickly. A user needs to pay a substantial amount of time to load a configuration only on initialization and a tiny amount of time on a context-switch. Self-reconfiguration moves the initiative for a configuration change from a global controller down to the level of individual blocks.

11.4.1 Early Configurable Computing Machines

The YUPPIE chip, PAM, and Splash-2 were three early implementations of reconfigurable systems. The YUPPIE chip was in the direction of an HVR-Mesh implementation (see Section 3.1.1), while the other two had the ability to change configurations as a central principle, though not at run-time.

The **YUPPIE** (Yorktown Ultra Parallel Polymorphic Image Engine) system was built around an array of bit-serial processing elements (PEs) connected by a torus. Each PE had four ports and could fuse pairs of opposite ports. In this manner, it could form horizontal and vertical buses. PEs operated in SIMD fashion, with each containing a one-bit ALU and a few one-bit registers. The YUPPIE chip contained a 4×4 array of PEs.

The **PAM** (Programmable Active Memories) system is a reconfigurable co-processor (Figure 11.19). The name arises because the processor can write to and read from the PAM, like a memory, but the PAM processes data between the write and read operations, hence, it is active. Its DECPeRLe-1 realization included 23 FPGAs—a 4×4 computational core and the others used for switching and control. It also included some RAM to buffer and reorder local data. Since the computational core is made up of FPGAs, its processing can change with a change in configuration bitstream, so this is programmable—or reconfigurable in our terminology. Like RTR systems since, PAM found its best applications in problems with high computing power requirements (such as a heat equation solver, Viterbi decoder, and sound synthesizer), real-time constraints (such as a calorimeter and stereoscopic vision system), or non-standard data formats.

Splash-2 operated as an attached processor appended to a host computer via an expansion bus. It contained 17 FPGAs. Sixteen of these serve as the computing surface, operating on 32-bit data with four tag

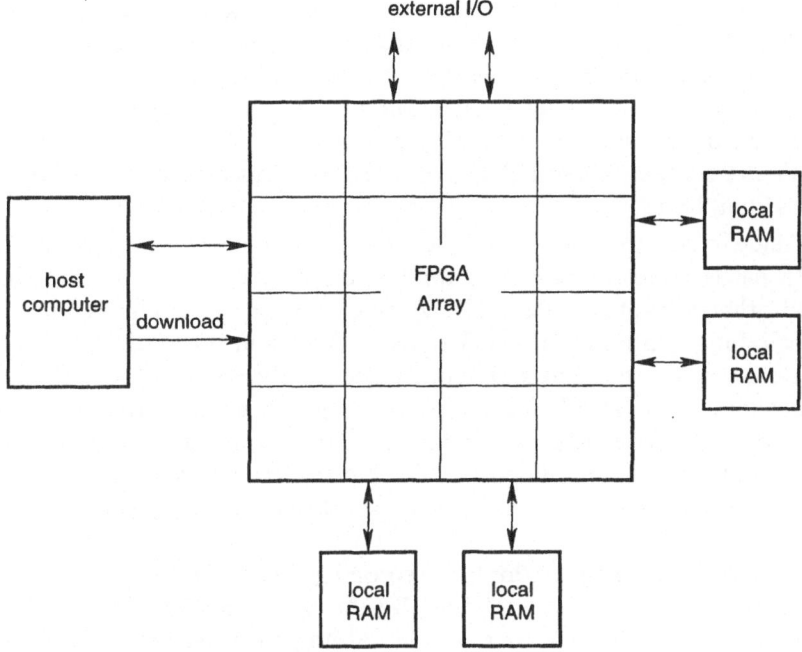

Figure 11.19. Programmable active memories (PAM) structure.

bits. These FPGAs connect through a crossbar, controlled by the 17th FPGA. One can preload up to eight configurations to the crossbar and switch among them quickly. The crossbar also contains a broadcast capability. It was capable of expansion to fifteen processor boards, with each containing 17 FPGAs as described above.

11.4.2 Other Directions in RTR

In this section we will first look at three general, sometimes combined, directions for future RTR systems. One of these, self reconfiguration, could prove useful in implementing dynamically reconfigurable models such as the R-Mesh (Section 11.5). Afterward, we will survey several recent hardware implementations tuned to RTR.

Coarse-Grained Architectures. These architectures do not in themselves facilitate reconfiguration at run-time, but they aim for improved performance on the applications for which RTR is used. Such applications often manipulate integers and so are better served by 4-bit or 8-bit data paths and operators rather than the individual bit manipulation allowed and required by FPGAs. They trade the fine flexibility of FPGAs for size and speed advantages on their target applications. (By the way, in the FPGA context, fine-grained typically refers to function blocks with a few logic gates and coarse-grained typically refers to function blocks with many logic gates or four- or five-input LUTs. In the RTR context, these FPGAs are all fine-grained as they manipulate individual bits.)

Aside from improved size and faster operation by having operators and data paths more tuned to the application, coarse-grained architectures hold other advantages for RTR. They require fewer configuration bits. Specifying a route from point A to point B for four bits of data in a 4-bit word-size coarse-grained architecture needs only one route specification, while doing so on an FPGA requires stating four separate routes, one for each bit. Consequently, reconfiguration times are faster. Furthermore, place-and-route is simplified by the coarser structures. Adaptation to the application compensates for the loss of detailed manipulation.

Context-Switching.   This is the second general architectural enhancement with a purpose of evolving FPGAs in a direction more suitable to RTR. A context-switching chip has storage near each programmable element (function block and interconnection) to hold one or more alternative configurations to the configuration that is currently running on the chip. Furthermore, it can quickly replace the current configuration by a stored configuration. A clear cost of context-switching is the area required for the memory to store contexts on the chip. A clear advantage for RTR is the speed of switching configurations. Garp and Trumpet, described below, incorporate this idea in different forms.

Some context-switching chips load configurations initially and require the chip to stop running to load new configurations. These would work best for computations that cycle through a small number of phases. Others permit the user to change a stored configuration while another configuration is executing. This allows the user to implement RTR schemes that run one part of a circuit while reconfiguring a different part, as introduced early in this chapter. Faster reconfiguration times reached by context-switching afford a larger pool of applications for RTR and an increasing range of problem sizes for which RTR is beneficial.

Self-Reconfiguration.   This is the third general enhancement for RTR. This research direction aims to push the role of initiating a configuration change from a global controller to local function blocks. The setting is an FPGA or, more generally, an array of reconfigurable logic blocks with storage for multiple contexts local to the logic blocks. Self-reconfiguration allows a function block to modify its stored contexts itself. Self-reconfiguration also allows a function block to initiate a context-switch (for its own configuration) itself. These abilities speed up replacing contexts, since changing a context happens locally rather than being loaded from an external source and since multiple function blocks can change their contexts simultaneously. A function block can make changes in response to local input data and intermediate results. (A side effect of the increased ability of the function blocks is increased granularity; indeed, the term processing element (PE), rather than function block, is more common in self-reconfigurable architectures.) Overall, self-reconfiguration adds to the fast configuration swap of context-switching by permitting fast local revisions of stored contexts. Thus, it is ideally suited for RTR.

The notion of self-reconfiguration is also an important step in the direction of implementing models such as the R-Mesh that also reconfigure connections among processors on the basis of local information.

Garp. This architecture combines on the same die a processor with an array of reconfigurable hardware used as an accelerator (Figure 11.20). Rather than aiming for computations in predefined areas such as im-

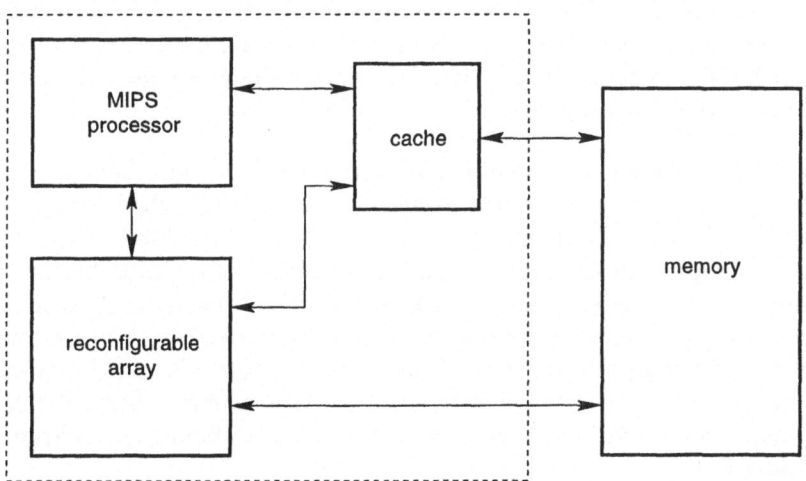

Figure 11.20. Garp structure.
Reprinted with permission from the *Proceedings of the IEEE Symposium on Field-Programmable Custom Computing Machines*, J. R. Hauser and J. Wawrzynek, "Garp: A MIPS Processor with a Reconfigurable Coprocessor," 1997, pp. 12–21 (© 2003 IEEE).

age processing, Garp is tailored to general-purpose computing. Specifically, the reconfigurable hardware accelerates loops of general-purpose programs. It features a high bandwidth, direct path between the reconfigurable array and memory that allows speedy access to precomputed configuration contexts. Furthermore, Garp can store several configurations in a configuration cache that holds recently replaced configurations so that it can reload them even more quickly.

The Garp project also aims for automatic compilation from standard C code. Its compiler is to identify sections of code that reconfigurable hardware can accelerate. For appropriate loops, it performs module mapping and placement, then generates detailed function block configuration data and routing.

PipeRench. This architecture targets pipelined computations. It virtualizes the reconfigurable hardware to overcome problems faced by conventional FPGAs applied to RTR. The pipeline reconfiguration idea is that of pipeline morphing presented earlier in Section 11.2.1. To attain single cycle reconfiguration time for a pipeline stage, PipeRench uses a wide, on-chip configuration buffer. It is structured in rows, called stripes, of processing elements with pass registers and interconnection. Each stripe corresponds to a pipeline stage.

The compiler for PipeRench aims for compilation speed over configuration size. Consequently, it uses a deterministic, linear time, greedy algorithm for place-and-route. It tailors circuit design to data width and performs constant propagation (partial evaluation, see page 424).

Trumpet. This is a test chip that incorporates on-chip memory; lack of on-chip memory often arises as an obstacle to RTR when using conventional FPGAs. Trumpet contains embedded DRAM banks with configurable logic. The design goal is an arrangement of function blocks (in compute pages) and memory blocks (in memory pages) connected by a "fat pyramid" network—a fat tree plus nearest neighbor connections. The core of a compute page is a 5-input look-up table. The on-chip memory blocks can serve as a high-bandwidth data memory, but they can also store configurations. Such storage enables configuration swapping in under 5 μs.

11.5   Designing Implementable R-Mesh Algorithms

In the preceding chapters we developed several techniques and algorithms for reconfigurable models, and explored issues such as scalability and power. These ideas provide a better understanding of the capabilities and limitations of dynamic reconfiguration and identify methods to harness this power. These ideas also implicitly outline certain algorithm design guidelines. For example, the fact that some models (such as the LR-Mesh) have optimal scaling simulations is an important consideration in selecting the underlying model for an algorithm. On the other hand, the fact that some models are less powerful than other must not be ignored. For instance, if a superfast connected components algorithm is the goal, then an LR-Mesh is unlikely to fit the bill.

In this section, we view algorithm design from a hardware implementability perspective. Our discussion addresses questions such as, what can the algorithm designer do to assist in realizing the underlying reconfigurable model? For example, we observed in Chapter 3 that the HVR-Mesh is easier to realize than other models. In this section, we will see why. We will also develop other ideas that that would provide the algorithm designer a better understanding of issues in realizing of reconfigurable models, and describe approaches that address some of these issues.

The power of reconfigurable models such as the R-Mesh stems from its ability to construct fast buses connecting a large number of processors in numerous bus configurations. This is also perhaps the most significant challenge in implementing a dynamically reconfigurable model. In this section we address this issue. In Section 11.5.1, we first discuss bus delay, perhaps the most important consideration for realizing buses in reconfigurable models. Then, we discuss three measures of bus delay (unit cost, log cost, and bends cost). In Section 11.5.2, we present a result for implementing a segmentable bus (Section 1.1) and use this implementation as a building block to realize the HVR-Mesh and the LR-Mesh. We then argue that the bends-cost measure accurately models the bus delay in these implementations. In Section 11.5.3, we revisit a standard LR-Mesh algorithm for adding bits (introduced in Chapters 1 and 2 with the unit-cost measure of bus delay that was adopted so far in this book). We outline a method to convert this algorithm to one that performs well with the bends-cost measure of bus delay. This suggests that (1) the unit-cost measure (the bus delay measure used in the preceding chapters of this book) plays a crucial role in initial stages of algorithm development in which the broad strategy takes shape, and (2) bends cost is a viable measure of bus delay.

11.5.1 Bus Delay

Functionally speaking, a bus is a medium shared by several processors. In the ideal, one processor (or more processors in a concurrent write model) may write to the bus and all processors connected to the bus could instantaneously read the information written. In this section, we consider only linear (non-branching), acyclic buses. Define the *length* of a linear bus β to be $length(\beta)$ = the number of processors connected to bus β (number of taps to the bus). Practical considerations limit bus length. Note that bus length, as defined above, reflects the number of taps to the bus, rather than the physical length of a bus.

A typical bus implementation connects processors to a set of wires (the bus) through input/output drivers. Here, the bus length is limited by the ability of a writer to maintain proper logic levels across all the readers. This arrangement works well as long as the bus length is not very high. Another important consideration is the input capacitances of the readers that limit the speed at which the bus can switch between a logic 0 and a logic 1; the higher the bus length, the greater the capacitance. The term *loading* collectively denotes these effects. An optical bus implementation generally replaces the wire with a waveguide (such as an optical fiber or a slab) and the drivers by optical couplers. Here, a large bus length could cause the energy from a writer to be spread too thinly among the readers; this has an effect similar to the limited driving capability of devices connected to an electrical bus.

In addition to loading, speed of operation is another factor limiting bus length. A reconfigurable bus system contains switches whose states collectively correspond to various bus configurations. The propagation delays of these switches accumulate along the data path of the bus and are the primary limiting factor for the bus length. A reconfigurable optical bus would use optical switches that attenuate the signal traversing them, reducing the amount of energy per unit time that is incident on a detector. In either case, the effect of a bus with large length is a reduced speed of operation. (For example, reconfiguring a bus too fast could alter a data path before information from all of its sources have reached their destinations. Another way bus delay affects speed is by requiring that successive writes to the same bus be separated by sufficient time for information from the first write to propagate to all readers.) We use the term *bus delay* to quantify the detrimental effect of a large bus length. Typically, the speed at which the reconfigurable architecture can operate is inversely proportional to the delay of its buses. The delay of a bus depends on the data path from the writer(s) to the readers. Since this quantity is difficult to ascertain precisely (as the bus configuration can change at each step), it is customary to use *bus delay measures* that estimate the bus delay. An ideal bus delay measure should be both accurate and easy to use. Later in this section we introduce various bus delay measures.

We assume that buses connect physically proximate processors with insignificant propagation delay due to the physical length of the wires or waveguides used in the bus (compared to "bus delay" as defined above).

We now discuss three measures of bus delay.

Let $D(\beta)$ denote the delay of bus β, under a bus delay measure D. For a given "step" of an R-Mesh algorithm, let $\mathcal{B}$ denote the set of buses. The time to perform this step under bus delay measure D is

$$\max \Big\{ D(\beta) \ : \ \beta \in \mathcal{B} \Big\}. \tag{11.1}$$

A conventional view of a linear, acyclic bus as a wire with multiple taps often evokes the "linear-cost" measure in which the delay of a bus is directly proportional to its length (number of processors/ports connected to it); that is for any bus β

$$\text{Linear-Cost}(\beta) = length(\beta). \tag{11.2}$$

Although the linear-cost assumption is simple to justify in practice, it renders most R-Mesh algorithms useless, as they will require at least linear time. A bus, however, is only an abstraction of a shared communication medium, whose implementation need not be restricted to the one described above. That is, other bus delay measures may also be useful. We now describe the unit-cost, log-cost, and bends-cost measures of bus delay. As noted earlier, we describe these measures for a linear, acyclic bus.

Unit Cost. The unit-cost measure of bus delay assumes unit bus delay, irrespective of the length of the bus. That is, for any bus β,

$$\text{Unit-Cost}(\beta) = 1. \tag{11.3}$$

Indeed, this is the measure assumed so far in this book. It has the advantage of simplicity and allows the algorithm designer to focus on reconfigurable computing techniques without having to grapple with details of bus delay. However under current technological constraints, it is not feasible to realize a bus whose delay is independent of its length.

Log Cost. The log-cost measure of bus delay assumes $\log L$ delay for a bus of length L. That is, for any bus β,

$$\text{Log-Cost}(\beta) = \log \Big(length(\beta) \Big). \tag{11.4}$$

Since most algorithms running on an R-Mesh with N processors use at least one bus whose length is polynomial in N, bus delay under the log-cost measure is typically $\Theta(\log N)$. Thus, the log-cost measure is pretty much like a "weighted unit-cost" measure with a $\Theta(\log N)$ weight per unit. It is possible to realize a length-L, segmentable bus with $O(\log L)$ delay (see Theorem 11.2). The log-cost measure also accurately models bus delay in a segmentable bus and an HVR-Mesh, whose buses are simply horizontal or vertical segmentable buses (see Theorem 11.3). A key property that makes this segmentable bus realization possible is that the bus spans a fixed sequence of processors (or ports). In a more general R-Mesh model such as the LR-Mesh (see page 73), a bus can span various combinations of processors, in numerous orders. Indeed under different bus configurations, an exponentially large number of different buses can traverse all processors of the LR-Mesh (see Problem 3.5). Consequently, selecting a realization from a set of all possible bus realizations is not a viable approach. In other words, the log-cost measure of bus delay, while offering simplicity, accurately models only a limited number of configurations.

Bends Cost.   Every linear bus is a sequence of alternating horizontal and vertical bus "pieces" with a bend joining adjacent pieces. Let $bends(\beta)$ denote the number of bends in bus β. With the bends-cost measure, the delay of bus β is

$$\text{Bends-Cost}(\beta) = 1 + bends(\beta). \qquad (11.5)$$

In the next section we show that it is possible to realize an LR-Mesh for which bends cost is an accurate measure of bus delay.

We now illustrate the three delay measures with the buses of Figure 11.21. Assuming unit cost, both buses have unit delay, and with log

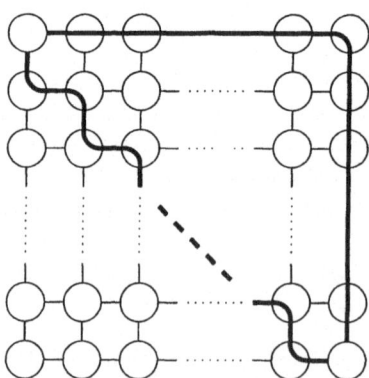

Figure 11.21.   An illustration of bus delay measures using two buses on an $N \times N$ R-Mesh. Both buses (shown bold) have $\Theta(N)$ length.

cost, both buses have $\Theta(\log N)$ delay. With bends cost, however, the bus traversing the perimeter of the R-Mesh has one bend and hence a delay of 2, while the other bus has $2N - 3$ bends and $2N - 2$ delay.

11.5.2 An LR-Mesh Implementation

An LR-Mesh (see page 73) permits each processor to configure itself so that no more than two ports connect to each other. This ensures that all buses in an LR-Mesh are linear (non-branching). In this section we outline an approach to implementing a cycle-free LR-Mesh (one in which each bus is acyclic).

The implementation will evolve in three stages. The first result we present is for a segmentable bus, which one can view as a one-dimensional LR-Mesh (or a one-dimensional HVR-Mesh). This result will easily translate to a corresponding result for a (two-dimensional) HVR-Mesh, a restricted form of the LR-Mesh. Finally, we will put the first two results together to realize the LR-Mesh. In the following results we use the term "actual bus delay" to distinguish it from delays estimated by the measures of Section 11.5.1.

A Segmentable Bus Implementation. Functionally speaking, an N processor segmentable bus (see Section 1.1) has N segment switches (one per processor) placed along the length of the bus. Each processor can set its segment switch to cut the bus between itself and the next processor, or reset its switch to place itself and the next processor on a contiguous portion of the bus. Each processor can read from and write to its sections of the bus. Two bus accesses (reads or writes) are considered concurrent if they are to a contiguous (unsegmented) portion of the bus. Typically, concurrent reads are allowed. If concurrent writes are also allowed, then the segmentable bus is called a CRCW segmentable bus. Key to the power of the segmentable bus is the fact that each processor can set or reset its segment switch independently of other processors' actions. The following result uses a binary tree to implement a segmentable bus.

THEOREM 11.2 *There exists an implementation of a CRCW segmentable bus with N processors for which the actual bus delay is $O(\log N)$.*

Remarks: The constants in the $O(\log N)$ delay are quite small. Since an N processor structure typically has processors of $\Omega(\log N)$ word-size, the above delay is of the order of a few clock cycles.

The following implementations of the HVR-Mesh and the LR-Mesh can use any segmentable bus implementation as a building block. To

capture the generality of the result we will denote the (worst case) actual
bus delay of a $2N$ processor segmentable bus by $\Delta(N)$. (The quantity
$2N$ arises from considering the two ports of each processor in an N
processor linear array as separate entities.) For the implementation of
Theorem 11.2, we have $\Delta(N) = \Theta(\log N)$.

An HVR-Mesh Implementation. An HVR-Mesh (see page 73) is
a two-dimensional R-Mesh in which each bus runs either along a row
or a column; that is, a bus cannot bend between a row and a column.
One way of viewing an HVR-Mesh is as a mesh with a segmentable bus
on each row and each column. This gives the obvious implementation
illustrated in Figure 11.22 and stated in the theorem below.

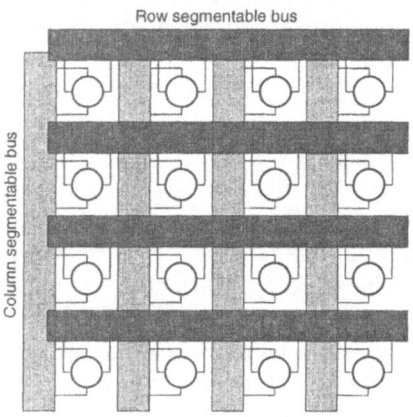

Figure 11.22.   Structure of a 4×4 HVR-Mesh implementation.

THEOREM 11.3 *There exists an implementation of a CRCW $N \times N$
HVR-Mesh for which the actual bus delay is at most $\Delta(N)$, the worst
case actual delay of a $2N$ processor segmentable bus.*

An LR-Mesh Implementation. An LR-Mesh (see page 73) is an
R-Mesh whose buses are all linear (non-branching). Here we assume
the LR-Mesh to also be cycle free (see Problem 3.4). To implement an
$N \times N$ LR-Mesh, first construct an $N \times N$ HVR-Mesh (Theorem 11.3).
Next, use switches within each processor to connect the E and W ports
to the N and S ports; the row (resp., column) segmentable buses control
connections between the E and W (resp., N and S) ports. Figure 11.23
illustrates these switches.

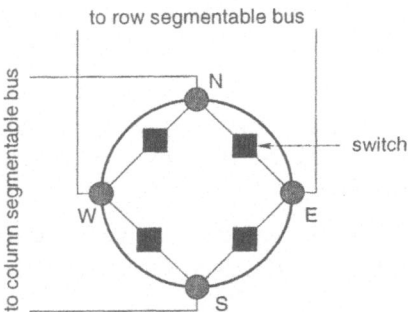

Figure 11.23. Switches within a processor in an LR-Mesh implementation.

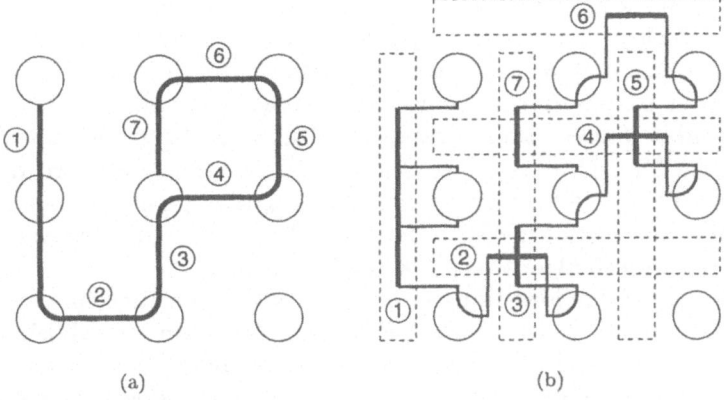

Figure 11.24. A bus delay example for the LR-Mesh implementation. Part (a) shows a sample bus with six bends and seven horizontal and vertical pieces. Part (b) shows the segmentable buses traversed by these pieces. Notice that two non-adjacent bus pieces (numbered 3 and 7) traverse different segments of the same segmentable bus.

A bus β in the above implementation that bends B times traverses $B + 1$ segmentable buses (in succession). (Figure 11.24(a) shows a bus with six bends that traverses seven horizontal or vertical pieces. Figure 11.24(b) shows the corresponding seven segmentable buses traversed in the the implementation.) The actual delay of bus β is (at most) $\Delta(N) \cdot (1 + B)$. Since $\Delta(N)$ usually depends only on the LR-Mesh size and is independent of the length of the bus or the number of bends in it, the above realization of an LR-Mesh has buses whose delay is proportional to that given by the bends-cost measure. Thus, there exists an LR-Mesh realization for which the bends-cost measure is an accurate yardstick of bus delay.

THEOREM 11.4 *There exists an implementation of an $N \times N$ cycle-free LR-Mesh for which the actual bus delay of a bus with B bends is at most $\Delta(N) \cdot (1 + B)$, where $\Delta(N)$ denotes the worst case actual delay of a $2N$ processor segmentable bus.*

Remark: The above result requires concurrent writes (if any) to be resolved by the ARBITRARY, COMMON, COLLISION, or COLLISION$^+$ rules.

11.5.3 Retooling Algorithms for the Bends-Cost Measure

In the preceding section we showed that the bends-cost measure is an accurate estimate of the actual bus delay of an LR-Mesh implementation. Thus, one way to realize a useful LR-Mesh algorithm is by employing buses with as few bends as possible. Given the large body of results for the unit-cost R-Mesh, a more useful approach is to adapt these algorithms to only use configurations whose buses have a limited number of bends. This section outlines a method to convert an LR-Mesh algorithm for adding bits (see Sections 1.2 and 2.3.2) to work within an acceptable bus delay (using buses with a limited number of bends). This approach is more general, however, and can be used to convert several other LR-Mesh algorithms in a similar manner.

The algorithm for adding N bits runs with a constant number of steps on an $(N + 1) \times N$ LR-Mesh. Key to this algorithm is establishing a bus (henceforth called the signal bus) with one end at the top row (row 0) and leftmost column of the LR-Mesh that moves down by one row for each 1 in the input. A signal written to this bus at row 0 reaches row i at the rightmost column of the LR-Mesh if the sum of the input bits is i. Figures 1.6, 2.7, and 11.25(a) show example configurations used by the algorithm with the signal bus in bold. For an instance with $\Theta(N)$ 1s among the N input bits, the signal bus has $\Theta(N)$ bends. In other words, although the algorithm runs in a constant number of steps, it employs buses with $\Omega(N)$ delay (in the worst case). We now describe a method to convert this algorithm to work using buses with at most B bends (hence, $O(B \cdot \Delta(N))$ actual delay), where the algorithm designer can select B to suit technological constraints.

The idea is to first partition the LR-Mesh into sub-LR-Meshes that are small enough to employ buses with at most B bends. For the algorithm for adding bits, this entails partitioning the $(N + 1) \times N$ LR-Mesh into $(N + 1) \times \left\lfloor \frac{B}{2} \right\rfloor$ *level-1 slices*, each with all rows and $\left\lfloor \frac{B}{2} \right\rfloor$ contiguous columns of the LR-Mesh. Cut buses crossing the border between two adjacent slices so that a bus in the original LR-Mesh configuration is broken into segments. Each segment lies within one slice and has at most B bends. Next determine the end points of each bus segment within its slice, and replace it with another bus segment with the same end points, but with only two bends. At this point, every bus segment in a slice has at most two bends. Collect each set of $\left\lfloor \frac{B}{2} \right\rfloor$ contiguous level-1 slices into a "level-2 slice," reconnecting buses across adjacent level-1 slices. Bus segments in a level-2 slice have at most B bends. Now process the level-2 slice in the same manner and replace its bus segments with new segments between the same end points, but with at most two bends. Collect each set of $\left\lfloor \frac{B}{2} \right\rfloor$ contiguous level-2 slices into a level-3 slice. Proceed in the same manner until the algorithm generates a slice that covers the entire N-column LR-Mesh and restricts every bus to at most B bends. It is easy to show that a level-$\Theta\left(\frac{\log N}{\log B}\right)$ slice covers the entire LR-Mesh. In this slice, the signal bus has the same end points as in the original algorithm, but has at most B bends.

Figure 11.25(a)–(c) (distributed over pages 460–462) illustrate this approach. Figure 11.25(a) shows the LR-Mesh configuration for adding input bits $1, 0, 1, 1, 1, 1, 0, 1, 0$. Let B, the maximum number of bends permitted per bus, be six. Observe that the buses of Figure 11.25(a) have many more bends. For example, the signal bus (shown in bold) has 12 bends. The algorithm first partitions the LR-Mesh into slices. For the example there are three slices shown separated by dashed lines in the figure. Each slice has three columns and can have a bus with at most six bends; in the example, the signal bus has six bends within the middle slice. Next, the algorithm determines, for example, that the signal bus spans rows 0–2 of the leftmost level-1 slice, rows 2–5 of the middle slice and rows 5 and 6 of the rightmost slice. As shown in Figure 11.25(b), the algorithm replaces each bus segment of level-1 slices by a bus segment with just two bends; moreover, this new segment spans the same rows as the original segment. To show that the new buses span the same set of rows as the original buses, segments are not shown separated between slices. Observe that only buses that could potentially carry a signal matter for the solution; thus each slice embeds only segments that originate from the leftmost column of the slice and terminate at the rightmost column of the slice. The situation in Figure 11.25(c) does not actually arise when six bends are permitted. We use the figure only to illustrate how the algorithm collects three level-1 slices of Figure 11.25(b) into one level-2 slice that covers the entire LR-Mesh and replaces each original bus by a new bus with at most two bends.

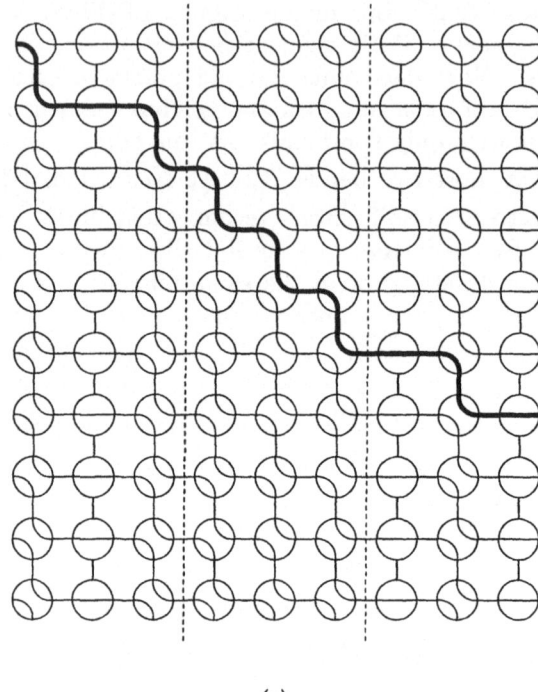

(a)

Figure 11.25.   An example configuration of an LR-Mesh for adding bits. The signal bus is in bold and the vertical dashed lines separate level-1 slices.

From the foregoing discussion it is clear that the algorithm runs in $\Theta\left(\frac{\log N}{\log B}\right)$ steps, each employing buses with at most B bends. With the LR-Mesh realization of Section 11.5.2 we have the following result.

THEOREM 11.5 *For any $B \geq \Delta(N)$, the sum of N bits can be computed on an $(N + 1) \times N$ LR-Mesh with buses of delay at most B in $O\left(\frac{\log N}{\log B - \log \Delta(N)}\right)$ time, where $\Delta(N)$ denotes the delay of a $2N$-element segmentable bus.*

An important observation is that if $B = N^\epsilon$ for $0 < \epsilon < 1$, then the algorithm implied by the above theorem runs in constant time on an implementable R-Mesh model whose bus delay is sublinear in the number of processors spanned by the bus.

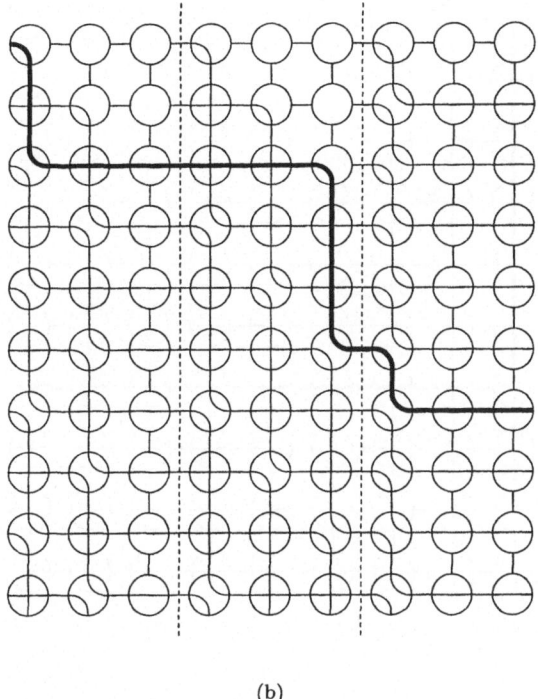

(b)

Figure 11.25 (continued)
The new configuration of level-1 slices (separated by dashed lines). The figure does not show buses segmented between slices.

Problems

11.1 How many different functions can be implemented on a k-input, 1-bit output LUT?

11.2 FPGAs F_1 and F_2 each have n configurable elements and one pin through which configuration bits (and other configuration information including addresses for partial reconfiguration) can be serially streamed into the chip. FPGA F_1 is fully reconfigurable, and FPGA F_2 is partially reconfigurable. Reconfiguring an element of F_1 requires one bit; reconfiguration here proceeds in a regular order, so no addresses are needed. FPGA F_2 has a set of k blocks, each with $\frac{n}{k}$ configurable elements. Any subset of these k blocks can be

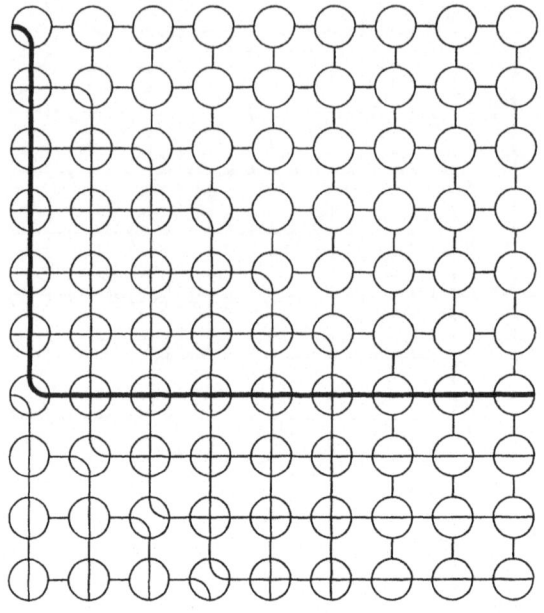

(c)

Figure 11.25 (continued)
A level-2 slice configuration in which each bus is transformed to have at most two
bends, but with the same end points as the original bus.

configured separately, but all $\frac{n}{k}$ elements within a block must be reconfigured when the block is reconfigured. Reconfiguring an element
of F_2 requires an address plus one reconfiguration bit.

Determine the maximum and minimum number of bits needed to
configure $1 \leq x \leq n$ elements of each of F_1 and F_2.

11.3   Design a circuit to add a constant value of 64 to any given 7-bit
       binary integer to produce an 8-bit sum. Assuming AND, OR, NOT,
       NAND, and NOR gates to have unit cost and delay and XOR and
       XNOR gates to have a cost and delay of two units each, compare
       your design with a standard 8-bit ripple-carry adder.

11.4   Repeat Problem 11.3 for constant 85 instead of 64.

11.5   Design an n-bit "constant term" adder to add constant $k > 0$ to any given input. Compare its speed and cost with that of a standard n-bit ripple-carry adder. Do certain values of k lead to simpler and faster constant term adders? Which values?

11.6   Use m-bit LUTs ($2^m \times n$ memories) and other hardware as required to construct an $n \times n$-bit KCM that multiplies an n-bit integer with a n-bit constant to produce a $2n$-bit result.

11.7   Let a traditional $n \times n$-bit multiplier have an^2 cost and $b \log n$ delay. Let the cost of a w-bit wide, n-bit LUT ($2^n \times b$ memory) be $cw2^n$ and let its delay be $d \cdot n$. Let an n-bit adder cost $e \cdot n$ and let its delay be $f \log n$.

Compare the cost and speed of a KCM constructed with b-bit wide, n-bit LUTs with those of a traditional multiplier.

11.8   (a) Construct a multiply-accumulate unit that includes (i) an $n \times n$-bit KCM that produces a $2n$-bit product and (ii) a $2n$-bit adder. Analyze the cost and delay of the multiply-accumulate unit using the parameters of Problem 11.7.

        (b) Construct a circuit comprising multiply-accumulate units to compute the inner product of input vectors with a given constant vector in a pipelined fashion.

11.9   Suppose an RTR solution on a partially reconfigurable FPGA uses m identical modules in each of n iterations. Each module needs to be reconfigured for a new iteration. Suppose the FPGA can hold M modules. Let t_i and t_r denote the times for each iteration and reconfiguration of all modules.

Calculate the total time and describe the method to efficiently perform the computation (ignore buffering, control, etc.) in each of the following cases.

        (a) $M \geq 2m$ and $t_i \geq t_r$

        (b) $m \leq M < 2m$ and $t_i \geq t_r$

        (c) $M < m$ and $t_i \geq t_r$

        (d) $M < m$ and $t_i < t_r$

11.10   An RTR application on a partially reconfigurable FPGA needs a p-stage pipeline. The FPGA can accommodate H units of hardware. Each pipeline stage needs h units of hardware. Each register (for storing partially pipelined quantities) uses g units of hardware. (Ignore hardware requirements for control and data movement.)

Explain how the FPGA runs the application when

(a) $H \geq ph$,

(b) $ph > H \geq \frac{p}{2}(h + g)$,

(c) $ph > H \geq \frac{ph}{2}$, and

(d) $\frac{p}{x}(h + (x-1)g) > H \geq \frac{p}{x+1}(h + xg)$, where $x \geq 2$ is an integer.

11.11   Consider the pipeline of Problem 11.10. Suppose each stage runs in t time and reconfigures in t' time. If n pieces of data are to pass through the pipeline, how long would the FPGA run? Consider all cases of Problem 11.10. Ignore control and register times. Assume that the FPGA can reconfigure while a part of it is running.

11.12   Design an RTR solution for an 8-tap adaptive FIR filter that will use pipelined multiply-accumulate (MAC) units (as opposed to a tree of adders as shown in Figure 11.10). Use parameters from Problems 11.10 and 11.11. Specify your solution for the case where the FPGA can hold eight MAC units and also for the case where the FPGA can hold only four MAC units.

11.13   Design a solution using pipelined MAC units for a two-dimensional (nonadaptive) FIR filter, such as for an image. Assume that the filter has a 3×3 window of filter coefficients that remain fixed for the duration of the computation.

11.14   Solve Problem 11.13 for the case of an adaptive FIR filter in which filter coefficients can change at each step.

11.15   An RTR application has five stages S_1, S_2, S_3, S_4, and S_5. Each stage has multiple possible implementations, for example, S_1^1 and S_1^2 for S_1 and S_2^1, S_2^2, and S_2^3 for S_2 (see Figure 11.26). The tables in Figure 11.27 give the time needed to reconfigure between the implementations of the stages.

Stage	Implementations							
	S_i^1		S_i^2		S_i^3		S_i^4	
S_i	area	time	area	time	area	time	area	time
S_1	110	30	90	35				
S_2	200	50	170	65	150	75		
S_3	310	17	280	21	250	25	200	32
S_4	320	60	300	70	250	90	200	110
S_5	290	45	250	60	200	80		

Figure 11.26. Resource requirements for possible implementations of stages in Problem 11.15.

to	S_2^1	S_2^2	S_2^3
from S_1^1	20	10	10
S_1^2	24	18	12

to	S_3^1	S_3^2	S_3^3	S_3^4
from S_2^1	31	14	18	15
S_2^2	33	25	12	16
S_2^3	30	25	15	20

to	S_4^1	S_4^2	S_4^3	S_4^4
from S_3^1	20	35	17	20
S_3^2	32	25	25	15
S_3^3	30	28	10	15
S_3^4	32	25	20	15

to	S_5^1	S_5^2	S_5^3
from S_4^1	15	25	15
S_4^2	25	22	18
S_4^3	29	18	10
S_4^3	25	20	10

Figure 11.27. Configuration times between possible implementations of stages in Problem 11.15.

Construct a sequence of configurations realizing one stage at a time for each of the following conditions. (Overall time includes computation time and time to reconfigure between stages.)

(a) Minimize overall time.

(b) Minimize area.

(c) Minimize overall time subject to the constraint of maximum area of 200.

(d) Minimize area subject to the constraint of maximum overall time of 340.

11.16   Section 11.2.3.1 on mapping loops to a sequence of RTR configura-
        tions states that a greedy approach can fail. Construct an example
        set of tasks, configurations, and reconfiguration costs such that, from
        configuration C_1, the greedy choice for next configuration is C_2, but
        this choice is not optimal.

11.17   To account for transitions from the last task of a loop to the first
        task in the next iteration of the loop, the method of Section 11.2.3.1
        unrolls the loop m times, where m is the number of configurations
        and is independent of the number of iterations. Explain why this is
        sufficient and why it is not necessary to unroll the loop q times if q
        is the number of iterations.

11.18   The end of Section 11.2.3.1 sketches a pair of heuristics to partition
        a task graph and arrange pipeline stages while constructing an RTR
        implementation of a loop. Describe the algorithm in detail.

11.19   In the DISC system (Section 11.3.1), each task spans the width of the
        FPGA, and the system performs a one-dimensional task allocation as
        new tasks arrive.

        (a)   Assume that the system does not hold information on tasks that
              have not yet arrived. Design an algorithm for task compaction
              on DISC to handle the case when a task arrives requesting r
              rows and r rows are free, but not contiguous.

        (b)   Design an algorithm with improved performance over that of
              part (a) for the case in which the system holds information on
              all tasks to arrive in the future. This information includes the
              size of the task, arrival time, and duration.

11.20   Prove that the reflexive closure of the "dominates" relation (page 445)
        is a partial order. Hence, prove that the visibility graph is acyclic.

11.21   Given a set of tasks placed on an FPGA as shown in Figure 11.28,
        construct the visibility graph for the tasks and compact them to the
        right according to the algorithm of Section 11.3.4.

11.22   What are the advantages and disadvantages of a coarse-grained ar-
        chitecture as compared to a fine-grained architecture? (You may wish
        to consider the issues in terms of speed and size for a 1-bit processing
        element vs. a b-bit processing element.)

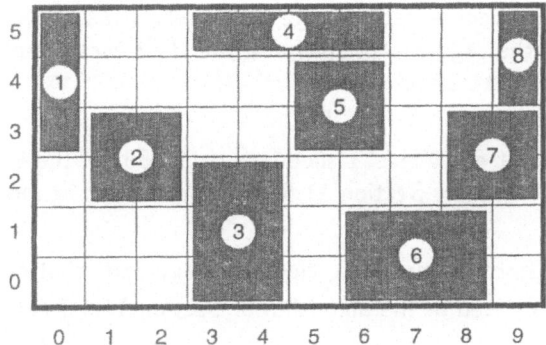

Figure 11.28. Tasks for Problem 11.21.

11.23 Use context-switching to sort by columnsort (Section 5.3.1.1). What is the smallest number of contexts needed?

11.24 Suppose technology limits to L the number of processors that one could physically connect to a wire (bus). Explain how you would construct a "virtual bus" that functions as a bus of length $N \geq L$ (in that it broadcasts a value written from any processor to all other processors). Express the length of a bus cycle on your virtual bus in terms of the length of a bus cycle of a bus of length L constructed by connecting L processors directly to a wire.

11.25 Explain a method to implement a segmentable bus whose delay is logarithmic in its length.

11.26 Generalize the concept of bus delay to non-linear buses. Is this concept different for electrical and optical non-linear buses?

11.27 Prove that the arrangement shown in Figure 11.22 works as a CRCW HVR-Mesh.

11.28 Prove that the implementation illustrated by Figures 11.22 and 11.23 works as an LR-Mesh.

11.29 Why will the implementation of Theorem 11.3 not work for a PRIORITY CRCW LR-Mesh?

11.30   Does the bends-cost measure accurately measure the actual bus delays of the segmentable bus and the HVR-Mesh implementations of Theorems 11.2 and 11.3?

11.31   Prove that every level-1 slice (see page 458) of the LR-Mesh used in the algorithm of Section 11.5.3 has buses with at most B bends.

11.32   Prove that the level of a slice (see page 458) that covers the entire LR-Mesh used in the algorithm of Section 11.5.3 is $\Theta\left(\frac{\log N}{\log B}\right)$.

11.33   Prove Theorem 11.5.

Bibliographic Notes

Several papers offer excellent introductions to configurable computing in general and RTR in particular [34, 43, 61, 79, 80, 112, 139, 196, 197, 339, 341]. In addition to work cited later in this note, some RTR applications work includes papers on image and video processing [114, 289, 307], cryptography [71], DSP [66], networking [42, 44, 88, 137, 138, 208], and neural networks [97, 143].

Papers by Brown and Rose [45] and Rose *et al.* [282] provide clear, detailed introductions to FPGA architecture. Hauck [131] examined the role of FPGAs in reprogrammable systems, with architectural details and a broad scope of configurable computing. FPGA manufacturers such as Xilinx [362, 364, 366] and Atmel [9, 10, 11] provide easy access to detailed information on their products.

Wirthlin and Hutchings [354] cited the range of reduction of reconfiguration bits moving from a fully reconfigurable FPGA to a partially reconfigurable FPGA. In addition to the partially reconfigurable FPGAs cited in Section 11.1, some of the partially reconfigurable FPGAs that have been produced previously are the Xilinx XC6200 family [363] and National Semiconductor's Configurable Logic Array (CLAy) chip [234], and the DynaChip DL6000 and DY6000 families [91, 92].

Bondalapati and Prasanna [35, 39] introduced the HySAM model of a configurable computing system.

Examples of hardware tailored to input data, as described in Section 11.2, include interconnections dependent on an encryption key in DES [175] and rotate distance in a hash function [294]. Examples of the use of constant coefficient multipliers include use in an encryption algorithm, DFT, and filter [51, 69, 358, 365]. Enzler *et al.* [106] described a method to estimate size and timing of relevant FPGA circuits. Additional examples of RTR constant propagation include template matching [206, 342, 356, 357], neural networks [121], and database search [294]. White [353] provided a good introduction to distributed arithmetic, focusing on designs for a multiply-accumulate operation; see also Taylor [311].

An RTR implementation of the IDEA encryption algorithm [358] provides a good example of reconfiguring while computing. Luk *et al.* [193] introduced the concept of pipeline morphing, also used by PipeRench [115].

The RTR solutions in Section 11.2.2 are from the following sources: FIR filtering is from Wojko and ElGindy [358], neural networks are from Hutchings and colleagues [97, 121, 122, 357], motion estimation is from Tanougast *et al.* [307], and database searching is from Shirazi *et al.* [294].

Bondalapati and Prasanna [35, 38] developed the work on mapping loops to reconfigurable architectures described in Section 11.2.3, while Dandalis *et al.* [68] designed generic techniques for RTR handling of graph problems. There are other useful resources on RTR for generic problems [33, 36, 37, 52, 192, 354, 369].

Several papers offer good introductions to hardware operating system-style support for RTR, including Diessel and Wigley [87], Fornaciari and Piuri [112], Robinson and Lysaght [281], and others [43, 49, 86, 149, 176, 295, 301]. Wirthlin and Hutchings [354, 355] created the DISC system; see also Villasenor and Hutchings [339]. Burns *et al.* [47] developed the RAGE system incorporating operating system-style services. Robinson and Lysaght [281] created the configuration controllers of Section 11.3.3, building on prior work of Shirazi *et al.* [295].

Additional researchers have begun looking at related aspects of this problem of controlling an FPGA as a shared computing resource [87, 112]. Diessel *et al.* [86] designed a multitasking operating system to share a board with eight FPGAs among up to eight users. Each user (each task) receives one entire FPGA, that is, each FPGA handles only one task at a time. Jean *et al.* [149] designed a resource manager to allocate and load configurations on a system with eight FPGA chips. Each task may request multiple chips, but without partial reconfiguration of a chip.

Diessel and ElGindy [84] devised the one-dimensional task compaction scheme described in Section 11.3.4. Tatineni and Trahan [310] extended this scheme to a real-time setting in which tasks have given service times and deadlines. Diessel *et al.* [85] investigated more flexible compaction schemes (hence, demanding more computation time) and heuristics for scheduling the task movements, comparing the ordered compaction scheme to local repacking and a genetic algorithm. ElGindy *et al.* [100] applied a genetic algorithm to handle task rearrangement and order of task movements in the setting of an application with input streams at constant data rates.

On the early reconfigurable systems in Section 11.4.1, Maresca and Li [202] introduced the YUPPIE chip in 1989. Vuillemin, Bertin, and others [26, 27, 344] presented Programmable Active Memories. Athanas, Abbott, Arnold, and others [6, 7, 8] introduced and applied Splash-2. AnyBoard [337] was another early reconfigurable system.

Hauser and Wawrzynek [132] and Callahan *et al.* [48] presented the Garp architecture, Goldstein *et al.* [115] described PipeRench, and Perissakis *et al.* [269] developed Trumpet, which embedded DRAM in a reconfigurable array.

Several examples of coarse-grained architectures aimed at RTR exist [70, 129, 130, 203]. Researchers have studied different structures to support context-switching [37, 129, 289]. Sidhu *et al.* [299, 300] described a self-reconfigurable array and its application to string matching.

Several other notable alternative structures for RTR have been proposed by researchers [209, 218, 226, 275, 327, 345].

A discussion of issues related to buses with a large number of taps (such as loading and delay) can be found in Slater [302], Feldman *et al.* [108], and Dharmasena and Vaidyanathan [81, 82, 83]. The unit cost and the log cost bus-delay measures were proposed by Miller *et al.* [213, 215, 216]. El-Boghdadi *et al.* [93, 94, 96] introduced the bends cost measure. They also designed algorithms for the bend cost delay measure, including the algorithm of Section 11.5.3. Details of segmentable bus implementations can be found in Bertossi and Mei [29] and El-Boghdadi *et al.* [93, 95].

References

[1] S. G. Akl and K. A. Lyons, *Parallel Computational Geometry*, Prentice Hall, Englewood Cliffs, New Jersey, 1993.

[2] E. Allender, M. C. Loui, and K. W. Regan, "Complexity Classes," in *CRC Handbook of Algorithms and Theory of Computation*, M. Atallah, ed., CRC Press, (1999).

[3] E. Allender, M. C. Loui, and K. W. Regan, "Reducibility and Completeness," in *CRC Handbook of Algorithms and Theory of Computation*, M. Atallah, ed., CRC Press, (1999).

[4] H. M. Alnuweiri, "A Fast Reconfigurable Network for Graph Connectivity and Transitive Closure," *Parallel Processing Letters*, vol. 4, nos. 1 & 2, (1994), pp. 105–115.

[5] H. M. Alnuweiri, "Parallel Constant-Time Connectivity Algorithms on a Reconfigurable Network of Processors," *IEEE Transactions on Parallel and Distributed Systems*, vol. 6, no. 1, (1995), pp. 105–110.

[6] J. M. Arnold, D. A. Buell, and E. G. Davis, "SPLASH 2," *Proc. 4th Symposium on Parallel Algorithms and Architectures*, (1992), pp. 316–322.

[7] P. M. Athanas and A. L. Abbott, "Image Processing on a Custom Computing Platform," *Proc. 4th International Workshop on Field-Programmable Logic and Applications (Springer-Verlag Lecture Notes in Computer Science vol. 849)*, (1994), pp. 156–167.

[8] P. M. Athanas and A. L. Abbott, "Addressing the Computational Requirements of Image Processing with a Custom Computing Machine: An Overview," *Proc. 2nd Reconfigurable Architectures Workshop*, (1995).

[9] Atmel Corp., "AT6000 Series Configuration," configuration guide, 1999.

[10] Atmel Corp., AT40K FPGAs, data sheet, 2002.

[11] Atmel Corp. web site, http://www.atmel.com

[12] Y. Azar and U. Vishkin, "Tight Comparison Bounds on the Complexity of Parallel Sorting," *SIAM Journal on Computing*, vol. 16, no. 3, (1987), pp. 458–464.

[13] P. Baglietto, M. Maresca, and M. Migliardi, "Pure SIMD Processor Arrays with a Two-Dimensional Reconfigurable Network Do Not Support Virtual Parallelism," *Proc. 1st Reconfigurable Architectures Workshop*, (1994).

[14] P. Baglietto, M. Maresca, and M. Migliardi, "A Parallel Algorithm for Minimum Cost Path Computation on Polymorphic Processor Array," *Proc. 5th Reconfigurable Architectures Workshop (Springer-Verlag Lecture Notes in Computer Science vol. 1388)*, (1998), pp. 13–18.

[15] K. Batcher, "Sorting Networks and Their Applications," *Proc. AFIPS Spring Joint Computing Conference*, (1968), pp. 307–314.

[16] P. Beame and J. Hastad, "Optimal Bounds for Decision Problems on the CRCW PRAM," *Journal of the ACM*, vol. 36, (1989), pp. 643–670.

[17] Y. Ben-Asher, D. Gordon, and A. Schuster, "Efficient Self Simulation Algorithms for Reconfigurable Arrays," *Journal of Parallel and Distributed Computing*, vol. 30, no. 1, (1995), pp. 1–22.

[18] Y. Ben-Asher, K.-J. Lange, D. Peleg, and A. Schuster, "The Complexity of Reconfiguring Network Models," *Information and Computation*, vol. 121, no. 1, (1995), pp. 41–58.

[19] Y. Ben-Asher, D. Peleg, R. Ramaswami, and A. Schuster, "The Power of Reconfiguration," *Journal of Parallel and Distributed Computing*, vol. 13, (1991), pp. 139–153.

[20] Y. Ben-Asher and A. Schuster, "Ranking on Reconfigurable Networks," *Parallel Processing Letters*, vol. 1, no. 2, (1991), pp. 149–156.

[21] Y. Ben-Asher and A. Schuster, "The Complexity of Data Reduction on a Reconfigurable Linear Array," *Journal of Algorithms*, vol. 18, (1995), pp. 322–357.

[22] Y. Ben-Asher and A. Schuster, "Time-Size Tradeoffs for Reconfigurable Meshes," *Parallel Processing Letters*, vol. 6, no. 2, (1996), pp. 231–245.

[23] Y. Ben-Asher and A. Schuster, "Single Step Undirected Reconfigurable Networks," *VLSI Design*, special issue on High Performance Bus-Based Architectures, S. Olariu, ed.; also in *Proc. International Conference on High Performance Computing*, (1997), Bangalore, India.

[24] Y. Ben-Asher and E. Stein, "Basic Algorithms for the Asynchronous Reconfigurable Mesh," *9th Reconfigurable Architectures Workshop* in *Proc. International Parallel and Distributed Processing Symposium*, (2002).

[25] P. Berthomé, T. Hagerup, I. Newman, and A. Schuster, "Self-Simulation for the Passive Optical Star," *Journal of Algorithms*, vol. 34, no. 1, (2000), pp. 128–147.

[26] P. Bertin, D. Roncin, and J. Vuillemin, "Programmable Active Memories: A Performance Assessment," *Proc. Parallel Architectures and Their Efficient Use (Proc. 1st Heinz Nixdorf Symposium, Springer-Verlag Lecture Notes in Computer Science vol. 678)*, (1992), pp. 119–130.

[27] P. Bertin and H. Touati, "PAM Programming Environments: Practice and Experience," *Proc. Workshop on FPGAs for Custom Computing Machines*, (1994), pp. 133–138.

[28] A. A. Bertossi and A. Mei, "A Residue Number System on Reconfigurable Mesh with Applications to Prefix Sums and Approximate String Matching," *IEEE Transactions on Parallel and Distributed Systems*, vol. 11, no. 11, (2000), pp. 1186–1199.

[29] A. A. Bertossi and A. Mei, "Optimal Segmented Scan and Simulation of Reconfigurable Architectures on Fixed Connection Networks," *Proc. IEEE/ACM International Conference on High Performance Computing*, (2000), pp. 51–60.

[30] M. Blum, R. W. Floyd, V. R. Pratt, R. L. Rivest, and R. E. Tarjan, "Time Bounds for Selection," *Journal of Computer and System Sciences*, vol. 7, (1973), pp. 448–461.

[31] V. Bokka, H. Gurla, S. Olariu, and J. L. Schwing, "Constant-Time Convexity Problems on Reconfigurable Meshes," *Journal of Parallel and Distributed Computing*, vol. 27, (1995), pp. 86–99.

[32] V. Bokka, H. Gurla, S. Olariu, and J. L. Schwing, "Constant-Time Algorithms for Constrained Triangulations on Reconfigurable Meshes," *IEEE Transactions on Parallel and Distributed Systems*, vol. 9, no. 11, (1998), pp. 1057–1072.

[33] K. Bondalapati, P. Diniz, P. Duncan, J. Granacki, M. Hall, R. Jain, and H. Zeigler, "DEFACTO: A Design Environment for Adaptive Computing Technology," *Proc. 6th Reconfigurable Architectures Workshop, (Springer-Verlag Lecture Notes in Computer Science vol. 1586)*, (1999), pp. 570–578.

[34] K. Bondalapati and V. K. Prasanna, "Reconfigurable Meshes: Theory and Practice," *Proc. 4th Reconfigurable Architectures Workshop* in *Reconfigurable Architectures: High Performance by Configware*, R. W. Hartenstein and V. K. Prasanna, eds., (1997).

[35] K. Bondalapati and V. K. Prasanna, "Mapping Loops onto Reconfigurable Architectures," *Proc. 8th International Workshop on Field-Programmable Logic and Applications (Springer-Verlag Lecture Notes in Computer Science vol. 1482)*, (1998), pp. 268–277.

[36] K. Bondalapati and V. K. Prasanna, "DRIVE: An Interpretive Simulation and Visualization Environment for Dynamically Reconfigurable Systems," *Proc. 9th International Workshop on Field-Programmable Logic and Applications (Springer-Verlag Lecture Notes in Computer Science vol. 1673)*, (1999), pp. 31–40.

[37] K. Bondalapati and V. K. Prasanna, "Hardware Object Selection for Mapping Loops onto Reconfigurable Architectures," *Proc. International Conference on Parallel and Distributed Processing Techniques and Applications*, (1999).

[38] K. Bondalapati and V. K. Prasanna, "Loop Pipelining and Optimization for Run Time Reconfiguration," *Proc. 7th Reconfigurable Architectures Workshop (Springer-Verlag Lecture Notes in Computer Science vol. 1800)*, (2000), pp. 906–915.

[39] K. Bondalapati and V. K. Prasanna, "Reconfigurable Computing Systems," *Proc. IEEE*, vol. 90, no. 7, (2002), pp. 1201–1217.

[40] A. G. Bourgeois and J. L. Trahan, "Relating Two-Dimensional Reconfigurable Meshes with Optically Pipelined Buses," *International Journal of Foundations of Computer Science*, vol. 11, no. 4, (2000), pp. 553–571.

[41] A. G. Bourgeois and J. L. Trahan, "Fault Tolerant Algorithms for a Linear Array with a Reconfigurable Pipelined Bus System," to appear in *Parallel Algorithms and Applications*.

[42] F. Braun, J. Lockwood, and M. Waldvogel, "Protocol Wrappers for Layered Network Packet Processing in Reconfigurable Hardware," *IEEE Micro*, vol. 22, no. 1, (2002), pp. 66–74.

[43] G. Brebner, "Field-Programmable Logic: Catalyst for New Computing Paradigms," *Proc. 8th International Workshop on Field-Programmable Logic and Applications (Springer-Verlag Lecture Notes in Computer Science vol. 1482)*, (1998), pp. 49–58.

[44] G. Brebner, "Single-Chip Gigabit Mixed-Version IP Router on Virtex-II Pro," *Proc. IEEE Symposium on Field-Programmable Custom Computing Machines*, (2002), pp. 35–44.

[45] S. Brown and J. Rose, "FPGA and CPLD Architectures: A Tutorial," *IEEE Design and Test of Computers*, vol. 13, (1996), pp. 42–57.

[46] J. Bruck, L. De Coster, N. Dewulf, C.-T. Ho, and R. Lauwereins, "On the Design and Implementation of Broadcast and Global Combine Operations Using the Postal Model," *IEEE Transactions on Parallel and Distributed Systems*, vol. 7, no. 3, (1996), pp. 256–265.

[47] J. Burns, A. Donlin, J. Hogg, S. Singh, and M. de Wit, "A Dynamic Reconfiguration Run-Time System," *Proc. Workshop on FPGAs for Custom Computing Machines*, (1997), pp. 66–75.

[48] T. J. Callahan, J. R. Hauser, and J. Wawrzynek, "The Garp Architecture and C Compiler," *IEEE Computer*, vol. 33, no. 4, (2000), pp. 62–69.

[49] E. Caspi, M. Chu, R. Huang, J. Yeh, J. Wawrzynek, and A. DeHon, "Stream Computations Organized for Reconfigurable Execution (SCORE)," *Proc. 10th International Workshop on Field-Programmable Logic and Applications (Springer-Verlag Lecture Notes in Computer Science vol. 1896)*, (2000), pp. 605–614.

[50] C.-C. Chao, W.-T. Chen, and G.-H. Chen, "Multiple Search Problem on Reconfigurable Meshes," *Information Processing Letters*, vol. 58, (1996), pp. 65–69.

[51] K. Chapman, "Constant Coefficient Multipliers for the XC4000E," Xilinx Application Note XAPP 054, 1996.

[52] K. S. Chatha and R. Vemuri, "Hardware-Software Codesign for Dynamically Reconfigurable Architectures," *Proc. 9th International Workshop on Field-Programmable Logic and Applications (Springer-Verlag Lecture Notes in Computer Science vol. 1673)*, (1999), pp. 175–184.

[53] G.-H. Chen, S. Olariu, J. L. Schwing, B.-F. Wang, and J. Zheng, "Constant-Time Tree Algorithms on Reconfigurable Meshes on Size $n \times n$," *Journal of Parallel and Distributed Computing*, vol. 26, (1995), pp. 137–150.

[54] G.-H. Chen, B.-F. Wang, and C.-J Lu, "On the Parallel Computation of the Algebraic Path Problem," *IEEE Transactions on Parallel and Distributed Systems*, vol. 3, no. 2, (1992), pp. 251–256.

[55] G.-H. Chen, B.-F. Wang, and H. Lu, "Deriving Algorithms on Reconfigurable Networks Based on Function Decomposition," *Theoretical Computer Science*, vol. 120, no. 2, (1993), pp. 215–227.

[56] Y.-C Chen and W.-T Chen, "Constant Time Sorting on Reconfigurable Meshes," *IEEE Transactions on Computers*, vol. 43, no. 6, (1994), pp. 749–751.

[57] K.-L. Chung, "Computing Horizontal/Vertical Convex Shape's Moments on Reconfigurable Meshes," *Pattern Recognition*, vol. 29, no. 10, (1996), pp. 1713–1717.

[58] K.-L. Chung, "Image Template Matching on Reconfigurable Meshes," *Parallel Processing Letters*, vol. 6, no. 3, (1996), pp. 345–353.

[59] J. Cogolludo and S. Rajasekaran, "Permutation Routing on Reconfigurable Meshes," *Proc. 4th International Symposium on Algorithms and Computation (Springer-Verlag Lecture Notes in Computer Science vol. 762)*, (1993), pp. 157–166.

[60] R. Cole and U. Vishkin, "Deterministic Coin Tossing with Applications to Optimal Parallel List Ranking," *Information and Control*, vol. 70, no. 1, (1986), pp. 32–53.

[61] K. Compton and S. Hauck, "Reconfigurable Computing: A Survey of Systems and Software," *ACM Computing Surveys*, vol. 34, no. 2, (2002), pp. 171–210.

[62] A. Condon, R. E. Ladner, J. Lampe, and R. Sinha, "Complexity of Sub-Bus Mesh Computations," Technical Report UW-CSE-93-1-02, Department of Computer Science, University of Washington, Seattle, 1993.

[63] S. A. Cook, C. Dwork, and R. Reischuk, "Upper and Lower Time Bounds for Parallel Random Access Machines without Simultaneous Writes," *SIAM Journal on Computing*, vol. 15, no. 1, (1986), pp. 87–97.

[64] D. Coppersmith and S. Winograd, "Matrix Multiplication via Arithmetic Progressions," *Journal of Symbolic Computation*, vol. 9, (1990), pp. 251–280.

[65] T. H. Cormen, C. E. Leiserson, R. L. Rivest, and C. Stein, *Introduction to Algorithms*, 2nd ed., McGraw-Hill, Boston, Massachusetts, 2001.

[66] T. Courtney, R. Turner, and R. Woods, "An Investigation of Reconfigurable Multipliers for Use in Adaptive Signal Processing," *Proc. IEEE IEEE Symposium on Field-Programmable Custom Computing Machines*, (2000), pp. 341–343.

[67] A. Czumaj, F. Meyer auf der Heide, and V. Stemann, "Simulating Shared Memory in Real Time: On the Computation Power of Reconfigurable Architectures," *Information and Computation*, vol. 137, no. 2, (1997), pp. 103–120.

[68] A. Dandalis, A. Mei, and V. K. Prasanna, "Domain Specific Mapping for Solving Graph Problems on Reconfigurable Devices," *Proc. 6th Reconfigurable Architectures Workshop (Springer-Verlag Lecture Notes in Computer Science vol. 1586)*, (1999), pp. 652–660.

[69] A. Dandalis and V. K. Prasanna, "Fast Parallel Implementation of DFT Using Configurable Devices," *Proc. 7th International Workshop on Field-Programmable Logic and Applications (Springer-Verlag Lecture Notes in Computer Science vol. 1304)*, (1997), pp. 314–323.

[70] A. Dandalis and V. K. Prasanna, "Space-efficient Mapping of 2D-DCT onto Dynamically Configurable Coarse-Grained Architectures," *Proc. 8th International Workshop on Field-Programmable Logic and Applications (Springer-Verlag Lecture Notes in Computer Science vol. 1482)*, (1998), pp. 471–475.

[71] A. Dandalis, V. K. Prasanna, and J. D. P. Rolim, "An Adaptive Cryptographic Engine for IPSec Architectures," *Proc. IEEE IEEE Symposium on Field-Programmable Custom Computing Machines*, (2000), pp. 132–141.

[72] A. Datta, "Constant-Time Algorithm for Medial Axis Transform on the Reconfigurable Mesh," *Proc. 13th International Parallel Processing Symposium & 10th Symposium on Parallel and Distributed Processing*, (1999), pp. 431–435.

[73] A. Datta, "Efficient Graph Algorithms on a Linear Array with a Reconfigurable Pipelined Bus System," *Proc. International Parallel and Distributed Processing Symposium*, (2001).

[74] A. Datta, R. Owens, and S. Soundaralakshmi, "Fast Sorting on a Linear Array with a Reconfigurable Pipelined Bus System," *Proc. Workshop on Optics and Computer Science (Springer-Verlag Lecture Notes in Computer Science vol. 1800)*, (2000), pp. 1110–1117.

[75] A. Datta and S. Soundaralakshmi, "Fast and Scalable Algorithms for the Euclidean Distance Transform on the LARPBS," *Proc. Workshop on Advances in Parallel and Distributed Computational Models*, (2001).

[76] A. Datta and S. Soundaralakshmi, "Constant-Time Algorithm for the Euclidean Distance Transform on Reconfigurable Meshes," *Journal of Parallel and Distributed Computing*, vol. 61, no. 10, (2001), pp. 1439–1455.

[77] A. Datta, S. Soundaralakshmi, and R. Owens, "Fast Sorting Algorithms on a Linear Array with a Reconfigurable Pipelined Bus System," *IEEE Transactions on Parallel and Distributed Systems*, vol. 13, no. 3, (2002), pp. 212–222.

[78] H. Davenport, "The Prime Number Theorem," in *Multiplicative Number Theory*, Springer-Verlag, New York, pp. 111-114, 1980.

[79] A. DeHon, "The Density Advantage of Configurable Computing," *IEEE Computer*, vol. 33, no. 4, (2000), pp. 41–49.

[80] A. DeHon and J. Wawrzynek, "Reconfigurable Computing: What, Why, and Implications for Design Automation," *Proc. Design Automation Conference*, (1999), pp. 610–615.

[81] H. P. Dharmasena "Multiple-Bus Networks for Binary-Tree Algorithms," Ph.D Thesis, Department of Electrical & Computer Engineering, Louisiana State University, (2000).

[82] H. P. Dharmasena and R. Vaidyanathan, "An Optimal Multiple Bus Networks for Fan-in Algorithms," *Proc. International Conference on Parallel Processing*, (1997), pp. 100–103.

[83] H. P. Dharmasena and R. Vaidyanathan, "Lower Bound on the Loading of Degree-2 Multiple Bus Networks for Binary-Tree Algorithms," *Proc. International Parallel Processing Symposium*, (1999), pp. 21–25.

[84] O. Diessel and H. ElGindy, "Run-Time Compaction of FPGA Designs," *Proc. 7th International Workshop on Field-Programmable Logic and Applications (Springer-Verlag Lecture Notes in Computer Science vol. 1304)*, (1997), pp. 131–140.

[85] O. Diessel, H. ElGindy, M. Middendorf, H. Schmeck, and B. Schmidt, "Dynamic Scheduling of Tasks on Partially Reconfigurable FPGAs," *IEE Proceedings-Computers and Digital Techniques*, vol. 147, no. 3, (2000), pp. 181–188.

[86] O. Diessel, D. Kearney, and G. Wigley, "A Web-Based Multiuser Operating System for Reconfigurable Computing," *Proc. 6th Reconfigurable Architectures Workshop (Springer-Verlag Lecture Notes in Computer Science vol. 1586)*, (1999), pp. 579–587.

[87] O. Diessel and G. Wigley, "Opportunities for Operating Systems Research in Reconfigurable Computing," Technical Report ACRC-99-018, School of Computer and Information Science, University of South Australia, 1999.

[88] J. Ditmar, K. Torkelsson, and A. Jantsch, "A Dynamically Reconfigurable FPGA-Based Content Addressable Memory for Internet Protocol Characterization," *Proc. 10th International Workshop on Field-Programmable Logic and Applications (Springer-Verlag Lecture Notes in Computer Science vol. 1896)*, (2000), pp. 19–28.

[89] D. P. Doctor and D. Krizanc, "Three Algorithms for Selection on the Reconfigurable Mesh," Technical Report TR-219, School of Computer Science, Carleton University, 1993.

[90] J. Duato, S. Yalmanchili, and L. Ni, *Interconnection Networks: An Engineering Approach*, IEEE Computer Scoiety Press, Los Alamitos, California, 1997.

[91] DynaChip, "DL6000 Family Fast Field Programmable Gate Array," data sheet, 1998.

[92] DynaChip, "DY6000 Family Fast Field Programmable Gate Array," data sheet, 1999.

[93] H. M. El-Boghdadi "On Implementing Dynamically Reconfigurable Architectures," Ph.D. Thesis, Department of Electrical and Computer Engineering, Louisiana State University, (2003).

[94] H. M. El-Boghdadi, R. Vaidyanathan, J. L. Trahan, and S. Rai, "Implementing Prefix Sums and Multiple Addition Algorithms for the Reconfigurable Mesh on the Reconfigurable Tree Architecture," *Proc. International Conference on Parallel and Distributed Processing Techniques and Applications*, (2002), pp. 1068–1074.

[95] H. M. El-Boghdadi, R. Vaidyanathan, J. L. Trahan, and S. Rai, "On the Communication Capability of the Self-Reconfigurable Gate Array Architecture," *9th Reconfigurable Architectures Workshop* in *Proc. International Parallel and Distributed Processing Symposium*, (2002).

[96] H. M. El-Boghdadi, R. Vaidyanathan, J. L. Trahan, and S. Rai, "On Designing Implementable Algorithms for the Linear Reconfigurable Mesh," *Proc. International Conference on Parallel and Distributed Processing Techniques and Applications*, (2002), pp. 241–246.

[97] J. G. Eldredge and B. L. Hutchings, "Run-Time Reconfiguration: A Method for Enhancing the Functional Density of SRAM-Based FPGAs," *Journal VLSI Signal Processing*, vol. 12, (1996), pp. 67–86.

[98] H. ElGindy, "A Sparse Matrix Multiplication Algorithm for the Reconfigurable Mesh Architecture," Technical Report 96-08, Department of Computer Science and Software Engineering, University of Newcastle, Australia, 1996.

[99] H. ElGindy, "An Improved Sorting Algorithm for Linear Arrays with Optical Buses," Manuscript, 1998.

[100] H. ElGindy, M. Middendorf, H. Schmeck, and B. Schmidt, "Task Rearrangement of Partially Reconfigurable FPGAs with Restricted Buffer," *Proc. 10th International Workshop on Field-Programmable Logic and Applications (Springer-Verlag Lecture Notes in Computer Science vol. 1896)*, (2000), pp. 379–388.

[101] H. ElGindy and S. Rajasekaran, "Sorting and Selection on a Linear Array with Optical Bus System," *Parallel Processing Letters*, vol. 9, no. 3, (1999), pp. 373–383.

[102] H. ElGindy, A. K. Somani, H. Schroder, H. Schmeck, and A. Spray, "RMB – A Reconfigurable Multiple Bus Network," *Proc. 2nd High Performance Computer Architecture Symposium*, (1996), pp. 108–117.

[103] H. ElGindy and L. Węgrowicz, "Selection on the Reconfigurable Mesh," *Proc. International Conference on Parallel Processing*, (1991), vol. III, pp. 26–33.

[104] H. ElGindy and L. Wetherall, "An L_1 Voronoi Diagram Algorithm for a Reconfigurable Mesh," *Proc. 2nd Reconfigurable Architectures Workshop*, (1995).

[105] H. ElGindy and L. Wetherall, "A Simple Voronoi Diagram Algorithm for a Reconfigurable Mesh," *IEEE Transactions on Parallel and Distributed Systems*, vol. 8, (1997), pp. 1133–1142.

[106] R. Enzler, T. Jeger, D. Cottet, and G. Tröster, "High-Level Area and Performance Estimation of Hardware Building Blocks on FPGAs," *Proc. 10th International Workshop on Field-Programmable Logic and Applications (Springer-Verlag Lecture Notes in Computer Science vol. 1896)*, (2000), pp. 525–534.

[107] F. Ercal and H. C. Lee, "Time-Efficient Maze Routing Algorithms on Reconfigurable Mesh Architectures," *Journal of Parallel and Distributed Computing*, vol. 44, no. 2, (1997), pp. 133–140.

[108] M. Feldman, R. Vaidyanathan, and A. El-Amawy, "High Speed, High Capacity Bused Interconnects Using Optical Slab Waveguides," *Proc. Workshop on Optics and Computer Science (Springer-Verlag Lecture Notes in Computer Science vol. 1586)*, (1999), pp. 924–937.

[109] J. A. Fernández-Zepeda, R. Vaidyanathan, and J. L. Trahan, "Scalability of the FR-Mesh under Different Concurrent Write Rules," *Proc. World Multiconference on Systemics, Cybernetics and Informatics*, (1997), vol. 1, pp. 437–444.

[110] J. A. Fernández-Zepeda, R. Vaidyanathan, and J. L. Trahan, "Scaling Simulation of the Fusing-Restricted Reconfigurable Mesh," *IEEE Transactions on Parallel and Distributed Systems*, vol. 9, no. 9, (1998), pp. 861–871.

[111] J. A. Fernández-Zepeda, R. Vaidyanathan, and J. L. Trahan, "Using Bus Linearization to Scale the Reconfigurable Mesh," *Journal of Parallel and Distributed Computing*, vol. 62, no. 4, (2002), pp. 495–516.

[112] W. Fornaciari and V. Piuri, "Virtual FPGAs: Some Steps Behind the Physical Barriers," *Proc. 5th Reconfigurable Architectures Workshop (Springer-Verlag Lecture Notes in Computer Science vol. 1388)*, (1998), pp. 7–12.

[113] P. Fragopoulou, "On Efficient Summation of N Numbers on an N-Processor Reconfigurable Mesh," *Parallel Processing Letters*, vol. 3, no. 1, (1993), pp. 71–78.

[114] J. Gause, P. Y. K. Cheung, and W. Luk, "Reconfigurable Shape-Adaptive Template Matching Architectures," *Proc. IEEE Symposium on Field-Programmable Custom Computing Machines (FCCM '02)*, (2002), pp. 98–107.

[115] S. C. Goldstein, H. Schmit, M. Budiu, S. Cadambi, M. Moe, and R. R. Taylor, "PipeRench: A Reconfigurable Architecture and Compiler," *IEEE Computer*, vol. 33, no. 4, (2000), pp. 70–77.

[116] S. A. Guccione, D. Levi, and D. Downs, "A Reconfigurable Content Address-able Memory," *Proc. 7th Reconfigurable Architectures Workshop (Springer-Verlag Lecture Notes in Computer Science vol. 1800)*, (2000), pp. 882–889.

[117] J. Gunnels, C. Lin, G. Morrow, and R. van de Geijn, "A Flexible Class of Parallel Matrix Multiplication Algorithms," *Proc. 12th International Parallel Processing Symposium & 9th Symposium on Parallel and Distributed Process-ing*, (1998), pp. 110–116.

[118] Z. Guo, "Sorting on Array Processors with Pipelined Buses," *Proc. International Conference on Parallel Processing*, (1992), pp. 289–292.

[119] Z. Guo, "Optically Interconnected Processor Arrays with Switching Ca-pability," *Journal of Parallel and Distributed Computing*, vol. 23, (1994), pp. 314–329.

[120] Z. Guo, R. Melhem, R. Hall, D. Chiarulli, and S. Levitan, "Pipelined Com-munications in Optically Interconnected Arrays," *Journal of Parallel and Dis-tributed Computing*, vol. 12, (1991), pp. 269–282.

[121] J. D. Hadley and B. L. Hutchings, "Design Methodologies for Partially Re-configured Systems," *Proc. Workshop on FPGAs for Custom Computing Ma-chines*, (1995), pp. 78–84.

[122] J. D. Hadley and B. L. Hutchings, "Designing a Partially Reconfigured Sys-tem," *Field Programmable Gate Arrays (FPGAs) for Fast Board Development and Reconfigurable Computing*, J. Schewel, ed., *Proceedings of SPIE*, vol. 2607, (1995), pp. 210–220.

[123] T. Hagerup, "Towards Optimal Parallel Bucket Sorting," *Information and Computation*, vol. 75, (1987), pp. 39–51.

[124] T. Hagerup, "Constant-Time Parallel Integer Sorting," *Proc. ACM Symposium on the Theory of Computing*, (1991), pp. 299–306.

[125] M. Hamdi and Y. Pan, "Efficient Parallel Algorithms on Optically Intercon-nected Arrays of Processors," *IEE Proceedings-Computers and Digital Tech-niques*, vol. 142, no. 2, (1995), pp. 87–92.

[126] Y. Han, Y. Pan, and H. Shen, "Sublogarithmic Deterministic Selection on Arrays with a Reconfigurable Optical Bus," *IEEE Transactions on Parallel and Distributed Systems*, vol. 51, no. 6, (2002), pp. 702–707.

[127] E. Hao, P. D. MacKenzie, and Q. Stout, "Selection on the Reconfigurable Mesh," *Proc. IEEE Symposium on the Frontiers of Massively Parallel Com-putation*, (1992), pp. 38–45.

[128] G. H. Hardy and E. M. Wright, "Statement of the Prime Number Theorem," in *An Introduction to the Theory of Numbers*, Clarendon Press, Oxford, pp. 9–10, 1979.

[129] R. W. Hartenstein, M. Herz, T. Hoffman, and U. Nageldinger, "On Recon-figurable Co-processing Units," *Proc. 5th Reconfigurable Architectures Work-shop (Springer-Verlag Lecture Notes in Computer Science vol. 1388)*, (1998), pp. 67–72.

[130] R. W. Hartenstein, R. Kress, and H. Reinig, "A New FPGA Architecture for Word-Oriented Datapaths," *Proc. 4th International Workshop on Field-Programmable Logic and Applications (Springer-Verlag Lecture Notes in Computer Science vol. 849)*, (1994), pp. 144–155.

[131] S. Hauck, "The Roles of FPGA's in Reprogrammable Systems," *Proceedings of the IEEE*, vol. 86, no. 4, (1998), pp. 615–638.

[132] J. Hauser and J. Wawrzynek, "Garp: A MIPS Processor with a Reconfigurable Coprocessor," *Proc. IEEE Symposium on Field-Programmable Custom Computing Machines*, (1997), pp. 12–21.

[133] T. Hayashi, K. Nakano, and S. Olariu, "An $O((\log \log n)^2)$ Time Algorithm to Compute the Convex Hull on Reconfigurable Meshes," *IEEE Transactions on Parallel and Distributed Systems*, vol. 9, no. 12, (1998), pp. 1167–1179.

[134] T. Hayashi, K. Nakano, and S. Olariu, "Efficient List Ranking on the Reconfigurable Mesh, with Applications," *Theory of Computing Systems*, vol. 31, no. 5, (1999), pp. 593–611.

[135] M. C. Herbordt, J. C. Corbett, and C. C. Weems, "Practical Algorithms for Online Routing on Fixed and Reconfigurable Meshes," *Journal of Parallel and Distributed Computing*, vol. 20, no. 3, (1993), pp. 341–356.

[136] J. E. Hopcroft, R. Motwani, and J. D. Ullman, *Introduction to Automata Theory, Languages, and Computation*, 2nd ed., Addison Wesley, Boston, Massachusetts, 2001.

[137] E. L. Horta and S. T. Kofuji, "A Run-Time Reconfigurable ATM Switch," *9th Reconfigurable Architectures Workshop* in *Proc. International Parallel and Distributed Processing Symposium*, (2002).

[138] B. L. Hutchings, R. Franklin, and D. Carver, "Assisting Network Intrusion Detection with Reconfigurable Hardware," *Proc. IEEE Symposium on Field-Programmable Custom Computing Machines (FCCM '02)*, (2002), pp. 111–120.

[139] B. L. Hutchings and M. J. Wirthlin, "Implementation Approaches for Reconfigurable Logic Applications," *Proc. 5th International Workshop on Field-Programmable Logic and Applications (Springer-Verlag Lecture Notes in Computer Science vol. 975)*, (1995), pp. 419–428.

[140] N. Imlig, T. Shiozawa, K. Nagami, Y. Nakane, R. Konishi, H. Ito, and A. Nagoya, "Scalable Space/Time-Shared Stream Processing on the Run-Time Reconfigurable PCA Architecture," *8th Reconfigurable Architectures Workshop* in *Proc. International Parallel and Distributed Processing Symposium*, (2001).

[141] A. E. Ingham, *The Distribution of Prime Numbers*, Cambridge University Press, Cambridge, UK, 1990.

[142] J. JáJá, *An Introduction to Parallel Algorithms*, Addison-Wesley Publishing Co., Reading, Massachusetts, 1992.

482 DYNAMIC RECONFIGURATION

[143] P. James-Roxby and B. Blodget, "Adapting Constant Multipliers in a Neural Network Implementation," *Proc. IEEE IEEE Symposium on Field-Programmable Custom Computing Machines*, (2000), pp. 335–336.

[144] J.-W. Jang, M. Nigam, V. K. Prasanna, and S. Sahni, "Constant Time Algorithms for Computational Geometry on the Reconfigurable Mesh," *IEEE Transactions on Parallel and Distributed Systems*, vol. 8, (1997), pp. 1–12.

[145] J. Jang, H. Park, and V. Prasanna, "A Bit Model of Reconfigurable Mesh," *Proc. 1st Reconfigurable Architectures Workshop*, (1994).

[146] J. Jang, H. Park, and V. Prasanna, "A Fast Algorithm for Computing a Histogram on Reconfigurable Mesh," *IEEE Transactions on Pattern Analysis and Machine Intelligence*, vol. 17, no. 2, (1995), pp. 97–106.

[147] J. Jang, H. Park, and V. Prasanna, "An Optimal Multiplication Algorithm on Reconfigurable Mesh," *IEEE Transactions on Parallel and Distributed Systems*, vol. 8, no. 5, (1997), pp. 521–532.

[148] J.-w. Jang and V. K. Prasanna, "An Optimal Sorting Algorithm on Reconfigurable Mesh," *Journal of Parallel and Distributed Computing*, vol. 25, no. 1, (1995), pp. 31–41.

[149] J. S. N. Jean, K. Tomko, V. Yavagal, J. Shah, and R. Cook, "Dynamic Reconfiguration to Support Concurrent Applications," *IEEE Transactions on Computers*, vol. 48, no. 6, (1999), pp. 591–602.

[150] J. Jenq and S. Sahni, "Image Shrinking and Expanding on a Pyramid," *IEEE Transactions on Parallel and Distributed Systems*, vol. 4, no. 11, (1993), pp. 1291–1296.

[151] D. S. Johnson, "A Catalog of Complexity Classes," in *Handbook of Theoretical Computer Science, Vol. A: Algorithms and Complexity*, J. van Leeuwen, ed., MIT Press, (1990), pp. 67–162.

[152] P. Jordan, "Reconfigurable Computing Aims at Signal Processing," *EE Times* on-line, (2002), http://www.eetimes.com/story/OEG20020208S0064.

[153] T.-W. Kao, S.-J. Horng, and H.-R. Tsai, "Computing Connected Components and Some Related Applications on a RAP," *Proc. International Conference on Parallel Processing*, (1993), vol. III, pp. 57–64.

[154] T.-W. Kao, S.-J. Horng, and Y.-L. Wang, "An $O(1)$ Time Algorithms for Computing Histogram and Hough Transform on a Cross-bridge Reconfigurable Array of Processors," *IEEE Transactions on Systems, Man and Cybernetics*, vol. 25, no. 4, (1995), pp. 681–687.

[155] A. Kapoor, H. Shröder, and B. Beresford-Smith, "Deterministic Permutation Routing on a Reconfigurable Mesh," *Proc. International Parallel Processing Symposium*, (1994), pp. 536–540.

[156] R. M. Karp and V. Ramachandran, "Parallel Algorithms for Shared-Memory Machines," in *Handbook of Theoretical Computer Science, Vol. A: Algorithms and Complexity*, J. van Leeuwen, ed., MIT Press, (1990), pp. 869–941.

[157] M. Kaufman, H. Shröder, and J. F. Sibeyn, "Routing and Sorting on Reconfigurable Meshes," *Parallel Processing Letters*, vol. 5, no. 1, (1995), pp. 81–95.

[158] H.-G. Kim and Y.-K. Cho, "Point Visibility of a Simple Polygon on Reconfigurable Mesh," *Proc. 5th IEEE Symposium on Parallel and Distributed Processing*, (1993), pp. 748–751.

[159] M. Kim and J.-W. Jang, "Fast Quadtree Building on a Reconfigurable Mesh," *Proc. 3rd Reconfigurable Architectures Workshop*, (1996).

[160] S. K. Kim, "Constant-Time RMESH Algorithms for the Range Minima and Co-Minima Problems," *Parallel Processing Letters*, vol. 24, (1998), pp. 965–977.

[161] I. Koren, *Computer Arithmetic Algorithms*, Prentice Hall, Englewood Cliffs, New Jersey, 1993.

[162] R. Kreuger, "Virtex-EM FIR Filter for Video Applications," Xilinx application note XAPP241, (2000).

[163] C. Kruskal, "Searching, Merging, and Sorting in Parallel Computation," *IEEE Transactions on Computers*, vol. C-32, no. 10, (1983), pp. 942–946.

[164] J. B. Kruskal, "On the Shortest Spanning Subtree of a Graph and the Traveling Salesman Problem," *Proceedings of the American Mathematical Society*, vol. 7, (1956), pp. 48–50.

[165] V. Kumar, A. Grama, A. Gupta, and G. Karypis, *Introduction to Parallel Algorithms*, Benjamin/Cummins Publishing Co., Redwood City, California, 1994.

[166] M. Kunde, "Lower Bounds for Sorting on Mesh-Connected Architectures," *Acta Informatica*, vol. 24, (1987), pp. 121–130.

[167] M. Kunde and K. Gürtzig, "Efficient Sorting and Routing on Reconfigurable Meshes Using Restricted Bus Length," *Proc. International Parallel Processing Symposium*, (1997), pp. 713–720.

[168] T. H. Lai and M.-J. Sheng, "Constructing Euclidean Minimum Spanning Trees and All Nearest Neighbors on Reconfigurable Meshes," *IEEE Transactions on Parallel and Distributed Systems*, vol. 7, no. 8, (1996), pp. 806–817.

[169] S.-S. Lee, S.-J. Horng, H.-R. Tsai, and S.-S. Tsai, "Building a Quadtree and Its Applications on a Reconfigurable Mesh," *Pattern Recognition*, vol. 29, no. 9, (1996), pp. 1571–1579.

[170] R. S. Lehman, "On the Difference $\pi(x) - \text{li}(x)$," *Acta Arithmetica*, vol. 11, (1966), pp. 397–410.

[171] D. J. Lehmann, "Algebraic Structures for Transitive Closure," *Theoretical Computer Science*, vol. 4, no. 1, (1977), pp. 59–76.

[172] T. Leighton, *Complexity Issues in VLSI*, MIT Press, Cambridge, Massachusetts, 1983.

[173] T. Leighton, "Tight Bounds on the Complexity of Parallel Sorting," *IEEE Transactions on Computers*, vol. 34, (1985), pp. 344–354.

[174] T. Leighton, *Introduction to Parallel Algorithms and Architectures: Arrays · Trees · Hypercubes*, Morgan Kaufmann Publishers, San Mateo, California, 1992.

[175] J. Leonard and W. H. Mangione-Smith, "A Case Study of Partially Evaluated Hardware Circuits: Key-Specific DES," *Proc. 7th International Workshop on Field-Programmable Logic and Applications (Springer-Verlag Lecture Notes in Computer Science vol. 1304)*, (1997), pp. 151–160.

[176] L. Levinson, R. Männer, M. Sessler, and H. Simmler, "Preemptive Multitasking on FPGAs," *Proc. IEEE IEEE Symposium on Field-Programmable Custom Computing Machines*, (2000), pp. 301–302.

[177] S. Levitan, D. Chiarulli, and R. Melhem, "Coincident Pulse Techniques for Multiprocessor Interconnection Structures," *Applied Optics*, vol. 29, no. 14, (1990), pp. 2024–2039.

[178] P. S. Lewis and S. Y. Kung, "Dependence Graph Based Design of Systolic Arrays for the Algebraic Path Problem," *Proc. 12th Asilomar Conference on Signals, Systems, and Computers*, (1986), pp. 13–18.

[179] H. Li and M. Maresca, "Polymorphic Torus Architecture for Computer Vision," *IEEE Transactions on Pattern Analysis and Machine Intelligence*, vol. 11, (1989), pp. 233–243.

[180] H. Li and M. Maresca, "Polymorphic Torus Network," *IEEE Transactions on Computers*, vol. 38, (1989), pp. 1345–1351.

[181] H. Li and Q. F. Stout, "Reconfigurable SIMD Massively Parallel Processors," *Proceedings of the IEEE*, vol. 79, no. 4, (1991), pp. 429–443.

[182] K. Li, "Fast and Scalable Parallel Matrix Computations with Optical Buses," *Proc. Workshop on Optics and Computer Science (Springer-Verlag Lecture Notes in Computer Science vol. 1800)*, (2000), pp. 1053–1062.

[183] K. Li, Y. Pan, and S. Q. Zheng, "Fast and Efficient Parallel Matrix Multiplication Algorithms on a Linear Array with a Reconfigurable Pipelined Bus System," *IEEE Transactions on Parallel and Distributed Systems*, vol. 9, no. 8, (1998), pp. 705–720.

[184] K. Li, Y. Pan, and S. Q. Zheng, "Parallel Matrix Computations Using a Reconfigurable Pipelined Optical Bus," *Journal of Parallel and Distributed Computing*, vol. 59, no. 1, (1999), pp. 13–30.

[185] K. Li, Y. Pan, and S. Q. Zheng, "Efficient Deterministic and Probabilistic Simulations of PRAMs on Linear Arrays with Reconfigurable Pipelined Bus Systems," *Journal of Supercomputing*, vol. 15, no. 2, (2000), pp. 163–181.

[186] Y. Li, Y. Pan, and S. Q. Zheng, "Pipelined Time-Division Multiplexing Optical Bus with Conditional Delays," *Optical Engineering*, vol. 36, no. 9, (1997), pp. 2417–2424.

[187] R. Lin, "Fast Algorithms for Lowest Common Ancestors on a Processor Array with Reconfigurable Buses," *Information Processing Letters*, vol. 40, (1991), pp. 223–230.

[188] R. Lin and S. Olariu, "Reconfigurable Buses with Shift Switching: Concepts and Applications," *IEEE Transactions on Parallel and Distributed Systems*, vol. 6, no. 1, (1995), pp. 93–102.

[189] R. Lin and S. Olariu, "An Efficient VLSI Architecture for Columnsort," *IEEE Transactions on VLSI Systems*, vol. 7, (1999), pp. 135–139.

[190] R. Lin, S. Olariu, J. L. Schwing, and J. Zhang, "Sorting in $O(1)$ Time on an $n \times n$ Reconfigurable Mesh," *Proc. 9th European Workshop on Parallel Computing*, (1992), pp. 16–27.

[191] Y.-W. Lu, J. B. Burr, and A. M. Peterson, "Permutation on a Mesh with Reconfigurable Bus: Algorithm and Practical Consideration," *Proc. 7th International Parallel Processing Symposium*, (1993), pp. 298–308.

[192] W. Luk, A. Derbyshire, S. Guo, and D. Siganos, "Serial Hardware Libraries for Reconfigurable Designs," *Proc. 9th International Workshop on Field-Programmable Logic and Applications (Springer-Verlag Lecture Notes in Computer Science vol. 1673)*, (1999), pp. 186–194.

[193] W. Luk, N. Shirazi, S. R. Guo, and P. Y. K. Cheung, "Pipeline Morphing and Virtual Pipelines," *Proc. 7th International Workshop on Field-Programmable Logic and Applications (Springer-Verlag Lecture Notes in Computer Science vol. 1304)*, (1997), pp. 111–120.

[194] P. D. MacKenzie, "A Separation Between Reconfigurable Mesh Models," *Parallel Processing Letters*, vol. 5, no. 1, (1995), pp. 15–22.

[195] B. M. Maggs and S. A. Plotkin, "Minimum-Cost Spanning Tree as a Path Finding Problem," *Information Processing Letters*, vol. 26, no. 6, (1988), pp. 291–293.

[196] W. H. Mangione-Smith and B. L. Hutchings, "Configurable Computing: The Road Ahead," *Proc. 4th Reconfigurable Architectures Workshop* in *Reconfigurable Architectures: High Performance by Configware*, R. W. Hartenstein and V. K. Prasanna, eds., (1997).

[197] W. H. Mangione-Smith, B. Hutchings, D. Andrews, A. DeHon, C. Ebeling, R. Hartenstein, O. Mencer, J. Morris, K. Palem, V. K. Prasanna, and H. A. E. Spaanenburg, "Seeking Solutions in Configurable Computing," *IEEE Computer*, vol. 30, no. 12, (1997), pp. 38–43.

[198] Y. Maon, B. Schieber, and U. Vishkin, "Parallel Ear Decomposition Search (EDS) and st-Numbering in Graphs," *Theoretical Computer Science*, vol. 47, no. 3, (1986), pp. 277–296.

[199] J. M. Marberg and E. Gafni, "Sorting in Constant Number of Row and Column Phases on a Mesh," *Algorithmica*, vol. 3, (1988), pp. 561–572.

[200] M. Maresca, "Polymorphic Processor Arrays," *IEEE Transactions on Parallel and Distributed Systems*, vol. 4, no. 5, (1993), pp. 490–506.

[201] M. Maresca and P. Baglietto, "Transitive Closure and Graph Component Labeling on Realistic Processor Arrays Based on Reconfigurable Mesh Network," *Proc. IEEE International Conference on Computer Design: VLSI in Computers and Processors*, (1991), pp. 229–232.

[202] M. Maresca and H. Li, "Connection Autonomy in SIMD Computers: A VLSI Implementation," *Journal of Parallel and Distributed Computing*, vol. 7, (1989), pp. 302–320.

[203] A. Marshall, T. Stansfield, I. Kostarnov, J. Vuillemin, and B. Hutchings, "A Reconfigurable Arithmetic Array for Multimedia Applications," *Proc. 1999 ACM/SIGDA 7th International Symposium on Field Programmable Gate Arrays*, (1999), pp. 135–143.

[204] Y. Matias and A. Schuster, "Fast, Efficient Mutual and Self Simulations for Shared Memory and Reconfigurable Mesh," *Parallel Algorithms and Applications*, vol. 8, (1996), pp. 195–221.

[205] S. Matsumae and N. Tokura, "Simulation Algorithms Among Enhanced Mesh Models," *Institute of Electronics, Information and Communication Engineers (IEICE) Transactions on Information and Systems*, vol. E82-D, no. 10, (1999), pp. 1324–1337.

[206] G. McGregor and P. Lysaght, "Self Controlling Dynamic Reconfiguration: A Case Study," *Proc. 9th International Workshop on Field-Programmable Logic and Applications (Springer-Verlag Lecture Notes in Computer Science vol. 1673)*, (1999), pp. 144–154.

[207] R. Melhem, D. Chiarulli, and S. Levitan, "Space Multiplexing of Waveguides in Optically Interconnected Multiprocessor Systems," *The Computer Journal*, vol. 32, no. 4, (1989), pp. 362–369.

[208] G. Memik, S. O. Memik, and W. H. Mangione-Smith, "Design and Analysis of a Layer Seven Network Processor Accelerator using Reconfigurable Logic," *Proc. IEEE Symposium on Field-Programmable Custom Computing Machines (FCCM '02)*, (2002), pp. 131–140.

[209] S. Memik and M. Sarrafzadeh, "Strategically Programmable Systems," *8th Reconfigurable Architectures Workshop* in *Proc. International Parallel and Distributed Processing Symposium*, (2001).

[210] M. Middendorf and H. ElGindy, "Matrix Multiplication on Processor Arrays with Optical Buses," *Informatica*, vol. 22, (1999), pp. 255–262.

[211] M. Middendorf, H. Schmeck, and G. Turner, "Sparse Matrix Multiplication on a Reconfigurable Mesh," *Australian Computer Journal*, vol. 27, no. 2, (1995), pp. 37–40.

[212] G. L. Miller and V. Ramachandran, "Efficient Parallel Ear Decomposition with Applications," manuscript, Mathematical Sciences Research Institute, Berkeley, CA, 1986.

[213] R. Miller, V. K. Prasanna-Kumar, D. I. Reisis, and Q. F. Stout, "Parallel Computations on Reconfigurable Meshes," Technical Report TR IRIS#229, Department of Computer Science, University of Southern California, 1987.

[214] R. Miller, V. K. Prasanna-Kumar, D. I. Reisis, and Q. F. Stout, "Data Movement Operations and Applications on Reconfigurable VLSI Arrays," *Proc. International Conference on Parallel Processing*, (1988), vol. 1, pp. 205–208.

[215] R. Miller, V. K. Prasanna-Kumar, D. I. Reisis, and Q. F. Stout, "Meshes with Reconfigurable Buses," *Proc. 5th MIT Conference on Advanced Research in VLSI*, (1988), pp. 163–178.

[216] R. Miller, V. Prasanna-Kumar, D. Reisis, and Q. Stout, "Parallel Computing on Reconfigurable Meshes," *IEEE Transactions on Computers*, vol. 42, no. 6, (1993), pp. 678–692.

[217] D. S. Mitrinović, *Analytic Inequalities*, Springer-Verlag, New York, 1970.

[218] C. A. Moritz, D. Yeung, and A. Agarwal, "Exploring Optimal Performance-Cost Designs for Raw Microprocessors," *Proc. Symposium on FPGAs for Custom Computing Machines*, (1998), pp. 12–27.

[219] J. M. Moshell and J. Rothstein, "Bus Automata and Immediate Languages," *Information and Control*, vol. 40, (1979), pp. 88–121.

[220] R. Motwani and P. Raghavan, *Randomized Algorithms*, Cambridge University Press, Cambridge, UK, 1995.

[221] J. I. Munro and M. S. Paterson, "Selection and Sorting with Limited Storage," *Theoretical Computer Science*, vol. 12, (1980), pp. 315–323.

[222] M. M. Murshed "The Reconfigurable Mesh: Programming Model, Self-Simulation, Adaptablility, Optimality, and Applications," Ph.D. Thesis, The Australian National University, (1999).

[223] M. M. Murshed and R. P. Brent, "Constant Time Algorithms for Computing the Contour of Maximal Elements on the Reconfigurable Mesh," *Proc. International Conference on Parallel and Distributed Systems*, (1997), pp. 172–177.

[224] M. M. Murshed and R. P. Brent, "Adaptive AT^2 Optimal Algorithms on Reconfigurable Meshes," Technical Report TR-CS-98-02, Department of Computer Science, Australian National University, 1998.

[225] H. Nagano, A. Matsura, and A. Nagoya, "An Efficient Implementation Method of Fractal Image Compression on Dynamically Reconfigurable Architecture," *Proc. 6th Reconfigurable Architectures Workshop (Springer-Verlag Lecture Notes in Computer Science vol. 1586)*, (1999), pp. 670–678.

[226] H. Nakada, K. Oguri, N. Imlig, M. Inamori, R. Konishi, H. Ito, K. Nagami, and T. Shiozawa, "Plastic Cell Architecture: A Dynamically Reconfigurable Hardware-based Computer," *Proc. 6th Reconfigurable Architectures Workshop (Springer-Verlag Lecture Notes in Computer Science vol. 1586)*, (1999), pp. 679–687

[227] K. Nakano, "Prefix-Sums Algorithms on Reconfigurable Meshes," *Parallel Processing Letters*, vol. 5, no. 1, (1995), pp. 23–35.

[228] K. Nakano, "Computation of the Convex Hull for Sorted Points on a Reconfigurable Mesh," *Parallel Algorithms and Applications*, vol. 8, (1996), pp. 243–250.

[229] K. Nakano, T. Masuzawa, and N. Tokura, "A Sub-Logarithmic Time Sorting Algorithm on a Reconfigurable Arrray," *Institute of Electronics, Information and Communication Engineers (IEICE) Transactions*, vol. E-74, no. 11, (1991), pp. 3894–3901.

[230] K. Nakano and S. Olariu, "An Optimal Algorithm for the Angle-Restricted All Nearest Neighbor Problem on the Reconfigurable Mesh, with Applications," *IEEE Transactions on Parallel and Distributed Systems*, vol. 8, no. 9, (1997), pp. 983–990.

[231] K. Nakano and S. Olariu, "An Efficient Algorithm for Row Minima Computations on Basic Reconfigurable Meshes," *IEEE Transactions on Parallel and Distributed Systems*, vol. 9, no. 6, (1998), pp. 561–569.

[232] K. Nakano and K. Wada, "Integer Summing Algorithms on Reconfigurable Meshes," *Theoretical Computer Science*, vol. 197, nos. 1-2, (1998), pp. 57–77.

[233] D. Nassimi and S. Sahni, "Bitonic Sort on a Mesh-Connected Parallel Computer," *IEEE Transactions on Computers*, vol. 28, no. 1, (1979), pp. 2–7.

[234] National Semiconductor, "Configurable Logic Array (CLAy) Data Sheet," 1993.

[235] M. Nigam and S. Sahni, "Sorting n Numbers on $n \times n$ Reconfigurable Meshes with Buses," *Journal of Parallel and Distributed Computing*, vol. 23, (1994), pp. 37–48.

[236] N. Nisan and A. Ta-Shma, "Symmetric Logspace is Closed Under Complement," *Proc. 27th ACM Symposium on the Theory of Computing*, (1995), pp. 140–146.

[237] D. R. O'Hallaron, "Uniform Approach for Solving Some Classical Problems on a Linear Array," *Proc. International Conference on Parallel Processing*, (1989), vol. 3, pp. 161–168.

[238] S. Olariu, M. Overstreet, and Z. Wen, "Reconstructing a Binary Tree from its Traversals in Doubly Logarithmic CREW Time," *Journal of Parallel and Distributed Computing*, vol. 27, (1995), pp. 100–105.

[239] S. Olariu and J. L. Schwing, "A Novel Deterministic Sampling Scheme with Applications to Broadcast-Efficient Sorting on the Reconfigurable Mesh," *Journal of Parallel and Distributed Computing*, vol. 32, (1996), pp. 215–222.

[240] S. Olariu, J. L. Schwing, W. Shen, L. Wilson, and J. Zhang, "A Simple Selection Algorithm for Reconfigurable Meshes," *Parallel Algorithms and Applications*, vol. 1, (1993), pp. 29–41.

[241] S. Olariu, J. L. Schwing, and J. Zhang, "Fundamental Algorithms on Reconfigurable Meshes," *Proc. 29th Allerton Conference on Communication, Control and Computing,* (1991), pp. 811–820.

[242] S. Olariu, J. L. Schwing, and J. Zhang, "On the Power of Two-Dimensional Processor Arrays with Reconfigurable Bus Systems," *Parallel Processing Letters,* vol. 1, no. 1, (1991), pp. 29–34.

[243] S. Olariu, J. L. Schwing, and J. Zhang, "Fast Computer Vision Algorithms for Reconfigurable Meshes," *Image and Vision Computing,* vol. 10, (1992), pp. 610–616.

[244] S. Olariu, J. L. Schwing, and J. Zhang, "Fundamental Data Movement Algorithms for Reconfigurable Meshes," *Proc. 11th International Phoenix Conference on Computers and Communications,* (1992), pp. 472–479.

[245] S. Olariu, J. Schwing, and J. Zhang, "Applications of Reconfigurable Meshes to Constant Time Computations," *Parallel Computing,* vol. 19, no. 2, (1993), pp. 229–237.

[246] S. Olariu, J. L. Schwing, and J. Zhang, "Integer Problems on Reconfigurable Meshes, with Applications," *Journal of Computer and Software Engineering,* vol. 1, no. 1, (1993), pp. 33–45.

[247] S. Olariu, J. L. Schwing, and J. Zhang, "Optimal Convex Hull Algorithms on Enhanced Meshes," *BIT,* vol. 33, no. 3, (1993), pp. 396–410.

[248] J. O'Rourke, *Computational Geometry in C,* Cambridge University Press, Cambridge, UK, 1994.

[249] T.-T. Pan and S.-S. Lin, "Constant-Time Algorithms for Minimum Spanning Tree and Related Problems on Processor Array with Reconfigurable Bus Systems," *The Computer Journal,* vol. 45, no. 2, (2002), pp. 174–186.

[250] V. Pan and J. Reif, "Efficient Parallel Solution of Linear Systems," *Proc. ACM Symposium on the Theory of Computing,* (1985), pp. 143–152.

[251] Y. Pan, "Hough Transform on Arrays with an Optical Bus," *Proc. 5th IASTED International Conference on Parallel and Distributed Computing and Systems,* (1992), pp. 161–166.

[252] Y. Pan, "Order Statistics on a Linear Array with a Reconfigurable Bus," *Future Generation Computer Systems,* vol. 11, no. 3, (1995), pp. 321–328.

[253] Y. Pan, "Constant-Time Hough Transform on a 3D Reconfigurable Mesh Using Fewer Processors," *Proc. 7th Reconfigurable Architectures Workshop (Springer-Verlag Lecture Notes in Computer Science vol. 1800),* (2000), pp. 966–973.

[254] Y. Pan and M. Hamdi, "Singular Value Decomposition on Processor Arrays with a Pipelined Bus System," *Journal of Network and Computer Applications,* vol. 19, no. 3, (1996), pp. 235–248.

[255] Y. Pan, M. Hamdi, and K. Li, "Efficient and Scalable Quicksort on a Linear Array with a Reconfigurable Pipelined Bus System," *Future Generation Computer Systems,* vol. 13, no. 6, (1998), pp. 501–513.

[256] Y. Pan, M. Hamdi, and K. Li, "Euclidean Distance Transform for Binary Images on Reconfigurable Mesh-Connected Computers," *IEEE Transactions on Systems, Man and Cybernetics-Part B:Cybernetics*, vol. 30, no. 1, (2000), pp. 240–244.

[257] Y. Pan, J. Li, and R. Vemuri, "Continuous Wavelet Transform on Reconfigurable Meshes," *Proc. Workshop on Parallel and Distributed Computing in Image Processing, Video Processing, and Multimedia*, (2001).

[258] Y. Pan and K. Li, "Linear Array with a Reconfigurable Pipelined Bus System: Concepts and Applications," *Information Sciences*, vol. 106, nos. 3/4, (1998), pp. 237–258.

[259] Y. Pan, K. Li, and S. Q. Zheng, "Fast Nearest Neighbor Algorithms on a Linear Array with a Reconfigurable Pipelined Bus System," *Parallel Algorithms and Applications*, vol. 13, (1998), pp. 1–25.

[260] Y. Pan, J. L. Trahan, and R. Vaidyanathan, "A Scalable and Efficient Algorithm for Computing the City Block Distance Transform on Reconfigurable Meshes," *The Computer Journal*, vol. 40, no. 7, (1997), pp. 435–440.

[261] Y. Pan, S. Q. Zheng, K. Li, and H. Shen, "An Improved Generalization of Mesh-Connected Computers with Multiple Buses," *IEEE Transactions on Parallel and Distributed Systems*, vol. 12, no. 3, (2001), pp. 293–305.

[262] S. Pavel "Computation and Communication Aspects of Arrays with Optical Pipelined Buses," Ph.D. Thesis, Department of Computing and Information Sciences, Queen's University, Kingston, Ontario, Canada, (1996).

[263] S. Pavel and S. G. Akl, "Integer Sorting and Routing in Arrays with Reconfigurable Optical Buses," *Proc. International Conference on Parallel Processing*, (1996), pp. III-90–III-94.

[264] S. Pavel and S. G. Akl, "Matrix Operations Using Arrays with Reconfigurable Optical Buses," *Parallel Algorithms and Applications*, vol. 8, (1996), pp. 223–242.

[265] S. Pavel and S. G. Akl, "On the Power of Arrays with Optical Pipelined Buses," *Proc. International Conference on Parallel and Distributed Processing Techniques and Applications*, (1996), pp. 1443–1454.

[266] S. Pavel and S. G. Akl, "Integer Sorting and Routing in Arrays with Reconfigurable Optical Buses," *International Journal of Foundations of Computer Science*, vol. 9, (1998), pp. 99–120.

[267] H. Park, H. J. Kim, and V. Prasanna, "An O(1) Time Optimal Algorithm for Multiplying Matrices on Reconfigurable Mesh," *Information Processing Letters*, vol. 47, (1993), pp. 109–113.

[268] H. Park, V. Prasanna, and J. Jang, "Fast Arithmetic on Reconfigurable Meshes," *Proc. International Conference on Parallel Processing*, (1993), pp. 236–243.

[269] S. Perissakis, Y. Joo, J. Ahn, A. DeHon, and J. Wawrzynek, "Embedded DRAM for a Reconfigurable Array," *Proc. 1999 Symposium on VLSI Circuits*, (1999).

[270] F. P. Preparata and M. I. Shamos, *Computational Geometry: An Introduction*, Springer-Verlag, New York, 1985.

[271] F. P. Preparata and J. E. Vuillemin, "Area-Time Optimal VLSI Networks for Multiplying Matrices," *Information Processing Letters*, vol. 11, (1980), pp. 77–80.

[272] C. Qiao, "On Designing Communication-Intensive Algorithms for a Spanning Optical Bus Based Array," *Parallel Processing Letters*, vol. 5, no. 3, (1995), pp. 499–511.

[273] C. Qiao and R. Melhem, "Time-Division Optical Communications in Multiprocessor Arrays," *IEEE Transactions on Computers*, vol. 42, no. 5, (1993), pp. 577–590.

[274] C. Qiao, R. Melhem, D. Chiarulli, and S. Levitan, "Optical Multicasting in Linear Arrays," *International Journal of Optical Computing*, vol. 2, no. 1, (1991), pp. 31–48.

[275] B. Radunovic and V. Milutinovic, "A Survey of Reconfigurable Computing Architectures," *Proc. 8th International Workshop on Field-Programmable Logic and Applications (Springer-Verlag Lecture Notes in Computer Science vol. 1482)*, (1998), pp. 376–385.

[276] S. Rajasekaran, "Mesh Connected Computers with Fixed and Reconfigurable Buses: Packet Routing, Sorting, and Selection," *IEEE Transactions on Computers*, vol. 45, no. 5, (1996), pp. 529–539.

[277] S. Rajasekaran and S. Sahni, "Sorting, Selection, and Routing on the Array with Reconfigurable Optical Buses," *IEEE Transactions on Parallel and Distributed Systems*, vol. 8, no. 11, (1997), pp. 1123–1132.

[278] A. G. Ranade, "How to Emulate Shared Memory," *Journal of Computer and System Sciences*, vol. 42, (1991), pp. 307–324.

[279] J. H. Reif, ed., *Synthesis of Parallel Algorithms*, Morgan Kaufmann Publishers, San Mateo, California, 1993.

[280] Y. Robert and D. Trystsam, "Systolic Solution of the Algebraic Path Problem," in *Systolic Arrays*, W. Moore, A. McCabe, and R. Urquhart, ed., Hilger, Bristol, England, (1986), pp. 171–180.

[281] D. Robinson and P. Lysaght, "Modelling and Synthesis of Configuration Controllers for Dynamically Reconfigurable Logic Systems Using the DCS CAD Framework," *Proc. 9th International Workshop on Field-Programmable Logic and Applications (Springer-Verlag Lecture Notes in Computer Science vol. 1673)*, (1999), pp. 41–50.

[282] J. Rose, A. El Gamal, and A. Sangiovanni-Vincentelli, "Architecture of Field-Programmable Gate Arrays," *Proceedings of the IEEE*, vol. 81, no. 7, (1993), pp. 1013–1029.

[283] A. L. Rosenberg, V. Scarano, and R. Sitaraman, "The Reconfigurable Ring of Processors: Efficient Algorithms via Hypercube Simulation," *Parallel Processing Letters*, vol. 5, no. 1, (1995), pp. 37–48.

[284] G. Rote, "A Systolic Array Algorithm for the Algebraic Path Problem," *Computing*, vol. 34, (1985), pp. 191–219.

[285] J. Rothstein, "Bus Automata, Brains and Mental Models," *IEEE Transactions on Systems, Man and Cybernetics*, vol. 18, no. 4, (1988), pp. 522–531.

[286] S. Sahni, "Computing on Reconfigurable Bus Architectures," in *Computer Systems & Education*, Tata McGraw-Hill Publishing Co., (1994), pp. 386–398

[287] S. Sahni, "Data Manipulation on the Distributed Memory Bus Computer," *Parallel Processing Letters*, vol. 5, no. 1, (1995), pp. 3–14.

[288] J. E. Savage, "Area-Time Tradeoffs for Matrix Multiplication and Related Problems in VLSI Models," *Journal of Computer and System Sciences*, vol. 22, no. 2, (1981), pp. 230–242.

[289] S. M. Scalera, J. J. Murray, and S. Lease, "A Mathematical Benefit Analysis of Context Switching Reconfigurable Computing," *Proc. 5th Reconfigurable Architectures Workshop (Springer-Verlag Lecture Notes in Computer Science vol. 1388)*, (1998), pp. 73–78.

[290] C. P. Schnorr and A. Shamir, "An Optimal Sorting Algorithm for Mesh-Connected Computers," *Proc. 18th ACM Symposium on the Theory of Computing*, (1986), pp. 255–261.

[291] A. Schuster "Dynamic Reconfiguring Networks for Parallel Computers: Algorithms and Complexity Bounds," Ph.D. Thesis, Dept. of Computer Science, Hebrew University, Israel, (1991).

[292] A Selberg, "An Elementary Proof of the Prime Number Theorem," *Annals of Mathematics*, vol. 50, (1949), pp. 305–313.

[293] N. Shankar and V. Ramachandran, "Efficient Parallel Circuits and Algorithms for Division," *Information Processing Letters*, vol. 29, no. 6, (1988), pp. 307–313.

[294] N. Shirazi, W. Luk, D. Benyamin, and P. Y. K. Cheung, "Quantitative Analysis of Run-Time Reconfigurable Database Search," *Proc. 9th International Workshop on Field-Programmable Logic and Applications (Springer-Verlag Lecture Notes in Computer Science vol. 1673)*, (1999), pp. 253–263.

[295] N. Shirazi, W. Luk, and P. Y. K. Cheung, "Run-Time Management of Dynamically Reconfigurable Designs," *Proc. 8th International Workshop on Field-Programmable Logic and Applications (Springer-Verlag Lecture Notes in Computer Science vol. 1482)*, (1998), pp. 59–68.

[296] D. B. Shu, L. W. Chow, J. G. Nash, and C. Weems, "A Content Address-able, Bit-Serial Associate Processor," *Proc. IEEE Workshop on VLSI Signal Processing*, (1988), vol. III, R. W. Brodersen and H. S. Moscovitz, eds., pp. 120–128.

[297] D. B. Shu and J. G. Nash, "The Gated Interconnection Network for Dynamic Programming," in *Concurrent Computations*, S. K. Tewksbury *et al.*, eds., Plenum Publishers, New York, 1988, pp. 645–658.

[298] D. B. Shu, J. G. Nash, and K. Kim, "Parallel Implementation of Image Understanding Tasks on Gated-Connection Networks," *Proc. 5th International Parallel Processing Symposium*, (1991), pp. 216–223.

[299] R. P. S. Sidhu, A. Mei, and V. K. Prasanna, "String Matching on Multicontext FPGAs using Self-Reconfiguration," *Proc. 1999 ACM/SIGDA 7th International Symposium on Field Programmable Gate Arrays*, (1999), pp. 217–226.

[300] R. Sidhu, S. Wadhwa, A. Mei, and V. K. Prasanna, "A Self-Reconfigurable Gate Array Architecture," *Proc. 10th International Workshop on Field-Programmable Logic and Applications (Springer-Verlag Lecture Notes in Computer Science vol. 1896)*, (2000), pp. 106–120.

[301] H. Simmler, L. Levinson, and R. Männer, "Multitasking on FPGA Coprocessors," *Proc. 10th International Workshop on Field-Programmable Logic and Applications (Springer-Verlag Lecture Notes in Computer Science vol. 1896)*, (2000), pp. 121–130.

[302] M. Slater, *Microprocessor Based Design: A Comprehensive Guide to Hardware Design*, Prentice Hall Inc., Englewood Cliffs, New Jersey, 1989.

[303] L. Snyder, "Introduction to the Configurable Highly Parallel Computer," *IEEE Computer*, vol. 15, (1982), pp. 47–56.

[304] L. Stockmeyer and U. Vishkin, "Simulation of Parallel Random Access Machines by Circuits," *SIAM Journal on Computing*, vol. 13, no. 2, (1984), pp. 409–422.

[305] Q. F. Stout, "Mesh-Connected Computer with Broadcasting," *IEEE Transactions on Computers*, vol. 32, (1983), pp. 826–829.

[306] C. P. Subbaraman, J. L. Trahan, and R. Vaidyanathan, "List Ranking and Graph Algorithms on the Reconfigurable Multiple Bus Machine," *Proc. International Conference on Parallel Processing*, (1993), vol. 3, pp. 244–247.

[307] C. Tanougast, Y. Berviller, and S. Weber, "Optimization of Motion Estimator for Run-Time-Reconfiguration Implementation," *Proc. 7th Reconfigurable Architectures Workshop (Springer-Verlag Lecture Notes in Computer Science vol. 1800)*, (2000), pp. 959–965.

[308] R. E. Tarjan, "A Unified Approach to Path Problems," *Journal of the ACM*, vol. 28, no. 3, (1981), pp. 577–593.

[309] R. E. Tarjan and U. Vishkin, "Finding Biconnected Components and Computing Tree Functions in Logarithmic Parallel Time," *SIAM Journal on Computing*, vol. 14, no. 4, (1985), pp. 862–874.

[310] S. Tatineni and J. L. Trahan, "Scheduling and Compacting Real-Time Tasks on FPGAs," manuscript, 2003.

[311] F J. Taylor, *Digital Filter Design Handbook*, Marcel Dekker, New York, 1983.

[312] T. Thangavel and V. P. Muthuswamy, "A Parallel Algorithm to Generate n-ary Reflected Gray Codes in a Linear Array with a Reconfigurable Bus System," *Parallel Processing Letters*, vol. 3, no. 2, (1993), pp. 157–164.

[313] T. Thangavel and V. P. Muthuswamy, "Parallel Algorithms for Addition and Multiplication on Processor Arrays with Reconfigurable Bus Systems," *Information Processing Letters*, vol. 46, no. 2, (1993), pp. 89–94.

[314] R. K. Thiruchelvan, J. L. Trahan, and R. Vaidyanathan, "Sorting on Reconfigurable Multiple Bus Machines," *Proc. 36th Midwest Symposium on Circuits and Systems*, (1993), pp. 554–557.

[315] C. D. Thompson and H. T. Kung, "Sorting on a Mesh-Connected Parallel Computer," *Communications of the ACM*, vol. 20, no. 4, (1977), pp. 263–271.

[316] J. L. Trahan, A. G. Bourgeois, Y. Pan, and R. Vaidyanathan, "Optimally Scaling Permutation Routing on Reconfigurable Linear Arrays with Optical Buses," *Journal of Parallel and Distributed Computing*, vol. 60, no. 9, (2000), pp. 1125–1136.

[317] J. L. Trahan, A. G. Bourgeois, and R. Vaidyanathan, "Tighter and Broader Complexity Results for Reconfigurable Models," *Parallel Processing Letters*, vol. 8, no. 3, (1998), pp. 271–282.

[318] J. L. Trahan, M. C. Loui, and V. Ramachandran, "Multiplication, Division, and Shift Instructions in Parallel Random Access Machines," *Theoretical Computer Science*, vol. 100, no. 1, (1992), pp. 1–44.

[319] J. L. Trahan, C.-m. Lu, and R. Vaidyanathan, "Integer and Floating Point Matrix-Vector Multiplication on the Reconfigurable Mesh," *Proc. 10th International Parallel Processing Symposium*, (1996), pp. 702–706.

[320] J. L. Trahan, Y. Pan, R. Vaidyanathan, and A. G. Bourgeois, "Scalable Basic Algorithms on a Linear Array with a Reconfigurable Pipelined Bus System," *Proc. 10th ISCA International Conference on Parallel and Distributed Computing and Systems*, (1997), pp. 564–569.

[321] J. L. Trahan and R. Vaidyanathan, "Relative Scalability of the Reconfigurable Multiple Bus Machine," *Proc. 3rd Reconfigurable Architectures Workshop*, (1996).

[322] J. L. Trahan, R. Vaidyanathan, and U. K. K. Manchikatla, "Maximum Finding on the Reconfigurable Mesh," manuscript, 1996.

[323] J. L. Trahan, R. Vaidyanathan, and C. P. Subbaraman, "Constant Time Graph and Poset Algorithms on the Reconfigurable Multiple Bus Machine," *Proc. International Conference on Parallel Processing,* (1994), vol. 3, pp. 214–217.

[324] J. L. Trahan, R. Vaidyanathan, and C. P. Subbaraman, "Constant Time Graph Algorithms on the Reconfigurable Multiple Bus Machine," *Journal of Parallel and Distributed Computing,* vol. 46, no. 1, (1997), pp. 1–14.

[325] J. L. Trahan, R. Vaidyanathan, and R. K. Thiruchelvan, "On the Power of Segmenting and Fusing Buses," *Journal of Parallel and Distributed Computing,* vol. 34, no. 1, (1996), pp. 82–94.

[326] H.-R. Tsai, S.-J. Horng, S.-S. Lee, S.-S. Tsai, and T.-W. Kao, "Parallel Hierarchical Clustering Algorithms on Processor Arrays with a Reconfigurable Bus System," *Pattern Recognition,* vol. 30, no. 5, (1997), pp. 801–815.

[327] W. Tsu, K. Macy, A. Joshi, R. Huang, N. Walker, T. Tung, O. Rowhani, V. George, J. Wawrzynek, and A. DeHon, "HSRA: High-Speed, Hierarchical Synchronous Reconfigurable Array," *Proc. ACM/SIGDA 7th International Symposium on Field Programmable Gate Arrays,* (1999), pp. 125–134.

[328] G. Turner and H. Schröder, "Fast Token Distribution on Reconfigurable meshes," Technical Report TR 95-10, Department of Computer Science, University of Newcastle, 1995.

[329] R. Vaidyanathan "The R-PRAM: A New Model of Parallel Computation and its Application to Sorting," Ph.D Thesis, Department of Electrical and Computer Engineering, Syracuse University, (1990).

[330] R. Vaidyanathan, "Sorting on PRAMs with Reconfigurable Buses," *Information Processing Letters,* vol. 42, no. 4, (1992), pp. 203–208.

[331] R. Vaidyanathan, C. R. P. Hartmann, and P. K. Varshney, "PRAMs with Variable Memory Word-Size," *Information Processing Letters,* vol. 42, (1992), pp. 217–222.

[332] R. Vaidyanathan and J. L. Trahan, "Optimal Simulation of Multidimensional Reconfigurable Meshes by Two-Dimensional Reconfigurable Meshes," *Information Processing Letters,* vol. 47, no. 5, (1993), pp. 267–273.

[333] R. Vaidyanathan, J. L. Trahan, and C-m. Lu, "Degree of Scalability: Scalable Reconfigurable Mesh Algorithms for Multiple Addition and Matrix-Vector Multiplication," *Parallel Computing,* vol. 29, no. 1, (2003), pp. 95–109.

[334] L. G. Valiant, "Parallelism in Comparison Problems," *SIAM Journal on Computing,* vol. 4, (1975), pp. 348–355.

[335] L. G. Valiant, "A Bridging Model for Parallel Computation," *Communications of the ACM,* vol. 33, no. 8, (1990), pp. 103–111.

[336] L. G. Valiant, "General Purpose Parallel Architectures," in *Handbook of Theoretical Computer Science, Vol. A: Algorithms and Complexity,* J. van Leeuwen, ed., MIT Press, (1990), pp. 943–972.

[337] D. E. Van den Bout, J. N. Morris, D. Thomae, S. Labrozzi, S. Wingo, and D. Hallman, "AnyBoard: An FPGA-Based, Reconfigurable System," *IEEE Design and Test of Computers*, vol. 9, no. 3, (1992), pp. 21–30.

[338] H. Venkateswaran, "Properties that Characterize LOGCFL," *Journal of Computer and System Sciences*, vol. 43, no. 2, (1991), pp. 380–404.

[339] J. Villasenor and B. Hutchings, "The Flexibility of Configurable Computing," *IEEE Signal Processing Magazine*, vol. 15, no. 5, (1998), pp. 67–84.

[340] J. Villasenor, C. Jones, and B. Schoner, "Video Communications Using Rapidly Reconfigurable Hardware," *IEEE Transactions on Circuits and Systems for Video Technology*, vol. 5, no. 6, (1995), pp. 565–567.

[341] J. Villasenor and W. H. Mangione-Smith, "Configurable Computing," *Scientific American*, vol. 276, no. 6, (1997), pp. 66–71.

[342] J. Villasenor, B. Schoner, K. Chia, and C. Zapata, "Configurable Computing Solutions for Automatic Target Recognition," *Proc. Workshop on FPGAs for Custom Computing Machines*, (1996), pp. 70–79.

[343] U. Vishkin, "Structural Parallel Algorithmics," *Proc. International Colloquium on Automata, Languages and Programming*, (1991), pp. 363–380.

[344] J. Vuillemin, P. Bertin, D. Roncin, M. Shand, H. Touati, and P. Boucard, "Programmable Active Memories: Reconfigurable Systems Come of Age," *IEEE Transactions on VLSI Systems*, vol. 4, no. 1, (1996), pp. 56–69.

[345] E. Waingold, M. Taylor, D. Srikrishna, V. Sarkar, W. Lee, V. Lee, J. Kim, M. Frank, P. Finch, R. Barua, J. Babb, S. Amarasinghe, and A. Agarwal, "Baring It All to Software: Raw Machines," *IEEE Transactions on Computers*, vol. 30, no. 9, (1997), pp. 86–93.

[346] B. F. Wang and G. H. Chen, "Constant Time Algorithms for the Transitive Closure and Some Related Graph Problems on Processor Arrays with Reconfigurable Bus Systems," *IEEE Transactions on Parallel and Distributed Systems*, vol. 1, no. 4, (1990), pp. 500–507.

[347] B. F. Wang and G. H. Chen, "Two-Dimensional Processor Array with a Reconfigurable Bus System is at Least as Powerful as CRCW Model," *Information Processing Letters*, vol. 36, (1990), pp. 21–36.

[348] B. F. Wang, G. H. Chen, and H. Li, "Configurational Computation: A New Computation Method on Processor Arrays with Reconfigurable Bus Systems," *Proc. International Conference on Parallel Processing*, (1991), vol. III, pp. 42–49.

[349] B. F. Wang, G. H. Chen, and H. Li, "Fast Algorithms for Some Arithmetic and Logic Operations," *Proc. National Computer Symposium*, (1991), pp. 178–183.

[350] B. F. Wang, G. H. Chen, and F. C. Lin, "Constant Time Sorting on a Processor Array with a Reconfigurable Bus System," *Information Processing Letters*, vol. 34, (1990), pp. 187–192.

[351] Y.-R. Wang and S.-J. Horng, "An O(1) Time Parallel Algorithm for the 3D Euclidean Distance Transform on the AROB," *Proc. International Conference on Parallel and Distributed Processing Techniques and Applications*, (2002), pp. 1120–1126.

[352] C. C. Weems, S. P. Levitan, A. R. Hanson, E. M. Riseman, D. B. Shu, and J. G. Nash, "The Image Understanding Architecture," *International Journal of Computer Vision*, vol. 2, (1989), pp. 251–282.

[353] S. A. White, "Applications of Distributed Arithmetic to Digital Signal Processing: A Tutorial Review," *IEEE ASSP Magazine*, vol. 6, no. 3, (1989), pp. 4–19.

[354] M. J. Wirthlin and B. L. Hutchings, "DISC: The Dynamic Instruction Set Computer," in *Field Programmable Gate Arrays (FPGAs) for Fast Board Development and Reconfigurable Computing*, J. Schewel, ed., *Proceedings of SPIE*, vol. 2607, (1995), pp. 92–103.

[355] M. J. Wirthlin and B. L. Hutchings, "Sequencing Run-Time Reconfigured Hardware with Software," *Proc. ACM/SIGDA International Symposium on Field Programmable Gate Arrays*, (1996), pp. 122–128.

[356] M. J. Wirthlin and B. L. Hutchings, "Improving Functional Density Through Run-Time Constant Propagation," *Proc. ACM/SIGDA International Symposium on Field Programmable Gate Arrays*, (1997), pp. 86–92.

[357] M. J. Wirthlin and B. L. Hutchings, "Improving Functional Density Using Run-Time Circuit Reconfiguration," *IEEE Transactions on VLSI Systems*, vol. 6, no. 2, (1998), pp. 247–256.

[358] M. Wojko and H. ElGindy, "Configuration Sequencing with Self-Configurable Binary Multipliers," *Proc. 6th Reconfigurable Architectures Workshop (Springer-Verlag Lecture Notes in Computer Science vol. 1586)*, (1999), pp. 643–651.

[359] C.-H. Wu and S.-J. Horng, "L_2 Vector Median Filters on Arrays with Reconfigurable Optical Buses," *IEEE Transactions on Parallel and Distributed Systems*, vol. 12, no. 12, (2001), pp. 1281–1292.

[360] C.-H. Wu, S.-J. Horng, and H.-R. Tsai, "Efficient Parallel Algorithms for Hierarchical Clustering on Arrays with Reconfigurable Optical Buses," *Journal of Parallel and Distributed Computing*, vol. 60, no. 9, (2000), pp. 1137–1153.

[361] C.-H. Wu, S.-J Horng, and H.-R. Tsai, "Optimal Parallel Algorithms for Computer Vision Problems," *Journal of Parallel and Distributed Computing*, vol. 62, no. 6, (2002), pp. 1021–1041.

[362] Xilinx, Inc., "XC4000XLA/XV Series Field Programmable Gate Arrays," product specification, 1999.

[363] Xilinx, Inc., "XC6200 Field Programmable Gate Arrays," data sheet, 1997.

[364] Xilinx, Inc., Virtex Series FPGAs, data sheet, 2002.

[365] Xilinx, Inc., "Constant (k) Coefficient Multiplier Generator for Virtex," application note, 1999.

[366] Xilinx, Inc. web site, http://www.xilinx.com

[367] S. Yalmanchili and J. K. Aggarwal, "Reconfigurable Strategies for Parallel Architectures," *IEEE Computer*, vol. 18, no. 12, (1985), pp. 44–61.

[368] S. Q. Zheng and Y. Li, "Pipelined Asynchronous Time-Division Multiplexing Optical Bus," *Optical Engineering*, vol. 36, (1997), pp. 3392–3400.

[369] X. Zhou and M. Martonosi, "Augmenting Modern Superscalar Architectures with Configurable Extended Instructions," *Proc. 7th Reconfigurable Architectures Workshop (Springer-Verlag Lecture Notes in Computer Science vol. 1800)*, (2000), pp. 941–950.

Index